D1506872

Course	Strategic Management
Course Number	**22:620:588**
Instructor	Edward Hubbard
	Rutgers University
	MBA Program

http://create.mcgraw-hill.com

ISBN-10: 1121812104   ISBN-13: 9781121812109

Contents

Credits

Chapter 1. Strategic Managment:Creating Competive Advantage

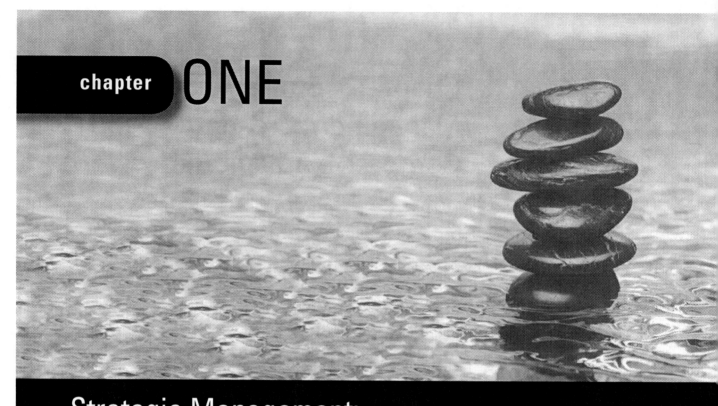

chapter ONE

Strategic Management:

Creating Competitive Advantages

After reading this chapter, you should have a good understanding of:

LO1.1   The definition of strategic management and its four key attributes.

LO1.2   The strategic management process and its three interrelated and principal activities.

LO1.3   The vital role of corporate governance and stakeholder management as well as how "symbiosis" can be achieved among an organization's stakeholders.

LO1.4   The importance of social responsibility, including environmental sustainability, and how it can enhance a corporation's innovation strategy.

LO1.5   The need for greater empowerment throughout the organization.

LO1.6   How an awareness of a hierarchy of strategic goals can help an organization achieve coherence in its strategic direction.

LEARNING OBJECTIVES

PART 1: STRATEGIC ANALYSIS

We define strategic management as *consisting of the analyses, decisions, and actions an organization undertakes in order to create and sustain competitive advantages.* At the heart of strategic management is the question: How and why do some firms outperform others? Thus, the challenge to managers is to decide on strategies that provide advantages that can be sustained over time. There are four key attributes of strategic management. It is directed at overall organizational goals, includes multiple stakeholders, incorporates short-term as well as long-term perspectives, and recognizes trade-offs between effectiveness and efficiency. We discuss the above definition and the four key attributes in the first section.

The second section addresses the strategic management process. The three major processes are strategy analysis, strategy formulation, and strategy implementation. These three components parallel the analyses, decisions, and actions in the above definition. We discuss how each of the 12 chapters addresses these three processes and provide examples from each chapter.

The third section discusses two important and interrelated concepts: corporate governance and stakeholder management. Corporate governance addresses the issue of who "governs" the corporation and determines its direction. It consists of three primary participants: stockholders (owners), management (led by the chief executive officer), and the board of directors (elected to monitor management). Stakeholder management recognizes that the interests of various stakeholders, such as owners, customers, and employees, can often conflict and create challenging decision-making dilemmas for managers. However, we discuss how some firms have been able to achieve "symbiosis" among stakeholders wherein their interests are considered interdependent and can be achieved simultaneously. We also discuss the important role of social responsibility and explain the concept of "shared value." Further, we emphasize the need for corporations to incorporate environmental sustainability in their strategic actions.

The fourth section addresses factors in the business environment that have increased the level of unpredictable change for today's leaders. Such factors have also created the need for a greater strategic management perspective and reinforced the role of empowerment throughout the organization.

The final section focuses on the need for organizations to ensure consistency in their vision, mission, and strategic objectives which, collectively, form a hierarchy of goals. While visions may lack specificity, they must evoke powerful and compelling mental images. Strategic objectives are much more specific and are essential for driving toward overall goals.

⚏⚏ Learning from Mistakes

What makes the study of strategic management so interesting? For one, struggling firms can become stars, while high flyers can become earthbound very rapidly. As colorfully noted by Arthur Martinez, Sears' former chairman: "Today's peacock is tomorrow's feather duster." Consider, for example, the change in membership on the prestigious *Fortune 500* list of the largest U.S. firms:[1]

- Of the 500 companies that appeared on the first list in 1955, only 62, ranked by revenue, have appeared on the list every year since.
- Some of the most powerful companies on today's list—businesses like Intel, Apple, and Google—grew from nothing to great on the strength of new technologies, bumping venerable old companies off the list.
- Nearly 2,000 companies have appeared on the list since its inception, and most are long gone from it. Just making the list guarantees nothing about your ability to endure.
- In 2009 and 2010, admittedly more volatile years than most, 71 companies—including Bear Stearns, Circuit City, Merrill Lynch, and Tribune—dropped off the 500.

Let's take a look at another fallen star, Nokia, the Finnish phone manufacturer. Nokia captured the emerging market for mobile phones and built the industry's most powerful brand in the 1990s.[2] Its handsets virtually defined the industry from the time it launched the first GSM phone in 1992. Then from 1996 to 2001, its revenues increased almost fivefold, and in 1998 it was the world's largest mobile manufacturer. In 2005 it sold its billionth handset, an 1100 model, to a customer in Nigeria. Unfortunately, Nokia's market dominance was short-lived. What happened?

While Nokia focused on emerging markets, it took its eye off the ball in developed economies, where the smartphone revolution was on its way. Nokia's focus on mobile phones for voice communication turned out to be their most disastrous call in the past 10 years. In addition to voice communications, customers also demanded interactive applications, Web browsing, and global positioning systems—as provided by Apple's iPhone and RIM's BlackBerry. As noted in *The Economist:* "Apple's iPhone and Google's Android range compete on 'cool.' BlackBerry is synonymous with business. But what does Nokia stand for?"

Nokia's inability to meet customer needs in both established and emerging markets resulted in a significant drop in its market share. It dropped from almost 51 percent in the fourth quarter of 2007 to less than 41 percent in the fourth quarter of 2008.

Since Apple introduced its first iPhone on January 9, 2007, Nokia's stock dropped 45 percent over the next three years—wiping out about $77 billion in the firm's market capitalization. Over the same period, Apple's shares soared 234 percent! Further, the 2010 global brands ranking by Millward Brown Optimor, placed Nokia in 43rd place, i.e., 30 places down compared to its position in 2009. Its profit margins had also been shrinking, along with its market share and the average price of its phones. Finally, at its peak, Nokia accounted for 4 percent of Finland's gross national product—by 2009, that share was down to only 1.6 percent, according to Helsinki-based economic research institute, ETLA.

Nokia also suffered from its location. Building a mobile telephone giant in Finland was a great achievement. However, Nokia wasn't surrounded by Internet companies or consumer electronics manufacturers. It wasn't exposed to a culture of innovation which would have forced it to question its assumptions and business decisions. Maybe in short, Nokia needed to be where the action was, that is, in the middle of the computer industry as well as the film, music, and Internet businesses. As suggested by *Bloomberg BusinessWeek*:

> Nokia should have relocated to California a decade ago. It would have caused an outcry in Finland, and probably Brussels as well. And it would have been worth it. Nokia needed to pitch itself into the cauldron of technological change. Maybe that way it could have held onto its brand leadership, rather than surrender it to a computer manufacturer that looked dead on its feet a decade ago.

> The cruel truth—for all its residual market share—is that Nokia misread the way the mobile phone industry was merging with the computer industry and social networking. And now, maybe it's too late to turn that around.

Today's leaders, such as those at Nokia, face a large number of complex challenges in the global marketplace. In considering how much credit (or blame) they deserve, two perspectives of leadership come immediately to mind: the "romantic" and "external control" perspectives.[3] First, let's look at the **romantic view of leadership.** Here, the implicit assumption is that the leader is the key force in determining an organization's success—or lack thereof.[4] This view dominates the popular press in business magazines such as *Fortune, BusinessWeek,* and *Forbes,* wherein the CEO is either lauded for his or her firm's success or chided for the organization's demise.[5] Consider, for example, the credit that has been bestowed on leaders such as Jack Welch, Andrew Grove, and Herb Kelleher for the tremendous accomplishments of their firms, General Electric, Intel, and Southwest Airlines, respectively.

romantic view of leadership situations in which the leader is the key force determining the organization's success—or lack thereof.

Similarly, Apple's success in the last decade has been attributed almost entirely to Steve Jobs, its CEO.[6] Apple's string of hit products such as iMac computers, iPods, and iPhones are testament to his genius for developing innovative, user-friendly, and aesthetically pleasing products. In addition to being a perfectionist in product design, Jobs also is a master showman with a cult following. On January 14, 2009, he announced that he was taking a medical leave through June. Perhaps not surprisingly, Apple's stock immediately dropped 10 percent. And, almost exactly two years later, on January 17, 2011, Jobs announced that he was taking another medical leave. The immediate reaction: Apple's shares went down 6 percent the following week—this reflects a drop of around $20 billion in the firm's market value.[7]

● The BP oil spill in April 2010, severely affected many industries along the Gulf Coast.

Finally, consider how George Buckley reinvigorated 3M's focus on innovation. 3M, with $23 billion in 2010 revenues, produces an astonishing 55,000 different products. Its goal has always been to generate 30 percent of its sales from products introduced in the past five years. However, when the board asked Buckley in 2005 to assume the CEO position, this benchmark had dropped to only 21 percent. Strategy Spotlight 1.1 describes Buckley's strong initiatives to accelerate 3M's rate of innovation.

strategy spotlight

How CEO George Buckley Turned Around 3M

Why is innovation important to 3M? As their older products become outmoded or become commodities, they must be replaced. According to Larry Wendling, head of 3M's corporate research, "Our business model is literally new-product innovation." However, when James McNerney left the company to become Boeing's CEO, the percentage had slid to 21 percent. And, what's worse, much of the new product revenue came from a single category: optical films.

The board went outside the firm for its new CEO and appointed George Buckley, who had previously served as CEO of Brunswick, an Illinois company known for bowling gear and boats. What is perhaps most important to know about Buckley, however, is that he has a Ph.D. in electrical engineering and is a scientist at heart, with several patents to his name. He states: "This is to me an engineer's and scientist's Toys'R'Us," and "There is no company like it in America. There is no company like it in the world."

When Buckley took over 3M, he quickly set some clear business goals for the company. He wanted his managers to protect and strengthen 3M's core businesses, which included abrasives, optical film, and industrial tapes. He also wanted 3M to develop lower-cost

products to compete in emerging markets, as well as for the firm to play a key role in future growth markets such as renewable energy, water infrastructure, and mobile digital media.

Perhaps most important, Buckley has been an outspoken champion for 3M's labs. In 2009, despite the deep recession, he kept R&D spending at more than $1 billion and asserted that "even in the worst economic times in memory, we released over 1,000 new products." He also removed the stringent focus on efficiency, particularly in basic research. This had a huge psychic payoff for staff at the science-centric company. Ram Charan, a world-famous consultant who advises the firm claims "George has accelerated the innovation machine by devoting his personal time, his energy, his focus, to empowering the researchers, opening up their minds and urging them to restore the luster of 3M." Buckley's results are impressive: The percentage of 3M's revenue from products introduced in the past five years is back to 30 percent and is expected to reach the mid-30s by 2012.

In closing, Marc Gunther, a contributing editor at *Fortune* magazine, provides some interesting personal insights: "Buckley is a charming and, above all, enthusiastic guy . . . who, in his spare time, likes taking apart and putting together old motorcycles or restoring Victorian furniture . . . While he surely needs traditional management skills to oversee a global company of 75,000 people, my sense is that his scientific curiosity about how the world works and boyish delight in how things get invented make him a perfect fit for 3M."

Sources: Gunther, M. 2010. 3M's innovation revival. *Fortune.* September 27: 73–76; Hindo, B. 2007. 3M chief plants a money tree. *www.businessweek.com.* June 11: np; and, Gunther, M. Why 3M is unique. *theenergycollective.com.* December 10: np.

On the other hand, when things don't go well, much of the failure of an organization can also, rightfully, be attributed to the leader.[8] Nokia's leadership failed to see the changes taking place in the mobile phone industry. In contrast, Apple fully capitalized on the emerging trend toward sophisticated smartphones.

The contrasting fortunes of Hewlett-Packard under two different CEOs also demonstrate the influence leadership has on firm performance.[9] When Carly Fiorina was fired as CEO of the firm, HP enjoyed an immediate increase in its stock price of 7 percent—hardly a strong endorsement of her leadership! Her successor, Mark Hurd, led the firm to five years of outstanding financial results. Interestingly, when he abruptly resigned on August 6, 2010, the firm's stock dropped 12 percent almost instantly! (To provide some perspective, this represents a decrease in HP's market value of about $12 billion.)

However, this reflects only part of the picture. Consider another perspective called the **external control view of leadership.** Here, rather than making the implicit assumption that the leader is the most important factor in determining organizational outcomes, the focus is on external factors that may positively (or negatively) affect a firm's success. We don't have to look far to support this perspective. Developments in the general environment,

external control view of leadership situations in which external forces—where the leader has limited influence—determine the organization's success.

such as economic downturns, governmental legislation, or an outbreak of major internal conflict or war, can greatly restrict the choices that are available to a firm's executives. In addition, major unanticipated developments can often have very negative consequences for businesses regardless of how well formulated their strategies are.

Let's look at a few recent examples:[10]

- Hurricane Katrina in 2007 had a disastrous effect on businesses located along the Gulf Coast.
- The financial meltdown of 2008 and the resultant deep recession during the following two years forced once proud corporations like General Motors and Citigroup to ask for government bailouts. Others, such as Merrill Lynch and Washington Mutual, had to be acquired by other firms.
- In the aftermath of BP's disastrous oil well explosion on April 20, 2010, the fishing and tourism industries in the region suffered significant downturns. BP itself was forced to pay a $20 billion fine to the U.S. government.
- In April 2010, a volcanic eruption in Iceland disrupted air traffic all over Europe for well over a week. It is estimated that major airlines lost approximately $1.7 billion.
- On March 11, 2011, a 9.0 earthquake and tsunami devastated Japan and resulted in the loss of more than 20,000 lives. During the next two trading days, the country's stock exchange (Nikkei) suffered its biggest loss in 40 years. The disaster hit nearly every industry hard—especially energy companies. For example, Tokyo Electric Power Co., which operates a nuclear power plant that was severly damaged, fell 24.7 percent, and Toshiba Corp., a maker of nuclear power plants, slid 19.5 percent. Firms as diverse as Toyota, Honda, and Sony were forced to halt production because extensive damage to roads and distribution systems made it nearly impossible to move products.

Before moving on, it is important to point out that successful executives are often able to navigate around the difficult circumstances that they face. At times it can be refreshing to see the optimistic position they take when they encounter seemingly insurmountable odds. Of course, that's not to say that one should be naïve or Pollyannaish. Consider, for example, how one CEO is handling trying times:[11]

Name a general economic woe, and the chances are that Charles Needham is dealing with it.

- Market turmoil has knocked 80 percent off the shares of South Africa's Metorex, the mining company that he heads.
- The plunge in global commodities is slamming prices for the copper, cobalt, and other minerals Metorex unearths across Africa. The credit crisis makes it harder to raise money.
- And fighting has again broken out in the Democratic Republic of Congo, where Metorex has a mine and several projects in development.

Such problems might send many executives to the window ledge. Yet Needham appears unruffled as he sits down at a conference table in the company's modest offices in a Johannesburg suburb. The combat in northeast Congo, he notes, is far from Metorex's mine. Commodity prices are still high, in historical terms. And Needham is confident he can raise enough capital, drawing on relationships with South African banks. "These are the kinds of things you deal with, doing business in Africa," he says.

What Is Strategic Management?

Given the many challenges and opportunities in the global marketplace, today's managers must do more than set long-term strategies and hope for the best.[12] They must go beyond what some have called "incremental management," whereby they view their job as making

strategic management the analyses, decisions, and actions an organization undertakes in order to create and sustain competitive advantages.

a series of small, minor changes to improve the efficiency of their firm's operations.[13] That is fine if your firm is competing in a very stable, simple, and unchanging industry. But there aren't many of those left. The pace of change is accelerating, and the pressure on managers to make both major and minor changes in a firm's strategic direction is increasing.

Rather than seeing their role as merely custodians of the status quo, today's leaders must be proactive, anticipate change, and continually refine and, when necessary, make dramatic changes to their strategies. The strategic management of the organization must become both a process and a way of thinking throughout the organization.

Defining Strategic Management

>LO1.1

The definition of strategic management and its four key attributes.

Strategic management consists of the analyses, decisions, and actions an organization undertakes in order to create and sustain competitive advantages. This definition captures two main elements that go to the heart of the field of strategic management.

First, the strategic management of an organization entails three ongoing processes: *analyses*, *decisions*, and *actions*. Strategic management is concerned with the *analysis* of strategic goals (vision, mission, and strategic objectives) along with the analysis of the internal and external environment of the organization. Next, leaders must make strategic decisions. These *decisions*, broadly speaking, address two basic questions: What industries should we compete in? How should we compete in those industries? These questions also often involve an organization's domestic and international operations. And last are the *actions* that must be taken. Decisions are of little use, of course, unless they are acted on. Firms must take the necessary actions to implement their **strategies.** This requires leaders to allocate the necessary resources and to design the organization to bring the intended strategies to reality.

strategy The ideas, decisions, and actions that enable a firm to succeed.

Second, the essence of strategic management is the study of why some firms outperform others.[14] Thus, managers need to determine how a firm is to compete so that it can obtain advantages that are sustainable over a lengthy period of time. That means focusing on two fundamental questions:

competitive advantage A firm's resources and capabilities that enable it to overcome the competitive forces in its industry(ies).

- *How should we compete in order to create **competitive advantages** in the marketplace?* Managers need to determine if the firm should position itself as the low-cost producer or develop products and services that are unique and will enable the firm to charge premium prices. Or should they do some combination of both?
- *How can we create competitive advantages in the marketplace that are unique, valuable, and difficult for rivals to copy or substitute?* That is, managers need to make such advantages sustainable, instead of temporary.

Rivals almost always copy ideas that work. In the 1980s, American Airlines tried to establish a competitive advantage by introducing the frequent flyer program. Within weeks, all the airlines did the same thing. Overnight, frequent flyer programs became a necessary tool for competitive parity instead of a competitive advantage. The challenge, therefore, is to create competitive advantages that are sustainable.

operational effectiveness performing similar activities better than rivals.

Sustainable competitive advantage cannot be achieved through operational effectiveness alone.[15] The popular management innovations of the last two decades—total quality, just-in-time, benchmarking, business process reengineering, outsourcing—are all about operational effectiveness. **Operational effectiveness** means performing similar activities better than rivals. Each of these is important, but none lead to sustainable competitive advantage because everyone is doing them. Strategy is all about being different. Sustainable competitive advantage is possible only by performing different activities from rivals or performing similar activities in different ways. Companies such as Walmart, Southwest Airlines, and IKEA have developed unique, internally consistent, and difficult-to-imitate activity systems that have provided them with sustained competitive advantages. A company with a good strategy must make clear choices about what it wants to accomplish. Trying to do everything that your rivals do eventually leads to mutually destructive price competition, not long-term advantage.

The Four Key Attributes of Strategic Management

Before discussing the strategic management process, let's briefly talk about four attributes of strategic management.[16] It should become clear how this course differs from other courses that you have had in functional areas, such as accounting, marketing, operations, and finance. Exhibit 1.1 provides a definition and the four attributes of strategic management.

First, strategic management is *directed toward overall organizational goals and objectives.* That is, effort must be directed at what is best for the total organization, not just a single functional area. Some authors have referred to this perspective as "organizational versus individual rationality."[17] That is, what might look "rational" or ideal for one functional area, such as operations, may not be in the best interest of the overall firm. For example, operations may decide to schedule long production runs of similar products to lower unit costs. However, the standardized output may be counter to what the marketing department needs to appeal to a demanding target market. Similarly, research and development may "overengineer" the product to develop a far superior offering, but the design may make the product so expensive that market demand is minimal. Therefore, in this course you will look at cases and strategic issues from the perspective of the organization rather than that of the functional area(s) in which you have the strongest background.

Second, strategic management *includes multiple stakeholders in decision making.*[18] **Stakeholders** are those individuals, groups, and organizations who have a "stake" in the success of the organization, including owners (shareholders in a publicly held corporation), employees, customers, suppliers, the community at large, and so on. (We'll discuss this in more detail later in this chapter.) Managers will not be successful if they focus on a single stakeholder. For example, if the overwhelming emphasis is on generating profits for the owners, employees may become alienated, customer service may suffer, and the suppliers may resent demands for pricing concessions. However, many organizations can satisfy multiple stakeholder needs simultaneously. For example, financial performance may increase because employees who are satisfied with their jobs work harder to enhance customer satisfaction—leading to higher profits.

Third, strategic management *requires incorporating both short-term and long-term perspectives.*[19] Peter Senge, a leading strategic management author, has referred to this need as a "creative tension."[20] That is, managers must maintain both a vision for the future of the organization as well as a focus on its present operating needs. However, financial

> **stakeholders** individuals, groups, and organizations who have a stake in the success of the organization, including owners (shareholders in a publicly held corporation), employees, customers, suppliers, and the community at large.

Definition: Strategic management consists of the analyses, decisions, and actions an organization undertakes in order to create and sustain competitive advantages.

Exhibit 1.1
Strategic Management Concepts

Key Attributes of Strategic Management

- Directs the organization toward overall goals and objectives.
- Includes multiple stakeholders in decision making.
- Needs to incorporate short-term and long-term perspectives.
- Recognizes trade-offs between efficiency and effectiveness.

markets can exert significant pressures on executives to meet short-term performance targets. Studies have shown that corporate leaders often take a short-term approach to the detriment of creating long-term shareholder value. Consider the following:

> According to recent studies, only 59 percent of financial executives say they would pursue a positive net present value project if it meant missing the quarter's consensus earnings per-share estimate. Worse, 78 percent say they would sacrifice value—often a great deal of value—to smooth earnings. Similarly, managers are more likely to cut R&D to reverse an earning slide if a significant amount of the company's equity is owned by institutions with high portfolio turnover. Many companies have the same philosophy about long-term investments such as infrastructure and employee training.[21]

effectiveness tailoring actions to the needs of an organization rather than wasting effort, or "doing the right thing."

Fourth, strategic management *involves the recognition of trade-offs between effectiveness and efficiency.* Some authors have referred to this as the difference between "doing the right thing" (**effectiveness**) and "doing things right" (**efficiency**).[22] While managers must allocate and use resources wisely, they must still direct their efforts toward the attainment of overall organizational objectives. Managers who only focus on meeting short-term budgets and targets may fail to attain the broader goals. Consider the following amusing story told by Norman Augustine, former CEO of defense giant Martin Marietta (now Lockheed Martin):

efficiency performing actions at a low cost relative to a benchmark, or "doing things right."

> I am reminded of an article I once read in a British newspaper which described a problem with the local bus service between the towns of Bagnall and Greenfields. It seemed that, to the great annoyance of customers, drivers had been passing long queues of would-be passengers with a smile and a wave of the hand. This practice was, however, clarified by a bus company official who explained, "It is impossible for the drivers to keep their timetables if they must stop for passengers."[23]

Clearly, the drivers who were trying to stay on schedule had ignored the overall mission. As Augustine noted, "Impeccable logic but something seems to be missing!"

Successful managers must make many trade-offs. It is central to the practice of strategic management. At times, managers must focus on the short term and efficiency; at other times the emphasis is on the long term and expanding a firm's product-market scope in order to anticipate opportunities in the competitive environment. For example, consider Kevin Sharer's perspective. He is CEO of Amgen, the giant $15 billion biotechnology firm:

ambidexterity the challenge managers face of both aligning resources to take advantage of existing product markets as well as proactively exploring new opportunities.

> A CEO must always be switching between what I call different altitudes—tasks of different levels of abstraction and specificity. At the highest altitude you're asking the big questions: What are the company's mission and strategy? Do people understand and believe in these aims? Are decisions consistent with them? At the lowest altitude, you're looking at on-the-ground operations: Did we make that sale? What was the yield on that last lot in the factory? How many days of inventory do we have for a particular drug? And then there's everything in between: How many chemists do we need to hire this quarter? What should we pay for a small biotech company that has a promising new drug? Is our production capacity adequate to roll out a product in a new market?[24]

strategic management process strategy analysis, strategy formulation, and strategy implementation

Some authors have developed the concept of **"ambidexterity"** which refers to a manager's challenge to both align resources to take advantage of existing product markets as well as proactively explore new opportunities.[25] Strategy Spotlight 1.2 discusses ambidextrous behaviors that are required for success in today's challenging marketplace.

> **>LO 1.2**
> The strategic management process and its three interrelated and principal activities.

The Strategic Management Process

We've identified three ongoing processes—analyses, decisions, and actions—that are central to strategic management. In practice, these three processes—often referred to as strategy analysis, strategy formulation, and strategy implementation—are highly interdependent and do not take place one after the other in a sequential fashion in most companies.

1.2   strategy spotlight

Ambidextrous Behaviors: Combining Alignment and Adaptability

A recent study involving 41 business units in 10 multinational companies identified four ambidextrous behaviors in individuals. Such behaviors are the essence of ambidexterity, and they illustrate how a dual capacity for alignment and adaptability can be woven into the fabric of an organization at the individual level.

They take time and are alert to opportunities beyond the confines of their own jobs. A large computer company's sales manager became aware of a need for a new software module that nobody currently offered. Instead of selling the customer something else, he worked up a business case for the new module. With management's approval, he began working full time on its development.

They are cooperative and seek out opportunities to combine their efforts with others. A marketing manager for Italy was responsible for supporting a newly acquired subsidiary. When frustrated about the limited amount of contact she had with her peers in other countries, she began discussions with them. This led to the creation of a European marketing forum which meets quarterly to discuss issues, share best practices, and collaborate on marketing plans.

They are brokers, always looking to build internal networks. When visiting the head office in St. Louis, a Canadian plant manager heard about plans for a $10 million investment for a new tape manufacturing plant. After inquiring further about the plans and returning to

Canada, he contacted a regional manager in Manitoba, who he knew was looking for ways to build his business. With some generous support from the Manitoba government, the regional manager bid for, and ultimately won, the $10 million investment.

They are multitaskers who are comfortable wearing more than one hat. Although an operations manager for a major coffee and tea distributor was charged with running his plant as efficiently as possible, he took it upon himself to identify value-added services for his clients. By developing a dual role, he was able to manage operations and develop a promising electronic module that automatically reported impending problems inside a coffee vending machine. With corporate funding, he found a subcontractor to develop the software, and he then piloted the module in his own operations. It was so successful that it was eventually adopted by operations managers in several other countries.

A recent *Harvard Business Review* article provides some useful insights on how one can become a more ambidextrous leader. Consider the following questions:

- **Do you meet your numbers?**
- **Do you help others?**
- **What do you do for your peers?** Are you just their in-house competitor?
- **When you manage up, do you bring problems—or problems with possible solutions?**
- **Are you transparent?** Managers who get a reputation for spinning events gradually lose the trust of peers and superiors.
- **Are you developing a group of senior-managers who know you and are willing to back your original ideas with resources?**

Source: Birkinshaw, J. & Gibson, C. 2004. Building ambidexterity into an organization. *MIT Sloan Management Review,* 45(4): 47–55; and, Bower, J. L. 2007. Solve the succession crisis by growing inside-out leaders. *Harvard Business Review,* 85(11): 90–99.

Intended versus Realized Strategies

Henry Mintzberg, a management scholar at McGill University, argues that viewing the strategic management process as one in which analysis is followed by optimal decisions and their subsequent meticulous implementation neither describes the strategic management process accurately nor prescribes ideal practice.[26] He sees the business environment as far from predictable, thus limiting our ability for analysis. Further, decisions are seldom based on optimal rationality alone, given the political processes that occur in all organizations.[27]

Taking into consideration the limitations discussed above, Mintzberg proposed an alternative model. As depicted in Exhibit 1.2, decisions following from analysis, in this model, constitute the ***intended*** strategy of the firm. For a variety of reasons, the intended strategy rarely survives in its original form. Unforeseen environmental developments,

intended strategy
strategy in which organizational decisions are determined only by analysis.

Exhibit 1.2   Realized Strategy and Intended Strategy: Usually Not the Same

Source: From Mintzberg, H. & Waters, J. A., "Of Strategies: Deliberate and Emergent," *Strategic Management Journal*, Vol. 6, 1985, pp. 257–272. Copyright © John Wiley & Sons Limited. Reproduced with permission.

unanticipated resource constraints, or changes in managerial preferences may result in at least some parts of the intended strategy remaining *unrealized*. On the other hand, good managers will want to take advantage of a new opportunity presented by the environment, even if it was not part of the original set of intentions. For example, consider the wind energy industry.

> In October 2008, the United States Congress extended a key wind tax credit and many states have mandates requiring utilities to tap renewable energy. Such legislation, combined with falling clean energy costs and wildly cyclical prices for coal, oil, and gas, has created a surge in demand for companies such as GE Wind Energy, which makes large turbines and fan blades. Not surprisingly, such businesses have increased hiring and research and development, as well as profit and revenue forecasts.[28]

realized strategy strategy in which organizational decisions are determined by both analysis and unforeseen environmental developments, unanticipated resource constraints, and/or changes in managerial preferences.

Thus, the final **realized strategy** of any firm is a combination of deliberate and emergent strategies.

Next, we will address each of the three key strategic management processes: strategy analysis, strategy formulation, and strategy implementation and provide a brief overview of the chapters.

Exhibit 1.3 depicts the strategic management process and indicates how it ties into the chapters in the book. Consistent with our discussion above, we use two-way arrows to convey the interactive nature of the processes.

Strategy Analysis

strategy analysis study of firms' external and internal environments, and their fit with organizational vision and goals.

Strategy analysis may be looked upon as the starting point of the strategic management process. It consists of the "advance work" that must be done in order to effectively formulate and implement strategies. Many strategies fail because managers may want to formulate and implement strategies without a careful analysis of the overarching goals of the organization and without a thorough analysis of its external and internal environment.

Analyzing Organizational Goals and Objectives (Chapter 1)   A firm's vision, mission, and strategic objectives form a hierarchy of goals that range from broad statements of intent and bases for competitive advantage to specific, measurable strategic objectives.

Analyzing the External Environment of the Firm (Chapter 2)   Managers must monitor and scan the environment as well as analyze competitors. Two frameworks of the external environment are provided: (1) the general environment consists of several elements, such as demographic, technological, and economic segments, and (2) the industry environment consists of competitors and other organizations that may threaten the success of a firm's products and services.

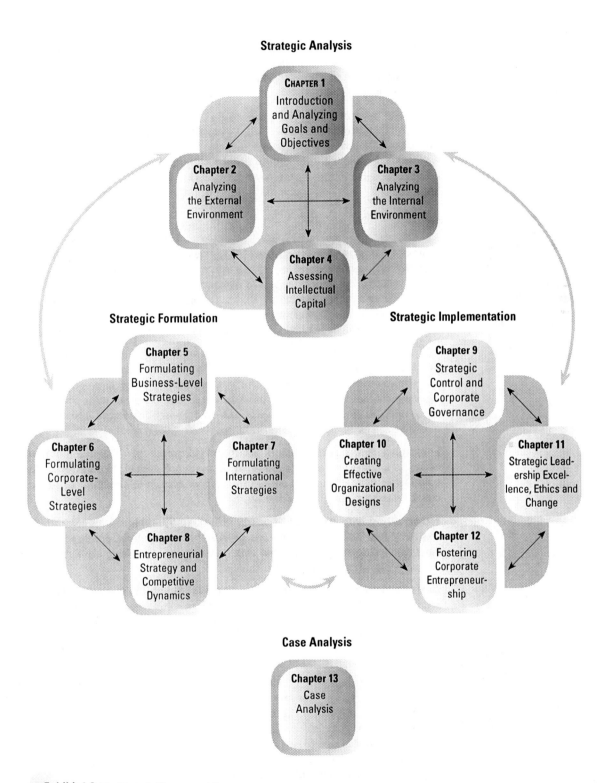

Exhibit 1.3 The Strategic Management Process

Assessing the Internal Environment of the Firm (Chapter 3)   Analyzing the strengths and relationships among the activities that constitute a firm's value chain (e.g., operations, marketing and sales, and human resource management) can be a means of uncovering potential sources of competitive advantage for the firm.[29]

Assessing a Firm's Intellectual Assets (Chapter 4)   The knowledge worker and a firm's other intellectual assets (e.g., patents, trademarks) are becoming increasingly important as the drivers of competitive advantages and wealth creation. We also assess how well the organization creates networks and relationships as well as how technology can enhance collaboration among employees and provide a means of accumulating and storing knowledge.[30]

Strategy Formulation

strategy formulation
decisions made by firms regarding investments, commitments, and other aspects of operations that create and sustain competitive advantage.

A firm's strategy formulation is developed at several levels. First, business-level strategy addresses the issue of how to compete in a given business to attain competitive advantage. Second, corporate-level strategy focuses on two issues: (a) what businesses to compete in and (b) how businesses can be managed to achieve synergy; that is, they create more value by working together than if they operate as stand-alone businesses. Third, a firm must determine the best method to develop international strategies as it ventures beyond its national boundaries. Fourth, managers must formulate effective entrepreneurial initiatives.

Formulating Business-Level Strategy (Chapter 5)   The question of how firms compete and outperform their rivals and how they achieve and sustain competitive advantages goes to the heart of strategic management. Successful firms strive to develop bases for competitive advantage, which can be achieved through cost leadership and/or differentiation as well as by focusing on a narrow or industrywide market segment.[31]

Formulating Corporate-Level Strategy (Chapter 6)   Corporate-level strategy addresses a firm's portfolio (or group) of businesses. It asks (1) What business (or businesses) should we compete in? and (2) How can we manage this portfolio of businesses to create synergies among the businesses?

Formulating International Strategy (Chapter 7)   When firms enter foreign markets, they face both opportunities and pitfalls.[32] Managers must decide not only on the most appropriate entry strategy but also how they will go about attaining competitive advantages in international markets.[33]

Entrepreneurial Strategy and Competitive Dynamics (Chapter 8)   Entrepreneurial activity aimed at new value creation is a major engine for economic growth. For entrepreneurial initiatives to succeed viable opportunities must be recognized and effective strategies must be formulated.

Strategy Implementation

strategy implementation
actions made by firms that carry out the formulated strategy, including strategic controls, organizational design, and leadership.

Clearly, sound strategies are of no value if they are not properly implemented.[34] Strategy implementation involves ensuring proper strategic controls and organizational designs, which includes establishing effective means to coordinate and integrate activities within the firm as well as with its suppliers, customers, and alliance partners.[35] Leadership plays a central role, including ensuring that the organization is committed to excellence and ethical behavior. It also promotes learning and continuous improvement and acts entrepreneurially in creating and taking advantage of new opportunities.

Strategic Control and Corporate Governance (Chapter 9)   Firms must exercise two types of strategic control. First, informational control requires that organizations continually monitor and scan the environment and respond to threats and opportunities.

Second, behavioral control involves the proper balance of rewards and incentives as well as cultures and boundaries (or constraints). Further, successful firms (those that are incorporated) practice effective corporate governance.

Creating Effective Organizational Designs (Chapter 10)   To succeed, firms must have organizational structures and designs that are consistent with their strategy. And, in today's rapidly changing competitive environments, firms must ensure that their organizational boundaries—those internal to the firm and external—are more flexible and permeable.[36] Often, organizations develop strategic alliances to capitalize on the capabilities of other organizations.

Creating a Learning Organization and an Ethical Organization (Chapter 11) Effective leaders set a direction, design the organization, and develop an organization that is committed to excellence and ethical behavior. In addition, given rapid and unpredictable change, leaders must create a "learning organization" to ensure that the entire organization can benefit from individual and collective talents.

Fostering Corporate Entrepreneurship (Chapter 12)   With rapid and unpredictable change in the global marketplace, firms must continually improve and grow as well as find new ways to renew their organizations. Corporate entrepreneurship and innovation provide firms with new opportunities, and strategies should be formulated that enhance a firm's innovative capacity.

Chapter 13, "Analyzing Strategic Management Cases," provides guidelines and suggestions on how to evaluate cases in this course. Thus, the concepts and techniques discussed in these 12 chapters can be applied to real-world organizations.

Let's now address two concepts—corporate governance and stakeholder management—that are critical to the strategic management process.

The Role of Corporate Governance and Stakeholder Management

Most business enterprises that employ more than a few dozen people are organized as corporations. As you recall from your finance classes, the overall purpose of a corporation is to maximize the long-term return to the owners (shareholders). Thus, we may ask: Who is really responsible for fulfilling this purpose? Robert Monks and Neil Minow provide a useful definition of **corporate governance** as "the relationship among various participants in determining the direction and performance of corporations. The primary participants are (1) the shareholders, (2) the management (led by the chief executive officer), and (3) the board of directors."[37] This relationship is illustrated in Exhibit 1.4.

The board of directors (BOD) are the elected representatives of the shareholders charged with ensuring that the interests and motives of management are aligned with those of the owners (i.e., shareholders). In many cases, the BOD is diligent in fulfilling its purpose. For example, Intel Corporation, the giant $43 billion maker of microprocessor chips, is widely recognized as an excellent example of sound governance practices. Its BOD follows guidelines to ensure that its members are independent (i.e., not members of the executive management team and do not have close personal ties to top executives) so that they can provide proper oversight, it has explicit guidelines on the selection of director candidates (to avoid "cronyism"), and it provides detailed procedures for formal evaluations of directors and the firm's top officers.[38] Such guidelines serve to ensure that management is acting in the best interests of shareholders.[39]

Recently, there has been much criticism as well as cynicism by both citizens and the business press about the poor job that management and the BODs of large corporations are doing. We only have to look at the scandals at firms such as Arthur Andersen, WorldCom,

>LO1.3
The vital role of corporate governance and stakeholder management as well as how "symbiosis" can be achieved among an organization's stakeholders.

corporate governance the relationship among various participants in determining the direction and performance of corporations. The primary participants are (1) the shareholders, (2) the management (led by the chief executive officer), and (3) the board of directors.

Management
(Headed by the chief executive officer)

Shareholders
(Owners)

Board of Directors
(Elected by the shareholders
to represent their interests)

Exhibit 1.4 **The Key Elements of Corporate Governance**

Enron, Tyco, and ImClone Systems.[40] Such malfeasance has led to an erosion of the public's trust in the governance of corporations. For example, a recent Gallup poll found that 90 percent of Americans felt that people leading corporations could not be trusted to look after the interests of their employees, and only 18 percent thought that corporations looked after their shareholders. Forty-three percent, in fact, believed that senior executives were in it only for themselves. In Britain, that figure, according to another poll, was an astonishing 95 percent.[41] Perhaps worst of all, in another study, 60 percent of directors (the very people who decide how much executives should earn) felt that executives were "dramatically overpaid"![42]

It is now clear that much of the bonus pay awarded to executives on Wall Street in the past few years was richly undeserved.[43] In the three years that led up to the recent collapse of seven big financial institutions, the chief executives of those firms collected a total of $80 million in performance bonuses and raked in $210 million in severance pay and earnings from stock sales. Let's take a closer look at a few of these payouts (the amounts below represent bonus pay, severance, and gains from stock sales from 2005 to late 2008):

- Richard Fuld, Lehman Brothers ($172 million)
- Kerry Killinger, Washington Mutual ($37 million)
- Martin Sullivan, American International Group ($36 million)
- Michael Perry, Indymac, Federal Bank ($20 million)
- Kenneth Thompson, Wachovia Corporation ($14 million)

Clearly, there is a strong need for improved corporate governance, and we will address this topic in Chapter 9.[44] We focus on three important mechanisms to ensure effective corporate governance: an effective and engaged board of directors, shareholder activism, and proper managerial rewards and incentives.[45] In addition to these internal controls, a key role is played by various external control mechanisms.[46] These include the auditors, banks, analysts, an active financial press, and the threat of hostile takeovers.

Alternative Perspectives of Stakeholder Management

stakeholder management a firm's strategy for recognizing and responding to the interests of all its salient stakeholders.

Generating long-term returns for the shareholders is the primary goal of a publicly held corporation.[47] As noted by former Chrysler vice chairman Robert Lutz, "We are here to serve the shareholder and create shareholder value. I insist that the only person who owns the company is the person who paid good money for it."[48]

Despite the primacy of generating shareholder value, managers who focus solely on the interests of the owners of the business will often make poor decisions that lead to negative, unanticipated outcomes.[49] For example, decisions such as mass layoffs to increase profits, ignoring issues related to conservation of the natural environment to save money, and exerting excessive pressure on suppliers to lower prices can certainly harm the firm in the long run. Such actions would likely lead to negative outcomes such as alienated employees, increased governmental oversight and fines, and disloyal suppliers.

Clearly, in addition to *shareholders,* there are other *stakeholders* (e.g. suppliers, customers) who must be explicitly taken into account in the strategic management process.[50] A stakeholder can be defined as an individual or group, inside or outside the company, that has a stake in and can influence an organization's performance. Each stakeholder group makes various claims on the company.[51] Exhibit 1.5 provides a list of major stakeholder groups and the nature of their claims on the company.

Zero Sum or Symbiosis?   There are two opposing ways of looking at the role of stakeholder management in the strategic management process.[52] The first one can be termed "zero sum." In this view, the role of management is to look upon the various stakeholders as competing for the organization's resources. In essence, the gain of one individual or group is the loss of another individual or group. For example, employees want higher wages (which drive down profits), suppliers want higher prices for their inputs and slower, more flexible delivery times (which drive up costs), customers want fast deliveries and higher quality (which drive up costs), the community at large wants charitable contributions (which take money from company goals), and so on. This zero-sum thinking is rooted, in part, in the traditional conflict between workers and management, leading to the formation of unions and sometimes ending in adversarial union–management negotiations and long, bitter strikes.

Consider, for example, the many stakeholder challenges facing Walmart, the world's largest retailer.

Walmart strives to ramp up growth while many stakeholders are watching nervously: employees and trade unions; shareholders, investors, and creditors; suppliers and joint venture partners; the governments of the U.S. and other nations where the retailer operates; and customers. In addition many non-governmental organizations (NGOs), particularly in countries where the retailer buys its products, are closely monitoring Walmart. Walmart's stakeholders have different interests, and not all of them share the firm's goals. Each group has the ability, in various degrees, to influence the firm's choices and results. Clearly, this wasn't the case when Sam Walton built his first store in Rogers, Arkansas, in 1962![53]

Exhibit 1.5
An Organization's Key Stakeholders and the Nature of Their Claims

Stakeholder Group	Nature of Claim
Stockholders	Dividends, capital appreciation
Employees	Wages, benefits, safe working environment, job security
Suppliers	Payment on time, assurance of continued relationship
Creditors	Payment of interest, repayment of principal
Customers	Value, warranties
Government	Taxes, compliance with regulations
Communities	Good citizenship behavior such as charities, employment, not polluting the environment

There will always be conflicting demands on organizations. However, organizations can achieve mutual benefit through stakeholder symbiosis, which recognizes that stakeholders are dependent upon each other for their success and well-being.[54] Consider Procter & Gamble's "laundry detergent compaction," a technique for compressing even more cleaning power into ever smaller concentrations.

In the early 2000s, P&G perfected a technique that could compact two or three times as much cleaning powder into a liquid concentration. This remarkable breakthrough has led to a change not only in consumer shopping habits, but also a revolution in industry supply-chain economics. Let's look at how several key stakeholders are affected along the supply chain:[55]

> *Consumers* love concentrated liquids because they are easier to carry, pour, and store. *Retailers,* meanwhile, prefer them because they take up less floor and shelf space, which leads to higher sales-per-square-foot—a big deal for Walmart, Target, and other big retailers. *Shipping and wholesalers,* meanwhile, prefer reduced-sized products because smaller bottles translate into reduced fuel consumption and improved warehouse space utilization. And, finally, *environmentalists* favor such products because they use less packaging and produce less waste than conventional products.

Strategy Spotlight 1.3 discusses the role of NGOs and their potential influence on companies' operations. While some organizations have been confronted for their controversial impact on the environment, others have made environmental concerns part of their business strategies and have been praised by watchdog groups for being proactive.

Crowdsourcing: Stakeholders Can Fulfill Multiple Roles   Thus far, we have implicitly assumed that stakeholders' roles are fixed. That is, a stakeholder is . . . pick one: a customer, supplier, employee, competitor, and so fourth. However, in practice, that is certainly not the case. Consider Shaw Industries, a vertically integrated carpet producer (which we discuss in Chapter 6). It acquired Amoco's polypropylene fiber manufacturing facilities, which provide carpet fibers for both internal use and sale to other manufacturers. Thus, some of Shaw's competitors are also its customers. Similarly, a retailer may share space on tractor trailers that it uses to ship products to its stores. This helps to decrease everyone's logistics costs—hence rivals become customers (or collaborators). And rivals can become key allies (within the boundaries of the same firm) when a firm acquires competitors to consolidate an industry—as has been the case in a myriad of industries such as finance, defense, and funeral homes.

crowdsourcing
practice wherein the Internet is used to tap a broad range of individuals and groups to generate ideas and solve problems.

To show how stakeholder roles are becoming more fluid, we'd like to introduce a concept that will be a theme through the text: **crowdsourcing.**[56] When and where did the term originate? In January 2006, open sourcing was, for most businesspeople, little more than an online curiosity. At that time, Jeff Howe of *Wired* magazine started to write an article about the phenomenon. However, he soon discovered a far more important story to be told: Large—as well as small—companies in a wide variety of industries had begun farming out serious tasks to individuals and groups on the Internet. Together with his editor, Mark Robinson, they coined a new term to describe the phenomenon. In June 2006, the article appeared in which *crowdsourcing* was defined as the tapping of the "latent talent of the (online) crowd." It has become the term of choice for a process that is infiltrating many aspects of business life.

Clearly, *crowdsourcing* has claimed some well-known successes, particularly on the product development front: Consider:

- The Linux operating system, created as an open-source alternative to Windows and UNIX, can be downloaded free and altered to suit any user's needs. And, with all the firepower brought to bear by the online open-source community, bugs in the system get fixed in a matter of hours.

1.3

strategy spotlight

NGOs: A Key Stakeholder Group

Although the number of NGOs worldwide is hard to determine, according to a recent study there are at least 40,000 multinational NGOs. In addition, there are also hundreds of thousands based in individual countries. The focus of most of these is, at least partially, on the welfare of the environment.

What are NGOs? NGOs describe a wide array of groups and organizations—from activist groups "reclaiming the streets" to development organizations delivering aid and providing essential public services. Other NGOs are research-driven policy organizations, looking to engage with decision makers. Still others see themselves as watchdogs, casting a critical eye over current events.

The largest NGOs are multinational operations with enormous reach and influence. They include well-established organizations such as Greenpeace, Sierra Club, World Wildlife Fund, Nature Conservancy, Environmental Defense, Natural Resources Defense Council, Conservation International, Friends of the Earth, and National Wildlife Federation. Many of these established groups have been around for more than 30 years and can still have a major public influence. In fact, according to a recent study that polled opinion leaders, 55 percent trust NGOs, versus only 6 percent that trust businesses.

Sources: Esty, D. C. & Winston, A. S. 2009. *Green to Gold.* Hoboken, NJ: Wiley: 69–70; Anonymous. 2009. Timberland Steps It Up a Notch, Commit to Amazon Protections. *www.greenpeace.org.* July 29: np; and, Anonymous. undated. The Rise and Role of NGOs in Sustainable Development. *www.iisd.org.* np.

Some of these organizations are confrontational, taking a range of actions to reach their goals, from making waves in courts (the National Resources Defense Council), to boarding oil rigs (Greenpeace), to illegal activities, exemplified by arsonists' actions in the Colorado mountain resort of Vail. It is impossible for firms to predict all potential actions, especially irrational ones. However, they can reduce the odds of being attacked. In contrast to Vail, other ski resorts, such as Aspen, have confronted environmental issues and made them a central focus of their business strategies. For example, Aspen ski company decided to rely solely on wind power to power all of its operations. As a result, the company was rated as the number one ski resort in the West in addressing environmental issues by respected watchdog groups. Vail, on the other hand, is still trying to catch up.

As another example of a firm's environmentally sensitive behavior, Nike recently announced that it would not source any leather from the Amazon until deforestation for cattle expansion is halted. Their announcement, coupled with a similar one by Timberland, followed the release of a Greenpeace report entitled "Slaughtering the Amazon." It documented a three-year investigation that tracked beef, leather, and other cattle products from ranches involved in deforestation at the heart of the Amazon rainforest.

ethics

- One of Amazon's smartest moves was to invite their customers to write online reviews. The customers are neither paid nor controlled by the company, but the content that they create adds enormous value to other customers and, therefore, to Amazon.
- Roughly five million users per month swear by Wikipedia, the free online encyclopedia created and updated by Internet volunteers to the tune of roughly two million articles and counting.

Throughout the book, we will introduce examples of *crowdsourcing* to show its relevance to key strategy concepts. For example, in Chapter 3, we describe how RYZ, a tiny high-end sneaker company, relies on its customers to both design and market its products. Chapter 5 discusses Netflix, which recently awarded a $1 million prize to a group of programming experts who built a system that was 10 percent better than Cinematch—its in-house system to personalize movie recommendations. And, in Chapter 6, we discuss how a strategic alliance helped two firms more effectively cultivate and create animation content using the internet.

strategy spotlight   1.4

How Goldcorp Used Crowdsourcing to Strike Gold!

A little over a decade ago, Toronto-based gold mining company Goldcorp was in big trouble. Besieged by strikes, lingering debts, and an exceedingly high cost of production, the firm had terminated mining operations. Conditions in the marketplace were quite poor and the gold market was contracting. Most analysts assumed that the company's 50-year-old mine in Red Lake, Ontario, was nearly dead. Without solid evidence of substantial new gold deposits, Goldcorp was likely to fold.

Clearly, CEO Robert McEwen needed a miracle. He was frustrated with his in-house geologists' reliability in estimating the value and location of gold on his property. He did something that was unprecedented in the industry: He published his geological data on the Web for all to see and he challenged the world to do the prospecting. The "Goldcorp Challenge" posted a total of $575,000 in prize money to be awarded to the participants who submitted the best methods and estimates.

His reasoning: If he could attract the attention of world-class talent to the problem of finding more gold in Red Lake, just as Linux managed to attract world-class programmers to the cause of better software, he could tap into thousands of minds that he wouldn't otherwise

have access to. He could also speed up exploration and improve his odds of discovery.

Although his geologists were appalled at the idea of exposing their super-secret data to the world, the response was immediate. More than 1,400 scientists, engineers, and geologists from 50 countries downloaded the company's data and started their viral exploration. Says McEwen: "We had math, advanced physics, intelligent systems, computer graphics, and organic solutions to inorganic problems. There were capabilities I had never seen before in the industry. When I saw the computer graphics, I almost fell out of my chair."

The panel of five judges was astonished by the creativity of the submissions. The top winner, which won $105,000, was a collaboration by two groups in Australia: Fractal Graphics, of West Perth, and Taylor Wall & Associates, in Queensland, which together had developed a powerful 3-D graphical depiction of the mine. One of the team members humorously stated: "I've never been to a mine. I'd never even been to Canada." Overall, the contestants identified 110 targets on the Red Lake property, more than 80 percent of which yielded substantial quantities of gold. In fact, since the challenge was initiated, an astounding 8 million ounces of gold have been found—worth well over $3 billion (given gold's fluctuating market value). Not a bad return on a half million dollar investment.

As of early 2011, Goldcorp had annual revenues of $3 billion and a market value of $33 billion! Not bad for a once failing firm . . .

Sources: de Castella, T. 2010. Should We Trust the Wisdom of Crowds? *news.bbc.co.uk*. July 5: np; Libert, B. & Spector, J. 2008. *We Are Smarter Than Me.* Philadelphia, PA: Wharton School Publishing; Tapscott, D. & Williams, A. D. 2007. Innovation in the Age of Mass Collaboration. *www.businessweek.com*. February 1: np; and, Tischler, L. 2002. He Struck Gold on the Net (Really). *fastcompany.com*. May 2: np.

crowdsourcing

Strategy Spotlight 1.4 describes how Goldcorp, a Toronto-based mining company, crowdsourced the expertise required to identify the best location to mine gold on the firm's property. Goldcorp invited geologists around the world to compete for $575,000 in prize money for analyzing its geological data. It was a remarkable success!

Social Responsibility and Environmental Sustainability: Moving beyond the Immediate Stakeholders

Organizations cannot ignore the interests and demands of stakeholders such as citizens and society in general that are beyond its immediate constituencies—customers, owners, suppliers, and employees. The realization that firms have multiple stakeholders and that evaluating their performance must go beyond analyzing their financial results has led to a new way of thinking about businesses and their relationship to society. We address this important issue in the following three sections.

First, *social responsibility* recognizes that businesses must respond to society's expectations regarding their obligations to society. Second, an emerging perspective, *shared value,* views social responsibility not just as an added cost to businesses. Instead, it views businesses as creators of value that they then share with society in a mutually beneficial relationship. Finally, we discuss the *triple bottom line approach* to evaluating a firm's performance. This perspective takes into account financial, social, and environmental performance.

Social Responsibility is the expectation that businesses or individuals will strive to improve the overall welfare of society.[57] From the perspective of a business, this means that managers must take active steps to make society better by virtue of the business being in existence.[58] Similar to norms and values, actions that constitute socially responsible behavior tend to change over time. In the 1970s affirmative action was a high priority and during the 1990s and up to the present time, the public has been concerned about environmental quality. Many firms have responded to this by engaging in recycling and reducing waste. And in the wake of terrorist attacks on New York City and the Pentagon, as well as the continuing threat from terrorists worldwide, a new kind of priority has arisen: the need to be vigilant concerning public safety.

> **social responsibility** the expectation that businesses or individuals will strive to improve the overall welfare of society.

Today, demands for greater corporate responsibility have accelerated.[59] These include corporate critics, social investors, activists, and, increasingly, customers who claim to assess corporate responsibility when making purchasing decisions. Such demands go well beyond product and service quality.[60] They include a focus on issues such as labor standards, environmental sustainability, financial and accounting reporting, procurement, and environmental practices.[61] At times, a firm's reputation can be tarnished by exceedingly poor judgment on the part of one of its managers. For example, BP CEO Tony Hayward's decision to withhold information from the public about the magnitude of the oil spill in the Gulf of Mexico further damaged the firm's reputation.

> **>LO1.4**
> The importance of social responsibility, including environmental sustainability, and how it can enhance a corporation's innovation strategy.

A key stakeholder group that appears to be particularly susceptible to corporate social responsibility (CSR) initiatives is customers.[62] Surveys indicate a strong positive relationship between CSR behaviors and consumers' reactions to a firm's products and services.[63] For example:

- Corporate Citizenship's poll conducted by Cone Communications found that "84 percent of Americans say they would be likely to switch brands to one associated with a good cause, if price and quality are similar."[64]
- Hill & Knowlton/Harris's Interactive poll reveals that "79 percent of Americans take corporate citizenship into account when deciding whether to buy a particular company's product and 37 percent consider corporate citizenship an important factor when making purchasing decisions."[65]

Such findings are consistent with a large body of research that confirms the positive influence of CSR on consumers' company evaluations and product purchase intentions across a broad range of product categories.

The Concept of "Shared Value" Capitalism is typically viewed as an unparalleled vehicle for meeting human needs, improving efficiency, creating jobs, and building wealth.[66] However, a narrow conceptualization of capitalism has prevented business from harnessing its full potential to meet society's broader challenges. The opportunities have always been there but have been overlooked. It is increasingly acknowledged that businesses acting as businesses, not as charitable donors, are the most powerful force for addressing the pressing issues that we face. This new conception of capitalism redefines the purpose of the corporation as creating shared value, not just profit per se. This will drive the next wave of innovation and productivity growth in the global economy.

Shared value can be defined as policies and operating practices that enhance the competitiveness of a company while simultaneously advancing the economic and social conditions in which it operates. Shared value creation focuses on identifying and expanding the connections between societal and economic progress.[67]

Shared value is not about personal values. Nor is it about "sharing" the value created by firms—a redistribution approach. Instead, it is about expanding the total pool of economic and social value. A good example of this difference is the fair trade movement:

> Fair trade aims to increase the proportion of revenue that goes to poor farmers by paying them higher prices for the same crops. Though this may be a noble sentiment, fair trade is mostly about redistribution rather than expanding the overall amount of value created.

> A shared value perspective, however, focuses on improving growing techniques and strengthening the local cluster of supporting suppliers and other institutions in order to increase farmers' efficiency, yields, product quality, and sustainability. This leads to a bigger pie of revenue and profits that benefits both farmers and the companies that buy from them. Early studies of cocoa farmers in the Ivory Coast, for example, suggest that while fair trade can increase farmers' incomes by 10 to 20 percent, shared value investments can raise their incomes by more than 300 percent! Initial investment and time may be required to implement new procurement practices and develop the cluster. However, the return will be greater economic value and broader strategic benefits for all participants.

A firm's value chain inevitably affects—and is affected by—numerous societal issues. Opportunities to create shared value arise because societal problems can create economic costs in the firm's value chain. Such external factors inflict internal costs to the firm, even in the absence of regulation or resource taxes. For example, excess product packaging and greenhouse gases are not just costly to the environment but also costly to businesses.

The shared value perspective acknowledges that the congruence between societal progress and value chain productivity is far greater than traditionally believed. The synergy increases when firms consider societal issues from a shared value perspective and invent new ways of operating to address them. So far, however, relatively few firms have reaped the full productivity benefits.

Let's look at what a few companies are doing to reap "win-win" benefits by addressing societal challenges and, in so doing, enjoying higher productivity and profitability:

- Hindustan Unilever is creating a new direct-to-home distribution system. It is operated by underprivileged female entrepreneurs in Indian villages of fewer than 2,000 people. The firm provides microcredit and training and has more than 45,000 entrepreneurs covering about 100,000 villages across 15 Indian states. Project Shakti, the name of the distribution system, provides benefits to communities not only by giving women skills that often double their household income but also by reducing the spread of communicable diseases through increased access to hygiene products. Thus, the unique ability of business to market to hard-to-reach consumers can benefit society by getting life-altering products into the hands of people that need them. Project Shakti now accounts for 5 percent of Unilever's total revenues in India. It has also extended the company's reach into rural areas and built its brand in media-dark regions, creating major economic value for the company.
- Leading companies have learned that because of lost workdays and diminished employee productivity, poor health costs them far more than health benefits do. For example, Johnson & Johnson has helped employees stop smoking (a two-thirds reduction in the past 15 years) and has implemented many other new wellness programs. Such initiatives have saved the company $250 million on health care costs, a return of $2.71 for every dollar spent on wellness from 2002 to 2008. Further, Johnson & Johnson has benefited from a more present and productive workforce.

- Olam International, a leading cashew producer, traditionally shipped its nuts from Africa to Asia for processing. By opening local processing plants and training workers in Tanzania, Mozambique, Nigeria, and the Ivory Coast, Olam cut its processing and shipping costs by as much as 25 percent and greatly reduced carbon emissions! Further, Olam built preferred relationships with local farmers. It has provided direct employment to 17,000 people—95 percent of whom are women—and indirect employment to an equal number of people, in rural areas where jobs otherwise were not available.

The Triple Bottom Line: Incorporating Financial as Well as Environmental and Social Costs   Many companies are now measuring what has been called a **"triple bottom line."** This involves assessing financial, social, and environmental performance. Shell, NEC, Procter & Gamble, and others have recognized that failing to account for the environmental and social costs of doing business poses risks to the company and its community.[68]

> **triple bottom line** assessment of a firm's financial, social, and environmental performance.

The environmental revolution has been almost four decades in the making.[69] In the 1960s and 1970s, companies were in a state of denial regarding their firms' impact on the natural environment. However, a series of visible ecological problems created a groundswell for strict governmental regulation. In the U.S., Lake Erie was "dead," and in Japan, people died of mercury poisoning. Clearly, the effects of global warming are being felt throughout the world. Some other examples include the following:

- Ice roads are melting, so Canadian diamond miners must airlift equipment at great cost instead of trucking it in.
- More severe storms and rising seas mean oil companies must build stronger rigs, and cities must build higher seawalls.
- The loss of permafrost and protective sea ice may force villages like Alaska's Shismaref to relocate.
- Yukon River salmon and fisheries are threatened by a surge of parasites associated with a jump in water temperature.
- Later winters have let beetles spread in British Columbia, killing 22 million acres of pine forests, an area the size of Maine.

● Windpower is a more sustainable, environmentally friendly option than nuclear power plants or coal- or oil-fired power plants.

- In Mali, Africa, crops are threatened. The rainy season is now too short for rice, and the dry season is too hot for potatoes.[70]

Stuart Hart, writing in the *Harvard Business Review,* addresses the magnitude of problems and challenges associated with the natural environment:

> The challenge is to develop a *sustainable global economy:* an economy that the planet is capable of supporting indefinitely. Although we may be approaching ecological recovery in the developed world, the planet as a whole remains on an unsustainable course. Increasingly, the scourges of the late twentieth century—depleted farmland, fisheries, and forests; choking urban pollution; poverty; infectious disease; and migration—are spilling over geopolitical borders. The simple fact is this: in meeting our needs, we are destroying the ability of future generations to meet theirs . . . corporations are the only organizations with the resources, the technology, the global reach, and, ultimately, the motivation to achieve sustainability.[71]

Environmental sustainability is now a value embraced by the most competitive and successful multinational companies.[72] The McKinsey Corporation's survey of more than 400 senior executives of companies around the world found that 92 percent agreed with former Sony President Akio Morita's contention that the environmental challenge will be one of the central issues in the 21st century.[73] Virtually all executives acknowledged their firm's responsibility to control pollution, and 83 percent agreed that corporations have an environmental responsibility for their products even after they are sold.

For many successful firms, environmental values are now becoming a central part of their cultures and management processes.[74] And, as noted earlier, environmental impacts are being audited and accounted for as the "third bottom line." According to one 2004 corporate report, "If we aren't good corporate citizens as reflected in a Triple Bottom Line that takes into account social and environmental responsibilities along with financial ones—eventually our stock price, our profits, and our entire business could suffer."[75] Also, a CEO survey on sustainability by Accenture debunks the notion that sustainability and profitability are mutually exclusive corporate goals. The study found that sustainability is being increasingly recognized as a source of cost efficiencies and revenue growth. In fact, 80 percent of the more than 760 CEOs surveyed indicated that the recent deep recession has only served to heighten the importance of sustainability for their businesses.[76]

Let's take a look at how Dell is making money and helping their customers at the end of their product's technology life cycle:[77]

> Since computers generally have a rather short life cycle, companies are faced with real challenges over environmental and data liabilities when they need to dispose of obsolete equipment. Dell's Asset Recovery System helps customers deal with both the software and environmental cleanup they need.
>
> For about $25 for a piece of equipment, Dell comes to your office and takes your computer away. They first perform a "destructive data overwrite" to eliminate all digital information on the computer, and then they dismantle the machine. Dell refurbishes and reuses some of the parts, and recycles the plastic. In the end, only 1 percent of the old computer's volume goes to a landfill.
>
> This environmentally sustainable service enhances customer relationships and helps to drive sales. Dell discovered that the take-back role comes, conveniently, when Dell is delivering the next generation of equipment. Dell's executives would be happy if this service was just breaking even—but they are turning a profit on it. As noted by Daniel Esty and Andrew Winston in their book *Green to Gold,* "They seem a bit sheepish about doing so. We see no need to apologize."

Clearly, there are many other examples of how firms have profited by investing in socially responsible behavior, including those activities that enhance environmental sustainability. However, how do such "socially responsible" companies fare in terms of shareholder returns compared to benchmarks such as the Standard & Poor's 500 index? Strategy Spotlight 1.5 focuses on this issue.

>LO1.5
The need for greater empowerment throughout the organization.

The Strategic Management Perspective: An Imperative throughout the Organization

Strategic management requires managers to take an integrative view of the organization and assess how all of the functional areas and activities fit together to help an organization achieve its goals and objectives. This cannot be accomplished if only the top managers in the organization take an integrative, strategic perspective of issues facing the firm and everyone else "fends for themselves" in their independent, isolated functional areas. Instead, people throughout the organization must strive toward overall goals.

1.5

Socially Responsible Investing (SRI): Can You Do Well by Doing Good?

SRI is a broad-based approach to investing that now encompasses an estimated $3.07 trillion out of $25.2 trillion in the U.S. investment marketplace today. SRI recognizes that corporate responsibility and societal concerns are valid parts of investment decisions. With SRI, investors have the opportunity to put their money to work to build a more sustainable world while earning competitive returns both today and over time.

And, as the saying goes, nice guys don't have to finish last. The ING SRI, which tracks the stocks of 50 companies, enjoyed a 47.4 percent return in 2009. That easily beat the 26.5 percent gain of the Standard & Poor's 500-stock index. And a review of the 145 socially responsible equity mutual and exchange-traded funds tracked by Morningstar shows that 65 percent of them outperformed the S&P 500 last year.

Sources: Kaahwarski, T. 2010. It Pays to Be Good. *Bloomberg BusinessWeek.* February 1 & 8: 69; Anonymous. undated. Performance and Socially Responsible Investments. *www.socialinvest.org.* np; Anonymous. Socially Responsible Investing Facts. *www.socialinvest.* np.

strategy spotlight

Many socially responsible investing funds shun alcohol, tobacco, gambling, and defense companies—while embracing tech. Thus, they clearly benefited from the 2009 returns of popular holdings, including Cisco (+46.9%), Microsoft (+60.5%), Google (+101.5%), and Intel (+43.9%). Over the recent 10-year period, Parnassus Equity Income and New Alternatives gained nearly 7 percent a year, on average, versus a 9 percent cumulative loss for the S&P 500 over the same period.

Another indication of the competitive performance of SRI funds is the performance of SRI indices over the long term. The longest running SRI index, the FTSE KLD 400, was started in 1990. Since that time, it has continued to perform competitively. It returned an average of 9.51 percent a year from inception through December 31, 2009, compared to 8.66 percent for the S&P 500 over the same period.

ethics

The need for such a perspective is accelerating in today's increasingly complex, interconnected, ever-changing, global economy. As noted by Peter Senge of MIT, the days when Henry Ford, Alfred Sloan, and Tom Watson (top executives at Ford, General Motors, and IBM, respectively) "learned for the organization are gone." He goes on to say:

> In an increasingly dynamic, interdependent, and unpredictable world, it is simply no longer possible for anyone to "figure it all out at the top." The old model, "the top thinks and the local acts," must now give way to integrating thinking and acting at all levels. While the challenge is great, so is the potential payoff. "The person who figures out how to harness the collective genius of the people in his or her organization," according to former Citibank CEO Walter Wriston, "is going to blow the competition away."[78]

To develop and mobilize people and other assets, leaders are needed throughout the organization.[79] No longer can organizations be effective if the top "does the thinking" and the rest of the organization "does the work." Everyone must be involved in the strategic management process. There is a critical need for three types of leaders:

- *Local line leaders* who have significant profit-and-loss responsibility.
- *Executive leaders* who champion and guide ideas, create a learning infrastructure, and establish a domain for taking action.
- *Internal networkers* who, although they have little positional power and formal authority, generate their power through the conviction and clarity of their ideas.[80]

Sally Helgesen, author of *The Web of Inclusion: A New Architecture for Building Great Organizations,* also expressed the need for leaders throughout the organization. She asserted that many organizations "fall prey to the heroes-and-drones syndrome, exalting the value of those in powerful positions while implicitly demeaning the contributions of those who fail to achieve top rank."[81] Culture and processes in which leaders emerge at all levels, both up and down as well as across the organization, typify today's high-performing firms.[82]

Top-level executives are key in setting the tone for the empowerment of employees. Consider Richard Branson, founder of the Virgin Group, whose core businesses include retail operations, hotels, communications, and an airline. He is well known for creating a culture and an informal structure where anybody in the organization can be involved in generating and acting upon new business ideas. In an interview, he stated,

> [S]peed is something that we are better at than most companies. We don't have formal board meetings, committees, etc. If someone has an idea, they can pick up the phone and talk to me. I can vote "done, let's do it." Or, better still, they can just go ahead and do it. They know that they are not going to get a mouthful from me if they make a mistake. Rules and regulations are not our forte. Analyzing things to death is not our kind of thing. We very rarely sit back and analyze what we do.[83]

To inculcate a strategic management perspective throughout the organization, managers must often make a major effort to effect transformational change. This involves extensive communication, incentives, training, and development. For example, under the direction of Nancy Snyder, a corporate vice president, Whirlpool, the world's largest producer of household appliances, brought about a significant shift in the firm's reputation as an innovator.[84] This five-year initiative included both financial investments in capital spending as well as a series of changes in management processes, including training innovation mentors, making innovation a significant portion of leadership development programs, enrolling all salaried employees in online courses in business innovation, and providing employees with an innovation portal that allows them access to multiple innovation tools and data.

We'd like to close with our favorite example of how inexperience can be a virtue. It further reinforces the benefits of having broad involvement throughout the organization in the strategic management process (see Strategy Spotlight 1.6).

hierarchy of goals
organizational goals ranging from, at the top, those that are less specific yet able to evoke powerful and compelling mental images, to, at the bottom, those that are more specific and measurable.

Ensuring Coherence in Strategic Direction

Employees and managers throughout the organization must strive toward common goals and objectives.[85] By specifying desired results, it becomes much easier to move forward. Otherwise, when no one knows what the firm is striving to accomplish, they have no idea of what to work toward.

Organizations express priorities best through stated goals and objectives that form a **hierarchy of goals,** which includes its vision, mission, and strategic objectives.[86] What visions may lack in specificity, they make up for in their ability to evoke powerful and compelling mental images. On the other hand, strategic objectives tend to be more specific and provide a more direct means of determining if the organization is moving toward broader, overall goals.[87] Visions, as one would expect, also have longer time horizons than either mission statements or strategic objectives. Exhibit 1.6 depicts the hierarchy of goals and its relationship to two attributes: general versus specific and time horizon.

>LO1.6
How an awareness of a hierarchy of strategic goals can help an organization achieve coherence in its strategic direction.

Organizational Vision

vision
organizational goal(s) that evoke(s) powerful and compelling mental images.

A **vision** is a goal that is "massively inspiring, overarching, and long term."[88] It represents a destination that is driven by and evokes passion. A vision may or may not succeed; it depends on whether everything else happens according to a firm's strategy. As Mark Hurd, Hewlett-Packard's CEO, humorously pointed out, "Without execution, vision is just another word for hallucination."[89]

1.6   strategy spotlight

Strategy and the Value of Inexperience

Peter Gruber, chairman of Mandalay Entertainment, explained how his firm benefited from the creative insights of an inexperienced intern.

Sometimes life is all about solving problems. In the movie business, at least, there seems to be one around every corner. One of the most effective lessons I've learned about tackling problems is to start by asking not "How to?" but rather "What if?" I learned that lesson from a young woman who was interning on a film I was producing. She actually saved the movie from being shelved by the studio.

The movie, *Gorillas in the Mist*, had turned into a logistical nightmare. We wanted to film at an altitude of 11,000 feet, in the middle of the jungle, in Rwanda—then on the verge of a revolution—and to use more than 200 animals. Warner Brothers, the studio financing the movie, worried that we would exceed our budget. But our biggest problem was that the screenplay required the gorillas to do what we wrote—in other words, to "act." If they couldn't or wouldn't, we'd have to fall back on a formula that the studio had seen fail before: using dwarfs in gorilla suits on a soundstage.

We called an emergency meeting to solve these problems. In the middle of it, a young intern asked, "What if you let the gorillas write the story?" Everyone laughed and wondered what she was doing in the meeting with experienced filmmakers. Hours later, someone casually asked her what she had meant. She said, "What if you sent a really good cinematographer into the jungle with a ton of film to shoot the gorillas. Then you could write a story around what the gorillas did on film." It was a brilliant idea. And we did exactly what she suggested: We sent Alan Root, an Academy Award–nominated cinematographer, into the jungle for three weeks. He came back with phenomenal footage that practically wrote the story for us. We shot the film for $20 million—half of the original budget!

This woman's inexperience enabled her to see opportunities where we saw only boundaries. This experience taught me three things. First, ask high-quality questions, like "What if?" Second, find people who add new perspectives and create new conversations. As experienced filmmakers, we believed that our way was the only way—and that the intern lacked the experience to have an opinion. Third, pay attention to those with new voices. If you want unlimited options for solving a problem, engage the what if before you lock onto the how to. You'll be surprised by what you discover.

Source: Gruber, P. 1998. My greatest lesson. *Fast Company* 15: 88, 90.

Leaders must develop and implement a vision. In a survey of executives from 20 different countries, respondents were asked what they believed were a leader's key traits.[90] Ninety-eight percent responded that "a strong sense of vision" was the most important. Similarly, when asked about the critical knowledge skills, the leaders cited "strategy formulation to achieve a vision" as the most important skill. In other words, managers need

Exhibit 1.6   **A Hierarchy of Goals**

to have not only a vision but also a plan to implement it. Regretfully, 90 percent reported a lack of confidence in their own skills and ability to conceive a vision. For example, T. J. Rogers, CEO of Cypress Semiconductor, an electronic chipmaker that faced some difficulties in 1992, lamented that his own shortsightedness caused the danger, "I did not have the 50,000-foot view, and got caught."[91]

One of the most famous examples of a vision is Disneyland's: "To be the happiest place on earth." Other examples are:

- "Restoring patients to full life." (Medtronic)
- "We want to satisfy all of our customers' financial needs and help them succeed financially." (Wells Fargo)
- "Our vision is to be the world's best quick service restaurant." (McDonald's)
- "To organize the world's information and make it universally accessible and useful." (Google)

Although such visions cannot be accurately measured by a specific indicator of how well they are being achieved, they do provide a fundamental statement of an organization's values, aspirations, and goals. Such visions go well beyond narrow financial objectives, of course, and strive to capture both the minds and hearts of employees.

The vision statement may also contain a slogan, diagram, or picture—whatever grabs attention.[92] The aim is to capture the essence of the more formal parts of the vision in a few words that are easily remembered, yet that evoke the spirit of the entire vision statement. In its 20-year battle with Xerox, Canon's slogan, or battle cry, was "Beat Xerox." Motorola's slogan is "Total Customer Satisfaction." Outboard Marine Corporation's slogan is "To Take the World Boating."

Clearly, vision statements are not a cure-all. Sometimes they backfire and erode a company's credibility. Visions fail for many reasons, including the following:[93]

The Walk Doesn't Match the Talk   An idealistic vision can arouse employee enthusiasm. However, that same enthusiasm can be quickly dashed if employees find that senior management's behavior is not consistent with the vision. Often, vision is a sloganeering campaign of new buzzwords and empty platitudes like "devotion to the customer," "teamwork," or "total quality" that aren't consistently backed by management's action.

Irrelevance   Visions created in a vacuum—unrelated to environmental threats or opportunities or an organization's resources and capabilities—often ignore the needs of those who are expected to buy into them. Employees reject visions that are not anchored in reality.

Not the Holy Grail   Managers often search continually for the one elusive solution that will solve their firm's problems—that is, the next "holy grail" of management. They may have tried other management fads only to find that they fell short of their expectations. However, they remain convinced that one exists. A vision simply cannot be viewed as a magic cure for an organization's illness.

Too Much Focus Leads to Missed Opportunities   The downside of too much focus is that in directing people and resources toward a grandiose vision, losses can be devastating. Consider, Samsung's ambitious venture into automobile manufacturing:

> In 1992, Kun-Hee Lee, chairman of South Korea's Samsung Group, created a bold strategy to become one of the 10 largest car makers by 2010. Seduced by the clarity of the vision, Samsung bypassed staged entry through a joint venture or initial supply contract. Instead, Samsung borrowed heavily to build a state-of-the-art research and design facility and erect a greenfield factory, complete with cutting-edge robotics. Samsung Auto suffered operating losses and crushing interest charges from the beginning. And within a few years the business was divested for a fraction of the initial investment.[94]

An Ideal Future Irreconciled with the Present   Although visions are not designed to mirror reality, they must be anchored somehow in it. People have difficulty identifying with a vision that paints a rosy picture of the future but does not account for the often hostile environment in which the firm competes or that ignores some of the firm's weaknesses.

Mission Statements

A company's **mission statement** differs from its vision in that it encompasses both the purpose of the company as well as the basis of competition and competitive advantage.

Exhibit 1.7 contains the vision statement and mission statement of WellPoint Health Network, a giant $63 billion managed health care organization. Note that while the vision statement is broad based, the mission statement is more specific and focused on the means by which the firm will compete.

Effective mission statements incorporate the concept of stakeholder management, suggesting that organizations must respond to multiple constituencies. Customers, employees, suppliers, and owners are the primary stakeholders, but others may also play an important role. Mission statements also have the greatest impact when they reflect an organization's enduring, overarching strategic priorities and competitive positioning. Mission statements also can vary in length and specificity. The two mission statements below illustrate these issues.

> **mission statement**
> a set of organizational goals that include both the purpose of the organization, its scope of operations, and the basis of its competitive advantage.

- To produce superior financial returns for our shareholders as we serve our customers with the highest quality transportation, logistics, and e-commerce. (Federal Express)
- To be the very best in the business. Our game plan is status go . . . we are constantly looking ahead, building on our strengths, and reaching for new goals. In our quest of these goals, we look at the three stars of the Brinker logo and are reminded of the basic values that are the strength of this company . . . People, Quality and Profitability. Everything we do at Brinker must support these core values. We also look at the eight golden flames depicted in our logo, and are reminded of the fire that ignites our mission and makes up the heart and soul of this incredible company. These flames are: Customers, Food, Team, Concepts, Culture, Partners, Community, and Shareholders. As keeper of these flames, we will continue to build on our strengths and work together to be the best in the business. (Brinker International, whose restaurant chains include Chili's and On the Border)[95]

Few mission statements identify profit or any other financial indicator as the sole purpose of the firm. Indeed, many do not even mention profit or shareholder return.[96]

Exhibit 1.7
Comparing WellPoint Health Network's Vision and Mission

Vision

WellPoint *will redefine our industry:*
Through a new generation of consumer-friendly products that put individuals back in control of their future.

Mission

The WellPoint companies provide health *security* by offering a *choice* of quality branded health and related financial services *designed* to meet the *changing* expectations of individuals, families, and their sponsors throughout a *lifelong* relationship.

Source: WellPoint Health Network company records.

Employees of organizations or departments are usually the mission's most important audience. For them, the mission should help to build a common understanding of purpose and commitment to nurture.

A good mission statement, by addressing each principal theme, must communicate why an organization is special and different. Two studies that linked corporate values and mission statements with financial performance found that the most successful firms mentioned values other than profits. The less successful firms focused almost entirely on profitability.[97] In essence, profit is the metaphorical equivalent of oxygen, food, and water that the body requires. They are not the point of life, but without them, there is no life.

Vision statements tend to be quite enduring and seldom change. However, a firm's mission can and should change when competitive conditions dramatically change or the firm is faced with new threats or opportunities.

The transformation of the James Irvine Foundation is described in Strategy Spotlight 1.7. It changed from a philanthropic foundation with the broad mission of "promoting the welfare of the people of California" to a narrow mission that focuses on the education of youths ages 14 to 24.

strategic objectives
A set of organizational goals that are used to operationalize the mission statement and that are specific and cover a well-defined time frame.

Strategic Objectives

Strategic objectives are used to operationalize the mission statement.[98] That is, they help to provide guidance on how the organization can fulfill or move toward the "higher goals" in the goal hierarchy—the mission and vision. Thus, they are more specific and cover a more well-defined time frame. Setting objectives demands a yardstick to measure the fulfillment of the objectives.[99]

Exhibit 1.8 lists several firms' strategic objectives—both financial and nonfinancial. While most of them are directed toward generating greater profits and returns for the owners of the business, others are directed at customers or society at large.

Exhibit 1.8
Strategic Objectives

Strategic Objectives (Financial)

- Increase sales growth 6 percent to 8 percent and accelerate core net earnings growth from 13 percent to 15 percent per share in each of the next 5 years. (Procter & Gamble)
- Generate Internet-related revenue of $1.5 billion. (AutoNation)
- Increase the contribution of Banking Group earnings from investments, brokerage, and insurance from 16 percent to 25 percent. (Wells Fargo)
- Cut corporate overhead costs by $30 million per year. (Fortune Brands)

Strategic Objectives (Nonfinancial)

- We want a majority of our customers, when surveyed, to say they consider Wells Fargo the best financial institution in the community. (Wells Fargo)
- We want to operate 6,000 stores by 2010—up from 3,000 in the year 2000. (Walgreen's)
- We want to be the top-ranked supplier to our customers. (PPG)
- Reduce greenhouse gases by 10 percent (from a 1990 base) by 2010. (BP Amoco)

Sources: Company documents and annual reports.

1.7

strategy spotlight

How the James Irvine Foundation Redefined Its Mission

Several years ago the James Irvine Foundation, with a $1.5 billion endowment, undertook its first comprehensive strategic planning effort in more than a decade. Its leaders continued to embrace the broad mission that had been set by real estate magnate James Irvine in 1937: to promote the welfare of the people of California.

Over time, however, this inspirational statement had led to a sprawling portfolio of grants, and the foundation's leaders had come to recognize that it was far too open-ended to be useful in making program and funding decisions. To decide where the foundation could have the most lasting impact, they commissioned research on a broad range of issues facing Californians, including education, health, and the environment. Through its research, the foundation found that changing demographics, technology, and audience expectations would influence dramatically how art museums, symphony orchestras, and theaters would run their establishments.

Source: Ditkoff, S. W., & Colby, S. J. 2009. Galvanizing Philanthropy. *Harvard Business Review.* 87(11): 109; Anonymous. undated. A Conversation with John Jenks, Irvine's Chief Investment Officer. *www.irvine.org.* np; and, Emerling, S. 2009. James Irvine Foundation Rewards the Innovators. *www.articles.latimes .com,* June 17: np.

The senior team was soon flooded in data. Some findings leaped out—the significant challenges facing California's youth, for one. But given the magnitude of the state's needs, the team quickly realized that numbers alone could justify a large variety of funding decisions. So it honed in on three critical organizational values: addressing the root causes rather than crises; enabling Californians to help themselves; and working on problems that might attract like-minded partners or funders. Guided by both values and data, the team redefined its mission and selected youths ages 14 to 24 as the primary beneficiaries of its funding, and education as the primary lever for change. Saying yes to those criteria meant exiting other investments in, for example, civic culture and sustainable communities. It was a difficult choice.

The Irvine Foundation had to make some hard decisions: What, for instance, should it do about its long-standing commitment to the arts? The arts did not emerge from the data as a critical challenge, but decades of investment there had given Irvine unique assets in the form of reputation and relationships. Furthermore, its exit would have a disproportionately harsh impact on the field. So the foundation's leaders continued arts funding, albeit at a much lower level.

For objectives to be meaningful, they need to satisfy several criteria. They must be:

- *Measurable.* There must be at least one indicator (or yardstick) that measures progress against fulfilling the objective.
- *Specific.* This provides a clear message as to what needs to be accomplished.
- *Appropriate.* It must be consistent with the organization's vision and mission.
- *Realistic.* It must be an achievable target given the organization's capabilities and opportunities in the environment. In essence, it must be challenging but doable.
- *Timely.* There must be a time frame for achieving the objective. As the economist John Maynard Keynes once said, "In the long run, we are all dead!"

When objectives satisfy the above criteria, there are many benefits. First, they help to channel all employees' efforts toward common goals. This helps the organization concentrate and conserve valuable resources and work collectively in a timely manner.

Second, challenging objectives can help to motivate and inspire employees to higher levels of commitment and effort. Much research has supported the notion that people work harder when they are striving toward specific goals instead of being asked simply to "do their best."

Third, as we noted earlier in the chapter, there is always the potential for different parts of an organization to pursue their own goals rather than overall company goals. Although well intentioned, these may work at cross-purposes to the organization as a whole. Meaningful objectives thus help to resolve conflicts when they arise.

Finally, proper objectives provide a yardstick for rewards and incentives. They will ensure a greater sense of equity or fairness when rewards are allocated.

In summary, an organization must take care to ensure consistency throughout in how it implements strategic objectives. Consider how Textron, an $11 billion conglomerate, ensures that its corporate goals are effectively implemented:

> At Textron, each business unit identifies "improvement priorities" that it must act upon to realize the performance outlined in the firm's overall strategic plan. Each improvement priority is translated into action items with clearly defined accountabilities, timetables, and key performance indicators (KPIs) that enable executives to tell how a unit is delivering on a priority. Improvement priorities and action items cascade to every level at the firm—from the management committee (consisting of Textron's top five executives) down to the lowest levels in each of the company's 10 business units. Says Lewis Campbell, Textron's CEO, "Everyone needs to know: 'If I have only one hour to work, here's what I'm going to focus on.' Our goal deployment process makes each individual's accountabilities and priorities clear."[100]

As indicated in this example, organizations have lower-level objectives that are more specific than strategic objectives. These are often referred to as short-term objectives—essential components of a firm's "action plan" that are critical in implementing the firm's chosen strategy. We discuss these issues in detail in Chapter 9.

Reflecting on Career Implications . . .

- **Attributes of Strategic Management:** How do your activities and actions contribute to the goals of your organization? Observe the decisions you make on the job. What are the short-term and long-term implications of your decisions and actions? Have you recently made a decision that might yield short-term profits but might negatively impact the long-term goals of the organization (e.g., cutting maintenance expenses to meet a quarterly profit target)?
- **Intended versus Emergent Strategies:** Don't be too inflexible in your career strategies; strive to take advantage of new opportunities as they arise. Many promising career opportunities may "emerge" that were not part of your intended career strategy or your specific job assignment. Take initiative by pursuing opportunities to get additional training (e.g., learn a software or a statistical package), volunteering for a short-term overseas assignment, etc.
- **Ambidexterity:** Avoid defining your role in the organization too narrowly; look for opportunities to leverage your talents and your organization's resources to create value for your organization. This often involves collaborating with people in other departments or with your organization's customers and suppliers.
- **Strategic Coherence:** Focus your efforts on the "big picture" in your organization. In doing this, you should always strive to assure that your efforts are directed toward your organization's vision, mission, and strategic objectives.

Summary

We began this introductory chapter by defining strategic management and articulating some of its key attributes. Strategic management is defined as "consisting of the analyses, decisions, and actions an organization undertakes to create and sustain competitive advantages." The issue of how and why some firms outperform others in the marketplace is central to the study of strategic management. Strategic management has four key attributes: It is directed at overall organizational goals, includes multiple stakeholders, incorporates both short-term and long-term perspectives, and incorporates trade-offs between efficiency and effectiveness.

The second section discussed the strategic management process. Here, we paralleled the above definition of strategic management and focused on three core activities in the strategic management process—strategy analysis, strategy formulation, and strategy implementation. We noted how each of these activities is highly interrelated to and interdependent on the others. We also discussed how each of the 12 chapters in this text fits into the three core activities.

Next, we introduced two important concepts—corporate governance and stakeholder management—which must be taken into account throughout the strategic management process. Governance mechanisms can be broadly divided into two groups: internal and external. Internal governance mechanisms include shareholders (owners), management (led by the chief executive officer), and the board of directors. External control is exercised by auditors, banks, analysts, and an active business press as well as the threat of takeovers. We identified five key stakeholders in all organizations: owners, customers, suppliers, employees, and society at large. Successful firms go beyond an overriding focus on satisfying solely the interests of owners. Rather, they recognize the inherent conflicts that arise among the demands of the various stakeholders as well as the need to endeavor to attain "symbiosis"—that is, interdependence and mutual benefit—among the various stakeholder groups. The emerging practice of crowdsourcing, wherein the Internet is used to generate ideas and solve problems, is leading to an evolution in stakeholder roles. Managers must also recognize the need to act in a socially responsible manner which, if done effectively, can enhance a firm's innovativeness. The "shared value" approach represents an innovative perspective on creating value for the firm and society at the same time. The managers also should recognize and incorporate issues related to environmental sustainability in their strategic actions.

In the fourth section, we discussed factors that have accelerated the rate of unpredictable change that managers face today. Such factors, and the combination of them, have increased the need for managers and employees throughout the organization to have a strategic management perspective and to become more empowered.

The final section addressed the need for consistency among a firm's vision, mission, and strategic objectives. Collectively, they form an organization's hierarchy of goals. Visions should evoke powerful and compelling mental images. However, they are not very specific. Strategic objectives, on the other hand, are much more specific and are vital to ensuring that the organization is striving toward fulfilling its vision and mission.

Summary Review Questions

1. How is "strategic management" defined in the text, and what are its four key attributes?
2. Briefly discuss the three key activities in the strategic management process. Why is it important for managers to recognize the interdependent nature of these activities?
3. Explain the concept of "stakeholder management." Why shouldn't managers be solely interested in stockholder management, that is, maximizing the returns for owners of the firm—its shareholders?
4. What is "corporate governance"? What are its three key elements and how can it be improved?
5. How can "symbiosis" (interdependence, mutual benefit) be achieved among a firm's stakeholders?
6. Why do firms need to have a greater strategic management perspective and empowerment in the strategic management process throughout the organization?
7. What is meant by a "hierarchy of goals"? What are the main components of it, and why must consistency be achieved among them?

Key Terms

romantic view of leadership, 05
external control view of leadership, 06
strategic management, 08
strategy, 08
competitive advantage, 08
operational effectiveness, 08
stakeholders, 09
effectiveness, 10
efficiency, 10
ambidexterity, 10
strategic management process, 10
intended strategy, 11
realized strategy, 12
strategy analysis, 12
strategy formulation, 14

strategy implementation, 14	stakeholder management, 16
corporate governance, 15	crowdsourcing, 18

social responsibility, 21	vision, 26
triple bottom line, 23	mission statement, 29
hierarchy of goals, 26	strategic objectives, 30

Experiential Exercise

Using the Internet or library sources, select four organizations—two in the private sector and two in the public sector. Find their mission statements. Complete the following exhibit by identifying the stakeholders that are mentioned. Evaluate the differences between firms in the private sector and those in the public sector.

Name			
Mission Statement			
Stakeholders (✓ = mentioned)			
1. Customers			
2. Suppliers			
3. Managers/employees			
4. Community-at-large			
5. Owners			
6. Others?			
7. Others?			

Application Questions & Exercises

1. Go to the Internet and look up one of these company sites: *www.walmart.com*, *www.ge.com*, or *www. fordmotor.com*. What are some of the key events that would represent the "romantic" perspective of leadership? What are some of the key events that depict the "external control" perspective of leadership?

2. Select a company that competes in an industry in which you are interested. What are some of the recent demands that stakeholders have placed on this company? Can you find examples of how the company is trying to develop "symbiosis" (interdependence and mutual benefit) among its stakeholders? (Use the Internet and library resources.)

3. Provide examples of companies that are actively trying to increase the amount of empowerment in the strategic management process throughout the organization. Do these companies seem to be having positive outcomes? Why? Why not?

4. Look up the vision statements and/or mission statements for a few companies. Do you feel that they are constructive and useful as a means of motivating employees and providing a strong strategic direction? Why? Why not? (*Note:* Annual reports, along with the Internet, may be good sources of information.)

Ethics Questions

1. A company focuses solely on short-term profits to provide the greatest return to the owners of the business (i.e., the shareholders in a publicly held firm). What ethical issues could this raise?

2. A firm has spent some time—with input from managers at all levels—in developing a vision statement and a mission statement. Over time, however, the behavior of some executives is contrary to these statements. Could this raise some ethical issues?

References

1. Gunther, M. 2010. Fallen angels. *Fortune,* November 1: 75–78.

2. Sidhu, I. 2010. *Doing both.* East Saddle River, NJ & London: FT Press; ben-Aaron, D. 2010. After Nokia, can angry birds propel Finland? *Bloomberg BusinessWeek.* December 6–December 12: 48–50; ben-Aaron, D. 2010. Nokia board faces call for change on $77 billion lost value. *http://www.bloomberg.com/news.* July 15: np; Anonymous. 2010. The curse of the alien boss. *The Economist.* August 7: 65; and, Lynn, M. 2010. The fallen king of Finland. *Bloomberg BusinessWeek.* September 26: 6–7. We thank Pratik Kapadia for his valued contribution.

3. For a discussion of the "romantic" versus "external control" perspective, refer to Meindl, J. R. 1987. The romance of leadership and the evaluation of organizational performance. *Academy of Management Journal* 30: 92–109; and Pfeffer, J. & Salancik, G. R. 1978. *The external control of organizations: A resource dependence perspective.* New York: Harper & Row.

4. A recent perspective on the "romantic view" of leadership is provided by Mintzberg, H. 2004. Leadership and management development: An afterword. *Academy of Management Executive,* 18(3): 140–142.

5. For a discussion of the best and worst managers for 2008, read: Anonymous. 2009. The best managers. *BusinessWeek,* January 19: 40–41; and, The worst managers. On page 42 in the same issue.

6. Burrows, P. 2009. Apple without its core? *BusinessWeek.* January 26/February 2: 31.

7. For an insightful discussion of Steve Jobs's impact on Apple, read: Satariano, A. 2011. The essence of Apple. *Bloomberg BusinessWeek.* January 24–January 30: 6–8.

8. For a study on the effects of CEOs on firm performance, refer to: Kor, Y. Y. & Misangyi, V. F. 2008. *Strategic Management Journal,* 29(11):1357–1368.

9. Charan, R. & Colvin, G. 2010. Directors: A harsh new reality. *money.cnn.com.* October 6: np.

10. Dobson, C. 2010. Global airlines lost $1.7 billion due to Iceland ash cloud. *www.theepochtimes.com.* May 23: np, and Pylas, P. 2011. Nikkei slides 11 percent on radiation fears. *www.finance.yahoo.com.* March 14: np.

11. Ewing, J. 2008. South Africa emerges from the shadows. *BusinessWeek.* December 15: 52–56.

12. For an interesting perspective on the need for strategists to maintain a global mind-set, refer to Begley, T. M. & Boyd, D. P. 2003. The need for a global mind-set. *MIT Sloan Management Review* 44(2): 25–32.

13. Porter, M. E. 1996. What is strategy? *Harvard Business Review* 74(6): 61–78.

14. See, for example, Barney, J. B. & Arikan, A. M. 2001. The resource-based view: Origins and implications. In Hitt, M. A., Freeman, R. E., & Harrison, J. S. (Eds.), *Handbook of strategic management:* 124–189. Malden, MA: Blackwell.

15. Porter, M. E. 1996. What is strategy? *Harvard Business Review,* 74(6): 61–78; and Hammonds, K. H. 2001. Michael Porter's big ideas. *Fast Company,* March: 55–56.

16. This section draws upon Dess, G. G. & Miller, A. 1993. *Strategic management.* New York: McGraw-Hill.

17. See, for example, Hrebiniak, L. G. & Joyce, W. F. 1986. The strategic importance of managing myopia. *Sloan Management Review,* 28(1): 5–14.

18. For an insightful discussion on how to manage diverse stakeholder groups, refer to Rondinelli, D. A. & London, T. 2003. How corporations and environmental groups cooperate: Assessing cross-sector alliances and collaborations. *Academy of Management Executive,* 17(1): 61–76.

19. Some dangers of a short-term perspective are addressed in: Van Buren, M. E. & Safferstone, T. 2009. The quick wins paradox. *Harvard Business Review,* 67(1): 54–61.

20. Senge, P. 1996. Leading learning organizations: The bold, the powerful, and the invisible. In Hesselbein, F., Goldsmith, M., & Beckhard, R.

(Eds.), *The leader of the future:* 41–58. San Francisco: Jossey-Bass.

21. Samuelson, J. 2006. A critical mass for the long term. *Harvard Business Review,* 84(2): 62, 64; and, Anonymous. 2007. Power play. *The Economist,* January 20: 10–12.

22. Loeb, M. 1994. Where leaders come from. *Fortune,* September 19: 241 (quoting Warren Bennis).

23. Address by Norman R. Augustine at the Crummer Business School, Rollins College, Winter Park, FL, October 20, 1989.

24. Hemp, P. 2004. An Interview with CEO Kevin Sharer. *Harvard Business Review,* 82(7/8): 66–74.

25. New perspectives on "management models" are addressed in: Birkinshaw, J. & Goddard, J. 2009. What is your management model? *MIT Sloan Management Review,* 50(2): 81–90.

26. Mintzberg, H. 1985. Of strategies: Deliberate and emergent. *Strategic Management Journal,* 6: 257–272.

27. Some interesting insights on decision-making processes are found in: Nutt, P. C. 2008. Investigating the success of decision making processes. *Journal of Management Studies,* 45(2): 425–455.

28. Aston, A. 2009. How to bet on cleantech. *BusinessWeek,* January 5: 70–71.

29. A study investigating the sustainability of competitive advantage is: Newbert, S. L. 2008. Value, rareness, competitive advantages, and performance: A conceptual-level empirical investigation of the resource-based view of the firm. *Strategic Management Journal,* 29(7): 745–768.

30. Good insights on mentoring are addressed in: DeLong, T. J., Gabarro, J. J., & Lees, R. J. 2008. Why mentoring matters in a hypercompetitive world. *Harvard Business Review,* 66(1): 115–121.

31. A unique perspective on differentiation strategies is: Austin, R. D. 2008. High margins and the quest for aesthetic coherence. *Harvard Business Review,* 86(1): 18–19.

32. Some insights on partnering in the global area are discussed in: MacCormack, A. & Forbath, T. 2008. *Harvard Business Review*, 66(1): 24, 26.

33. For insights on how firms can be successful in entering new markets in emerging economies, refer to: Eyring, M. J., Johnson, M. W. & Nair, H. 2011. New business models in emerging markets. *Harvard Business Review*, 89(1/2): 88–95.

34. An interesting discussion of the challenges of strategy implementation is: Neilson, G. L., Martin, K. L., & Powers, E. 2008. The secrets of strategy execution. *Harvard Business Review*, 86(6): 61–70.

35. Interesting perspectives on strategy execution involving the link between strategy and operations are addressed in: Kaplan, R. S. & Norton, D. P. 2008. Mastering the management system. *Harvard Business Review*, 66(1): 62–77.

36. An innovative perspective on organizational design is found in: Garvin, D. A. & Levesque, L. C. 2008. The multiunit enterprise. *Harvard Business Review*, 86(6): 106–117.

37. Monks, R. & Minow, N. 2001. *Corporate governance* (2nd ed.). Malden, MA: Blackwell.

38. Intel Corp. 2007. *Intel corporation board of directors guidelines on significant corporate governance issues.* www.intel.com

39. Jones, T. J., Felps, W., & Bigley, G. A. 2007. Ethical theory and stakeholder-related decisions: The role of stakeholder culture. *Academy of Management Review*, 32(1): 137–155.

40. For example, see The best (& worst) managers of the year, 2003. *BusinessWeek*, January 13: 58–92; and Lavelle, M. 2003. Rogues of the year. *Time*, January 6: 33–45.

41. Handy, C. 2002. What's a business for? *Harvard Business Review*, 80(12): 49–55.

42. Anonymous, 2007. In the money. *Economist*, January 20: 3–6.

43. Hessel, E. & Woolley, S. 2008. Your money or your life. *Forbes*, October 27: 52.

44. Some interesting insights on the role of activist investors can be found in: Greenwood, R. & Schol, M. 2008. When (not) to listen to activist investors. *Harvard Business Review*, 66(1): 23–24.

45. For an interesting perspective on the changing role of boards of directors, refer to Lawler, E. & Finegold, D. 2005. Rethinking governance. *MIT Sloan Management Review*, 46(2): 67–70.

46. Benz, M. & Frey, B. S. 2007. Corporate governance: What can we learn from public governance? *Academy of Management Review*, 32(1): 92–104.

47. The salience of shareholder value is addressed in: Carrott, G. T. & Jackson, S. E. 2009. Shareholder value must top the CEO's agenda. *Harvard Business Review*, 67(1): 22–24.

48. Stakeholder symbiosis. 1998. *Fortune*, March 30: S2.

49. An excellent review of stakeholder management theory can be found in: Laplume, A. O., Sonpar, K., & Litz, R. A. 2008. Stakeholder theory: Reviewing a theory that moves us. *Journal of Management*, 34(6): 1152–1189.

50. For a definitive, recent discussion of the stakeholder concept, refer to Freeman, R. E. & McVae, J. 2001. A stakeholder approach to strategic management. In Hitt, M. A., Freeman, R. E., & Harrison, J. S. (Eds.). *Handbook of strategic management*: 189–207. Malden, MA: Blackwell.

51. Harrison, J. S., Bosse, D. A. & Phillips, R. A. 2010. Managing for stakeholders, stakeholder utility functions, and competitive advantage. *Strategic Management Journal*, 31(1): 58–74.

52. For an insightful discussion on the role of business in society, refer to Handy, op. cit.

53. Camillus, J. 2008. Strategy as a wicked problem. *Harvard Business Review*, 86(5): 100–101.

54. Stakeholder symbiosis. op. cit., p. S3.

55. Sidhu, I. 2010. *Doing both*. FT Press: Upper Saddle River, NJ: 7–8.

56. Our discussion of crowdsourcing draws on the first two books that have

addressed this concept: Libert, B. & Spector, J. 2008. *We are smarter than me*. Philadelphia: Wharton Publishing; and, Howe, J. 2008. *Crowdsourcing*. New York: Crown Business. Eric von Hippel has addressed similar ideas in his earlier book (2005. *Democratizing innovation*. Cambridge, MA: MIT Press).

57. Thomas, J. G. 2000. Macroenvironmetal forces. In Helms, M. M. (Ed.), *Encyclopedia of management*. (4th ed.): 516–520. Farmington Hills, MI: Gale Group.

58. For a strong advocacy position on the need for corporate values and social responsibility, read Hollender, J. 2004. What matters most: Corporate values and social responsibility. *California Management Review*, 46(4): 111–119.

59. Waddock, S. & Bodwell, C. 2004. Managing responsibility: What can be learned from the quality movement. *California Management Review*, 47(1): 25–37.

60. For a discussion of the role of alliances and collaboration on corporate social responsibility initiatives, refer to Pearce, J. A. II. & Doh, J. P. 2005. The high impact of collaborative social initiatives. *MIT Sloan Management Review*, 46(3): 30–40.

61. Insights on ethical behavior and performance are addressed in: Trudel, R. & Cotte, J. 2009. *MIT Sloan Management Review*, 50(2): 61–68.

62. Bhattacharya, C. B. & Sen, S. 2004, Doing better at doing good: When, why, and how consumers respond to corporate social initiatives. *California Management Review*, 47(1): 9–24.

63. For some findings on the relationship between corporate social responsibility and firm performance, see: Margolis, J. D. & Elfenbein, H. A. 2008. *Harvard Business Review*, 86(1): 19–20.

64. Cone Corporate Citizenship Study, 2002, www.coneinc.com.

65. Refer to www.bsr.org.

66. This section draws on: Porter, M. E. & Kramer, M. R. 2011. Creating shared value. *Harvard Business Review*, 89 (1/2): 62–77.

67. A similar concept is conscious capitalism. Refer, for example, to: Sheth, J. N. 2007. *Firms of endearment: How world-class companies profit from passion and purpose.* Philadelphia, PA: Wharton Publishing.

68. An insightful discussion of the risks and opportunities associated with global warming, refer to: Lash, J. & Wellington, F. 2007. Competitive advantage on a warming planet. *Harvard Business Review*, 85(3): 94–102.

69. This section draws on Hart, S. L. 1997. Beyond greening: Strategies for a sustainable world. *Harvard Business Review*, 75(1): 66–76, and Berry, M. A. & Rondinelli, D. A. 1998. Proactive corporate environmental management: A new industrial revolution. *Academy of Management Executive*, 12(2): 38–50.

70. Carey, J. 2006. Business on a warmer planet. *BusinessWeek*, July 17: 26–29.

71. Hart, op. cit., p. 67.

72. For a creative perspective on environmental sustainability and competitive advantage as well as ethical implications, read Ehrenfeld, J. R. 2005. The roots of sustainability. *MIT Sloan Management Review*, 46(2): 23–25.

73. McKinsey & Company. 1991. *The corporate response to the environmental challenge.* Summary Report, Amsterdam: McKinsey & Company.

74. Delmas, M. A. & Montes-Sancho, M. J. 2010. Voluntary agreements to improve environmental quality: Symbolic and substantive cooperation. *Strategic Management Journal*, 31(6): 575–601.

75. Vogel, D. J. 2005. Is there a market for virtue? The business case for corporate social responsibility. *California Management Review*, 47(4): 19–36.

76. Walsh, D. T. 2010. Harness the profit motive to deliver environmental sustainability. *www.huffingtonpost.com.* November 5: np.

77. Esty, D. C. & Winston, A. S. 2009. *Green to gold.* Hoboken, NJ: Wiley: 124–125.

78. Senge, P. M. 1990. The leader's new work: Building learning organizations. *Sloan Management Review*, 32(1): 7–23.

79. For an interesting perspective on the role of middle managers in the strategic management process, refer to Huy, Q. H. 2001. In praise of middle managers. *Harvard Business Review*, 79(8): 72–81.

80. Senge, 1996, op. cit., pp. 41–58.

81. Helgesen, S. 1996. Leading from the grass roots. In Hesselbein, F., Goldsmith, M., & Beckhard, R. (Eds.), *The leader of the future:* 19–24. San Francisco: Jossey-Bass.

82. Wetlaufer, S. 1999. Organizing for empowerment: An interview with AES's Roger Sant and Dennis Blake. *Harvard Business Review*, 77(1): 110–126.

83. Kets de Vries, M. F. R. 1998. Charisma in action: The transformational abilities of Virgin's Richard Branson and ABB's Percy Barnevik. *Organizational Dynamics*, 26(3): 7–21.

84. Hamel, G. 2006. The why, what, and how of management innovation. *Harvard Business Review*, 84(2): 72–84.

85. An interesting discussion on how to translate top management's goals into concrete actions is found in: Bungay, S. 2011. How to make the most of your company's strategy. *Harvard Business Review*, 89(1/2): 132–40.

86. An insightful discussion about the role of vision, mission, and strategic objectives can be found in: Collis, D. J. & Rukstad, M. G. 2008. Can you say what your strategy is? *Harvard Business Review*, 66(4): 82–90.

87. Our discussion draws on a variety of sources. These include Lipton, M. 1996. Demystifying the development of an organizational vision. *Sloan Management Review*, 37(4): 83–92; Bart, C. K. 2000. Lasting inspiration. *CA Magazine*, May: 49–50; and Quigley, J. V. 1994. Vision: How leaders develop it, share it, and sustain it. *Business Horizons*, September–October: 37–40.

88. Lipton, op. cit.

89. Hardy, Q. 2007. The uncarly. *Forbes*, March 12: 82–90.

90. Some interesting perspective on gender differences in organizational vision are discussed in: Ibarra, H. & Obodaru, O. 2009. Women and the vision thing. *Harvard Business Review*, 67(1): 62–70.

91. Quigley, op. cit.

92. Ibid.

93. Lipton, op. cit. Additional pitfalls are addressed in this article.

94. Sull, D. N. 2005. Strategy as active waiting. *Harvard Business Review*, 83(9): 120–130.

95. Company records.

96. Lipton, op. cit.

97. Sexton, D. A. & Van Aukun, P. M. 1985. A longitudinal study of small business strategic planning. *Journal of Small Business Management*, January: 8–15, cited in Lipton, op. cit.

98. For an insightful perspective on the use of strategic objectives, refer to Chatterjee, S. 2005. Core objectives: Clarity in designing strategy. *California Management Review*, 47(2): 33–49.

99. Ibid.

100. Mankins, M. M. & Steele, R. 2005. Turning great strategy into great performance. *Harvard Business Review*, 83(5): 66–73.

Chapter 2. Analyzing the External Environment of the Firm

chapter TWO

Analyzing the External Environment of the Firm

Creating Competitive Advantages

After reading this chapter, you should have a good understanding of:

LO2.1   The importance of developing forecasts of the business environment.

LO2.2   Why environmental scanning, environmental monitoring, and collecting competitive intelligence are critical inputs to forecasting.

LO2.3   Why scenario planning is a useful technique for firms competing in industries characterized by unpredictability and change.

LO2.4   The impact of the general environment on a firm's strategies and performance.

LO2.5   How forces in the competitive environment can affect profitability, and how a firm can improve its competitive position by increasing its power vis-à-vis these forces.

LO2.6   How the Internet and digitally based capabilities are affecting the five competitive forces and industry profitability.

LO2.7   The concept of strategic groups and their strategy and performance implications.

LEARNING OBJECTIVES

S trategies are not and should not be developed in a vacuum. They must be responsive to the external business environment. Otherwise, your firm could become, in effect, the most efficient producer of buggy whips, leisure suits, or typewriters. To avoid such strategic mistakes, firms must become knowledgeable about the business environment. One tool for analyzing trends is forecasting. In the development of forecasts, environmental scanning and environmental monitoring are important in detecting key trends and events. Managers also must aggressively collect and disseminate competitor intelligence. The information gleaned from these three activities is invaluable in developing forecasts and scenarios to minimize present and future threats as well as to exploit opportunities. We address these issues in the first part of this chapter. We also introduce a basic tool of strategy analysis—the concept of SWOT analysis (strengths, weaknesses, opportunities, and threats).

In the second part of the chapter, we present two frameworks for analyzing the external environment—the general environment and the competitive environment. The general environment consists of six segments—demographic, sociocultural, political/legal, technological, economic, and global. Trends and events in these segments can have a dramatic impact on your firm.

The competitive environment is closer to home. It consists of five industry-related factors that can dramatically affect the average level of industry profitability. An awareness of these factors is critical in making decisions such as which industries to enter and how to improve your firm's current position within an industry. This is helpful in neutralizing competitive threats and increasing power over customers and suppliers. We also address how industry and competitive practices are being affected by the capabilities provided by Internet technologies. In the final part of this section, we place firms within an industry into strategic groups based on similarities in resources and strategies. As we will see, the concept of strategic groups has important implications for the intensity of rivalry and how the effects of a given environmental trend or event differ across groups.

Learning from Mistakes

The emerging middle-class market in China has grown rapidly, and its appetite for consumerism and savings has skyrocketed.[1] Currently the upper tier of China's wealthiest account for 25 percent of Chinese household savings and will continue to control the bulk of the nation's accumulated wealth—60 percent by 2025. Their importance to banks and other financial-services firms will therefore increase. As the first foreign bank—and now the largest foreign financial institution in Hong Kong—Citibank Hong Kong was counting on over 100 years of successful, award-winning business strategies to help it grow along with China's economy and its increasing consumer financial needs. But it suffered from a misstep . . .

The company expected favorable results after launching a 15 percent customer discount program in partnership with a restaurant chain. However, Citibank found itself in the hot seat, or bowl for that matter, with many environmentally conscious customers. In a matter of days, social media campaigns had sprung up condemning the promotion. Citibank Hong Kong quickly removed the promotion after being inundated with emails and calls to action. So how did this shining example of a foreign company tarnish its reputation abroad?

Well . . . the cultural delicacy item that Citibank Hong Kong promoted (with partner Maxim's Chinese Cuisine outlets) was shark fin soup, a soup that is increasingly known for contributing to an estimated 90–100 million shark deaths per year due to definning. The prized fins are collected from live sharks by removing them and then throwing the sharks back in the ocean to die. The company tried to promote a rare, high-status item (US$150/bowl), but ignored the growing sensitivity the market had toward shark fin soup. Citibank Hong Kong lost sight of its environmentally informed market and paid the price when this issue was widely publicized.

Successful managers must recognize opportunities and threats in their firm's external environment. They must be aware of what's going on outside their company. If they focus exclusively on the efficiency of internal operations, the firm may degenerate into the world's most efficient producer of buggy whips, typewriters, or carbon paper. But if they miscalculate the market, opportunities will be lost—hardly an enviable position for their firm. As we saw from the Citibank Hong Kong example, misreading the market can lead to negative consequences—and even adversely affect a firm's reputation.

● Citibank Hong Kong paid a stiff price for promoting shark fin soup for a sales promotion in China.

In *Competing for the Future,* Gary Hamel and C. K. Prahalad suggest that "every manager carries around in his or her head a set of biases, assumptions, and presuppositions about

the structure of the relevant 'industry,' about how one makes money in the industry, about who the competition is and isn't, about who the customers are and aren't, and so on."[2] Environmental analysis requires you to continually question such assumptions. Peter Drucker labeled these interrelated sets of assumptions the "theory of the business."[3] The sudden reversal in Nokia's fortunes (chapter 1) clearly illustrates that if a company does not keep pace with changes in the external environment, it becomes difficult to sustain competitive advantages and deliver strong financial results.

A firm's strategy may be good at one point in time, but it may go astray when management's frame of reference gets out of touch with the realities of the actual business situation. This results when management's assumptions, premises, or beliefs are incorrect or when internal inconsistencies among them render the overall "theory of the business" invalid. As Warren Buffett, investor extraordinaire, colorfully notes, "Beware of past performance 'proofs.' If history books were the key to riches, the Forbes 400 would consist of librarians."

In the business world, many once successful firms have fallen. Consider the high-tech company Novell, which went head-to-head with Microsoft. Novell bought market-share loser WordPerfect to compete with Microsoft Word. The result? A $1.3 billion loss when Novell sold WordPerfect to Corel. And today we may wonder who will be the next Blockbuster, Circuit City, or *Encyclopaedia Britannica*.

Creating the Environmentally Aware Organization

So how do managers become environmentally aware?[4] We will now address three important processes—scanning, monitoring, and gathering competitive intelligence—used to develop forecasts.[5] Exhibit 2.1 illustrates relationships among these important activities. We also discuss the importance of scenario planning in anticipating major future changes in the external environment and the role of SWOT analysis.[6]

> **>LO2.1**
> The importance of developing forecasts of the business environment.

The Role of Scanning, Monitoring, Competitive Intelligence, and Forecasting

Environmental Scanning   **Environmental scanning** involves surveillance of a firm's external environment to predict environmental changes and detect changes already under way.[7,8] This alerts the organization to critical trends and events before changes develop a discernible pattern and before competitors recognize them.[9] Otherwise, the firm may be forced into a reactive mode.[10]

> **>LO2.2**
> Why environmental scanning, environmental monitoring, and collecting competitive intelligence are critical inputs to forecasting.

Experts agree that spotting key trends requires a combination of knowing your business and your customer as well as keeping an eye on what's happening around you.[11] Such a big-picture/small-picture view enables you to better identify the emerging trends that will affect your business. We suggest a few tips in Exhibit 2.2.

Leading firms in an industry can also be a key indicator of emerging trends.[11] For example, with its wide range of household goods, Procter & Gamble is a barometer for consumer spending. Any sign that it can sell more of its premium products without cutting prices sharply indicates that shoppers may finally be becoming less price-sensitive with

> **environmental scanning** surveillance of a firm's external environment to predict environmental changes and detect changes already under way.

Exhibit 2.1   **Inputs to Forecasting**

Exhibit 2.2
Some Suggestions on How to Spot Hot Trends

- **Listen.** Ask your customers questions about your products and services. Ask what they are looking for next. Find out what media they're watching and what they think of current events.
- **Pay attention.** Read trade publications related to your industry to identify key issues. Watch industries that are always on the cutting edge, such as technology, music, and fashion, in order to discover emerging trends that may affect your business.
- **Follow trends online.** Trend-hunting websites such as trendhunter.com and jwtintelligence.com offer up the trends du jour. Add them to your regular Web-surfing itinerary.
- **Go old school.** Ask your customers what they think. Organize online or in-person focus groups to find out what people are thinking. You can also launch social media groups or chat rooms to gather feedback from your audience.

Source: Moran, G. 2008. Be Your Own Trendspotter. *Entrepreneur,* December: 17.

everyday purchases. In particular, investors will examine the performance of beauty products like Olay moisturizers and CoverGirl cosmetics for evidence that spending on small, discretionary pick-me-ups is improving.

Strategy Spotlight 2.1 addresses how Zara, a Spanish fashion retailer, keeps abreast of trends and promising opportunities.

environmental monitoring a firm's analysis of the external environment that tracks the evolution of environmental trends, sequences of events, or streams of activities.

Environmental Monitoring   **Environmental monitoring** tracks the evolution of environmental trends, sequences of events, or streams of activities. They may be trends that the firm came across by accident or ones that were brought to its attention from outside the organization.[12] Monitoring enables firms to evaluate how dramatically environmental trends are changing the competitive landscape.

One of the authors of this text has conducted on-site interviews with executives from several industries to identify indicators that firms monitor as inputs to their strategy process. Examples of such indicators included:

- *A Motel 6 executive.* The number of rooms in the budget segment of the industry in the United States and the difference between the average daily room rate and the consumer price index (CPI).
- *A Pier 1 Imports executive.* Net disposable income (NDI), consumer confidence index, and housing starts.
- *A Johnson & Johnson medical products executive.* Percentage of gross domestic product (GDP) spent on health care, number of active hospital beds, and the size and power of purchasing agents (indicates the concentration of buyers).

Such indices are critical for managers in determining a firm's strategic direction and resource allocation.

competitive intelligence a firm's activities of collecting and interpreting data on competitors, defining and understanding the industry, and identifying competitors' strengths and weaknesses.

Competitive Intelligence   **Competitive intelligence** (CI) helps firms define and understand their industry and identify rivals' strengths and weaknesses.[13] This includes the intelligence gathering associated with collecting data on competitors and interpreting such data. Done properly, competitive intelligence helps a company avoid surprises by anticipating competitors' moves and decreasing response time.[14]

Examples of competitive analysis are evident in daily newspapers and periodicals such as *The Wall Street Journal, BusinessWeek,* and *Fortune.* For example, banks continually track home loan, auto loan, and certificate of deposit (CD) interest rates charged by rivals. Major airlines change hundreds of fares daily in response to competitors' tactics.

2.1

strategy spotlight

How Zara, a Spanish Retailer, Spots Opportunities

After massive investments in sophisticated IT systems, many companies continue to miss market shifts that their rivals exploit. With IT investments, however, it's not how much you spend but how you spend it. To continually identify gaps in the market, firms need real-time data and the ability to share it widely throughout the organization. Those hard data must be supplemented with direct observations from the field.

Consider Spanish retailer, Zara, whose success is often attributed to its flexible supply chain. Equally impressive is Zara's ability to spot changing preferences among its fickle customers—despite spending only one-quarter of the industry average on IT. Zara's designers, marketing managers, and buyers work side by side in the company's sprawling headquarters. The open office plan fosters frequent discussions and promotes the sharing of real-time data as well as field observations and anecdotes. By co-locating employees from different functions, Zara allows them to break out of their silos and develop a holistic feel for the market, see how their work fits, and sense new opportunities as they arise.

Source: Sull, D. 2010. Are You Ready to Rebound? *Harvard Business Review*. 88(3): 72; D'Aveni, R. A. 2010. *Beating the Commodity Trap*. Boston: Harvard Business Press; and, Caesar, J. 2010. Zara Launches Online Retail Store. *www.bbc.co.uk*. September 2: np.

For instance, in the summer of 2007, Zara launched a line of slim-fit clothes, including pencil skirts and tapered jeans, in response to catwalk trends and what celebrities were wearing. Marketing executives projected that the new items would fly off the racks, but the daily statistics revealed that the items were not selling. So Zara marketing managers immediately went into the field to see firsthand what was happening. They talked to managers, employees, and customers and quickly realized that women loved how the clothes looked but struggled to squeeze into their usual size in the dressing room. Zara responded by recalling the items and relabeling them one size smaller. The company then watched sales boom as customers happily fit into their usual size. The shared, real-time data supplemented with firsthand observation helped employees respond quickly and tip the balance from failure to success.

Zara has experienced tremendous growth and increasing market power. By 2007, it was the biggest fashion company in Europe, outpacing H&M as queen of cheap chic. It is committed to international expansion. In 2008, Korea, Ukraine, Montenegro, Egypt, and Honduras were conquered, and, in 2009, Zara announced a joint venture with India's Tata Group to open stores in India.

Finally, in September 2010, Zara launched its first online retail stores in France, Spain, Italy, Portugal, and the United Kingdom. Since Zara is "liked" by more than 4.5 million people who have signed up as fans on Facebook, the key to its success will now be to convert those fans to customers.

Car manufacturers are keenly aware of announced cuts or increases in rivals' production volume, sales, and sales incentives (e.g., rebates and low interest rates on financing). This information is used in their marketing, pricing, and production strategies.

The Internet has dramatically accelerated the speed at which firms can find competitive intelligence. Leonard Fuld, founder of the Cambridge, Massachusetts, training and consulting firm Fuld & Co., specializes in competitive intelligence.[15] His firm often profiles top company and business group managers and considers these issues: What is their background? What is their style? Are they marketers? Are they cost cutters? Fuld has found that the more articles he collects and the more biographies he downloads, the better he can develop profiles.

One of Fuld & Co.'s clients asked it to determine the size, strength, and technical capabilities of a privately-held company. Initially, it was difficult to get detailed information. Then one analyst used Deja News (*www.dejanews.com*), now part of Google, to tap into some online discussion groups. The analyst's research determined that the company had posted 14 job openings on one Usenet group. That posting was a road map to the competitor's development strategy.

At times, a firm's aggressive efforts to gather competitive intelligence may lead to unethical or illegal behaviors.[16] Strategy Spotlight 2.2 provides an example of a company, United Technologies, that has set clear guidelines to help prevent unethical behavior.

strategy spotlight

2.2

Ethical Guidelines on Competitive Intelligence: United Technologies

United Technologies (UT) is a $53 billion global conglomerate composed of world-leading businesses with rich histories of technological pioneering, such as Otis Elevator, Carrier Air Conditioning, and Sikorsky (helicopters). It was founded in 1853 and has an impressive history of technological accomplishments. UT built the first working helicopter, developed the first commercially available hydrogen cells, and designed complete life support systems for space shuttles. UT believes strongly in a robust code of ethics. In the last decade, they have clearly articulated their principles governing business conduct. These include an antitrust guide, an ethics guide when contracting with the U.S. government and foreign governments, a policy on accepting gifts from suppliers, and guidelines for proper usage of e-mail. One such document is the Code of Ethics Guide on Competitive Intelligence. This encourages managers and workers to ask themselves these five questions whenever they have ethical concerns.

1. Have I done anything that coerced somebody to share this information? Have I, for example,

threatened a supplier by indicating that future business opportunities will be influenced by the receipt of information with respect to a competitor?

2. Am I in a place where I should not be? If, for example, I am a field representative with privileges to move around in a customer's facility, have I gone outside the areas permitted? Have I misled anybody in order to gain access?

3. Is the contemplated technique for gathering information evasive, such as sifting through trash or setting up an electronic "snooping" device directed at a competitor's facility from across the street?

4. Have I misled somebody in a way that the person believed sharing information with me was required or would be protected by a confidentiality agreement? Have I, for example, called and misrepresented myself as a government official who was seeking some information for some official purpose?

5. Have I done something to evade or circumvent a system intended to secure or protect information?

Sources: Nelson, B. 2003. The thinker. *Forbes*, March 3: 62–64; and The Fuld war room—Survival kit 010. Code of ethics (printed 2/26/01); and *www.yahoo.com*.

ethics

A word of caution: Executives must be careful to avoid spending so much time and effort tracking the actions of traditional competitors that they ignore new competitors. Further, broad environmental changes and events may have a dramatic impact on a firm's viability. Peter Drucker, considered the father of modern management, wrote:

> Increasingly, a winning strategy will require information about events and conditions outside the institution: noncustomers, technologies other than those currently used by the company and its present competitors, markets not currently served, and so on.[17]

Consider the fall of the once-mighty *Encyclopaedia Britannica*.[18] Its demise was not caused by a traditional competitor in the encyclopedia industry. It was caused by new technology. CD-ROMs came out of nowhere and devastated the printed encyclopedia industry. Why? A full set of the *Encyclopaedia Britannica* sells for about $2,000, but an encyclopedia on CD-ROM, such as Microsoft *Encarta*, sells for about $50. To make matters worse, many people receive *Encarta* free with their personal computers.

environmental forecasting the development of plausible projections about the direction, scope, speed, and intensity of environmental change.

Environmental Forecasting Environmental scanning, monitoring, and competitive intelligence are important inputs for analyzing the external environment. **Environmental forecasting** involves the development of plausible projections about the direction, scope, speed, and intensity of environmental change.[19] Its purpose is to predict change.[20] It asks:

How long will it take a new technology to reach the marketplace? Will the present social concern about an issue result in new legislation? Are current lifestyle trends likely to continue?

Some forecasting issues are much more specific to a particular firm and the industry in which it competes. Consider how important it is for Motel 6 to predict future indicators, such as the number of rooms, in the budget segment of the industry. If its predictions are low, it will build too many units, creating a surplus of room capacity that would drive down room rates.

A danger of forecasting is that managers may view uncertainty as black and white and ignore important gray areas.[21] The problem is that underestimating uncertainty can lead to strategies that neither defend against threats nor take advantage of opportunities.

In 1977 one of the colossal underestimations in business history occurred when Kenneth H. Olsen, president of Digital Equipment Corp., announced, "There is no reason for individuals to have a computer in their home." The explosion in the personal computer market was not easy to detect in 1977, but it was clearly within the range of possibilities at the time. And, historically, there have been underestimates of the growth potential of new telecommunication services. The electric telegraph was derided by Ralph Waldo Emerson, and the telephone had its skeptics. More recently, an "infamous" McKinsey study in the early 1980s predicted fewer than 1 million cellular users in the United States by 2000. Actually, there were nearly 100 million.[22]

Obviously, poor predictions never go out of vogue. Consider some of the "gems" associated with the global financial crisis that began in 2008.[23]

>LO2.3
Why scenario planning is a useful technique for firms competing in industries characterized by unpredictability and change.

- "Freddie Mac and Fannie Mae are fundamentally sound. . . . I think they are in good shape going forward."—Barney Frank (D-Mass.), House Financial Services Committee Chairman, July 14, 2008. (*Two months later, the government forced the mortgage giants into conservatorships.*)
- "Existing home sales to trend up in 2008"—Headline of a National Association of Realtors press release, December 9, 2007. (*On December 23, 2007, the group said November sales were down 11 percent from a year earlier in the worst housing slump since the Great Depression.*)
- "I think you'll see $150 a barrel [of oil] by the end of the year."—T. Boone Pickens, June 20, 2008. (*Oil was then around $135 a barrel. By late December it was around $40.*)
- "I expect there will be some failures. . . . I don't anticipate any serious problems of that sort among the large internationally active banks."—Ben Bernanke, Federal Reserve Chairman, February 28, 2008. (*In September, Washington Mutual became the largest financial institution in U.S. history to fail. Citigroup needed an even bigger rescue in November.*)
- "In today's regulatory environment, it's virtually impossible to violate rules."—Bernard Madoff, money manager, October 20, 2007. (*On December 11, 2008, Madoff was arrested for allegedly running a Ponzi scheme that may have lost investors $50 billion. He was sentenced to 150 years in prison on July 29, 2009.*)

Scenario Analysis is a more in-depth approach to forecasting. It draws on a range of disciplines and interests, among them economics, psychology, sociology, and demographics. It usually begins with a discussion of participants' thoughts on ways in which societal trends, economics, politics, and technology may affect an issue.[24] For example, consider Lego. The popular Danish toy manufacturer has a strong position in the construction toys market. But what would happen if this broadly defined market should change dramatically? After all, Lego is competing not only with producers of similar

scenario analysis an in-depth approach to environmental forecasting that involves experts' detailed assessments of societal trends, economics, politics, technology, or other dimensions of the external environment.

strategy spotlight   2.3

Scenario Planning at PPG

PPG Industries, the Pittsburgh-based manufacturer of paints, coatings, optical products, specialty materials, chemicals, glass, and fiber glass, has paid dividends every year since 1899 and has maintained or increased dividends every year since 1972. With sales over $13 billion and operations in more than 60 countries, PPG is truly a global player. Although considered a very successful company, PPG has had its share of strategic errors. Realizing that business was slowing down in its core businesses, PPG acquired medical electronics businesses from Honeywell and Litton Industries in 1986 and from Allegheny International in 1987. However, these efforts at diversification proved to be failures, as the firm's competence in low-cost, standardized production in stable, mature industries was of little help in the highly volatile biomedical industry, where customization was vital. Seven years later, PPG exited the medical electronics business by selling off these units. To profit from the construction boom in China, PPG entered the Chinese market with a focus on glass. After years of losses, the company realized that it would have to focus on coatings.

These costly failures led PPG to a new emphasis on strategic planning. One of the key tools they use today is scenario planning. They have developed four alternative futures based on differing assumptions about two key variables: the cost of energy (because their manufacturing operations are energy intensive) and the extent of opportunity for growth in emerging markets. In the most favorable scenario, cost of energy will stay moderate and stable and opportunities for growth and differentiation will be fast and strong. In this scenario, they determined that their success will depend on having the resources to pursue new opportunities. On the other hand, in the worst case scenario, cost of energy will be high and opportunities for growth will be weak and slow. This scenario would call for a complete change in strategic direction. Between these two extremes lies the possibility of two mixed scenarios. First, opportunity for growth in emerging markets may be high, but cost of energy may be high and volatile. In this scenario, the company's success will depend on coming up with more efficient processes. Finally, cost of energy may remain moderate and stable, but opportunities for growth in emerging markets may remain weak and slow. In this situation, the most viable strategy may be one of capturing market share with new products.

Developing strategies based on possible future scenarios seems to be paying off for PPG Industries. The company currently boasts a return on equity of 19.1 percent and its stock has had a total return of over 43 percent over the most recent 52-week period.

Source: Camillus, J. C. 2008. Strategy as a Wicked Problem. *Harvard Business Review*, 86 (5): 98–106; *www.ppg.com.*; and *www.finance.yahoo.com.*

products but also on a much broader canvas for a share of children's playtime. In this market, Lego has a host of competitors, many of them computer based; still others have not yet been invented. Lego may end up with an increasing share of a narrow, shrinking market (much like IBM in the declining days of the mainframe computer). To avoid such a fate, managers must consider a wider context than their narrow, traditional markets, by laying down guidelines for at least 10 years in the future to anticipate rapid change. Strategy Spotlight 2.3 provides an example of scenario planning at PPG Industries.

SWOT Analysis

To understand the business environment of a particular firm, you need to analyze both the general environment and the firm's industry and competitive environment. Generally, firms compete with other firms in the same industry. An industry is composed of a set of firms that produce similar products or services, sell to similar customers, and use similar methods of production. Gathering industry information and understanding competitive dynamics among the different companies in your industry is key to successful strategic management.

One of the most basic techniques for analyzing firm and industry conditions is **SWOT analysis.** SWOT stands for strengths, weaknesses, opportunities, and threats. It provides "raw material"—a basic listing of conditions both inside and surrounding your company.

The Strengths and Weaknesses refer to the internal conditions of the firm—where your firm excels (strengths) and where it may be lacking relative to competitors (weaknesses). Opportunities and Threats are environmental conditions external to the firm. These could be factors either in the general or competitive environment. In the general environment, one might experience developments that are beneficial for most companies such as improving economic conditions, that lower borrowing costs or trends that benefit some companies and harm others. An example is the heightened concern with fitness, which is a threat to some companies (e.g., tobacco) and an opportunity to others (e.g., health clubs). Opportunities and threats are also present in the competitive environment among firms competing for the same customers.

The general idea of SWOT analysis is that a firm's strategy must:

- build on its strengths,
- remedy the weaknesses or work around them,
- take advantage of the opportunities presented by the environment, and,
- protect the firm from the threats.

Despite its apparent simplicity, the SWOT approach has been very popular. First, it forces managers to consider both internal and external factors simultaneously. Second, its emphasis on identifying opportunities and threats makes firms act proactively rather than reactively. Third, it raises awareness about the role of strategy in creating a match between the environmental conditions and the firm's internal strengths and weaknesses. Finally, its conceptual simplicity is achieved without sacrificing analytical rigor. (We will also address some of the limitations of SWOT analysis in Chapter 3.)

The General Environment

The **general environment** is composed of factors that can have dramatic effects on firm strategy.[25] Typically, a firm has little ability to predict trends and events in the general environment and even less ability to control them. When listening to CNBC, for example, you can hear many experts espouse different perspectives on what action the Federal Reserve Board may take on short-term interest rates—an action that can have huge effects on the valuation of entire economic sectors. Also, it's difficult to predict future political events such as the ongoing Middle East peace negotiations and tensions on the Korean peninsula. Dramatic innovations in information technology (e.g., the Internet) have helped keep inflation in check by lowering the cost of doing business in the United States at the beginning of the 21st century.[26]

We divide the general environment into six segments: demographic, sociocultural, political/legal, technological, economic, and global. Exhibit 2.3 provides examples of key trends and events in each of the six segments of the general environment.

The Demographic Segment

Demographics are the most easily understood and quantifiable elements of the general environment. They are at the root of many changes in society. Demographics include elements such as the aging population,[27] rising or declining affluence, changes in ethnic composition, geographic distribution of the population, and disparities in income level.[28]

The impact of a demographic trend, like all segments of the general environment, varies across industries. Rising levels of affluence in many developed countries bode well

SWOT analysis a framework for analyzing a company's internal and external environment and that stands for strengths, weaknesses, opportunities, and threats.

general environment factors external to an industry, and usually beyond a firm's control, that affect a firm's strategy.

>LO2.4
The impact of the general environment on a firm's strategies and performance.

demographic segment of the general environment genetic and observable characteristics of a population, including the levels and growth of age, density, sex, race, ethnicity, education, geographic region, and income.

Exhibit 2.3
General Environment: Key Trends and Events

Demographic

- Aging population
- Rising affluence
- Changes in ethnic composition
- Geographic distribution of population
- Greater disparities in income levels

Sociocultural

- More women in the workforce
- Increase in temporary workers
- Greater concern for fitness
- Greater concern for environment
- Postponement of family formation

Political/Legal

- Tort reform
- Americans with Disabilities Act (ADA) of 1990
- Repeal of Glass-Steagall Act in 1999 (banks may now offer brokerage services)
- Deregulation of utility and other industries
- Increases in federally mandated minimum wages
- Taxation at local, state, federal levels
- Legislation on corporate governance reforms in bookkeeping, stock options, etc. (Sarbanes-Oxley Act of 2002)

Technological

- Genetic engineering
- Emergence of Internet technology
- Computer-aided design/computer-aided manufacturing systems (CAD/CAM)
- Research in synthetic and exotic materials
- Pollution/global warming
- Miniaturization of computing technologies
- Wireless communications
- Nanotechnology

Economic

- Interest rates
- Unemployment rates
- Consumer Price Index
- Trends in GDP
- Changes in stock market valuations

Global

- Increasing global trade
- Currency exchange rates
- Emergence of the Indian and Chinese economies
- Trade agreements among regional blocs (e.g., NAFTA, EU, ASEAN)
- Creation of WTO (leading to decreasing tariffs/free trade in services)
- Increased risks associated with terrorism

2.4

strategy spotlight

China's Growing Middle Class Helps Cargo Carriers Rebound from the Recession

Increasingly, wealthy Chinese consumers eat more imported fresh fish, lobster, and cheese and wear imported fashions. One implication: They are helping global air cargo revenue rebound from the decline in 2009, the worst year in five decades.

China, with its soaring demand for luxury goods and perishable foods from overseas will lead an 18.5 percent recovery in air shipments in 2010, according to the International Air Transport Association. "China has attracted more investment and luxury brands, as purchasing power has gotten much stronger," said Kelvin Lau, an equity analyst at Daiwa Institute of Research in Hong Kong. For example, Cathay Pacific, the biggest carrier in Hong Kong,

is flying 100 tons of lobster and 150 tons of grouper to China and Hong Kong every month from Australia and Indonesia. It also increased shipments of sashimi-grade fish to the country from Tokyo by 60 percent in the first four months of 2010.

The size of China's middle class could rise to 46 percent of all households by 2020, from 32 percent in 2010, claims the research firm Euromonitor International. The firm defines middle-class households as those with annual disposable incomes equivalent to $5,000 to $15,000.

United Parcel Service, the world's largest package-delivery firm, has added two cargo planes in Hong Kong and one in Shanghai in 2010. FedEx, the world's largest air cargo carrier, is planning to buy more air freighters for its longest routes to Asia.

Shanghai International Port, China's largest port group, had a throughput of 428 million tons in 2010—up from 365 tons the previous year. And Global Logistic Properties Ltd., a logistics company whose customers include Walmart China and FedEx, expects cargo demand through the Beijing airport to increase by 15 percent a year from 2010 to 2015.

Source: Leung, W. & Ling, C. S. 2010. Chinese Consumers' Appetites Fatten Air Shippers. *International Herald Tribune.* July 30: 15; Wong, F. & Lian, R. 2011. Shanghai International Port Posts 44 Percent Jump in 2010 Net. *www.reuters. com.* January 11: np; and, Park, K. 2011. Global Logistic to Expand in Smaller China Cities to Tap on Rental Growth. *www.bloomberg.com.* January 4: np.

for brokerage services as well as for upscale pets and supplies. However, this trend may adversely affect fast-food restaurants because people can afford to dine at higher-priced restaurants. Fast-food restaurants depend on minimum-wage employees to operate efficiently, but the competition for labor intensifies as more attractive employment opportunities become prevalent, thus threatening the employment base for restaurants. Let's look at the details of one of these trends.

The aging population in the United States and other developed countries has important implications. The U.S. Bureau of Statistics states that only 18 percent of American workers were 55 and older in 2008.[29] However, by 2012 that figure will increase to 24 percent, or about one in four, of all U.S. workers. At the same time, the United States is expected to experience a significant drop in younger workers aged 25 to 44 from 68 percent to 64 percent by 2018, making it increasingly important for employers to recruit and retain older workers.

Strategy Spotlight 2.4 discusses how the increasing appetite for high-end consumer goods by China's growing middle class has boosted the revenues for air cargo carriers. This comes at a time when many western economies are still reeling from a recession.

The Sociocultural Segment

Sociocultural forces influence the values, beliefs, and lifestyles of a society. Examples include a higher percentage of women in the workforce, dual-income families, increases in the number of temporary workers, greater concern for healthy diets and physical fitness, greater interest in the environment, and postponement of having children. Such forces enhance sales of products and services in many industries but depress sales in others. The increased number

sociocultural segment of the general environment the values, beliefs, and lifestyles of a society.

of women in the workforce has increased the need for business clothing merchandise but decreased the demand for baking product staples (since people would have less time to cook from scratch). This health and fitness trend has helped industries that manufacture exercise equipment and healthful foods but harmed industries that produce unhealthful foods.

Increased educational attainment by women in the workplace has led to more women in upper management positions.[30] Given such educational attainment, it is hardly surprising that companies owned by women have been one of the driving forces of the U.S. economy; these companies (now more than 9 million in number) account for 40 percent of all U.S. businesses and have generated more than $3.6 trillion in annual revenue. In addition, women have a tremendous impact on consumer spending decisions. Not surprisingly, many companies have focused their advertising and promotion efforts on female consumers. Consider, for example, Lowe's efforts to attract female shoppers:

> Lowe's has found that women prefer to do larger home-improvement projects with a man—be it a boyfriend, husband, or neighbor. As a result, in addition to its "recipe card classes" (that explain various projects that take only one weekend), Lowe's offers co-ed store clinics for projects like sink installation. "Women like to feel they're given the same attention as a male customer," states Lowe's spokesperson Julie Valeant-Yenichek, who points out that most seminar attendees, whether male or female, are inexperienced.[31]

Home Depot recently spent millions of dollars to add softer lighting and brighter signs in 300 stores. Why? It is an effort to match rival Lowe's appeal to women.

The Political/Legal Segment

political/legal segment of the general environment how a society creates and exercises power, including rules, laws, and taxation policies.

Political processes and legislation influence environmental regulations with which industries must comply.[32,33] Some important elements of the political/legal arena include tort reform, the Americans with Disabilities Act (ADA) of 1990, the repeal of the Glass-Steagall Act in 1999 (banks may now offer brokerage services), deregulation of utilities and other industries, and increases in the federally mandated minimum wage.[34]

Government legislation can also have a significant impact on the governance of corporations. The U.S. Congress passed the Sarbanes-Oxley Act in 2002, which greatly increases the accountability of auditors, executives, and corporate lawyers. This act responded to the widespread perception that existing governance mechanisms failed to protect the interests of shareholders, employees, and creditors. Clearly, Sarbanes-Oxley has also created a tremendous demand for professional accounting services.

Legislation can also affect firms in the high-tech sector of the economy by expanding the number of temporary visas available for highly skilled foreign professionals.[35] For example, a bill passed by the U.S. Congress in October 2000 allowed 195,000 H-1B visas for each of the following three years—up from a cap of 115,000. However, beginning in 2006 and continuing through 2010, the annual cap on H-1B visas has shrunk to only 65,000—with an additional 20,000 visas available for foreigners with a Master's or higher degree from a U.S. institution. Many of the visas are for professionals from India with computer and software expertise. As one would expect, this is a political "hot potato" for industry executives as well as U.S. labor and workers' right groups. The key arguments against increases in H-1B visas are that H-1B workers drive down wages and take jobs from Americans.

Strategy Spotlight 2.5 discusses one of the proactive steps that Microsoft has taken to address this issue.

The Technological Segment

technological segment of the general environment innovation and state of knowledge in industrial arts, engineering, applied sciences, and pure science; and their interaction with society.

Developments in technology lead to new products and services and improve how they are produced and delivered to the end user.[36] Innovations can create entirely new industries and alter the boundaries of existing industries.[37] Technological developments and trends include genetic engineering, Internet technology, computer-aided design/computer-aided

2.5

strategy spotlight

How Microsoft "Gets Around" H-1B Visa Restrictions

In March 2008, Microsoft Chairman Bill Gates took one of his company's most problematic issues to the U.S. Senate. During his testimony, he criticized U.S. immigration policy that limits the H-1B visas issued to skilled workers from foreign countries—workers that Microsoft would urgently like to hire. Gates told the lawmakers: "It makes no sense to tell well-trained, highly skilled individuals—many of whom are educated at top universities—that the U.S. does not welcome or value them" and that the U.S. "will find it far more difficult to maintain its competitive edge over the next 50 years if it excludes those who are able and willing to help

Sources: Elliott, M. 2010. Opinion. *Fortune.* June 14: 56; MacDonald, I. 2008. Finesse the visa crisis with a worker-mobility plan. *Harvard Business Review,* 86(11): 28–29; Greene, J. 2008. Case study: Microsoft's Canadian solution. *BusinessWeek,* January 28: 51; MacDonald, I. 2008. Tech firms get creative in employing foreigners. *Dallas Morning News,* November 16: 5D; and, Anonymous. 2007. Microsoft to open Canada center in response to U.S. immigration. *www.workpermit.com,* July 10: np.

us compete." Gates also claimed that Microsoft hires four Americans in supporting roles for every high-skilled H-1B visa holder it hires. (This claim was also made in a June 2010 editorial in *Fortune* magazine.) Despite his efforts, the senators ignored his pleas and the visa policy went unchanged.

What to do? Six months later, Microsoft opened an office in Richmond, British Columbia, a suburb of Vancouver. Here, it hopes to place hundreds of workers unable to obtain U.S. visas. Placing workers in the same time zone will help them to collaborate—given that the facility is located just 130 miles north of Microsoft's Redmond, Washington, campus. And it is just a 2½ hour drive on Interstate 5 if one needs face time. It certainly doesn't hurt that Canada does not place limits on visas for skilled workers. An unusually pointed press release by Microsoft stated: "The Vancouver area is a global gateway with a diverse population, is close to Microsoft's offices in Redmond, and allows the company to recruit and retain highly skilled people affected by immigration issues in the U.S."

---

manufacturing (CAD/CAM), research in artificial and exotic materials, and, on the downside, pollution and global warming.[38] Petroleum and primary metals industries spend significantly to reduce their pollution. Engineering and consulting firms that work with polluting industries derive financial benefits from solving such problems.

Nanotechnology is becoming a very promising area of research with many potentially useful applications.[39] Nanotechnology takes place at industry's tiniest stage: one billionth of a meter. Remarkably, this is the size of 10 hydrogen atoms in a row. Matter at such a tiny scale behaves very differently. Familiar materials—from gold to carbon soot—display startling and useful new properties. Some transmit light or electricity. Others become harder than diamonds or turn into potent chemical catalysts. What's more, researchers have found that a tiny dose of nanoparticles can transform the chemistry and nature of far bigger things.

However, transforming the power of new technologies to commercially viable products can be difficult.[40] For example, the East Japan Railway Company tried to capture tiny amounts of energy from the footsteps of the thousands of commuters who passed through their gates. Unfortunately, they found out that all the energy generated in a day at the station was miniscule: enough to light a 100-watt bulb for a few minutes!

The Economic Segment

The economy affects all industries, from suppliers of raw materials to manufacturers of finished goods and services, as well as all organizations in the service, wholesale, retail, government, and nonprofit sectors.[41] Key economic indicators include interest rates, unemployment rates, the Consumer Price Index, the gross domestic product, and net disposable income.[42] Interest-rate increases have a negative impact on the residential home construction industry but a negligible (or neutral) effect on industries that produce consumer necessities such as prescription drugs or common grocery items.

economic segment of the general environment characteristics of the economy, including national income and monetary conditions.

Other economic indicators are associated with equity markets. Perhaps the most watched is the Dow Jones Industrial Average (DJIA), which is composed of 30 large industrial firms. When stock market indexes increase, consumers' discretionary income rises and there is often an increased demand for luxury items such as jewelry and automobiles. But when stock valuations decrease, demand for these items shrinks. For example, Exhibit 2.4 shows that the sales of value-priced liquor, wine, and beer actually went up, while sales of higher priced alcoholic beverages did not fare so well during the recent recession.

The Global Segment

global segment of the general environment influences from foreign countries, including foreign market opportunities, foreign-based competition, and expanded capital markets.

More firms are expanding their operations and market reach beyond the borders of their "home" country. Globalization provides both opportunities to access larger potential markets and a broad base of production factors such as raw materials, labor, skilled managers, and technical professionals. However, such endeavors also carry many political, social, and economic risks.[43]

Examples of key elements include currency exchange rates, increasing global trade, the economic emergence of China, trade agreements among regional blocs (e.g., North American Free Trade Agreement, European Union), and the General Agreement on Tariffs and Trade (GATT) (lowering of tariffs).[44] Increases in trade across national boundaries also provide benefits to air cargo and shipping industries but have a minimal impact on service industries such as bookkeeping and routine medical services. The emergence of China as an economic power has benefited many industries, such as construction, soft drinks, and computers. However, it has had a negative impact on the defense industry in the United States as diplomatic relations between the two nations improve.

A key factor in the global economy is the rapid rise of the middle class in emerging countries. By 2015, for the first time, the number of consumers in Asia's middle class will equal those in Europe and North America combined. An important implication of this trend is the dramatic change in hiring practices of U.S. multinationals. In 2010, for example, American companies have created 1.4 million jobs overseas—but only 1 million in the United States.[45]

Also, consider the cost of terrorism. A recent survey indicates that for S&P 500 firms, the threat has caused direct and indirect costs of $107 billion a year. This figure includes extra spending (on insurance and redundant capacity, for instance) as well as lost revenues (from fearful consumers' decreased activity).[46]

Relationships among Elements of the General Environment

In our discussion of the general environment, we see many relationships among the various elements.[47] For example, a demographic trend in the United States, the aging of the population, has important implications for the economic segment (in terms of tax policies to

Exhibit 2.4
Alcoholic Beverage Sales during the Recession: Low End versus Premium Products

Percentage changes in dollar sales compared to a year earlier (52 weeks ended March 6, 2010)	
Spirits Increase in value-priced liquors	+1.4%
Top-shelf spirits	Flat
Wine Growth of $9–$12 bottles of table wine	+6%
Decline of $20 bottles of table wine	−1.6%
Beer Growth of cheapest beer segment	+7.3%
Decline in sales of imported beers	−3.8%

Source: Kalwarski, T. 2010. No Recession Hangover for the Booze Business. *Bloomberg Businessweek*, April, 19: 17.

provide benefits to increasing numbers of older citizens). Another example is the emergence of information technology as a means to increase the rate of productivity gains in the United States and other developed countries. Such use of IT results in lower inflation (an important element of the economic segment) and helps offset costs associated with higher labor rates.

The effects of a trend or event in the general environment vary across industries. Governmental legislation (political/legal) to permit the importation of prescription drugs from foreign countries is a very positive development for drugstores but a very negative event for U.S. drug manufacturers. Exhibit 2.5 provides other examples of how the impact of trends or events in the general environment can vary across industries.

Exhibit 2.5   The Impact of General Environmental Trends on Various Industries

Segment/Trends and Events	Industry	Positive	Neutral	Negative
Demographic				
Aging population	Health care	✓		
	Baby products			✓
Rising affluence	Brokerage services	✓		
	Fast foods			✓
	Upscale pets and supplies	✓		
Sociocultural				
More women in the workforce	Clothing	✓		
	Baking products (staples)			✓
Greater concern for health and fitness	Home exercise equipment	✓		
	Meat products			✓
Political/legal				
Tort reform	Legal services			✓
	Auto manufacturing	✓		
Americans with Disabilities Act (ADA)	Retail			✓
	Manufacturers of elevators, escalators, and ramps	✓		
Technological				
Genetic engineering	Pharmaceutical	✓		
	Publishing		✓	
Pollution/global warming	Engineering services	✓		
	Petroleum			✓
Economic				
Interest rate increases	Residential construction			✓
	Most common grocery products		✓	
Global				
Increasing global trade	Shipping	✓		
	Personal service		✓	
Emergence of China as an economic power	Soft drinks	✓		
	Defense			✓

strategy spotlight   2.6

The Internet and Digital Technologies: Affecting Many Environmental Segments

The Internet has dramatically changed the way business is conducted in every corner of the globe. According to digital economy visionary Don Tapscott:

> The Net is much more than just another technology development; the Net represents something qualitatively new—an unprecedented, powerful, universal communications medium. Far surpassing radio and television, this medium is digital, infinitely richer, and interactive. . . . Mobile computing devices, broadband access, wireless networks, and computing power embedded in everything from refrigerators to automobiles are converging into a global network that will enable people to use the Net just about anywhere and anytime.

The Internet provides a platform or staging area for the application of numerous technologies, rapid advances in knowledge, and unprecedented levels of global communication and commerce. Even technologies that don't require the Internet to function, such as wireless phones and GPS, rely on the Internet for data transfer and communications.

Sources: Anonymous. 2005. SMBs believe in the Web. *eMarketer.com, www. emarketer.com*, May 16. Downes, L. & Mui, C. 1998. *Unleashing the killer app.* Boston: Harvard Business School Press. Green, H. 2003. Wi-Fi means business. *BusinessWeek*, April 28: 86–92; McGann, R. 2005. Broadband: High speed, high spend. *ClickZ Network, www.clickz.com*, January 24; Tapscott, D. 2001. Rethinking strategy in a Networked World. *Strategy and Business*, Third Quarter: 34–41; and, Yang, C. 2003. Beyond wi-fi: A new wireless age. *BusinessWeek*, December 15: 84–88.

Growth in Internet usage has surged in recent years both among individual users as well as businesses. Exhibit 2.6 illustrates (2000–2010) worldwide growth trends in Internet use. Business use of the Internet has become nearly ubiquitous throughout the economy. Major corporations all have a Web presence, and many companies use the Internet to interact with key stakeholders. For example, some companies have direct links with suppliers through online procurement systems that automatically reorder inventories and supplies. Companies such as Cisco Systems even interact with their own employees using the Internet to update employment records, such as health care information and benefits.

Small and medium-sized enterprises (SMEs) are also relying on the Internet more than ever. A recent study found that 87 percent of SMEs are receiving monthly revenue from their Web site, and 42 percent derive more than a quarter of their monthly revenue from their Internet presence. According to Joel Kocher, CEO of Interland, "We are getting to the point in most small-business categories where it will soon be safe to say that if you're not online, you're not really serious about being in business."

Despite these advances, the Internet and digital technologies still face numerous challenges. For example, international standards for digital and wireless communications are still in flux. As a result, cell phones and other devices that work in the United States are often useless in many parts of Europe and Asia. And, unlike analog systems, electronic bits of data that are zooming through space can be more easily lost, stolen, or manipulated. However, even with these problems, Internet and digital technologies will continue to be a growing global phenomenon. As Andy Grove, former chairman of Intel, stated, "The world now runs on Internet time."

Geographic Regions	Internet Users, 2000 (1000s)	Internet Users, 2010 (1000s)	Population Penetration	Usage Growth, 2000–2010
Africa	4,514	110,932	10.9%	2,357%
Asia	114,304	825,094	21.5%	622%
Europe	105,096	475,069	58.4%	352%
Middle East	3,285	63,241	29.8%	1,825%
North America	108,097	266,225	77.4%	146%
Latin America/Caribbean	18,069	204,690	34.5%	1,033%
Oceania/Australia	7,620	21,264	61.3%	179%
World Total	360,985	1,966,515	28.7%	445%

Source: *www.internetworldstats.com*

Exhibit 2.6   Growth in Internet Activity

Before moving on, let's consider the Internet. The Internet has been a leading and highly visible component of a broader technological phenomenon—the emergence of digital technology. These technologies are altering the way business is conducted and having an impact on nearly every business domain. Strategy Spotlight 2.6 addresses the impact of the Internet and digital technologies on the business environment.

The Competitive Environment

Managers must consider the competitive environment (also sometimes referred to as the task or industry environment). The nature of competition in an industry, as well as the profitability of a firm, is often more directly influenced by developments in the competitive environment.

The **competitive environment** consists of many factors that are particularly relevant to a firm's strategy. These include competitors (existing or potential), customers, and suppliers. Potential competitors may include a supplier considering forward integration, such as an automobile manufacturer acquiring a rental car company, or a firm in an entirely new industry introducing a similar product that uses a more efficient technology.

Next, we will discuss key concepts and analytical techniques that managers should use to assess their competitive environments. First, we examine Michael Porter's five-forces model that illustrates how these forces can be used to explain an industry's profitability.[48] Second, we discuss how the five forces are being affected by the capabilities provided by Internet technologies. Third, we address some of the limitations, or "caveats," that managers should be familiar with when conducting industry analysis. Finally, we address the concept of strategic groups, because even within an industry it is often useful to group firms on the basis of similarities of their strategies. As we will see, competition tends to be more intense among firms *within* a strategic group than between strategic groups.

Porter's Five-Forces Model of Industry Competition

The "five-forces" model developed by Michael E. Porter has been the most commonly used analytical tool for examining the competitive environment. It describes the competitive environment in terms of five basic competitive forces.[49]

1. The threat of new entrants.
2. The bargaining power of buyers.
3. The bargaining power of suppliers.
4. The threat of substitute products and services.
5. The intensity of rivalry among competitors in an industry.

Each of these forces affects a firm's ability to compete in a given market. Together, they determine the profit potential for a particular industry. The model is shown in Exhibit 2.7. A manager should be familiar with the five-forces model for several reasons. It helps you decide whether your firm should remain in or exit an industry. It provides the rationale for increasing or decreasing resource commitments. The model helps you assess how to improve your firm's competitive position with regard to each of the five forces.[50] For example, you can use insights provided by the five-forces model to create higher entry barriers that discourage new rivals from competing with you.[51] Or you may develop strong relationships with your distribution channels. You may decide to find suppliers who satisfy the price/performance criteria needed to make your product or service a top performer.

The Threat of New Entrants   The threat of new entrants refers to the possibility that the profits of established firms in the industry may be eroded by new competitors.[52] The extent of the threat depends on existing barriers to entry and the combined reactions from existing competitors.[53] If entry barriers are high and/or the newcomer can

---

>LO2.5
How forces in the competitive environment can affect profitability, and how a firm can improve its competitive position by increasing its power vis-à-vis these forces.

industry
a group of firms that produce similar goods or services.

competitive environment
factors that pertain to an industry and affect a firm's strategies.

Porter's five-forces model of industry competition
a tool for examining the industry-level competitive environment, especially the ability of firms in that industry to set prices and minimize costs.

threat of new entrants the possibility that the profits of established firms in the industry may be eroded by new competitors.

Exhibit 2.7   Porter's Five-Forces Model of Industry Competition

Source: Adapted and reprinted with permission of The Free Press, a division of Simon & Schuster Adult Publishing Group, from *Competitive Strategy: Techniques for Analyzing Industries and Competitors* by Michael E. Porter. Copyright © 1980, 1998 by The Free Press. All rights reserved.

anticipate a sharp retaliation from established competitors, the threat of entry is low. These circumstances discourage new competitors. There are six major sources of entry barriers.

economies of scale decreases in cost per unit as absolute output per period increases.

Economies of Scale Economies of scale refers to spreading the costs of production over the number of units produced. The cost of a product per unit declines as the absolute volume per period increases. This deters entry by forcing the entrant to come in at a large scale and risk strong reaction from existing firms or come in at a small scale and accept a cost disadvantage. Both are undesirable options.

product differentiation the degree that a product has strong brand loyalty or customer loyalty.

Product Differentiation When existing competitors have strong brand identification and customer loyalty, differentiation creates a barrier to entry by forcing entrants to spend heavily to overcome existing customer loyalties.

Capital Requirements The need to invest large financial resources to compete creates a barrier to entry, especially if the capital is required for risky or unrecoverable up-front advertising or research and development (R&D).

Switching Costs A barrier to entry is created by the existence of one-time costs that the buyer faces when switching from one supplier's product or service to another.

switching cost one-time costs that a buyer/supplier faces when switching from one supplier/buyer to another.

Access to Distribution Channels The new entrant's need to secure distribution for its product can create a barrier to entry.

Cost Disadvantages Independent of Scale Some existing competitors may have advantages that are independent of size or economies of scale. These derive from:

- Proprietary products
- Favorable access to raw materials
- Government subsidies
- Favorable government policies

In an environment where few, if any, of these entry barriers are present, the threat of new entry is high. For example, if a new firm can launch its business with a low capital investment and operate efficiently despite its small scale of operation, it is likely to be a threat. One company that failed because of low entry barriers in an industry is ProCD.[54] You probably never heard of this company. It didn't last very long. ProCD provides an example of a firm that failed because it entered an industry with very low entry barriers.

The story begins in 1986 when Nynex (a former Baby Bell company) issued the first electronic phone book, a compact disk containing all listings for the New York City area. It charged $10,000 per copy and sold the CDs to the FBI, IRS, and other large commercial and government organizations. James Bryant, the Nynex executive in charge of the project, smelled a fantastic business opportunity. He quit Nynex and set up his own firm, ProCD, with the ambitious goal of producing an electronic directory covering the entire United States.

The telephone companies, fearing an attack on their highly profitable Yellow Pages business, refused to license digital copies of their listings. Bryant was not deterred. He hired Chinese workers at $3.50 a day to type every listing from every U.S. telephone book into a database. The result contained more than 70 million phone numbers and was used to create a master disk that enabled ProCD to make hundreds of thousands of copies. Each CD sold for hundreds of dollars and cost less than a dollar each to produce.

It was a profitable business indeed! However, success was fleeting. Competitors such as Digital Directory Assistance and American Business Information quickly launched competing products with the same information. Since customers couldn't tell one product from the next, the players were forced to compete on price alone. Prices for the CD soon plummeted to a few dollars each. A high-priced, high-margin product just months earlier, the CD phone book became little more than a cheap commodity.

The Bargaining Power of Buyers   Buyers threaten an industry by forcing down prices, bargaining for higher quality or more services, and playing competitors against each other. These actions erode industry profitability.[55] The power of each large buyer group depends on attributes of the market situation and the importance of purchases from that group compared with the industry's overall business. A buyer group is powerful when:

> **bargaining power of buyers** the threat that buyers may force down prices, bargain for higher quality or more services, and play competitors against each other.

- *It is concentrated or purchases large volumes relative to seller sales.* If a large percentage of a supplier's sales are purchased by a single buyer, the importance of the buyer's business to the supplier increases. Large-volume buyers also are powerful in industries with high fixed costs (e.g., steel manufacturing).
- *The products it purchases from the industry are standard or undifferentiated.* Confident they can always find alternative suppliers, buyers play one company against the other, as in commodity grain products.
- *The buyer faces few switching costs.* Switching costs lock the buyer to particular sellers. Conversely, the buyer's power is enhanced if the seller faces high switching costs.
- *It earns low profits.* Low profits create incentives to lower purchasing costs. On the other hand, highly profitable buyers are generally less price sensitive.
- *The buyers pose a credible threat of backward integration.* If buyers are either partially integrated or pose a credible threat of backward integration, they are typically able to secure bargaining concessions.
- *The industry's product is unimportant to the quality of the buyer's products or services.* When the quality of the buyer's products is not affected by the industry's product, the buyer is more price sensitive.

At times, a firm or set of firms in an industry may increase its buyer power by using the services of a third party. FreeMarkets Online is one such third party.[56] Pittsburgh-based FreeMarkets has developed software enabling large industrial buyers to organize online auctions for qualified suppliers of semistandard parts such as fabricated components,

strategy spotlight   2.7

Tuition Increases: Sometimes Students Have Low Bargaining Power

Students at the University of California at Berkeley got hit with a 32 percent tuition fee increase in 2010. They protested by taking over a classroom building. As noted by *Forbes* writer Asher Hawkins: "It was a futile effort. Students who are already embarked on a four-year program are something of a captive audience, and California's state coffers are empty."

After the increase, the tuition and fees for in-state undergraduate students will come to about $10,000 for the academic year. (This represents a compound annual increase of nearly 10 percent over the past decade.) Although this may still seem like a reasonable price for a high-quality education, there could be more price increases ahead.

At some state schools, the risk of sharp tuition increases is quite high. *Forbes* conducted a study that analyzed university financial data, state budgets, and tuition levels to come up with a "danger list." These are state schools that are most likely to raise tuition or cut the quality of the educational experience over the next four-year period. It should be something for students to consider when deciding where to go for undergraduate school.

Five of the 10 schools on the high-risk short list were part of the University of California system. A big contributing factor is the state's enormous budget deficit. And since Berkeley and UCLA have 10 to 12 applicants for every available spot, they are easy targets for legislators looking for ways to balance the budget. A spokesman for the UC system, Peter King, agrees: "The factors employed by *Forbes* to generate this ranking list capture well the perfect storm that has enveloped the University of California system."

On January 8, 2011, California Governor Jerry Brown proposed cutting a combined $1 billion from the University of California and California State systems, which had a combined $5.6 billion general fund budget in 2010. Mark Yudof, president of the UC system stated, "The collective tuition payments made by UC students for the first time in history would exceed what the state contributes to the system's general fund."

Sources: Staley, O. 2011. California universities feel the squeeze. *Bloomberg Businessweek*. January 24–January 30: 29–30; Hawkins, A. 2010. Tuition risk. *Forbes*. May 10: 36; and, Woo, S. 2011. California governor unveils spending plan. *www.wsj.com*. January 11: np.

packaging materials, metal stampings, and services. By aggregating buyers, FreeMarkets increases the buyers' bargaining power. The results are impressive. In its first 48 auctions, most participating companies saved over 15 percent; some saved as much as 50 percent.

Although a firm may be tempted to take advantage of its suppliers because of high buyer power, it must be aware of the potential long-term backlash from such actions. A recent example (Strategy Spotlight 2.7) is the growing resentment that students have toward state universities in California because of steep increases in tuition. Unfortunately, students are essentially a captive market and have relatively little bargaining power.

bargaining power of suppliers the threat that suppliers may raise prices or reduce the quality of purchased goods and services.

The Bargaining Power of Suppliers   Suppliers can exert bargaining power by threatening to raise prices or reduce the quality of purchased goods and services. Powerful suppliers can squeeze the profitability of firms so far that they can't recover the costs of raw material inputs.[57] The factors that make suppliers powerful tend to mirror those that make buyers powerful. A supplier group will be powerful when:

- *The supplier group is dominated by a few companies and is more concentrated (few firms dominate the industry) than the industry it sells to.* Suppliers selling to fragmented industries influence prices, quality, and terms.
- *The supplier group is not obliged to contend with substitute products for sale to the industry.* The power of even large, powerful suppliers can be checked if they compete with substitutes.
- *The industry is not an important customer of the supplier group.* When suppliers sell to several industries and a particular industry does not represent a significant fraction of its sales, suppliers are more prone to exert power.

- *The supplier's product is an important input to the buyer's business.* When such inputs are important to the success of the buyer's manufacturing process or product quality, the bargaining power of suppliers is high.
- *The supplier group's products are differentiated or it has built up switching costs for the buyer.* Differentiation or switching costs facing the buyers cut off their options to play one supplier against another.
- *The supplier group poses a credible threat of forward integration.* This provides a check against the industry's ability to improve the terms by which it purchases.

The Threat of Substitute Products and Services   All firms within an industry compete with industries producing substitute products and services.[58] Substitutes limit the potential returns of an industry by placing a ceiling on the prices that firms in that industry can profitably charge. The more attractive the price/performance ratio of substitute products, the tighter the lid on an industry's profits.

Identifying substitute products involves searching for other products or services that can perform the same function as the industry's offerings. This may lead a manager into businesses seemingly far removed from the industry. For example, the airline industry might not consider video cameras much of a threat. But as digital technology has improved and wireless and other forms of telecommunication have become more efficient, teleconferencing has become a viable substitute for business travel. That is, the rate of improvement in the price–performance relationship of the substitute product (or service) is high.

Teleconferencing can save both time and money, as IBM found out with its "Manager Jam" idea.[59] With 319,000 employees scattered around six continents, it is one of the world's largest businesses (including 32,000 managers) and can be a pretty confusing place. The shift to an increasingly mobile workplace means many managers supervise employees they rarely see face-to-face. To enhance coordination, Samuel Palmisano, IBM's new CEO, launched one of his first big initiatives: a two-year program exploring the role of the manager in the 21st century. "Manager Jam," as the project was nicknamed, was a 48-hour real-time Web event in which managers from 50 different countries swapped ideas and strategies for dealing with problems shared by all of them, regardless of geography. Some 8,100 managers logged on to the company's intranet to participate in the discussion forums.

Renewable energy resources are also a promising substitute product and are rapidly becoming more economically competitive with fossil fuels. Strategy Spotlight 2.8 addresses this critical issue.

The Intensity of Rivalry among Competitors in an Industry   Firms use tactics like price competition, advertising battles, product introductions, and increased customer service or warranties. Rivalry occurs when competitors sense the pressure or act on an opportunity to improve their position.[60]

Some forms of competition, such as price competition, are typically highly destabilizing and are likely to erode the average level of profitability in an industry.[61] Rivals easily match price cuts, an action that lowers profits for all firms. On the other hand, advertising battles expand overall demand or enhance the level of product differentiation for the benefit of all firms in the industry. Rivalry, of course, differs across industries. In some instances it is characterized as warlike, bitter, or cutthroat, whereas in other industries it is referred to as polite and gentlemanly. Intense rivalry is the result of several interacting factors, including the following:

- *Numerous or equally balanced competitors.* When there are many firms in an industry, the likelihood of mavericks is great. Some firms believe they can make moves without being noticed. Even when there are relatively few firms, and they are nearly equal in size and resources, instability results from fighting among companies having the resources for sustained and vigorous retaliation.

threat of substitute products and services the threat of limiting the potential returns of an industry by placing a ceiling on the prices that firms in that industry can profitably charge without losing too many customers to substitute products.

substitute products and services products and services outside the industry that serve the same customer needs as the industry's products and services.

intensity of rivalry among competitors in an industry the threat that customers will switch their business to competitors within the industry.

strategy spotlight   2.8

The Growing Viability of Renewable Resources as Substitutes for Fossil Fuels

Renewable resources currently provide just over 6 percent of total U.S. energy. However, that figure could increase rapidly in the years ahead, according to a joint report issued in September 2006 by the Worldwatch Institute and the Center for Progress, entitled "American Energy: The Renewable Path to Energy Security."

The report indicates that many of the new technologies that harness renewables are, or soon will be, economically competitive with fossil fuels. Dynamic growth rates are driving down costs and spurring rapid advances in technologies. And, since 2000, global wind energy generation has more than tripled, solar cell production has risen six-fold, production of fuel ethanol from crops has more than doubled, and biodiesel production has expanded nearly four-fold. Annual global investment in "new" renewable energy has risen almost six-fold since 1995, with cumulative investment over the period nearly $180 billion.

A November 2006 study by the RAND Corporation is consistent with the aforementioned report. It asserts that

the economy of the United States would likely benefit, rather than be slowed, if the nation attained the goal of supplying 25 percent of its energy needs from renewable sources by 2025. Such developments would also reduce U.S. dependence on oil, which would mean a substantial start on capping greenhouse gas emissions, which most scientists link to global warming.

Deep Patel, founder of Los Angeles–based online clean-energy technologies retailer *GoGreenSolar.com*, provides some practical insights:

- *Clean energy is regional:* Think solar in sunny climates like California, geothermal in Nevada, and wind in blustery states such as Oklahoma.

- *Big corporations tend to hire established, renewable energy companies.* "But no one's paying as much attention to smaller businesses and homeowners that want to go solar. For entrepreneurs, that represents the biggest untapped market."

- *Consumers need help "taking a staged approach to going solar."* At GoGreenSolar, a "Plug N Play Solar Power Kit" starts consumers off with two solar panels that they can add to later. Patel's prediction: more such modular solutions will become available.

Sources: Anonymous. 2008. Clean Energy. *Entrepreneur,* December: 59; Clayton, M. 2006. Greener, cleaner . . . and competitive. *www.csmonitor.com.* December 4; and, Anonymous. 2006. Renewables becoming cost-competitive with fossil fuels in the U.S. *www.worldwatch.org.* September 18.

 environmental sustainability

- *Slow industry growth.* Slow industry growth turns competition into a fight for market share, since firms seek to expand their sales.
- *High fixed or storage costs.* High fixed costs create strong pressures for all firms to increase capacity. Excess capacity often leads to escalating price cutting.
- *Lack of differentiation or switching costs.* Where the product or service is perceived as a commodity or near commodity, the buyer's choice is typically based on price and service, resulting in pressures for intense price and service competition. Lack of switching costs, described earlier, has the same effect.
- *Capacity augmented in large increments.* Where economies of scale require that capacity must be added in large increments, capacity additions can be very disruptive to the industry supply/demand balance.
- *High exit barriers.* Exit barriers are economic, strategic, and emotional factors that keep firms competing even though they may be earning low or negative returns on their investments. Some exit barriers are specialized assets, fixed costs of exit, strategic interrelationships (e.g., relationships between the business units and others within a company in terms of image, marketing, shared facilities, and so on), emotional barriers, and government and social pressures (e.g., governmental discouragement of exit out of concern for job loss).

Rivalry between firms is often based solely on price, but it can involve other factors. Take Pfizer's market position in the impotence treatment market. Pfizer was the first pharmaceutical firm to develop Viagra, a highly successful drug that treats impotence.

In several countries, the United Kingdom among them, Pfizer faced a lawsuit by Eli Lilly & Co. and Icos Corp. challenging its patent protection. These two pharmaceutical firms recently entered into a joint venture to market Cialis, a drug to compete with Viagra. The U.K. courts agreed and lifted the patent.

This opened the door for Eli Lilly and Icos to proceed with challenging Pfizer's market position. Because Cialis has fewer side effects than Viagra, the drug has the potential to rapidly decrease Pfizer's market share in the United Kingdom if physicians switch prescriptions from Viagra to Cialis. If future patent challenges are successful, Pfizer may see its sales of Viagra erode rapidly.[62] But Pfizer is hardly standing still. It recently doubled its advertising expenditures on Viagra.

Exhibit 2.8 summarizes our discussion of industry five-forces analysis. It points out how various factors such as economies of scale and capital requirements affect each "force."

> **Internet** a global network of linked computers that use a common transmission format, exchange information and store data.

How the Internet and Digital Technologies Are Affecting the Five Competitive Forces

The Internet and other digital technologies are having a significant impact on nearly every industry. These technologies have fundamentally changed the ways businesses interact with each other and with consumers. In most cases, these changes have affected industry forces in ways that have created many new strategic challenges. In this section, we will evaluate Michael Porter's five-forces model in terms of the actual use of the Internet and the new technological capabilities that it makes possible.

> **>LO2.6**
> How the Internet and digitally based capabilities are affecting the five competitive forces and industry profitability.

The Threat of New Entrants In most industries, the threat of new entrants has increased because digital and Internet-based technologies lower barriers to entry. For example, businesses that reach customers primarily through the Internet may enjoy savings on other traditional expenses such as office rent, sales-force salaries, printing, and postage. This may encourage more entrants who, because of the lower start-up expenses, see an opportunity to capture market share by offering a product or performing a service more efficiently than existing competitors. Thus, a new cyber entrant can use the savings provided by the Internet to charge lower prices and compete on price despite the incumbent's scale advantages.

Alternatively, because digital technologies often make it possible for young firms to provide services that are equivalent or superior to an incumbent, a new entrant may be able to serve a market more effectively, with more personalized services and greater attention to product details. A new firm may be able to build a reputation in its niche and charge premium prices. By so doing, it can capture part of an incumbent's business and erode profitability. Consider Voice Over Internet Protocol (VOIP), a fast growing alternative to traditional phone service, which is expected to reach 25 million U.S. households by 2012.[63] Savings of 20 to 30 percent are common for VOIP consumers. This is driving prices down and lowering telecom industry profits. More importantly it threatens the value of the phone line infrastructure that the major carriers have invested in so heavily.

Another potential benefit of Web-based business is access to distribution channels. Manufacturers or distributors that can reach potential outlets for their products more efficiently by means of the Internet may enter markets that were previously closed to them. Access is not guaranteed, however, because strong barriers to entry exist in certain industries.[64]

The Bargaining Power of Buyers The Internet and wireless technologies may increase buyer power by providing consumers with more information to make buying decisions and by lowering switching costs. But these technologies may also suppress the power

Threat of New Entrants Is High When:	High	Low
Economies of scale are		X
Product differentiation is		X
Capital requirements are		X
Switching costs are		X
Incumbent's control of distribution channels is		X
Incumbent's proprietary knowledge is		X
Incumbent's access to raw materials is		X
Incumbent's access to government subsidies is		X

Power of Buyers Is High When:	High	Low
Concentration of buyers relative to suppliers is	X	
Switching costs are		X
Product differentiation of suppliers is		X
Threat of backward integration by buyers is	X	
Extent of buyer's profits is		X
Importance of the supplier's input to quality of buyer's final product is		X

Power of Suppliers Is High When:	High	Low
Concentration relative to buyer industry is	X	
Availability of substitute products is		X
Importance of customer to the supplier is		X
Differentiation of the supplier's products and services is	X	
Switching costs of the buyer are	X	
Threat of forward integration by the supplier is	X	

Threat of Substitute Products Is High When:	High	Low
The differentiation of the substitute product is	X	
Rate of improvement in price–performance relationship of substitute product is	X	

Intensity of Competitive Rivalry Is High When:	High	Low
Number of competitors is	X	
Industry growth rate is		X
Fixed costs are	X	
Storage costs are	X	
Product differentiation is		X
Switching costs are		X
Exit barriers are	X	
Strategic stakes are	X	

Exhibit 2.8 Competitive Analysis Checklist

of traditional buyer channels that have concentrated buying power in the hands of a few, giving buyers new ways to access sellers. To sort out these differences, let's first distinguish between two types of buyers: end users and buyer channel intermediaries.

End users are the final customers in a distribution channel. Internet sales activity that is labeled "B2C"—that is, business-to-consumer—is concerned with end users. The Internet is likely to increase the power of these buyers for several reasons. First, the Internet provides large amounts of consumer information. This gives end users the information they need to shop for quality merchandise and bargain for price concessions. The automobile industry provides an excellent example. For a small fee, agencies such as Consumers Union (publishers of *Consumer Reports*) will provide customers with detailed information about actual automobile manufacturer costs.[65] This information, available online, can be used to bid down dealers' profits. Second, an end user's switching costs are also potentially much lower because of the Internet. Switching may involve only a few clicks of the mouse to find and view a competing product or service online.

In contrast, the bargaining power of distribution channel buyers may decrease because of the Internet. *Buyer channel intermediaries* are the wholesalers, distributors, and retailers who serve as intermediaries between manufacturers and end users. In some industries, they are dominated by powerful players that control who gains access to the latest goods or the best merchandise. The Internet and wireless communications, however, make it much easier and less expensive for businesses to reach customers directly. Thus, the Internet may increase the power of incumbent firms relative to that of traditional buyer channels. Strategy Spotlight 2.9 illustrates some of the changes brought on by the Internet that have affected the industry's two types of buyers.

The Bargaining Power of Suppliers   Use of the Internet and digital technologies to speed up and streamline the process of acquiring supplies is already benefiting many sectors of the economy. But the net effect of the Internet on supplier power will depend on the nature of competition in a given industry. As with buyer power, the extent to which the Internet is a benefit or a detriment also hinges on the supplier's position along the supply chain.

The role of suppliers involves providing products or services to other businesses. The term "B2B"—that is, business-to-business—often refers to businesses that supply or sell to other businesses. The effect of the Internet on the bargaining power of suppliers is a double-edged sword. On the one hand, suppliers may find it difficult to hold onto customers because buyers can do comparative shopping and price negotiations so much faster on the Internet. This is especially damaging to supply-chain intermediaries, such as product distributors, who cannot stop suppliers from directly accessing other potential business customers. In addition, the Internet inhibits the ability of suppliers to offer highly differentiated products or unique services. Most procurement technologies can be imitated by competing suppliers, and the technologies that make it possible to design and customize new products rapidly are being used by all competitors.

On the other hand, several factors may also contribute to stronger supplier power. First, the growth of new Web-based business may create more downstream outlets for suppliers to sell to. Second, suppliers may be able to create Web-based purchasing arrangements that make purchasing easier and discourage their customers from switching. Online procurement systems directly link suppliers and customers, reducing transaction costs and paperwork.[66] Third, the use of proprietary software that links buyers to a supplier's website may create a rapid, low-cost ordering capability that discourages the buyer from seeking other sources of supply. *Amazon.com*, for example, created and patented One-Click purchasing technology that speeds up the ordering process for customers who enroll in the service.[67]

Finally, suppliers will have greater power to the extent that they can reach end users directly without intermediaries. Previously, suppliers often had to work through intermediaries who brought their products or services to market for a fee. But a process known as

strategy spotlight   2.9

Buyer Power in the Book Industry: The Role of the Internet

The $25 billion book publishing industry illustrates some of the changes brought on by the Internet that have affected buying power among two types of buyers—end users and buyer channel intermediaries. Prior to the Internet, book publishers worked primarily through large distributors. These intermediaries such as Tennessee-based Ingram, one of the largest and most powerful distributors, exercised strong control over the movement of books from publishers to bookstores. This power was especially strong relative to small, independent publishers who often found it difficult to get their books into bookstores and in front of potential customers.

Sources: Healy, M. 2009. Book Industry Trends 2009 shows publishers' net revenues rose 1.0 percent in 2007 to reach $40.3 billion. *www.bisg.org.* May 29: np; Books "most popular online buy." 2008. *newsvote.bbc.co.uk.* January 29: np. Hoynes, M. 2002. Is it the same for book sales? *BookWeb.org, www.bookweb.org.* March 20; *www.parapublishing.com;* Teague, D. 2005. U.S. book production reaches new high of 195,000 titles in 2004; Fiction soars.*Bowker.com, www.bowker.com,* May 24; and Teicher, C. M. 2007. March of the small presses. *Publishers Weekly, www.publishersweekly.com,* March 26; and The Nielsen Company, 2010. Global trends in online: A Nielsen global consumer report.

The Internet has significantly changed these relationships. Publishers can now negotiate distribution agreements directly with online retailers such as Amazon and Books-A-Million. Such online bookstores now account for about $4 billion in annual sales. And small publishers can use the Internet to sell directly to end users and publicize new titles, without depending on buyer channel intermediaries to handle their books. By using the Internet to appeal to niche markets, 63,000 small publishers with revenues of less than $50 million each generated $14.2 billion in sales in 2005—over half of the industry's total sales.

Future trends for the industry do not look favorable. The Book Industry Study Group (BISG) released figures in May 2009 which estimated that publishers' revenues in 2008 reached $40.3 billion, up 1 percent from 2007's total. BISG expects revenues to increase to $43.5 billion by the end of 2012. There is also good news for online book sellers: According to results from a 2010 worldwide survey by Nielsen Online, 44 percent of users had bought books online—up from 34 percent just three years earlier.

disintermediation is removing the organizations or business process layers responsible for intermediary steps in the value chain of many industries.[68] Just as the Internet is eliminating some business functions, it is creating an opening for new functions. These new activities are entering the value chain by a process known as *reintermediation*—the introduction of new types of intermediaries. Many of these new functions are affecting traditional supply chains. For example, delivery services are enjoying a boom because of the Internet. Many more consumers are choosing to have products delivered to their door rather than going out to pick them up.

The Threat of Substitutes   Along with traditional marketplaces, the Internet has created a new marketplace and a new channel. In general, therefore, the threat of substitutes is heightened because the Internet introduces new ways to accomplish the same tasks.

Consumers will generally choose to use a product or service until a substitute that meets the same need becomes available at a lower cost. The economies created by Internet technologies have led to the development of numerous substitutes for traditional ways of doing business. For example, a company called Conferenza is offering an alternative way to participate in conferences for people who don't want to spend the time and money to attend. Conferenza's website provides summaries of many conference events, quality ratings using an "event intelligence" score, and schedules of upcoming events.[69]

Another example of substitution is in the realm of electronic storage. With expanded desktop computing, the need to store information electronically has increased dramatically. Until recently, the trend has been to create increasingly larger desktop storage capabilities and techniques for compressing information that create storage efficiencies. But a viable substitute has recently emerged: storing information digitally on the Internet. Companies such as My Docs Online Inc. are providing Web-based storage that firms can access simply by leasing space online. Since these storage places are virtual, they can be accessed anywhere the Web can be accessed. Travelers can access important documents and files without transporting them physically from place to place. Cyberstorage is not free, but it is cheaper and more convenient than purchasing and carrying disk storage.[70]

The Intensity of Competitive Rivalry   Because the Internet creates more tools and means for competing, rivalry among competitors is likely to be more intense. Only those competitors that can use digital technologies and the Web to give themselves a distinct image, create unique product offerings, or provide "faster, smarter, cheaper" services are likely to capture greater profitability with the new technology. Such gains are hard to sustain, however, because in most cases the new technology can be imitated quickly. Thus, the Internet tends to increase rivalry by making it difficult for firms to differentiate themselves and by shifting customer attention to issues of price.

Rivalry is more intense when switching costs are low and product or service differentiation is minimized. Because the Internet makes it possible to shop around, it has "commoditized" products that might previously have been regarded as rare or unique. Since the Internet reduces the importance of location, products that previously had to be sought out in geographically distant outlets are now readily available online. This makes competitors in cyberspace seem more equally balanced, thus intensifying rivalry.

The problem is made worse for marketers by the presence of shopping robots ("bots") and infomediaries that search the Web for the best possible prices. Consumer websites like mySimon and PriceSCAN seek out all the Web locations that sell similar products and provide price comparisons.[71] Obviously, this focuses the consumer exclusively on price. Some shopping infomediaries, such as BizRate and CNET, not only search for the lowest prices on many different products but also rank the customer service quality of different sites that sell similarly priced items.[72] Such infomediary services are good for consumers because they give them the chance to compare services as well as price. For businesses, however, they increase rivalry by consolidating the marketing message that consumers use to make a purchase decision into a few key pieces of information over which the selling company has little control.

Exhibit 2.9 summarizes many of the ways the Internet is affecting industry structure. These influences will also change how companies develop and deploy strategies to generate above-average profits and sustainable competitive advantage.

Using Industry Analysis: A Few Caveats

For industry analysis to be valuable, a company must collect and evaluate a wide variety of information. As the trend toward globalization accelerates, information on foreign markets as well as on a wider variety of competitors, suppliers, customers, substitutes, and potential new entrants becomes more critical. Industry analysis helps a firm not only to evaluate the profit potential of an industry but also consider various ways to strengthen its position vis-à-vis the five forces. However, we'd like to address a few caveats.

First, *managers must not always avoid low profit industries (or low profit segments in profitable industries).*[73] Such industries can still yield high returns for some players who pursue sound strategies. As examples, consider Paychex, a payroll-processing company, and WellPoint Health Network, a huge health care insurer:[74]

> Paychex, with $2 billion in revenues, became successful by serving small businesses. Existing firms had ignored them because they assumed that such businesses could not afford the service. When Paychex's founder, Tom Golisano, failed to convince his bosses at Electronic Accounting Systems that they were missing a great opportunity, he launched the firm. It now serves nearly 600,000 clients in the United States and Germany. Paychex's after-tax-return on sales is a stunning 24 percent.

Exhibit 2.9   How the Internet and Digital Technologies Influence Industry

	Benefits to Industry (+)	Disadvantages to Industry (−)
Threat of New Entrants		• Lower barriers to entry increase number of new entrants. • Many Internet-based capabilities can be easily imitated.
Bargaining Power of Buyers	• Reduces the power of buyer intermediaries in many distribution channels.	• Switching costs decrease. • Information availability online empowers end users.
Bargaining Power of Suppliers	• Online procurement methods can increase bargaining power over suppliers.	• The Internet gives suppliers access to more customers and makes it easier to reach end users. • Online procurement practices deter competition and reduce differentiating features.
Threat of Substitutes	• Internet-based increases in overall efficiency can expand industry sales.	• Internet-based capabilities create more opportunities for substitution.
Intensity of Rivalry		• Since location is less important, the number of competitors increases. • Differences among competitors are harder to perceive online. • Rivalry tends to focus on price and differentiating features are minimized.

Sources: Bodily, S. & Venkataraman, S. 2004. Not walls, windows: Capturing value in the digital age. *Journal of Business Strategy.* 25(3): 15–25; Lumpkin, G. T., Droege, S. B., & Dess, G. G. 2002. E-commerce strategies: Achieving sustainable competitive advantage and avoiding pitfalls. *Organizational Dynamics*, 30 (Spring): 1–17.

In 1986, WellPoint Health Network (when it was known as Blue Cross of California) suffered a loss of $160 million. That year, Leonard Schaeffer became CEO and challenged the conventional wisdom that individuals and small firms were money losers. (This was certainly "heresy" at the time—the firm was losing $5 million a year insuring 65,000 individuals!) However, by the early 1990s, the health insurer was leading the industry in profitability. The firm has continued to grow and outperform its rivals even during economic downturns. By 2010, its revenues and profits were $65 billion and $4.8 billion, respectively—each figure representing an *annual* increase of over 18 percent for the most recent four-year period.

zero-sum game a situation in which multiple players interact, and winners win only by taking from other players.

Second, five-forces analysis implicitly *assumes a zero-sum game, determining how a firm can enhance its position relative to the forces.* Yet such an approach can often be short-sighted; that is, it can overlook the many potential benefits of developing constructive win–win relationships with suppliers and customers. Establishing long-term mutually beneficial relationships with suppliers improves a firm's ability to implement just-in-time (JIT) inventory systems, which let it manage inventories better and respond quickly to market demands. A recent study found that if a company exploits its powerful position against a supplier, that action may come back to haunt the company.[75] Consider, for example, General Motors' heavy-handed dealings with its suppliers:[76]

> GM has a reputation for particularly aggressive tactics. Although it is striving to crack down on the most egregious of these, it continues to rank dead last in the annual supplier satisfaction survey. "It's a brutal process," says David E. Cole, who is head of the Center for Automotive Research in Ann Arbor. "There are bodies lying by the side of the road."
>
> Suppliers point to one particularly nasty tactic: shopping their technology out the back door to see if rivals can make it cheaper. In one case, a GM purchasing manager showed a supplier's new brake design to Delphi Corporation. He was fired. However, in a recent survey, parts executives said they tend to bring hot new technology to other carmakers first. This is yet another reason GM finds it hard to compete in an intensely competitive industry.

Third, the five-forces analysis also has been criticized for *being essentially a static analysis*. External forces as well as strategies of individual firms are continually changing the structure of all industries. The search for a dynamic theory of strategy has led to greater use of game theory in industrial organization economics research and strategy research.

Based on game-theoretic considerations, Brandenburger and Nalebuff recently introduced the concept of the value net,[77] which in many ways is an extension of the five-forces analysis. It is illustrated in Exhibit 2.10. The value net represents all the players in the game and analyzes how their interactions affect a firm's ability to generate and appropriate value. The vertical dimension of the net includes suppliers and customers. The firm has direct transactions with them. On the horizontal dimension are substitutes and complements, players with whom a firm interacts but may not necessarily transact. The concept of complementors is perhaps the single most important contribution of value net analysis and is explained in more detail below.

Complements typically are products or services that have a potential impact on the value of a firm's own products or services. Those who produce complements are usually referred to as complementors.[78] Powerful hardware is of no value to a user unless there is software that runs on it. Similarly, new and better software is possible only if the hardware on which it can be run is available. This is equally true in the video game industry, where the sales of game

complements
products or services that have an impact on the value of a firm's products or services.

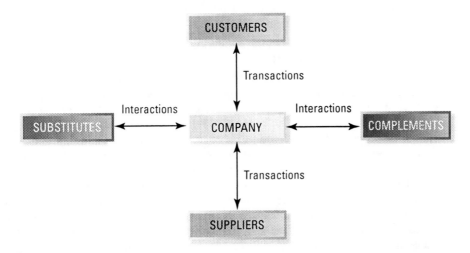

Exhibit 2.10 **The Value Net**

Source: Reprinted by permission of *Harvard Business Review*. Exhibit from "The Right Game: Use Game Theory to Shape Strategy," by A. Brandenburger and B. J. Nalebuff, July–August 1995. Copyright © 1995 by the Harvard Business School Publishing Corporation. All rights reserved.

consoles and video games complement each other. Nintendo's success in the early 1990s was a result of their ability to manage their relationship with their complementors. They built a security chip into the hardware and then licensed the right to develop games to outside firms. These firms paid a royalty to Nintendo for each copy of the game sold. The royalty revenue enabled Nintendo to sell game consoles at close to their cost, thereby increasing their market share, which, in turn, caused more games to be sold and more royalties to be generated.[79]

Despite efforts to create win–win scenarios, conflict among complementors is inevitable.[80] After all, it is naive to expect that even the closest of partners will do you the favor of abandoning their own interests. And even the most successful partnerships are seldom trouble free. Power is a factor that comes into play as we see in Strategy Spotlight 2.10 with the example of Apple's iPod—an enormously successful product.

We would like to close this section with some recent insights from Michael Porter, the originator of the five-forces analysis.[81] He addresses two critical issues in conducting a good industry analysis, which will yield an improved understanding of the root causes of profitability: (1) choosing the appropriate time frame and (2) a rigorous quantification of the five forces.

- *Good industry analysis looks rigorously at the structural underpinnings of profitability. A first step is to understand the time horizon.* One of the essential tasks in industry analysis is to distinguish short-term fluctuations from structural changes. A good guideline for the appropriate time horizon is the full business cycle for the particular industry. For most industries, a three- to five-year horizon is appropriate. However, for some industries with long lead times, such as mining, the appropriate horizon may be a decade or more. It is average profitability over this period, not profitability in any particular year, which should be the focus of analysis.

- *The point of industry analysis is not to declare the industry attractive or unattractive but to understand the underpinnings of competition and the root causes of profitability.* As much as possible, analysts should look at industry structure quantitatively, rather than be satisfied with lists of qualitative factors. Many elements of five forces can be quantified: the percentage of the buyer's total cost accounted for by the industry's product (to understand buyer price sensitivity); the percentage of industry sales required to fill a plant or operate a logistical network to efficient scale (to help assess barriers to entry); and the buyer's switching cost (determining the inducement an entrant or rival must offer customers).

Strategic Groups within Industries

In an industry analysis, two assumptions are unassailable: (1) No two firms are totally different, and (2) no two firms are exactly the same. The issue becomes one of identifying groups of firms that are more similar to each other than firms that are not, otherwise known as **strategic groups**.[82] This is important because rivalry tends to be greater among firms that are alike. Strategic groups are clusters of firms that share similar strategies. After all, is Kmart more concerned about Nordstrom or Walmart? Is Mercedes more concerned about Hyundai or BMW? The answers are straightforward.[83]

These examples are not meant to trivialize the strategic groups concept.[84] Classifying an industry into strategic groups involves judgment. If it is useful as an analytical tool, we must exercise caution in deciding what dimensions to use to map these firms. Dimensions include breadth of product and geographic scope, price/quality, degree of vertical integration, type of distribution (e.g., dealers, mass merchandisers, private label), and so on. Dimensions should also be selected to reflect the variety of strategic combinations in an industry. For example, if all firms in an industry have roughly the same level of product differentiation (or R&D intensity), this would not be a good dimension to select.

What value is the strategic groups concept as an analytical tool? *First, strategic groupings help a firm identify barriers to mobility that protect a group from attacks by other*

strategic groups
clusters of firms that share similar strategies.

>LO2.7
The concept of strategic groups and their strategy and performance implications.

2.10

strategy spotlight

Apple's iPod: Relationships with Its Complementors

In 2002, Steve Jobs began his campaign to cajole the major music companies into selling tracks to iPod users through the iTunes Music Store, an online retail site. Most industry executives, after being burned by illegal file-sharing services like Napster and Kazaa, just wanted digital music to disappear. However, Jobs's passionate vision persuaded them to climb on board. He promised to reduce the risks that they faced by offering safeguards against piracy, as well as a hip product (iPod and iPad Touch) that would drive sales.

However, Apple had a much stronger bargaining position when its contracts with the music companies came up for renewal in April 2005. By then, iTunes had captured 80 percent of the market for legal downloads. The music companies, which were receiving between 60 and 70 cents per download, wanted more. Their reasoning: If the iTunes Music Store would only charge $1.50 or $2.00 per track, they could double or triple their revenues and profits. Since Jobs knew that he could sell more iPods if the music was cheap, he was determined to keep the price of a download at 99 cents and to maintain Apple's

Source: Hesseldahl, A. 2008. Now that we all have iPods. *BusinessWeek*, December 15: 36; Apple Computer Inc. 10-K, 2010; and, Yoffie, D. B. & Kwak, M. 2006. With friends like these: The art of managing complementors. *Harvard Business Review*, 84(9): 88–98.

margins. Given iTunes' dominant position, the music companies had little choice but to relent.

Apple's foray into music has been tremendously successful. Between 2006 and 2009, iPod sales increased from $7.7 billion to $9.4 billion—a 22 percent increase. And, other music related products and services soared from $4 billion to $5 billion over the same period. Despite tough competition, Apple still dominates the music player business.

● The iPod is largely responsible for Apple's recent stellar financial performance.

groups.[85] Mobility barriers are factors that deter the movement of firms from one strategic position to another. For example, in the chainsaw industry, the major barriers protecting the high-quality/dealer-oriented group are technology, brand image, and an established network of servicing dealers.

The second value of strategic grouping is that it *helps a firm identify groups whose competitive position may be marginal or tenuous.* We may anticipate that these competitors may exit the industry or try to move into another group. In recent years in the retail department store industry, firms such as JCPenney and Sears have experienced extremely difficult times because they were stuck in the middle, neither an aggressive discount player like Walmart nor a prestigious upscale player like Neiman Marcus.

Third, strategic groupings *help chart the future directions of firms' strategies.* Arrows emanating from each strategic group can represent the direction in which the group (or a firm within the group) seems to be moving. If all strategic groups are moving in a similar direction, this could indicate a high degree of future volatility and intensity of competition. In the automobile industry, for example, the competition in the minivan and sport utility segments has intensified in recent years as many firms have entered those product segments.

Fourth, strategic groups are *helpful in thinking through the implications of each industry trend for the strategic group as a whole.* Is the trend decreasing the viability of a group? If so, in what direction should the strategic group move? Is the trend increasing or decreasing entry barriers? Will the trend decrease the ability of one group to separate itself from other groups? Such analysis can help in making predictions about industry evolution. A sharp increase in interest rates, for example, tends to have less impact on providers of higher-priced goods (e.g., Porsches) than on providers of lower-priced goods (e.g., Chevrolet Cobalt) whose customer base is much more price sensitive.

Exhibit 2.11 provides a strategic grouping of the worldwide automobile industry.[86] The firms in each group are representative; not all firms are included in the mapping. We have identified four strategic groups. In the top left-hand corner are high-end luxury automakers who focus on a very narrow product market. Most of the cars produced by the members of this group cost well over $100,000. Some cost many times that amount. The 2010 45B Ferrari Italia starts at $225,000, and the 2010 Lamborghini Gallardo will set you back about $221,000 (in case you were wondering how to spend your employment signing bonus). Players in this market have a very exclusive clientele and face little rivalry from other strategic groups. At the other extreme, in the lower left-hand corner is a strategic group that has low-price/quality attributes and targets a narrow market. These players, Hyundai and Kia, limit competition from other strategic groups by pricing their products very low. The third group (near the middle) consists of firms high in product pricing/quality and average in their product-line breadth. The final group (at the far right) consists of firms with a broad range of products and multiple price points. These firms have entries that compete at both the lower end of the market (e.g., the Ford Focus) and the higher end (e.g., Chevrolet Corvette).

The auto market has been very dynamic and competition has intensified in recent years.[87] Many firms in different strategic groups compete in the same product markets, such as minivans and sport utility vehicles. In the late 1990s Mercedes entered the fray with its M series, and Porsche has a recent entry as well with its Cayenne, a 2004 model.

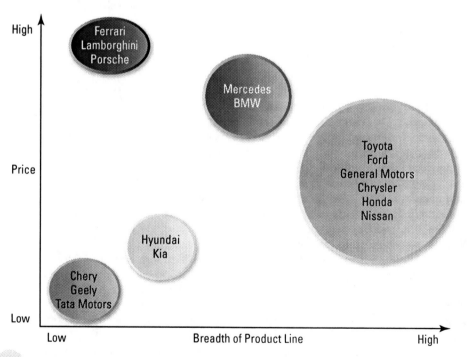

Exhibit 2.11   **The World Automobile Industry: Strategic Groups**

Note: Members of each strategic group are not inclusive, only illustrative.

Some players are also going more upscale with their product offerings. Recently, Hyundai introduced its Genesis, starting at $33,000. This brings Hyundai into direct competition with entries from other strategic groups such as Toyota's Camry and Honda's Accord. Hyundai is offering an extensive warranty (10 years, 100,000 miles) in an effort to offset customer perceptions of their lower quality. To further intensify competition, some key automakers are providing offerings in lower-priced segments. BMW, with their 1-series, is a well-known example. Such cars, priced in the low $30,000s, compete more directly with products from broad-line manufacturers like Ford, General Motors, and Toyota.

Such models are competing in an industry that has experienced relatively flat unit sales in the first half of the last decade. However, in recent years things have turned increasingly sour. U.S. automobile sales dropped from 13.2 million units in 2008 to only 10.4 million units in 2009 (the fewest units since 1982) and 11.3 million units in 2010. This compares to an average of 16.4 million units between 2000 and 2007. And J. D. Power predicts sales of only 13.2 million units for 2011, as the economy emerges from the recession.[88] One can certainly expect incentive-laden offerings to appear on dealer lots for some time to come.

Our discussion would not be complete, of course, without paying some attention to recent entries in the automobile industry that will likely lead to the formation of a new strategic group—placed at the bottom left corner of the grid in Exhibit 2.11. Three firms—China's Zhejiang Geely Holding Company, China's Chery Automobile Company, and India's Tata Motors—have introduced models that bring new meaning to the term "subcompact."[89] Let's take a look at these econoboxes.

Chery's QQ model sells for between $4,000 and $7,000 in the Chinese market and sports horsepower in the range of 51 to 74. Geely's best-selling four-door sedan, the Free Cruiser, retails from $6,300 and $6,900. The firm is planning to go more upscale with the Geely KingKong ($7,500–$10,000), a four-door 1.5- to 1.8-liter sedan, and the Vision ($9,700–$15,300), a 1.8-liter four-door sedan. But, for price-points, India's Tata Motors has everyone beat. In January 2008, it unveiled the Nano with an astonishing retail price of only $2,500. It is a four-door, five-seat hatchback that gets 54 miles per gallon. But before you order one—keep in mind that it only comes with a 30 horsepower engine.

Reflecting on Career Implications...

- *Creating the Environmentally Aware Organization:* In your career, what are some ways in which you can engage in scanning, monitoring, and intelligence gathering for future job opportunities? Consider, for example, subscribing to your field's professional publications and becoming actively involved in relevant professional organizations.
- *SWOT Analysis:* From a career standpoint, periodically evaluate your strengths and weaknesses as well as potential opportunities and threats to your career. In addition, strive to seek input from trusted peers and superiors.
- *General Environment:* Carefully evaluate the elements of the general environment facing your firm. Identify factors (e.g., rapid technological change) that can provide promising career opportunities as well as possibilities for you to add value for your organization. In doing this, don't focus solely on "internal factors" of your organization.
- *Five-Forces Analysis:* Consider the five forces affecting the industry within which your organization competes. If the "forces" are unfavorable, the long-term profit potential of the industry may be unattractive. And, there will likely be fewer resources available and—all other things being equal—fewer career opportunities.

Summary

Managers must analyze the external environment to minimize or eliminate threats and exploit opportunities. This involves a continuous process of environmental scanning and monitoring as well as obtaining competitive intelligence on present and potential rivals. These activities provide valuable inputs for developing forecasts. In addition, many firms use scenario planning to anticipate and respond to volatile and disruptive environmental changes.

We identified two types of environments: the general environment and the competitive environment. The six segments of the general environment are demographic, sociocultural, political/legal, technological, economic, and global. Trends and events occurring in these segments, such as the aging of the population, higher percentages of women in the workplace, governmental legislation, and increasing (or decreasing) interest rates, can have a dramatic effect on a firm. A given trend or event may have a positive impact on some industries and a negative, neutral, or no impact at all on others.

The competitive environment consists of industry-related factors and has a more direct impact than the general environment. Porter's five-forces model of industry analysis includes the threat of new entrants, buyer power, supplier power, threat of substitutes, and rivalry among competitors. The intensity of these factors determines, in large part, the average expected level of profitability in an industry. A sound awareness of such factors, both individually and in combination, is beneficial not only for deciding what industries to enter but also for assessing how a firm can improve its competitive position. We discuss how many of the changes brought about by the digital economy can be understood in the context of five-forces analysis. The limitations of five-forces analysis include its static nature and its inability to acknowledge the role of complementors. Although we addressed the general environment and competitive environment in separate sections, they are quite interdependent. A given environmental trend or event, such as changes in the ethnic composition of a population or a technological innovation, typically has a much greater impact on some industries than on others.

The concept of strategic groups is also important to the external environment of a firm. No two organizations are completely different nor are they exactly the same. The question is how to group firms in an industry on the basis of similarities in their resources and strategies. The strategic groups concept is valuable for determining mobility barriers across groups, identifying groups with marginal competitive positions, charting the future directions of firm strategies, and assessing the implications of industry trends for the strategic group as a whole.

Summary Review Questions

1. Why must managers be aware of a firm's external environment?
2. What is gathering and analyzing competitive intelligence and why is it important for firms to engage in it?
3. Discuss and describe the six elements of the external environment.
4. Select one of these elements and describe some changes relating to it in an industry that interests you.
5. Describe how the five forces can be used to determine the average expected profitability in an industry.
6. What are some of the limitations (or caveats) in using five-forces analysis?
7. Explain how the general environment and industry environment are highly related. How can such interrelationships affect the profitability of a firm or industry?
8. Explain the concept of strategic groups. What are the performance implications?

Key Terms

environmental scanning, 41
environmental monitoring, 42
competitive intelligence, 42
environmental forecasting, 44
scenario analysis, 45
SWOT analysis, 47
general environment, 47
demographic segment of the general environment, 47
sociocultural segment of the general environment, 49
political/legal segment of the general environment, 50
technological segment of the general environment, 50
economic segment of the general environment, 51
global segment of the general environment, 52
industry, 55
competitive environment, 55
Porter's five-forces model of industry competition, 55
threat of new entrants, 55
economies of scale, 56
product differentiation, 56
switching cost, 56
bargaining power of buyers, 57
bargaining power of suppliers, 58

Experiential Exercise

Select one of the following industries: personal computers, airlines, or automobiles. For this industry, evaluate the strength of each of Porter's five forces as well as complementors.

Industry Force	High? Medium? Low?	Why?
1. Threat of new entrants		
2. Power of buyers		
3. Power of suppliers		
4. Power of substitutes		
5. Rivalry among competitors		
6. Complementors		

Application Questions & Exercises

1. Imagine yourself as the CEO of a large firm in an industry in which you are interested. Please (1) identify major trends in the general environment, (2) analyze their impact on the firm, and (3) identify major sources of information to monitor these trends. (Use Internet and library resources.)

2. Analyze movements across the strategic groups in the U.S. retail industry. How do these movements within this industry change the nature of competition?

3. What are the major trends in the general environment that have impacted the U.S. pharmaceutical industry?

4. Go to the Internet and look up *www.kroger.com*. What are some of the five forces driving industry competition that are affecting the profitability of this firm?

Ethics Questions

1. What are some of the legal and ethical issues involved in collecting competitor intelligence in the following situations?

   a. Hotel A sends an employee posing as a potential client to Hotel B to find out who Hotel B's major corporate customers are.

   b. A firm hires an MBA student to collect information directly from a competitor while claiming the information is for a course project.

   c. A firm advertises a nonexistent position and interviews a rival's employees with the intention of obtaining competitor information.

2. What are some of the ethical implications that arise when a firm tries to exploit its power over a supplier?

References

1. Heimbuch, J. 2010. Hooray! Hawaii outlaws shark fin soup. *www.treehugger.com,* October 27: np.; Anonymous. 2006. The value of China's emerging middle class. *www.mkq preview.com.* June: np; and, Wassener, B. 2010. A shark fin promotion backfires. *www.green.blogs.nytimes.com.* July 22: np; and, *www.citigroup.com.* We thank Kimberly Kentfield for her valued contributions.

2. Hamel, G. & Prahalad, C. K. 1994. *Competing for the future.* Boston: Harvard Business School Press.

3. Drucker, P. F. 1994. Theory of the business. *Harvard Business Review,* 72: 95–104.

4. For an insightful discussion on managers' assessment of the external environment, refer to Sutcliffe, K. M. & Weber, K. 2003. The high cost of accurate knowledge. *Harvard Business Review,* 81(5): 74–86.

5. For insights on recognizing and acting on environmental opportunities, refer to: Alvarez, S. A. & Barney, J. B. 2008. Opportunities, organizations, and entrepreneurship: Theory and debate. *Strategic Entrepreneurship Journal,* 2(3): entire issue.

6. Charitou, C. D. & Markides, C. C. 2003. Responses to disruptive strategic innovation. *MIT Sloan Management Review,* 44(2): 55–64.

7. Our discussion of scanning, monitoring, competitive intelligence, and forecasting concepts draws on several sources. These include Fahey, L. & Narayanan, V. K. 1983. *Macroenvironmental analysis for strategic management.* St. Paul, MN: West; Lorange, P., Scott, F. S., & Ghoshal,

S. 1986. *Strategic control.* St. Paul, MN: West; Ansoff, H. I. 1984. *Implementing strategic management.* Englewood Cliffs, NJ: Prentice Hall; and Schreyogg, G. & Stienmann, H. 1987. Strategic control: A new perspective. *Academy of Management Review,* 12: 91–103.

8. An insightful discussion on how leaders can develop "peripheral vision" in environmental scanning is found in: Day, G. S. & Schoemaker, P. J. H. 2008. Are you a "vigilant leader"? *MIT Sloan Management Review,* 49 (3): 43–51.

9. Elenkov, D. S. 1997. Strategic uncertainty and environmental scanning: The case for institutional influences on scanning behavior. *Strategic Management Journal,* 18: 287–302.

10. For an interesting perspective on environmental scanning in emerging economies see May, R. C., Stewart, W. H., & Sweo, R. 2000. Environmental scanning behavior in a transitional economy: Evidence from Russia. *Academy of Management Journal,* 43(3): 403–27.

11. Bryon, E. 2010. For insight into P&G, check Olay numbers. *Wall Street Journal.* October 27: C1.

12. Tang, J. 2010. How entrepreneurs discover opportunities in China: An institutional view. *Asia Pacific Journal of Management.* 27(3): 461–480.

13. Walters, B. A. & Priem, R. L. 1999. Business strategy and CEO intelligence acquisition. *Competitive Intelligence Review,* 10(2): 15–22.

14. Prior, V. 1999. The language of competitive intelligence, Part 4. *Competitive Intelligence Review,* 10(1): 84–87.

15. Zahra, S. A. & Charples, S. S. 1993. Blind spots in competitive analysis. *Academy of Management Executive* 7(2): 7–27.

16. Wolfenson, J. 1999. The world in 1999: A battle for corporate honesty. *The Economist* 38: 13–30.

17. Drucker, P. F. 1997. The future that has already happened. *Harvard Business Review,* 75(6): 22.

18. Evans, P. B. & Wurster, T. S. 1997. Strategy and the new economics of information. *Harvard Business Review,* 75(5): 71–82.

19. Fahey & Narayanan, op. cit., p. 41.

20. Insights on how to improve predictions can be found in: Cross, R., Thomas, R. J., & Light, D. A. 2009. The prediction lover's handbook. *MIT Sloan Management Review,* 50 (2): 32–34.

21. Courtney, H., Kirkland, J., & Viguerie, P. 1997. Strategy under uncertainty. *Harvard Business Review,* 75(6): 66–79.

22. Odlyzko, A. 2003. False hopes. *Red Herring,* March: 31.

23. Coy, P. 2009. Worst predictions about 2008. *BusinessWeek,* January 12: 15–16.

24. For an interesting perspective on how Accenture practices and has developed its approach to scenario planning, refer to Ferguson, G., Mathur, S., & Shah, B. 2005. Evolving from information to insight. *MIT Sloan Management Review,* 46(2): 51–58.

25. Dean, T. J., Brown, R. L., & Bamford, C. E. 1998. Differences in large and small firm responses to environmental context: Strategic implications from a comparative analysis of business formations. *Strategic Management Journal,* 19: 709–728.

26. Some insights on management during economic downturns are in: Colvin, G. 2009. How to manage your business in a recession. *Fortune,* January 19: 88–93.

27. Colvin, G. 1997. How to beat the boomer rush. *Fortune,* August 18: 59–63.

28. Porter, M. E. 2010. Discovering—and lowering—the real costs of health care. *Harvard Business Review,* 89 (1/2): 49–50.

29. U.S. Bureau of Labor Statistics. 2009. *Occupational handbook, 2010–2011 edition.* December 19. *www.bls.gov/oco/oco203.htm.*

30. Challenger, J. 2000. Women's corporate rise has reduced relocations. *Lexington (KY) Herald-Leader,* October 29: D1.

31. Tsao, A. 2005. Retooling home improvement, *Businesssweek.com,* February, 14; and, Grow, B. 2004.

Who wears the wallet in the family? *BusinessWeek,* August 16:10.

32. Watkins, M. D. 2003. Government games. *MIT Sloan Management Review* 44(2): 91–95.

33. A discussion of the political issues surrounding caloric content on meals is in: Orey, M. 2008. A food fight over calorie counts. *BusinessWeek,* February 11: 36.

34. For a discussion of the linkage between copyright law and innovation, read: Guterman, J. 2009. Does copyright law hinder innovation? *MIT Sloan Management Review,* 50(2): 14–15.

35. Davies, A. 2000. The welcome mat is out for nerds. *BusinessWeek,* May 21: 17; Broache, A. 2007. Annual H-1B visa cap met—already. *news.cnet.com,* April 3: np; and, Anonymous. Undated. Cap count for H-1B and H-2B workers for fiscal year 2009. *www.uscis.gov:* np.

36. Hout, T. M., Ghemawat, P. 2010. China vs. the world: Whose technology is it? *Harvard Business Review,* 88(12): 94–103.

37. Anonymous. Business ready for Internet revolution. 1999. *Financial Times,* May 21: 17.

38. A discussion of an alternate energy—marine energy—is the topic of: Boyle, M. 2008. Scottish power. *Fortune.* March 17: 28.

39. Baker, S. & Aston, A. 2005. The business of nanotech. *BusinessWeek,* February 14: 64–71.

40. Morse, G. 2009. The power of unwitting workers. *Harvard Business Review,* 87(10): 26.

41. For an insightful discussion of the causes of the global financial crisis, read: Johnson, S. 2009. The global financial crisis—What really precipitated it? *MIT Sloan Management Review.* 50(2): 16–18.

42. Tyson, L. D. 2011. A better stimulus for the U.S. economy. *Harvard Business Review,* 89(1/2): 53.

43. A interesting and balanced discussion on the merits of multinationals to the U.S. economy is found in: Mandel, M. 2008. Multinationals: Are they good for America? *BusinessWeek,* March 10: 41–64.

44. Insights on risk perception across countries are addressed in: Purda, L. D. 2008. Risk perception and the financial system. *Journal of International Business Studies*, 39(7): 1178–1196.

45. Gogoi, P. 2010. Many U.S. companies are hiring . . . overseas. *www.msn.com*. December 28: np.

46. Byrnes, N. 2006. The high cost of fear. *BusinessWeek*, November 6: 16.

47. Goll, I. & Rasheed, M. A. 1997. Rational decision-making and firm performance: The moderating role of environment. *Strategic Management Journal*, 18: 583–591.

48. This discussion draws heavily on Porter, M. E. 1980. *Competitive strategy:* Chapter 1. New York: Free Press.

49. Ibid.

50. Rivalry in the airline industry is discussed in: Foust, D. 2009. Which airlines will disappear in 2009? *BusinessWeek*, January 19: 46–47.

51. Fryer, B. 2001. Leading through rough times: An interview with Novell's Eric Schmidt. *Harvard Business Review*, 78(5): 117–123.

52. For a discussion on the importance of barriers to entry within industries, read Greenwald, B. & Kahn, J. 2005. *Competition demystified: A radically simplified approach to business strategy*. East Rutherford, NJ: Portfolio.

53. A discussion of how the medical industry has erected entry barriers that have resulted in lawsuits is found in: Whelan, D. 2008. Bad medicine. *BusinessWeek*, March 10: 86–98.

54. The ProCD example draws heavily upon Shapiro, C. & Varian, H. R. 2000. Versioning: The smart way to sell information. *Harvard Business Review*, 78(1): 106–114.

55. Wise, R. & Baumgarter, P. 1999. Go downstream: The new profit imperative in manufacturing. *Harvard Business Review*, 77(5): 133–141.

56. Salman, W. A. 2000. The new economy is stronger than you think. *Harvard Business Review*, 77(6): 99–106.

57. Mudambi, R. & Helper, S. 1998. The "close but adversarial" model of supplier relations in the U.S. auto industry. *Strategic Management Journal*, 19: 775–792.

58. Trends in the solar industry are discussed in: Carey, J. 2009. Solar: The sun will come out tomorrow. *BusinessWeek*, January 12: 51.

59. Tischler, L. 2002. IBM: Manager jam. *Fast Company*, October: 48.

60. An interesting analysis of self-regulation in an industry (chemical) is in: Barnett, M. L. & King, A. A. 2008. Good fences make good neighbors: A longitudinal analysis of an industry self-regulatory institution. *Academy of Management Journal*, 51(6): 1053–1078.

61. For an interesting perspective on the intensity of competition in the supermarket industry, refer to Anonymous. 2005. Warfare in the aisles. *The Economist*, April 2: 6–8.

62. Marcial, G. 2000. Giving Viagra a run for its money. *BusinessWeek*, October 23: 173.

63. McGann, R. 2005. VOIP poised to take flight? *ClickZ.com*, February 23, *www.clickz.com*.

64. For an interesting perspective on changing features of firm boundaries, refer to Afuah, A. 2003. Redefining firm boundaries in the face of Internet: Are firms really shrinking? *Academy of Management Review*, 28(1): 34–53.

65. *www.consumerreports.org*.

66. Time to rebuild. 2001. *Economist*, May 19: 55–56.

67. *www.amazon.com*.

68. For more on the role of the Internet as an electronic intermediary, refer to Carr, N. G. 2000. Hypermediation: Commerce as clickstream. *Harvard Business Review*, 78(1): 46–48.

69. Olofson, C. 2001. The next best thing to being there. *Fast Company*, April: 175; and *www.conferenza.com*.

70. Lelii, S. R. 2001. Free online storage a thing of the past ? *eWEEK*, April 22.

71. *www.mysimon.com*; and *www.pricescan.com*.

72. *www.cnet.com*; and *www.bizrate.com*.

73. For insights into strategies in a low-profit industry, refer to: Hopkins, M. S. 2008. The management lessons of a beleaguered industry. *MIT Sloan Management Review*, 50(1): 25–31.

74. Foust, D. 2007. The best performers. *BusinessWeek*, March 26: 58–95; Rosenblum, D., Tomlinson, D., & Scott, L. 2003. Bottom-feeding for blockbuster businesses. *Harvard Business Review*, 81(3): 52–59; Paychex 2006 Annual Report; and, WellPoint Health Network 2005 Annual Report.

75. Kumar, N. 1996. The power of trust in manufacturer-retailer relationship. *Harvard Business Review*, 74(6): 92–110.

76. Welch, D. 2006. Renault-Nissan: Say hello to Bo. *BusinessWeek*, July 31: 56–57.

77. Brandenburger, A. & Nalebuff, B. J. 1995. The right game: Use game theory to shape strategy. *Harvard Business Review*, 73(4): 57–71.

78. For a scholarly discussion of complementary assets and their relationship to competitive advantage, refer to Stieglitz, N. & Heine, K. 2007. Innovations and the role of complementarities in a strategic theory of the firm. *Strategic Management Journal*, 28(1): 1–15.

79. A useful framework for the analysis of industry evolution has been proposed by Professor Anita McGahan of Boston University. Her analysis is based on the identification of the core activities and the core assets of an industry and the threats they face. She suggests that an industry may follow one of four possible evolutionary trajectories—radical change, creative change, intermediating change, or progressive change—based on these two types of threats of obsolescence. Refer to: McGahan, A. M. 2004. How industries change. *Harvard Business Review*, 82(10): 87–94.

80. Yoffie, D. B. & Kwak, M. 2006. With friends like these: The art of managing complementors. *Harvard Business Review*, 84(9): 88–98.

81. Porter, M. I. 2008. The five competitive forces that shape strategy. *Harvard Business Review*, 86 (1): 79–93.

82. Peteraf, M. & Shanley, M. 1997. Getting to know you: A theory of strategic group identity. *Strategic Management Journal*, 18 (Special Issue): 165–186.

83. An interesting scholarly perspective on strategic groups may be found in

Dranove, D., Perteraf, M., & Shanley, M. 1998. Do strategic groups exist? An economic framework for analysis. *Strategic Management Journal,* 19(11): 1029–1044.

84. For an empirical study on strategic groups and predictors of performance, refer to Short, J. C., Ketchen, D. J., Jr., Palmer, T. B., & Hult, T. M. 2007. Firm, strategic group, and industry influences on performance. *Strategic Management Journal,* 28(2): 147–167.

85. This section draws on several sources, including Kerwin, K. R. & Haughton, K. 1997. Can Detroit make cars that baby boomers like? *BusinessWeek,* December 1: 134–148; and Taylor, A., III. 1994. The new golden age of autos. *Fortune,* April 4: 50–66.

86. Csere, C. 2001. Supercar supermarket. *Car and Driver,* January: 118–127.

87. For a discussion of the extent of overcapacity in the worldwide automobile industry, read: Roberts, D., Matlack, C., Busyh, J., & Rowley, I. 2009. A hundred factories too many. *BusinessWeek,* January 19: 42–43.

88. Naughton, K. 2010. HIS auto trims 2010 U.S. vehicle sales forecast to 11.3 million units. *www.bloomberg.com/news.* September 27: np; and, Woodall, B. 2011. J. D. Power lowers U.S. auto sales forecast. *www.reuters.com.* August 10: np.

89. This discussion draws on: Wojdyla, B. 2008. The $2500 Tata Nano, unveiled in India. *jalopnik.com,* January 10: np; Roberts, D. 2008. China's Geely has global auto ambitions. *businessweek.com,* July 27: np; and, Fairclough, G. 2007. In China, Chery automobile drives an industry shift. *The Wall Street Journal,* December 4: A1, A17.

Chapter 3., Assessing the internal Environment of the Firm

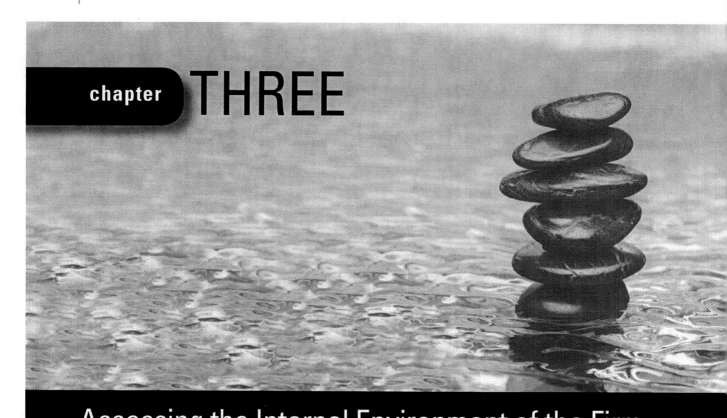

chapter THREE

Assessing the Internal Environment of the Firm

After reading this chapter, you should have a good understanding of:

LO3.1   The benefits and limitations of SWOT analysis in conducting an internal analysis of the firm.

LO3.2   The primary and support activities of a firm's value chain.

LO3.3   How value-chain analysis can help managers create value by investigating relationships among activities within the firm and between the firm and its customers and suppliers.

LO3.4   The resource-based view of the firm and the different types of tangible and intangible resources, as well as organizational capabilities.

LO3.5   The four criteria that a firm's resources must possess to maintain a sustainable advantage and how value created can be appropriated by employees and managers.

LO3.6   The usefulness of financial ratio analysis, its inherent limitations, and how to make meaningful comparisons of performance across firms.

LO3.7   The value of the "balanced scorecard" in recognizing how the interests of a variety of stakeholders can be interrelated.

LO3.8   How firms are using Internet technologies to add value and achieve unique advantages. (Appendix)

LEARNING OBJECTIVES

Two firms compete in the same industry and both have many strengths in a variety of functional areas: marketing, operations, logistics, and so on. However, one of these firms outperforms the other by a wide margin over a long period of time. How can this be so? This chapter endeavors to answer that question.

We begin with two sections that include frameworks for gaining key insights into a firm's internal environment: value-chain analysis and the resource-based view of the firm. In value-chain analysis, we divide a firm's activities into a series of value-creating steps. We then explore how individual activities within the firm add value, and also how *interrelationships* among activities within the firm, and between the firm and its suppliers and customers, create value.

In the resource-based view of the firm, we analyze the firm as a collection of tangible and intangible resources as well as organizational capabilities. Advantages that tend to be sustainable over time typically arise from creating *bundles* of resources and capabilities that satisfy four criteria: they are valuable, rare, difficult to imitate, and difficult to substitute. Not all of the value created by a firm will necessarily be kept (or appropriated) by the owners. We discuss the four key factors that determine how profits will be distributed between owners as well as employees and managers.

In the closing sections, we discuss how to evaluate a firm's performance and make comparisons across firms. We emphasize both the inclusion of financial resources and the interests of multiple stakeholders. Central to our discussion is the concept of the balanced scorecard, which recognizes that the interests of different stakeholders can be interrelated. We also consider how a firm's performance evolves over time and how it compares with industry norms and key competitors.

In an appendix to this chapter, we explore how Internet-based businesses and incumbent firms are using digital technologies to add value. We consider four activities—search, evaluation, problem solving, and transaction—as well as three types of content—customer feedback, expertise, and entertainment programming. Such technology-enhanced capabilities are providing new means with which firms can achieve competitive advantages.

▄▄▄ Learning from Mistakes

Toyota Motor Company had developed an industry-leading strategy that focused on value innovation and cost reduction.[1] For many years it was a solid strategy for both the company and its customers. Over the years, Toyota built a reputation for engineering excellence and cost cutting. Its engineers collaborated with suppliers to extract cost-savings without compromising quality. Yet, by the middle of the last decade, Toyota's virtue had become a vice and eventually led to recalled vehicles, lawsuits, and a damaged reputation. What went wrong?

Toyota's problems stemmed from an overwhelming desire to cut costs. This, in turn, led to a product that did not meet the same high quality that its customers had come to expect. When a North American parts supplier interested in working with the automaker did a teardown of a 2007 Camry, its engineers were surprised by how much the traditional Toyota craftsmanship had been watered down by years of nips and tucks. One example of this came to light in 2006, when a redesigned Camry revealed an embarrassing flaw in its headliner (the lining that covers the inside of the roof). Under pressure to cut costs, a Toyota affiliate chose a carbon fiber material that had not yet been approved by Toyota engineers. Unfortunately, the new carbon fiber material required so much heat to mold during production that it would catch fire. Thus, as many as 30 percent of the parts were scrapped—compared to a normal scrap rate for headliners of about 5 percent.

The worst of Toyota's problems came in early 2010 when the company recalled around 3.8 million vehicles. The problem with these vehicles occurred when customers complained that their car would suddenly accelerate to speeds of over 100 mph without warning. This recall included America's most popular passenger vehicle, the Camry, and the best-selling gas-electric hybrid, the Prius. Recalls came after the National Highway Traffic Safety Administration received reports of 102 incidents in which the accelerator became stuck. However, safety analysts estimated that there were approximately 2,000 cases in which owners of Toyota vehicles, including Camry, Prius, and Lexus, experienced "runaway cars."

A well-publicized incident that further tarnished Toyota's reputation was the tragic death of the Saylor family. On August 28, 2009, Mark Saylor died alongside his wife Cleofe, and their daughter Mahala, 13, and Mrs. Saylor's brother, Chris Lastrella when the Lexus they had rented accelerated out of control on a highway in San Diego. In the emergency call, Mr. Lastrella was heard saying: "We're in a Lexus . . . and we're going north on 125 and our accelerator is stuck . . . there's no brakes . . . we're approaching the intersection . . . Hold on . . . hold on and pray . . . pray."

Clearly, Toyota got carried away chasing high-speed growth, market share, and productivity gains year in and year out. This focus slowly dulled the commitment to quality embedded in Toyota's corporate culture. In February 2010, Kiichiro Toyoda, the grandson of the company's founder, told a congressional committee: "I fear the pace at which we have grown may have been too quick . . . Priorities became confused, and we were not able to stop, think and make improvements as much as we were able to do before."

Toyota aggressively tried to cut costs at a rate their product could not keep up with. By ignoring key aspects of the value chain, such as operations and R&D, quality was sacrificed within Toyota. This led to products that were faulty as well as a recall that has cost them billions of dollars in repairs and lost revenue—plus a damaged reputation.

In this chapter we will place heavy emphasis on the value-chain concept. That is, we focus on the key value-creating activities (e.g., operations, marketing and sales, and procurement) that a firm must effectively manage and integrate in order to attain competitive advantages in the marketplace. However, firms must not only pay close attention to their own value-creating activities but must also maintain close and effective relationships with key organizations outside the firm boundaries such as suppliers, customers, and alliance partners. Clearly, Toyota's overemphasis on cost cutting—both within the firm and with their suppliers—eroded the quality of their cars as well as their reputation with customers.

Before moving to value-chain analysis, let's briefly revisit the benefits and limitations of SWOT analysis. As discussed in Chapter 2, a SWOT analysis consists of a careful listing of a firm's strengths, weaknesses, opportunities, and threats. While we believe SWOT analysis is very helpful as a starting point, it should not form the primary basis for evaluating a firm's internal strengths and weaknesses or the opportunities and threats in the environment. Strategy Spotlight 3.1 elaborates on the limitations of the traditional SWOT approach.

We will now turn to value-chain analysis. As you will see, it provides greater insights into analyzing a firm's competitive position than SWOT analysis does by itself.

>LO3.1
The benefits and limitations of SWOT analysis in conducting an internal analysis of the firm.

Value-Chain Analysis

Value-chain analysis views the organization as a sequential process of value-creating activities. The approach is useful for understanding the building blocks of competitive advantage and was described in Michael Porter's seminal book *Competitive Advantage*.[2] Value is the amount that buyers are willing to pay for what a firm provides them and is measured by total revenue, a reflection of the price a firm's product commands and the quantity it can sell. A firm is profitable when the value it receives exceeds the total costs involved in creating its product or service. Creating value for buyers that exceeds the costs of production (i.e., margin) is a key concept used in analyzing a firm's competitive position.

Porter described two different categories of activities. First, five **primary activities**—inbound logistics, operations, outbound logistics, marketing and sales, and service—contribute to the physical creation of the product or service, its sale and transfer to the buyer, and its service after the sale. Second, **support activities**—procurement, technology development, human resource management, and general administration—either add value by themselves or add value through important relationships with both primary activities and other support activities. Exhibit 3.1 illustrates Porter's value chain.

value-chain analysis a strategic analysis of an organization that uses value-creating activities.

primary activities sequential activities of the value chain that refer to the physical creation of the product or service, its sale and transfer to the buyer, and its service after sale, including inbound logistics, operations, outbound logistics, marketing and sales, and service.

Exhibit 3.1 **The Value Chain: Primary and Support Activities**

Source: Reprinted with the permission of Free Press, a division of Simon & Schuster Inc., from *Competitive Advantage: Creating and Sustaining Superior Performance* by Michael E. Porter. Copyright © 1985, 1998 The Free Press. All rights reserved.

support activities activities of the value chain that either add value by themselves or add value through important relationships with both primary activities and other support activities; including procurement, technology development, human resource management, and general administration.

strategy spotlight   3.1

The Limitations of SWOT Analysis

SWOT analysis is a tried-and-true tool of strategic analysis. SWOT (strengths, weaknesses, opportunities, threats) analysis is used regularly in business to initially evaluate the opportunities and threats in the business environment as well as the strengths and weaknesses of a firm's internal environment. Top managers rely on SWOT to stimulate self-reflection and group discussions about how to improve their firm and position it for success.

But SWOT has its limitations. It is just a starting point for discussion. By listing the firm's attributes, managers have the raw material needed to perform more in-depth strategic analysis. However, SWOT cannot show them how to achieve a competitive advantage. They must not make SWOT analysis an end in itself, temporarily raising awareness about important issues but failing to lead to the kind of action steps necessary to enact strategic change.

Consider the ProCD example from Chapter 2, page 57. A brief SWOT analysis might include the following:

Strengths	Opportunities
First-mover advantage	Demand for electronic phone books
Low labor cost	Sudden growth in use of digital technology

Weaknesses	Threats
Inexperienced new company	Easily duplicated product
No proprietary information	Market power of incumbent firms

The combination of low production costs and an early-mover advantage in an environment where demand for CD-based phone books was growing rapidly seems to indicate that ProCD founder James Bryant had a golden opportunity. But the SWOT analysis did not reveal how to turn those strengths into a competitive advantage, nor did it highlight how rapidly the environment would change, allowing imitators to come into the market and erode his first-mover advantage. Let's look at some of the limitations of SWOT analysis.

Strengths May Not Lead to an Advantage

A firm's strengths and capabilities, no matter how unique or impressive, may not enable it to achieve a competitive advantage in the marketplace. It is akin to recruiting a concert pianist to join a gang of thugs—even though such

an ability is rare and valuable, it hardly helps the organization attain its goals and objectives! Similarly, the skills of a highly creative product designer would offer little competitive advantage to a firm that produces low-cost commodity products. Indeed, the additional expense of hiring such an individual could erode the firm's cost advantages. If a firm builds its strategy on a capability that cannot, by itself, create or sustain competitive advantage, it is essentially a wasted use of resources. ProCD had several key strengths, but it did not translate them into lasting advantages in the marketplace.

SWOT's Focus on the External Environment Is Too Narrow

Strategists who rely on traditional definitions of their industry and competitive environment often focus their sights too narrowly on current customers, technologies, and competitors. Hence they fail to notice important changes on the periphery of their environment that may trigger the need to redefine industry boundaries and identify a whole new set of competitive relationships. Reconsider the example from Chapter 2 of *Encyclopaedia Britannica*, whose competitive position was severely eroded by a "nontraditional" competitor—CD-based encyclopedias (e.g., Microsoft *Encarta*) that could be used on home computers.

SWOT Gives a One-Shot View of a Moving Target

A key weakness of SWOT is that it is primarily a static assessment. It focuses too much of a firm's attention on one moment in time. Essentially, this is like studying a single frame of a motion picture. You may be able to identify the principal actors and learn something about the setting, but it doesn't tell you much about the plot. Competition among organizations is played out over time. As circumstances, capabilities, and strategies change, static analysis techniques do not reveal the dynamics of the competitive environment. Clearly, ProCD was unaware that its competitiveness was being eroded so quickly.

SWOT Overemphasizes a Single Dimension of Strategy

Sometimes firms become preoccupied with a single strength or a key feature of the product or service they are offering and ignore other factors needed for competitive success. For example, Toyota, the giant automaker, paid a heavy price for its excessive emphasis on cost control. The resulting problems with quality and the negative publicity led to severe financial losses and an erosion of its reputation in many markets.

SWOT analysis has much to offer, but only as a starting point. By itself, it rarely helps a firm develop competitive advantages that it can sustain over time.

Sources: Shapiro, C. & Varian, H. R. 2000. Versioning: The Smart Way to Sell Information. *Harvard Business Review,* 78(1): 99–106; and Picken, J. C. & Dess, G. G. 1997. *Mission Critical.* Burr Ridge, IL: Irwin Professional Publishing.

To get the most out of value-chain analysis, view the concept in its broadest context, without regard to the boundaries of your own organization. That is, place your organization within a more encompassing value chain that includes your firm's suppliers, customers, and alliance partners. Thus, in addition to thoroughly understanding how value is created within the organization, be aware of how value is created for other organizations in the overall supply chain or distribution channel.[3]

Next, we'll describe and provide examples of each of the primary and support activities. Then, we'll provide examples of how companies add value by means of relationships among activities within the organization as well as activities outside the organization, such as those activities associated with customers and suppliers.[4]

> **>LO3.2**
> The primary and support activities of a firm's value chain.

Primary Activities

Five generic categories of primary activities are involved in competing in any industry, as shown in Exhibit 3.2. Each category is divisible into a number of distinct activities that depend on the particular industry and the firm's strategy.[5]

Inbound Logistics   Inbound logistics is primarily associated with receiving, storing, and distributing inputs to the product. It includes material handling, warehousing, inventory control, vehicle scheduling, and returns to suppliers.

> **inbound logistics** receiving, storing, and distributing inputs of a product.

Just-in-time (JIT) inventory systems, for example, were designed to achieve efficient inbound logistics. In essence, Toyota epitomizes JIT inventory systems, in which parts deliveries arrive at the assembly plants only hours before they are needed. JIT systems will play a vital role in fulfilling Toyota's commitment to fill a buyer's new car order in just five days.[6] This standard is in sharp contrast to most competitors that require approximately 30 days' notice to build vehicles. Toyota's standard is three times faster than even Honda Motors, considered to be the industry's most efficient in order follow-through. The five

---

Exhibit 3.2
The Value Chain: Some Factors to Consider in Assessing a Firm's Primary Activities

Inbound Logistics

- Location of distribution facilities to minimize shipping times.
- Warehouse layout and designs to increase efficiency of operations for incoming materials.

Operations

- Efficient plant operations to minimize costs.
- Efficient plant layout and workflow design.
- Incorporation of appropriate process technology.

Outbound Logistics

- Effective shipping processes to provide quick delivery and minimize damages.
- Shipping of goods in large lot sizes to minimize transportation costs.

Marketing and Sales

- Innovative approaches to promotion and advertising.
- Proper identification of customer segments and needs.

Service

- Quick response to customer needs and emergencies.
- Quality of service personnel and ongoing training.

Source: Adapted from Porter, M.E. 1985. *Competitive Advantage: Creating and Sustaining Superior Performance.* New York: Free Press.

days represent the time from the company's receipt of an order to the time the car leaves the assembly plant. Actual delivery may take longer, depending on where a customer lives. How can Toyota achieve such fast turnaround?

- Its 360 key suppliers are now linked to the company by way of computer on a virtual assembly line.
- Suppliers load parts onto trucks in the order in which they will be installed.
- Parts are stacked on trucks in the same place each time to help workers unload them quickly.
- Deliveries are required to meet a rigid schedule with as many as 12 trucks a day and no more than four hours between trucks.

operations all activities associated with transforming inputs into the final product form.

Operations   Operations include all activities associated with transforming inputs into the final product form, such as machining, packaging, assembly, testing, printing, and facility operations.

Creating environmentally friendly manufacturing is one way to use operations to achieve competitive advantage. Shaw Industries (now part of Berkshire Hathaway), a world-class competitor in the floor-covering industry, is well known for its concern for the environment.[7] It has been successful in reducing the expenses associated with the disposal of dangerous chemicals and other waste products from its manufacturing operations. Its environmental endeavors have multiple payoffs. Shaw has received many awards for its recycling efforts—awards that enhance its reputation.

outbound logistics collecting, storing, and distributing the product or service to buyers.

Outbound Logistics   Outbound logistics is associated with collecting, storing, and distributing the product or service to buyers. These activities include finished goods, warehousing, material handling, delivery vehicle operation, order processing, and scheduling.

● Despite superb logistics and excellent manufacturing operations, Dell's competitive position in personal computers—including desktops and laptops—has eroded in recent years.

Campbell Soup uses an electronic network to facilitate its continuous-replenishment program with its most progressive retailers.[8] Each morning, retailers electronically inform Campbell of their product needs and of the level of inventories in their distribution centers. Campbell uses that information to forecast future demand and to determine which products require replenishment (based on the inventory limits previously established with each retailer). Trucks leave Campbell's shipping plant that afternoon and arrive at the retailers' distribution centers the same day. The program cuts the inventories of participating retailers from about a four- to a two-weeks' supply. Campbell Soup achieved this improvement because it slashed delivery time and because it knows the inventories of key retailers and can deploy supplies when they are most needed.

The Campbell Soup example also illustrates the win–win benefits of exemplary value-chain activities. Both the supplier (Campbell) and its buyers (retailers) come out ahead. Since the retailer makes more money on Campbell products delivered through continuous replenishment, it has an incentive to carry a broader line and give the company greater shelf space. After Campbell introduced the program, sales of its products grew twice as fast through participating retailers as through all other retailers. Not surprisingly, supermarket chains love such programs.

3.2

strategy spotlight

Security Risks in Mexico Have Led to Higher Shipping Costs

A report in January 2009 by the U.S. Joint Forces Command caught some by surprise with its warning about Mexico's political instability. It stated: "In terms of worst-case scenarios for the Joint Force and indeed the world, two large and important states bear consideration for a rapid and sudden collapse: Pakistan and Mexico." While the report stated that a collapse in Mexico was considered less likely, it went on to say, "The government, its politicians and judicial infrastructure are all under sustained assault and pressure by criminal gangs and drug cartels. How that internal conflict turns out over the next several years will have a major impact on the stability of the Mexican state."

A December 17, 2010, *Wall Street Journal* article also claimed that fights between drug cartels claimed more than 31,000 lives over the most recent four-year period—including 11,000 lives in 2010. Further, crimes such as robbery, extortion, and kidnapping increased. For some companies—especially those that don't yet have operations in Mexico—the violence has become daunting.

Sources: Casey, N., & Hagerty, J. R. 2010. Companies Shun Violent Mexico. *www.wsj.com*. December 17: np; Anonymous. 2009. Just How Risky Has Mexico Become as a Sourcing Location? *www.scdigest.com*. February 9: np; and Villagran, L. 2010. Companies Grapple with Mexico Security Risks. *Dallas Morning News*. August 20: 1D, 3D.

Not surprisingly, such instability has implications for quality of life and economic development—as well as the cost of doing business. Let's take a look at how logistics costs are affected.

Ryder Systems, for example, doesn't take any chances when it comes to securing its shipping operations in Mexico. It uses GPS to track every one of its trucks moving manufactured goods in Mexico to the border. Private security agents escort every container before it heads to Texas or elsewhere. It handles about 3,000 border crossings weekly. And if a load arrives late, alarms are raised and the dogs do their inspections—not once, but three times.

Faced with the threat of smuggling attempts by criminal organizations in Mexico, foreign companies are simply forced to do more and spend more. In the process, they are charging consumers more to shore up security in a country where killings, extortions, and kidnappings have become part of daily life. While it is difficult to define the full scope of the problem, those who provide risk analysis can offer some insights.

The share of corporate operating costs dedicated to security has risen by roughly a third in the past two years, according to Julio Millan, a Mexico City–based business consultant. He estimates that security spending in 2010 accounted for 3 percent of corporate operating costs in the northern part of the country, versus only 2 percent in 2009. "That's a huge jump," claims Millan. "The public is paying the cost of security through the price of products."

Many U.S. companies with manufacturing plants in Mexico took advantage of low labor costs. However, they have experienced a sharp increase in their shipping costs. This is because they have been forced to spend more on security as a result of increasing drug-related violence (see Strategy Spotlight 3.2).

Marketing and Sales   These activities are associated with purchases of products and services by end users and the inducements used to get them to make purchases.[9] They include advertising, promotion, sales force, quoting, channel selection, channel relations, and pricing.[10,11]

It is not always enough to have a great product.[12] The key is to convince your channel partners that it is in their best interests not only to carry your product but also to market it in a way that is consistent with your strategy.[13] Consider Monsanto's efforts at educating distributors to improve the value proposition of its line of Saflex® windows.[14] The products had a superior attribute: The window design permitted laminators to form an exceptional type of glass by sandwiching a plastic sheet interlayer between two pieces of glass. This product is not only stronger and offers better ultraviolet protection than regular glass, but also when cracked, it adheres to the plastic sheet—an excellent safety feature for both cars and homes.

> **marketing and sales** activities associated with purchases of products and services by end users and the inducements used to get them to make purchases.

Despite these benefits, Monsanto had a hard time convincing laminators and window manufacturers to carry these products. According to Melissa Toledo, brand manager at Monsanto, "Saflex was priced at a 30 percent premium above traditional glass, and the various stages in the value chain (distributors and retailers) didn't think there would be a demand for such an expensive glass product." What did Monsanto do? It reintroduced Saflex as KeepSafe® and worked to coordinate the product's value propositions. By analyzing the experiences of all of the players in the supply chain, it was able to create marketing programs that helped each build a business aimed at selling its products. Said Toledo, "We want to know how they go about selling those types of products, what challenges they face, and what they think they need to sell our products. This helps us a lot when we try to provide them with these needs."[15]

At times, a firm's marketing initiatives may become overly aggressive and lead to actions that are both unethical and illegal.[16] For example:

- *Burdines.* This department store chain is under investigation for allegedly adding club memberships to its customers' credit cards without prior approval.
- *Fleet Mortgage.* This company has been accused of adding insurance fees for dental coverage and home insurance to its customers' mortgage loans without the customers' knowledge.
- *HCI Direct.* Eleven states have accused this direct-mail firm with charging for panty hose samples that customers did not order.
- *Juno Online Services.* The Federal Trade Commission brought charges against this Internet service provider for failing to provide customers with a telephone number to cancel service.

Strategy Spotlight. 3.3 discusses RYZ, a company which has almost no marketing costs. Why? It relies exclusively on social media such as Myspace and Facebook to create demand for its products.

service actions associated with providing service to enhance or maintain the value of the product.

Service   This primary activity includes all actions associated with providing service to enhance or maintain the value of the product, such as installation, repair, training, parts supply, and product adjustment.

Let's see how two retailers are providing exemplary customer service. At Sephora.com, a customer service representative taking a phone call from a repeat customer has instant access to what shade of lipstick she likes best. This will help the rep cross-sell by suggesting a matching shade of lip gloss. CEO Jim Wiggett expects such personalization to build loyalty and boost sales per customer. Nordstrom, the Seattle-based department store chain, goes even a step further. It offers a cyber-assist: A service rep can take control of a customer's Web browser and literally lead her to just the silk scarf that she is looking for. CEO Dan Nordstrom believes that such a capability will close enough additional purchases to pay for the $1 million investment in software.

Support Activities

Support activities in the value chain can be divided into four generic categories, as shown in Exhibit 3.3. Each category of the support activity is divisible into a number of distinct value activities that are specific to a particular industry. For example, technology development's discrete activities may include component design, feature design, field testing, process engineering, and technology selection. Similarly, procurement may include activities such as qualifying new suppliers, purchasing different groups of inputs, and monitoring supplier performance.

procurement the function of purchasing inputs used in the firm's value chain, including raw materials, supplies, and other consumable items as well as assets such as machinery, laboratory equipment, office equipment, and buildings.

Procurement   Procurement refers to the function of purchasing inputs used in the firm's value chain, not to the purchased inputs themselves.[17] Purchased inputs include raw materials, supplies, and other consumable items as well as assets such as machinery, laboratory equipment, office equipment, and buildings.[18,19]

3.3

strategy spotlight

Crowdsourcing: RYZ's Potential Customers Become Its Marketing and Design Staff

What happens when a company lets consumers design and vote on their own products? Quite often, the firm's overhead goes down and profits go up. This business model is an example of using crowdsourcing as a means of community-based design.

One of these companies is RYZ, founded in 2008, with over $1 million in revenues. It doesn't need a large marketing or design staff. Rather, it relies on potential customers for that. Would-be designers use a template from the company's website to create a pair of high-rise sneakers. The designs are posted online, and viewers vote on which ones they like. Winning designs are produced, and designers get $1,000 plus 1 percent of royalties for their efforts.

RYZ runs a weekly contest to cherry pick the best submitted sneaker design, which is then manufactured in a limited edition and sold for $54.99 to $99. And encouraging winners to promote their work makes sense: After all, you are more likely to try to make your design a success when you've invested time and effort. As an additional inducement, the winners get their picture on the company's website—along with a statement touting their work.

Not surprisingly, marketing costs are virtually nil, and relying on customers for design and market research enables the firm to move much more quickly, claims Rob Langstaff, the firm's founder and CEO. Previously head of Adidas North America, he says that it would take about 12 months and a substantial investment to get a design to market in the traditional, large shoe companies. In contrast, he asserts that RYZ can go from design to final product in only about six weeks.

Sources: Britten, F. 2010. The Youdesign Movement. *www.nyt.com*. February 25: np; Kaufman, W. 2009. Crowdsourcing Turns Business on Its Head. *www.npr.org*. August 20: np; and *RYZwear.com*.

crowdsourcing

Exhibit 3.3 The Value Chain: Some Factors to Consider in Assessing a Firm's Support Activities

General Administration

- Effective planning systems to attain overall goals and objectives.
- Excellent relationships with diverse stakeholder groups.
- Effective information technology to integrate value-creating activities.

Human Resource Management

- Effective recruiting, development, and retention mechanisms for employees.
- Quality relations with trade unions.
- Reward and incentive programs to motivate all employees.

Technology Development

- Effective R&D activities for process and product initiatives.
- Positive collaborative relationships between R&D and other departments.
- Excellent professional qualifications of personnel.

Procurement

- Procurement of raw material inputs to optimize quality and speed and to minimize the associated costs.
- Development of collaborative win-win relationships with suppliers.
- Analysis and selection of alternative sources of inputs to minimize dependence on one supplier.

Source: Adapted from Porter, M.E. 1985. *Competitive Advantage: Creating and Sustaining Superior Performance*. New York: Free Press.

Microsoft has improved its procurement process (and the quality of its suppliers) by providing formal reviews of its suppliers. One of Microsoft's divisions has extended the review process used for employees to its outside suppliers.[20] The employee services group, which is responsible for everything from travel to 401(k) programs to the on-site library, outsources more than 60 percent of the services it provides. Unfortunately, the employee services group was not providing them with enough feedback. This was feedback that the suppliers wanted to get and that Microsoft wanted to give.

The evaluation system that Microsoft developed helped clarify its expectations to suppliers. An executive noted: "We had one supplier—this was before the new system—that would have scored a 1.2 out of 5. After we started giving this feedback, and the supplier understood our expectations, its performance improved dramatically. Within six months, it scored a 4. If you'd asked me before we began the feedback system, I would have said that was impossible."

technology development
activities associated with the development of new knowledge that is applied to the firm's operations.

Technology Development   Every value activity embodies technology.[21] The array of technologies employed in most firms is very broad, ranging from technologies used to prepare documents and transport goods to those embodied in processes and equipment or the product itself.[22] Technology development related to the product and its features supports the entire value chain, while other technology development is associated with particular primary or support activities.

The Allied Signal and Honeywell merger brought together roughly 13,000 scientists and an $870 million R&D budget that should lead to some innovative products and services in two major areas: performance materials and control systems. Some of the possible innovations include:

- *Performance materials.* The development of uniquely shaped fibers with very high absorption capability. When employed in the company's Fram oil filters, they capture 50 percent more particles than ordinary filters. This means that cars can travel further with fewer oil changes.
- *Control systems.* Working with six leading oil companies, Honeywell developed software using "self-learning" algorithms that predict when something might go wrong in an oil refinery before it actually does. Examples include a faulty gas valve or hazardous spillage.[23]

human resource management
activities involved in the recruiting, hiring, training, development and compensation of all types of personnel.

Human Resource Management   Human resource management consists of activities involved in the recruiting, hiring, training, development, and compensation of all types of personnel.[24] It supports both individual primary and support activities (e.g., hiring of engineers and scientists) and the entire value chain (e.g., negotiations with labor unions).[25]

Like all great service companies, JetBlue Airways Corporation is obsessed with hiring superior employees.[26] But they found it difficult to attract college graduates to commit to careers as flight attendants. JetBlue developed a highly innovative recruitment program for flight attendants—a one-year contract that gives them a chance to travel, meet lots of people, and then decide what else they might like to do. They also introduced the idea of training a friend and employee together so that they could share a job. With such employee-friendly initiatives, JetBlue has been very successful in attracting talent.

Jeffrey Immelt, GE's chairman, addresses the importance of effective human resource management:[27]

Human resources has to be more than a department. GE recognized early on—50 or 60 years ago—that in a multibusiness company, the common denominators are people and culture. From an employee's first day at GE, she discovers that she's in the people-development business as much as anything else. You'll find that most good companies have the same basic HR processes that we have, but they're discrete. HR at GE is not an agenda item; it is the agenda.

3.4

strategy spotlight

Removing Individual Metrics in Performance Evaluations

ITT China President William Taylor wanted to know why employee turnover was so high in the Shanghai sales office. The local manager knew the answer: If the sales manager gave workers an average "3" on the 1-5 performance scale, they'd stop talking to him and, in some cases, quit shortly thereafter. The manager lamented: "They're losing face in the organization. It would be great if we could do something about the scores."

Comments like that popped up around the world. For example, in southern Europe, the focus on individual performance didn't sit well with the region's more "collective

ethos," claims James Duncan, director of ITT's talent development. And in Scandinavia, where there's more of "a sense of equality between bosses and workers," says Duncan, some workers asked, "What gives you the right to rate me a 3?" That led ITT to make the radical decision to ditch performance ratings altogether.

Most employees, who still require a detailed evaluation, cheered the changes. In one of the ITT plants in Shenyang, China, the new system has helped to cut the plant's attrition rate in half. The change isn't as popular in the U.S., where some metrics-loving engineers in the defense business remain attached to the old rankings. Still, most people have come around. Says Duncan, "It's not just Asia and Europe." No matter what culture you are from, everyone "likes the fact that they're treated like an adult in this discussion."

Source: McGregor, J. 2008. Case study: To Adapt, ITT Lets Go of Unpopular Ratings. *BusinessWeek*, January 28: 46.

Strategy Spotlight 3.4 discusses a rather unique approach to individual performance evaluations: eliminate the metrics!

General Administration   General administration consists of a number of activities, including general management, planning, finance, accounting, legal and government affairs, quality management, and information systems. Administration (unlike the other support activities) typically supports the entire value chain and not individual activities.[28]

Although general administration is sometimes viewed only as overhead, it can be a powerful source of competitive advantage. In a telephone operating company, for example, negotiating and maintaining ongoing relations with regulatory bodies can be among the most important activities for competitive advantage. Also, in some industries top management plays a vital role in dealing with important buyers.[29]

The strong and effective leadership of top executives can also make a significant contribution to an organization's success. As we discussed in Chapter 1, chief executive officers (CEOs) such as Herb Kelleher, Andrew Grove, and Jack Welch have been credited with playing critical roles in the success of Southwest Airlines, Intel, and General Electric.

Information systems can also play a key role in increasing operating efficiencies and enhancing a firm's performance.[30] Consider Walgreen Co.'s introduction of Intercom Plus, a computer-based prescription management system. Linked by computer to both doctors' offices and third-party payment plans, the system automates telephone refills, store-to-store prescription transfers, and drug reordering. It also provides information on drug interactions and, coupled with revised workflows, frees up pharmacists from administrative tasks to devote more time to patient counseling.[31]

Interrelationships among Value-Chain Activities within and across Organizations

We have defined each of the value-chain activities separately for clarity of presentation. Managers must not ignore, however, the importance of relationships among value-chain

>LO3.3
How value-chain analysis can help managers create value by investigating relationships among activities within the firm and between the firm and its customers and suppliers.

general administration
general management, planning, finance, accounting, legal and government affairs, quality management, and information systems; activities that support the entire value chain and not individual activities.

interrelationships
collaborative and strategic exchange relationships between value-chain activities either (a) within firms or (b) between firms. Strategic exchange relationships involve exchange of resources such as information, people, technology, or money that contribute to the success of the firm.

activities.[32] There are two levels: (1) **interrelationships** among activities within the firm and (2) relationships among activities within the firm and with other stakeholders (e.g., customers and suppliers) that are part of the firm's expanded value chain.[33]

With regard to the first level, consider AT&T's innovative Resource Link program. Here, employees who have reached their plateau may apply for temporary positions in other parts of the organization. Clearly, this program has the potential to benefit all activities within the firm's value chain because it creates opportunities for top employees to lend their expertise to all of the organization's value-creating activities.

With regard to the second level, Campbell Soup's use of electronic networks enabled it to improve the efficiency of outbound logistics.[34] However, it also helped Campbell manage the ordering of raw materials more effectively, improve its production scheduling, and help its customers better manage their inbound logistics operations.

Strategy Spotlight 3.5 discusses an innovative initiative by Timberland, a leading shoe manufacturer, to eliminate toxic adhesives from its shoes. This effort has the potential for long-term cost savings for their suppliers as well as increased market share for their product line.

The "Prosumer" Concept: Integrating Customers into the Value Chain

When addressing the value-chain concept, it is important to focus on the interrelationship between the organization and its most important stakeholder—its customers.[35] A key to success for some leading-edge firms is to team up with their customers to satisfy their particular need(s). As stated in a recent IBM Global CEO Study:

> In the future, we will be talking more and more about the "prosumer"—a customer/ producer who is even more extensively integrated into the value chain. As a consequence, production processes will be customized more precisely and individually.[36]

Including customers in the actual production process can create greater satisfaction among them. It also has the potential to result in significant cost savings and to generate innovative ideas for the firm, which can be transferred to the customer in terms of lower prices and higher quality products and services.

In terms of how a firm views its customers, the move to create the prosumer stands in rather stark contrast to the conventional marketing approach in which the customer merely consumes the products produced by the company. Another area where this approach differs from conventional thinking concerns the notion of tying the customer into the company through, for example, loyalty programs and individualized relationship marketing.

How Procter & Gamble Embraced the Prosumer Concept   In the early 2000s P&G's people were not clearly oriented toward any common purpose. The corporate mission "To meaningfully improve the everyday lives of the customers" had not been explicitly or inspirationally rolled out to the employees. To more clearly focus everyone's efforts, P&G expanded the mission to include the idea that "the consumer is the boss." This philosophy became one in which people who buy and use P&G products are valued not just for their money but also as *a rich source of information and direction*. "The consumer is the boss" became far more than a slogan in P&G. It became a clear, simple, and inclusive cultural priority for both employees and the external stakeholders such as suppliers.

The P&G efforts in the fragrance areas are one example. P&G transformed this small underperforming business area into a global leader and the world's largest fine fragrance company. They accomplished this by clearly and precisely defining the target consumer for each fragrance brand and by identifying subgroups of consumers for some brands. P&G still kept the partnerships with established fashion houses such as Dolce & Gabbana, Gucci, and Lacoste. However, the main point was to make the consumer the boss, focusing on innovations that were meaningful to consumers, including, for instance, fresh new

3.5

strategy spotlight

Timberland's Detoxification Initiative

Making shoes is a surprisingly toxic business. Both the materials and the adhesives that connect them are made of chemicals that are known dangers to the cardiac, respiratory, and nervous systems. One pair of running shoes will hardly harm you. However, workers in the industry face real risks.

Timberland, the second largest company in the outdoor industry, with $1.3 billion in revenues, realized that it needed to rethink the industry's traditional reliance on toxic chemicals. It became the first footwear company to test new water-based adhesives on nonathletic shoes. (Nike and others had already taken the initiatives in the "white shoe," or athletic, part of the industry.) Making such a change required the firm to work closely with Asian suppliers. According to Timberland's website, the company released its long-term strategy in 2008, which included its goal to create products at lower cost and with less harm to the environment. The strategy included eliminating polyvinylchloride (PVC) from its product line and increasing the use of water-based adhesives in its footwear in order to reduce the use of solvents.

Common sense would suggest that Timberland's detoxification efforts would be very costly for its suppliers. And during the test phase it was quite expensive. The new adhesives cost more because economies of scale hadn't yet been achieved. However, over time, Timberland fully expects the process to be at least cost neutral for its business and a money maker for the full value chain.

Sources: Esty, D. C. & Winston, A. S. *Green to Gold*. Hoboken, NJ: Wiley, p: 112–113; *www.community.timberland.com*; and *finance.yahoo.com*.

Why? Water-based adhesives eliminate almost entirely the supplier's expense for handling hazardous materials, including waste disposal, insurance, and training. Manufacturing expenses had already declined during the testing phase, because water-based adhesives go on with one coat instead of two, and the application equipment requires less cleaning. Thus, suppliers can run

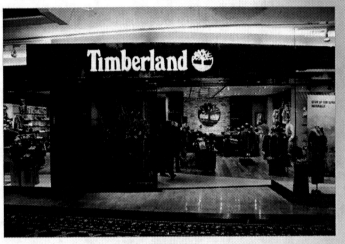

● Timberland is well known for their environmental sustainability initiatives.

longer without interruption. The change also improves worker safety as well as reduces both labor costs and time.

Sounds good. But will Timberland be able to capture these supplier savings down the road? Probably not, but over time this strategy should help the firm win market share and drive revenues.

 environmental sustainability

---

scents, distinctive packaging, and proactive marketing. In addition, P&G streamlined the supply chain to reduce complexity and lower its cost structure.

"The consumer is the boss" idea goes even further. It also means that P&G tries to build social connections through digital media and other forms of interactions (thus incorporating the crowdsourcing concept that we introduced in Chapter 1). Baby diapers are one example. P&G used to use handmade diapers for its product tests. Today, however, this product is shown digitally and created in alternatives in an on-screen virtual world. Changes can be made immediately as new ideas emerge, and it can be redesigned on screen. Thus, P&G is creating a social system with the consumers (and potential consumers) that enable the firm to co-design and co-engineer new innovations with buyers. At P&G the philosophy of "the consumer is the boss" set a new standard.

Applying the Value Chain to Service Organizations

The concepts of inbound logistics, operations, and outbound logistics suggest managing the raw materials that might be manufactured into finished products and delivered to customers. However, these three steps do not apply only to manufacturing. They correspond to any transformation process in which inputs are converted through a work process into outputs that add value. For example, accounting is a sort of transformation process that converts daily records of individual transactions into monthly financial reports. In this example, the transaction records are the inputs, accounting is the operation that adds value, and financial statements are the outputs.

What are the "operations," or transformation processes, of service organizations? At times, the difference between manufacturing and service is in providing a customized solution rather than mass production as is common in manufacturing. For example, a travel agent adds value by creating an itinerary that includes transportation, accommodations, and activities that are customized to your budget and travel dates. A law firm renders services that are specific to a client's needs and circumstances. In both cases, the work process (operation) involves the application of specialized knowledge based on the specifics of a situation (inputs) and the outcome that the client desires (outputs).

The application of the value chain to service organizations suggests that the value-adding process may be configured differently depending on the type of business a firm is engaged in. As the preceding discussion on support activities suggests, activities such as procurement and legal services are critical for adding value. Indeed, the activities that may only provide support to one company may be critical to the primary value-adding activity of another firm.

Exhibit 3.4 provides two models of how the value chain might look in service industries. In the retail industry, there are no manufacturing operations. A firm, such as Best Buy, adds value by developing expertise in the procurement of finished goods and by displaying them in their stores in a way that enhances sales. Thus, the value chain makes procurement activities (i.e., partnering with vendors and purchasing goods) a primary rather than a support activity. Operations refer to the task of operating Best Buy's stores.

Exhibit 3.4 Some Examples of Value Chains in Service Industries

For an engineering services firm, research and development provides inputs, the transformation process is the engineering itself, and innovative designs and practical solutions are the outputs. Arthur D. Little, for example, is a large consulting firm with offices in 20 countries. In its technology and innovation management practice, A. D. Little strives to make the best use of the science, technology and knowledge resources available to create value for a wide range of industries and client sectors. This involves activities associated with research and development, engineering, and creating solutions as well as downstream activities such as marketing, sales, and service. How the primary and support activities of a given firm are configured and deployed will often depend on industry conditions and whether the company is service and/or manufacturing oriented.

Resource-Based View of the Firm

The **resource-based view (RBV) of the firm** combines two perspectives: (1) the internal analysis of phenomena within a company and (2) an external analysis of the industry and its competitive environment.[37] It goes beyond the traditional SWOT (strengths, weaknesses, opportunities, threats) analysis by integrating internal and external perspectives. The ability of a firm's resources to confer competitive advantage(s) cannot be determined without taking into consideration the broader competitive context. A firm's resources must be evaluated in terms of how valuable, rare, and hard they are for competitors to duplicate. Otherwise, the firm attains only competitive parity.

As noted earlier (in Strategy Spotlight 3.1), a firm's strengths and capabilities—no matter how unique or impressive—do not necessarily lead to competitive advantages in the marketplace. The criteria for whether advantages are created and whether or not they can be sustained over time will be addressed later in this section. Thus, the RBV is a very useful framework for gaining insights as to why some competitors are more profitable than others. As we will see later in the book, the RBV is also helpful in developing strategies for individual businesses and diversified firms by revealing how core competencies embedded in a firm can help it exploit new product and market opportunities.

In the two sections that follow, we will discuss the three key types of resources that firms possess (summarized in Exhibit 3.5): tangible resources, intangible resources, and organizational capabilities. Then we will address the conditions under which such assets and capabilities can enable a firm to attain a sustainable competitive advantage.[38]

It is important to note that resources by themselves typically do not yield a competitive advantage. Even if a basketball team recruited an all-star center, there would be little chance of victory if the other members of the team were continually outplayed by their opponents or if the coach's attitude was so negative that everyone, including the center, became unwilling to put forth their best efforts.

In a business context, a firm's excellent value-creating activities (e.g., logistics) would not be a source of competitive advantage if those activities were not integrated with other important value-creating activities such as marketing and sales. Thus, a central theme of the resource-based view of the firm is that competitive advantages are created (and sustained) through the bundling of several resources in unique combinations.[39]

Types of Firm Resources

Firm resources are all assets, capabilities, organizational processes, information, knowledge, and so forth, controlled by a firm that enable it to develop and implement value-creating strategies.

Tangible Resources These are assets that are relatively easy to identify. They include the physical and financial assets that an organization uses to create value for its

resource-based view of the firm perspective that firms' competitive advantages are due to their endowment of strategic resources that are valuable, rare, costly to imitate, and costly to substitute.

>LO3.4
The resource-based view of the firm and the different types of tangible and intangible resources, as well as organizational capabilities.

tangible resources organizational assets that are relatively easy to identify, including physical assets, financial resources, organizational resources, and technological resources.

Exhibit 3.5
The Resource-Based View of the Firm: Resources and Capabilities

Tangible Resources	
Financial	• Firm's cash account and cash equivalents.
	• Firm's capacity to raise equity.
	• Firm's borrowing capacity.
Physical	• Modern plant and facilities.
	• Favorable manufacturing locations.
	• State-of-the-art machinery and equipment.
Technological	• Trade secrets.
	• Innovative production processes.
	• Patents, copyrights, trademarks.
Organizational	• Effective strategic planning processes.
	• Excellent evaluation and control systems.

Intangible Resources	
Human	• Experience and capabilities of employees.
	• Trust.
	• Managerial skills.
	• Firm-specific practices and procedures.
Innovation and creativity	• Technical and scientific skills.
	• Innovation capacities.
Reputation	• Brand name.
	• Reputation with customers for quality and reliability.
	• Reputation with suppliers for fairness, non–zero-sum relationships.

Organizational Capabilities

- Firm competencies or skills the firm employs to transfer inputs to outputs.
- Capacity to combine tangible and intangible resources, using organizational processes to attain desired end.

EXAMPLES:
  - Outstanding customer service.
  - Excellent product development capabilities.
  - Innovativeness of products and services.
  - Ability to hire, motivate, and retain human capital.

Source: Adapted from Barney, J. B. 1991. Firm Resources and Sustained Competitive Advantage. *Journal of Management:* 17: 101; Grant, R. M. 1991. *Contemporary Strategy Analysis:* 100–102. Cambridge England: Blackwell Business and Hitt, M. A., Ireland, R. D., & Hoskisson, R. E. 2001. *Strategic Management: Competitiveness and Globalization* (4th ed.). Cincinnati: South-Western College Publishing.

customers. Among them are financial resources (e.g., a firm's cash, accounts receivables, and its ability to borrow funds); physical resources (e.g., the company's plant, equipment, and machinery as well as its proximity to customers and suppliers); organizational resources (e.g., the company's strategic planning process and its employee development, evaluation, and reward systems); and technological resources (e.g., trade secrets, patents, and copyrights).

Many firms are finding that high-tech, computerized training has dual benefits: It develops more effective employees and reduces costs at the same time. Employees at FedEx take computer-based job competency tests every 6 to 12 months.[40] The 90-minute computer-based tests identify areas of individual weakness and provide input to a computer database of employee skills—information the firm uses in promotion decisions.

Intangible Resources   Much more difficult for competitors (and, for that matter, a firm's own managers) to account for or imitate are **intangible resources**, which are typically embedded in unique routines and practices that have evolved and accumulated over time. These include human resources (e.g., experience and capability of employees, trust, effectiveness of work teams, managerial skills), innovation resources (e.g., technical and scientific expertise, ideas), and reputation resources (e.g., brand name, reputation with suppliers for fairness and with customers for reliability and product quality).[41] A firm's culture may also be a resource that provides competitive advantage.[42]

For example, you might not think that motorcycles, clothes, toys, and restaurants have much in common. Yet Harley-Davidson has entered all of these product and service markets by capitalizing on its strong brand image—a valuable intangible resource.[43] It has used that image to sell accessories, clothing, and toys, and it has licensed the Harley-Davidson Café in New York City to provide further exposure for its brand name and products.

Strategy Spotlight 3.6 discusses how various social networking sites have the potential to play havoc with a firm's reputation.

Organizational Capabilities   **Organizational capabilities** are not specific tangible or intangible assets, but rather the competencies or skills that a firm employs to transform inputs into outputs.[44] In short, they refer to an organization's capacity to deploy tangible and intangible resources over time and generally in combination, and to leverage those capabilities to bring about a desired end.[45] Examples of organizational capabilities are outstanding customer service, excellent product development capabilities, superb innovation processes, and flexibility in manufacturing processes.[46]

In the case of Apple, the majority of components used in their products can be characterized as proven technology, such as touch screen and MP3 player functionality.[47] However, Apple combines and packages these in new and innovative ways while also seeking to integrate the value chain. This is the case with iTunes, for example, where suppliers of downloadable music are a vital component of the success Apple has enjoyed with their iPod series of MP3 players. Thus, Apple draws on proven technologies and their ability to offer innovative combinations of these.

Firm Resources and Sustainable Competitive Advantages

As we have mentioned, resources alone are not a basis for competitive advantages, nor are advantages sustainable over time.[48] In some cases, a resource or capability helps a firm to increase its revenues or to lower costs but the firm derives only a temporary advantage because competitors quickly imitate or substitute for it.[49] Many e-commerce businesses in the early 2000s saw their profits seriously eroded because new (or existing) competitors easily duplicated their business model. For example, Priceline.com, expanded its offerings from enabling customers to place bids online for airline tickets to a wide variety of other products. However, it was easy for competitors (e.g., a consortium of major airlines) to duplicate Priceline's products and services. Ultimately, its market capitalization had plummeted roughly 98 percent from its all-time high.

For a resource to provide a firm with the potential for a sustainable competitive advantage, it must have four attributes.[50] First, the resource must be valuable in the sense that it exploits opportunities and/or neutralizes threats in the firm's environment. Second, it must be rare among the firm's current and potential competitors. Third, the resource must be difficult for competitors to imitate. Fourth, the resource must have no strategically equivalent

intangible resources organizational assets that are difficult to identify and account for and are typically embedded in unique routines and practices, including human resources, innovation resources, and reputation resources.

organizational capabilities the competencies and skills that a firm employs to transform inputs into outputs.

strategic resources (also firm resources or organizational resources) firms' capabilities that are valuable, rare, costly to imitate, and costly to substitute.

>LO3.5
The four criteria that a firm's resources must possess to maintain a sustainable advantage and how value created can be appropriated by employees and managers.

strategy spotlight   3.6

Blogs, Social Networking Sites, and Corporate Reputations: A Lethal Combination?

Customers are now connecting with and drawing power from one another. The mechanism: online social technologies such as blogs, social networking sites like MySpace, user-generated content sites like YouTube, and countless communities across the web. They are defining their own perspective on companies and brands—a perspective that is often at odds with the image a company wants to project. This groundswell of people using technologies to get the things they need from one another, rather than from the companies, has tilted the balance of power from company to customer.

Let's look at an example: Brian Finkelstein, a law student, had trouble with the cable modem in his home. A Comcast Cable repairman arrived to fix the problem. However, when the technician had to call the home office for a key piece of information, he was put on hold for so long that he fell asleep on Finkelstein's couch. Outraged, Finkelstein made a video of the sleeping technician and posted it on YouTube. The clip became a hit—with more than a million viewings. And, to this day, it continues to undermine Comcast's efforts to improve its reputation for customer service.

Source: Bernoff, J. & Li, C. 2008. Harnessing the Power of the Oh-So-Social Web. *MIT Sloan Management Review*, 49(3): 36–42; and, Stelter, B. 2008. Griping Online? Comcast Hears and Talks Back. nytimes.com, July 25: np.

But Comcast is working hard to improve its reputation. It has a lot of work to do—after all, the company was ranked at the bottom of a recent American Customer Satisfaction Index, which tracks consumer opinions of more than 200 companies. And hundreds of customers have filed grievances on a site called comcastmustdie.com.

One of Comcast's initiatives to try to turn things around is headed by Frank Eliason, its digital care manager. He uses readily available online tools to monitor public comments on blogs, message boards, and social networks for any mention of Comcast. When Eliason sees a complaint, he contacts the source and tries to defuse the problem. "When you're having a two-way conversation, you really get to clear the air," says Eliason.

Comcast says the online outreach is part of a larger effort to revamp its customer service. In just five months, Eliason, whose job redefines customer service, has reached out to well over 1,000 customers online.

Comcast is not the only company trying to reach out to customers online. Using the social messaging service Twitter, Southwest Airlines answers customer questions about ticket prices and flight delays, Whole Foods Market posts details about discounts, and the chief executive of the online shoe store Zappos shares details of his life with 7,200 "followers." Many other companies also monitor online discussion groups. But given its track record, Comcast felt they needed to take the extra step: contacting customers who are discussing the company online.

---

substitutes. These criteria are summarized in Exhibit 3.6. We will now discuss each of these criteria. Then, we will examine how Dell's competitive advantage, which seemed secure as late as 2006, has eroded.

Is the Resource Valuable?   Organizational resources can be a source of competitive advantage only when they are valuable. Resources are valuable when they enable a firm to formulate and implement strategies that improve its efficiency or effectiveness. The SWOT framework suggests that firms improve their performance only when they exploit opportunities or neutralize (or minimize) threats.

The fact that firm attributes must be valuable in order to be considered resources (as well as potential sources of competitive advantage) reveals an important complementary relationship among environmental models (e.g., SWOT and five-forces analyses) and the resource-based model. Environmental models isolate those firm attributes that exploit opportunities and/or neutralize threats. Thus, they specify what firm attributes may be considered as resources. The resource-based model then suggests what additional characteristics these resources must possess if they are to develop a sustained competitive advantage.

Is the resource or capability . . .	Implications
Valuable?	• Neutralize threats and exploit opportunities
Rare?	• Not many firms possess
Difficult to imitate?	• Physically unique
	• Path dependency (how accumulated over time)
	• Causal ambiguity (difficult to disentangle what it is or how it could be re-created)
	• Social complexity (trust, interpersonal relationships, culture, reputation)
Difficult to substitute?	• No equivalent strategic resources or capabilities

Exhibit 3.6
Four Criteria for Assessing Sustainability of Resources and Capabilities

Is the Resource Rare? If competitors or potential competitors also possess the same valuable resource, it is not a source of a competitive advantage because all of these firms have the capability to exploit that resource in the same way. Common strategies based on such a resource would give no one firm an advantage. For a resource to provide competitive advantages, it must be uncommon, that is, rare relative to other competitors.

This argument can apply to bundles of valuable firm resources that are used to formulate and develop strategies. Some strategies require a mix of multiple types of resources—tangible assets, intangible assets, and organizational capabilities. If a particular bundle of firm resources is not rare, then relatively large numbers of firms will be able to conceive of and implement the strategies in question. Thus, such strategies will not be a source of competitive advantage, even if the resource in question is valuable.

Can the Resource Be Imitated Easily? Inimitability (difficulty in imitating) is a key to value creation because it constrains competition.[51] If a resource is inimitable, then any profits generated are more likely to be sustainable.[52] Having a resource that competitors can easily copy generates only temporary value.[53] This has important implications. Since managers often fail to apply this test, they tend to base long-term strategies on resources that are imitable. IBP (Iowa Beef Processors) became the first meatpacking company in the United States to modernize by building a set of assets (automated plants located in cattle-producing states) and capabilities (low-cost "disassembly" of carcasses) that earned returns on assets of 1.3 percent in the 1970s. By the late 1980s, however, ConAgra and Cargill had imitated these resources, and IBP's profitability fell by nearly 70 percent, to 0.4 percent.

Monster.com entered the executive recruiting market by providing, in essence, a substitute for traditional bricks-and-mortar headhunting firms. Although Monster.com's resources are rare and valuable, they are subject to imitation by new rivals—other dot-com firms. Why? There are very low entry barriers for firms wanting to try their hand at recruitment. For example, many job search dot-coms have emerged in recent years, including jobsearch.com, headhunter.com, nationjob.com, and hotjobs.com. In all, there are more than 40,000 online job boards available to job seekers. It would be most difficult for a firm to attain a sustainable advantage in this industry.

Clearly, an advantage based on inimitability won't last forever. Competitors will eventually discover a way to copy most valuable resources. However, managers can forestall them and sustain profits for a while by developing strategies around resources that have at least one of the following four characteristics.[54]

Physical Uniqueness The first source of inimitability is physical uniqueness, which by definition is inherently difficult to copy. A beautiful resort location, mineral rights, or Pfizer's pharmaceutical patents simply cannot be imitated. Many managers believe that several of their resources may fall into this category, but on close inspection, few do.

path dependency
a characteristic of resources that is developed and/or accumulated through a unique series of events.

Path Dependency A greater number of resources cannot be imitated because of what economists refer to as **path dependency.** This simply means that resources are unique and therefore scarce because of all that has happened along the path followed in their development and/or accumulation. Competitors cannot go out and buy these resources quickly and easily; they must be built up over time in ways that are difficult to accelerate.

The Gerber Products Co. brand name for baby food is an example of a resource that is potentially inimitable. Re-creating Gerber's brand loyalty would be a time-consuming process that competitors could not expedite, even with expensive marketing campaigns. Similarly, the loyalty and trust that Southwest Airlines employees feel toward their firm and its cofounder, Herb Kelleher, are resources that have been built up over a long period of time. Also, a crash R&D program generally cannot replicate a successful technology when research findings cumulate. Clearly, these path-dependent conditions build protection for the original resource. The benefits from experience and learning through trial and error cannot be duplicated overnight.

causal ambiguity
a characteristic of a firm's resources that is costly to imitate because a competitor cannot determine what the resource is and/or how it can be re-created.

Causal Ambiguity The third source of inimitability is termed **causal ambiguity.** This means that would-be competitors may be thwarted because it is impossible to disentangle the causes (or possible explanations) of either what the valuable resource is or how it can be re-created. What is the root of 3M's innovation process? You can study it and draw up a list of possible factors. But it is a complex, unfolding (or folding) process that is hard to understand and would be hard to imitate.

Often, causally ambiguous resources are organizational capabilities, involving a complex web of social interactions that may even depend on particular individuals. When Continental and United tried to mimic the successful low-cost strategy of Southwest Airlines, the planes, routes, and fast gate turnarounds were not the most difficult aspects for them to copy. Those were all rather easy to observe and, at least in principle, easy to duplicate. However, they could not replicate Southwest's culture of fun, family, frugality, and focus since no one can clearly specify exactly what that culture is or how it came to be.

Strategy Spotlight 3.7 describes Amazon's continued success as the world's largest online marketplace. Competitors recently tried to imitate Amazon's free shipping strategy, but with limited success. The reason is that Amazon has developed an array of interrelated elements of strategy which their rivals find too difficult to imitate.

social complexity
a characteristic of a firm's resources that is costly to imitate because the social engineering required is beyond the capability of competitors, including interpersonal relations among managers, organizational culture, and reputation with suppliers and customers.

Social Complexity A firm's resources may be imperfectly inimitable because they reflect a high level of **social complexity.** Such phenomena are typically beyond the ability of firms to systematically manage or influence. When competitive advantages are based on social complexity, it is difficult for other firms to imitate them.

A wide variety of firm resources may be considered socially complex. Examples include interpersonal relations among the managers in a firm, its culture, and its reputation with its suppliers and customers. In many of these cases, it is easy to specify how these socially complex resources add value to a firm. Hence, there is little or no causal ambiguity surrounding the link between them and competitive advantage. But an understanding that certain firm attributes, such as quality relations among managers, can improve a firm's efficiency does not necessarily lead to systematic efforts to imitate them. Such social engineering efforts are beyond the capabilities of most firms.

Although complex physical technology is not included in this category of sources of imperfect inimitability, the exploitation of physical technology in a firm typically involves the use of socially complex resources. That is, several firms may possess the same physical technology, but only one of them may have the social relations, culture, group norms, and so on to fully exploit the technology in implementing its strategies. If such complex social resources are not subject to imitation (and assuming they are valuable and rare and no substitutes exist), this firm may obtain a sustained competitive advantage from exploiting its physical technology more effectively than other firms.

3.7

Amazon Prime: Very Difficult for Rivals to Copy

strategy spotlight

Amazon Prime is a free shipping service which guarantees delivery of products within two days for an annual fee of $79. According to *Bloomberg Businessweek,* it may be the most ingenious and effective customer loyalty program in all of e-commerce, if not retail in general. It converts casual shoppers, who gorge on the gratification of having purchases reliably appear two days after they order, into Amazon addicts. Analysts describe Prime as one of the main factors driving Amazon's stock price—up nearly 300 percent from 2008 to 2010. Also, it is one of the main reasons why Amazon's sales grew 30 percent during the recession while other retailers suffered.

Analysts estimate that Amazon Prime has more than 4 million members in the United States, a small slice of Amazon's 121 million active buyers worldwide. However, analysts claim that Prime members increase their purchases on the site by about 150 percent after they join and may be responsible for as much as 20 percent of Amazon's overall sales in the United States. Such shoppers are considered the "whales" of the $140 billion U.S. e-commerce market, one of the fastest-growing parts of U.S. retail. And, according to Hudson Square Research, Amazon, with a hefty 8 percent of the U.S. e-commerce market, is the single biggest online retailer in the United States.

Source: Stone, B. 2010. What's in the box? Instant gratification. *Bloomberg Businessweek.* November 29-December 5: 39–40; Klein, E. 2010. The genius of Amazon Prime. *www.voices.washingtonpost.com.* November 29: np; and Fowler, G. A. 2010. Retailers team up against Amazon. *www.wsj.com.* October 6: np.

Prime was introduced in 2004. It was the result of a years-long search for the right loyalty program. An Amazon software engineer named Charlie Ward first suggested the idea of a free shipping service via a suggestion box feature on Amazon's internal website. Bing Gordon, an Amazon board member and venture capitalist, came up with the "Prime" name. Other executives, including Chief Executive Jeffrey Bezos, devised the two-day shipping offer—which exploited Amazon's ability to accelerate the handling of individual items in its distribution centers.

Amazon Prime has proven to be extremely hard for rivals to copy. Why? It enables Amazon to exploit its wide selection, low prices, network of third-party merchants, and finely tuned distribution system. All that while also keying off that faintly irrational human need to maximize the benefits of a club that you have already paid to join.

Now, several years after the program's creation, rivals—both online and off—have realized the increasing threat posed by Prime and are rushing to try to respond. For example, in October 2010, a consortium of more than 20 retailers, including Barnes & Noble, Sports Authority, and Toys 'R' Us, banded together to offer their own copycat $79, two-day shipping program, ShopRunner, which applies to products across their websites. However, as noted by Fiona Dias, the executive who administers the program, "As Amazon added more merchandising categories to Prime, retailers started feeling the pain. They have finally come to understand that Amazon is an existential threat and that Prime is the fuel of the engine."

Strategy Spotlight 3.8 describes how a Chinese beverage firm captured a significant market share in rural China by establishing close relationships with its distributors.

Are Substitutes Readily Available?   The fourth requirement for a firm resource to be a source of sustainable competitive advantage is that there must be no strategically equivalent valuable resources that are themselves not rare or inimitable. Two valuable firm resources (or two bundles of resources) are strategically equivalent when each one can be exploited separately to implement the same strategies.

Substitutability may take at least two forms. First, though it may be impossible for a firm to imitate exactly another firm's resource, it may be able to substitute a similar resource that enables it to develop and implement the same strategy. Clearly, a firm seeking to imitate another firm's high-quality top management team would be unable to copy the team exactly. However, it might be able to develop its own unique management team. Though these two teams would have different ages, functional backgrounds, experience, and so on, they could be strategically equivalent and thus substitutes for one another.

strategy spotlight   3.8

How a Chinese Beverage Company Succeeded by Creating Close Partnerships with Its Distributors

In 1998, when Hangzhou Wahaha Co. Ltd (Wahaha), the largest Chinese beverage producer, decided to take on Coca-Cola and PepsiCo, they began their attack in the rural areas of China. Why? They believed that they possessed a competitive advantage over the international giants because of the partnerships that they had built with the distributors across the more remote locations in China. ("Wa ha ha," which sounds like a child laughing, comes from a children's folk song.)

Four years prior to the launch of the "Wahaha Future Cola," the firm developed a policy for how to tie in "channel members" over the long term as a response to the increasing problem of accounts receivable and bad debt. This policy provided incentives for the channel members to pay an annual deposit in advance to cover any potential future bad debt and to operate according to Wahaha's payment policy.

Sounds OK, but what did the distributors get in return? They received an interest rate from Wahaha that was superior to the bank rate. In addition, further discounts were offered for early payment, and annual bonuses were awarded to distributors that met the criterion for prompt payment.

Wahaha implemented this model over a two-year period. It effectively struck financial partnerships with existing distributors that led to higher commitment from distributors. This creative strategy became instrumental to Wahaha's success and their ability to deliver products to the rural areas of China. Here, logistics often create unique challenges.

Wahaha's distribution network now consists of about 4,000 first-tier domestic wholesalers and a large number of second- and third-tier wholesalers and outlets to ensure that Wahaha's products reach millions of retailers nationwide within one week of leaving the factory—no small feat with China's vast rural areas and provinces as far out as Xinjiang and Tibet. As CEO Zong Qinghou colorfully points out: "Our rapid and sound network serves as human blood vessels which circulate the bloodstream to every part of the body once the products are ready."

In contrast, domestic and multinational companies established their own distribution networks—not partnerships with local distributors as Wahaha had done. Not surprisingly, Wahaha has managed to capture impressive market share increases in markets traditionally dominated by Coca-Cola and PepsiCo. And its financial results have been stunning. From 2003 to 2009, its revenues have increased from $1.24 billion to $5.2 billion, and its profits have increased from $165 million to $1.5 billion. These figures represent annual compound rate increases of 27 and 45 percent, respectively!

Source: Anonymous. 2010. Wahaha . . . China's leading beverage producer. *www.chinabevnews.com.* April 11: np; Andersen, M. M., Froholdt, M. & Poulfelt, F. 2010. *Return on Strategy.* New York: Routledge; and Miller, P. M. 2004. The Chinese beverage company's expansion is no laughing matter. *www.chinabuisnessreview.* September–October: np.

Second, very different firm resources can become strategic substitutes. For example, Internet booksellers such as Amazon.com compete as substitutes for bricks-and-mortar booksellers such as B. Dalton. The result is that resources such as premier retail locations become less valuable. In a similar vein, several pharmaceutical firms have seen the value of patent protection erode in the face of new drugs that are based on different production processes and act in different ways, but can be used in similar treatment regimes. The coming years will likely see even more radical change in the pharmaceutical industry as the substitution of genetic therapies eliminates certain uses of chemotherapy.[55]

To recap this section, recall that resources and capabilities must be rare and valuable as well as difficult to imitate or substitute in order for a firm to attain competitive advantages that are sustainable over time.[56] Exhibit 3.7 illustrates the relationship among the four criteria of sustainability and shows the competitive implications.

In firms represented by the first row of Exhibit 3.7, managers are in a difficult situation. When their resources and capabilities do not meet any of the four criteria, it would be difficult to develop any type of competitive advantage, in the short or long term. The

Exhibit 3.7
Criteria for Sustainable
Competitive Advantage
and Strategic
Implications

Is a resource or capability ...				
Valuable?	Rare?	Difficult to Imitate?	Without Substitutes?	Implications for Competitiveness?
No	No	No	No	Competitive disadvantage
Yes	No	No	No	Competitive parity
Yes	Yes	No	No	Temporary competitive advantage
Yes	Yes	Yes	Yes	Sustainable competitive advantage

Source: Adapted from Barney, J. B. 1991. Firm Resources and Sustained Competitive Advantage. *Journal of Management*, 17: 99–120.

resources and capabilities they possess enable the firm neither to exploit environmental opportunities nor neutralize environmental threats. In the second and third rows, firms have resources and capabilities that are valuable as well as rare, respectively. However, in both cases the resources and capabilities are not difficult for competitors to imitate or substitute. Here, the firms could attain some level of competitive parity. They could perform on par with equally endowed rivals or attain a temporary competitive advantage. But their advantages would be easy for competitors to match. It is only in the fourth row, where all four criteria are satisfied, that competitive advantages can be sustained over time. Next, let's look at Dell and see how its competitive advantage, which seemed to be sustainable for a rather long period of time, has eroded.

Dell's Eroding (Sustainable?) Competitive Advantage   In 1984, Michael Dell started Dell Inc. in a University of Texas dorm room with an investment of $1,000.[57] By 2006, Dell had attained annual revenues of $56 billion and a net income of $3.6 billion—making Michael Dell one of the richest people in the world. Dell achieved this meteoric growth by differentiating itself through the direct sales approach that it pioneered. Its user-configurable products met the diverse needs of its corporate and institutional customer base. Exhibit 3.8 summarizes how Dell achieved its remarkable success by integrating its tangible resources, intangible resources, and organizational capabilities.

Dell continued to maintain this competitive advantage by strengthening its value-chain activities and interrelationships that are critical to satisfying the largest market opportunities. It achieved this by (1) implementing e-commerce direct sales and support processes that accounted for the sophisticated buying habits of the largest markets and (2) matching its inventory management to its extensive supplier network. Dell also sustained these advantages by investing in intangible resources, such as proprietary assembly methods and packaging configurations, that helped to protect against the threat of imitation.

Dell recognized that the PC is a complex product with components sourced from several different technologies and manufacturers. Thus, in working backward from the customer's purchasing habits, Dell saw that the company could build valuable solutions by organizing its resources and capabilities around build-to-specification tastes, making both the sales and integration processes flexible, and passing on overhead expenses to its suppliers. Even as the PC industry became further commoditized, Dell was one of the few competitors that was able to retain solid margins. It accomplished this by adapting its manufacturing and assembly capabilities to match the PC market's trend toward user compatibility.

For many years, it looked as if Dell's competitive advantage over its rivals would be sustainable for a very long period of time. However, by early 2007, Dell began falling

| Resource | Competitive Advantage |

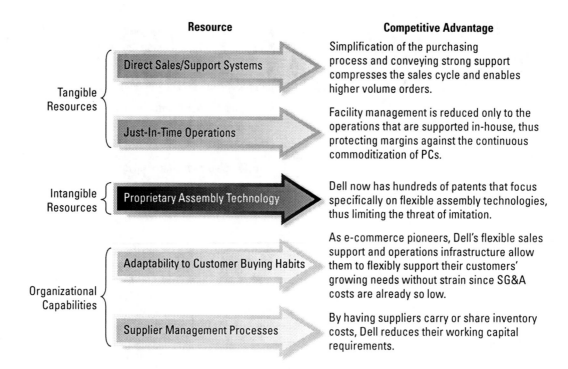

Tangible Resources

Direct Sales/Support Systems → Simplification of the purchasing process and conveying strong support compresses the sales cycle and enables higher volume orders.

Just-In-Time Operations → Facility management is reduced only to the operations that are supported in-house, thus protecting margins against the continuous commoditization of PCs.

Intangible Resources

Proprietary Assembly Technology → Dell now has hundreds of patents that focus specifically on flexible assembly technologies, thus limiting the threat of imitation.

Organizational Capabilities

Adaptability to Customer Buying Habits → As e-commerce pioneers, Dell's flexible sales support and operations infrastructure allow them to flexibly support their customers' growing needs without strain since SG&A costs are already so low.

Supplier Management Processes → By having suppliers carry or share inventory costs, Dell reduces their working capital requirements.

Exhibit 3.8 Dell's Tangible Resources, Intangible Resources, and Organizational Capabilities

behind its rivals in market share. This led to a significant decline in its stock price—followed by a complete shake-up of the top management team. But what led to Dell's competitive decline in the first place?[58]

- Dell had become so focused on cost that it failed to pay attention to the design of the brand. Customers increasingly began to see the product as a commodity.
- Much of the growth in the PC industry today is in laptops. Customers demand a sleeker, better-designed machine instead of just the cheapest laptop. Also, they often want to see the laptop before they buy it.
- When Dell outsourced its customer service function to foreign locations, it led to a decline in customer support. This eroded Dell's brand value.
- Dell's efforts to replicate its made-to-order, no middleman strategy to other products such as printers and storage devices proved to be a failure. This is because customers saw little need for customization of these products.
- Rivals such as HP have been improving their product design and reducing their costs.[59] Thus, they now have cost parity with Dell, while enjoying a better brand image and the support of an extensive dealer network.

Not surprisingly, Dell's performance has suffered. Between 2006 and 2010, its revenues and net income have slumped from $56 billion to $53 billion and $3.6 billion and $1.4 billion, respectively. Inder Sidhu, the author of *Doing Both* (2010), provides a succinct summary of the central lesson in the Dell story:[60]

> Dell illustrates what can happen when a company emphasizes optimization to the exclusion of reinvention. Dell's obsession with operational excellence prevented it from delivering innovations that the market wanted, costing it a great deal of goodwill and prestige. When *Fortune* announced its annual list of "Most Admired Companies" in 2009, Dell, the leader from just four years prior, wasn't even mentioned in the top 50.

The Generation and Distribution of a Firm's Profits: Extending the Resource-Based View of the Firm

The resource-based view of the firm has been useful in determining when firms will create competitive advantages and enjoy high levels of profitability. However, it has not been developed to address how a firm's profits (often referred to as "rents" by economists) will be distributed to a firm's management and employees or other stakeholders such as customers, suppliers, or governments.[61] This becomes an important issue because firms may be successful in creating competitive advantages that can be sustainable for a period of time. However, much of the profits can be retained (or "appropriated") by its employees and managers or other stakeholders instead of flowing to the owners of the firm (i.e., the stockholders).*

Consider Viewpoint DataLabs International, a Salt Lake City–based company that makes sophisticated three-dimensional models and textures for film production houses, video games, and car manufacturers. This example will help to show how employees are often able to obtain (or "appropriate") a high proportion of a firm's profits:

> Walter Noot, head of production, was having trouble keeping his highly skilled Generation X employees happy with their compensation. Each time one of them was lured away for more money, everyone would want a raise. "We were having to give out raises every six months—30 to 40 percent—then six months later they'd expect the same. It was a big struggle to keep people happy."[62]

At Viewpoint DataLabs, much of the profits are being generated by the highly skilled professionals working together. They are able to exercise their power by successfully demanding more financial compensation. In part, management has responded favorably because they are united in their demands, and their work involves a certain amount of social complexity and causal ambiguity—given the complex, coordinated efforts that their work entails.

Four factors help explain the extent to which employees and managers will be able to obtain a proportionately high level of the profits that they generate:[63]

- **Employee Bargaining Power.** If employees are vital to forming a firm's unique capability, they will earn disproportionately high wages. For example, marketing professionals may have access to valuable information that helps them to understand the intricacies of customer demands and expectations, or engineers may understand unique technical aspects of the products or services. Additionally, in some industries such as consulting, advertising, and tax preparation, clients tend to be very loyal to individual professionals employed by the firm, instead of to the firm itself. This enables them to "take the clients with them" if they leave. This enhances their bargaining power.
- **Employee Replacement Cost.** If employees' skills are idiosyncratic and rare (a source of resource-based advantages), they should have high bargaining power based on the high cost required by the firm to replace them. For example, Raymond Ozzie, the software designer who was critical in the development of Lotus Notes, was able to dictate the terms under which IBM acquired Lotus.
- **Employee Exit Costs.** This factor may tend to reduce an employee's bargaining power. An individual may face high personal costs when leaving the organization. Thus, that individual's threat of leaving may not be credible. In addition, an employee's expertise may be firm-specific and of limited value to other firms. Causal ambiguity may make it difficult for the employee to explain his or her specific contribution to a given project. Thus, a rival firm might be less likely to pay a high wage premium since it would be unsure of the employee's unique contribution.

---

* Economists define rents as profits (or prices) in excess of what is required to provide a normal return.

- *Manager Bargaining Power.* Managers' power is based on how well they create resource-based advantages. They are generally charged with creating value through the process of organizing, coordinating, and leveraging employees as well as other forms of capital such as plant, equipment, and financial capital (addressed further in Chapter 4). Such activities provide managers with sources of information that may not be readily available to others. Thus, although managers may not know as much about the specific nature of customers and technologies, they are in a position to have a more thorough, integrated understanding of the total operation.

Chapter 9 addresses the conditions under which top-level managers (such as CEOs) of large corporations have been, at times, able to obtain levels of total compensation that would appear to be significantly disproportionate to their contributions to wealth generation as well as to top executives in peer organizations. Here, corporate governance becomes a critical control mechanism. For example, William Esrey and Ronald T. LeMay (the former two top executives at Sprint Corporation) earned more than $130 million in stock options because of "cozy" relationships with members of their board of directors, who tended to approve with little debate huge compensation packages.[64]

Such diversion of profits from the owners of the business to top management is far less likely when the board members are truly independent outsiders (i.e., they do not have close ties to management). In general, given the external market for top talent, the level of compensation that executives receive is based on factors similar to the ones just discussed that determine the level of their bargaining power.[65]

In addition to employees and managers, other stakeholder groups can also appropriate a portion of the rents generated by a firm. If, for example, a critical input is controlled by a monopoly supplier or if a single buyer accounts for most of a firm's sales, their bargaining power can greatly erode the potential profits of a firm. Similarly, excessive taxation by governments can also reduce what is available to a firm's stockholders.

Evaluating Firm Performance: Two Approaches

This section addresses two approaches to use when evaluating a firm's performance. The first is financial ratio analysis, which, generally speaking, identifies how a firm is performing according to its balance sheet, income statement, and market valuation. As we will discuss, when performing a financial ratio analysis, you must take into account the firm's performance from a historical perspective (not just at one point in time) as well as how it compares with both industry norms and key competitors.[66]

The second perspective takes a broader stakeholder view. Firms must satisfy a broad range of stakeholders, including employees, customers, and owners, to ensure their long-term viability. Central to our discussion will be a well-known approach—the balanced scorecard—that has been popularized by Robert Kaplan and David Norton.[67]

financial ratio analysis a technique for measuring the performance of a firm according to its balance sheet, income statement, and market valuation.

Financial Ratio Analysis

The beginning point in analyzing the financial position of a firm is to compute and analyze five different types of financial ratios:

- Short-term solvency or liquidity
- Long-term solvency measures
- Asset management (or turnover)
- Profitability
- Market value

Exhibit 3.9 summarizes each of these five ratios.

I. Short-term solvency, or liquidity, ratios

$$\text{Current ratio} = \frac{\text{Current assets}}{\text{Current liabilities}}$$

$$\text{Quick ratio} = \frac{\text{Current assets} - \text{Inventory}}{\text{Current liabilities}}$$

$$\text{Cash ratio} = \frac{\text{Cash}}{\text{Current liabilities}}$$

II. Long-term solvency, or financial leverage, ratios

$$\text{Total debt ratio} = \frac{\text{Total assets} - \text{Total equity}}{\text{Total assets}}$$

Debt-equity ratio = Total debt/Total equity

Equity multiplier = Total assets/Total equity

$$\text{Times interest earned ratio} = \frac{\text{EBIT}}{\text{Interest}}$$

$$\text{Cash coverage ratio} = \frac{\text{EBIT} + \text{Depreciation}}{\text{Interest}}$$

III. Asset utilization, or turnover, ratios

$$\text{Inventory turnover} = \frac{\text{Cost of goods sold}}{\text{Inventory}}$$

$$\text{Days' sales in inventory} = \frac{365 \text{ days}}{\text{Inventory turnover}}$$

$$\text{Receivables turnover} = \frac{\text{Sales}}{\text{Accounts receivable}}$$

$$\text{Days' sales in receivables} = \frac{365 \text{ days}}{\text{Receivables turnover}}$$

$$\text{Total asset turnover} = \frac{\text{Sales}}{\text{Total assets}}$$

$$\text{Capital intensity} = \frac{\text{Total assets}}{\text{Sales}}$$

IV. Profitability ratios

$$\text{Profit margin} = \frac{\text{Net income}}{\text{Sales}}$$

$$\text{Return on assets (ROA)} = \frac{\text{Net income}}{\text{Total assets}}$$

$$\text{Return on equity (ROE)} = \frac{\text{Net income}}{\text{Total equity}}$$

$$\text{ROE} = \frac{\text{Net income}}{\text{Sales}} \times \frac{\text{Sales}}{\text{Assets}} \times \frac{\text{Assets}}{\text{Equity}}$$

V. Market value ratios

$$\text{Price-earnings ratio} = \frac{\text{Price per share}}{\text{Earnings per share}}$$

$$\text{Market-to-book ratio} = \frac{\text{Market value per share}}{\text{Book value per share}}$$

Exhibit 3.9 A Summary of Five Types of Financial Ratios

Appendix 1 to Chapter 13 (the Case Analysis chapter) provides detailed definitions for and discussions of each of these types of ratios as well as examples of how each is calculated. Refer to pages 491 to 500.

A meaningful ratio analysis must go beyond the calculation and interpretation of financial ratios.[68] It must include how ratios change over time as well as how they are interrelated. For example, a firm that takes on too much long-term debt to finance operations will see an immediate impact on its indicators of long-term financial leverage. The additional debt will negatively affect the firm's short-term liquidity ratio (i.e., current and quick ratios) since the firm must pay interest and principal on the additional debt each year until it is retired. Additionally, the interest expenses deducted from revenues reduce the firm's profitability.

A firm's financial position should not be analyzed in isolation. Important reference points are needed. We will address some issues that must be taken into account to make financial analysis more meaningful: historical comparisons, comparisons with industry norms, and comparisons with key competitors.

>LO3.6
The usefulness of financial ratio analysis, its inherent limitations, and how to make meaningful comparisons of performance across firms.

Historical Comparisons When you evaluate a firm's financial performance, it is very useful to compare its financial position over time. This provides a means of evaluating trends. For example, Apple Inc. reported revenues of $65 billion and net income of $14 billion in 2010. Virtually all firms would be very happy with such financial success. These

Exhibit 3.10
Historical Trends: Return on Sales (ROS) for a Hypothetical Company

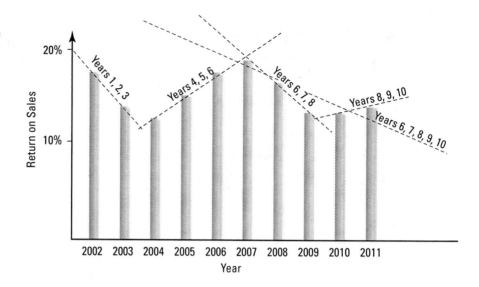

figures represent a stunning annual growth in revenue and net income of 100 percent and 190 percent, respectively, for the 2008 to 2010 time period. Had Apple's revenues and net income in 2010 been $40 billion and $6 billion, respectively, it would still be a very large and highly profitable enterprise. However, such performance would have significantly damaged Apple's market valuation and reputation as well as the careers of many of its executives.

Exhibit 3.10 illustrates a 10-year period of return on sales (ROS) for a hypothetical company. As indicated by the dotted trend lines, the rate of growth (or decline) differs substantially over time periods.

Comparison with Industry Norms   When you are evaluating a firm's financial performance, remember also to compare it with industry norms. A firm's current ratio or profitability may appear impressive at first glance. However, it may pale when compared with industry standards or norms.

Comparing your firm with all other firms in your industry assesses relative performance. Banks often use such comparisons when evaluating a firm's creditworthiness. Exhibit 3.11 includes a variety of financial ratios for three industries: semiconductors, grocery stores, and skilled-nursing facilities. Why is there such variation among the financial ratios for these three industries? There are several reasons. With regard to the collection period, grocery stores operate mostly on a cash basis, hence a very short collection period. Semiconductor manufacturers sell their output to other manufacturers (e.g., computer makers) on terms such as 2/15 net 45, which means they give a 2 percent discount on bills paid within 15 days and start charging interest after 45 days. Skilled-nursing facilities also have a longer collection period than grocery stores because they typically rely on payments from insurance companies.

The industry norms for return on sales also highlight differences among these industries. Grocers, with very slim margins, have a lower return on sales than either skilled-nursing facilities or semiconductor manufacturers. But how might we explain the differences between skilled-nursing facilities and semiconductor manufacturers? Health care facilities, in general, are limited in their pricing structures by Medicare/Medicaid regulations and by insurance reimbursement limits, but semiconductor producers have pricing structures determined by the market. If their products have superior performance, semiconductor manufacturers can charge premium prices.

Exhibit 3.11
**How Financial Ratios
Differ across Industries**

Financial Ratio	Semiconductors	Grocery Stores	Skilled-Nursing Facilities
Quick ratio (times)	1.9	0.6	1.2
Current ratio (times)	3.9	1.9	1.6
Total liabilities to net worth (%)	30.2	71.4	156.9
Collection period (days)	49.0	2.6	30.3
Assets to sales (%)	147.3	19.5	113.9
Return on sales (%)	24	1.1	2.4

Source: Dun & Bradstreet. *Industry Norms and Key Business Ratios, 2007–2008.* One Year Edition, SIC #3600–3699 (Semiconductors); SIC #5400–5499 (Grocery Stores); SIC #8000–8099 (Skilled-Nursing Facilities). New York: Dun & Bradstreet Credit Services.

Comparison with Key Competitors   Recall from Chapter 2 that firms with similar strategies are members of a strategic group in an industry. Furthermore, competition is more intense among competitors within groups than across groups. Thus, you can gain valuable insights into a firm's financial and competitive position if you make comparisons between a firm and its most direct rivals. Consider a firm trying to diversify into the highly profitable pharmaceutical industry. Even if it was willing to invest several hundred million dollars, it would be virtually impossible to compete effectively against industry giants such as Pfizer and Merck. These two firms have 2010 revenues of $68 billion and $46 billion, respectively, and R&D budgets of $9 billion and $11 billion, respectively.[69]

Integrating Financial Analysis and Stakeholder Perspectives: The Balanced Scorecard

It is useful to see how a firm is performing over time in terms of several ratios. However, such traditional approaches to performance assessments can be a double-edged sword.[70] Many important transactions that managers make—investments in research and development, employee training and development, and, advertising and promotion of key brands— may greatly expand a firm's market potential and create significant long-term shareholder value. But such critical investments are not reflected positively in short-term financial reports. Financial reports typically measure expenses, not the value created. Thus, managers may be penalized for spending money in the short term to improve their firm's long-term competitive viability!

Now consider the other side of the coin. A manager may destroy the firm's future value by dissatisfying customers, depleting the firm's stock of good products coming out of R&D, or damaging the morale of valued employees. Such budget cuts, however, may lead to very good short-term financials. The manager may look good in the short run and even receive credit for improving the firm's performance. In essence, such a manager has mastered "denominator management," whereby decreasing investments makes the return on investment (ROI) ratio larger, even though the actual return remains constant or shrinks.

The Balanced Scorecard: Description and Benefits   To provide a meaningful integration of the many issues that come into evaluating a firm's performance, Kaplan and Norton developed a **"balanced scorecard."**[71] This provides top managers with a fast but comprehensive view of the business. In a nutshell, it includes financial measures that reflect the results of actions already taken, but it complements these indicators with measures of customer satisfaction, internal processes, and the organization's innovation and improvement activities—operational measures that drive future financial performance.

> **>LO3.7**
> The value of the "balanced scorecard" in recognizing how the interests of a variety of stakeholders can be interrelated.

balanced scorecard
a method of evaluating a firm's performance using performance measures from the customers', internal, innovation and learning, and financial perspectives.

Exhibit 3.12
The Balanced Scorecard's Four Perspectives

- How do customers see us? (customer perspective)
- What must we excel at? (internal business perspective)
- Can we continue to improve and create value? (innovation and learning perspective)
- How do we look to shareholders? (financial perspective)

customer perspective measures of firm performance that indicate how well firms are satisfying customers' expectations.

internal business perspective measures of firm performance that indicate how well firms' internal processes, decisions and actions are contributing to customer satisfaction.

innovation and learning perspective measures of firm performance that indicate how well firms are changing their product and service offerings to adapt to changes in the internal and external environments.

financial perspective measures of firms' financial performance that indicate how well strategy, implementation and execution are contributing bottom-line improvement.

The balanced scorecard enables managers to consider their business from four key perspectives: customer, internal, innovation and learning, and financial. These are briefly described in Exhibit 3.12.

Customer Perspective Clearly, how a company is performing from its customers' perspective is a top priority for management. The balanced scorecard requires that managers translate their general mission statements on customer service into specific measures that reflect the factors that really matter to customers. For the balanced scorecard to work, managers must articulate goals for four key categories of customer concerns: time, quality, performance and service, and cost. For example, lead time may be measured as the time from the company's receipt of an order to the time it actually delivers the product or service to the customer.

Internal Business Perspective Customer-based measures are important. However, they must be translated into indicators of what the firm must do internally to meet customers' expectations. Excellent customer performance results from processes, decisions, and actions that occur throughout organizations in a coordinated fashion, and managers must focus on those critical internal operations that enable them to satisfy customer needs. The internal measures should reflect business processes that have the greatest impact on customer satisfaction. These include factors that affect cycle time, quality, employee skills, and productivity. Firms also must identify and measure the key resources and capabilities they need for continued success.

Innovation and Learning Perspective Given the rapid rate of markets, technologies, and global competition, the criteria for success are constantly changing. To survive and prosper, managers must make frequent changes to existing products and services as well as introduce entirely new products with expanded capabilities. A firm's ability to improve, innovate, and learn is tied directly to its value. Simply put, only by developing new products and services, creating greater value for customers, and increasing operating efficiencies can a company penetrate new markets, increase revenues and margins, and enhance shareholder value. A firm's ability to do well from an innovation and learning perspective is more dependent on its intangible than tangible assets. Three categories of intangible assets are critically important: human capital (skills, talent, and knowledge), information capital (information systems, networks), and organization capital (culture, leadership).

Financial Perspective Measures of financial performance indicate whether the company's strategy, implementation, and execution are indeed contributing to bottom-line improvement. Typical financial goals include profitability, growth, and shareholder value. Periodic financial statements remind managers that improved quality, response time, productivity, and innovative products benefit the firm only when they result in improved sales, increased market share, reduced operating expenses, or higher asset turnover.[72]

Consider how Sears, the huge retailer, found a strong causal relationship between employee attitudes, customer attitudes, and financial outcomes.[73] Through an ongoing study, Sears developed (and continues to refine) what it calls its total performance indicators, or

TPI—a set of indicators for assessing their performance with customers, employees, and investors. Sears's quantitative model has shown that a 5.0 percent improvement in employee attitudes leads to a 1.3 percent improvement in customer satisfaction, which in turn drives a 0.5 percent improvement in revenue. Thus, if a single store improved its employee attitude by 5.0 percent, Sears could predict with confidence that if the revenue growth in the district as a whole were 5.0 percent, the revenue growth in this particular store would be 5.5 percent. Interestingly, Sears's managers consider such numbers as rigorous as any others that they work with every year. The company's accounting firm audits management as closely as it audits the financial statements.

A key implication is that managers do not need to look at their job as balancing stakeholder demands. They must avoid the following mind-set: "How many units in employee satisfaction do I have to give up to get some additional units of customer satisfaction or profits?" Instead, the balanced scorecard provides a win–win approach—increasing satisfaction among a wide variety of organizational stakeholders, including employees (at all levels), customers, and stockholders.

Limitations and Potential Downsides of the Balanced Scorecard   There is general agreement that there is nothing inherently wrong with the concept of the balanced scorecard.[74] The key limitation is that some executives may view it as a "quick fix" that can be easily installed. However, implementing a balanced metrics system is an evolutionary process. It is not a one-time task that can be quickly checked off as "completed." If managers do not recognize this from the beginning and fail to commit to it long term, the organization will be disappointed. Poor execution becomes the cause of such performance outcomes. And organizational scorecards must be aligned with individuals' scorecards to turn the balanced scorecards into a powerful tool for sustained performance.[*]

In a recent study of 50 Canadian medium-size and large organizations, the number of users expressing skepticism about scorecard performance was much greater than the number claiming positive results. However, the overwhelming perspective was that balanced scorecards can be worthwhile in clarifying an organization's strategy, and if this can be accomplished, better results will follow. A few companies stated categorically that scorecards have improved their firm's financial results. For example, one respondent claimed that "We did not meet our financial goals previously, but since implementing our balanced scorecard, we have now met our goals three years running."

On the other hand, a greater number of respondents agreed with the statement "Balanced scorecards don't really work." Some representative comments included: "It became just a number-crunching exercise by accountants after the first year," "It is just the latest management fad and is already dropping lower on management's list of priorities as all fads eventually do," and "If scorecards are supposed to be a measurement tool, why is it so hard to measure their results?" There is much work to do before scorecards can become a viable framework to measure sustained strategic performance.

Problems often occur in the balanced scorecard implementation efforts when there is an insufficient commitment to learning and the inclusion of employees' personal ambitions. Without a set of rules for employees that address continuous process improvement and the personal improvement of individual employees, there will be limited employee buy-in and insufficient cultural change. Thus, many improvements may be temporary and superficial. Often, scorecards that failed to attain alignment and improvements dissipated

---

[*] Building on the concepts that are the foundation of the balanced scorecard approach, Kaplan and Norton have recently developed a useful tool called the strategy map. Strategy maps show the cause and effect links by which specific improvements in different areas lead to a desired outcome. Strategy maps also help employees see how their jobs are related to the overall objectives of the organization. They also help us understand how an organization can convert its assets—both tangible and intangible—into tangible outcomes. Refer to Kaplan, R. S. & Norton, D. P. 2000. Having Trouble with Your Strategy? Then Map It. *Harvard Business Review,* 78(10): 167–176.

Exhibit 3.13
Potential Limitations of the Balanced Scorecard

Most agree that the balanced scorecard concept is a useful and an appropriate management tool. However, there are many design and implementation issues that may short circuit its value, including the following:

- *Lack of a Clear Strategy.* A scorecard can be developed without the aid of a strategy. However, it then becomes a key performance indicator or stakeholder system, lacking in many of the attributes offered from a true balanced scorecard.

- *Limited or Ineffective Executive Sponsorship.* Although training and education are important, without tenacious leadership and support of a scorecard project, the effort is most likely doomed.

- *Too Much Emphasis on Financial Measures Rather than Nonfinancial Measures.* This leads to measures that do not connect to the drivers of the business and are not relevant to performance improvement.

- *Poor Data on Actual Performance.* This can negate most of the effort invested in defining performance measures because a company can't monitor actual changes in results from changes in behavior.

- *Inappropriate Links of Scorecard Measures to Compensation.* Although this can focus managerial and employee attention, exercising it too soon can produce many unintended side effects such as dysfunctional decision making by managers looking to cash in.

- *Inconsistent or Inappropriate Terminology.* Everyone must speak the same language if measurement is to be used to guide change within an organization. Translating strategy into measures becomes even more difficult if everyone cannot agree on (or understand) the same language and terminology.

Sources: Angel, R. & Rampersad, H. 2005. Do Scorecards Add Up? *Camagazine.com.* May: np; and Niven, P. 2002. *Balanced Scorecard Step by Step: Maximizing Performance and Maintaining Results.* New York: John Wiley & Sons.

very quickly. And, in many cases, management's efforts to improve performance were seen as divisive and were viewed by employees as aimed at benefiting senior management compensation. This fostered a "what's in it for me?" attitude. Exhibit 3.13 summarizes some of the potential downsides of the balanced scorecard.

Reflecting on Career Implications . . .

- *The Value Chain:* Carefully analyze where you can add value in your firm's value chain. How might your firm's support activities (e.g., information technology, human resource practices) help you accomplish your assigned tasks more effectively?
- *The Value Chain:* Consider important relationships among activities both within your firm as well as between your firm and its suppliers, customers, and alliance partners.
- *Resource-Based View of the Firm:* Are your skills and talents rare, valuable, difficult to imitate, and have few substitutes? If so, you are in a better position to add value for your firm—and earn rewards and incentives. How can your skills and talents be enhanced to help satisfy these criteria to a greater extent? More training? Change positions within the firm? Consider career options at other organizations?
- *Balanced Scorecard:* In your decision making, strive to "balance" the four perspectives: customer, internal business, innovation and learning, and financial. Do not focus too much on short-term profits. Do your personal career goals provide opportunities to develop your skills in all four directions?

Summary

In the traditional approaches to assessing a firm's internal environment, the primary goal of managers would be to determine their firm's relative strengths and weaknesses. Such is the role of SWOT analysis, wherein managers analyze their firm's strengths and weaknesses as well as the opportunities and threats in the external environment. In this chapter, we discussed why this may be a good starting point but hardly the best approach to take in performing a sound analysis. There are many limitations to SWOT analysis, including its static perspective, its potential to overemphasize a single dimension of a firm's strategy, and the likelihood that a firm's strengths do not necessarily help the firm create value or competitive advantages.

We identified two frameworks that serve to complement SWOT analysis in assessing a firm's internal environment: value-chain analysis and the resource-based view of the firm. In conducting a value-chain analysis, first divide the firm into a series of value-creating activities. These include primary activities such as inbound logistics, operations, and service as well as support activities such as procurement and human resources management. Then analyze how each activity adds value as well as how *interrelationships* among value activities in the firm and among the firm and its customers and suppliers add value. Thus, instead of merely determining a firm's strengths and weaknesses per se, you analyze them in the overall context of the firm and its relationships with customers and suppliers—the value system.

The resource-based view of the firm considers the firm as a bundle of resources: tangible resources, intangible resources, and organizational capabilities. Competitive advantages that are sustainable over time generally arise from the creation of bundles of resources and capabilities. For advantages to be sustainable, four criteria must be satisfied: value, rarity, difficulty in imitation, and difficulty in substitution. Such an evaluation requires a sound knowledge of the competitive context in which the firm exists. The owners of a business may not capture all of the value created by the firm. The appropriation of value created by a firm between the owners and employees is determined by four factors: employee bargaining power, replacement cost, employee exit costs, and manager bargaining power.

An internal analysis of the firm would not be complete unless you evaluate its performance and make the appropriate comparisons. Determining a firm's performance requires an analysis of its financial situation as well as a review of how well it is satisfying a broad range of stakeholders, including customers, employees, and stockholders. We discussed the concept of the balanced scorecard, in which four perspectives must be addressed: customer, internal business, innovation and learning, and financial. Central to this concept is the idea that the interests of various stakeholders can be interrelated. We provide examples of how indicators of employee satisfaction lead to higher levels of customer satisfaction, which in turn lead to higher levels of financial performance. Thus, improving a firm's performance does not need to involve making trade-offs among different stakeholders. Assessing the firm's performance is also more useful if it is evaluated in terms of how it changes over time, compares with industry norms, and compares with key competitors.

In the Appendix to Chapter 3, we discuss how Internet and digital technologies have created new opportunities for firms to add value. Four value-adding activities that have been enhanced by Internet capabilities are search, evaluation, problem solving, and transaction. These four activities are supported by three different types of content that Internet businesses often use—customer feedback, expertise, and entertainment programming. Seven business models have been identified that are proving successful for use by Internet firms. These include commission, advertising, markup, production, referral, subscription, and fee-for-service–based models. Firms also are finding that combinations of these business models can contribute to greater success.

Summary Review Questions

1. SWOT analysis is a technique to analyze the internal and external environment of a firm. What are its advantages and disadvantages?
2. Briefly describe the primary and support activities in a firm's value chain.
3. How can managers create value by establishing important relationships among the value-chain activities both within their firm and between the firm and its customers and suppliers?
4. Briefly explain the four criteria for sustainability of competitive advantages.
5. Under what conditions are employees and managers able to appropriate some of the value created by their firm?
6. What are the advantages and disadvantages of conducting a financial ratio analysis of a firm?
7. Summarize the concept of the balanced scorecard. What are its main advantages?

Key Terms

value-chain analysis, 81
primary activities, 81
support activities, 81
inbound logistics, 83
operations, 84
outbound logistics, 84
marketing and sales, 85
service, 86
procurement, 86
technology
  development, 88
human resource
  management, 88
general
  administration, 89
interrelationships, 90
resource-based view of the
  firm, 93

tangible resources, 93
intangible resources, 95
organizational
  capabilities, 95
strategic resources
  (also firm resources
  or organizational
  resources), 95
path dependency, 98
causal ambiguity, 98
social complexity, 98
financial ratio
  analysis, 104
balanced scorecard, 107
customer
  perspective, 108
internal perspective, 108
innovation and learning

perspective, 108
financial
  perspective, 108
search activities, 117
evaluation activities, 117

problem-solving
  activities, 117
transaction
  activities, 118
business model, 119

Experiential Exercise

Dell Computer is a leading firm in the personal computer industry, with annual revenues of $53 billion during its 2010 fiscal year. Dell had created a very strong competitive position via its "direct model," whereby it manufactures its personal computers to detailed customer specifications. However, its advantage has been eroded recently by strong rivals such as HP.

Below we address several questions that focus on Dell's value-chain activities and interrelationships among them as well as whether they are able to attain sustainable competitive advantage(s). (We discuss Dell in this chapter on pages 101–102.)

1. Where in Dell's value chain are they creating value for their customer?

Value-Chain Activity	Yes/No	How Does Dell Create Value for the Customer?
Primary:		
Inbound logistics		
Operations		
Outbound logistics		
Marketing and sales		
Service		
Support:		
Procurement		
Technology development		
Human resource management		
General administration		

2. What are the important relationships among Dell's value-chain activities? What are the important interdependencies? For each activity, identify the relationships and interdependencies.

	Inbound logistics	Operations	Outbound logistics	Marketing and sales	Service	Procurement	Technology development	Human resource management	General administration
Inbound logistics									
Operations									
Outbound logistics									
Marketing and sales									
Service									
Procurement									
Technology development									
Human resource management									
General administration									

3. What resources, activities, and relationships enable Dell to achieve a sustainable competitive advantage?

Resource/Activity	Is It Valuable?	Is It Rare?	Are There Few Substitutes?	Is It Difficult to Make?
Inbound logistics				
Operations				
Outbound logistics				
Marketing and sales				
Service				
Procurement				
Technology development				
Human resource management				
General administration				

Application Questions & Exercises

1. Using published reports, select two CEOs who have recently made public statements regarding a major change in their firm's strategy. Discuss how the successful implementation of such strategies requires changes in the firm's primary and support activities.

2. Select a firm that competes in an industry in which you are interested. Drawing upon published financial reports, complete a financial ratio analysis. Based on changes over time and a comparison with industry norms, evaluate the firm's strengths and weaknesses in terms of its financial position.

3. How might exemplary human resource practices enhance and strengthen a firm's value-chain activities?

4. Using the Internet, look up your university or college. What are some of its key value-creating activities that provide competitive advantages? Why?

Ethics Questions

1. What are some of the ethical issues that arise when a firm becomes overly zealous in advertising its products?

2. What are some of the ethical issues that may arise from a firm's procurement activities? Are you aware of any of these issues from your personal experience or businesses you are familiar with?

References

1. Anonymous. 2010. 'There's no brakes . . . hold on and pray': Last words of man before he and his family died in Toyota Lexus crash. www.dailymail.co.uk. February 3: np. Ohnsman, A. 2010. The Humbling of Toyota. BusinessWeek, March 22: 32–36; Anonymous. 2009. Toyota recalls 3.8 million vehicles, www.msnbc.com. September 29: np; Ross, B. 2009. Owners of Toyota cars in rebellion over series of accidents caused by sudden acceleration, Part one. www.abcnews.go.com. November 3: np; and, Ohnsman, A. 2009. Toyota recall crisis said to lie in cost cuts, growth ambitions, www.bloomberg.com. February 26: np. We thank Jason Hirsch for his valued contributions.

2. Our discussion of the value chain will draw on Porter, M. E. 1985. Competitive advantage: chap. 2. New York: Free Press.

3. Dyer, J. H. 1996. Specialized supplier networks as a source of competitive advantage: Evidence from the auto industry. Strategic Management Journal, 17: 271–291.

4. For an insightful perspective on value-chain analysis, refer to Stabell, C. B. & Fjeldstad, O. D. 1998. Configuring value for competitive advantage: On chains, shops, and networks. Strategic Management Journal, 19: 413–437. The authors develop concepts of value chains, value shops, and value networks to extend the value-creation

logic across a broad range of industries. Their work builds on the seminal contributions of Porter, 1985, op. cit., and others who have addressed how firms create value through key interrelationships among value-creating activities.

5. Ibid.

6. Maynard, M. 1999. Toyota promises custom order in 5 days. USA Today, August 6: B1.

7. Shaw Industries. 1999. Annual report: 14–15.

8. Fisher, M. L. 1997. What is the right supply chain for your product? Harvard Business Review, 75(2): 105–116.

9. Jackson. M. 2001. Bringing a dying brand back to life. Harvard Business Review, 79(5): 53–61.

10. Anderson, J. C. & Nmarus, J. A. 2003. Selectively pursuing more of your customer's business. MIT Sloan Management Review, 44(3): 42–50.

11. Insights on advertising are addressed in: Rayport, J. F. 2008. Where is advertising? Into 'stitials. Harvard Business Review, 66(5): 18–20.

12. An insightful discussion of the role of identity marketing—that is, the myriad labels that people use to express who they are—in successful marketing activities is found in Reed, A., II & Bolton, L. E. 2005. The complexity of identity. MIT Sloan Management Review, 46(3): 18–22.

13. Insights on the usefulness of off-line ads are the focus of: Abraham, M.

2008. The off-line impact of online ads. Harvard Business Review, 66(4): 28.

14. Berggren, E. & Nacher, T. 2000. Why good ideas go bust. Management Review, February: 32–36.

15. For an insightful perspective on creating effective brand portfolios, refer to Hill, S., Ettenson, R., & Tyson, D. 2005. Achieving the ideal brand portfolio. MIT Sloan Management Review, 46(2): 85–90.

16. Haddad, C. & Grow, B. 2001. Wait a second—I didn't order that! BusinessWeek, July 16: 45.

17. For a scholarly discussion on the procurement of technology components, read Hoetker, G. 2005. How much you know versus how well I know you: Selecting a supplier for a technically innovative component. Strategic Management Journal, 26(1): 75–96.

18. For a discussion on criteria to use when screening suppliers for back-office functions, read Feeny, D., Lacity, M., & Willcocks, L. P. 2005. Taking the measure of outsourcing providers. MIT Sloan Management Review, 46(3): 41–48.

19. For a study investigating sourcing practices, refer to: Safizadeh, M. H., Field, J. M., & Ritzman, L. P. 2008. Sourcing practices and boundaries of the firm in the financial services industry. Strategic Management Journal, 29(1): 79–92.

20. Imperato, G. 1998. How to give good feedback. *Fast Company,* September: 144–156.

21. Bensaou, B. M. & Earl, M. 1998. The right mindset for managing information technology. *Harvard Business Review,* 96(5): 118–128.

22. A discussion of R&D in the pharmaceutical industry is in: Garnier, J-P. 2008. Rebuilding the R&D engine in big pharma. *Harvard Business Review,* 66(5): 68–76.

23. Donlon, J. P. 2000. Bonsignore's bid for the big time. *Chief Executive,* March: 28–37.

24. Ulrich, D. 1998. A new mandate for human resources. *Harvard Business Review,* 96(1): 124–134.

25. A study of human resource management in China is: Li, J., Lam, K., Sun, J. J. M., & Liu, S. X. Y. 2008. Strategic resource management, institutionalization, and employment modes: An empirical study in China. *Strategic Management Journal,* 29(3): 337–342.

26. Wood, J. 2003. Sharing jobs and working from home: The new face of the airline industry. AviationCareer. net, February 21.

27. Green, S., Hasan, F., Immelt, J. Marks, M., & Meiland, D. 2003. In search of global leaders. *Harvard Business Review,* 81(8): 38–45.

28. For insights on the role of information systems integration in fostering innovation refer to: Cash, J. I. Jr., Earl, M. J., & Morison, R. 2008. Teaming up to crack innovation and enterprise integration. *Harvard Business Review,* 66(11): 90–100.

29. For a cautionary note on the use of IT, refer to McAfee, A. 2003. When too much IT knowledge is a dangerous thing. *MIT Sloan Management Review,* 44(2): 83–90.

30. Walgreen Co. 1996. *Information technology and Walgreens: Opportunities for employment,* January; and Dess, G. G. & Picken, J. C. 1997. *Beyond productivity.* New York: AMACOM.

31. The important role in IT for a Japanese bank is addressed in: Upton, D. M. & Staats, B. R. 2008. Radically simple IT. *Harvard Business Review,* 66(3): 118–124.

32. For an interesting perspective on some of the potential downsides of close customer and supplier relationships, refer to Anderson, E. & Jap, S. D. 2005. The dark side of close relationships. *MIT Sloan Management Review,* 46(3): 75–82.

33. Day, G. S. 2003. Creating a superior customer-relating capability. *MIT Sloan Management Review,* 44(3): 77–82.

34. To gain insights on the role of electronic technologies in enhancing a firm's connections to outside suppliers and customers, refer to Lawrence, T. B., Morse, E. A., & Fowler, S. W. 2005. Managing your portfolio of connections. *MIT Sloan Management Review,* 46(2): 59–66.

35. This section draws on Andersen, M. M., Froholdt, M. & Poulfelt, F. 2010. *Return on strategy.* New York: Routledge: 96–100.

36. Quote from Hartmut Jenner, CEO, Alfred Karcher GmbH, IBM Global CEO Study, P. 27.

37. Collis, D. J. & Montgomery, C. A. 1995. Competing on resources: Strategy in the 1990's. *Harvard Business Review,* 73(4): 119–128; and Barney, J. 1991. Firm resources and sustained competitive advantage. *Journal of Management,* 17(1): 99–120.

38. For recent critiques of the resource-based view of the firm, refer to: Sirmon, D. G., Hitt, M. A., & Ireland, R. D. 2007. Managing firm resources in dynamic environments to create value: Looking inside the black box. *Academy of Management Review,* 32(1): 273–292; and Newbert, S. L. Empirical research on the resource-based view of the firm: An assessment and suggestions for future research. *Strategic Management Journal,* 28(2): 121–146.

39. For insights into research findings on the linkage between resources and performance, refer to: Crook, T. R., Ketchen, D. J., Jr., Combs, J. G., & Todd, S. Y. 2008. Strategic resources and performance: A meta-analysis. *Strategic Management Journal,* 29(11): 1141–1154.

40. Henkoff, R. 1993. Companies that train the best. *Fortune,* March 22: 83; and Dess & Picken, *Beyond productivity,* p. 98.

41. Gaines-Ross, L. 2010. Reputation warfare. *Harvard Business Review,* 88(12): 70–76.

42. Barney, J. B. 1986. Types of competition and the theory of strategy: Towards an integrative framework. *Academy of Management Review,* 11(4): 791–800.

43. Harley-Davidson. 1993. Annual report.

44. For a rigorous, academic treatment of the origin of capabilities, refer to Ethiraj, S. K., Kale, P., Krishnan, M. S., & Singh, J. V. 2005. Where do capabilities come from and how do they matter? A study of the software services industry. *Strategic Management Journal,* 26(1): 25–46.

45. For an academic discussion on methods associated with organizational capabilities, refer to Dutta, S., Narasimhan, O., & Rajiv, S. 2005. Conceptualizing and measuring capabilities: Methodology and empirical application. *Strategic Management Journal,* 26(3): 277–286.

46. Lorenzoni, G. & Lipparini, A. 1999. The leveraging of interfirm relationships as a distinctive organizational capability: A longitudinal study. *Strategic Management Journal,* 20: 317–338.

47. Andersen, M. M. op. cit. 209.

48. A study investigating the sustainability of competitive advantage is: Newbert, S. L. 2008. Value, rareness, competitive advantages, and performance: A conceptual-level empirical investigation of the resource-based view of the firm. *Strategic Management Journal,* 29(7): 745–768.

49. Arikan, A. M. & McGahan, A. M. 2010. The development of capabilities in new firms. *Strategic Management Journal,* 31(1): 1–18.

50. Barney, J. 1991. Firm resources and sustained competitive advantage. *Journal of Management,* 17(1): 99–120.

51. Barney, 1986, op. cit. Our discussion of inimitability and substitution draws upon this source.

52. A study that investigates the performance implications of imitation is: Ethiraj, S. K. & Zhu, D. H. 2008. Performance effects of imitative

entry. *Strategic Management Journal,* 29(8): 797–818.

53. Sirmon, D. G., Hitt, M. A., Arregale, J.-L. & Campbell, J. T. 2010. The dynamic interplay of capability strengths and weaknesses: Investigating the bases of temporary competitive advantage. *Strategic Management Journal,* 31(13): 1386–1409.

54. Deephouse, D. L. 1999. To be different, or to be the same? It's a question (and theory) of strategic balance. *Strategic Management Journal,* 20: 147–166.

55. Yeoh, P. L. & Roth, K. 1999. An empirical analysis of sustained advantage in the U.S. pharmaceutical industry: Impact of firm resources and capabilities. *Strategic Management Journal,* 20: 637–653.

56. Robins, J. A. & Wiersema, M. F. 2000. Strategies for unstructured competitive environments: Using scarce resources to create new markets. In Bresser, R. F., et al., (Eds.), *Winning strategies in a deconstructing world:* 201–220. New York: John Wiley.

57. For an insightful case on how Dell was able to build its seemingly sustainable competitive advantage in the marketplace, refer to "Matching Dell" by Jan W. Rivkin and Michael E. Porter, Harvard Business School Case 9-799-158 (June 6, 1999).

58. Byrnes, N. & Burrows, P. 2007. Where Dell went wrong. *BusinessWeek,* February 18: 62–63; and Smith, A. D. 2007. Dell's moves create buzz. *Dallas Morning News.* February 21: D1.

59. For an insightful perspective on how HP has increased its market share and profitability in the personal computer

market, refer to: Edwards, C. 2008. How HP got the wow! back. *BusinessWeek,* December 22: 60–61. HP surpassed Dell in fall 2006 to become the world's largest PC manufacturer, and it increased its market share from 14.5 percent to 18.8 percent between June 2005 and September 2008.

60. Sidhu, I. op. cit., 61.

61. Amit, R. & Schoemaker, J. H. 1993. Strategic assets and organizational rent. *Strategic Management Journal,* 14(1): 33–46; Collis, D. J. & Montgomery, C. A. 1995. Competing on resources: Strategy in the 1990's. *Harvard Business Review,* 73(4): 118–128; Coff, R. W. 1999. When competitive advantage doesn't lead to performance: The resource-based view and stakeholder bargaining power. *Organization Science,* 10(2): 119–133; and Blyler, M. & Coff, R. W. 2003. Dynamic capabilities, social capital, and rent appropriation: Ties that split pies. *Strategic Management Journal,* 24: 677–686.

62. Munk, N. 1998. The new organization man. *Fortune,* March 16: 62–74.

63. Coff, op. cit.

64. Lavelle, L. 2003. Sprint's board needs a good sweeping, too. *BusinessWeek,* February 24: 40; Anonymous. 2003. Another nail in the coffin. *The Economist,* February 15: 69–70; and Byrnes, N., Dwyer, P., & McNamee, M. 2003. Hacking away at tax shelters, *BusinessWeek,* February 24: 41.

65. We have focused our discussion on how internal stakeholders (e.g., employees, managers, and top executives) may appropriate a firm's profits (or rents).

For an interesting discussion of how a firm's innovations may be appropriated by external stakeholders (e.g., customers, suppliers) as well as competitors, refer to Grant, R. M. 2002. *Contemporary strategy analysis* (4th ed.): 335–340. Malden, MA: Blackwell.

66. Luehrman, T. A. 1997. What's it worth? A general manager's guide to valuation. *Harvard Business Review,* 45(3): 132–142.

67. See, for example, Kaplan, R. S. & Norton, D. P. 1992. The balanced scorecard: Measures that drive performance. *Harvard Business Review,* 69(1): 71–79.

68. Hitt, M. A., Ireland, R. D., & Stadter, G. 1982. Functional importance of company performance: Moderating effects of grand strategy and industry type. *Strategic Management Journal,* 3: 315–330.

69. *finance.yahoo.com.*

70. Kaplan & Norton, op. cit.

71. Ibid.

72. For a discussion of the relative value of growth versus increasing margins, read Mass, N. J. 2005. The relative value of growth. *Harvard Business Review,* 83(4): 102–112.

73. Rucci, A. J., Kirn, S. P., & Quinn, R. T. 1998. The employee-customer-profit chain at Sears. *Harvard Business Review,* 76(1): 82–97.

74. Our discussion draws upon: Angel, R. & Rampersad, H. 2005. Do scorecards add up? *camagazine.com.* May: np.; and Niven, P. 2002. *Balanced scorecard step by step: Maximizing performance and maintaining results.* New York: John Wiley & Sons.

APPENDIX TO CHAPTER 3

>LO3.8

How firms are using Internet technologies to add value and achieve unique advantages. (Appendix)

How the Internet and Digital Technologies Add Value

The Internet has changed the way business is conducted. By providing new ways to interact with customers and using digital technologies to streamline operations, the Internet is helping companies create new value propositions. Let's take a look at several ways these changes have added new value. Exhibit 3A.1 illustrates four related activities that are being revolutionized by the Internet—search, evaluation, problem solving, and transactions.[1]

[1] The ideas in this section draw on several sources, including Zeng, M. & Reinartz, W. 2003. Beyond Online Search: The Road to Profitability. *California Management Review,* Winter: 107–130; and Stabell, C. B. & Fjeldstad, O. D. 1998. Configuring Value for Competitive Advantage: On Chains, Shops, and Networks. *Strategic Management Journal,* 19: 413–437.

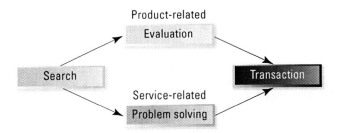

Exhibit 3A.1 Internet Activities that Add Value

Sources: Adapted from Zeng, M., & Reinartz, W. 2003. Beyond online search: The road to profitability. *California Management Review.* Winter: 107–130; and Stabell, C. B., & Fjeldstad, O. D. 1998. Configuring value for competitive advantage: On chains, shops, and networks. *Strategic Management Journal,* 19: 413–437.

Search Activities

Search refers to the process of gathering information and identifying purchase options. The Internet has enhanced both the speed of information gathering and the breadth of information that can be accessed. This enhanced search capability is one of the key reasons the Internet has lowered switching costs—by decreasing the cost of search. These efficiency gains have greatly benefited buyers. Suppliers also have benefited. Small suppliers that had difficulty getting noticed can be found more easily, and large suppliers can publish thousands of pages of information for a fraction of the cost that hard-copy catalogs once required. Additionally, online search engines such as Google, Yahoo and Bing have accelerated the search process to incredible speeds.

> **search activities** a way that digital technologies and the Internet have added value to firms' operations by enhancing the gathering of information and identifying purchase options.

Evaluation Activities

Evaluation refers to the process of considering alternatives and comparing the costs and benefits of various options. Online services that facilitate comparative shopping, provide product reviews, and catalog customer evaluations of performance have made the Internet a valuable resource.[2] For example, BizRate.com offers extensive product ratings that can help evaluate products. Sites such as CNET that provide comparative pricing have helped lower prices even for quality products that have traditionally maintained premium prices. Opinion-based sites such as ePinions.com and PlanetFeedback.com provide reports of consumer experiences with various vendors.

> **evaluation activities** a way that digital technologies and the Internet have added value to firms' operations by facilitating the comparison of the costs and benefits of various options.

Many Internet businesses, according to digital business experts Ming Zeng and Werner Reinartz, could improve their performance by making a stronger effort to help buyers evaluate purchases.[3] Even so, only certain types of products can be evaluated online. Products such as CDs that appeal primarily to the sense of sound sell well on the Internet. But products that appeal to multiple senses are harder to evaluate online. This explains why products such as furniture and fashion have never been strong online sellers. It's one thing to look at a leather sofa, but to be able to sit on it, touch, and smell the leather online are impossible.

Problem-Solving Activities

Problem solving refers to the process of identifying problems or needs and generating ideas and action plans to address those needs. Whereas evaluation is primarily product-related, problem solving is typically used in the context of services. Customers usually have unique problems that are handled one at a time. For example, online travel services such as Travelocity help customers select from many options to form a unique travel package. Furthermore, problem solving often involves providing answers immediately (compared to the creation of a new product). Firms in industries such as medicine, law, and engineering are using the Internet and digital technologies to deliver many new solutions.

> **problem-solving activities** a way that digital technologies and the Internet have added value to firms' operations by identifying problems or needs and generating ideas and action plans to address those needs.

[2] For an interesting discussion of how successful Internet-based companies are using evaluation to add value see Weiss, L. M., Capozzi, M. M., & Prusak, L. 2004. Learning from the Internet Giants. *Sloan Management Review,* 45(4): 79–84.
[3] Zeng & Reinartz, op.cit.

Many products involve both a service and a product component; therefore, both problem solving and evaluation may be needed. Dell Computer's website is an example of a site that has combined the benefits of both. By creating a website that allows for customization of individual computers, they address the unique concerns of customers "one computer at a time." But the site also features a strong evaluative component because it allows users to compare the costs and features of various options. Shoppers can even compare their customized selection to refurbished Dell computers that are available at a substantially lower cost.

Transaction Activities

transaction activities a way that digital technologies and the Internet have added value to firms' operations by completing sales efficiently, including negotiating and agreeing contractually, making payments, and taking delivery.

Transaction refers to the process of completing the sale, including negotiating and agreeing contractually, making payments, and taking delivery. Numerous types of Internet-enabled activities have contributed to lowering this aspect of overall transaction costs. Auctions of various sorts, from raw materials used in manufacturing to collectibles sold on eBay, facilitate the process of arriving at mutually agreed-on prices. Services such as PayPal provide a third-party intermediary that facilitates transactions between parties who never have (and probably never will) meet. Amazon.com's One-Click technology allows for very rapid purchases, and Amazon's overall superiority in managing order fulfillment has made its transactions process rapid and reliable. Amazon's success today can be attributed to a large extent to its having sold this transaction capability to other companies such as Target, Toys "R" Us and even Borders (another bookseller!).[4]

Other Sources of Competitive Advantage

There are other factors that can be important sources of competitive advantage. One of the most important of these is content. The Internet makes it possible to capture vast amounts of content at a very low cost. Three types of content can improve the value proposition of a website—customer feedback, expertise, and entertainment programming.

- *Customer Feedback.* Buyers often trust what other buyers say more than a company's promises. One type of content that can enhance a website is customer testimonials. Remember the leather sofa online? The testimonials of other buyers can build confidence and add to the chances that the purchaser will buy online sight unseen. This is one way that content can be a source of competitive advantage. Being able to interact with like-minded customers by reading their experiences or hearing how they have responded to a new product offering builds a sense of belonging that is otherwise hard to create.

- *Expertise.* The Internet has emerged as a tremendously important learning tool. Fifty-one percent of users compare the Internet to a library.[5] The prime reason many users go to the Web is to gain expertise. Websites that provide new knowledge or unbiased information are highly valuable. Additionally the problem-solving function often involves educating consumers regarding options and implications of various choices. For example, LendingTree.com, the online loan company, provides a help center that includes extensive information and resources about obtaining loans, maintaining good credit, and so forth. Further, the expertise function is not limited to consumer sites. In the case of B2B businesses, websites that facilitate sharing expert knowledge help build a sense of community in industry or professional groups.

- *Entertainment Programming.* The Internet is being used by more and more people as an entertainment medium. With technologies such as streaming media, which allows the Internet to send televisionlike images and sound, computers can provide everything from breaking news to video games to online movies. A study by the Pew Internet and American Life Project indicates that among people using high-speed broadband service, TV viewing is down and online activity has increased. One reason is that the technology is interactive, which means that viewers don't just passively watch, but they use the Web to create art or play online games. Businesses have noticed this trend, of course, and are creating Web content that is not just informative but entertaining.

These three types of content—customer feedback, expertise, and entertainment programming—are potential sources of competitive advantage. That is, they create advantages by making the value creation process even stronger. Or, if they are handled poorly, they diminish performance.

[4] Bayers, C. 2002. The Last Laugh. *Business 2.0,* September: 86–93.
[5] Greenspan, R. 2003. Internet Not for Everyone. *CyberAtlas,* April 16, *www.cyberatlas.com.*

Business Models

The Internet provides a unique platform or staging area for business activity, which has become, in some ways, like a new marketplace. How do firms conduct business in this new arena? One way of addressing this question is by describing various Internet business models. A business model is a method and a set of assumptions that explain how a business creates value and earns profits in a competitive environment. Some of these models are quite simple and traditional even when applied in an Internet context. Others have features that are unique to the digitally networked, online environment. In this section, we discuss seven Internet business models that account for the vast majority of business conducted online.[6]

- *Commission-Based* **Models** are used by businesses that provide services for a fee. The business is usually a third-party intermediary, and the commission charged is often based on the size of the transaction. The most common type is a brokerage service, such as a stockbroker (e.g., Schwab.com), real estate broker (e.g., Remax.com), or transaction broker (e.g., PayPal.com). This category also includes auction companies such as eBay. In exchange for putting buyers and sellers together, eBay earns a commission.
- *Advertising-Based* **Models** are used by companies that provide content and/or services to visitors and sell advertising to businesses that want to reach those visitors. It is similar to the broadcast television model, in which viewers watch shows produced with advertising dollars. A key difference is that online visitors can interact with both the ads and the content. Large portals such as Yahoo.com are in this category as well as specialty portals such as iNest.com, which provides services for buyers of newly constructed homes. Epinions.com, a recommender system, is just one example of the many types of content that are often available.
- *Markup-Based* **Models** are used by businesses that add value in marketing and sales (rather than production) by acquiring products, marking up the price, and reselling them at a profit. Also known as the merchant model, it applies to both wholesalers and retailers. Amazon.com is the best-known example in this category. It also includes bricks-and-mortar companies such as Walmart, which has a very successful online operation, and vendors whose products are purely digital such as Fonts.com, which sells downloadable fonts and photographs.
- *Production-Based* **Models** are used by companies that add value in the production process by converting raw materials into value-added products. Thus, it is also referred to as the manufacturing model. The Internet adds value to this model in two key ways. First, it lowers marketing costs by enabling direct contact with end users. Second, such direct contact facilitates customization and problem solving. Dell's online ordering system is supported by a state-of-the-art customized manufacturing process. Travelocity uses its rich database of travel options and customer profiles to identify, produce, and deliver unique solutions.
- *Referral-Based* **Models** are used by firms that steer customers to another company for a fee. One type is the affiliate model, in which a vendor pays an affiliate a fee each time a visitor clicks through the affiliate's website and makes a purchase from the vendor. Many name-brand companies use affiliate programs. For example, WeddingChannel.com, which provides a bridal registry where wedding guests can buy gifts from companies such as Tiffany's, Macy's, or Crate & Barrel, receives a fee each time a sale is made through its website. Another referral-based example is Yesmail.com, which generates leads using e-mail marketing.
- *Subscription-Based* **Models** are used by businesses that charge a flat fee for providing either a service or proprietary content. Internet service providers are one example of this model. Companies such as America Online and Earthlink supply Internet connections for fees that are charged whether buyers use the service or not. Subscription-based models are also used by content creators such as the *Economist* or the *New York Times*. Although these recognizable brands often provide free content, only a small portion is available free. The *Economist,* for example, advertises that 70 percent of its content is available only to subscribers.
- *Fee-for-Service–Based* **Models** are used by companies that provide ongoing services similar to a utility company. Unlike the commission-based model, the fee-for-service model involves a pay-as-you-go system. That is, activities are metered and companies pay only for the amount of service used. Application service providers fall in this category. For example, eProject.com

> **business model** a method and a set of assumptions that explain how a business creates value and earns profits in a competitive environment.

---

[6] Afuah, A. & Tucci, C.L. 2003. *Internet Business Models and Strategies* (2nd ed). New York: McGraw-Hill; and, Timmers, P. 1999. *Electronic Commerce.* New York: Wiley.

provides virtual work space where people in different physical locations can collaborate online. Users essentially rent Internet space, and a host of tools that make it easy to interact, for a fee based on their usage.

Exhibit 3A.2 summarizes the key feature of each Internet business model, suggests what role content may play in the model, and addresses how the four value-adding activities—search, evaluation, problem solving, and transaction—can be sources of competitive advantage.

Exhibit 3A.2
Internet Business Models

Type	Features and Content	Sources of Competitive Advantage
Commission-Based	Charges commissions for brokerage or intermediary services. Adds value by providing expertise and/or access to a wide network of alternatives.	Search Evaluation Problem solving Transaction
Advertising-Based	Web content paid for by advertisers. Adds value by providing free or low-cost content—including customer feedback, expertise, and entertainment programming—to audiences that range from very broad (general content) to highly targeted (specialized content).	Search Evaluation
Markup-Based	Resells marked-up merchandise. Adds value through selection, through distribution efficiencies, and by leveraging brand image and reputation. May use entertainment programming to enhance sales.	Search Transaction
Production-Based	Sells manufactured goods and custom services. Adds value by increasing production efficiencies, capturing customer preferences, and improving customer service.	Search Problem solving
Referral-Based	Charges fees for referring customers. Adds value by enhancing a company's product or service offering, tracking referrals electronically, and generating demographic data. Expertise and customer feedback often included with referral information.	Search Problem solving Transaction
Subscription-Based	Charges fees for unlimited use of service or content. Adds value by leveraging strong brand name, providing high-quality information to specialized markets, or providing access to essential services. May consist entirely of entertainment programming.	Evaluation Problem solving
Fee-for-Service–Based	Charges fees for metered services. Adds value by providing service efficiencies, expertise, and practical outsourcing solutions.	Problem solving Transaction

Sources: Afuah, A. & Tucci, C. L. 2003. *Internet Business Models and Strategies* (2nd ed). New York: McGraw-Hill; Rappa, M. 2005. *Business Models on the Web,* digitalenterprise.org/models/models.html; and Timmers, P. 1999. *Electronic Commerce.* New York: Wiley.

chapter 4. Recognizing a Firm's Intellectual Assests: Moving beyond a Firm's Tangible

chapter FOUR

Recognizing a Firm's Intellectual Assets:

Moving beyond a Firm's Tangible Resources

After reading this chapter, you should have a good understanding of:

LO4.1   Why the management of knowledge professionals and knowledge itself are so critical in today's organizations.

LO4.2   The importance of recognizing the interdependence of attracting, developing, and retaining human capital.

LO4.3   The key role of social capital in leveraging human capital within and across the firm.

LO4.4   The importance of social networks in knowledge management and in promoting career success.

LO4.5   The vital role of technology in leveraging knowledge and human capital.

LO4.6   Why "electronic" or "virtual" teams are critical in combining and leveraging knowledge in organizations and how they can be made more effective.

LO4.7   The challenge of protecting intellectual property and the importance of a firm's dynamic capabilities.

LEARNING OBJECTIVES

One of the most important trends that managers must consider is the significance of the knowledge worker in today's economy. Managers must both recognize the importance of top talent and provide mechanisms to leverage human capital to innovate and, in the end, develop products and services that create value.

The first section addresses the increasing role of knowledge as the primary means of wealth generation in today's economy. A company's value is not derived solely from its physical assets, such as plant, equipment, and machinery. Rather, it is based on knowledge, know-how, and intellectual assets—all embedded in people.

The second section discusses the key resource itself, human capital, which is the foundation of intellectual capital. We explore ways in which the organization can attract, develop, and retain top talent—three important, interdependent activities. With regard to attracting human capital, we address issues such as "hiring for attitude, training for skill." One of the issues regarding developing human capital is encouraging widespread involvement throughout the organization. Our discussion on retaining human capital addresses issues such as the importance of having employees identify with an organization's mission and values. We also address the value of a diverse workforce.

The attraction, development, and retention of human capital are necessary but not sufficient conditions for organizational success. In the third section we address social capital—networks of relationships among a firm's members. This is especially important where collaboration and sharing information are critical. We address why social capital can be particularly important in attracting human capital and making teams effective. We also address the vital role of social networks—both in improving knowledge management and in promoting career success.

The fourth section addresses the role of technology in leveraging human capital. Examples range from e-mail and the use of networks to facilitate collaboration among individuals to more complex forms of technologies, such as sophisticated knowledge management systems. We discuss how electronic teams can be effectively managed. We also address how technology can help to retain knowledge.

The last section discusses the differences between protection of physical property and intellectual property. We suggest that the development of dynamic capabilities may be one of the best ways that a firm can protect its intellectual property.

▇▇ Learning from Mistakes

Hitachi Ltd., a Japanese multinational corporation, is the world's third largest tech firm.[1] Its first president, Namihei Odaira, believed that "inventions are an engineer's lifeblood," and, not surprisingly, he focused on the company's inventions from the very beginning. He demanded that his tech people apply their engineering skills toward generating inventions and patents. This, he felt, could be the key to value creation and competitive advantage. Sounds good . . . but what problems arose?

In 1970 alone, Hitachi filed 20,000 patent applications. Unfortunately, the emphasis was on the sheer number rather than the quality of each patent. At that time, the company earned a mere $5 million in licensing income but paid out $95 million in licensing fees.

In 1979, Hitachi faced major patent litigation. Westinghouse charged Hitachi, a Hitachi-GE joint venture, and a few other companies with patent infringement and petitioned the U.S. International Trade Commission to block the import of circuit breakers from Japan. By then, Hitachi already had several dozen U.S. patents for electrical power transmission equipment. However, it found that they were all patents for features distinctive to Hitachi products and were not the type that other companies could use. Thus, there were no grounds for countersuing Westinghouse for patent infringement.

Hitachi's second big patent problem occurred in 1986. Texas Instruments sued a total of nine Japanese and Korean semiconductor manufacturers in the U.S. International Trade Commission and Texas courts, arguing that its licensing fee was too low and that it could not renew Hitachi's contract at the terms proposed. It demanded to set the licensing fee for DRAM manufacturing technology at 10 percent of sales.

These were bitter lessons for Hitachi. It initiated four campaigns to double its number of "strategic patents" in 1981, 1985, 1990, and 1995, respectively. The goal was to focus their resources on patents that would create the most value for the firm as well as to gain global patent coverage for the company's world-class products and technologies.

Patents can be very valuable. However, a company must effectively use them to create value. Hitachi realized that there was no point in obtaining a mountain of patents if they were not going to help the company compete in the competitive marketplace.

Managers are always looking for stellar professionals who can take their organizations to the next level. However, attracting talent is a necessary but *not* sufficient condition for success. In today's knowledge economy, it does not matter how big your stock of resources is—whether it be top talent, physical resources, or financial capital. Rather, the question becomes: How good is the organization at attracting top talent and leveraging that talent to produce a stream of products and services valued by the marketplace?

We also address issues associated with intellectual property (IP) and its potential to create value for the firm. The Hitachi example shows how heavy investment in IP alone is insufficient for value creation in the competitive marketplace.

> **>LO4.1**
> Why the management of knowledge professionals and knowledge itself are so critical in today's organizations.

The Central Role of Knowledge in Today's Economy

Central to our discussion is an enormous change that has accelerated over the past few decades and its implications for the strategic management of organizations.[2] For most of the 20th century, managers focused on tangible resources such as land, equipment, and money as well as intangibles such as brands, image, and customer loyalty. Efforts were directed more toward the efficient allocation of labor and capital—the two traditional factors of production.

How times have changed. Today, more than 50 percent of the gross domestic product (GDP) in developed economies is knowledge-based; it is based on intellectual assets and intangible people skills.[3] In the U.S., intellectual and information processes create most of the value for firms in large service industries (e.g., software, medical care, communications, and education), which make up 77 percent of the U.S. GDP. In the manufacturing sector, intellectual activities like R&D, process design, product design, logistics, marketing, and technological innovation produce the preponderance of value added.[4] To drive home the point, Gary Hamel and the late C. K. Prahalad, two leading writers in strategic management state:

> The machine age was a physical world. It consisted of things. Companies made and distributed things (physical products). Management allocated things (capital budgets); management invested in things (plant and equipment).
>
> In the machine age, people were ancillary, and things were central. In the information age, things are ancillary, knowledge is central. A company's value derives not from things, but from knowledge, know-how, intellectual assets, competencies—all embedded in people.[5]

In the **knowledge economy,** wealth is increasingly created by effective management of knowledge workers instead of by the efficient control of physical and financial assets. The growing importance of knowledge, coupled with the move by labor markets to reward knowledge work, tells us that investing in a company is, in essence, buying a set of talents, capabilities, skills, and ideas—intellectual capital—not physical and financial resources.[6]

Let's provide a few examples. People don't buy Microsoft's stock because of its software factories; it doesn't own any. Rather, the value of Microsoft is bid up because it sets standards for personal-computing software, exploits the value of its name, and forges alliances with other companies. Similarly, Merck didn't become the "Most Admired" company, for seven consecutive years in *Fortune*'s annual survey, because it can manufacture pills, but because its scientists can discover medicines. P. Roy Vagelos, who was CEO of Merck, the $44 billion pharmaceutical giant, during its long run atop the "Most Admired" survey, said, "A low-value product can be made by anyone anywhere. When you have knowledge no one else has access to—that's dynamite. We guard our research even more carefully than our financial assets."[7]

To apply some numbers to our arguments, let's ask, What's a company worth?[8] Start with the "big three" financial statements: income statement, balance sheet, and statement of cash flow. If these statements tell a story that investors find useful, then a company's market value* should roughly (but not precisely, because the market looks forward and the books look backward) be the same as the value that accountants ascribe to it—the book value of the firm. However, this is not the case. A study compared the market value with the book value of 3,500 U.S. companies over a period of two decades. In 1978 the two were similar: Book value was 95 percent of market value. However, market values and book values have diverged significantly. Within 20 years, the S&P industrials were—on average—trading at 2.2 times book value.[9] Robert A. Howell, an expert on the changing role of finance and accounting, muses that "The big three financial statements . . . are about as useful as an 80-year-old Los Angeles road map."

The gap between a firm's market value and book value is far greater for knowledge-intensive corporations than for firms with strategies based primarily on tangible assets.[10] Exhibit 4.1 shows the ratio of market-to-book value for some well-known companies. In

knowledge economy an economy where wealth is created through the effective management of knowledge workers instead of by the efficient control of physical and financial assets.

---

* The market value of a firm is equal to the value of a share of its common stock times the number of shares outstanding. The book value of a firm is primarily a measure of the value of its tangible assets. It can be calculated by the formula: total assets − total liabilities.

intellectual capital the difference between the market value of the firm and the book value of the firm, including assets such as reputation, employee loyalty and commitment, customer relationships, company values, brand names, and the experience and skills of employees.

firms where knowledge and the management of knowledge workers are relatively important contributors to developing products and services—and physical resources are less critical—the ratio of market-to-book value tends to be much higher.

As shown in Exhibit 4.1, firms such as Apple, Google, Microsoft, and Oracle have very high market value to book value ratios because of their high investment in knowledge resources and technological expertise. In contrast, firms in more traditional industry sectors such as International Paper, Nucor, and Southwest Airlines have relatively low market to book ratios. This reflects their greater investments in physical resources and lower investment in knowledge resources. A firm like Intel has a market to book value ratio that falls between the above two groups of firms. This is because their high level of investment in knowledge resources is matched by a correspondingly huge investment in plant and equipment. For example, in 2007, Intel invested $3 billion to build a fabrication facility in Chandler, Arizona.[11]

Many writers have defined **intellectual capital** as the difference between a firm's market value and book value—that is, a measure of the value of a firm's intangible assets.[12] This broad definition includes assets such as reputation, employee loyalty and commitment, customer relationships, company values, brand names, and the experience and skills of employees.[13] Thus, simplifying, we have:

$$\text{Intellectual capital} = \text{Market value of firm} - \text{Book value of the firm}$$

human capital the individual capabilities, knowledge, skills, and experience of a company's employees and managers.

How do companies create value in the knowledge-intensive economy? The general answer is to attract and leverage human capital effectively through mechanisms that create products and services of value over time.

First, **human capital** is the "*individual* capabilities, knowledge, skills, and experience of the company's employees and managers."[14] This knowledge is relevant to the task at hand, as well as the capacity to add to this reservoir of knowledge, skills, and experience through learning.[15]

social capital the network of friendships and working relationships between talented people both inside and outside the organization.

Second, **social capital** is "the network of relationships that individuals have throughout the organization." Relationships are critical in sharing and leveraging knowledge and in acquiring resources.[16] Social capital can extend beyond the organizational boundaries to include relationships between the firm and its suppliers, customers, and alliance partners.[17]

Exhibit 4.1 Ratio of Market Value to Book Value for Selected Companies

Company	Annual Sales ($ billions)	Market Value ($ billions)	Book Value ($ billions)	Ratio of Market to Book Value
Apple	65.2	314.6	47.8	6.6
Google	20.9	196.4	36.0	5.4
Microsoft	65.8	241.3	46.2	5.2
Oracle	32.0	157.0	30.8	5.1
Intel	42.7	116.1	41.7	2.8
International Paper	24.6	12.3	6.0	2.1
Nucor	14.9	13.8	7.4	1.9
Southwest Airlines	11.7	9.9	5.5	1.8

Note: The data on market valuations are as of January 11, 2011. All other financial data are based on the most recently available balance sheets and income statements.

Source: www.finance.yahoo.com.

Third is the concept of "knowledge," which comes in two different forms. First, there is **explicit knowledge** that is codified, documented, easily reproduced, and widely distributed, such as engineering drawings, software code, and patents.[18] The other type of knowledge is **tacit knowledge.** That is in the minds of employees and is based on their experiences and backgrounds.[19] Tacit knowledge is shared only with the consent and participation of the indivivdual.

New knowledge is constantly created through the continual interaction of explicit and tacit knowledge. Consider, two software engineers working together on a computer code. The computer code is the explicit knowledge. By sharing ideas based on each individual's experience—that is, their tacit knowledge—they create new knowledge when they modify the code. Another important issue is the role of "socially complex processes," which include leadership, culture, and trust.[20] These processes play a central role in the creation of knowledge.[21] They represent the "glue" that holds the organization together and helps to create a working environment where individuals are more willing to share their ideas, work in teams, and, in the end, create products and services of value.[22]

Numerous books have been written on the subject of knowledge management and the central role that it has played in creating wealth in organizations and countries throughout the developed world.[23] Here, we focus on some of the key issues that organizations must address to compete through knowledge.

We will now turn our discussion to the central resource itself—human capital—and some guidelines on how it can be attracted/selected, developed, and retained.[24] Tom Stewart, editor of the *Harvard Business Review,* noted that organizations must also undergo significant efforts to protect their human capital. A firm may "diversify the ownership of vital knowledge by emphasizing teamwork, guard against obsolescence by developing learning programs, and shackle key people with golden handcuffs."[25] In addition, people are less likely to leave an organization if there are effective structures to promote teamwork and information sharing, strong leadership that encourages innovation, and cultures that demand excellence and ethical behavior. Such issues are central to this chapter. Although we touch on these issues throughout this chapter, we provide more detail in later chapters. We discuss organizational controls (culture, rewards, and boundaries) in Chapter 9, organization structure and design in Chapter 10, and a variety of leadership and entrepreneurship topics in Chapters 11 and 12.

explicit knowledge
knowledge that is codified, documented, easily reproduced, and widely distributed.

tacit knowledge
knowledge that is in the minds of employees and is based on their experiences and backgrounds.

Human Capital: The Foundation of Intellectual Capital

Organizations must recruit talented people—employees at all levels with the proper sets of skills and capabilities coupled with the right values and attitudes. Such skills and attitudes must be continually developed, strengthened, and reinforced, and each employee must be motivated and her efforts focused on the organization's goals and objectives.[26]

The rise to prominence of knowledge workers as a vital source of competitive advantage is changing the balance of power in today's organization.[27] Knowledge workers place professional development and personal enrichment (financial and otherwise) above company loyalty. Attracting, recruiting, and hiring the "best and the brightest," is a critical first step in the process of building intellectual capital. At a symposium for CEOs, Bill Gates said, "The thing that is holding Microsoft back . . . is simply how [hard] we find it to go out and recruit the kind of people we want to grow our research team."[28]

Hiring is only the first of three processes in which all successful organizations must engage to build and leverage their human capital. Firms must also *develop* employees to fulfill their full potential to maximize their joint contributions.[29] Finally, the first two processes are for naught if firms can't provide the working environment and intrinsic and extrinsic rewards to *retain* their best and brightest.[30]

>LO4.2

The importance of recognizing the interdependence of attracting, developing, and retaining human capital.

These activities are highly interrelated. We would like to suggest the imagery of a three-legged stool (see Exhibit 4.2).[31] If one leg is weak or broken, the stool collapses.

To illustrate such interdependence, poor hiring impedes the effectiveness of development and retention processes. In a similar vein, ineffective retention efforts place additional burdens on hiring and development. Consider the following anecdote, provided by Jeffrey Pfeffer of the Stanford University Business School:

> Not long ago, I went to a large, fancy San Francisco law firm—where they treat their associates like dog doo and where the turnover is very high. I asked the managing partner about the turnover rate. He said, "A few years ago, it was 25 percent, and now we're up to 30 percent." I asked him how the firm had responded to that trend. He said, "We increased our recruiting." So I asked him, "What kind of doctor would you be if your patient was bleeding faster and faster, and your only response was to increase the speed of the transfusion?"[32]

Clearly, stepped-up recruiting is a poor substitute for weak retention.[33] Although there are no simple, easy-to-apply answers, we can learn from what leading-edge firms are doing to attract, develop, and retain human capital in today's highly competitive marketplace.[34] Before moving on, Strategy Spotlight 4.1 addresses the importance of a firm's "green" or environmental sustainability strategy in attracting young talent.

Attracting Human Capital

All we can do is bet on the people we pick. So my whole job is picking the right people.

Jack Welch, former chairman, General Electric Company[35]

The first step in the process of building superior human capital is input control: attracting and selecting the right person.[36] Human resource professionals often approach employee selection from a "lock and key" mentality—that is, fit a key (a job candidate) into a lock (the job). Such an approach involves a thorough analysis of the person and the job. Only then can the right decision be made as to how well the two will fit together. How can you fail, the theory goes, if you get a precise match of knowledge, ability, and skill profiles? Frequently, however, the precise matching approach places its emphasis on task-specific skills (e.g., motor skills, specific information processing capabilities, and communication skills) and puts less emphasis on the broad general knowledge and experience, social skills, values, beliefs, and attitudes of employees.[37]

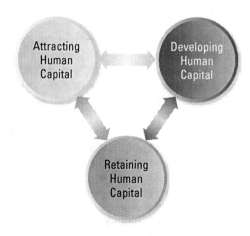

Exhibit 4.2 **Human Capital: Three Interdependent Activities**

4.1

Going "Green" Helps Attract Talent

When companies go "green," they often find that the benefits extend beyond the environment. Eco-friendly strategies can also help attract young talent and reduce costs. According to Lindsey Pollack, author of *Getting from College to Career:*

> Students are looking to work for companies that care about the environment. They are almost expecting greenness like they expect work-life balance, ethnic diversity, and globalization.

A recent poll on green employment by Monster-TRAK.com, a job website geared toward students and entry-level hires, found that 80 percent of young professionals are interested in securing a job that has a positive impact on the environment, and 92 percent would be more inclined to work for a company that is environmentally friendly. And, in another survey, 68 percent of Millennials said they would refuse to work for an employer that is not socially responsible.

In response, paper maker NewPage Corp. distributes a brochure that highlights the firm's commitment to environmental responsibility when it recruits on campuses. It showcases the company's new corporate headquarters, in Miamisburg, Ohio, that uses 28 percent to 39 percent less energy than a standard office building and is furnished with environmentally friendly materials. Says NewPage CEO Mark Sunwyn, "At the end of the day, we are competing with everyone else for the best talent, and this is a generation that is very concerned with the environment."

To meet the growing demand for students interested in working for green companies, MonsterTRAK, a unit of the giant employment firm Monster.com, launched GreenCareers. It was the first online recruitment service that focuses on green employment. EcoAmerica and the Environmental Defense Fund, two environmental nonprofits, are adding their expertise in partnership with MonsterTRAK. "EcoAmerica approached MonsterTRAK to create GreenCareers because there is an urgent need to reach and educate environmentally 'agnostic' audiences, in this case college students, about the ways they can address climate change and other serious environmental problems," claims Mark Charnock, vice president and general manager at MonsterTRAK.

Sources: Luhby, T. 2008. How to Lure Gen Y Workers? *CNNMoney.com*, August 17: np; Mattioli. 2007. How Going Green Draws Talent, Cut Costs. *Wall Street Journal*, November 13: B10; and, Odell, A. M. 2007. Working for the Earth: Green Companies and Green Jobs Attract Employees. *www. socialfunds.com*, October 9: np.

**environmental
sustainability**

Many have questioned the precise matching approach. They argue that firms can identify top performers by focusing on key employee mind-sets, attitudes, social skills, and general orientations. If they get these elements right, the task-specific skills can be learned quickly. (This does not imply, however, that task-specific skills are unimportant; rather, it suggests that the requisite skill sets must be viewed as a necessary but not sufficient condition.) This leads us to a popular phrase today that serves as the title of the next section.

"Hire for Attitude, Train for Skill" Organizations are increasingly emphasizing general knowledge and experience, social skills, values, beliefs, and attitudes of employees.[38] Consider Southwest Airlines' hiring practices, which focus on employee values and attitudes. Given its strong team orientation, Southwest uses an "indirect" approach. For example, the interviewing team asks a group of employees to prepare a five-minute presentation about themselves. During the presentations, interviewers observe which candidates enthusiastically support their peers and which candidates focus on polishing their own presentations while the others are presenting.[39] The former are, of course, favored.

Alan Cooper, president of Cooper Software, Inc., in Palo Alto, California, goes further. He cleverly *uses technology* to hone in on the problem-solving ability of his applicants and their attitudes before an interview even takes place. He has devised a "Bozo

Filter," an online test that can be applied to any industry. Before you spend time on whether job candidates will work out satisfactorily, find out how their minds work. Cooper advised, "Hiring was a black hole. I don't talk to bozos anymore, because 90 percent of them turn away when they see our test. It's a self-administering bozo filter."[40] How does it work?

> The online test asks questions designed to see how prospective employees approach problem-solving tasks. For example, one key question asks software engineer applicants to design a table-creation software program for Microsoft Word. Candidates provide pencil sketches and a description of the new user interface. Another question used for design communicators asks them to develop a marketing strategy for a new touch-tone phone—directed at consumers in the year 1850. Candidates e-mail their answers back to the company, and the answers are circulated around the firm to solicit feedback. Only candidates with the highest marks get interviews.

Sound Recruiting Approaches and Networking   Companies that take hiring seriously must also take recruiting seriously. The number of jobs that successful knowledge-intensive companies must fill is astonishing. Ironically, many companies still have no shortage of applicants. For example, Google, ranked fourth on *Fortune*'s 2011 "100 Best Companies to Work For," is planning to hire thousands of employees—even though its hiring rate has slowed.[41] The challenge becomes having the right job candidates, not the greatest number of them.

GE Medical Systems, which builds CT scanners and magnetic resonance imaging (MRI) systems, relies extensively on networking. They have found that current employees are the best source for new ones. Recently, Steven Patscot, head of staffing and leadership development, made a few simple changes to double the number of referrals. First, he simplified the process—no complex forms, no bureaucracy, and so on. Second, he increased incentives. Everyone referring a qualified candidate received a gift certificate from Sears. For referrals who were hired, the "bounty" increases to $2,000. Although this may sound like a lot of money, it is "peanuts" compared to the $15,000 to $20,000 fees that GE typically pays to headhunters for each person hired.[42] Also, when someone refers a former colleague or friend for a job, his or her credibility is on the line. Thus, employees will be careful in recommending people for employment unless they are reasonably confident that these people are good candidates. This provides a good "screen" for the firm in deciding whom to hire. Hiring the right people makes things a lot easier: fewer rules and regulations, less need for monitoring and hierarchy, and greater internalization of organizational norms and objectives.

Consider some of the approaches that companies are currently using to recruit and retain young talent. As baby boomers retire, people in this demographic group are becoming more and more important in today's workforce. We also provide some "tips" on how to get hired. We address these issues in Exhibit 4.3.

Developing Human Capital

It is not enough to hire top-level talent and expect that the skills and capabilities of those employees remain current throughout the duration of their employment. Rather, training and development must take place at all levels of the organization.[43] For example, Solectron assembles printed circuit boards and other components for its Silicon Valley clients.[44] Its employees receive an average of 95 hours of company-provided training each year. Chairman Winston Chen observed, "Technology changes so fast that we estimate 20 percent of an engineer's knowledge becomes obsolete each year. Training is an obligation we owe to our employees. If you want high growth and high quality, then training is a big part of the equation." Although the financial returns on training may be hard to calculate, most experts believe it is essential. One company that has calculated the benefit from training is Motorola. Every dollar spent on training returns $30 in productivity gains over the following three years.

Exhibit 4.3
**What Companies Are
Doing to Attract and
Retain Young Talent . . .
and What You Should Do
to Get Hired**

Here are some "best practices" that companies are using to help recruit and retain today's high-maintenance Millennials. This generation has also been termed "Generation Y" or "Echo Boom" and includes people born after 1982:

- ***Don't fudge the sales pitch.*** High-tech presentations and one-on-one attention may be attractive to undergrads, but the pitch had better match the experience. Today's ultraconnected students can get the lowdown on a company by spending five minutes on a social networking site.

- ***Let them have a life.*** Wary of their parents' 80-hour workweeks, Millennials strive for more balance, so liberal vacations are a must. They also want assurances they'll be able to use it. At KPMG, 80 percent of employees used 40 hours of paid time off in the six months through May 2006.

- ***No time clocks, please.*** Recent grads don't mind long hours if they can work them on their own time. Lockheed Martin allows employees to work nine-hour days and take every other Friday off.

- ***Give them responsibility.*** A chance to work on fulfilling projects and develop ones of their own is important to Millennials. Google urges entry-level employees to spend 20 percent of their time developing new ideas. PepsiCo allows promising young employees to manage small teams in six months.

- ***Feedback and more feedback.*** Career planning advice and frequent performance appraisals are keys to holding on to young hires. Lehman Brothers provides new hires with two mentors—a slightly older peer to help them get settled and a senior employee to give long-term guidance.

- ***Giving back matters.*** Today's altruistic young graduates expect to have opportunities for community service. Wells Fargo encourages its employees to teach financial literacy classes in the community. Accenture and Bain allow employees to consult for nonprofits.

Some advice on how to get hired (based on Fortune's "100 Best Companies to Work For"):

- **It helps to know someone.** Almost all of the "Best Companies" rely extensively on employee referrals. Principal Financial Group and many others get about 40 percent of new hires this way.

- **Do creative research.** Know more about the place and the industry than your rivals. A Google search is not viewed as a form of "creative research." Says Jay Jones, a recruiting manager for Alcon Laboratories: "Detailed research, including talking to customers, is so rare it will almost guarantee you get hired."

- **Unleash your inner storyteller.** By far the most popular interview style is what's known as behavioral, meaning that you will be asked to describe troublesome situations in past jobs and tell exactly how you handled them.

- **No lone rangers need apply.** By and large, team players are wanted. "I actually count the number of times a candidates says 'I' in an interview," says Adobe's recruiting director, Jeff Vijungco. "We'd rather hear 'we.'"

- **Be open to learning new things.** Showing passion is a must, and most of the "100 Best" pride themselves on creating "learning environments." Thus, talk about the skills you'd like to acquire or polish. Declaring that you're already the best at what you do is a turnoff.

Source: Fisher, A. 2008. How to Get Hired by a "Best" Company. *Fortune*, February 4: 96; and Gerdes, L. 2006. The Top 50 Employers for New College Grads. *BusinessWeek*, September 18: 64–81.

In addition to training and developing human capital, firms must encourage widespread involvement, monitor and track employee development, and evaluate human capital.[45]

Encouraging Widespread Involvement   Developing human capital requires the active involvement of leaders at all levels. It won't be successful if it is viewed only as the responsibility of the human resources department. Each year at General Electric, 200 facilitators, 30 officers, 30 human resource executives, and many young managers actively participate in GE's orientation program at Crotonville, its training center outside New York City. Topics include global competition, winning on the global playing field, and personal examination of the new employee's core values vis-à-vis GE's values. As a senior manager once commented, "There is nothing like teaching Sunday school to force you to confront your own values."

Similarly, A. G. Lafley, Procter & Gamble's former CEO, claimed that he spent 40 percent of his time on personnel.[46] Andy Grove, who was previously Intel's CEO, required all senior people, including himself, to spend at least a week a year teaching high flyers. And Nitin Paranjpe, CEO of Hindustan Unilever, recruits people from campuses and regularly visits high-potential employees in their offices.

Transferring Knowledge   Often in our lives, we need to either transfer our knowledge to someone else (a child, a junior colleague, a peer) or access accumulated bits of wisdom—someone else's tacit knowledge.[47] This is a vital aspect of developing human capital.[48] However, before we can even begin to plan such a transfer, we need to understand how our brains process incoming information. According to Dorothy A. Leonard of Harvard University:

> Our existing tacit knowledge determines how we assimilate new experiences. Without receptors—hooks on which to hang new information—we may not be able to perceive and process the information. It is like being sent boxes of documents but having no idea how they could or should be organized.

This cognitive limitation also applies to the organizational level. When GE Healthcare sets up or transfers operations, it appoints an experienced manager as the "pitcher" and a team in the receiving plant as the "catcher." These two teams work together, often over a period of years—first at the pitcher's location and then at the catcher's. To ensure a smooth transition, the pitching team needs to be sensitive to the catching team's level of experience and familiarity with GE Healthcare procedures.

Strategy Spotlight 4.2 discusses an emerging trend in organizations—reverse mentoring. Here, Internet savvy new hires mentor seasoned executives.

Monitoring Progress and Tracking Development   Whether a firm uses on-site formal training, off-site training (e.g., universities), or on-the-job training, tracking individual progress—and sharing this knowledge with both the employee and key managers—becomes essential. Like many leading-edge firms, GlaxoSmithKline (GSK) places strong emphasis on broader experiences over longer time periods. Dan Phelan, senior vice president and director of human resources, explained, "We ideally follow a two-plus-two-plus-two formula in developing people for top management positions." This reflects the belief that GSK's best people should gain experience in two business units, two functional units (such as finance and marketing), and in two countries.

Evaluating Human Capital   In today's competitive environment, collaboration and interdependence are vital to organizational success. Individuals must share their knowledge and work constructively to achieve collective, not just individual, goals. However, traditional systems evaluate performance from a single perspective (i.e., "top down") and generally don't address the "softer" dimensions of communications and social skills, values, beliefs, and attitudes.[49]

4.2

strategy spotlight

Time Warner's Reverse Mentoring Program

Time Warner recently developed a mentoring program that engages people on both ends of their careers. In this case, some of the company's senior executives were challenged to stay at the forefront of a rapidly evolving new-media landscape. To raise awareness of digital media, Time Warner launched Digital Reverse Mentoring—a program in which tech-savvy college students mentor senior executives on emerging digital trends and technologies such as Facebook, Twitter, and other Web 2.0 applications. Gen Y mentors meet with senior executives for

Source: Hewlett, S. A., Sherbin, L. & Sumberg, K. 2009. How Gen Y & Boomers will reshape your agenda. *Harvard Business Review,* 87(7/8): 76.

one-on-one meetings about writing blogs, posting videos on YouTube, and making imaginative use of new media. The program helps them not only to better understand how new technologies are affecting Time Warner but also to obtain fresh ideas on optimizing the firm's online presence. In addition to imparting technical skills, Gen Y mentors provide Boomer mentees with insights into the values, consumer behaviors, and communication styles of the younger generation.

Time Warner enjoys the immeasurable benefits of a more market-attuned leadership team. In a broader sense, however, programs like these pay off by proving that a company is part of a new breed of employer—one that respects educated workers' increasing desires for flexibility, personal growth, connectivity, and a chance to give back.

To address the limitations of the traditional approach, many organizations use 360-degree evaluation and feedback systems.[50] Here, superiors, direct reports, colleagues, and even internal and external customers rate a person's performance.[51] Managers rate themselves to have a personal benchmark. The 360-degree feedback system complements teamwork, employee involvement, and organizational flattening. As organizations continue to push responsibility downward, traditional top-down appraisal systems become insufficient.[52] For example, a manager who previously managed the performance of 3 supervisors might now be responsible for 10 and is less likely to have the in-depth knowledge needed to appraise and develop them adequately. Exhibit 4.4 provides a portion of GE's 360-degree system.

Evaluation systems must also ensure that a manager's success does not come at the cost of compromising the organization's core values. Such behavior generally leads to only short-term wins for both the manager and the organization. The organization typically suffers long-term losses in terms of morale, turnover, productivity, and so on. Accordingly, Merck's former chairman, Ray Gilmartin, told his employees, "If someone is achieving results but not demonstrating the core values of the company, at the expense of our people, that manager does not have much of a career here."

> **360-degree evaluation and feedback systems** superiors, direct reports, colleagues, and even external and internal customers rate a person's performance.

Retaining Human Capital

It has been said that talented employees are like "frogs in a wheelbarrow."[53] They can jump out at any time! By analogy, the organization can either try to force employees to stay in the firm or try to keep them from jumping out by creating incentives.[54] In other words, today's leaders can either provide the work environment and incentives to keep productive employees and management from wanting to bail out, or they can use legal means such as employment contracts and noncompete clauses.[55] Firms must prevent the transfer of valuable and sensitive information outside the organization. Failure to do so would be the neglect of a leader's fiduciary responsibility to shareholders. However, greater efforts should be directed at the former (e.g., good work environment and incentives), but, as we all know, the latter (e.g., employment contracts and noncompete clauses) have their place.[56]

Exhibit 4.4
An Excerpt from General Electric's 360-Degree Leadership Assessment Chart

Vision	•	Has developed and communicated a clear, simple, customer-focused vision/direction for the organization.
	•	Forward-thinking, stretches horizons, challenges imaginations.
	•	Inspires and energizes others to commit to Vision. Captures minds. Leads by example.
	•	As appropriate, updates Vision to reflect constant and accelerating change affecting the business.

Customer/Quality Focus

Integrity

Accountability/Commitment

Communication/Influence

Shared Ownership/Boundaryless

Team Builder/Empowerment

Knowledge/Expertise/Intellect

Initiative/Speed

Global Mind-Set

Source: Adapted from Slater, R. 1994. *Get Better or Get Beaten:* 152–155. Burr Ridge, IL: Irwin Professional Publishing.

Note: This evaluation system consists of 10 "characteristics"—Vision, Customer/Quality Focus, Integrity, and so on. Each of these characteristics has four "performance criteria." For illustrative purposes, the four performance criteria of "Vision" are included.

Identifying with an Organization's Mission and Values   People who identify with and are more committed to the core mission and values of the organization are less likely to stray or bolt to the competition. For example, take the perspective of Steve Jobs, Apple's widely admired CEO:[57]

> When I hire somebody really senior, competence is the ante. They have to be really smart. But the real issue for me is: Are they going to fall in love with Apple? Because if they fall in love with Apple, everything else will take care of itself. They'll want to do what's best for Apple, not what's best for them, what's best for Steve, or anyone else.

"Tribal loyalty" is another key factor that links people to the organization.[58] A tribe is not the organization as a whole (unless it is very small). Rather, it is teams, communities of practice, and other groups within an organization or occupation.

Brian Hall, CEO of Values Technology in Santa Cruz, California, documented a shift in people's emotional expectations from work. From the 1950s on, a "task first" relationship—"tell me what the job is, and let's get on with it"—dominated employee attitudes. Emotions and personal life were checked at the door. In the past few years, a "relationship-first" set of values has challenged the task orientation. Hall believes that it will become dominant. Employees want to share attitudes and beliefs as well as workspace.

Challenging Work and a Stimulating Environment   Arthur Schawlow, winner of the 1981 Nobel Prize in physics, was asked what made the difference between highly creative and less creative scientists. His reply: "The labor of love aspect is very important. The most successful scientists often are not the most talented.[59] But they are the ones impelled by curiosity. They've got to know what the answer is."[60] Such insights highlight the importance of intrinsic motivation: the motivation to work on something because it is exciting, satisfying, or personally challenging.[61]

One way firms keep highly mobile employees motivated and challenged is through opportunities that lower barriers to an employee's mobility within a company. For example, Shell Oil Company has created an "open sourcing" model for talent. Jobs are listed on Shell's intranet, and, with a two-month notice, employees can go to work on anything that interests them. Monsanto[62] has developed a similar approach. According to one executive:

> Because we don't have a lot of structure, people will flow toward where success and innovation are taking place. We have a free-market system where people can move, so you have an outflow of people in areas where not much progress is being made. Before, the HR function ran processes like management development and performance evaluation. Now it also facilitates this movement of people.

Financial and Nonfinancial Rewards and Incentives   Financial rewards are a vital organizational control mechanism (as we will discuss in Chapter 9). Money—whether in the form of salary, bonus, stock options, and so forth—can mean many different things to people. It might mean security, recognition, or a sense of freedom and independence.

Paying people more is seldom the most important factor in attracting and retaining human capital.[63] Most surveys show that money is not the most important reason why people take or leave jobs, and that money, in some surveys, is not even in the top 10. Consistent with these findings, Tandem Computers (part of Hewlett-Packard) typically doesn't tell people being recruited what their salaries would be. People who asked were told that their salaries were competitive. If they persisted along this line of questioning, they would not be offered a position. Why? Tandem realized a rather simple idea: People who come for money will leave for money.

Another nonfinancial reward is accommodating working families with children. Balancing demands of family and work is a problem at some point for virtually all employees.

Exhibit 4.5 describes strategies used by three leading-edge firms to retain their key employees—even during difficult economic times.

Exhibit 4.5
Retention Rules: How Three Companies Are Keeping Their Best during Tough Times

Start a Talent Agency: Yum Brands started a Talent Scout program to recruit outsiders. Selected top performers nominate at least 25 people, and they get cash when a recruit is hired. Global talent VP John Kurnick says 25 percent of the finance team's recent hires came from this program. Although it wasn't designed for retention, "it's been the most gratifying for the scout," says Kurnick, and it encourages the scout to stay with the company.

Change Up Bonus Time: Software maker Intuit moved its annual restricted stock grant up from July to February to address the economic uncertainties that the employees felt. Intuit's human resources team wanted the grant to make a big impact. Program manager Eileen Fagan claims: "It took one more worry off people's plates. It was a huge incentive for feeling good about the company."

Send Them Abroad—If It Fits: During recessionary times, global opportunities can energize top performers, says Ari Bousbib, former executive VP of United Technologies. During the downturn, he says, the company offered more expatriate assignments (for those whose family situations allowed it) as bonuses came under pressure.

Source: McGregor, J. & Dubey, R. 2010. Giving Back to Your Stars. *Fortune.* November 1: 53–54.

Enhancing Human Capital: The Role of Diversity in the Workforce

A combination of demographic trends and accelerating globalization of business has made the management of cultural differences a critical issue.[64] Workforces, which reflect demographic changes in the overall population, will be increasingly heterogeneous along dimensions such as gender, race, ethnicity, and nationality.[65] Demographic trends in the United States indicate a growth in Hispanic Americans from 6.9 million in 1960 to over 35 million in 2000, an expected increase to over 59 million by 2020 and 102 million by 2050. Similarly, the Asian-American population should grow to 20 million in 2020 from 12 million in 2000 and only 1.5 million in 1970. And the African-American population is becoming more ethnically heterogeneous. Census estimates project that in 2010 as many as 10 percent of Americans of African descent were immigrants from Africa or the Caribbean.[66]

Such demographic changes have implications not only for the labor pool but also for customer bases, which are also becoming more diverse.[67] This creates important organizational challenges and opportunities.

The effective management of diversity can enhance the social responsibility goals of an organization.[68] However, there are many other benefits as well. Six other areas where sound management of diverse workforces can improve an organization's effectiveness and competitive advantages are: (1) cost, (2) resource acquisition, (3) marketing, (4) creativity, (5) problem-solving, and (6) organizational flexibility.

- *Cost Argument.* As organizations become more diverse, firms effective in managing diversity will have a cost advantage over those that are not.
- *Resource Acquisition Argument.* Firms with excellent reputations as prospective employers for women and ethnic minorities will have an advantage in the competition for top talent. As labor pools shrink and change in composition, such advantages will become even more important.
- *Marketing Argument.* For multinational firms, the insight and cultural sensitivity that members with roots in other countries bring to marketing efforts will be very useful. A similar rationale applies to subpopulations within domestic operations.
- *Creativity Argument.* Less emphasis on conformity to norms of the past and a diversity of perspectives will improve the level of creativity.
- *Problem-Solving Argument.* Heterogeniety in decision-making and problem-solving groups typically produces better decisions because of a wider range of perspectives as well as more thorough analysis. Jim Schiro, former CEO of PriceWaterhouse Coopers, explains, "When you make a genuine commitment to diversity, you bring a greater diversity of ideas, approaches, and experiences and abilities that can be applied to client problems. After all, six people with different perspectives have a better shot at solving complex problems than sixty people who all think alike."[69]
- *Organizational Flexibility Argument.* With effective programs to enhance workplace diversity, systems become less determinant, less standardized, and therefore more fluid. Such fluidity should lead to greater flexibility to react to environmental changes. Reactions should be faster and less costly.

Consider how MTV Networks (part of Viacom) has benefited from a diverse workforce.[70]

One cross-cultural group discovered marketing opportunities in the similarities between North American country music and Latin American music, which use many of the same instruments, feature singers with similar vocal styles, and—in the U.S. Sunbelt—appeal to much the same audience. Other groups have influenced the multicultural content of Nickelodeon's children's programming. Says Tom Freston, MTV's former CEO, "Those teams are diverse by design to generate innovation. The probability that you will get a good, original, innovative idea with that type of chemistry is simply much higher."

The Vital Role of Social Capital

>LO4.3
The key role of social capital in leveraging human capital within and across the firm.

Successful firms are well aware that the attraction, development, and retention of talent *is a necessary but not sufficient condition* for creating competitive advantages.[71] In the knowledge economy, it is not the stock of human capital that is important, but the extent to which it is combined and leveraged.[72] In a sense, developing and retaining human capital becomes less important as key players (talented professionals, in particular) take the role of "free agents" and bring with them the requisite skill in many cases. Rather, the development of social capital (that is, the friendships and working relationships among talented individuals) gains importance, because it helps tie knowledge workers to a given firm.[73] Knowledge workers often exhibit greater loyalties to their colleagues and their profession than their employing organization, which may be "an amorphous, distant, and sometimes threatening entity."[74] Thus, a firm must find ways to create "ties" among its knowledge workers.

Let's look at a hypothetical example. Two pharmaceutical firms are fortunate enough to hire Nobel Prize–winning scientists.[75] In one case, the scientist is offered a very attractive salary, outstanding facilities and equipment, and told to "go to it!" In the second case, the scientist is offered approximately the same salary, facilities, and equipment plus one additional ingredient: working in a laboratory with 10 highly skilled and enthusiastic scientists. Part of the job is to collaborate with these peers and jointly develop promising drug compounds. There is little doubt as to which scenario will lead to a higher probability of retaining the scientist. The interaction, sharing, and collaboration will create a situation in which the scientist will develop firm-specific ties and be less likely to "bolt" for a higher salary offer. Such ties are critical because knowledge-based resources tend to be more tacit in nature, as we mentioned early in this chapter. Therefore, they are much more difficult to protect against loss (i.e., the individual quitting the organization) than other types of capital, such as equipment, machinery, and land.

Another way to view this situation is in terms of the resource-based view of the firm that we discussed in Chapter 3. That is, competitive advantages tend to be harder for competitors to copy if they are based on "unique bundles" of resources.[76] So, if employees are working effectively in teams and sharing their knowledge and learning from each other, not only will they be more likely to add value to the firm, but they also will be less likely to leave the organization, because of the loyalties and social ties that they develop over time.

How Social Capital Helps Attract and Retain Talent

The importance of social ties among talented professionals creates a significant challenge (and opportunity) for organizations. In *The Wall Street Journal*, Bernard Wysocki described the increase in a type of "Pied Piper Effect," in which teams or networks of people are leaving one company for another.[77] The trend is to recruit job candidates at the crux of social relationships in organizations, particularly if they are seen as having the potential to bring with them valuable colleagues.[78] This is a process that is referred to as "hiring via personal networks." Let's look at one instance of this practice.

> Gerald Eickhoff, founder of an electronic commerce company called Third Millennium Communications, tried for 15 years to hire Michael Reene. Why? Mr. Eickhoff says that he has "these Pied Piper skills." Mr. Reene was a star at Andersen Consulting in the 1980s and at IBM in the 1990s. He built his businesses and kept turning down overtures from Mr. Eickhoff.
>
> However, in early 2000, he joined Third Millennium as chief executive officer, with a salary of just $120,000 but with a 20 percent stake in the firm. Since then, he has brought in a raft of former IBM colleagues and Andersen subordinates. One protégé from his time

at Andersen, Mary Goode, was brought on board as executive vice president. She promptly tapped her own network and brought along former colleagues.

Wysocki considers the Pied Piper effect one of the underappreciated factors in the war for talent today. This is because one of the myths of the New Economy is rampant individualism, wherein individuals find jobs on the Internet career sites and go to work for complete strangers. Perhaps, instead of Me Inc., the truth is closer to We Inc.[79]

Another example of social relationships causing human capital mobility is the emigration of talent from an organization to form start-up ventures. Microsoft is perhaps the best-known example of this phenomenon.[80] Professionals frequently leave Microsoft en masse to form venture capital and technology start-ups, called "Baby Bills," built around teams of software developers. For example, Ignition Corporation, of Bellevue, Washington, was formed by Brad Silverberg, a former Microsoft senior vice president. Eight former Microsoft executives, among others, founded the company.

Social relationships can provide an important mechanism for obtaining both resources and information from individuals and organizations outside the boundary of a firm.[81] Strategy Spotlight 4.3 describes how alumni programs for recently laid-off employees benefit both the individuals and the firm.

Social Networks: Implications for Knowledge Management and Career Success

>LO4.4
The importance of social networks in knowledge management and in promoting career success.

Managers face many challenges driven by such factors as rapid changes in globalization and technology. Leading a successful company is more than a one-person job. As Tom Malone recently put it in *The Future of Work,* "As managers, we need to shift our thinking from command and control to coordinate and cultivate—the best way to gain power is sometimes to give it away."[82] The move away from top-down bureaucratic control to more open, decentralized network models makes it more difficult for managers to understand how work is actually getting done, who is interacting with whom both within and outside the organization, and the consequences of these interactions for the long-term health of the organization.[83] In short, coordination, cultivation, and collaboration are increasingly becoming the mode of work at every level.[84]

social network analysis analysis of the pattern of social interactions among individuals.

But how can this be done? **Social network analysis** depicts the pattern of interactions among individuals and helps to diagnose effective and ineffective patterns.[85] It helps identify groups or clusters of individuals that comprise the network, individuals who link the clusters, and other network members. It helps diagnose communication patterns and, consequently, communication effectiveness.[86] Such analysis of communication patterns is helpful because the configuration of group members' social ties within and outside the group affects the extent to which members connect to individuals who:

- convey needed resources,
- have the opportunity to exchange information and support,
- have the motivation to treat each other in positive ways, and,
- have the time to develop trusting relationships that might improve the groups' effectiveness.

However, such relationships don't "just happen."[87] Developing social capital requires interdependence among group members. Social capital erodes when people in the network become independent. And increased interactions between members aid in the development and maintenance of mutual obligations in a social network.[88] Social networks such as Facebook may facilitate increased interactions between members in a social network via Internet-based communications.

Let's take a brief look at a simplified network analysis to get a grasp of the key ideas. In Exhibit 4.6, the links are used to depict informal relationships among individuals involving

4.3

strategy spotlight

Don't Go Away Mad . . . Now You Are a Valued Alum!

Traditionally, when an employee is laid off, the relationship between the company and that person comes to a bitter end. Increasingly, leading-edge companies such as Dow Chemical and JPMorgan Chase are trying to maintain ties with their "alumni," even if they are moving on to other companies. What benefits do these efforts provide to the company and its ex-employees?

Source: Baker, S. 2009. You're Fired—But Stay in Touch. *BusinessWeek.* May 4: 53–55.

These alumni networks, which are often organized on Facebook or LinkedIn, offer their members valuable benefits such as free job ads and connections to others who might help them in finding new jobs or facilitating entrepreneurial opportunities. For the firm, these networks constitute a laboratory for learning. Former employees who have nice things to say about a company are essentially "brand ambassadors" who can help in future recruiting efforts. The companies can also track the discussions in the network to identify hot topics, companies, products, and technologies. Best of all, when the economy recovers, this is an enormous talent pool for recruiting workers who are already familiar with the company and socialized into its culture.

communication flows, personal support, and advice networks. There may be some individuals with literally no linkages, such as Fred. These individuals are typically labeled "isolates." However, most people do have some linkages with others.

To simplify, there are two primary types of mechanisms through which social capital will flow: *closure relationships* (depicted by Bill, Frank, George, and Susan) and *bridging relationships* (depicted by Mary). As we can see, in the former relationships one member is central to the communication flows in a group. In contrast, in the latter relationship, one person "bridges" or brings together groups that would have been otherwise unconnected.

Both closure and bridging relationships have important implications for the effective flow of information in organizations and for the management of knowledge. We will now briefly discuss each of these types of relationships. We will also address some of the implications that understanding social networks has for one's career success.

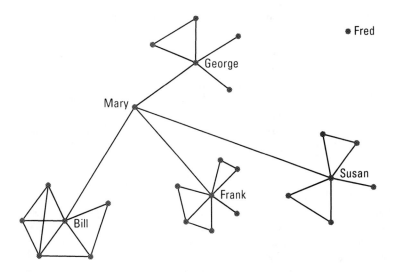

Exhibit 4.6 A Simplified Social Network

closure the degree to which all members of a social network have relationships (or ties) with other group members.

Closure   With **closure,** many members have relationships (or ties) with other members. As indicated in Exhibit 4.6, Bill's group would have a higher level of closure than Frank, Susan, or George's groups because more group members are connected to each other. Through closure, group members develop strong relationships with each other, high levels of trust, and greater solidarity. High levels of trust help to ensure that informal norms in the group are easily enforced and there is less "free riding." Social pressure will prevent people from withholding effort or shirking their responsibilities. In addition, people in the network are more willing to extend favors and "go the extra mile" on a colleague's behalf because they are confident that their efforts will be reciprocated by another member in their group. Another benefit of a network with closure is the high level of emotional support. This becomes particularly valuable when setbacks occur that may destroy morale or an unexpected tragedy happens that might cause the group to lose its focus. Social support helps the group to rebound from misfortune and get back on track.

But high levels of closure often come with a price. Groups that become too closed can become insular. They cut themselves off from the rest of the organization and fail to share what they are learning from people outside their group. Research shows that while managers need to encourage closure up to a point, if there is too much closure, they need to encourage people to open up their groups and infuse new ideas through bridging relationships.[89]

bridging relationships relationships in a social network that connect otherwise disconnected people.

Bridging Relationships   The closure perspective rests on an assumption that there is a high level of similarity among group members. However, members can be quite heterogeneous with regard to their positions in either the formal or informal structures of the group or the organization. Such heterogeneity exists because of, for example, vertical boundaries (different levels in the hierarchy) and horizontal boundaries (different functional areas).

Bridging relationships, in contrast to closure, stresses the importance of ties connecting people. Employees who bridge disconnected people tend to receive timely, diverse information because of their access to a wide range of heterogeneous information flows. Such bridging relationships span a number of different types of boundaries.

structural holes social gaps between groups in a social network where there are few relationships bridging the groups.

The University of Chicago's Ron Burt originally coined the term **"structural holes"** to refer to the social gap between two groups. Structural holes are common in organizations. When they occur in business, managers typically refer to them as "silos" or "stovepipes." Sales and engineering are a classic example of two groups whose members traditionally interact with their peers rather than across groups.

A study that Burt conducted at Raytheon, a $25 billion U.S. electronics company and military contractor, provides further insight into the benefits of bridging.[90]

> Burt studied several hundred managers in Raytheon's supply chain group and asked them to write down ideas to improve the company's supply chain management. Then he asked two Raytheon executives to rate the ideas. The conclusion: *The best suggestions consistently came from managers who discussed ideas outside their regular work group.*
>
> Burt found that Raytheon managers were good at thinking of ideas but bad at developing them. Too often, Burt said, the managers discussed their ideas with colleagues already in their informal discussion network. Instead, he said, they should have had discussions outside their typical contacts, particularly with an informal boss, or someone with enough power to be an ally but not an actual supervisor.

Before we address how to overcome barriers to collaboration and the implications of social network theory for managers' career success, one might ask: Which is the more valuable mechanism to develop and nurture social capital—closure or bridging relationships? As with many aspects of strategic management, the answer becomes: "It all depends." So let's look at a few contingent issues.[91]

First, consider firms in competitive environments characterized by rapidly changing technologies and markets. Such firms should bridge relationships across networks because they need a wide variety of timely sources of information. Also, innovation is facilitated if there are multiple, interdisciplinary perspectives. On the other hand, firms competing in a stable environment would typically face less unpredictability. Thus, the cohesive ties associated with network closure would help to ensure the timely and effective implementation of strategies.

A second contingent factor would be the type of business strategies that a firm may choose to follow (a topic that we address next in Chapter 5). Managers with social networks characterized by closure would be in a preferred position if their firm is following an overall low cost strategy.[92] Here, there is a need for control and coordination to implement strategies that are rather constrained by pressures to reduce costs. Alternatively, the uncertainties generally associated with differentiation strategies (i.e., creating products that are perceived by customers as unique and highly valued) would require a broad range of information sources and inputs. Social networks characterized by bridging relationships across groups would access the diverse informational sources needed to deal with more complex, multifaceted strategies.

A caveat: In both contingencies that we have discussed—competitive environment and business strategy—closure and bridging relationships across groups are necessary. Our purpose is to address where one type should be more dominant.

Developing Social Capital: Overcoming Barriers to Collaboration

Social capital within a group or organization develops through repeated interactions among its members and the resulting collaboration.[93] However, collaboration does not "just happen." People don't collaborate for various reasons. Effective collaboration requires overcoming four barriers:

- The not-invented-here barrier (people aren't willing to provide help)
- The hoarding barrier (people aren't willing to provide help)
- The search barrier (people are unable to find what they are looking for)
- The transfer barrier (people are unable to work with the people they don't know well)

All four barriers need to be low before effective collaboration can take place. Each one is enough to prevent people from collaborating well. The key is to identify which barriers are present in an organization and then to devise appropriate ways to overcome them.

Different barriers require different solutions. Motivational barriers require leaders to pull levers that make people more willing to collaborate. Ability barriers mean that leaders need to pull levers that enable motivated people to collaborate throughout the organization.

To be effective, leaders can choose a mix of three levers. First, when motivation is the problem, they can use the *unification lever,* wherein they craft compelling common goals, articulate a strong value of cross-company teamwork, and encourage collaboration in order to send strong signals to lift people's sights beyond their narrow interests toward a common goal.

Second, with the *people lever,* the emphasis isn't on getting people to collaborate more. Rather, it's on getting the right people to collaborate on the right projects. This means cultivating what may be called *T-shaped management:* people who simultaneously focus on the performance of their unit (the vertical part of the T) and across boundaries (the horizontal part of the T). People become able to collaborate when needed but are disciplined enough to say no when it's not required.

Third, by using the *network lever,* leaders can build nimble interpersonal networks across the company so that employees are better able to collaborate. Interpersonal networks are more effective than formal hierarchies. However, there is a dark side to networks: When people spend more time networking than getting work done, collaboration can adversely affect results.

---

unification lever method for making people more willing to collaborate by crafting compelling common goals articulating a strong value of cross-company teamwork, and encouraging collaboration in order to send strong signals to lift people's sights beyond their narrow interests towards a common goal.

network lever method for making people more willing to collaborate by building nimble interpersonal networks across the company.

T-shaped management people's dual focus on the performance of their unit (the vertical part of the T) and across boundaries (the horizontal part of the T).

people lever method for making people more willing to collaborate by getting the right people to work on the right projects.

strategy spotlight   4.4

Picasso versus van Gogh: Who Was More Successful and Why?

Vincent van Gogh and Pablo Picasso are two of the most iconoclastic—and famous—artists of modern times. Paintings by both of them have fetched over $100 million. And both of them were responsible for some of the most iconic images in the art world: Van Gogh's *Self-Portrait* (the one sans the earlobe) and *Starry Night* and Picasso's *The Old Guitarist* and *Guernica*. However, there is an important difference between van Gogh and Picasso. Van Gogh died penniless. Picasso's estate was estimated at $750 million when he died in 1973. What was the difference?

Van Gogh's primary connection to the art world was through his brother. Unfortunately, this connection didn't feed directly into the money that could have turned him into a living success. In contrast, Picasso's myriad connections provided him with access to commercial riches. As noted by Gregory Berns in his book *Iconoclast: A Neuroscientist Reveals How to Think Differently*, "Picasso's wide ranging social network, which included artists, writers, and politicians, meant that he was never more than a few people away from anyone of importance in the world."

In effect, van Gogh was a loner, and the charismatic Picasso was an active member of multiple social circles. In social networking terms, van Gogh was a solitary "node" who had few connections. Picasso, on the other hand, was a "hub" who embedded himself in a vast network

● Picasso was far more financially successful during his lifetime than van Gogh largely because of his extensive social network.

that stretched across various social lines. Where Picasso smoothly navigated multiple social circles, van Gogh had to struggle just to maintain connections with even those closest to him. Van Gogh inhabited an alien world, whereas Picasso was a social magnet. And because he knew so many people, the world was at Picasso's fingertips. From his perspective, the world was smaller.

Sources: Hayashi, A. M. 2008. Why Picasso Out Earned van Gogh. *MIT Sloan Management Review*, 50(1): 11–12; and Berns, G. 2008. *A Neuroscientist Reveals How to Think Differently*. Boston, MA: Harvard Business Press.

---

private information
information that is not available from public sources, and is usually communicated in the context of personal relationships.

public information
information that is available from public sources such as the internet.

Implications for Career Success   Let's go back in time in order to illustrate the value of social networks in one's career success. Consider two of the most celebrated artists of all time: Vincent van Gogh and Pablo Picasso. Strategy Spotlight 4.4 points out why these two artists enjoyed sharply contrasting levels of success during their lifetimes.

Effective social networks provide many advantages for the firm.[94] They can play a key role in an individual's career advancement and success. One's social network potentially can provide three unique advantages: private information, access to diverse skill sets, and power.[95] Managers see these advantages at work every day but might not consider how their networks regulate them.

Private Information We make judgments, using both public and private information. Today, public information is available from many sources, including the Internet. However, since it is so accessible, public information offers less competitive advantage than it used to.

In contrast, private information from personal contacts can offer something not found in publicly available sources, such as the release date of a new product or knowledge about what a particular interviewer looks for in candidates. Private information can give managers an edge, though it is more subjective than public information since it cannot be easily verified by independent sources, such as Dunn & Bradstreet. Consequently the value of your private information to others—and the value of others' private information to you—depends on how much trust exists in the network of relationships.

Access to Diverse Skill Sets Linus Pauling, one of only two people to win a Nobel Prize in two different areas and considered one of the towering geniuses of the 20th century, attributed his creative success not to his immense brainpower or luck but to his diverse contacts. He said, "The best way to have a good idea is to have a lot of ideas."

While expertise has become more specialized during the past 15 years, organizational, product, and marketing issues have become more interdisciplinary. This means that success is tied to the ability to transcend natural skill limitations through others. Highly diverse network relationships, therefore, can help you develop more complete, creative, and unbiased perspectives on issues. Trading information or skills with people whose experiences differ from your own, provides you with unique, exceptionally valuable resources. It is common for people in relationships to share their problems. If you know enough people, you will begin to see how the problems that another person is struggling with can be solved by the solutions being developed by others. If you can bring together problems and solutions, it will greatly benefit your career.

Power Traditionally, a manager's power was embedded in a firm's hierarchy. But, when corporate organizations became flatter, more like pancakes than pyramids, that power was repositioned in the network's brokers (people who bridged multiple networks), who could adapt to changes in the organization, develop clients, and synthesize opposing points of view. Such brokers weren't necessarily at the top of the hierarchy or experts in their fields, but they linked specialists in the firm with trustworthy and informative relationships.[96]

Most personal networks are highly clustered; that is, an individual's friends are likely to be friends with one another as well. Most corporate networks are made up of several clusters that have few links between them. Brokers are especially powerful because they connect separate clusters, thus stimulating collaboration among otherwise independent specialists.

Before moving on, Strategy Spotlight 4.5 discusses an interesting research study. It points out how women may differ from men in how they develop their social networks.

The Potential Downside of Social Capital

We'd like to close our discussion of social capital by addressing some of its limitations. First, some firms have been adversely affected by very high levels of social capital because it may breed **"groupthink"**—a tendency not to question shared beliefs.[97] Such thinking may occur in networks with high levels of closure where there is little input from people outside of the network. In effect, too many warm and fuzzy feelings among group members prevent people from rigorously challenging each other. People are discouraged from engaging in the "creative abrasion" that Dorothy Leonard of Harvard University describes as a key source of innovation.[98] Two firms that were well known for their collegiality, strong sense of employee membership, and humane treatment—Digital Equipment (now part of Hewlett-Packard) and Polaroid—suffered greatly from market misjudgments and strategic errors. The aforementioned aspects of their culture contributed to their problems.

Second, if there are deep-rooted mindsets, there would be a tendency to develop dysfunctional human resource practices. That is, the organization (or group) would continue to

groupthink a tendency in an organization for individuals not to question shared beliefs.

strategy spotlight

Developing Social Capital: Do Women and Men Differ?

Several years ago, Boris Groysberg conducted a study in which he warned managers about the risks associated with hiring star performers away from companies. His research investigated more than 1,000 star stock analysts, and he found that when one of them switches companies, not only does the star's performance plunge, but also the market value of the star's new company declines. In addition, the players don't tend to stay with their new firms very long—despite the generous pay packages that lured them in the first place. So everyone loses out.

However, when Groysberg further analyzed the data, he gained some new insights. One group of analysts maintained their stardom after changing employers: women. Unlike their male counterparts, female stars who switched firms performed just as well, in aggregate, as those who stayed put.

Why the gender discrepancy? There were two explanations. *First, the best female analysts appear to have built their franchises on portable, external relationships with clients and companies they covered—rather than on relationships within their firms.* In contrast, male analysts

Source: Groysberg, B . 2008. How Star Women Build Portable Skills. *Harvard Business Review*, 86(2): 74–81.

built up greater firm- and team-specific human capital. That is, they invested more in internal networks and unique capabilities and resources of the firms where they worked.

Second, women took greater care when assessing a prospective employer. They evaluated their options more carefully and analyzed a wider range of factors than men did before deciding to uproot themselves from a firm where they had been successful. Female star analysts, it seems, take their work environment more seriously yet rely on it less than male stars do. And they tend to look for a firm that will allow them to keep building their successful franchise their own way.

There is a clear explanation as to why the female analysts spent more time developing their external networks. Most salespeople, traders, and investment bankers are men. And men tend to spend more time with other men. Not surprisingly, the star women in the study were generally thwarted in their efforts to integrate themselves into the existing power structure. Thus, they went to greater lengths to cultivate relationships with clients and contacts at the companies they covered. Their decision to maintain such an external focus rested on four main factors: uneasy in-house relationships, poor mentorships, neglect by colleagues, and a vulnerable position in the labor market.

hire, reward, and promote like-minded people who tend to further intensify organizational inertia and erode innovation. Such homogeneity would increase over time and decrease the effectiveness of decision-making processes.

Third, the socialization processes (orientation, training, etc.) can be expensive in terms of both financial resources and managerial commitment. Such investments can represent a significant opportunity cost that should be evaluated in terms of the intended benefits. If such expenses become excessive, profitability would be adversely affected.

Finally, individuals may use the contacts they develop to pursue their own interests and agendas that may be inconsistent with the organization's goals and objectives. Thus, they may distort or selectively use information to favor their preferred courses of action or withhold information in their own self-interest to enhance their power to the detriment of the common good. Drawing on our discussion of social networks, this is particularly true in an organization that has too many bridging relationships but not enough closure relationships. In high closure groups, it is easier to watch each other to ensure that illegal or unethical acts don't occur. By contrast, bridging relationships make it easier for a person to play one group or individual off on another, with no one being the wiser.[99] We will discuss some behavioral control mechanisms in Chapter 9 (rewards, control, boundaries) that reduce such dysfunctional behaviors and actions.[100]

Using Technology to Leverage Human Capital and Knowledge

Sharing knowledge and information throughout the organization can be a means of conserving resources, developing products and services, and creating new opportunities. In this section we will discuss how technology can be used to leverage human capital and knowledge within organizations as well as with customers and suppliers beyond their boundaries.

> **>LO4.5**
> The vital role of technology in leveraging knowledge and human capital.

Using Networks to Share Information

As we all know, e-mail is an effective means of communicating a wide variety of information. It is quick, easy, and almost costless. Of course, it can become a problem when employees use it extensively for personal reasons. And we all know how fast jokes or rumors can spread within and across organizations!

Below is an example of how a CEO curbed what he felt was excessive e-mail use in his firm.[101]

> Scott Dockter, CEO of PBD Worldwide Fulfillment Services in Alpharetta, Georgia, launched "no e-mail Friday." Why? He suspected that overdependence on e-mail at PBD, which offers services such as call center management and distribution, was hurting productivity and, perhaps, sales. Accordingly, he instructed his 275 employees to pick up the phone or meet in person each Friday, and reduce e-mail use the rest of the time.
>
> That was tough to digest, especially for the younger staffers. "We discovered a lot of introverts . . . who had drifted into a pattern of communicating by e-mail," says Dockter. "However, in less than four months, the simple directive resulted in quicker problem-solving, better teamwork, and, best of all, happier customers." "Our relationship with PBD is much stronger," says Cynthia Fitzpatrick of Crown Financial Ministries. "You can't get to know someone through e-mail."

E-mail can also cause embarrassment if one is not careful. Consider the plight of a potential CEO—as recalled by Marshall Goldsmith, a well-known executive coach:[102]

> I witnessed a series of e-mails between a potential CEO and a friend inside the company. The first e-mail to the friend provided an elaborate description of "why the current CEO is an idiot." The friend sent a reply. Several rounds of e-mails followed. Then the friend sent an e-mail containing a funny joke. The potential CEO decided that the current CEO would love this joke and forwarded it to him. You can guess what happened next. The CEO scrolled down the e-mail chain and found the "idiot" message. The heir apparent was gone in a week.

E-mail can, however, be a means for top executives to communicate information efficiently. For example, Martin Sorrell, chairman of WPP Group PLC, a $2.4 billion advertising and public relations firm, is a strong believer in the use of e-mail.[103] He e-mails all of his employees once a month to discuss how the company is doing, address specific issues, and offer his perspectives on hot issues, such as new business models for the Internet. He believes that it keeps people abreast of what he is working on.

Technology can also enable much more sophisticated forms of communication in addition to knowledge sharing. Buckman Laboratories is a $505 million specialty chemicals company based in Memphis, Tennessee, with approximately 1,500 employees in over 100 countries. Buckman has successfully used its global knowledge-sharing network—known as K'Netix—to enhance its competitive advantages:[104]

> Here's an example of how the network can be applied. One of Buckman's paper customers in Michigan realized that the peroxide it was adding to remove ink from old magazines

was no longer working. A Buckman sales manager presented this problem to the knowledge network. Within two days, salespeople from Belgium and Finland identified a likely cause: Bacteria in the paper slurry was producing an enzyme that broke down the peroxide. The sales manager recommended a chemical to control the bacteria, solving the problem. You can imagine how positive the customer felt about Buckman. And with the company and the customer co-creating knowledge, a new level of trust and value can emerge.

Electronic Teams: Using Technology to Enhance Collaboration

>LO4.6
Why "electronic" or "virtual" teams are critical in combining and leveraging knowledge in organizations and how they can be made more effective.

Technology enables professionals to work as part of electronic, or virtual, teams to enhance the speed and effectiveness with which products are developed. For example, Microsoft has concentrated much of its development on **electronic teams** (or e-teams) that are networked together.[105] This helps to accelerate design and testing of new software modules that use the Windows-based framework as their central architecture. Microsoft is able to foster specialized technical expertise while sharing knowledge rapidly throughout the firm. This helps the firm learn how its new technologies can be applied rapidly to new business ventures such as cable television, broadcasting, travel services, and financial services.

What are electronic teams (or e-teams)? There are two key differences between e-teams and more traditional teams:[106]

electronic teams a team of individuals that completes tasks primarily through e-mail communication.

- E-team members either work in geographically separated work places or they may work in the same space but at different times. E-teams may have members working in different spaces and time zones, as is the case with many multinational teams.
- Most of the interactions among members of e-teams occur through electronic communication channels such as fax machines and groupware tools such as e-mail, bulletin boards, chat, and videoconferencing.

E-teams have expanded exponentially in recent years.[107] Organizations face increasingly high levels of complex and dynamic change. E-teams are also effective in helping businesses cope with global challenges. Most e-teams perform very complex tasks and most knowledge-based teams are charged with developing new products, improving organizational processes, and satisfying challenging customer problems. For example, Eastman Kodak's e-teams design new products, Hewlett Packard's e-teams solve clients' computing problems, and Sun Microsystems' (part of oracle) e-teams generate new business models.

Advantages   There are multiple advantages of e-teams.[108] In addition to the rather obvious use of technology to facilitate communications, the potential benefits parallel the other two major sections in this chapter—human capital and social capital.

First, e-teams are less restricted by the geographic constraints that are placed on face-to-face teams. Thus, e-teams have the potential to acquire a broader range of "human capital" or the skills and capacities that are necessary to complete complex assignments. So, e-team leaders can draw upon a greater pool of talent to address a wider range of problems since they are not constrained by geographic space. Once formed, e-teams can be more flexible in responding to unanticipated work challenges and opportunities because team members can be rotated out of projects when demands and contingencies alter the team's objectives.

Second, e-teams can be very effective in generating "social capital"—the quality of relationships and networks that form. Such capital is a key lubricant in work transactions and operations. Given the broader boundaries associated with e-teams, members and leaders generally have access to a wider range of social contacts than would be typically available in more traditional face-to-face teams. Such contacts are often connected to a broader scope of clients, customers, constituents, and other key stakeholders.

Challenges   However, there are challenges associated with making e-teams effective. Successful action by both traditional teams and e-teams requires that:

- Members *identify* who among them can provide the most appropriate knowledge and resources, and,
- E-team leaders and key members know how to *combine* individual contributions in the most effective manner for a coordinated and appropriate response.

Group psychologists have termed such activities "identification and combination" activities and teams that fail to perform them face a "process loss."[109] Process losses prevent teams from reaching high levels of performance because of inefficient interaction dynamics among team members. Such poor dynamics require that some collective energy, time, and effort be devoted to dealing with team inefficiencies, thus diverting the team away from its objectives. For example, if a team member fails to communicate important information at critical phases of a project, other members may waste time and energy. This can lead to conflict and resentment as well as to decreased motivation to work hard to complete tasks.

The potential for process losses tends to be more prevalent in e-teams than in traditional teams because the geographical dispersion of members increases the complexity of establishing effective interaction and exchanges. Generally, teams suffer process loss because of low cohesion, low trust among members, a lack of appropriate norms or standard operating procedures, or a lack of shared understanding among team members about their tasks. With e-teams, members are more geographically or temporally dispersed, and the team becomes more susceptible to the risk factors that can create process loss. Such problems can be exacerbated when team members have less than ideal competencies and social skills. This can erode problem-solving capabilities as well as the effective functioning of the group as a social unit.

A variety of technologies, from e-mail and Internet groups to Skype (acquired by eBay in 2005) and Cisco's Umi TelePresence, have facilitated the formation and effective functioning of e-teams as well as a wide range of collaborations within companies. Strategy Spotlight 4.6 highlights Cisco's efforts to use technology to enable such communication. Such technologies greatly enhance the collaborative abilities of employees and managers within a company at a reasonable cost—despite the distances that separate them.

Codifying Knowledge for Competitive Advantage

There are two different kinds of knowledge. Tacit knowledge is embedded in personal experience and shared only with the consent and participation of the individual. Explicit (or codified) knowledge, on the other hand, is knowledge that can be documented, widely distributed, and easily replicated. One of the challenges of knowledge-intensive organizations is to capture and codify the knowledge and experience that, in effect, resides in the heads of its employees. Otherwise, they will have to constantly "reinvent the wheel," which is both expensive and inefficient. Also, the "new wheel" may not necessarily be superior to the "old wheel."[110]

Once a knowledge asset (e.g., a software code or processes) is developed and paid for, it can be reused many times at very low cost, assuming that it doesn't have to be substantially modified each time. Let's take the case of a consulting company, such as Accenture (formerly Andersen Consulting).[111] Since the knowledge of its consultants has been codified and stored in electronic repositories, it can be employed in many jobs by a huge number of consultants. Additionally, since the work has a high level of standardization (i.e., there are strong similarities across the numerous client engagements), there is a rather high ratio of consultants to partners. For example, the ratio of consultants to partners is roughly 30, which is quite high. As one might expect, there must be extensive training of the newly hired consultants for such an approach to work. The recruits are trained at Accenture's

strategy spotlight 4.6

Videoconferencing: Allowing Employees to Communicate Face-to-Face over Long Distances

Cisco Systems has recognized that collaboration is the biggest technological trend of the next decade, driving productivity gains of 5 to 10 percent per year. It has created a strong portfolio of collaboration technologies, including TelePresence; WebEx; phones that run over the Internet; devices that produce, distribute, and archive videos; and hardware that can carry, distribute, and manage communications traffic no matter the origin or destination.

Internally, the use of these technologies has helped make Cisco's workforce one of the most distributed, connected, and productive in the world. Employees have experienced—and driven—a cultural revolution of not only information-sharing, but also teamwork and transparency.

Sources: Copeland, M. V. 2010. The New Global Worker Gadget: Videophones. *Fortune,* November 15: 36; Sidhu, I. 2010. *Doing Both.* Boston: Harvard Business Press; and Baig, E. C. 2010. Umi TelePresence Brings Videoconferencing Home. *www.usatoday.com.* December 2: np.

In a recent year, for example, TelePresence usage has increased 10 times, while WebEx conferencing usage has soared by 25 times. In addition, video postings have grown by more than 11 times on the company's website.

Cisco recently launched a new videoconferencing product, Umi TelePresence, that is aimed at the consumer market. It costs $599 (for the camera, console, cables, and remote control that constitute the system) and comes with an unlimited calling plan that runs $25 a month. What makes the product more expensive is that you might have to purchase a second or third Umi for family members, simply because it takes at least "two to tango" when it comes to videoconferencing. However, corporations could also use such home systems to allow global employees to connect with headquarters during business hours. As noted by Srinath Narasimhan, CEO of Tata Communications, remote employees are loath to go to the office for a 3 A.M. call in a video "suite." However, with a home setup, these employees could stumble out of bed and into a meeting—as long as they remember to comb their hair first!

Center for Professional Education, a 150-acre campus in St. Charles, Illinois. Using the center's knowledge-management respository, the consultants work through many scenarios designed to improve business processes. In effect, the information technologies enable the consultants to be "implementers, not inventors."

Access Health, a call-in medical center, also uses technology to capture and share knowledge. When someone calls the center, a registered nurse uses the company's "clinical decision architecture" to assess the caller's symptoms, rule out possible conditions, and recommend a home remedy, doctor's visit, or trip to the emergency room. The company's knowledge repository contains algorithms of the symptoms of more than 500 illnesses. According to CEO Joseph Tallman, "We are not inventing a new way to cure disease. We are taking available knowledge and inventing processes to put it to better use." The software algorithms were very expensive to develop, but the investment has been repaid many times over. The first 300 algorithms that Access Health developed have each been used an average of 8,000 times a year. Further, the company's paying customers—insurance companies and provider groups—save money because many callers would have made expensive trips to the emergency room or the doctor's office had they not been diagnosed over the phone.

The user community can be a major source of knowledge creation for a firm. Strategy Spotlight 4.7 highlights how SAP, in an example of effective crowdsourcing, has been able to leverage the expertise and involvement of its users to develop new knowledge and transmit it to their entire user community.

4.7   strategy spotlight

Crowdsourcing: How SAP Taps Knowledge Well beyond Its Boundaries

Traditionally, organizations built and protected their knowledge stocks—proprietary resources that no one else could access. However, the more the business environment changes, the faster the value of what you know at any point in time diminishes. In today's world, success hinges on the ability to access a growing variety of knowledge flows in order to rapidly replenish the firm's knowledge stocks. For example, when an organization tries to improve cycle times in a manufacturing process, it finds far more value in problem solving shaped by the diverse experiences, perspectives, and learning of a tightly knit team (shared through knowledge flows) than in a training manual (knowledge stocks) alone.

Knowledge flows can help companies gain competitive advantage in an age of near-constant disruption. The software company SAP, for example, routinely taps the more than 1.5 million participants in its Developer Network, which extends well beyond the boundaries of the firm. Those who post questions for the network community to address will receive a response in 17 minutes, on average, and 85 percent of all questions posted to date have been rated as "resolved." By providing a virtual platform for customers, developers, system integrators, and service vendors to create and exchange knowledge, SAP has significantly increased the productivity of all the participants in its ecosystem.

The site is open to everyone, regardless of whether you are an SAP customer, partner, or newcomer who needs to work with SAP technology. The site offers technical articles, Web-based training, code samples, evaluation systems, discussion forums, and excellent blogs for community experts.

Source: Hagel, J., III., Brown, J. S., & Davison, L. 2009. The Big Shift: Measuring the Forces of Change. *Harvard Business Review*, 87(4): 87; and Anonymous. undated. SAP Developer Network. *sap.sys-con.com*. np.

crowdsourcing

We close this section with a series of questions managers should consider in determining (1) how effective their organization is in attracting, developing, and retaining human capital and (2) how effective they are in leveraging human capital through social capital and technology. These questions, included in Exhibit 4.7, summarize some of the key issues addressed in this chapter.

Protecting the Intellectual Assets of the Organization: Intellectual Property and Dynamic Capabilities

>LO4.7
The challenge of protecting intellectual property and the importance of a firm's dynamic capabilities.

In today's dynamic and turbulent world, unpredictability and fast change dominate the business environment. Firms can use technology, attract human capital, or tap into research and design networks to get access to pretty much the same information as their competitors. So what would give firms a sustainable competitive advantage?[112] Protecting a firm's intellectual property requires a concerted effort on the part of the company. After all, employees become disgruntled and patents expire. The management of intellectual property (IP) involves, besides patents, contracts with confidentiality and noncompete clauses, copyrights, and the development of trademarks. Moreover, developing dynamic capabilities is the only avenue providing firms with the ability to reconfigure their knowledge and activities to achieve a sustainable competitive advantage.

Intellectual Property Rights

Intellectual property rights are more difficult to define and protect than property rights for physical assets (e.g., plant, equipment, and land). However, if intellectual property

intellectual property rights intangible property owned by a firm in the forms of patents, copyrights, trademarks, or trade secrets.

Exhibit 4.7   Issues to Consider in Creating Value through Human Capital, Social Capital, and Technology

Human Capital

Recruiting "Top-Notch" Human Capital

- Does the organization assess attitude and "general makeup" instead of focusing primarily on skills and background in selecting employees at all levels?
- How important are creativity and problem-solving ability? Are they properly considered in hiring decisions?
- Do people throughout the organization engage in effective networking activities to obtain a broad pool of worthy potential employees? Is the organization creative in such endeavors?

Enhancing Human Capital through Employee Development

- Does the development and training process inculcate an "organizationwide" perspective?
- Is there widespread involvement, including top executives, in the preparation and delivery of training and development programs?
- Is the development of human capital effectively tracked and monitored?
- Are there effective programs for succession at all levels of the organization, especially at the top-most levels?
- Does the firm effectively evaluate its human capital? Is a 360-degree evaluation used? Why? Why not?
- Are mechanisms in place to assure that a manager's success does not come at the cost of compromising the organization's core values?

Retaining the Best Employees

- Are there appropriate financial rewards to motivate employees at all levels?
- Do people throughout the organization strongly identify with the organization's mission?
- Are employees provided with a stimulating and challenging work environment that fosters professional growth?
- Are valued amenities provided (e.g., flex time, child-care facilities, telecommuting) that are appropriate given the organization's mission, strategy, and how work is accomplished?
- Is the organization continually devising strategies and mechanisms to retain top performers?

Social Capital

- Are there positive personal and professional relationships among employees?
- Is the organization benefiting (or being penalized) by hiring (or by voluntary turnover) en masse?
- Does an environment of caring and encouragement rather than competition enhance team performance?
- Do the social networks within the organization have the appropriate levels of closure and bridging relationships?
- Does the organization minimize the adverse effects of excessive social capital, such as excessive costs and "groupthink"?

Technology

- Has the organization used technologies such as e-mail and networks to develop products and services?
- Does the organization effectively use technology to transfer best practices across the organization?
- Does the organization use technology to leverage human capital and knowledge both within the boundaries of the organization and among its suppliers and customers?
- Has the organization effectively used technology to codify knowledge for competitive advantage?
- Does the organization try to retain some of the knowledge of employees when they decide to leave the firm?

Source: Adapted from Dess, G. G., & Picken, J. C. 1999. *Beyond Productivity:* 63–64. New York: AMACON.

rights are not reliably protected by the state, there will be no incentive to develop new products and services. Property rights have been enshrined in constitutions and rules of law in many countries. In the information era, though, adjustments need to be made to accommodate the new realities of knowledge. Knowledge and information are fundamentally different assets from the physical ones that property rights have been designed to protect.

The protection of intellectual rights raises unique issues, compared to physical property rights. IP is characterized by significant development costs and very low marginal costs. Indeed, it may take a substantial investment to develop a software program, an idea, or a digital music tune. Once developed, though, their reproduction and distribution cost may be almost zero, especially if the Internet is used. Effective protection of intellectual property is necessary before any investor will finance such an undertaking. Appropriation of their returns is harder to police since possession and deployment are not as readily observable. Unlike physical assets, intellectual property can be stolen by simply broadcasting it. Recall Napster and MP3 as well as the debates about counterfeit software, music CDs, and DVDs coming from developing countries such as China. Part of the problem is that using an idea does not prevent others from simultaneously using it for their own benefit, which is typically impossible with physical assets. Moreover, new ideas are frequently built on old ideas and are not easily traceable.

Strategy Spotlight 4.8 describes the many legal battles fought by a Canadian firm, Research in Motion of Waterloo, the developer of the popular BlackBerry. This example illustrates the high stakes that ride on intellectual property rights.

Countries are attempting to pass new legislation to cope with developments in new pharmaceutical compounds, stem cell research, and biotechnology. However, a firm that is faced with this challenge today cannot wait for the legislation to catch up. New technological developments, software solutions, electronic games, online services, and other products and services contribute to our economic prosperity and the creation of wealth for those entrepreneurs who have the idea first and risk bringing it to the market.

Dynamic Capabilities

Dynamic capabilities entail the capacity to build and protect a competitive advantage.[113] This rests on knowledge, assets, competencies, and complementary assets and technologies as well as the ability to sense and seize new opportunities, generate new knowledge, and reconfigure existing assets and capabilities.[114] According to David Teece, an economist at the University of California at Berkeley, dynamic capabilities are related to the entrepreneurial side of the firm and are built within a firm through its environmental and technological "sensing" apparatus, its choices of organizational form, and its collective ability to strategize. Dynamic capabilities are about the ability of an organization to challenge the conventional wisdom within its industry and market, learn and innovate, adapt to the changing world, and continuously adopt new ways to serve the evolving needs of the market.[115]

Examples of dynamic capabilities include product development, strategic decision making, alliances, and acquisitions.[116] Some firms have clearly developed internal processes and routines that make them superior in such activities. For example, 3M and Apple are ahead of their competitors in product development. Cisco Systems has made numerous acquisitions over the years. They seem to have developed the capability to identify and evaluate potential acquisition candidates and seamlessly integrate them once the acquisition is completed. Other organizations can try to copy Cisco's practices. However, Cisco's combination of the resources of the acquired companies and their reconfiguration that Cisco has already achieved places them well ahead of their competitors. As markets become

dynamic capabilities a firm's capacity to build and protect a competitive advantage, which rests on knowledge, assets, competencies, complementary assets, and technologies. Dynamic capabilities include the ability to sense and seize new opportunities, generate new knowledge, and reconfigure existing assets and capabilities.

strategy spotlight   4.8

Research in Motion, Maker of the BlackBerry, Loses an Intellectual Property Lawsuit

Research in Motion (RIM) is a Waterloo, Ontario–based company that is best known for developing the Black-Berry, a wireless device that integrates the functionalities of a cell phone with the ability to receive e-mail messages. During its brief history, it has become one of the fastest growing companies in North America. Founded by Mike Lazaridis, a former University of Waterloo student in 1984, Research in Motion was a competent but obscure technology firm until 1999 when the first BlackBerry was released. Through the development of integrated hardware, software, and services that support multiple wireless network standards, the BlackBerry has enabled RIM to grow from less than $50 million in sales revenue in 1999 to $15 billion by 2010. Even more impressive, by early 2011 the company boasted a market capitalization in excess of $30 billion. RIM's commitment to their slogan "always on, always connected" has won them a legion of dedicated followers around the globe.

Interestingly, legal challenges have been the biggest obstacles that Research in Motion has faced in the eight years since the introduction of the first BlackBerry. In 2000, NTP, a pure patent-holding company, filed suit against RIM for violation of five of its patents and petitioned the court for an injunction on the sale and support of BlackBerry devices. The case dragged on for years, and RIM felt relatively secure that no injunction would be

Sources: Henkel, J. & Reitzig, M. 2008. Patent Sharks. *Harvard Business Review,* 86(6): 129–133; Hesseldahl, A. 2006. RIM's Latest Patent Problem. *BusinessWeek Online,* May 2: np; Anonymous. 2006. Settlement Reached in BlackBerry Patent Case. (The Associated Press) MSNBC.Com. March 3: np; Wolk, M . 2006. RIM Pays Up, Taking "One for the Team." MSNBC.Com. March 3; and *finance.yahoo.com.*

● Research in Motion (RIM) has faced litigation over its highly successful BlackBerry.

issued. On February 24, 2006, things dramatically changed. U.S. District Court Judge James Spencer indicated that he was inclined to grant the injunction and that his ruling was imminent. Faced with the acute risk of an unfavorable decision, RIM settled only one week later for $612.5 million. It wound up paying a fortune for rights that were dubious at best—given that all five NTP patents had already been preliminarily invalidated by the U.S. Patent and Trademark Office and that two of them then received a final rejection.

increasingly dynamic, traditional sources of long-term competitive advantage become less relevant. In such markets, all that a firm can strive for are a series of temporary advantages. Dynamic capabilities allow a firm to create this series of temporary advantages through new resource configurations.[117]

Reflecting on Career Implications . . .

- *Human Capital:* Does your organization effectively attract, develop, and retain talent? If not, you may have fewer career opportunities to enhance your human capital at your organization. Do you take advantage of your organization's human resource programs such as tuition reimbursement, mentoring, etc.
- *Human Capital:* Does your organization value diversity? What kinds of diversity seem to be encouraged (e.g., age-based or ethnicity-based)? If not, there may be limited perspectives on strategic and operational issues and a career at this organization may be less attractive to you.
- *Social Capital:* Does your organization have effective programs to build and develop social capital such that professionals develop strong "ties" to the organization? Alternatively, is social capital so strong that you see effects occur such as "groupthink"? From your perspective, how might you better leverage social capital towards pursuing other career opportunities?
- *Technology:* Does your organization provide and effectively use technology (e.g., groupware, knowledge management systems) to help you leverage your talents and expand your knowledge base?

Summary

Firms throughout the industrial world are recognizing that the knowledge worker is the key to success in the marketplace. However, we also recognize that human capital, although vital, is still only a necessary, but not a sufficient, condition for creating value. We began the first section of the chapter by addressing the importance of human capital and how it can be attracted, developed, and retained. Then we discussed the role of social capital and technology in leveraging human capital for competitive success. We pointed out that intellectual capital—the difference between a firm's market value and its book value—has increased significantly over the past few decades. This is particularly true for firms in knowledge-intensive industries, especially where there are relatively few tangible assets, such as software development.

The second section of the chapter addressed the attraction, development, and retention of human capital. We viewed these three activities as a "three-legged stool"—that is, it is difficult for firms to be successful if they ignore or are unsuccessful in any one of these activities. Among the issues we discussed in *attracting* human capital were "hiring for attitude, training for skill" and the value of using social networks to attract human capital. In particular, it is important to attract employees who can collaborate with others, given the importance of collective efforts such as teams and task forces. With regard to *developing* human capital, we discussed the need to encourage widespread involvement throughout the organization, monitor progress and track the development of human capital, and evaluate human capital. Among the issues that are widely practiced in evaluating human capital is the 360-degree evaluation system. Employees are evaluated by their superiors, peers, direct reports, and even internal and external customers. We also addressed the value of maintaining a diverse workforce. Finally, some mechanisms for retaining human capital are employees' identification with the organization's mission and values, providing challenging work and a stimulating environment, the importance of financial and nonfinancial rewards and incentives, and providing flexibility and amenities. A key issue here is that a firm should not overemphasize financial rewards. After all, if individuals join an organization for money, they also are likely to leave for money. With money as the primary motivator, there is little chance that employees will develop firm-specific ties to keep them with the organization.

The third section of the chapter discussed the importance of social capital in leveraging human capital. Social capital refers to the network of relationships that individuals have throughout the organization as well as with customers and suppliers. Such ties can be critical in obtaining both information and resources. With regard to recruiting, for example, we saw how some firms are able to hire en masse groups of individuals who are part of social networks. Social relationships can also be very important in the effective functioning of groups. Finally, we discussed some of the potential downsides of social capital. These include the expenses that firms may bear when promoting social and working relationships among individuals as well as the potential for "groupthink," wherein individuals are reluctant to express divergent (or opposing) views on an issue because of social pressures to conform. We also introduced the concept of social networks. The relative advantages of being central in a network versus bridging multiple networks was discussed. We addressed the key role that social networks can play in both improving knowledge management and promoting career success.

The fourth section addressed the role of technology in leveraging human capital. We discussed relatively simple means of using technology, such as e-mail and networks where individuals can collaborate by way of personal computers. We provided suggestions and guidelines on how electronic teams can be effectively managed. We also addressed more sophisticated uses of technology, such as sophisticated management systems. Here knowledge can be codified and reused at very low cost, as we saw in the examples of firms in the consulting, health care, and high-technology industries.

In the last section we discussed the increasing importance of protecting a firm's intellectual property. Although traditional approaches such as patents, copyrights, and trademarks are important, the development of dynamic capabilities may be the best protection in the long run.

Summary Review Questions

1. Explain the role of knowledge in today's competitive environment.

2. Why is it important for managers to recognize the interdependence in the attraction, development, and retention of talented professionals?

3. What are some of the potential downsides for firms that engage in a "war for talent"?

4. Discuss the need for managers to use social capital in leveraging their human capital both within and across their firm.

5. Discuss the key role of technology in leveraging knowledge and human capital.

Key Terms

knowledge economy, 125
intellectual capital, 126
human capital, 126
social capital, 126
explicit knowledge, 127
tacit knowledge, 127
social network analysis, 138
360-degree evaluation and feedback systems, 133
closure, 140
bridging relationships, 140

structural holes, 140
unification lever, 141
people lever, 141
T-shaped management, 141
networth lever, 141
private information, 142
public information, 142
groupthink, 143
electronic teams, 146
intellectual property rights, 149
dynamic capabilities, 151

Experiential Exercise

Pfizer, a leading health care firm with $68 billion in revenues, is often rated as one of *Fortune*'s "Most Admired Firms." It is also considered an excellent place to work and has generated high return to shareholders. Clearly, they value their human capital. Using the Internet and/or library resources, identify some of the actions/strategies Pfizer has taken to attract, develop, and retain human capital. What are their implications?

Activity	Actions/Strategies	Implications
Attracting human capital		
Developing human capital		
Retaining human capital		

Application Questions & Exercises

1. Look up successful firms in a high-technology industry as well as two successful firms in more traditional industries such as automobile manufacturing and retailing. Compare their market values and book values. What are some implications of these differences?

2. Select a firm for which you believe its social capital— both within the firm and among its suppliers and customers—is vital to its competitive advantage. Support your arguments.

3. Choose a company with which you are familiar. What are some of the ways in which it uses technology to leverage its human capital?

4. Using the Internet, look up a company with which you are familiar. What are some of the policies and procedures that it uses to enhance the firm's human and social capital?

Ethics Questions

1. Recall an example of a firm that recently faced an ethical crisis. How do you feel the crisis and management's handling of it affected the firm's human capital and social capital?

2. Based on your experiences or what you have learned in your previous classes, are you familiar with any companies that used unethical practices to attract talented professionals? What do you feel were the short-term and long-term consequences of such practices?

References

1. Farmbrough, R. 2010. List of the largest global technology companies: Part 1. *www.wikipedia.org*. November 1: np; and Arai, H. 2000. *Intellectual Property Policies for the Twenty-First Century: The Japanese Experience in Wealth Creation*. WIPO Publication No. 834 (E). We thank Pratik Kapadia for his valued contribution.

2. Parts of this chapter draw upon some of the ideas and examples from Dess, G. G. & Picken, J. C. 1999. *Beyond productivity*. New York: AMACOM.

3. An acknowledged trend: The world economic survey. 1996. *The Economist*, September 2(8): 25–28.

4. Quinn, J. B., Anderson, P., & Finkelstein, S. 1996. Leveraging intellect. *Academy of Management Executive*, 10(3): 7–27; and *https://www.cia.gov/library/publications/the=world=factbook/geos/us.html*.

5. Hamel, G. & Prahalad, C. K. 1996. Competing in the new economy: Managing out of bounds. *Strategic Management Journal*, 17: 238.

6. Stewart, T. A. 1997. *Intellectual capital: The new wealth of organizations*. New York: Doubleday/Currency.

7. Leif Edvisson and Michael S. Malone have a similar, more detailed definition of *intellectual capital*: "the combined knowledge, skill, innovativeness, and ability to meet the task at hand." They consider intellectual capital to equal human capital plus structural capital. *Structural capital* is defined as "the hardware, software, databases, organization structure, patents, trademarks, and everything else of organizational capability that supports those employees' productivity—in a word, everything left at the office when the employees go home." Edvisson, L. & Malone, M. S. 1997. *Intellectual capital: Realizing your company's true value by finding its hidden brainpower:* 10–14. New York: HarperBusiness.

8. Stewart, T. A. 2001. Accounting gets radical. *Fortune*, April 16: 184–194.

9. Adams, S. & Kichen, S. 2008. Ben Graham then and now. *Forbes*, November 10: 56.

10. An interesting discussion of Steve Jobs's impact on Apple's valuation is in: Lashinsky, A. 2009. Steve's leave—what does it really mean? *Fortune*, February 2: 96–102.

11. Anonyous. 2007. Intel opens first high volume 45 nm microprocessor manufacturing factory. *www.intel.com*. October 25: np.

12. Thomas Stewart has suggested this formula in his book *Intellectual capital*. He provides an insightful discussion on pages 224–225, including some of the limitations of this approach to measuring intellectual capital. We recognize, of course, that during the late 1990s and in early 2000, there were some excessive market valuations of high-technology and Internet firms. For an interesting discussion of the extraordinary market valuation of Yahoo!, an Internet company, refer to Perkins, A. B. 2001. The Internet bubble encapsulated: Yahoo! *Red Herring*, April 15: 17–18.

13. Roberts, P. W. & Dowling, G. R. 2002. Corporate reputation and sustained superior financial performance. *Strategic Management Journal*, 23(12): 1077–1095.

14. For a recent study on the relationships between human capital, learning, and sustainable competitive advantage, read Hatch, N. W. & Dyer, J. H. 2005. Human capital and learning as a source of sustainable competitive advantage. *Strategic Management Journal*, 25: 1155–1178.

15. One of the seminal contributions on knowledge management is Becker, G. S. 1993. *Human capital: A theoretical and empirical analysis with special reference to education* (3rd ed.). Chicago: University of Chicago Press.

16. For an excellent overview of the topic of social capital, read Baron, R. A. 2005. Social capital. In Hitt, M. A. & Ireland, R. D. (Eds.), *The Blackwell encyclopedia of management* (2nd ed.): 224–226. Malden, MA: Blackwell.

17. For an excellent discussion of social capital and its impact on organizational performance, refer to Nahapiet, J. & Ghoshal, S. 1998. Social capital, intellectual capital, and the organizational advantage. *Academy of Management Review,* 23: 242–266.

18. An interesting discussion of how knowledge management (patents) can enhance organizational performance can be found in Bogner, W. C. & Bansal, P. 2007. Knowledge management as the basis of sustained high performance. *Journal of Management Studies,* 44(1): 165–188.

19. Polanyi, M. 1967. *The tacit dimension.* Garden City, NY: Anchor Publishing.

20. Barney, J. B. 1991. Firm resources and sustained competitive advantage. *Journal of Management,* 17: 99–120.

21. For an interesting perspective of empirical research on how knowledge can adversely affect performance, read Haas, M. R. & Hansen, M. T. 2005. When using knowledge can hurt performance: The value of organizational capabilities in a management consulting company. *Strategic Management Journal,* 26(1): 1–24.

22. New insights on managing talent are provided in: Cappelli, P. 2008. Talent management for the twenty-first century. *Harvard Business Review,* 66(3): 74–81.

23. Some of the notable books on this topic include Edvisson & Malone, op. cit.; Stewart, op. cit.; and Nonaka, I. & Takeuchi, I. 1995. *The knowledge creating company.* New York: Oxford University Press.

24. Segalla, M. & Felton, N. 2010. Find the real power in your organization. *Harvard Business Review,* 88(5): 34–35.

25. Stewart, T. A. 2000. Taking risk to the marketplace. *Fortune,* March 6: 424.

26. Insights on the Generation X's perspective on the workplace are in:

Erickson, T. J. 2008. Task, not time: Profile of a Gen Y job. *Harvard Business Review,* 86(2): 19.

27. Pfeffer, J. 2010. Building sustainable organizations: The human factor. *The Academy of Management Perspectives,* 24(1): 34–45.

28. Dutton, G. 1997. Are you technologically competent? *Management Review,* November: 54–58.

29. Some workplace implications for the aging workforce are addressed in: Strack, R., Baier, J., & Fahlander, A. 2008. Managing demographic risk. *Harvard Business Review,* 66(2): 119–128.

30. For a discussion of attracting, developing, and retaining top talent, refer to Goffee, R. & Jones, G. 2007. Leading clever people. *Harvard Business Review,* 85(3): 72–89.

31. Dess & Picken, op. cit.: 34.

32. Webber, A. M. 1998. Danger: Toxic company. *Fast Company,* November: 152–161.

33. Martin, J. & Schmidt, C. 2010. How to keep your top talent. *Harvard Business Review,* 88(5): 54–61.

34. Some interesting insights on why home-grown American talent is going abroad is found in: Saffo, P. 2009. A looming American diaspora. *Harvard Business Review,* 87(2): 27.

35. Morris, B. 1997. Key to success: People, people, people. *Fortune,* October 27: 232.

36. Davenport, T. H., Harris, J. & Shapiro, J. 2010. Competing on talent analytics. *Harvard Business Review,* 88(10): 62–69.

37. Ployhart, R. E. & Moliterno, T. P. 2011. Emergence of the human capital resource: A multilevel model. *Academy of Management Review,* 36(1): 127–150.

38. For insights on management development and firm performance in several countries, refer to: Mabey, C. 2008. Management development and firm performance in Germany, Norway, Spain, and the UK. *Journal of International Business Studies,* 39(8): 1327–1342.

39. Martin, J. 1998. So, you want to work for the best. . . . *Fortune,* January 12: 77.

40. Cardin, R. 1997. Make your own Bozo Filter. *Fast Company,* October–November: 56.

41. Gallagher, L. 2011. 100 best companies to work for *money.cnn.com.* January 20: np.

42. Martin, op. cit.; Henkoff, R. 1993. Companies that train best. *Fortune,* March 22: 53–60.

43. An interesting perspective on developing new talent rapidly when they join an organization can be found in Rollag, K., Parise, S., & Cross, R. 2005. Getting new hires up to speed quickly. *MIT Sloan Management Review,* 46(2): 35–41.

44. Stewart, T. A. 1998. Gray flannel suit? moi? *Fortune,* March 18: 80–82.

45. An interesting perspective on how Cisco Systems develops its talent can be found in Chatman, J., O'Reilly, C., & Chang, V. 2005. Cisco Systems: Developing a human capital strategy. *California Management Review,* 47(2): 137–166.

46. Anonymous. 2011. Schumpeter: The tussle for talent. *The Economist.* January 8: 68.

47. This section is based on Leonard, D. A. & Swap, W. 2004. Deep smarts. *Harvard Business Review,* 82(9): 88–97.

48. Useful insights on coaching can be found in: Coutu, D. & Kauffman, C. 2009. What coaches can do for you? *Harvard Business Review,* 67(1): 91–97.

49. For an innovative perspective on the appropriateness of alternate approaches to evaluation and rewards, refer to Seijts, G. H. & Lathan, G. P. 2005. Learning versus performance goals: When should each be used? *Academy of Management Executive,* 19(1): 124–132.

50. The discussion of the 360-degree feedback system draws on the article UPS. 1997. 360-degree feedback: Coming from all sides. *Vision* (a UPS Corporation internal company publication), March: 3; Slater, R. 1994. *Get better or get beaten: Thirty-one leadership secrets from Jack Welch.* Burr Ridge, IL: Irwin; Nexon, M. 1997. General Electric: The secrets of the finest company in the world.

L'Expansion, July 23: 18–30; and Smith, D. 1996. Bold new directions for human resources. *Merck World* (internal company publication), October: 8.

51. Interesting insights on 360-degree evaluation systems are discussed in: Barwise, P. & Meehan, Sean. 2008. So you think you're a good listener. *Harvard Business Review,* 66(4): 22–23.

52. Insights into the use of 360-degree evaluation are in: Kaplan, R. E. & Kaiser, R. B. 2009. Stop overdoing your strengths. *Harvard Business Review,* 87(2): 100–103.

53. Kets de Vries, M. F. R. 1998. Charisma in action: The transformational abilities of Virgin's Richard Branson and ABB's Percy Barnevik. *Organizational Dynamics,* Winter: 20.

54. For an interesting discussion on how organizational culture has helped Zappos become number one in *Fortune's* 2009 survey of the best companies to work for, see: O'Brien, J. M. 2009. Zappos knows how to kick it. *Fortune,* February 2: 54–58.

55. We have only to consider the most celebrated case of industrial espionage in recent years, wherein José Ignacio Lopez was indicted in a German court for stealing sensitive product planning documents from his former employer, General Motors, and sharing them with his executive colleagues at Volkswagen. The lawsuit was dismissed by the German courts, but Lopez and his colleagues were investigated by the U.S. Justice Department. Also consider the recent litigation involving noncompete employment contracts and confidentiality clauses of *International Paper v. Louisiana-Pacific, Campbell Soup v. H. J. Heinz Co.,* and *PepsiCo v. Quaker Oats's Gatorade.* In addition to retaining valuable human resources and often their valuable network of customers, firms must also protect proprietary information and knowledge. For interesting insights, refer to Carley, W. M. 1998. CEO gets hard lesson in how not to keep his lieutenants. *The Wall Street Journal,* February 11: A1, A10; and Lenzner, R.

& Shook, C. 1998. Whose Rolodex is it, anyway? *Forbes,* February 23: 100–103.

56. For an insightful discussion of retention of knowledge workers in today's economy, read Davenport, T. H. 2005. *The care and feeding of the knowledge worker.* Boston, MA: Harvard Business School Press.

57. Fisher, A. 2008. America's most admired companies. *Fortune,* March 17: 74.

58. Stewart, T. A. 2001. *The wealth of knowledge.* New York: Currency.

59. For insights on fulfilling one's potential, refer to: Kaplan, R. S. 2008. Reaching your potential. *Harvard Business Review,* 66(7/8): 45–57.

60. Amabile, T. M. 1997. Motivating creativity in organizations: On doing what you love and loving what you do. *California Management Review,* Fall: 39–58.

61. For an insightful perspective on alternate types of employee–employer relationships, read Erickson, T. J. & Gratton, L. 2007. What it means to work here. *Harvard Business Review,* 85(3): 104–112.

62. Monsanto has been part of Pharmacia since 2002. *Hoover's Handbook of Am. Bus.* 2004: 562.

63. Pfeffer, J. 2001. Fighting the war for talent is hazardous to your organization's health. *Organizational Dynamics,* 29(4): 248–259.

64. Cox, T. L. 1991. The multinational organization. *Academy of Management Executive,* 5(2): 34–47. Without doubt, a great deal has been written on the topic of creating and maintaining an effective diverse workforce. Some excellent, recent books include: Harvey, C. P. & Allard, M. J. 2005. *Understanding and managing diversity: Readings, cases, and exercises.* (3rd ed.). Upper Saddle River, NJ: Pearson Prentice-Hall; Miller, F. A. & Katz, J. H. 2002. *The inclusion breakthrough: Unleashing the real power of diversity.* San Francisco: Berrett Koehler; and Williams, M. A. 2001. *The 10 lenses: Your guide to living and working in a multicultural world.* Sterling, VA: Capital Books.

65. For an interesting perspective on benefits and downsides of diversity in global consulting firms, refer to: Mors, M. L. 2010. Innovation in a global consulting firm: When the problem is too much diversity. *Strategic Management Journal,* 31(8): 841–872.

66. www.rand.org/publications/RB/RB/5050. U. S. Census Bureau. 1970, 1980, 1990, and 2000 decennial censuses. Population projections, July 1, 2000, to July 1, 2050.

67. Hewlett, S. A. & Rashid, R. 2010. The battle for female talent in emerging markets. *Harvard Business Review,* 88(5): 101–107.

68. This section, including the six potential benefits of a diverse workforce, draws on Cox, T. H. & Blake, S. 1991. Managing cultural diversity: Implications for organizational competitiveness. *Academy of Management Executive,* 5(3): 45–56.

69. *www.pwcglobal.com/us/eng/careers/diversity/index.html.*

70. Johansson, F. 2005. Masters of the multicultural. *Harvard Business Review,* 83(10): 18–19.

71. This discussion draws on Dess, G. G. & Lumpkin, G. T. 2001. Emerging issues in strategy process research. In Hitt, M. A., Freeman, R. E. & Harrison, J. S. (Eds.). *Handbook of strategic management:* 3–34. Malden, MA: Blackwell.

72. Wong, S.-S. & Boh, W. F. 2010. Leveraging the ties of others to build a reputation for trustworthiness among peers. *Academy of Management Journal,* 53(1): 129–148.

73. Adler, P. S. & Kwon, S. W. 2002. Social capital: Prospects for a new concept. *Academy of Management Review,* 27(1): 17–40.

74. Capelli, P. 2000. A market-driven approach to retaining talent. *Harvard Business Review,* 78(1): 103–113.

75. This hypothetical example draws on Peteraf, M. 1993. The cornerstones of competitive advantage. *Strategic Management Journal,* 14: 179–191.

76. Wernerfelt, B. 1984. A resource-based view of the firm. *Strategic Management Journal,* 5: 171–180.

77. Wysocki, B., Jr. 2000. Yet another hazard of the new economy: The Pied

Piper Effect. *The Wall Street Journal,* March 20: A1–A16.

78. Ideas on how managers can more effectively use their social network are addressed in: McGrath, C. & Zell, D. 2009. Profiles of trust: Who to turn to, and for what. *MIT Sloan Management Review,* 50(2): 75–80.

79. Ibid.

80. Buckman, R. C. 2000. Tech defectors from Microsoft resettle together. *The Wall Street Journal,* October: B1–B6.

81. An insightful discussion of the interorganizational aspects of social capital can be found in Dyer, J. H. & Singh, H. 1998. The relational view: Cooperative strategy and sources of interorganizational competitive advantage. *Academy of Management Review,* 23: 66–79.

82. A study of the relationship between social networks and performance in China is found in: Li, J. J., Poppo, L., & Zhou, K. Z. 2008. Do managerial ties in China always produce value? Competition, uncertainty, and domestic vs. foreign firms. *Strategic Management Journal,* 29(4): 383–400.

83. Aime, F., Johnson, S., Ridge, J. W. & Hill, A. D. 2010. The routine may be stable but the advantage is not: Competitive implications of key employee mobility. *Strategic Management Journal,* 31(1): 75–87.

84. Hoppe, B. 2005. Structural holes, Part one. *connectedness.blogspot.com.* January 18: np.

85. There has been a tremendous amount of theory building and empirical research in recent years in the area of social network analysis. Unquestionably, two of the major contributors to this domain have been Ronald Burt and J. S. Coleman. For excellent background discussions, refer to: Burt, R. S. 1992. *Structural holes: The social structure of competition.* Cambridge, MA: Harvard University Press; Coleman, J. S. 1990. *Foundations of social theory.* Cambridge, MA: Harvard University Press; and Coleman, J. S. 1988. Social capital in the creation of human capital. *American Journal of Sociology.* 94: S95–S120. For a more recent review and integration of current thought on

social network theory, consider: Burt, R. S. 2005. *Brokerage & closure: An introduction to social capital.* Oxford Press: New York.

86. Our discussion draws on the concepts developed by Burt, 1992, op. cit.; Coleman, 1990, op. cit.; Coleman, 1988, op. cit.; and Oh, H., Chung, M. & Labianca, G. 2004. Group social capital and group effectiveness: The role of informal socializing ties. *Academy of Management Journal,* 47(6): 860–875. We would like to thank Joe Labianca (University of Kentucky) for his helpful feedback and ideas in our discussion of social networks.

87. Arregle, J. L., Hitt, M. A., Sirmon, D. G., & Very, P. 2007. The development of organizational social capital: Attributes of family firms. *Journal of Management Studies,* 44(1): 73–95.

88. A novel perspective on social networks is in: Pentland, A. 2009. How social networks network best. *Harvard Business Review,* 87(2): 37.

89. Oh et al., op. cit.

90. Hoppe, op. cit.

91. The discussion of these two contingent factors draws on Dess, G. G. & Shaw, J. D. 2001. Voluntary turnover, social capital, and organizational performance. *Academy of Management Review,* 26(3): 446–456.

92. The business-level strategies of overall low cost and differentiation draws upon Michael E. Porter's classic work and will be discussed in more detail in Chapter 5. Source: Porter, M. E. 1985. *Competitive advantage.* Free Press: New York.

93. This section draws on: Hansen, M. T. 2009. *Collaboration: How leaders avoid the traps, create unity, and reap big results.* Boston, MA: Harvard Business Press.

94. Perspectives on how to use and develop decision networks are discussed in: Cross, R., Thomas, R. J., & Light, D. A. 2009. How "who you know" affects what you decide. *MIT Sloan Management Review,* 50(2): 35–42.

95. Our discussion of the three advantages of social networks draws on Uzzi, B. & Dunlap. S. 2005. How to

build your network. *Harvard Business Review,* 83(12): 53–60. For a recent, excellent review on the research exploring the relationship between social capital and managerial performance, read Moran, P. 2005. Structural vs. relational embeddedness: Social capital and managerial performance. *Strategic Management Journal,* 26(12): 1129–1151.

96. A perspective on personal influence is in: Christakis, N. A. 2009. The dynamics of personal influence. *Harvard Business Review,* 87(2): 31.

97. Prusak, L. & Cohen, D. 2001. How to invest in social capital. *Harvard Business Review,* 79(6): 86–93.

98. Leonard, D. & Straus, S. 1997. Putting your company's whole brain to work. *Harvard Business Review,* 75(4): 110–122.

99. For an excellent discussion of public (i.e., the organization) versus private (i.e., the individual manager) benefits of social capital, refer to Leana, C. R. & Van Buren, H. J. 1999. Organizational social capital and employment practices. *Academy of Management Review,* 24(3): 538–555.

100. The authors would like to thank Joe Labianca, University of Kentucky, and John Lin, University of Texas at Dallas, for their very helpful input in our discussion of social network theory and its practical implications.

101. Brady, D. 2006. !#?@ the e-mail. Can we talk?. *BusinessWeek,* December 4: 109.

102. Goldsmith, M. 2009. How not to lose the top job. *Harvard Business Review,* 87(1): 74.

103. Taylor, W. C. 1999. Whatever happened to globalization? *Fast Company,* December: 228–236.

104. Prahalad, C. K. & Ramaswamy, V. 2004. *The future of competition: Co-creating value with customers.* Boston: Harvard Business School Press.

105. Lei, D., Slocum, J., & Pitts, R. A. 1999. Designing organizations for competitive advantage: The power of unlearning and learning. *Organizational Dynamics,* Winter: 24–38.

106. This section draws upon Zaccaro, S. J. & Bader, P. 2002. E-Leadership and

the challenges of leading e-teams: Minimizing the bad and maximizing the good. *Organizational Dynamics,* 31(4): 377–387.

107. Kirkman, B. L., Rosen, B., Tesluk, P. E., & Gibson, C. B. 2004. The impact of team empowerment on virtual team performance: The moderating role of face-to-face interaction. *Academy of Management Journal,* 47(2): 175–192.

108. The discussion of the advantages and challenges associated with e-teams draws on Zacarro & Bader, op. cit.

109. For a recent study exploring the relationship between team empowerment, face-to-face interaction, and performance in virtual teams, read Kirkman, Rosen, Tesluk, & Gibson, op. cit.

110. For an innovative study on how firms share knowledge with competitors and the performance implications, read Spencer, J. W. 2003. Firms' knowledge sharing strategies in the global innovation system: Empirical evidence from the flat panel display industry. *Strategic Management Journal,* 24(3): 217–235.

111. The examples of Andersen Consulting and Access Health draw upon Hansen, M. T., Nohria, N., & Tierney, T. 1999. What's your strategy for managing knowledge? *Harvard Business Review,* 77(2): 106–118.

112. This discussion draws on Conley, J. G. 2005. *Intellectual capital management,* Kellogg School of Management and Schulich School of Business, York University, Toronto, KS 2003; Conley, J. G. & Szobocsan, J. 2001. Snow White shows the way. *Managing Intellectual Property,* June: 15–25; Greenspan, A. 2004. Intellectual property rights, The Federal Reserve Board, Remarks by the chairman, February 27; and Teece, D. J. 1998. Capturing value from knowledge assets, *California Management Review,* 40(3): 54–79. The authors would like to thank Professor Theo Peridis, York University, for his contribution to this section.

113. E. Danneels. 2011. Trying to become a different type of company: Dynamic capability at Smith Corona. *Strategic Management Journal,* 32(1): 1–31.

114. A study of the relationship between dynamic capabilities and related diversification is: Doving, E. & Gooderham, P. N. 2008. *Strategic Management Journal,* 29(8): 841–858.

115. A perspective on strategy in turbulent markets is in: Sull, D. 2009. How to thrive in turbulent markets. *Harvard Business Review,* 87(2): 78–88.

116. Lee, G. K. 2008. Relevance of organizational capabilities and its dynamics: What to learn from entrants' product portfolios about the determinants of entry timing. *Strategic Management Journal,* 29(12): 1257–1280.

117. Eisenhardt, K. M. & Martin, J. E. 2000. Dynamic capabilities: What are they? *Strategic Management Journal,* 21: 1105–1121.

Chapter 5. Business Level Strategy: Creating and Sustaining Competitive Advantages

chapter **FIVE**

Business-Level Strategy:

Creating and Sustaining Competitive Advantages

After reading this chapter, you should have a good understanding of:

LO5.1 The central role of competitive advantage in the study of strategic management, and the three generic strategies: overall cost leadership, differentiation, and focus.

LO5.2 How the successful attainment of generic strategies can improve a firm's relative power vis-à-vis the five forces that determine an industry's average profitability.

LO5.3 The pitfalls managers must avoid in striving to attain generic strategies.

LO5.4 How firms can effectively combine the generic strategies of overall cost leadership and differentiation.

LO5.5 What factors determine the sustainability of a firm's competitive advantage.

LO5.6 How Internet-enabled business models are being used to improve strategic positioning.

LO5.7 The importance of considering the industry life cycle to determine a firm's business-level strategy and its relative emphasis on functional area strategies and value-creating activities.

LO5.8 The need for turnaround strategies that enable a firm to reposition its competitive position in an industry.

LEARNING OBJECTIVES

How firms compete with each other and how they attain and sustain competitive advantages go to the heart of strategic management. In short, the key issue becomes: Why do some firms outperform others and enjoy such advantages over time? This subject, business-level strategy, is the focus of Chapter 5.

The first part of the chapter draws on Michael Porter's framework of generic strategies. He identifies three strategies—overall cost leadership, differentiation, and focus—that firms may apply to outperform their rivals in an industry. We begin by describing each of these strategies and providing examples of firms that have successfully attained them as a means of outperforming competitors in their industry. Next, we address how these strategies help a firm develop a favorable position vis-à-vis the "five forces," suggest some of the pitfalls that managers must avoid when pursuing these generic strategies, and discuss the conditions under which firms may effectively combine generic strategies to outperform rivals.

The second section discusses the factors that determine the sustainability of competitive advantages. Using an example from the manufacturing sector, we discuss whether or not a firm's competitive advantages may be sustained over a long period of time.

The third section addresses how competitive strategies should be revised and redeployed in light of the shifts in industry and competitive forces caused by Internet and digital strategies. Here, combination strategies are the most solid because they integrate the new capabilities with sound principles.

The fourth and final section discusses a vital consideration in the effective use of business-level strategies: industry life cycles. The four stages of the industry life cycle—introduction, growth, maturity, and decline—are indicative of an evolving management process that affects factors such as the market growth rate and the intensity of competition. Accordingly, the stages of an industry's life cycle are an important contingency that managers should take into account when making decisions concerning the optimal overall business-level strategies and the relative emphasis to place on functional capabilities and value-creating activities. At times, firms are faced with performance declines and must find ways to revitalize their competitive positions. The actions followed to do so are referred to as turnaround strategies, which may be needed at any stage of the industry life cycle. However, they occur more frequently during the maturity and decline stages.

Learning from Mistakes

Recently, a battle over strategy divided top management and franchise owners at KFC.[1] Many franchise owners became upset with KFC's new strategy that moved away from its Southern fried heritage and moved toward promoting grilled chicken and sandwiches. In early 2009, CEO Roger Eaton introduced grilled chicken in a move to target health-conscious consumers in today's changing society. However, many franchise owners were disappointed with this strategy. Why? What went wrong?

On January 2010, the KFC National Council and Advertising Cooperative (which represents all U.S. franchises) sued KFC to gain control of their own ad strategy. This "civil war" erupted when the company introduced grilled chicken with the slogan "Unthink KFC." To make matters worse, after a year in the market, reports stated that grilled chicken accounted for only about 16 percent of all "on the bone" chicken sold. Also, an internal survey of 642 franchisees showed almost 50 percent of the stores' grilled chicken was thrown away!

One glaring example of miscommunication regarding business strategy between management and franchise owners occurred when KFC launched a grilled chicken giveaway on *Oprah,* a wildly popular television program, in May 2009. Management told franchisees to expect a couple hundred customers to redeem online coupons at each store. However, thousands showed up expecting free grilled chicken. One franchise owner said, "The cost to the franchisee was much larger than they said," and that the promotion cost her almost $15,000! This started a continued downfall in trust between management and owners. KFC canceled the promotion, and CEO Eaton apologized to customers in an online video.

Disagreements between KFC management and franchise owners over strategy led to decreased sales and store closings. KFC's franchisees were upset with the decision to push grilled chicken and claimed that it hurts the brand. They sued KFC and now do a lot of their own advertising to promote fried chicken at their stores.

business-level strategy a strategy designed for a firm or a division of a firm that competes within a single business.

generic strategies an analysis of business strategy into basic types based on breadth of target market (industrywide versus narrow market segment) and type of competitive advantage (low cost versus uniqueness).

In order to create and sustain a competitive advantage, companies such as KFC should analyze the value chains of their customers and suppliers to see where they can add value. They should not focus only on their internal operations. By not listening to and consulting with franchise owners, KFC has ignored and angered a large part of their extended value chain. The battle over ad strategy within the company has hurt the brand and eroded KFC's competitive advantage.

Types of Competitive Advantage and Sustainability

>LO5.1
The central role of competitive advantage in the study of strategic management, and the three generic strategies: overall cost leadership, differentiation, and focus.

Michael Porter presented three generic strategies that a firm can use to overcome the five forces and achieve competitive advantage.[2] Each of Porter's generic strategies has the potential to allow a firm to outperform rivals in their industry. The first, *overall cost leadership,* is based on creating a low-cost-position. Here, a firm must manage the relationships throughout the value chain and lower costs throughout the entire chain. Second, *differentiation* requires a firm to create products and/or services that are unique and valued. Here, the primary emphasis is on "nonprice" attributes for which customers will gladly pay a premium.[3] Third, a *focus* strategy directs attention (or "focus") toward narrow product lines, buyer segments, or targeted geographic markets and they must attain advantages either through differentiation or cost leadership.[4] Whereas the overall cost leadership and differentiation strategies strive to attain advantages industrywide, focusers have a narrow target market in mind. Exhibit 5.1 illustrates these three strategies on two dimensions: competitive advantage and strategic target.

Competitive Advantage

Exhibit 5.1 Three Generic Strategies

Source: Adapted and reprinted with the permission of The Free Press, a division of Simon & Schuster Inc. from *Competitive Strategy: Techniques for Analyzing Industries and Competitors* Michael E. Porter. Copyright © 1980, 1998 by The Free Press. All rights reserved.

Both casual observation and research support the notion that firms that identify with one or more of the forms of competitive advantage outperform those that do not.[5] There has been a rich history of strategic management research addressing this topic. One study analyzed 1,789 strategic business units and found that businesses combining multiple forms of competitive advantage (differentiation and overall cost leadership) outperformed businesses that used only a single form. The lowest performers were those that did not identify with any type of advantage. They were classified as "stuck in the middle." Results of this study are presented in Exhibit 5.2.[6]

For an example of the dangers of being "stuck in the middle," consider Coach and Tiffany—two brands in the "affordable luxury" category.[7] Such brands target middle-class customers for whom a $300 bag is a splurge. After sales and stock declines, they are migrating away from the middle—and going either higher or lower:

> In early 2008, Coach said that it would turn 40 of its nearly 300 stores into a more upscale format that will offer higher-end bags and concierge services. Tiffany, on the other hand, took

Exhibit 5.2 Competitive Advantage and Business Performance

	Competitive Advantage					
	Differentiation and Cost	Differentiation	Cost	Differentiation and Focus	Cost and Focus	Stuck in the Middle
Performance						
Return on investment (%)	35.5	32.9	30.2	17.0	23.7	17.8
Sales growth (%)	15.1	13.5	13.5	16.4	17.5	12.2
Gain in market share (%)	5.3	5.3	5.5	6.1	6.3	4.4
Sample size	123	160	100	141	86	105

the opposite tack. A new store opening in California will not sell any of its $148,000 diamond necklaces and instead focus on less expensive products like its $200-and-under silver jewelry. Claims Pat Conroy, head of Deloitte & Touche's consumer products sector: "Being in the middle is not a good place to be. You get assaulted from everyone."

overall cost leadership a firm's generic strategy based on appeal to the industrywide market using a competitive advantage based on low cost.

Overall Cost Leadership

The first generic strategy is overall cost leadership. Overall cost leadership requires a tight set of interrelated tactics that include:

- Aggressive construction of efficient-scale facilities.
- Vigorous pursuit of cost reductions from experience.
- Tight cost and overhead control.

Exhibit 5.3 Value-Chain Activities: Examples of Overall Cost Leadership

Support Activities

Firm Infrastructure
- Few management layers to reduce overhead costs.
- Standardized accounting practices to minimize personnel required.

Human Resource Management
- Minimize costs associated with employee turnover through effective policies.
- Effective orientation and training programs to maximize employee productivity.

Technology Development
- Effective use of automated technology to reduce scrappage rates.
- Expertise in process engineering to reduce manufacturing costs.

Procurement
- Effective policy guidelines to ensure low-cost raw materials (with acceptable quality levels).
- Shared purchasing operations with other business units.

Primary Activities

Inbound Logistics
- Effective layout of receiving dock operations.

Operations
- Effective use of quality control inspectors to minimize rework.

Outbound Logistics
- Effective utilization of delivery fleets

Marketing and Sales
- Purchase of media in large blocks.
- Sales force utilization is maximized by territory management.

Service
- Thorough service repair guidelines to minimize repeat maintenance calls.
- Use of single type of vehicle to minimize repair costs.

Source: Adapted from: Porter, M.E. 1985. *Competitive Advantage: Creating and Sustaining Superior Performance.* New York: Free Press.

5.1

strategy spotlight

The Experience Curve

The experience curve, developed by the Boston Consulting Group in 1968, is a way of looking at efficiencies developed through a firm's cumulative experience. In its basic form, the experience curve relates production costs to production output. As output doubles, costs decline by 10 percent to 30 percent. For example, if it costs $1 per unit to produce 100 units, the per unit cost will decline to between 70 to 90 cents as output increases to 200 units.

What factors account for this increased efficiency? First, the success of an experience curve strategy depends on the industry life cycle for the product. Early stages of a product's life cycle are typically characterized by rapid gains in technological advances in production efficiency. Most experience curve gains come early in the product life cycle.

Second, the inherent technology of the product offers opportunities for enhancement through gained experience. High-tech products give the best opportunity for gains in production efficiencies. As technology is developed, "value engineering" of innovative production processes is implemented, driving down the per unit costs of production.

Third, a product's sensitivity to price strongly affects a firm's ability to exploit the experience curve. Cutting the price of a product with high demand elasticity—where demand increases when price decreases—rapidly creates consumer purchases of the new product. By cutting prices, a firm can increase demand for its product. The increased demand in turn increases product manufacture, thus increasing the firm's experience in the manufacturing process. So by decreasing price and increasing demand, a firm gains manufacturing experience in that particular product, which drives down per unit production costs.

Fourth, the competitive landscape factors into whether or not a firm might benefit from an experience curve strategy. If other competitors are well positioned in the market,

Sources: Ghemawat, P. 1985. Building Strategy on the Experience Curve. *Harvard Business Review*, March–April: 143–149; Porter, M. E. 1996. *On Competition*. Boston: Harvard Business Review Press; and Oster, S. M. 1994. *Modern Competitive Analysis* (2nd ed.). New York: Oxford University Press.

have strong capital resources, and are known to promote their product lines aggressively to gain market share, an experience curve strategy may lead to nothing more than a price war between two or more strong competitors. But if a company is the first to market with the product and has good financial backing, an experience curve strategy may be successful.

In an article in the *Harvard Business Review*, Pankaj Ghemawat recommended answering several questions when considering an experience curve strategy.

- Does my industry exhibit a significant experience curve?
- Have I defined the industry broadly enough to take into account interrelated experience?
- What is the precise source of cost reduction?
- Can my company keep cost reductions proprietary?
- Is demand sufficiently stable to justify using the experience curve?
- Is cumulated output doubling fast enough for the experience curve to provide much strategic leverage?
- Do the returns from an experience curve strategy warrant the risks of technological obsolescence?
- Is demand price-sensitive?
- Are there well-financed competitors who are already following an experience curve strategy or are likely to adopt one if my company does?

Michael Porter suggested, however, that the experience curve is not useful in all situations. Whether or not to base strategy on the experience curve depends on what specifically causes the decline in costs. For example, if costs drop from efficient production facilities and not necessarily from experience, the experience curve is not helpful. But as Sharon Oster pointed out in her book on competitive analysis, the experience curve can help managers analyze costs when efficient learning, rather than efficient machinery, is the source of cost savings.

- Avoidance of marginal customer accounts.
- Cost minimization in all activities in the firm's value chain, such as R&D, service, sales force, and advertising.

Exhibit 5.3 draws on the value-chain concept (see Chapter 3) to provide examples of how a firm can attain an overall cost leadership strategy in its primary and support activities.

Key to an overall cost leadership strategy is the **experience curve,** which refers to how business "learns" to lower costs as it gains experience with production processes. With experience, unit costs of production decline as output increases in most industries. The experience curve concept is discussed in Strategy Spotlight 5.1 and Exhibit 5.4.

experience curve
the decline in unit costs of production as cumulative output increases.

Exhibit 5.4 **Comparing Experience Curve Effects**

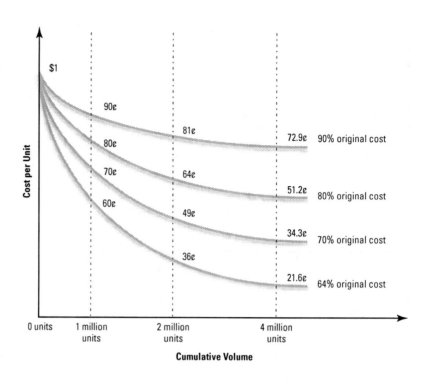

To generate above-average performance, a firm following an overall cost leadership position must attain **competitive parity** on the basis of differentiation relative to competitors.[8] In other words, a firm achieving parity is similar to its competitors, or "on par," with respect to differentiated products.[9] Competitive parity on the basis of differentiation permits a cost leader to translate cost advantages directly into higher profits than competitors. Thus, the cost leader earns above-average returns.[10]

The failure to attain parity on the basis of differentiation can be illustrated with an example from the automobile industry—the ill-fated Yugo. Below is an excerpt from a speech by J. W. Marriott, Jr., Chairman of the Marriott Corporation:[11]

> . . . money is a big thing. But it's not the only thing. In the 1980s, a new automobile reached North America from behind the Iron Curtain. It was called the Yugo, and its main attraction was price. About $3,000 each. But the only way they caught on was as the butt of jokes. Remember the guy who told his mechanic, "I want a gas cap for my Yugo." "OK," the mechanic replied, "that sounds like a fair trade."

Yugo was offering a lousy value proposition. The cars literally fell apart before your eyes. And the lesson was simple. Price is just one component of value. No matter how good the price, the most cost-sensitive consumer won't buy a bad product.

Next, we discuss some examples of how firms enhance cost leadership position.

While other managed care providers were having a string of weak years, WellPoint, based in Thousand Oaks, California, has had a number of banner years and recently enjoyed an annual profit growth of over 42 percent to $4.8 billion over the past three years.[12] Chairman Leonard Schaeffer credits the company's focus on innovation for both expanding revenues and cutting costs. For example, WellPoint asked the Food and Drug Administration (FDA) to make the allergy drug Claritin available over the counter. Surprisingly, this may be the first time that an insurer has approached the FDA with such a request. Schaeffer claimed, "They were kind of stunned," but the FDA agreed to consider it. It was a smart move for WellPoint. If approved as an over-the-counter drug, Claritin would reduce patient

competitive parity a firm's achievement of similarity, or being "on par," with competitors with respect to low cost, differentiation, or other strategic product characteristic.

5.2

strategy spotlight

Ryanair: A Highly Effective Overall Cost Leadership Strategy

Michael O'Leary, CEO of Ryanair Holdings PLC, makes no apologies for his penny-pinching. Want to check luggage? You'll pay up to $9.50 per bag for the privilege. Expecting free drinks and snacks? You'll be disappointed. Even a bottle of water will cost you $3.40. And it is not just the passengers who are affected. Flight crews buy their own uniforms, and staff at Ryanair's Spartan Dublin Airport headquarters must supply their own pens. After a customer sued Ryanair for charging $34 for the use of a wheelchair, the company added a 63 cent "wheelchair levy" to every ticket!

Low-fare U.S. carriers have taken the opposite approach of Ryanair by adding perks such as leather seats, live television, and business class. "All of the low-cost carriers' costs have gotten a little out of control," says Tim Sieber, general manager of The Boyd Group, an Evergreen (Colorado) aviation consultant. Clearly Ryanair hasn't followed its industry peers.

Ryanair has been extremely successful. It recently became the first airline in Europe to carry more than 7 million passengers in one month. As of late 2010, the company had a market capitalization of $7.2 billion, dwarfing competitors easyJet ($2.3 billion) and Ireland's legacy airline, Aer Lingus ($612 million), but it is still a bit short of Southwest ($8.29 billion) and Delta ($8.22 billion). Over the past decade, at a time when the global airline industry collectively lost nearly $50 billion, Ryanair turned healthy net profits in 9 out of the 10 years—earning $431 million in the most recent year. In the process, O'Leary has become one of Ireland's wealthiest citizens—the value of his Ryanair shares is nearly $300 million.

What is O'Leary's secret? He thinks like a retailer and charges for every little thing. Imagine the seat as a cell

phone: It comes free, or nearly free, but its owner winds up spending money on all sorts of services.

However, what O'Leary loses in seat revenue he more than makes up by turning both his planes and the Ryanair website into stores brimming with irresistible goodies, even as he charges for such "perks" as priority boarding and assigned seating.

Sounds outrageous? Probably so, but the strategy is clearly working. Although its average fare is $53, compared with $92 for Southwest Airlines, Ryanair's net margins are, at 18 percent—more than double the 7 percent achieved by Southwest. Says Nick van den Brul, an aviation analyst: "Ryanair is Walmart with wings." As O'Leary says, "You want luxury? Go somewhere else."

A few other Ryanair practices include:

- Flight attendants sell digital cameras ($137.50) and iPocket MP3 players ($165).

- The seats don't recline, seat-back pockets have been removed to cut cleaning time and speed turnaround of the planes, there's no entertainment, and seat-back trays will soon carry ads.

- Ryanair sells more than 98 percent of its tickets online. Its website offers insurance, hotels, car rentals, and more—even online bingo.

O'Leary is certainly a colorful person, and he has some "creative" or downright nutty ideas. Recently, he came up with the idea of replacing the last 10 rows with a standing cabin, outfitted with handrails, much like a New York City subway car, only without the benches and panhandlers. The increased capacity, he claims, would lower fares by 20 percent to 25 percent. He says: "In no plane ever operated by Ryanair will it be all standing. You will always have the choice of paying for the seat. The argument against it is that if there's ever a crash, people will be injured. If there's ever a crash, the people in the sit-down seats will be injured, too."

Sources: Gillete, F. 2010. The Duke of Discomfort. *Bloomberg, Business Week* September 12: 58–61; Ryanair Annual Report, 2008; Capell, K. 2006. Walmart with Wings. *BusinessWeek.* November 27: 44–45; Kumar, N. 2006. Strategies to Fight Low-Cost Rivals. *Harvard Business Review,* 84(12): 104–113; and *Ryanair Annual Report,* 2006.

visits to the doctor and eliminate the need for prescriptions—two reimbursable expenses for which WellPoint would otherwise be responsible.

Stephen Sanger, CEO of General Mills, recently came up with an idea that helped his firm cut costs.[13] To improve productivity, he sent technicians to watch pit crews during a NASCAR race. That experience inspired the techies to figure out how to reduce the time it takes to switch a plant line from five hours to 20 minutes. This provided an important lesson: Many interesting benchmarking examples can take place far outside of an industry. Often, process improvements involve identifying the best practices in other industries and adapting them for implementation in your own firm. After all, when firms benchmark competitors in their own industry, the end result is often copying and playing catch-up.[14]

A business that strives for a low-cost advantage must attain an absolute cost advantage relative to its rivals.[15] This is typically accomplished by offering a no-frills product or service to a broad target market using standardization to derive the greatest benefits from economies of scale and experience. However, such a strategy may fail if a firm is unable to attain parity on important dimensions of differentiation such as quick responses to customer requests for services or design changes. Strategy Spotlight 5.2 discusses Ryanair—a firm that has developed a very unique overall cost leadership strategy. One might say that it "one upped" Southwest Airlines!

>LO5.2

How the successful attainment of generic strategies can improve a firm's relative power vis-à-vis the five forces that determine an industry's average profitability.

Overall Cost Leadership: Improving Competitive Position vis-à-vis the Five Forces An overall low-cost position enables a firm to achieve above-average returns despite strong competition. It protects a firm against rivalry from competitors, because lower costs allow a firm to earn returns even if its competitors eroded their profits through intense rivalry. A low-cost position also protects firms against powerful buyers. Buyers can exert power to drive down prices only to the level of the next most efficient producer. Also, a low-cost position provides more flexibility to cope with demands from powerful suppliers for input cost increases. The factors that lead to a low-cost position also provide substantial entry barriers from economies of scale and cost advantages. Finally, a low-cost position puts the firm in a favorable position with respect to substitute products introduced by new and existing competitors.[16]

A few examples will illustrate these points. Ryanair's close attention to costs helps to protect them from buyer power and intense rivalry from competitors. Thus, they are able to drive down costs and enjoy relatively high power over their customers. By increasing productivity and lowering unit costs, General Mills (and its competitors in that industry) enjoy greater scale economies and erect higher entry barriers for others. Finally, as competitors such as WellPoint lower costs through means such as petitioning the FDA to make certain drugs available over the counter, they become less vulnerable to substitutes such as Internet-based competitors.

>LO5.3

The pitfalls managers must avoid in striving to attain generic strategies.

Potential Pitfalls of Overall Cost Leadership Strategies Potential pitfalls of overall cost leadership strategy include:

- *Too much focus on one or a few value-chain activities.* Would you consider a person to be astute if he cancelled his newspaper subscription and quit eating out to save money, but then "maxed out" several credit cards, requiring him to pay hundreds of dollars a month in interest charges? Of course not. Similarly, firms need to pay attention to all activities in the value chain.[17] Too often managers make big cuts in operating expenses, but don't question year-to-year spending on capital projects. Or managers may decide to cut selling and marketing expenses but ignore manufacturing expenses. Managers should explore *all* value-chain activities, including relationships among them, as candidates for cost reductions.

- *All rivals share a common input or raw material.* Here, firms are vulnerable to price increases in the factors of production. Since they're competing on costs, they are less able to pass on price increases, because customers can take their business to rivals who have lower prices. For example, consider manufacturing firms based in China which rely on a common input—low labor costs. Due to demographic factors, the supply of workers 16 to 24 years old has peaked and will drop by a third in the next 12 years, thanks to stringent family-planning policies that have sharply reduced China's population growth.[18] In one city, many factories are operating with vacancies of 15 to 20 percent, compelling some supervisors to cruise the streets in a desperate hiring quest during crunch times. Needless to say, there are strong demands for better working conditions and higher wages.

- *The strategy is imitated too easily.* One of the common pitfalls of a cost-leadership strategy is that a firm's strategy may consist of value-creating activities that are easy to imitate.[19] Such was the case with online brokers in recent years.[20] As of early 2001, there were about 140 online brokers, hardly symbolic of an industry where imitation is extremely difficult. But according to Henry McVey, financial services analyst at Morgan Stanley, "We think you need five to ten" online brokers.

What are some of the dynamics? First, although online brokers were geared up to handle 1.2 million trades a day, volume had shrunk to about 834,000—a 30 percent drop. Thus, competition for business intensified. Second, when the stock market is down, many investors trust their instincts less and seek professional guidance from brokerages that offer differentiated services. Eric Rajendra of A. T. Kearney, an international consulting company, claimed, "The current (online broker) model is inadequate for the pressures the industry is facing now."

- *A lack of parity on differentiation.* As noted earlier, firms striving to attain cost leadership advantages must obtain a level of parity on differentiation.[21] Firms providing online degree programs may offer low prices. However, they may not be successful unless they can offer instruction that is perceived as comparable to traditional providers. For them, parity can be achieved on differentiation dimensions such as reputation and quality and through signaling mechanisms such as accreditation agencies.

- *Erosion of cost advantages when the pricing information available to customers increases.* This is becoming a more significant challenge as the Internet dramatically increases both the quantity and volume of information available to consumers about pricing and cost structures. Life insurance firms offering whole life insurance provide an interesting example.[22] One study found that for each 10 percent increase in consumer use of the Internet, there is a corresponding reduction in insurance prices to consumers of 3 to 5 percent. Recently, the nationwide savings (or, alternatively, reduced revenues to providers) was between $115 and $125 million annually.

Differentiation

As the name implies, a **differentiation strategy** consists of creating differences in the firm's product or service offering by creating something that is perceived *industrywide* as unique and valued by customers.[23] Differentiation can take many forms:

- Prestige or brand image (Adam's Mark hotels, BMW automobiles).[24]
- Technology (Martin guitars, Marantz stereo components, North Face camping equipment).
- Innovation (Medtronic medical equipment, Apple's iPods).
- Features (Cannondale mountain bikes, Honda Goldwing motorcycles).
- Customer service (Nordstrom department stores, Sears lawn equipment retailing).
- Dealer network (Lexus automobiles, Caterpillar earthmoving equipment).

differentiation strategy a firm's generic strategy based on creating differences in the firm's product or service offering by creating something that is perceived *industrywide* as unique and valued by customers.

● Caterpillar is well known for its outstanding dealer network.

Exhibit 5.5
Value-Chain Activities:
Examples of
Differentiation

Support Activities
Firm Infrastructure
• Superior MIS—To integrate value-creating activities to improve quality.
• Facilities that promote firm image.
• Widely respected CEO enhances firm reputation.
Human Resource Management
• Programs to attract talented engineers and scientists.
• Provide training and incentives to ensure a strong customer service orientation.
Technology Development
• Superior material handling and sorting technology.
• Excellent applications engineering support.
Procurement
• Purchase of high-quality components to enhance product image.
• Use of most prestigious outlets.
Primary Activities
Inbound Logistics
• Superior material handling operations to minimize damage.
• Quick transfer of inputs to manufacturing process.
Operations
• Flexibility and speed in responding to changes in manufacturing specifications.
• Low defect rates to improve quality.
Outbound Logistics
• Accurate and responsive order processing.
• Effective product replenishment to reduce customer inventory.
Marketing and Sales
• Creative and innovative advertising programs.
• Fostering of personal relationship with key customers.
Service
• Rapid response to customer service requests.
• Complete inventory of replacement parts and supplies.

Source: Adapted from Porter, M.E. 1985. *Competitive Advantage: Creating and Sustaining Superior Performance.* New York: Free Press.

Exhibit 5.5 draws on the concept of the value chain as an example of how firms may differentiate themselves in primary and support activities.

Firms may differentiate themselves along several different dimensions at once.[25] For example, BMW is known for its high prestige, superior engineering, and high-quality automobiles. And Harley-Davidson differentiates on image and dealer services.[26]

Firms achieve and sustain differentiation advantages and attain above-average performance when their price premiums exceed the extra costs incurred in being unique.[27]

For example, both BMW and Harley-Davidson must increase consumer costs to offset added marketing expenses. Thus, a differentiator will always seek out ways of distinguishing itself from similar competitors to justify price premiums greater than the costs incurred by differentiating.[28] Clearly, a differentiator cannot ignore costs. After all, its premium prices would be eroded by a markedly inferior cost position. Therefore, it must attain a level of cost *parity* relative to competitors. Differentiators can do this by reducing costs in all areas that do not affect differentiation. Porsche, for example, invests heavily in engine design—an area in which its customers demand excellence—but it is less concerned and spends fewer resources in the design of the instrument panel or the arrangement of switches on the radio.[29]

Many companies successfully follow a differentiation strategy.[30] For example, FedEx's CEO and founder, Fred Smith, claims that the key to his firm's success is innovation.[31] He contends his management team didn't understand their real goal when they started the firm in 1971: "We thought that we were selling the transportation of goods; in fact, we were selling peace of mind." They now provide drivers with a handheld computer and a transmitting device so that customers can track their packages from their desktop PCs.

Lexus, a division of Toyota, provides an example of how a firm can strengthen its differentiation strategy by *achieving integration at multiple points along the value chain.*[32] Although the luxury car line was not introduced until the late 1980s, by the early 1990s the cars had already soared to the top of J. D. Power & Associates' customer satisfaction ratings.

> In the spirit of benchmarking, one of Lexus's competitors hired Custom Research Inc. (CRI), a marketing research firm, to find out why Lexus owners were so satisfied. CRI conducted a series of focus groups in which Lexus drivers eagerly offered anecdotes about the special care they experienced from their dealers. It became clear that, although Lexus was manufacturing cars with few mechanical defects, it was the extra care shown by the sales and service staff that resulted in satisfied customers. Such pampering is reflected in the feedback from one customer who claimed she never had a problem with her Lexus. However, upon further probing, she said, "Well, I suppose you could call the four times they had to replace the windshield a 'problem.' But frankly, they took care of it so well and always gave me a loaner car, so I never really considered it a problem until you mentioned it now." An insight gained in CRI's research is that perceptions of product quality (design, engineering, and manufacturing) can be strongly influenced by downstream activities in the value chain (marketing and sales, service).

Strategy Spotlight 5.3 addresses how Netflix, the successful Internet movie rental company, uses crowdsourcing to enhance its differentiation.

Differentiation: Improving Competitive Position vis-à-vis the Five Forces Differentiation provides protection against rivalry since brand loyalty lowers customer sensitivity to price and raises customer switching costs.[33] By increasing a firm's margins, differentiation also avoids the need for a low-cost position. Higher entry barriers result because of customer loyalty and the firm's ability to provide uniqueness in its products or services.[34] Differentiation also provides higher margins that enable a firm to deal with supplier power. And it reduces buyer power, because buyers lack comparable alternatives and are therefore less price sensitive.[35] Supplier power is also decreased because there is a certain amount of prestige associated with being the supplier to a producer of highly differentiated products and services. Last, differentiation enhances customer loyalty, thus reducing the threat from substitutes.[36]

Our examples illustrate these points. Lexus has enjoyed enhanced power over buyers because its top J. D. Power ranking makes buyers more willing to pay a premium price. This lessens rivalry, since buyers become less price-sensitive. The prestige associated with its brand name also lowers supplier power since margins are high. Suppliers would probably desire to be associated with prestige brands, thus lessening their incentives to drive up prices. Finally, the loyalty and "peace of mind" associated with a service provider such as FedEx makes such firms less vulnerable to rivalry or substitute products and services.

strategy spotlight   5.3

Crowdsourcing: How Netflix Boosts Its Differentiation

Netflix is well-known for its inviting online presentation and efficient distribution system. However, this highly successful movie-rental company prides itself on its capability to offer subscribers a compact list of films that they are likely to enjoy watching. And it must be working: Netflix sends 35,000 titles a day to its 7.5 million subscribers.

"Imagine that our website was a brick-and-mortar store," says Netflix vice president, James Bennett. "When people walk through the door, they see DVDs rearrange themselves. The movies that might interest them fly onto the shelves, and all the rest go to the back room."

The movies, of course, don't do the rearranging—that is done by the customers themselves, with an assist from a computer program called Cinematch, which Netflix developed in 2000. Customers are invited to rate each film they watch on a 1 to 5 scale. Cinematch analyzes these ratings, searches through 80,000 titles in inventory, and determines the list of films tailored to the taste of each of the firm's subscribers. By enticing them to rate films, Netflix achieves the latest in business innovation—getting customers to serve themselves.

Netflix is not unique in their use of so-called recommenders. Consider other online retailers such as Amazon, Apple, eBay, and Overstock. All of these rely on their customers for a helping hand in predicting what products the customers will prefer—whether the product is bedding, books, CDs, or DVDs. Customer ratings are used to rank corporate service providers as well.

For all these companies, the recommender system provides more than a chance to create an extra service. It helps them to establish a stronger connection with their customers. And studies have shown that it can substantially increase online sales.

Sources: Copeland, M.V. 2009. Tapping Tech's Beautiful Minds. *Fortune* October 12: 35–36; Libert, B. & Spector, J. 2008. *We Are Smarter Than Me*. Philadelphia: Wharton Publishing; and Howe, J. 2008. *Crowdsourcing*. New York: Crown Business.

The extent of Netflix's commitment to personalized movie recommendations was made clear in 2006 when it offered a $1 million prize to anyone who could build a system that was at least 10 percent better than Cinematch. In late 2009, it awarded the prize to a seven-person team of computer scientists, mathematicians, and statisticians who were from New Jersey, Israel, Quebec, and Austria. They built a system that was 20 percent better than Cinematch.

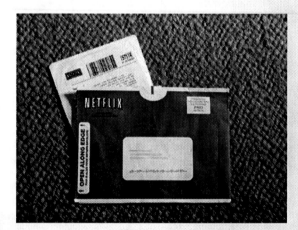

● Netflix generated a lot of favorable publicity with its $1 million prize competition.

Netflix has also developed another crowdsourcing feature called Friends. Here, subscribers see each other's list of films watched and compare the ratings they have awarded the films—in exchange for suggestions on other films to watch.

crowdsourcing

Potential Pitfalls of Differentiation Strategies   Potential pitfalls of a differentiation strategy include:

- *Uniqueness that is not valuable.* A differentiation strategy must provide unique bundles of products and/or services that customers value highly. It's not enough just to be "different." An example is Gibson's Dobro bass guitar. Gibson came up with a unique idea: Design and build an acoustic bass guitar with sufficient sound volume so that amplification wasn't necessary. The problem with other acoustic bass guitars was that they did not project enough volume because of the low-frequency bass notes. By adding a resonator plate on the body of the traditional acoustic bass, Gibson increased the sound volume. Gibson believed this product would serve a particular niche market—bluegrass and folk artists who played in small group "jams" with other acoustic musicians. Unfortunately, Gibson soon discovered that its targeted market was content with their existing options: an upright bass amplified with a microphone or an acoustic electric guitar. Thus, Gibson developed a unique product, but it was not perceived as valuable by its potential customers.[37]

- *Too much differentiation.* Firms may strive for quality or service that is higher than customers desire.[38] Thus, they become vulnerable to competitors who provide an appropriate level of quality at a lower price. For example, consider the expensive Mercedes-Benz S-Class, which ranges in price between $93,650 and $138,000 for the 2011 models.[39] *Consumer Reports* described it as "sumptuous," "quiet and luxurious," and a "delight to drive." The magazine also considered it to be the least reliable sedan available in the United States. According to David Champion, who runs their testing program, the problems are electronic. "The engineers have gone a little wild," he says. "They've put every bell and whistle that they think of, and sometimes they don't have the attention to detail to make these systems work." Some features include: a computer-driven suspension that reduces body roll as the vehicle whips around a corner; cruise control that automatically slows the car down if it gets too close to another car; and seats that are adjustable 14 ways and that are ventilated by a system that uses eight fans.

- *Too high a price premium.* This pitfall is quite similar to too much differentiation. Customers may desire the product, but they are repelled by the price premium. For example, Duracell (a division of Gillette) recently charged too much for batteries.[40] The firm tried to sell consumers on its superior quality products, but the mass market wasn't convinced. Why? The price differential was simply too high. At a CVS drugstore just one block from Gillette's headquarters, a four-pack of Energizer AA batteries was on sale at $2.99 compared with a Duracell four-pack at $4.59. Duracell's market share dropped 2 percent in a recent two-year period, and its profits declined over 30 percent. Clearly, the price/performance proposition Duracell offered customers was not accepted.

- *Differentiation that is easily imitated.* As we noted in Chapter 3, resources that are easily imitated cannot lead to sustainable advantages. Similarly, firms may strive for, and even attain, a differentiation strategy that is successful for a time. However, the advantages are eroded through imitation. Consider Cereality's innovative differentiation strategy of stores which offer a wide variety of cereals and toppings for around $4.00.[41] As one would expect, once their idea proved successful, competitors entered the market because much of the initial risk had already been taken. Rivals include an Iowa City restaurant named the Cereal Cabinet, the Cereal Bowl in Miami, and Bowls: A Cereal Joint in Gainesville, Florida. Says David Roth, one of Cereality's founders: "With any good business idea, you're faced with people who see you've cracked the code and who try to cash in on it."

- *Dilution of brand identification through product-line extensions.* Firms may erode their quality brand image by adding products or services with lower prices and less quality. Although this can increase short-term revenues, it may be detrimental in the long run. Consider Gucci.[42] In the 1980s Gucci wanted to capitalize on its prestigious brand name by launching an aggressive strategy of revenue growth. It added a set of lower-priced canvas goods to its product line. It also pushed goods heavily into department stores and duty-free channels and allowed its name to appear on a host of licensed items such as watches, eyeglasses, and perfumes. In the short term, this strategy worked. Sales soared. However, the strategy carried a high price. Gucci's

Exhibit 5.6 Potential Pitfalls of Overall Cost Leadership and Differentiation Strategies

Overall Cost Leadership:
- Too much focus on one or a few value-chain activities.
- All rivals share a common input or raw material.
- The strategy is imitated too easily.
- A lack of parity on differentiation.
- Erosion of cost advantages when the pricing information available to customers increases.

Differentiation:
- Uniqueness that is not valuable.
- Too much differentiation.
- The price premium is too high.
- Differentiation that is easily imitated.
- Dilution of brand identification through product-line extensions.
- Perceptions of differentiation may vary between buyers and sellers.

indiscriminate approach to expanding its products and channels tarnished its sterling brand. Sales of its high-end goods (with higher profit margins) fell, causing profits to decline.

- *Perceptions of differentiation may vary between buyers and sellers.* The issue here is that "beauty is in the eye of the beholder." Companies must realize that although they may perceive their products and services as differentiated, their customers may view them as commodities. Indeed, in today's marketplace, many products and services have been reduced to commodities.[43] Thus, a firm could overprice its offerings and lose margins altogether if it has to lower prices to reflect market realities.

Exhibit 5.6 summarizes the pitfalls of overall cost leadership and differentiation strategies. In addressing the pitfalls associated with these two generic strategies there is one common, underlying theme. Managers must be aware of the dangers associated with concentrating so much on one strategy that they fail to attain parity on the other.

Focus

focus strategy a firm's generic strategy based on appeal to a narrow market segment within an industry.

A **focus strategy** is based on the choice of a narrow competitive scope within an industry. A firm following this strategy selects a segment or group of segments and tailors its strategy to serve them. The essence of focus is the exploitation of a particular market niche. As you might expect, narrow focus itself (like merely "being different" as a differentiator) is simply not sufficient for above-average performance.

The focus strategy, as indicated in Exhibit 5.1, has two variants. In a cost focus, a firm strives to create a cost advantage in its target segment. In a differentiation focus, a firm seeks to differentiate in its target market. Both variants of the focus strategy rely on providing better service than broad-based competitors who are trying to serve the focuser's target segment. Cost focus exploits differences in cost behavior in some segments, while differentiation focus exploits the special needs of buyers in other segments.

Let's look at examples of two firms that have successfully implemented focus strategies. Network Appliance (NA) has developed a more cost-effective way to store and distribute computer files.[44] Its larger rival, EMC, makes mainframe-style products priced over $1 million that store files and accommodate Internet traffic. NA makes devices that cost under $200,000 for particular storage jobs such as caching (temporary storage) of Internet

5.4

strategy spotlight

If You Can't Afford an Extremely Expensive Car . . . You Can Rent One

If we assume that indulgence is best experienced in moderation, it should come as no surprise that the business of renting expensive sheet metal is soaring. Ken Kerzner, managing partner of Midway Car Rental in Los Angeles, has been renting high-end cars to business travelers, wealthy tourists, and movie moguls for 41 years.

He is having one of his best years. He claims that today's recession-weary customers are looking to try

Source: Callaway, S. 2010. Hot Rides for Rent. *Fortune.* September 6: 24.

new things while avoiding the headaches and overhead of ownerships. His 2,000-vehicle fleet offers just about everything. It ranges from the Smart car ($89 a day) to the Ferrari California and Lamborghini Gallardo at $2,850 and $2,999 a day, respectively. Don't want to spring for these two super-high-end cars? You can get a Porsche Targa 4S for *only* $1,499 a day.

Kerzner does have some serious competition. Beverly Hills Rent-a-Car, with locations in Los Angeles and Las Vegas, offers an even wider range. Interested in renting the $1.7 million Bugatti Veyron with an astonishing 1,001 horse power? You can find it here.

content. Focusing on such narrow segments has certainly paid off for NA; it has posted a remarkable 20 straight quarters of revenue growth.

Paccar, an $8 billion Bellevue, Washington–based heavy-truck manufacturer, has chosen a differentiation focus strategy.[45] The firm targets one group of customers: owner-operators. These are the drivers who own their trucks and contract directly with shippers or serve as subcontractors to larger trucking companies.

Paccar has invested heavily to develop a variety of features with owner-operators in mind: luxurious sleeper cabins, plush leather seats, noise-insulated cabins, sleek exterior styling, and so forth. At Paccar's extensive network of dealers, prospective buyers use software to select among thousands of options to put their personal signature on their trucks. These customized trucks are built to order, not to stock, and are delivered in eight weeks. Not surprisingly, customers are happy to pay Paccar a 10 percent premium, and its Kenworth and Peterbilt brands are considered status symbols at truck stops.

Strategy Spotlight 5.4 illustrates that you can pay as much as you want for some products or services. Case in point: car rentals.

Focus: Improving Competitive Position vis-à-vis the Five Forces Focus requires that a firm either have a low-cost position with its strategic target, high differentiation, or both. As we discussed with regard to cost and differentiation strategies, these positions provide defenses against each competitive force. Focus is also used to select niches that are least vulnerable to substitutes or where competitors are weakest.

Let's look at our examples to illustrate some of these points. First, Paccar experienced lower rivalry and greater bargaining power by providing products and services to a targeted market segment that was less price-sensitive. New rivals have difficulty attracting customers away from Paccar based only on lower prices. Similarly, the brand image and quality that this brand evoked heightened rivals' entry barriers. With regard to the strategy of cost focus, Network Appliances, the successful rival to EMC in the computer storage industry, was better able to absorb pricing increases from suppliers as a result of its lower cost structure, reducing supplier power.

Potential Pitfalls of Focus Strategies Potential pitfalls of focus strategies include:

* *Erosion of cost advantages within the narrow segment.* The advantages of a cost focus strategy may be fleeting if the cost advantages are eroded over time. For example, Dell's pioneering direct selling model in the personal computer industry has been

eroded by rivals such as Hewlett Packard as they gain experience with Dell's distribution method. Similarly, other firms have seen their profit margins drop as competitors enter their product segment.

- *Even product and service offerings that are highly focused are subject to competition from new entrants and from imitation.* Some firms adopting a focus strategy may enjoy temporary advantages because they select a small niche with few rivals. However, their advantages may be short-lived. A notable example is the multitude of dot-com firms that specialize in very narrow segments such as pet supplies, ethnic foods, and vintage automobile accessories. The entry barriers tend to be low, there is little buyer loyalty, and competition becomes intense. And since the marketing strategies and technologies employed by most rivals are largely nonproprietary, imitation is easy. Over time, revenues fall, profits margins are squeezed, and only the strongest players survive the shakeout.
- *Focusers can become too focused to satisfy buyer needs.* Some firms attempting to attain advantages through a focus strategy may have too narrow a product or service. Consider many retail firms. Hardware chains such as Ace and True Value are losing market share to rivals such as Lowe's and Home Depot that offer a full line of home and garden equipment and accessories. And given the enormous purchasing power of the national chains, it would be difficult for such specialty retailers to attain parity on costs.

Combination Strategies: Integrating Overall Low Cost and Differentiation

>LO5.4
How firms can effectively combine the generic strategies of overall cost leadership and differentiation.

Perhaps the primary benefit to firms that integrate low-cost and differentiation strategies is the difficulty for rivals to duplicate or imitate.[45] This strategy enables a firm to provide two types of value to customers: differentiated attributes (e.g., high quality, brand identification, reputation) and lower prices (because of the firm's lower costs in value-creating activities). The goal is thus to provide unique value to customers in an efficient manner.[46] Some firms are able to attain both types of advantages simultaneously.[47] For example, superior quality can lead to lower costs because of less need for rework in manufacturing, fewer warranty claims, a reduced need for customer service personnel to resolve customer complaints, and so forth. Thus, the benefits of combining advantages can be additive, instead of merely involving trade-offs. Next, we consider three approaches to combining overall low cost and differentiation.

combination strategies firms' integrations of various strategies to provide multiple types of value to customers.

Automated and Flexible Manufacturing Systems   Given the advances in manufacturing technologies such as CAD/CAM (computer aided design and computer aided manufacturing) as well as information technologies, many firms have been able to manufacture unique products in relatively small quantities at lower costs—a concept known as **mass customization.**[48]

mass customization a firm's ability to manufacture unique products in small quantities at low cost.

Let's consider Andersen Windows of Bayport, Minnesota—a $3 billion manufacturer of windows for the building industry.[49] Until about 20 years ago, Andersen was a mass producer, in small batches, of a variety of standard windows. However, to meet changing customer needs, Andersen kept adding to its product line. The result was catalogs of ever-increasing size and a bewildering set of choices for both homeowners and contractors. Over a 6-year period, the number of products tripled, price quotes took several hours, and the error rate increased. This not only damaged the company's reputation, but also added to its manufacturing expenses.

To bring about a major change, Andersen developed an interactive computer version of its paper catalogs that it sold to distributors and retailers. Salespersons can now customize each window to meet the customer's needs, check the design for structural soundness, and provide a price quote. The system is virtually error free, customers get exactly what

Exhibit 5.7 Effective Uses of Flexible Production Systems

- At Nikeid.com, customers can design an athletic or casual shoe to their specifications online, selecting almost every element of the shoe from the material of the sole to the color of the shoelace.

- Eleuria sells custom perfumes. Each product is created in response to a user profile constructed from responses to a survey about habits and preferences. Eleuria then provides a sample at modest cost to verify fit.

- Lands' End offers customized shirts and pants. Consumers specify style parameters, measurements, and fabrics through the firm's website. These settings are saved so that returning users can easily order a duplicate item.

- Cannondale permits consumers to specify the parameters that define a road bike frame, including custom colors and inscriptions. The user specifies the parameters on the firm's website and then arranges for delivery through a dealer.

Source: Randall, T., Terwiesch, C. & Ulrich, K. T. 2005. Principles for User Design of Custom Products. *California Management Review,* 47(4): 68–85.

they want, and the time to develop the design and furnish a quotation has been cut by 75 percent. Each showroom computer is connected to the factory, and customers are assigned a code number that permits them to track the order. The manufacturing system has been developed to use some common finished parts, but it also allows considerable variation in the final products. Despite its huge investment, Andersen has been able to lower costs, enhance quality and variety, and improve its response time to customers.

Exhibit 5.7 provides other examples of how flexible production systems have enabled firms to successfully engage in mass customization for their customers:[50]

Exploiting the Profit Pool Concept for Competitive Advantage   A profit pool is defined as the total profits in an industry at all points along the industry's value chain.[51] Although the concept is relatively straightforward, the structure of the profit pool can be complex.[52] The potential pool of profits will be deeper in some segments of the value chain than in others, and the depths will vary within an individual segment. Segment profitability may vary widely by customer group, product category, geographic market, or distribution channel. Additionally, the pattern of profit concentration in an industry is very often different from the pattern of revenue generation.

profit pool the total profits in an industry at all points along the industry's value chain.

Consider the automobile industry profit pool in Exhibit 5.8. Here we see little relationship between the generation of revenues and capturing of profits. While manufacturing generates most of the revenue, this value activity is far smaller profitwise than other value activities such as financing and extended warranty operations. So while a car manufacturer may be under tremendous pressure to produce cars efficiently, much of the profit (at least proportionately) can be captured in the aforementioned downstream operations. Thus, a carmaker would be ill-advised to focus solely on manufacturing and leave downstream operations to others through outsourcing.

Coordinating the "Extended" Value Chain by Way of Information Technology
Many firms have achieved success by integrating activities throughout the "extended value chain" by using information technology to link their own value chain with the value chains of their customers and suppliers. As noted in Chapter 3, this approach enables a firm to add value not only through its own value-creating activities, but also for its customers and suppliers.

Such a strategy often necessitates redefining the industry's value chain. A number of years ago, Walmart took a close look at its industry's value chain and decided to

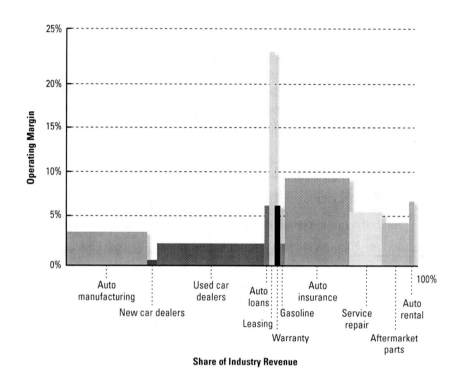

Exhibit 5.8 - graph axes: Operating Margin (y-axis) from 0% to 25%; Share of Industry Revenue (x-axis) to 100%. Categories: Auto manufacturing, New car dealers, Used car dealers, Auto loans, Leasing, Warranty, Gasoline, Auto insurance, Service repair, Aftermarket parts, Auto rental.

Exhibit 5.8 **The U.S. Automobile Industry's Profit Pool**

Source: Reprinted by permission of *Harvard Business Review*, Exhibit from "Profit Pools: A Fresh Look at Strategy," by O. Gadiesh and J. L. Gilbert, May–June 1999. Copyright © 1999 by the Harvard Business School Publishing Corporation; all rights reserved.

reframe the competitive challenge.[53] Although its competitors were primarily focused on retailing—merchandising and promotion—Walmart determined that it was not so much in the retailing industry as in the transportation logistics and communications industries. Here, linkages in the extended value chain became central. That became Walmart's chosen battleground. By redefining the rules of competition that played to its strengths, Walmart has attained competitive advantages and dominates its industry.

Integrated Overall Low-Cost and Differentiation Strategies: Improving Competitive Position vis-à-vis the Five Forces   Firms that successfully integrate both differentiation and cost advantages create an enviable position. For example, Walmart's integration of information systems, logistics, and transportation helps it to drive down costs and provide outstanding product selection. This dominant competitive position, serves to erect high entry barriers to potential competitors that have neither the financial nor physical resources to compete head-to-head. Walmart's size—over $400 billion in 2011 sales—provides the chain with enormous bargaining power over suppliers. Its low pricing and wide selection reduce the power of buyers (its customers), because there are relatively few competitors that can provide a comparable cost/value proposition. This reduces the possibility of intense head-to-head rivalry, such as protracted price wars. Finally, Walmart's overall value proposition makes potential substitute products (e.g., Internet competitors) a less viable threat.

Pitfalls of Integrated Overall Cost Leadership and Differentiation Strategies   The pitfalls of integrated overall cost leadership and differentiation include:

* *Firms that fail to attain both strategies may end up with neither and become "stuck in the middle."* A key issue in strategic management is the creation of competitive

advantages that enable a firm to enjoy above-average returns. Some firms may become "stuck in the middle" if they try to attain both cost and differentiation advantages. An example that we are all familiar with would be the Big 3 U.S. automobile makers. They have been plagued by expensive "legacy costs" associated with pension and health care obligations—a central issue in 2008 federal bailout legislation. And they suffer from long-term customer perceptions of mediocre quality—inferior to their European and Japanese rivals. The troubling quality perceptions persist despite the fact that the Big 3 has attained approximate parity with their Japanese and European competitors in recent J. D. Power surveys.

- *Underestimating the challenges and expenses associated with coordinating value-creating activities in the extended value chain.* Integrating activities across a firm's value chain with the value chain of suppliers and customers involves a significant investment in financial and human resources. Firms must consider the expenses linked to technology investment, managerial time and commitment, and the involvement and investment required by the firm's customers and suppliers. The firm must be confident that it can generate a sufficient scale of operations and revenues to justify all associated expenses.

- *Miscalculating sources of revenue and profit pools in the firm's industry.* Firms may fail to accurately assess sources of revenue and profits in their value chain. This can occur for several reasons. For example, a manager may be biased due to his or her functional area background, work experiences, and educational background. If the manager's background is in engineering, he or she might perceive that proportionately greater revenue and margins were being created in manufacturing, product, and process design than a person whose background is in a "downstream" value-chain activity such as marketing and sales. Or politics could make managers "fudge" the numbers to favor their area of operations. This would make them responsible for a greater proportion of the firm's profits, thus improving their bargaining position.

A related problem is directing an overwhelming amount of managerial time, attention, and resources to value-creating activities that produce the greatest margins—to the detriment of other important, albeit less profitable, activities. For example, a car manufacturer may focus too much on downstream activities, such as warranty fulfillment and financing operations, to the detriment of differentiation and cost of the cars themselves.

Can Competitive Strategies Be Sustained? Integrating and Applying Strategic Management Concepts

> **>LO5.5**
> What factors determine the sustainability of a firm's competitive advantage.

Thus far this chapter has addressed how firms can attain competitive advantages in the marketplace. We discussed the three generic strategies—overall cost leadership, differentiation, and focus—as well as combination strategies. Next we discussed the importance of linking value-chain activities (both those within the firm and those linkages between the firm's suppliers and customers) to attain such advantages. We also showed how successful competitive strategies enable firms to strengthen their position vis-à-vis the five forces of industry competition as well as how to avoid the pitfalls associated with the strategies.

Competitive advantages are, however, often short-lived. As we discussed in the beginning of Chapter 1, the composition of the firms that constitute the Fortune 500 list has experienced significant turnover in its membership over the years—reflecting the temporary nature of competitive advantages. And recall Dell's fall from grace (Chapter 3). Here was a firm whose advantages in the marketplace seemed unassailable in the early 2000s. In fact, it was *Fortune*'s "Most Admired Firm" in 2005. However, cracks began to appear in 2007, and its competitive position has recently been severely eroded by rivals such as Hewlett-Packard. In short, Dell focused so much on operational efficiency and perfecting its "direct model" that it failed to deliver innovations that an increasingly sophisticated market demanded. Also, Dell continues to face further pricing pressures as a result of the commoditization of the personal computer industry.[54]

Clearly, "nothing is forever" when it comes to competitive advantages. Rapid changes in technology, globalization, and actions by rivals from within—as well as outside—the industry can quickly erode a firm's advantages. It is becoming increasingly important to recognize that the duration of competitive advantages is declining, especially in technology intensive industries.[55] Even in industries which are normally viewed as "low tech," the increasing use of technology has suddenly made competitive advantages less sustainable.[56] Amazon's success in book retailing at the cost of Barnes & Noble, the former industry leader, as well as Blockbuster's struggle against Netflix in the video rental industry serve to illustrate how difficult it has become for industry leaders to sustain competitive advantages that they once thought would last forever.

In this section, we will discuss some factors that help determine whether a strategy is sustainable over a long period of time. We will draw on some strategic management concepts from the first five chapters. To illustrate our points, we will look at a company, Atlas Door, which created an innovative strategy in its industry and enjoyed superior performance for several years. Our discussion of Atlas Door draws on a *Harvard Business Review* article by George Stalk, Jr.[57]. It was published some time ago (1988), which provides us the benefit of hindsight to make our points about the sustainability of competitive advantage. After all, the strategic management concepts we have been addressing in the text are quite timeless in their relevance to practice. A brief summary follows:

Atlas Door: A Case Example

Atlas Door, a U.S.-based company, has enjoyed remarkable success. It has grown at an average annual rate of 15 percent in an industry with an overall annual growth rate of less than 5 percent. Recently, its pre-tax earnings were 20 percent of sales—about five times the industry average. Atlas is debt free and by its 10th year, the company achieved the number one competitive position in its industry.

Atlas produces industrial doors—a product with almost infinite variety, involving limitless choices of width and height and material. Given the importance of product variety, inventory is almost useless in meeting customer orders. Instead, most doors can be manufactured only after the order has been placed.

How Did Atlas Door Create Its Competitive Advantages in the Marketplace?   *First,* Atlas built just-in-time factories. Although simple in concept, they require extra tooling and machinery to reduce changeover times. Further, the manufacturing process must be organized by product and scheduled to start and complete with all of the parts available at the same time.

Second, Atlas reduced the time to receive and process an order. Traditionally, when customers, distributors, or salespeople called a door manufacturer with a request for price and delivery, they would have to wait more than one week for a response. In contrast, Atlas first streamlined and then automated its entire order-entry, engineering, pricing, and scheduling process. Atlas can price and schedule 95 percent of its incoming orders while the callers are still on the telephone. It can quickly engineer new special orders because it has preserved on computer the design and production data of all previous special orders—which drastically reduces the amount of reengineering necessary.

Third, Atlas tightly controlled logistics so that it always shipped only fully complete orders to construction sites. Orders require many components, and gathering all of them at the factory and making sure that they are with the correct order can be a time-consuming task. Of course, it is even more time-consuming to get the correct parts to the job site after the order has been shipped! Atlas developed a system to track the parts in production and the purchased parts for each order. This helped to ensure the arrival of all necessary parts at the shipping dock in time—a just-in-time logistics operation.

The Result?   When Atlas began operations, distributors had little interest in its product. The established distributors already carried the door line of a much larger competitor and saw little to no reason to switch suppliers except, perhaps, for a major price concession. But as a startup, Atlas was too small to compete on price alone. Instead, it positioned itself as the door supplier of last resort—the company people came to if the established supplier could not deliver or missed a key date.

Of course, with an average industry order fulfillment time of almost four months, some calls inevitably came to Atlas. And when it did get the call, Atlas commanded a higher price because of its faster delivery. Atlas not only got a higher price, but its effective integration of value-creating activities saved time and lowered costs. Thus, it enjoyed the best of both worlds.

In 10 short years, the company replaced the leading door suppliers in 80 percent of the distributors in the United States. With its strategic advantage, the company could be selective—becoming the supplier for only the strongest distributors.

Are Atlas Door's Competitive Advantages Sustainable?

We will now take both the "pro" and "con" position as to whether or not Atlas Door's competitive advantages will be sustainable for a very long time. It is important, of course, to assume that Atlas Door's strategy is unique in the industry, and the central issue becomes whether or not rivals will be able to easily imitate their strategy or create a viable substitute strategy.

"Pro" Position: The Strategy Is Highly Sustainable   Drawing on Chapter 2, it is quite evident that Atlas Door has attained a very favorable position vis-á-vis the five forces of industry competition. For example, it is able to exert power over its customers (distributors) because of its ability to deliver a quality product in a short period of time. Also, its dominance in the industry creates high entry barriers for new entrants. It is also quite evident that Atlas Door has been able to successfully integrate many value-chain activities within the firm—a fact that is integral to its just-in-time strategy. As noted in Chapter 3, such integration of activities provides a strong basis for sustainability, because rivals would have difficulty in imitating this strategy due to causal ambiguity and path dependency (i.e., it is difficult to build up in a short period of time the resources that Atlas Door has accumulated and developed as well as disentangle the causes of what the valuable resources are or how they can be re-created). Further, as noted in Chapter 4, Atlas Door benefits from the social capital that they have developed with a wide range of key stakeholders (Chapter 1) These would include customers, employees, and managers (a reasonable assumption, given how smoothly the internal operations flow and their long-term relationships with distributors). It would be very difficult for a rival to replace Atlas Door as the supplier of last resort—given the reputation that it has earned over time for "coming through in the clutch" on time-sensitive orders. Finally, we can conclude that Atlas Door has created competitive advantages in both overall low cost and differentiation (Chapter 5). Its strong linkages among value-chain activities—a requirement for its just-in-time operations—not only lowers costs but enables the company to respond quickly to customer orders. As noted in Exhibit 5.5 (page 170), many of the value-chain activities associated with a differentiation strategy reflect the element of speed or quick response.

"Con" Position: The Strategy Can Be Easily Imitated or Substituted   An argument could be made that much of Atlas Door's strategy relies on technologies that are rather well known and nonproprietary. Over time, a well-financed rival could imitate its strategy (via trial and error), achieve a tight integration among its value-creating activities, and implement a just-in-time manufacturing process. Because human capital is highly mobile (Chapter 4), a rival could hire away Atlas Door's talent, and these individuals could aid the rival in transferring Atlas Door's best practices. A new rival could also enter the industry with a large resource base, which might enable it to price its doors well under Atlas Door to build market share (but this would likely involve pricing below cost and would be a risky and nonsustainable strategy). Finally, a rival could potentially "leapfrog" the technologies and processes that Atlas Door has employed and achieve competitive superiority. With the benefit of hindsight, it could use the Internet to further speed up the linkages among its value-creating activities and the order entry processes with its customers and suppliers. (But even this could prove to be a temporary advantage, since rivals could relatively easily do the same thing.)

What Is the Verdict?   Both positions have merit. Over time, it would be rather easy to see how a new rival could achieve parity with Atlas Door—or even create a superior competitive position with new technologies or innovative processes. However, two factors make it extremely difficult for a rival to challenge Atlas Door in the short term: (1) the success that Atlas Door has enjoyed with its just-in-time scheduling and production systems—which involve the successful integration of many value-creating activities—helps the firm not only lower costs but also respond quickly to customer needs, and (2) the strong, positive reputational effects that it has earned with multiple stakeholders—especially its customers.

Finally, it is important to also understand that it is Atlas Door's ability to appropriate most of the profits generated by its competitive advantages that make it a highly successful company. As we discussed in Chapter 3, profits generated by resources can be appropriated by a number of stakeholders such as suppliers, customers, employees, or rivals. The structure of the industrial door industry makes such value appropriation difficult: the suppliers provide generic parts, no one buyer is big enough to dictate prices, the tacit nature of the knowledge makes imitation difficult, and individual employees may be easily replaceable. Still, even with the advantages that Atlas Door enjoys, they need to avoid becoming complacent or suffer the same fate as the dominant firm they replaced.

>LO5.6
How Internet-enabled business models are being used to improve strategic positioning.

How the Internet and Digital Technologies Affect the Competitive Strategies

Internet and digital technologies have swept across the economy and now have an impact on how nearly every company conducts its business. These changes have created new cost efficiencies and avenues for differentiation. However, the presence of these technologies is so widespread that it is questionable how any one firm can use them effectively in ways that genuinely set them apart from rivals. Thus, to stay competitive, firms must update their strategies to reflect the new possibilities and constraints that these phenomena represent. In this section, we address both the opportunities and the pitfalls that Internet and digital technologies offer to companies using overall cost leadership, differentiation, and focus strategies. We also briefly consider two major impacts that the Internet is having on business: lowering transaction costs and enabling mass customization.

digital technologies
information that is in numerical form, which facilitates its storage, transmission, analysis and manipulation.

Overall Cost Leadership

The Internet and digital technologies create new opportunities for firms to achieve low-cost advantages by enabling them to manage costs and achieve greater efficiencies. Managing costs, and even changing the cost structures of certain industries, is a key feature of the digital economy. Most analysts agree that the Internet's ability to lower transaction costs has transformed business. Broadly speaking, *transaction costs* refer to all the various expenses associated with conducting business. It applies not just to buy/sell transactions

Exhibit 5.9 Internet-Enabled Low-Cost Leader Strategies

- Online bidding and order processing eliminate the need for sales calls and minimize sales-force expenses.
- Online purchase orders have made many transactions paperless, thus reducing the costs of procurement and paper.
- Direct access to progress reports and the ability of customers to periodically check work in progress minimize rework.
- Collaborative design efforts using Internet technologies that link designers, materials suppliers, and manufacturers reduce the costs and speed the process of new product development.

but to the costs of interacting with every part of a firm's value chain, within and outside the firm. Think about it. Hiring new employees, meeting with customers, ordering supplies, addressing government regulations—all of these exchanges have some costs associated with them. Because business can be conducted differently on the Internet, new ways of saving money are changing the competitive landscape.

Other factors also help to lower transaction costs. The process of disintermediation (in Chapter 2) has a similar effect. Each time intermediaries are used in a transaction, additional costs are added. Removing intermediaries lowers transaction costs. The Internet reduces the costs to search for a product or service, whether it is a retail outlet (as in the case of consumers) or a trade show (as in the case of business-to-business shoppers). Not only is the need for travel eliminated but so is the need to maintain a physical address, whether it's a permanent retail location or a temporary presence at a trade show.

disintermediation the process of bypassing buyer channel intermediaries such as wholesalers, distributors, and retailers.

Exhibit 5.9 identifies several types of cost leadership strategies that are made possible by Internet and digital technologies. These cost savings are available throughout a firm's value chain, in both primary and support activities.

Potential Internet-Related Pitfalls for Low-Cost Leaders   One of the biggest threats to low-cost leaders is imitation. This problem is intensified for business done on the Internet. Most of the advantages associated with contacting customers directly, and even capabilities that are software driven (e.g., customized ordering systems or real-time access to the status of work in progress), can be duplicated quickly and without threat of infringement on proprietary information. Another pitfall relates to companies that become overly enamored with using the Internet for cost-cutting and thus jeopardize customer relations or neglect other cost centers.

Differentiation

For many companies, Internet and digital technologies have enhanced their ability to build brand, offer quality products and services, and achieve other differentiation advantages.[58] Among the most striking trends are new ways to interact with consumers. In particular, the Internet has created new ways of differentiating by enabling *mass customization*, which improves the response to customer wishes.

Mass customization has changed how companies go to market and has challenged some of the tried-and-true techniques of differentiation. Traditionally, companies reached customers using high-end catalogs, the showroom floor, personal sales calls and products using prestige packaging, celebrity endorsements, and charity sponsorships. All of these avenues are still available and may still be effective, depending on a firm's competitive environment. But many customers now judge the quality and uniqueness of a product or service by their ability to be involved in its planning and design, combined with speed of delivery and reliable results. Internet and digitally based capabilities are thus changing the

Exhibit 5.10 Internet-
Enabled Differentiation
Strategies

- Personalized online access provides customers with their own "site within a site" in which their prior orders, status of current orders, and requests for future orders are processed directly on the supplier's website.

- Online access to real-time sales and service information is being used to empower the sales force and continually update R&D and technology development efforts.

- Internet-based knowledge management systems that link all parts of the organization are shortening response times and accelerating organization learning.

- Quick online responses to service requests and rapid feedback to customer surveys and product promotions are enhancing marketing efforts.

way differentiators make exceptional products and achieve superior service. Such improvements are being made at a reasonable cost, allowing firms to achieve parity on the basis of overall cost leadership.

Exhibit 5.10 identifies differentiation activities that are made possible by Internet and digital technologies. Opportunities to differentiate are available in all parts of a company's value chain—both primary and support activities.

Potential Internet-Related Pitfalls for Differentiators   Traditional differentiation strategies such as building strong brand identity and prestige pricing have been undermined by Internet-enabled capabilities such as the ability to compare product features side-by-side or bid online for competing services. The sustainability of Internet-based gains from differentiation will deteriorate if companies offer differentiating features that customers don't want or create a sense of uniqueness that customers don't value. The result can be a failed value proposition—the value companies thought they were offering, does not translate into sales.

Focus

A focus strategy targets a narrow market segment with customized products and/or services. With focus strategies, the Internet offers new avenues in which to compete because they can access markets less expensively (low cost) and provide more services and features (differentiation). Some claim that the Internet has opened up a new world of opportunities for niche players who seek to access small markets in a highly specialized fashion.[59] Niche businesses are among the most active users of digital technologies and e-business solutions. According to the ClickZ.com division of Jupitermedia Corporation, 77 percent of small businesses agree that a website is essential for small business success. Small businesses also report that the Internet has helped them grow (58 percent), made them more profitable (51 percent), and helped reduce transaction costs (49 percent).[60] Clearly niche players and small businesses are using the Internet and digital technologies to create more viable focus strategies.

Many aspects of the Internet economy favor focus strategies because niche players and small firms have been able to extend their reach and effectively compete with larger competitors. For example, niche firms have been quicker than Fortune 1000 firms to adopt blogging as a way to create a community and gather customer feedback.[61] Effective use of blogs is an example of how focusers are using the new technology to provide the kinds of advantages that have been the hallmark of a focus strategy in the past—specialized knowledge, rapid response, and strong customer service. Thus, the Internet has provided many firms that pursue focus strategies with new tools for creating competitive advantages.

Exhibit 5.11 Internet-
Enabled Focus Strategies

- Permission marketing techniques are focusing sales efforts on specific customers who opt to receive advertising notices.

- Niche portals that target specific groups are providing advertisers with access to viewers with specialized interests.

- Virtual organizing and online "officing" are being used to minimize firm infrastructure requirements.

- Procurement technologies that use Internet software to match buyers and sellers are highlighting specialized buyers and drawing attention to smaller suppliers.

Exhibit 5.11 outlines several approaches to strategic focusing that are made possible by Internet and digital technologies. Both primary and support activities can be enhanced using the kind of singlemindedness that is characteristic of a focus strategy.

Potential Internet-Related Pitfalls for Focusers A key danger for focusers using the Internet relates to correctly assessing the size of the online marketplace. Focusers can misread the scope and interests of their target markets. This can cause them to focus on segments that are too narrow to be profitable or to lose their uniqueness in overly broad niches, making them vulnerable to imitators or new entrants.

What happens when an e-business focuser tries to overextend its niche? Efforts to appeal to a broader audience by carrying additional inventory, developing additional content, or offering additional services can cause it to lose the cost advantages associated with a limited product or service offering. Conversely, when focus strategies become too narrow, the e-business may have trouble generating enough activity to justify the expense of operating the website.

Are Combination Strategies the Key to E-Business Success?

Because of the changing dynamics presented by digital and Internet-based technologies, new strategic combinations that make the best use of the competitive strategies may hold the greatest promise.[62] Many experts agree that the net effect of the digital economy is *fewer* rather than more opportunities for sustainable advantages.[63] This means strategic thinking becomes more important.

More specifically, the Internet has provided all companies with greater tools for managing costs. So it may be that cost management and control will become more important management tools. In general, this may be good if it leads to an economy that makes more efficient use of its scarce resources. However, for individual companies, it may shave critical percentage points off profit margins and create a climate that makes it impossible to survive, much less achieve sustainable above-average profits.

Many differentiation advantages are also diminished by the Internet. The ability to comparison shop—to check product reviews and inspect different choices with a few clicks of the mouse—is depriving some companies, such as auto dealers, of the unique advantages that were the hallmark of their prior success. Differentiating is still an important strategy, of course. But how firms achieve it may change, and the best approach may be to combine differentiation with other competitive strategies.

Perhaps the greatest beneficiaries are the focusers who can use the Internet to capture a niche that previously may have been inaccessible. However, because the same factors that make it possible for a small niche player to be a contender may make that same niche attractive to a big company. That is, an incumbent firm that previously thought a niche

strategy spotlight   5.5

Liberty Mutual's Electronic Invoice System: Combining Low Cost and Differentiation Advantages

Boston-based Liberty Mutual Group is a leading global insurer and the sixth largest property and casualty insurer in the United States. Its largest line of business is personal automobile insurance. Liberty Mutual has $112.2 billion in assets and $33 billion in annual revenues—ranking the firm 71st on the Fortune 500 list of the largest corporations.

In 2000, Liberty Mutual became one of the first companies to experiment with electronic invoices. It set up a pilot program with a few law firms to submit its bills through a secured website. These firms, for the most part, handle claims litigation for Liberty, defending its policyholders in lawsuits. Its success with this program convinced Liberty that it could achieve significant cost savings and also pass along differentiating features to its customers and strategic partners. Liberty now processes nearly 400,000 electronic legal-services invoices a year—70 percent of the total invoices that the firm receives.

As expected, the initial transition was quite expensive. The company invested nearly $1 million in the first four years. However, Liberty estimates that the electronic invoice program saves the company $750,000 a year in direct costs by streamlining the distribution, payment, storage, and retrieval of invoices. E-invoices enable Liberty to move from intake to payment with half the staff that it had taken to process paper invoices. The firm has also created new efficiencies by cutting costs resulting from data entry errors, late payments, and overpayments. As a relatively minor issue, Liberty saves more than $20,000 per year on postage, photocopying, archiving, and retrieval costs.

The legal invoices are organized by litigation phase or task—for example, taking a deposition or reporting a witness statement. Work is diced into tiny increments of

six minutes or less. A single invoice that covers a month of complex litigation, for example, can include well over 1,000 lines. However, by building and mining a database of law firm billing practices, Liberty is able to generate a highly granular report card about law firm activities and performance. The new knowledge generated by this system not only increases internal effectiveness but also allows Liberty to provide detailed feedback to clients and other external stakeholders.

Online invoicing has also helped speed up both processing and response time. Liberty can instantaneously see how firms deploy and bill for partners, paralegals, and other staff, how they compare with each other on rates, hours, and case outcomes; and whether, how, and how often they send duplicate invoices or charge for inappropriate services. The system also allows Liberty to instantly review all of the time billed for a particular attorney across many cases, enabling the firm to reconstruct the total time billed to Liberty during a single day. More than once they have found that attorneys have billed more than 24 hours in a day. Liberty is also able to easily expose prohibited formula billing patterns (wherein, for example, they are billed a set amount for a service instead of actual time spent). In two cases in which formula billing was used, Liberty found that there were more than $28,000 in suspected overcharges.

Liberty Mutual is in the process of developing a large database of law firms' billing practices on different types of cases. The database should eventually enable Liberty to evaluate a law firm's billing activities and compare them to the norms of all of its partner firms. With such intelligence, it will be a rather straightforward matter to rate each firm's cost effectiveness in handling certain types of cases and match firms with cases accordingly.

Liberty's decision to use electronic invoices was initially based on the potential for cost savings. But the differentiating advantages it has achieved in terms of rapid feedback, decreased response time, and a knowledge trove in databases that can be electronically mined has provided the company with a fruitful combination of Internet-based strategic advantages.

Sources: Coyle, M., & Angevine, R. 2007. Liberty Mutual Group reports fourth quarter 2006 results. February 26, *www.libertymutual.com*; Smunt, T. L., & Sutcliffe, C. L., 2004. There's Gold in Them Bills. *Harvard Business Review*, 82(9): 24–25; and *www.libertymutualgroup.com*.

market was not worth the effort may use Internet technologies to enter that segment for a lower cost than in the past. The larger firm can then bring its market power and resources to bear in a way that a smaller competitor cannot match.

A combination strategy challenges a company to carefully blend alternative strategic approaches and remain mindful of the impact of different decisions on the firm's value-creating processes and its extended value-chain activities. Strong leadership is needed to maintain a bird's-eye perspective on a company's overall approach and to coordinate the multiple dimensions of a combination strategy.

Strategy Spotlight 5.5 describes the efforts of Liberty Mutual, a company that used Internet and digital technologies to successfully combine both differentiation and overall low-cost advantages.

Industry Life Cycle Stages: Strategic Implications

The **industry life cycle** refers to the stages of introduction, growth, maturity, and decline that occur over the life of an industry. In considering the industry life cycle, it is useful to think in terms of broad product lines such as personal computers, photocopiers, or long-distance telephone service. Yet the industry life cycle concept can be explored from several levels, from the life cycle of an entire industry to the life cycle of a single variation or model of a specific product or service.

Why are industry life cycles important?[64] The emphasis on various generic strategies, functional areas, value-creating activities, and overall objectives varies over the course of an industry life cycle. Managers must become even more aware of their firm's strengths and weaknesses in many areas to attain competitive advantages. For example, firms depend on their research and development (R&D) activities in the introductory stage. R&D is the source of new products and features that everyone hopes will appeal to customers. Firms develop products and services to stimulate consumer demand. Later, during the maturity phase, the functions of the product have been defined, more competitors have entered the market, and competition is intense. Managers then place greater emphasis on production efficiencies and process (as opposed to the product) engineering in order to lower manufacturing costs. This helps to protect the firm's market position and to extend the product life cycle because the firm's lower costs can be passed on to consumers in the form of lower prices, and price-sensitive customers will find the product more appealing.

Exhibit 5.12 illustrates the four stages of the industry life cycle and how factors such as generic strategies, market growth rate, intensity of competition, and overall objectives change over time. Managers must strive to emphasize the key functional areas during each of the four stages and to attain a level of parity in all functional areas and value-creating activities. For example, although controlling production costs may be a primary concern during the maturity stage, managers should not totally ignore other functions such as marketing and R&D. If they do, they can become so focused on lowering costs that they miss market trends or fail to incorporate important product or process designs. Thus, the firm may attain low-cost products that have limited market appeal.

It is important to point out a caveat. While the life cycle idea is analogous to a living organism (i.e., birth, growth, maturity, and death), the comparison has limitations.[65] Products and services go through many cycles of innovation and renewal. Typically, only fad products have a single life cycle. Maturity stages of an industry can be "transformed" or followed by a stage of rapid growth if consumer tastes change, technological innovations take place, or new developments occur. The cereal industry is a good example. When medical research indicated that oat consumption reduced a person's cholesterol, sales of Quaker Oats increased dramatically.[66]

Strategies in the Introduction Stage

In the **introduction stage,** products are unfamiliar to consumers.[67] Market segments are not well defined, and product features are not clearly specified. The early development of an industry typically involves low sales growth, rapid technological change, operating losses, and the need for strong sources of cash to finance operations. Since there are few players and not much growth, competition tends to be limited.

industry life cycle
the stages of introduction, growth, maturity, and decline that typically occur over the life of an industry.

>LO5.7
The importance of considering the industry life cycle to determine a firm's business-level strategy and its relative emphasis on functional area strategies and value-creating activities.

introduction stage
the first stage of the industry life cycle, characterized by (1) new products that are not known to customers, (2) poorly defined market segments, (3) unspecified product features, (4) low sales growth, (5) rapid technological change, (6) operating losses, and (7) a need for financial support.

Exhibit 5.12 Stages of the Industry Life Cycle

Stage Factor	Introduction	Growth	Maturity	Decline
Generic strategies	Differentiation	Differentiation	Differentiation Overall cost leadership	Overall cost leadership Focus
Market growth rate	Low	Very large	Low to moderate	Negative
Number of segments	Very few	Some	Many	Few
Intensity of competition	Low	Increasing	Very intense	Changing
Emphasis on product design	Very high	High	Low to moderate	Low
Emphasis on process design	Low	Low to moderate	High	Low
Major functional area(s) of concern	Research and development	Sales and marketing	Production	General management and finance
Overall objective	Increase market awareness	Create consumer demand	Defend market share and extend product life cycles	Consolidate, maintain, harvest, or exit

Success requires an emphasis on research and development and marketing activities to enhance awareness. The challenge becomes one of (1) developing the product and finding a way to get users to try it, and (2) generating enough exposure so the product emerges as the "standard" by which all other rivals' products are evaluated.

There's an advantage to being the "first mover" in a market.[68] It led to Coca-Cola's success in becoming the first soft-drink company to build a recognizable global brand and enabled Caterpillar to get a lock on overseas sales channels and service capabilities.

However, there can also be a benefit to being a "late mover." Target carefully considered its decision to delay its Internet strategy. Compared to its competitors Walmart and Kmart, Target was definitely an industry laggard. But things certainly turned out well:[69]

By waiting, Target gained a late mover advantage. The store was able to use competitors' mistakes as its own learning curve. This saved money, and customers didn't seem to mind the wait: When Target finally opened its website, it quickly captured market share from both Kmart and Walmart Internet shoppers. Forrester Research Internet analyst Stephen Zrike commented, "There's no question, in our mind, that Target has a far better understanding of how consumers buy online."

Examples of products currently in the introductory stages of the industry life cycle include electric vehicles, solar panels, and high-definition television (HDTV).

Strategies in the Growth Stage

The **growth stage** is characterized by strong increases in sales. Such potential attracts other rivals. In the growth stage, the primary key to success is to build consumer preferences for specific brands. This requires strong brand recognition, differentiated products, and the financial resources to support a variety of value-chain activities such as marketing and sales, and research and development. Whereas marketing and sales initiatives were mainly directed at spurring *aggregate* demand—that is, demand for all such products in the introduction stage—efforts in the growth stage are directed toward stimulating *selective* demand, in which a firm's product offerings are chosen instead of a rival's.

Revenues increase at an accelerating rate because (1) new consumers are trying the product and (2) a growing proportion of satisfied consumers are making repeat purchases.[70] In general, as a product moves through its life cycle, the proportion of repeat buyers to new purchasers increases. Conversely, new products and services often fail if there are relatively few repeat purchases. For example, Alberto-Culver introduced Mr. Culver's Sparklers, which were solid air fresheners that looked like stained glass. Although the product quickly went from the introductory to the growth stage, sales collapsed. Why? Unfortunately, there were few repeat purchasers because buyers treated them as inexpensive window decorations, left them there, and felt little need to purchase new ones. Examples of products currently in the growth stage include Internet servers and personal digital assistants (e.g., Palm Pilots).

> **growth stage** the second stage of the product life cycle, characterized by (1) strong increases in sales; (2) growing competition; (3) developing brand recognition; and (4) a need for financing complementary value-chain activities such as marketing, sales, customer service, and research and development.

Strategies in the Maturity Stage

In the **maturity stage** aggregate industry demand softens. As markets become saturated, there are few new adopters. It's no longer possible to "grow around" the competition, so direct competition becomes predominant.[71] With few attractive prospects, marginal competitors exit the market. At the same time, rivalry among existing rivals intensifies because of fierce price competition at the same time that expenses associated with attracting new buyers are rising. Advantages based on efficient manufacturing operations and process engineering become more important for keeping costs low as customers become more price sensitive. It also becomes more difficult for firms to differentiate their offerings, because users have a greater understanding of products and services.

An article in *Fortune* magazine that addressed the intensity of rivalry in mature markets was aptly titled "A Game of Inches." It stated, "Battling for market share in a slowing industry can be a mighty dirty business. Just ask laundry soap archrivals Unilever and Procter & Gamble."[72] These two firms have been locked in a battle for market share since 1965. Why is the competition so intense? There is not much territory to gain and industry sales were flat. An analyst noted, "People aren't getting any dirtier." Thus, the only way to win is to take market share from the competition. To increase its share, Procter & Gamble (P&G) spends $100 million a year promoting its Tide brand on television, billboards, buses, magazines, and the Internet. But Unilever isn't standing still. Armed with an $80 million budget, it launched a soap tablet product named Wisk Dual Action Tablets. For example, it delivered samples of this product to 24 million U.S. homes in Sunday

> **maturity stage** the third stage of the product life cycle, characterized by (1) slowing demand growth, (2) saturated markets, (3) direct competition, (4) price competition, and (5) strategic emphasis on efficient operations.

strategy spotlight   5.6

Reverse and Breakaway Positioning: How to Avoid Being Held Hostage to the Life-Cycle Curve

When firms adopt a reverse or breakaway positioning strategy, there is typically no pretense about what they are trying to accomplish. In essence, they subvert convention through unconventional promotions, prices, and attributes. That becomes a large part of their appeal—a cleverly positioned product offering. Next we discuss Commerce Bank's reverse positioning and Swatch's breakaway positioning.

Commerce Bank

While most banks offer dozens of checking and savings accounts and compete by trying to offer the highest interest rates, Commerce Bank takes a totally different approach. It pays among the lowest rates in its market. Further, it offers a very limited product line—just four checking accounts, for example. One would think that such a stingy approach would seem to scare off customers. However, Commerce Bank has been very successful. Between 1999 and 2005, it expanded from 120 to 373 branches and its total assets have soared from $5.6 billion to $39 billion.

How has it been so successful? It has stripped away all of what customers expect—lots of choices and peak interest rates and it has *reverse positioned* itself as "the most convenient bank in America." It's open seven days a week, including evenings until 8 p.m. You can get a debit card while you wait. And, when it rains, an escort with an umbrella will escort you to your car. Further, the bank offers free coffee, newspapers, and most of the branches

Sources: Moon, Y. 2005. Break Free from the Product Life Cycle. *Harvard Business Review*, 83(5): 87–94; Commerce Bancorp, Inc. *www.hoovers.com*; Swatch. *en.wikipedia.org*; and *www.commercebank.com*.

have free coin-counting machines that customers love (in one recent week, customers fed the machines a total of $28 million in loose change). Not too surprisingly, despite the inferior rates and few choices, new customers are flocking to the bank.

Swatch

Interestingly, the name "Swatch" is often misconstrued as a contraction of the words *Swiss watch*. However, Nicholas Hayek, Chairman, affirms that the original contraction was "Second Watch"—the new watch was introduced as a new concept of watches as casual, fun, and relatively disposable accessories. And therein lies Swatch's *breakaway positioning*.

When Swatch was launched in 1983, Swiss watches were marketed as a form of jewelry. They were serious, expensive, enduring, and discreetly promoted. Once a customer purchased one, it lasted a lifetime. Swatch changed all of that by defining its watches as playful fashion accessories which were showily promoted. They inspired impulse buying—customers would often purchase half a dozen in different designs. Their price—$40 when the brand was introduced—expanded Swatch's reach beyond its default category (watches as high-end jewelry) and moved it into the fashion accessory category, where it has different customers and competitors. Swatch was the official timekeeper of the 1996, 2000, and 2004 Summer Olympics.

Today, The Swatch Group is the largest watch company in the world. It has acquired many brands over the years including Omega, Longines, Calvin Klein, and Hamilton. Revenues have grown to $5.5 billion in 2009 and net income has increased to $753 million. These figures represent compound annual increases of 11 percent and 12 percent, respectively, over a four-year period.

---

reverse positioning a break in industry tendency to continuously augment products, characteristic of the product life cycle, by offering products with fewer product attributes and lower prices.

newspapers, followed by a series of TV ads. P&G launched a counteroffensive with Tide Rapid Action Tablets ads showed in side-by-side comparisons of the two products dropped into beakers of water. In the promotion, P&G claimed that its product is superior because it dissolves faster than Unilever's product.

Although this is only one example, many product classes and industries, including consumer products such as beer, automobiles, and televisions, are in maturity.

Firms do not need to be "held hostage" to the life-cycle curve. By positioning or repositioning their products in unexpected ways, firms can change how customers mentally categorize them. Thus, firms are able to rescue products floundering in the maturity phase of their life cycles and return them to the growth phase.

Two positioning strategies that managers can use to affect consumers' mental shifts are **reverse positioning**, which strips away "sacred" product attributes while adding new ones, and **breakaway positioning,** which associates the product with a radically different category.[73] We discuss each of these positioning strategies below and then provide an example of each in Strategy Spotlight 5.6.

Reverse Positioning   This assumes that although customers may desire more than the baseline product, they don't necessarily want an endless list of features. Such companies make the creative decision to step off the augmentation treadmill and shed product attributes that the rest of the industry considers sacred. Then, once a product is returned to its baseline state, the stripped-down product adds one or more carefully selected attributes that would usually be found only in a highly augmented product. Such an unconventional combination of attributes allows the product to assume a new competitive position within the category and move backward from maturity into a growth position on the life-cycle curve.

Breakaway Positioning   As noted above, with reverse positioning, a product establishes a unique position in its category but retains a clear category membership. However, with breakaway positioning, a product escapes its category by deliberately associating with a different one. Thus, managers leverage the new category's conventions to change both how products are consumed and with whom they compete. Instead of merely seeing the breakaway product as simply an alternative to others in its category, consumers perceive it as altogether different.

When a breakaway product is successful in leaving its category and joining a new one, it is able to redefine its competition. Similar to reverse positioning, this strategy permits the product to shift backward on the life-cycle curve, moving from the rather dismal maturity phase to a thriving growth opportunity.

Strategy Spotlight 5.6 provides examples of reverse and breakaway positioning.

Strategies in the Decline Stage

Although all decisions in the phases of an industry life cycle are important, they become particularly difficult in the **decline stage.** Firms must face up to the fundamental strategic choices of either exiting or staying and attempting to consolidate their position in the industry.[74]

The decline stage occurs when industry sales and profits begin to fall. Typically, changes in the business environment are at the root of an industry or product group entering this stage.[75] Changes in consumer tastes or a technological innovation can push a product into decline. Typewriters have entered into the decline stage because of the word processing capabilities of personal computers. Compact disks have forced cassette tapes into decline in the prerecorded music industry, and digital video disks (DVDs) are replacing compact disks. About 30 years earlier, of course, cassette tapes had led to the demise of long-playing records (LPs).

Products in the decline stage often consume a large share of management time and financial resources relative to their potential worth. Sales and profits decline. Also, competitors may start drastically cutting their prices to raise cash and remain solvent. The situation is further aggravated by the liquidation of assets, including inventory, of some of the competitors that have failed. This further intensifies price competition.

In the decline stage, a firm's strategic options become dependent on the actions of rivals. If many competitors leave the market, sales and profit opportunities increase. On the other hand, prospects are limited if all competitors remain.[76] If some competitors merge, their increased market power may erode the opportunities for the remaining players. Managers must carefully monitor the actions and intentions of competitors before deciding on a course of action.

Four basic strategies are available in the decline phase: *maintaining, harvesting, exiting,* or *consolidating.*[77]

breakaway positioning a break in industry tendency to incrementally improve products along specific dimensions, characteristic of the product life cycle, by offering products that are still in the industry but that are perceived by customers as being different.

decline stage the fourth stage of the product life cycle, characterized by (1) falling sales and profits, (2) increasing price competition, and (3) industry consolidation.

- *Maintaining* refers to keeping a product going without significantly reducing marketing support, technological development, or other investments, in the hope that competitors will eventually exit the market. Many offices, for example, still use typewriters for filling out forms and other purposes that cannot be completed on a PC. In some rural areas, rotary (or dial) telephones persist because of the older technology used in central switching offices. Thus, there may still be the potential for revenues and profits.

harvesting strategy a strategy of wringing as much profit as possible out of a business in the short to medium term by reducing costs.

- *Harvesting* involves obtaining as much profit as possible and requires that costs be reduced quickly. Managers should consider the firm's value-creating activities and cut associated budgets. Value-chain activities to consider are primary (e.g., operations, sales and marketing) and support (e.g., procurement, technology development). The objective is to wring out as much profit as possible.

- *Exiting the market* involves dropping the product from a firm's portfolio. Since a residual core of consumers exist, eliminating it should be carefully considered. If the firm's exit involves product markets that affect important relationships with other product markets in the corporation's overall portfolio, an exit could have repercussions for the whole corporation. For example, it may involve the loss of valuable brand names or human capital with a broad variety of expertise in many value-creating activities such as marketing, technology, and operations.

consolidation strategy a firm's acquiring or merging with other firms in an industry in order to enhance market power and gain valuable assets.

- *Consolidation* involves one firm acquiring at a reasonable price the best of the surviving firms in an industry. This enables firms to enhance market power and acquire valuable assets. One example of a consolidation strategy took place in the defense industry in the early 1990s. As the cliché suggests, "peace broke out" at the end of the Cold War and overall U.S. defense spending levels plummeted.[78] Many companies that make up the defense industry saw more than 50 percent of their market disappear. Only one-quarter of the 120,000 companies that once supplied the Department of Defense still serve in that capacity; the others have shut down their defense business or dissolved altogether. But one key player, Lockheed Martin, became a dominant rival by pursuing an aggressive strategy of consolidation. During the 1990s, it purchased 17 independent entities, including General Dynamics' tactical aircraft and space systems divisions, GE Aerospace, Goodyear Aerospace, and Honeywell ElectroOptics. These combinations enabled Lockheed Martin to emerge as the top provider to three governmental customers: the Department of Defense, the Department of Energy, and NASA.

Examples of products currently in the decline stage of the industry life cycle include automotive spark plugs (replaced by electronic fuel ignition), videocassette recorders (replaced by digital video disk recorders), and personal computer zip drives (replaced by compact disk read-write drives). And, as we mentioned previously, compact disks are being replaced by digital video disks (DVDs).

The introduction of new technologies and associated products does not always mean that old technologies quickly fade away. Research shows that in a number of cases, old technologies actually enjoy a very profitable "last gasp."[79] Examples include mainframe computers (versus minicomputers and PCs), coronary artery bypass graft surgery (versus angioplasty), and CISC (Complex Instruction Set Computing) architecture in computer processors versus RISC (Reduced Instruction Set Computing). In each case, the advent of new technology prompted predictions of the demise of the older technology, but each of these has proved to be resilient survivors. What accounts for their continued profitability and survival?

Retreating to more defensible ground is one strategy that firms specializing in technologies threatened with rapid obsolescence have followed. For example, while angioplasty may be appropriate for relatively healthier patients with blocked arteries, sicker, higher-risk patients seem to benefit more from coronary artery bypass graft surgery. This enabled the surgeons to concentrate on the more difficult cases and improve the technology itself. The advent of television unseated the radio as the major source of entertainment from American homes. However, the radio has survived and even thrived in venues where people are also engaged in other activities, such as driving.

Using the new to improve the old is a second approach. Carburetor manufacturers have improved the fuel efficiency of their product by incorporating electronic controls that were originally developed for electronic fuel injection systems. Similarly, CISC computer chip manufacturers have adopted many features from RISC chips.

Improving the price-performance trade-off is a third approach. IBM continues to make money selling mainframes long after their obituary was written. It retooled the technology using low-cost microprocessors and cut their prices drastically. Further, it invested and updated the software, enabling them to offer clients such as banks better performance and lower costs.

Clearly, "last gasps" may not necessarily translate into longer term gains, as the experience of the integrated steel mills suggests. When the first mini-mills appeared, integrated steel mills shifted to higher margin steel, but eventually mini-mills entered even the last strongholds of the integrated steel mills.

Turnaround Strategies

A **turnaround strategy** involves reversing performance decline and reinvigorating growth toward profitability.[80] A need for turnaround may occur at any stage in the life cycle but is more likely to occur during maturity or decline.

> **turnaround strategy** a strategy that reverses a firm's decline in performance and returns it to growth and profitability.

Most turnarounds require a firm to carefully analyze the external and internal environments.[81] The external analysis leads to identification of market segments or customer groups that may still find the product attractive.[82] Internal analysis results in actions aimed at reduced costs and higher efficiency. A firm needs to undertake a mix of both internally and externally oriented actions to effect a turnaround.[83] In effect, the cliché "you can't shrink yourself to greatness" applies.

A study of 260 mature businesses in need of a turnaround identified three strategies used by successful companies.[84]

> **>LO5.8**
> The need for turnaround strategies that enable a firm to reposition its competitive position in an industry.

- *Asset and cost surgery.* Very often, mature firms tend to have assets that do not produce any returns. These include real estate, buildings, etc. Outright sales or sale and leaseback free up considerable cash and improve returns. Investment in new plants and equipment can be deferred. Firms in turnaround situations try to aggressively cut administrative expenses and inventories and speed up collection of receivables. Costs also can be reduced by outsourcing production of various inputs for which market prices may be cheaper than in-house production costs.
- *Selective product and market pruning.* Most mature or declining firms have many product lines that are losing money or are only marginally profitable. One strategy is to discontinue such product lines and focus all resources on a few core profitable areas. For example, in the early 1980s, faced with possible bankruptcy, Chrysler Corporation sold off all its nonautomotive businesses as well as all its production facilities abroad. Focus on the North American market and identification of a profitable niche—namely, minivans—were keys to their eventual successful turnaround.
- *Piecemeal productivity improvements.* There are many ways in which a firm can eliminate costs and improve productivity. Although individually these are small gains, they cumulate over a period of time to substantial gains. Improving business processes by reengineering them, benchmarking specific activities against industry leaders, encouraging employee input to identify excess costs, increasing capacity utilization, and improving employee productivity lead to a significant overall gain.

Software maker Intuit is a case of a quick but well-implemented turnaround strategy. After stagnating and stumbling during the dot-com boom, Intuit, which is known for

strategy spotlight   5.7

Alan Mulally: Leading Ford's Extraordinary Turnaround

Shortly after Alan Mulally took over as Ford's CEO in September 2006, he organized a weekly meeting with his senior managers and asked them how things were going. Fine, fine, fine were the responses from around the table. To this, an incredulous Mulally exclaimed: "We are forecasting a $17 billion loss and no one has any problems!" Clearly, there were cultural issues at play (such as denial and executive rivalry) but also very serious strategic and financial problems as well.

What a change a few years can make! Ford's profits for 2010 were $6.6 billion and the firm has enjoyed seven straight quarters of profitability. This is quite a sharp contrast from its $14.7 billion loss in 2008—a time when high gasoline prices, bloated operations, and uncompetitive labor costs combined with the deep recession to create a perfect storm.

How did Mulally turn Ford around? It took many tough strategic decisions—involving not just company executives but Ford staff and the United Auto Workers (UAW). It involved downsizing, creating greater efficiency, improving quality, selling off the European luxury brands, and mortgaging assets to raise money. Ford's leaders and the United Auto Workers (UAW) also made transformational changes to lower the company's cost structure—a critical component to the company's long-term competitiveness.

Let's take a closer look at Mulally's strategic actions. We have to begin with the plan to undertake a dramatic refinancing of the business by raising bank loans secured against the company's assets. One of his first tasks was to finalize Ford's recovery plan and sell it to the banks. This financing enabled Ford to be the only major American automaker that avoided government-sponsored bankruptcy. And, as noted by Mulally, "The response that we received because we did not ask for the precious taxpayer's money has been tremendous." In fact, Jim Farley, head of marketing for Ford worldwide, estimates that Ford's standing on its own feet has been worth $1 billion in favorable publicity for the company and has attracted appreciative Americans into its dealers' showrooms.

Second, he decided that the firm would concentrate resources on the Ford brand and sell off the Premier Automotive Group (PAG) businesses—even if it meant taking a loss. Mulally had ridiculed the idea that top management could focus on Jaguar before breakfast, attend to Volvo or Land Rover before lunch, and then consider Ford and its Lincoln offshoot in North America in the afternoon. Accordingly, in 2007, Aston Martin was sold to private investors; Jaguar and Land Rover were sold to India's Tata Group in 2008; and a Chinese carmaker, Geely, bought Volvo in 2010. Further, the Mercury brand is being phased out.

Third, Mulally realized that in addition to fewer brands, Ford needed a much narrower range of cars, albeit higher quality ones, carrying its familiar blue oval logo in all segments of the market. At one point Ford's designers had to deal with 97 different models—that was cut to 36 and may go lower.

Fourth, along with rationalizing the product range, Mulally insisted on raising the aspiration level with regard to quality. Although Ford used to talk about claiming parity with Toyota's Camry, Mulally shifted the emphasis to trying to make each car that Ford sells "best in class." A number of new cars being created under the One Ford policy are coming from Europe. Quality has improved dramatically according to some of the industry's outside arbiters, such as J. D. Power.

Fifth, to ensure that regional stars such as the Focus could become global successes, 8 of Ford's 10 platforms (the floor pan and its underpinnings) are now global platforms. More shared platforms enables Ford to build different models more quickly and economically to account for regional tastes in cars and variations in regulations. For example, the various Fiesta-based cars may look different, but they share about two-thirds of their parts. Such actions are particularly important as Ford focuses (no pun intended) its efforts toward smaller, more fuel-efficient automobiles which traditionally have smaller margins. As noted by Lewis Booth, Ford's finance director, "Customers' tastes are converging. Fuel efficiency matters everywhere."

Sixth, Mulally had to make many painful restructuring decisions in order to match production to the number of cars that Ford could sell. Since 2006, Ford cut half of its shop-floor workforce in North America and a third of its office jobs. By the end of 2011, a total of 17 factories will have closed, and Ford's total employment will have fallen from 128,000 to 75,000. In addition, the number of dealers has been cut by a fifth. Helped by union concessions, Ford has shed about $14 billion in annual operational costs and now can compete with Japan's "transplant" factories in America.

Regarding Ford's successful transformation, Mulally cliams: "We have earned the right now to make a complete family of best-in-class vehicles right here in the United States with U.S. workers and competing with the very best in the world. That's not only good for Ford and our customers and our stakeholders but that's good for the United States of America." Without doubt, such a statement a few years ago would have been dismissed as hyperbole.

Sources: Linn, A. 2010. For Ford's Mulally, big bets are paying off. www. msnbc.com. October 26: nd; Anonymous. 2010. Epiphany in Dearborn. The Economist. December 11: 83–85; Reagan, J. Ford Motor's extraordinary turnaround. December 10: np; and www.finance.yahoo.com.

its Quickbook and Turbotax software, hired Stephen M. Bennett, a 22-year GE veteran, in 1999. He immediately discontinued Intuit's online finance, insurance, and bill-paying operations that were losing money. Instead, he focused on software for small businesses that employ less than 250 people. He also instituted a performance-based reward system that greatly improved employee productivity. Within a few years, Intuit was once again making substantial profits and its stock was up 42 percent.[85]

Even when an industry is in overall decline, pockets of profitability remain. These are segments with customers who are relatively price insensitive. For example, the replacement demand for vacuum tubes affords its manufacturers an opportunity to earn above normal returns although the product itself is technologically obsolete. Surprisingly, within declining industries, there may still be segments that are either stable or growing. Although fountain pens ceased to be the writing instrument of choice a long time ago, the fountain pen industry has successfully reconceptualized the product as a high margin luxury item that signals accomplishment and success. In the final analysis, every business has the potential for rejuvenation. But it takes creativity, persistence, and most of all a clear strategy to translate that potential into reality.

Strategy Spotlight 5.7 discusses Ford's remarkable turnaround under the direction of CEO Alan Mulally.

Reflecting on Career Implications . . .

- *Types of Competitive Advantage:* Always be aware of your organization's business-level strategy. What do you do to help your firm either increase differentiation or lower costs? What are some ways that your role in the firm can help realize these outcomes?
- *Combining Sources of Competitive Advantage:* Are you engaged in activities that simultaneously help your organization increase differentiation and lower costs?
- *Industry Life Cycle:* If your firm is in the mature stage of the industry life cycle, can you think of ways to enhance your firm's level of differentiation in order to make customers less price sensitive to your organization's goods and services?
- *Industry Life Cycle:* If you sense that your career is maturing (or in the decline phase!), what actions can you take to restore career growth and momentum (e.g., training, mentoring, professional networking)? Should you actively consider professional opportunities in other industries?

Summary

How and why firms outperform each other goes to the heart of strategic management. In this chapter, we identified three generic strategies and discussed how firms are able not only to attain advantages over competitors, but also to sustain such advantages over time. Why do some advantages become long-lasting while others are quickly imitated by competitors?

The three generic strategies—overall cost leadership, differentiation, and focus—form the core of this chapter. We began by providing a brief description of each

generic strategy (or competitive advantage) and furnished examples of firms that have successfully implemented these strategies. Successful generic strategies invariably enhance a firm's position vis-à-vis the five forces of that industry—a point that we stressed and illustrated with examples. However, as we pointed out, there are pitfalls to each of the generic strategies. Thus, the sustainability of a firm's advantage is always challenged because of imitation or substitution by new or existing rivals. Such competitor moves erode a firm's advantage over time.

We also discussed the viability of combining (or integrating) overall cost leadership and generic differentiation strategies. If successful, such integration can enable a firm to enjoy superior performance and improve its competitive position. However, this is challenging, and managers must be aware of the potential downside risks associated with such an initiative.

We addressed the challenges inherent in determining the sustainability of competitive advantages. Drawing on an example from a manufacturing industry, we discussed both the "pro" and "con" positions as to why competitive advantages are sustainable over a long period of time.

The way companies formulate and deploy strategies is changing because of the impact of the Internet and digital technologies in many industries. Further, Internet technologies are enabling the mass customization capabilities of greater numbers of competitors. Focus strategies are likely to increase in importance because the Internet provides highly targeted and lower-cost access to narrow or specialized markets. These strategies are not without their pitfalls, however, and firms need to understand the dangers as well as the potential benefits of Internet-based approaches.

The concept of the industry life cycle is a critical contingency that managers must take into account in striving to create and sustain competitive advantages. We identified the four stages of the industry life cycle—introduction, growth, maturity, and decline—and suggested how these stages can play a role in decisions that managers must make at the business level. These include overall strategies as well as the relative emphasis on functional areas and value—creating activities.

When a firm's performance severely erodes, turn-around strategies are needed to reverse its situation and enhance its competitive position. We have discussed three approaches—asset cost surgery, selective product and market pruning, and piecemeal productivity improvements.

Summary Review Questions

1. Explain why the concept of competitive advantage is central to the study of strategic management.
2. Briefly describe the three generic strategies—overall cost leadership, differentiation, and focus.
3. Explain the relationship between the three generic strategies and the five forces that determine the average profitability within an industry.
4. What are some of the ways in which a firm can attain a successful turnaround strategy?
5. Describe some of the pitfalls associated with each of the three generic strategies.

6. Can firms combine the generic strategies of overall cost leadership and differentiation? Why or why not?
7. Explain why the industry life cycle concept is an important factor in determining a firm's business-level strategy.

Key Terms

business-level strategy, 162
generic strategies, 162
overall cost leadership, 164
experience curve, 165
competitive parity, 166
differentiation strategy, 169
focus strategy, 174
combination strategies, 176
mass customization, 176
profit pool, 177
digital technologies, 182
disintermediation, 183
industry life cycle, 187
introduction stage, 187
growth stage, 189
maturity stage, 189
reverse positioning, 190
breakaway positioning, 191
decline stage, 191
consolidation strategy, 192
harvesting strategy, 192
turnaround strategy, 193

Experiential Exercise

What are some examples of primary and support activities that enable Nucor, a $19 billion steel manufacturer, to achieve a low-cost strategy? (Fill in table on the following page.)

Application Questions Exercises

1. Go to the Internet and look up www.walmart.com. How has this firm been able to combine overall cost leadership and differentiation strategies?
2. Choose a firm with which you are familiar in your local business community. Is the firm successful in following one (or more) generic strategies? Why or why not? What do you think are some of the challenges it faces in implementing these strategies in an effective manner?
3. Think of a firm that has attained a differentiation focus or cost focus strategy. Are their advantages sustainable? Why? Why not? (*Hint:* Consider its position vis-à-vis Porter's five forces.)
4. Think of a firm that successfully achieved a combination overall cost leadership and differentiation strategy. What can be learned from this example? Are these advantages sustainable? Why? Why not? (*Hint:* Consider its competitive position vis-à-vis Porter's five forces.)

Value-Chain Activity	Yes/No	How Does Nucor Create Value for the Customer?
Primary:		
Inbound logistics		
Operations		
Outbound logistics		
Marketing and sales		
Service		
Support:		
Procurement		
Technology development		
Human resource management		
General administration		

Ethics Questions

1. Can you think of a company that suffered ethical consequences as a result of an overemphasis on a cost leadership strategy? What do you think were the financial and nonfinancial implications?

2. In the introductory stage of the product life cycle, what are some of the unethical practices that managers could engage in to enhance their firm's market position? What could be some of the long-term implications of such actions?

References

1. Helm, B. 2010. At KFC, a battle among the chicken-hearted. *Bloomberg Businessweek.* August 16: 19; De Nies, Y. 2010. Kentucky fried fight. *www. abcnews.go.com.* August 17: np; and Morran, C. 2010. Squabble between KFC & franchisees over advertising goes to court. *www.consumerist.com.* September 20: np. We thank Jason Hirsch for his valued contributions.

2. For a recent perspective by Porter on competitive strategy, refer to Porter, M. E. 1996. What is strategy? *Harvard Business Review,* 74(6): 61–78.

3. For insights into how a start-up is using solar technology, see: Gimbel, B. 2009. Plastic power. *Fortune,* February 2: 34.

4. Useful insights on strategy in an economic downturn are in: Rhodes, D. & Stelter, D. 2009. Seize advantage in a downturn. *Harvard Business Review,* 87(2): 50–58.

5. Some useful ideas on maintaining competitive advantages can be found in Ma, H. & Karri, R. 2005. Leaders beware: Some sure ways to lose your competitive advantage. *Organizational Dynamics,* 343(1): 63–76.

6. Miller, A. & Dess, G. G. 1993. Assessing Porter's model in terms of its generalizability, accuracy, and simplicity. *Journal of Management Studies,* 30(4): 553–585.

7. Cendrowski, S. 2008. Extreme retailing. *Fortune,* March 31: 14.

8. For insights on how discounting can erode a firm's performance, read: Stibel, J. M. & Delgrosso, P. 2008. Discounts can be dangerous. *Harvard Business Review,* 66(12): 31.

9. For a scholarly discussion and analysis of the concept of competitive parity, refer to Powell, T. C. 2003. Varieties of competitive parity. *Strategic Management Journal,* 24(1): 61–86.

10. Rao, A. R., Bergen, M. E., & Davis, S. 2000. How to fight a price war. *Harvard Business Review,* 78(2): 107–120.

11. Marriot, J. W. Jr. Our competitive strength: Human capital. A speech given to the Detroit Economic Club on October 2, 2000.

12. Whalen, C. J., Pascual, A. M., Lowery, T., & Muller, J. 2001. The top 25 managers. *BusinessWeek,* January 8: 63.

13. Ibid.

14. For an interesting perspective on the need for creative strategies, refer to Hamel, G. & Prahalad, C. K. 1994. *Competing for the future.* Boston: Harvard Business School Press.

15. Interesting insights on Walmart's effective cost leadership strategy are found in: Palmeri, C. 2008. Wal-Mart is up for this downturn. *Business-Week,* November 6: 34.

16. An interesting perspective on the dangers of price discounting is: Mohammad, R. 2011. Ditch the discounts. *Harvard Business Review,* 89 (1/2): 23–25.

17. Dholakia, U. M. 2011. Why employees can wreck promotional offers. *Harvard Business Review,* 89(1/2): 28.

18. Jacobs, A. 2010. Workers in China voting with their feet. *International Herald Tribune.* July 13: 1, 14.

19. For a perspective on the sustainability of competitive advantages, refer to

Barney, J. 1995. Looking inside for competitive advantage. *Academy of Management Executive,* 9(4): 49–61.

20. Thornton, E., 2001, Why e-brokers are broker and broker. *BusinessWeek,* January 22: 94.

21. Mohammed, R. 2011. Ditch the discounts. *Harvard Business Review,* 89(1/2): 23–25.

22. Koretz, G. 2001. E-commerce: The buyer wins. *BusinessWeek,* January 8: 30.

23. For an "ultimate" in differentiated services, consider time shares in exotic automobiles such as Lamborghinis and Bentleys. Refer to: Stead, D. 2008. My Lamborghini—today, anyway. *BusinessWeek,* January 18:17.

24. For an interesting perspective on the value of corporate brands and how they may be leveraged, refer to Aaker, D. A. 2004, *California Management Review,* 46(3): 6–18.

25. A unique perspective on differentiation strategies is: Austin, R. D. 2008. High margins and the quest for aesthetic coherence. *Harvard Business Review,* 86(1): 18–19.

26. MacMillan, I. & McGrath, R. 1997. Discovering new points of differentiation. *Harvard Business Review,* 75(4): 133–145; Wise, R. & Baumgarter, P. 1999. Beating the clock: Corporate responses to rapid change in the PC industry. *California Management Review,* 42(1): 8–36.

27. For a discussion on quality in terms of a company's software and information systems, refer to Prahalad, C. K. & Krishnan, M. S. 1999. The new meaning of quality in the information age. *Harvard Business Review,* 77(5): 109–118.

28. The role of design in achieving differentiation is addressed in: Brown, T. 2008. Design thinking. *Harvard Business Review.* 86(6): 84–92.

29. Taylor, A., III. 2001. Can you believe Porsche is putting its badge on this car? *Fortune,* February 19: 168–172.

30. Ward, S., Light, L., & Goldstine, J. 1999. What high-tech managers need to know about brands. *Harvard Business Review,* 77(4): 85–95.

31. Rosenfeld, J. 2000. Unit of one. *Fast Company,* April: 98.

32. Markides, C. 1997. Strategic innovation. *Sloan Management Review,* 38(3): 9–23.

33. Bonnabeau, E., Bodick, N., & Armstrong, R. W. 2008. A more rational approach to new-product development. *Harvard Business Review.* 66(3): 96–102.

34. Insights on Google's innovation are in: Iyer, B. & Davenport, T. H. 2008. Reverse engineering Google's innovation machine. *Harvard Business Review.* 66(4): 58–68.

35. A discussion of how a firm used technology to create product differentiation is in: Mehta, S. N. 2009. Under Armor reboots. *Fortune.* February 2: 29–33 (5)

36. Bertini, M. & Wathieu, L. 2010. How to stop customers from fixating on price. *Harvard Business Review,* 88(5): 84–91.

37. The authors would like to thank Scott Droege, a faculty member at Western Kentucky University, for providing this example.

38. Dixon, M., Freeman, K. & Toman, N. 2010. Stop trying to delight your customers. *Harvard Business Review,* 88(7/8).

39. Flint, J. 2004. Stop the nerds. *Forbes,* July 5: 80; and, Fahey, E. 2004. Over-engineering 101. *Forbes,* December 13: 62.

40. Symonds, W. C. 2000. Can Gillette regain its voltage? *BusinessWeek,* October 16: 102–104.

41. Caplan, J. 2006. In a real crunch. *Inside Business,* July: A37–A38.

42. Gadiesh, O. & Gilbert, J. L. 1998. Profit pools: A fresh look at strategy. *Harvard Business Review,* 76(3): 139–158.

43. Colvin, G. 2000. Beware: You could soon be selling soybeans. *Fortune,* November 13: 80.

44. Whalen et al., op. cit.: 63. Porter, M. E. 2008. The five competitive forces that shape strategy. *Harvard Business Review,* 86(1): 78–97; and *www.finance.yahoo.com.*

45. Hall, W. K. 1980. Survival strategies in a hostile environment, *Harvard Business Review,* 58: 75–87; on the paint and allied products industry, see Dess, G. G. & Davis, P. S. 1984. Porter's (1980) generic strategies as determinants of strategic group membership and organizational performance. *Academy of Management Journal,* 27: 467–488; for the Korean electronics industry, see Kim, L. & Lim, Y. 1988. Environment, generic strategies, and performance in a rapidly developing country: A taxonomic approach. *Academy of Management Journal,* 31: 802–827; Wright, P., Hotard, D., Kroll, M., Chan, P., & Tanner, J. 1990. Performance and multiple strategies in a firm: Evidence from the apparel industry. In Dean, B. V. & Cassidy, J. C. (Eds.). *Strategic management: Methods and studies:* 93–110. Amsterdam: Elsevier-North Holland; and Wright, P., Kroll, M., Tu, H., & Helms, M. 1991. Generic strategies and business performance: An empirical study of the screw machine products industry. *British Journal of Management,* 2: 1–9.

46. Gilmore, J. H. & Pine, B. J., II. 1997. The four faces of customization. *Harvard Business Review,* 75(1): 91–101.

47. Heracleous, L. & Wirtz, J. 2010. Singapore Airlines' balancing act. *Harvard Business Review,* 88(7/8): 145–149.

48. Gilmore & Pine, op. cit. For interesting insights on mass customization, refer to Cattani, K., Dahan, E., & Schmidt, G. 2005. Offshoring versus "spackling." *MIT Sloan Management Review,* 46(3): 6–7.

49. Goodstein, L. D. & Butz, H. E. 1998. Customer value: The linchpin of organizational change. *Organizational Dynamics,* Summer: 21–34.

50. Randall, T., Terwiesch, C., & Ulrich, K. T. 2005. Principles for user design of customized products. *California Management Review,* 47(4): 68–85.

51. Gadiesh & Gilbert, op. cit.: 139–158.

52. Insights on the profit pool concept are addressed in: Reinartz, W. & Ulaga, W. 2008. How to sell services more profitably. *Harvard Business Review,* 66(5): 90–96.

53. This example draws on Dess & Picken. 1997. op. cit.

54. A rigorous and thorough discussion of the threats faced by industries due to the commoditization of products and services and what strategic actions firm should consider is found

in: D'Aveni, R. A. 2010. *Beating the commodity trap.* Boston: Harvard Business Press.

55. For an insightful, recent discussion on the difficulties and challenges associated with creating advantages that are sustainable for any reasonable period of time and suggested strategies, refer to: D'Aveni, R. A., Dagnino, G. B. & Smith, K. G. 2010. The age of temporary advantage. *Strategic Management Journal.* 31(13): 1371–1385. This is the lead article in a special issue of this journal that provides many ideas that are useful to both academics and practicing managers. For an additional examination of declining advantage in technologically intensive industries, see: Vaaler, P. M. & McNamara, G. 2010. Are technology-intensive industries more dynamically competitive? No and yes. *Organization Science.* 21: 271–289.

56. Rita McGrath provides some interesting ideas on possible strategies for firms facing highly uncertain competitive environments: McGrath, R. G. 2011. When your business model is in trouble. *Harvard Business Review,* 89(1/2); 96–98.

57. The Atlas Door example draws on: Stalk, G., Jr. 1988. Time—the next source of competitive advantage. *Harvard Business Review,* 66(4): 41–51.

58. Edelman, D. C. 2010. Branding in the digital age. *Harvard Business Review,* 88(12): 62–69.

59. Seybold, P. 2000. Niches bring riches. *Business 2.0,* June 13: 135.

60. Greenspan, R. 2004. Net drives profits to small biz. ClickZ.com, March 25, *www.clickz.com.* Greenspan, R. 2002. Small biz benefits from Internet tools. ClickZ.com, March 28, *www.clickz.com.*

61. Burns, E. 2006. Executives slow to see value of corporate blogging. ClickZ. com, May 9, *www.clickz.com.*

62. Empirical support for the use of combination strategies in an e-business context can be found in Kim, E., Nam, D., & Stimpert, J. L. 2004. The applicability of Porter's generic strategies in the Digital Age: Assumptions,

conjectures, and suggestions. *Journal of Management,* 30(5): 569–589.

63. Porter, M. E. 2001. Strategy and the Internet. *Harvard Business Review,* 79: 63–78.

64. For an interesting perspective on the influence of the product life cycle and rate of technological change on competitive strategy, refer to Lei, D. & Slocum, J. W. Jr. 2005. Strategic and organizational requirements for competitive advantage. *Academy of Management Executive,* 19(1): 31–45.

65. Dickson, P. R. 1994. *Marketing management:* 293. Fort Worth, TX: Dryden Press; Day, G. S. 1981. The product life cycle: Analysis and application. *Journal of Marketing Research,* 45: 60–67.

66. Bearden, W. O., Ingram, T. N., & LaForge, R. W. 1995. *Marketing principles and practices.* Burr Ridge, IL: Irwin.

67. MacMillan, I. C. 1985. Preemptive strategies. In Guth, W. D. (Ed.). *Handbook of business strategy:* 9-1–9-22. Boston: Warren, Gorham & Lamont; Pearce, J. A. & Robinson, R. B. 2000. *Strategic management* (7th ed.). New York: McGraw-Hill; Dickson, op. cit.: 295–296.

68. Bartlett, C. A. & Ghoshal, S. 2000. Going global: Lessons for late movers. *Harvard Business Review,* 78(2): 132–142.

69. Neuborne, E. 2000. E-tailers hit the relaunch key. *BusinessWeek,* October 17: 62.

70. Berkowitz, E. N., Kerin, R. A., & Hartley, S. W. 2000. *Marketing* (6th ed.). New York: McGraw-Hill.

71. MacMillan, op. cit.

72. Brooker, K. 2001. A game of inches. *Fortune,* February 5: 98–100.

73. Our discussion of reverse and breakaway positioning draws on Moon, Y. 2005. Break free from the product life cycle. *Harvard Business Review,* 83(5): 87–94. This article also discusses stealth positioning as a means of overcoming consumer resistance and advancing a product from the introduction to the growth phase.

74. MacMillan, op. cit.

75. Berkowitz et al., op. cit.

76. Bearden et al., op. cit.

77. The discussion of these four strategies draws on MacMillan, op. cit.; Berkowitz et al., op. cit.; and Bearden et al., op. cit.

78. Augustine, N. R. 1997. Reshaping an industry: Lockheed Martin's survival story. *Harvard Business Review,* 75(3): 83–94.

79. Snow, D. C. 2008. Beware of old technologies' last gasps. *Harvard Business Review,* January: 17–18. Lohr, S. 2008. Why old technologies are still kicking. *New York Times,* March 23: np; and McGrath, R. G. 2008. Innovation and the last gasps of dying technologies. ritamcgrath.com, March 18: np.

80. Coyne, K. P., Coyne, S. T. & Coyne, E. J. Sr. 2010. When you've got to cut costs—now. *Harvard Business Review,* 88(5): 74–83.

81. A study that draws on the resource-based view of the firm to investigate successful turnaround strategies is: Morrow, J. S., Sirmon, D. G., Hitt, M. A., & Holcomb, T. R. 2007. *Strategic Management Journal,* 28(3): 271–284.

82. For a study investigating the relationship between organizational restructuring and acquisition performance, refer to: Barkema, H. G. & Schijven, M. Toward unlocking the full potential of acquisitions: The role of organizational restructuring. *Academy of Management Journal,* 51(4): 696–722.

83. For some useful ideas on effective turnarounds and handling downsizings, refer to Marks, M. S. & De Meuse, K. P. 2005. Resizing the organization: Maximizing the gain while minimizing the pain of layoffs, divestitures and closings. *Organizational Dynamics,* 34(1): 19–36,

84. Hambrick, D. C. & Schecter, S. M. 1983. Turnaround strategies for mature industrial product business units. *Academy of Management Journal,* 26(2): 231–248.

85. Mullaney, T. J. 2002. The wizard of Intuit. *BusinessWeek,* October 28: 60–63.

Chapter 6. Corporate-Level Strategy: Creating Value through Diversification

chapter SIX

Corporate-Level Strategy:

Creating Value through Diversification

After reading this chapter, you should have a good understanding of:

LO6.1 The reasons for the failure of many diversification efforts.

LO6.2 How managers can create value through diversification initiatives.

LO6.3 How corporations can use related diversification to achieve synergistic benefits through economies of scope and market power.

LO6.4 How corporations can use unrelated diversification to attain synergistic benefits through corporate restructuring, parenting, and portfolio analysis.

LO6.5 The various means of engaging in diversification—mergers and acquisitions, joint ventures/strategic alliances, and internal development.

LO6.6 Managerial behaviors that can erode the creation of value.

LEARNING OBJECTIVES

Corporate-level strategy addresses two related issues: (1) what businesses should a corporation compete in, and (2) how can these businesses be managed so they create "synergy"—that is, more value by working together than if they were freestanding units? As we will see, these questions present a key challenge for today's managers. Many diversification efforts fail or, in many cases, provide only marginal returns to shareholders. Thus, determining how to create value through entering new markets, introducing new products, or developing new technologies is a vital issue in strategic management.

We begin by discussing why diversification initiatives, in general, have not yielded the anticipated benefits. Then, in the next three sections of the chapter, we explore the two key alternative approaches: related and unrelated diversification. With related diversification, corporations strive to enter product markets that share some resources and capabilities with their existing business units or increase their market power. Here we suggest four means of creating value: leveraging core competencies, sharing activities, pooled negotiating power, and vertical integration. With unrelated diversification, there are few similarities in the resources and capabilities among the firm's business units, but value can be created in multiple ways. These include restructuring, corporate parenting, and portfolio analysis approaches. Whereas the synergies to be realized with related diversification come from *horizontal relationships* among the business units, the synergies from unrelated diversification are derived from *hierarchical relationships* between the corporate office and the business units.

The last two sections address (1) the various means that corporations can use to achieve diversification and (2) managerial behaviors (e.g., self-interest) that serve to erode shareholder value. We address mergers and acquisitions (M&A), divestitures, joint ventures/strategic alliances, and internal development. Each of these involves the evaluation of important trade-offs. Detrimental managerial behaviors, often guided by a manager's self-interest, are "growth for growth's sake," egotism, and antitakeover tactics. Some of these behaviors raise ethical issues because managers, in some cases, are not acting in the best interests of a firm's shareholders.

Learning from Mistakes

Internet company AOL purchased the social networking firm Bebo in early 2008 for $850 million. In June 2010, it sold Bebo for the fire-sale price of $10 million. What went wrong?[1]

AOL was one of the biggest stars of the dotcom era, but its traditional business, dial-up Internet services, has steadily declined since its peak in 2001. The company tried to reinvent itself in 2008 by entering the social networking market by acquiring Bebo; the acquisition came shortly before AOL demerged from Time Warner in 2009. But in the words of Jeff Bewkes, Time Warner CEO at the time, from the get-go Bebo was seen as the "riskiest acquisition" the company made that year.

AOL's original rationale in purchasing Bebo was to tap into the phenomenon of online social networking by acquiring a presence in the rapidly growing community. The deal was part of AOL's strategy to shift from a subscription-based service for Internet connectivity to one focused on generating ad revenue by providing online media. The acquisition of Bebo pulled AOL away from their core strength of providing Internet service and placed the company in direct competition with social networking firms, such as Facebook. Unfortunately, Bebo proved to be an ineffective means of entering the online media industry.

In 2008, Bebo was a thriving, mainly European online social network community that was popular among teens, with about 40 million users. AOL's purchase of Bebo was intended to further the community's expansion into the U.S. market. Quite the opposite happened. In May of 2007, the firm had almost 9 million unique U.S. visitors, and a year later this number dropped to only 5 million unique visitors. (This was in contrast with their largest competitor in the social networking market, Facebook, who had 130.4 million unique U.S. visitors, showing continuous strong growth.)

One of the few actors that actually profited from Bebo was its founder, Michael Birch, who made $300 million from Bebo's original sale to AOL. According to Rory Cellan-Jones, BBC technology correspondent, AOL's decision to purchase Bebo was "one of the worst deals ever made in the dotcom era."

The acquisition was just one of a series of poor decisions that forced AOL to remove Randy Falco, the reigning CEO when the Bebo acquisition was made. They replaced him with Tim Armstrong, the one who divested it, in an effort to change strategies and bring the company back to profitability. According to Jim Clark, senior technology analyst at Mintel, the problems faced by AOL in integrating Bebo were a combination of paying too much in the first place as well as a lack of enough investment to make it profitable.*

* To make matters worse, in July 2010, AOL also sold ICQ instant messenger for $187.5 million, having purchased it for $400 million in 1998. The sales of Bebo and ICQ led to write-downs of $1.4 billion in the second quarter of 2010 and to a posted loss of $1.06 billion for the quarter.

>LO6.1
The reasons for the failure of many diversification efforts.

corporate-level strategy a strategy that focuses on gaining long-term revenue, profits, and market value through managing operations in multiple businesses.

AOL's experience with acquisitions is more the rule than the exception. Research shows that the vast majority of acquisitions result in value destruction rather than value creation. Many large multinational firms have also failed to effectively integrate their acquisitions, paid too high a premium for the target's common stock, or were unable to understand how the acquired firm's assets would fit with their own lines of business.[2] And, at times, top executives may not have acted in the best interests of shareholders. That is, the motive for the acquisition may have been to enhance the executives' power and prestige rather than to improve shareholder returns. At times, the only other people who may have benefited were the shareholders of the *acquired* firms—or the investment bankers who advise the acquiring firm, because they collect huge fees upfront regardless of what happens afterward![3]

Consider, for example, Pfizer's announcement on January 26, 2009, that it was acquiring Wyeth for $68 billion in cash and stock—which represented a 15 percent premium.[4] How did the market react? In rather typical fashion, Wyeth's stock went up 2 percent;

Pfizer's went down 9 percent. And, interestingly, the shares of Crucell, a Dutch biotech company, sank 10 percent after Wyeth pulled out of talks to buy it.

There have been several studies that were conducted over a variety of time periods that show how disappointing acquisitions have typically turned out. For example:

- A study evaluated the stock market reaction of 600 acquisitions over the period between 1975 and 1991. The results indicated that the acquiring firms suffered an average 4 percent drop in market value (after adjusting for market movements) in the three months following the acquisitions announcement.[5]
- In a study by Solomon Smith Barney of U.S. companies acquired since 1997 in deals for $15 billion or more, the stocks of the acquiring firms have, on average, underperformed the S&P stock index by 14 percentage points and underperformed their peer group by 4 percentage points after the deals were announced.[6]
- A study investigated 270 mergers that took place between 2000 and 2003 in multiple countries and regions. It found that after a merger, sales growth decreased by 6 percent, earnings growth dropped 9.4 percent, and market valuations declined 2.5 percent (figures are adjusted for industry trends and refer to three years pre- or postmerger).[7]
- A study that investigated 86 completed takeover bids that took place between 1993 and 2008 noted a negative return of 2 percent per month in long-term performance for the 3-year postacquisition period.[8]

Exhibit 6.1 lists some well-known examples of failed acquisitions and mergers. Recently there have been several acquisitions—often at fire sale prices—by financial services firms during the global financial crisis in 2008. For example, Bank of America bought

---

Exhibit 6.1
Some Well-Known M&A Blunders

Here are examples of some very expensive blunders:

- Sprint and Nextel merged in 2005. On January 31, 2008, the firm said it would take a merger-related charge of $31 billion. And, as of late-January, 2011, the stock has lost over 85 percent of its value since the merger.
- AOL paid $114 billion to acquire Time Warner in 2001. Over the next two years, AOL Time Warner lost $150 billion in market valuation.
- Conseco paid $5.8 billion to buy Green Tree, a mobile home mortgage lender, in 1998 though the company's net worth was not even $1 billion. In the next two years, Conseco lost 90 percent of its market value!
- Daimler Benz paid $36 billion to acquire Chrysler in 1998. After years of losses, it sold 80.1 percent of the unit to Cerberus Capital Management for $7.4 billion in 2007. And, as of 2009, Cerberus was trying to unload the unit.
- Quaker Oats' acquisition of the once high-flying Snapple for $1.8 billion in 1994 was followed by its divestment for $300 million three years later.
- AT&T bought computer equipment maker NCR for $7.4 billion in 1991, only to spin it off for $3.4 billion six years later.
- Sony acquired Columbia Pictures in 1989 for $4.8 billion although it had no competencies in movie production. Five years later, Sony was forced to take a $2.7 billion write-off on the acquisition.

Source: Ante, S.E. 2008. Sprint's Wake-Up Call. *Businessweek.com*. February 21: np; Gupta, P. 2008. Daimler May Sell Remaining Chrysler Stake. *www.reuters.com*, September 24: np; and Tully, S. 2006. The (Second) Worst Deal Ever. *Fortune*, October 16: 102–119.

Merrill Lynch, Wells Fargo purchased Wachovia, and JPMorgan acquired Washington Mutual. Only time will tell how well these turn out over the next few years.

Many acquisitions ultimately result in divestiture—an admission that things didn't work out as planned. In fact, some years ago, a writer for *Fortune* magazine lamented, "Studies show that 33 percent to 50 percent of acquisitions are later divested, giving corporate marriages a divorce rate roughly comparable to that of men and women."[9]

Admittedly, we have been rather pessimistic so far.[10] Clearly, many diversification efforts have worked out very well—whether through mergers and acquisitions, strategic alliances and joint ventures, or internal development. We will discuss many success stories throughout this chapter. Next, we will discuss the primary rationales for diversification.

>LO6.2

How managers can create value through diversification initiatives.

Making Diversification Work: An Overview

Clearly, not all diversification moves, including those involving mergers and acquisitions, erode performance. For example, acquisitions in the oil industry, such as British Petroleum's purchases of Amoco and Arco, are performing well as is the Exxon-Mobil merger. In the automobile industry, the Renault-Nissan alliance, under CEO Carlos Ghosn's leadership, has led to a quadrupling of its collective market capitalization—from $20.4 billion to $84.9 billion—by the end of 2006.[11] Many leading high-tech firms such as Microsoft, Cisco Systems, and Intel have dramatically enhanced their revenues, profits, and market values through a wide variety of diversification initiatives, including acquisitions, strategic alliances, and joint ventures, as well as internal development.*

So the question becomes: Why do some diversification efforts pay off and others produce poor results? This chapter addresses two related issues: (1) What businesses should a corporation compete in? and (2) How should these businesses be managed to jointly create more value than if they were freestanding units?

diversification the process of firms expanding their operations by entering new businesses.

Diversification initiatives—whether through mergers and acquisitions, strategic alliances and joint ventures, or internal development—must be justified by the creation of value for shareholders.[12] But this is not always the case.[13] Acquiring firms typically pay high premiums when they acquire a target firm. For example, in 2006 Freeport-McMoran paid a 30 percent premium to acquire Phelps Dodge in order to create the largest metals and mining concern in the U.S. In contrast, you and I, as private investors, can diversify our portfolio of stocks very cheaply. With an intensely competitive online brokerage industry, we can acquire hundreds (or thousands) of shares for a transaction fee of as little as $10.00 or less—a far cry from the 30 to 40 percent (or higher) premiums that corporations typically must pay to acquire companies.

Given the seemingly high inherent downside risks and uncertainties, one might ask: Why should companies even bother with diversification initiatives? The answer, in a word, is *synergy,* derived from the Greek word *synergos,* which means "working together." This can have two different, but not mutually exclusive, meanings.

First, a firm may diversify into *related* businesses. Here, the primary potential benefits to be derived come from *horizontal relationships;* that is, businesses sharing intangible resources (e.g., core competencies such as marketing) and tangible resources (e.g., production facilities, distribution channels).[14] Firms can also enhance their market power via

---

* Many high-tech firms, such as Motorola, IBM, Qualcomm, and Intel have also diversified through company-owned venture capital arms. Intel Capital, for example, has invested $4 billion in 1,000 companies over 15 years. Some 160 of those companies have been sold to other firms, while another 150 of them have been publicly listed. In 2006, Intel Capital's investments added $214 million to the parent company's net income. For an insightful discussion of how Apple might benefit from a venture capital initiative, refer to Hesseldahl, A. 2007. What to Do with Apple's Cash. *BusinessWeek,* March 19: 80.

pooled negotiating power and vertical integration. For example, Procter & Gamble enjoys many synergies from having businesses that share distribution resources.

Second, a corporation may diversify into *unrelated* businesses.[15] Here, the primary potential benefits are derived largely from *hierarchical relationships;* that is, value creation derived from the corporate office. Examples of the latter would include leveraging some of the support activities in the value chain that we discussed in Chapter 3, such as information systems or human resource practices. Cooper Industries has followed a successful strategy of unrelated diversification. There are few similarities in the products it makes or the industries in which it competes. However, the corporate office adds value through such activities as superb human resource practices and budgeting systems.

Please note that such benefits derived from horizontal (related diversification) and hierarchical (unrelated diversification) relationships are not mutually exclusive. Many firms that diversify into related areas benefit from information technology expertise in the corporate office. Similarly, unrelated diversifiers often benefit from the "best practices" of sister businesses even though their products, markets, and technologies may differ dramatically.

Exhibit 6.2 provides an overview of how we will address the various means by which firms create value through both related and unrelated diversification and also include a summary of some examples that we will address in this chapter.[16]

Exhibit 6.2
Creating Value through Related and Unrelated Diversification

Related Diversification: Economies of Scope

Leveraging core competencies

- 3M leverages its competencies in adhesives technologies to many industries, including automotive, construction, and telecommunications.

Sharing activities

- McKesson, a large distribution company, sells many product lines, such as pharmaceuticals and liquor, through its superwarehouses.

Related Diversification: Market Power

Pooled negotiating power

- The Times Mirror Company increases its power over customers by providing "one-stop shopping" for advertisers to reach customers through multiple media— television and newspapers—in several huge markets such as New York and Chicago.

Vertical integration

- Shaw Industries, a giant carpet manufacturer, increases its control over raw materials by producing much of its own polypropylene fiber, a key input to its manufacturing process.

Unrelated Diversification: Parenting, Restructuring, and Financial Synergies

Corporate restructuring and parenting

- The corporate office of Cooper Industries adds value to its acquired businesses by performing such activities as auditing their manufacturing operations, improving their accounting activities, and centralizing union negotiations.

Portfolio management

- Novartis, formerly Ciba-Geigy, uses portfolio management to improve many key activities, including resource allocation and reward and evaluation systems.

Related Diversification: Economies of Scope and Revenue Enhancement

related diversification a firm entering a different business in which it can benefit from leveraging core competencies, sharing activities, or building market power.

Related diversification enables a firm to benefit from horizontal relationships across different businesses in the diversified corporation by leveraging core competencies and sharing activities (e.g., production and distribution facilities). This enables a corporation to benefit from economies of scope. **Economies of scope** refers to cost savings from leveraging core competencies or sharing related activities among businesses in the corporation. A firm can also enjoy greater revenues if two businesses attain higher levels of sales growth combined than either company could attain independently.

economies of scope cost savings from leveraging core competencies or sharing related activities among businesses in a corporation.

For example, a sporting goods store with one or several locations may acquire retail stores carrying other product lines. This enables it to leverage, or reuse, many of its key resources—favorable reputation, expert staff and management skills, efficient purchasing operations—the basis of its competitive advantage(s), over a larger number of stores.[17]

Leveraging Core Competencies

>LO6.3
How corporations can use related diversification to achieve synergistic benefits through economies of scope and market power.

The concept of core competencies can be illustrated by the imagery of the diversified corporation as a tree.[18] The trunk and major limbs represent core products; the smaller branches are business units; and the leaves, flowers, and fruit are end products. The core competencies are represented by the root system, which provides nourishment, sustenance, and stability. Managers often misread the strength of competitors by looking only at their end products, just as we can fail to appreciate the strength of a tree by looking only at its leaves. Core competencies may also be viewed as the "glue" that binds existing businesses together or as the engine that fuels new business growth.

core competencies a firm's strategic resources that reflect the collective learning in the organization.

Core competencies reflect the collective learning in organizations—how to coordinate diverse production skills, integrate multiple streams of technologies, and market diverse products and services.[19] The knowledge necessary to put a radio on a chip does not in itself assure a company of the skill needed to produce a miniature radio approximately the size of a business card. To accomplish this, Casio, a giant electronic products producer, must synthesize know-how in miniaturization, microprocessor design, material science, and ultrathin precision castings. These are the same skills that it applies in its miniature card calculators, pocket TVs, and digital watches.

● Gillette's expertise in multiple competencies helps them develop superior shaving products.

For a core competence to create value and provide a viable basis for synergy among the businesses in a corporation, it must meet three criteria.[20]

- *The core competence must enhance competitive advantage(s) by creating superior customer value.* Every value-chain activity has the potential to provide a viable basis for building on a core competence.[21] At Gillette, for example, scientists developed the Fusion and Mach 3 after the introduction of the tremendously successful Sensor System because of a thorough understanding of several phenomena that underlie shaving. These include the physiology of facial hair and skin, the metallurgy of blade strength and sharpness, the dynamics of a cartridge moving across skin, and the physics of a razor blade severing hair. Such innovations are possible only with

6.1

strategy spotlight

Procter & Gamble Leverages Its Core Competence in Marketing and (Believe It or Not!) Franchising

Procter & Gamble, long dominant in detergents to wash clothes, wants to also dry clean them. The world's biggest consumer products company plans to roll out franchised Tide Dry Cleaners across America. P&G wants to put its brands to work selling services to boost U.S. revenue for its products.

Some think that their strategy could be a huge hit. For example, Andrew Cherng, founder of Panda Restaurant Group, which operates Chinese fast-food outlets in U.S. malls, plans to open around 150 Tide-branded dry cleaners over the next four years. He claims: "I wasn't around when McDonald's was taking franchisees. I'm not going to miss this one."

In 2007, the firm launched Mr. Clean Car Wash. Nine franchises are now in operation. The following year, P&G opened three test Tide Dry Cleaners in Kansas City. Having fine-tuned the concept, the firm is now going national. According to Michael Stone, P&G is moving into services

"that are virtually unbranded. One would think consumers would trust a Tide Dry Cleaners because they know P&G is behind it."

With more than 800,000 Facebook fans and legions of customers, P&G hopes that the Tide brand will draw people into franchise stores and that superior service—which includes drive-through service, 24-hour pickup, and cleaning methods it markets as environmentally safe—will keep them coming back. "The power of our brands represents disruptive innovation in these industries," claims Nathan Estruth, vice president for FutureWorks, P&G's entrepreneurial arm. "Imagine getting to start my new business with the power of Tide."

But . . . it won't be easy. Competition is fierce, and customers can be prickly: Woe to the dry cleaner that ruins a favorite suit or dress—even if it was cheaply made and decades old. Sanjiv Mehra, who headed Unilever's attempt to break into the dry-cleaning business about a decade ago, says that the key to success is in figuring out a way to do it cheaper or much better than the mom-and-pop stores that dominate the industry. At the end of the day, Unilever realized that it couldn't do either. He claims: "It comes back to, are you fundamentally changing the economics of the business?" adding that P&G's marketing muscle could turn out to be the difference. "That's where they will make a lot of money if they do it right."

Sources: Coleman-Lochner, L. & Clothier, M. 2010. P&G Puts Its Big Brands to Work in Franchises. *Bloomberg Businessweek.* September 6–12: 20; and Martin, A. 2010. Smelling an Opportunity. *www.nytimes.com.* December 8: np.

an understanding of such phenomena and the ability to combine such technologies into innovative products. Customers are willing to pay more for such technologically differentiated products.

- *Different businesses in the corporation must be similar in at least one important way related to the core competence.* It is not essential that the products or services themselves be similar. Rather, at least one element in the value chain must require similar skills in creating competitive advantage if the corporation is to capitalize on its core competence. At first glance you might think that cars and clothes have little in common. However, Strategy Spotlight 6.1 discusses how Procter & Gamble is leveraging its newfound competence in franchising to create a new revenue stream.

- *The core competencies must be difficult for competitors to imitate or find substitutes for.* As we discussed in Chapter 5, competitive advantages will not be sustainable if the competition can easily imitate or substitute them. Similarly, if the skills associated with a firm's core competencies are easily imitated or replicated, they are not a sound basis for sustainable advantages. Consider Sharp Corporation, a consumer electronics giant with 2010 revenues of $30 billion.[22] It has a set of specialized core competencies in optoelectronics technologies that are difficult to replicate and contribute to its competitive advantages in its core businesses. Its most successful technology has been liquid crystal displays (LCDs) that are critical components in nearly all of Sharp's products. Its expertise in this technology enabled Sharp to succeed in videocassette recorders (VCRs) with its innovative LCD viewfinder and led to the creation of its Wizard, a personal electronic organizer.

Steve Jobs provides insights on the importance of a firm's core competence. The Apple CEO is widely considered one of the world's most respected business leaders:[23]

> One of our biggest insights (years ago) was that we didn't want to get into any business where we didn't own or control the primary technology, because you'll get your head handed to you. We realized that for almost all future consumer electronics, the primary technology was going to be software. And we were pretty good at software. We could do the operating system software. We could write applications like iTunes on the Mac or even PC. And we could write the back-end software that runs on a cloud like iTunes. So we could write all these different kinds of software and tweed it all together and make it work seamlessly. And you ask yourself: What other companies can do that? It's a pretty short list.

Sharing Activities

As we saw above, leveraging core competencies involves transferring accumulated skills and expertise across business units in a corporation. Corporations also can achieve synergy by **sharing activities** across their business units. These include value-creating activities such as common manufacturing facilities, distribution channels, and sales forces. As we will see, sharing activities can potentially provide two primary payoffs: cost savings and revenue enhancements.

sharing activities having activities of two or more businesses' value chains done by one of the businesses.

Deriving Cost Savings   Typically, this is the most common type of synergy and the easiest to estimate. Peter Shaw, head of mergers and acquisitions at the British chemical and pharmaceutical company ICI, refers to cost savings as "hard synergies" and contends that the level of certainty of their achievement is quite high. Cost savings come from many sources, including the elimination of jobs, facilities, and related expenses that are no longer needed when functions are consolidated, or from economies of scale in purchasing. Cost savings are generally highest when one company acquires another from the same industry in the same country. Shaw Industries, recently acquired by Berkshire Hathaway, is the nation's largest carpet producer. Over the years, it has dominated the competition through a strategy of acquisition which has enabled Shaw, among other things, to consolidate its manufacturing operations in a few, highly efficient plants and to lower costs through higher capacity utilization.

Sharing activities inevitably involve costs that the benefits must outweigh such as the greater coordination required to manage a shared activity. Even more important is the need to compromise on the design or performance of an activity so that it can be shared. For example, a salesperson handling the products of two business units must operate in a way that is usually not what either unit would choose if it were independent. If the compromise erodes the unit's effectiveness, then sharing may reduce rather than enhance competitive advantage.

Enhancing Revenue and Differentiation   Often an acquiring firm and its target may achieve a higher level of sales growth together than either company could on its own. Shortly after Gillette acquired Duracell, it confirmed its expectation that selling Duracell batteries through Gillette's existing channels for personal care products would increase sales, particularly internationally. Gillette sold Duracell products in 25 new markets in the first year after the acquisition and substantially increased sales in established international markets. Also, a target company's distribution channel can be used to escalate the sales of the acquiring company's product. Such was the case when Gillette acquired Parker Pen. Gillette estimated that it could gain an additional $25 million in sales of its own Waterman pens by taking advantage of Parker's distribution channels.

Firms also can enhance the effectiveness of their differentiation strategies by means of sharing activities among business units. A shared order-processing system, for example, may permit new features and services that a buyer will value. Also, sharing can reduce the cost of differentiation. For instance, a shared service network may make more advanced, remote service technology economically feasible. To illustrate the potential for enhanced differentiation through sharing, consider $7 billion VF Corporation—producer of such well-known brands as Lee, Wrangler, Vanity Fair, and Jantzen.

> VF's acquisition of Nutmeg Industries and H. H. Cutler provided it with several large customers that it didn't have before, increasing its plant utilization and productivity. But more importantly, Nutmeg designs and makes licensed apparel for sports teams and organizations, while Cutler manufactures licensed brand-name children's apparel, including Walt Disney kids' wear. Such brand labeling enhances the differentiation of VF's apparel products. According to VF President Mackey McDonald, "What we're doing is looking at value-added knitwear, taking our basic fleece from Basset-Walker [one of its divisions], embellishing it through Cutler and Nutmeg, and selling it as a value-added product." Additionally, Cutler's advanced high-speed printing technologies will enable VF to be more proactive in anticipating trends in the fashion-driven fleece market. Claims McDonald, "Rather than printing first and then trying to guess what the customer wants, we can see what's happening in the marketplace and then print it up."[24]

As a cautionary note, managers must keep in mind that sharing activities among businesses in a corporation can have a negative effect on a given business's differentiation. For example, with the merger of Chrysler and Daimler-Benz, many consumers may lower their perceptions of Mercedes's quality and prestige because they felt that common production components and processes were being used across the two divisions. And Ford's Jaguar division was adversely affected as consumers came to understand that it shared many components with its sister divisions at Ford, including Lincoln. Perhaps, it is not too surprising that both Chrysler and Jaguar were divested by their parent corporations.

Related Diversification: Market Power

We now discuss how companies achieve related diversification through **market power.** We also address the two principal means by which firms achieve synergy through market power: *pooled negotiating power* and *vertical integration.* Managers do, however, have limits on their ability to use market power for diversification, because government regulations can sometimes restrict the ability of a business to gain very large shares of a particular market. Consider GE's attempt to acquire Honeywell:

market power firms' abilities to profit through restricting or controlling supply to a market or coordinating with other firms to reduce investment.

> When General Electric announced a $41 billion bid for Honeywell, the European Union stepped in. GE's market clout would have expanded significantly with the deal: GE would supply over one-half the parts needed to build several aircraft engines. The commission's concern, causing them to reject the acquisition, was that GE could use its increased market power to dominate the aircraft engine parts market and crowd out rivals.[25] Thus, while managers need to be aware of the strategic advantages of market power, they must at the same time be aware of regulations and legislation.

Pooled Negotiating Power

Similar businesses working together or the affiliation of a business with a strong parent can strengthen an organization's bargaining position relative to suppliers and customers and enhance its position vis-à-vis competitors. Compare, for example, the position of an independent food manufacturer with the same business within Nestlé. Being part of Nestlé provides the business with significant clout—greater bargaining power with suppliers and customers—since it is part of a firm that makes large purchases from suppliers

pooled negotiating power the improvement in bargaining position relative to suppliers and customers.

and provides a wide variety of products. Access to the parent's deep pockets increases the business's strength, and the Nestlé unit enjoys greater protection from substitutes and new entrants. Not only would rivals perceive the unit as a more formidable opponent, but the unit's association with Nestlé would also provide greater visibility and improved image.

Consolidating an industry can also increase a firm's market power.[26] This is clearly an emerging trend in the multimedia industry.[27] All of these mergers and acquisitions have a common goal: to control and leverage as many news and entertainment channels as possible.

When acquiring related businesses, a firm's potential for pooled negotiating power vis-à-vis its customers and suppliers can be very enticing. However, managers must carefully evaluate how the combined businesses may affect relationships with actual and potential customers, suppliers, and competitors. For example, when PepsiCo diversified into the fast-food industry with its acquisitions of Kentucky Fried Chicken, Taco Bell, and Pizza Hut (now part of Yum! Brands), it clearly benefited from its position over these units that served as a captive market for its soft-drink products. However, many competitors, such as McDonald's, have refused to consider PepsiCo as a supplier of its own soft-drink needs because of competition with Pepsi's divisions in the fast-food industry. Simply put, McDonald's did not want to subsidize the enemy! Thus, although acquiring related businesses can enhance a corporation's bargaining power, it must be aware of the potential for retaliation.

Strategy Spotlight 6.2 discusses how 3M's actions to increase its market power led to a lawsuit (which 3M lost) by a competitor.

Vertical Integration

vertical integration an expansion or extension of the firm by integrating preceding or successive production processes.

Vertical integration occurs when a firm becomes its own supplier or distributor. That is, it represents an expansion or extension of the firm by integrating preceding or successive production processes.[28] The firm incorporates more processes toward the original source of raw materials (backward integration) or toward the ultimate consumer (forward integration). For example, a car manufacturer might supply its own parts or make its own engines to secure sources of supply or control its own system of dealerships to ensure retail outlets for its products. Similarly, an oil refinery might secure land leases and develop its own drilling capacity to ensure a constant supply of crude oil. Or it could expand into retail operations by owning or licensing gasoline stations to guarantee customers for its petroleum products.

Clearly, vertical integration can be a viable strategy for many firms. Strategy Spotlight 6.3 discusses Shaw Industries, a carpet manufacturer that has attained a dominant position in the industry via a strategy of vertical integration. Shaw has successfully implemented strategies of both forward and backward integration. Exhibit 6.3 depicts the stages of Shaw's vertical integration.

Benefits and Risks of Vertical Integration   Vertical integration is a means for an organization to reduce its dependence on suppliers or its channels of distribution to end users. However, the benefits associated with vertical integration—backward or forward—must be carefully weighed against the risks.[29]

The *benefits* of vertical integration include (1) a secure supply of raw materials or distribution channels that cannot be "held hostage" to external markets where costs can fluctuate over time, (2) protection and control over assets and services required to produce and deliver valuable products and services, (3) access to new business opportunities and new forms of technologies, and (4) simplified procurement and administrative procedures since key activities are brought inside the firm, eliminating the need to deal with a wide variety of suppliers and distributors.

Winnebago, the leader in the market for drivable recreational vehicles with a 19.3 percent market share, illustrates some of vertical integration's benefits.[30] The word

6.2

strategy spotlight

How 3M's Efforts to Increase Its Market Power Backfired

In the spring and summer of 2006, 3M found itself in court facing three class-action lawsuits launched by consumers and retailers of transparent and invisible adhesive tape (often generically known as "Scotch tape"). The suits all alleged that 3M had unlawfully bullied its way into a monopoly position in the tape market and that, as a result, consumers had been deprived of their rightful amount of choice and often paid up to 40 percent too much for their tape.

One rival that was particularly interested in these cases is LaPage's Inc. of North York, Ontario—3M's only significant competitor in the home and office adhesive tape market. LaPage's has everything to gain from court penalties against 3M's selling practices. This includes greater access to the lucrative North American market. The Canadian company started 3M's legal travails in the first place: all of the current class-action suits were initiated by LePage's.

Back in 1997, LePage's (then based in Pittsburgh) filed a complaint in the Pennsylvania District Court against 3M's practice of selling its various tape products using what was called "bundled rebates." LePage's argued that it violated the Sherman Act, the century-old U.S. legislation that limited monopoly power. 3M's bundled rebate

program offered significant rebates—sometimes in the millions of dollars—to retailers as a reward for selling targeted amounts of six product lines. LePage's claimed that such selling targets were so large that retailers could only meet them by excluding competing products—in this case LePage's tape—from store shelves. For example, LePage's argued that Kmart, which had constituted 10% of LePage's sales dropped the account when 3M started offering the discount chain $1 million in rebates in return for selling more than $15 million worth of 3M products each year. Further, LePage's offered its own conspiracy theory: 3M introduced rebates not simply to grow its sales, but to eliminate LePage's—its only significant competitor.

A jury awarded LePage's $68.5 million in damages (the amount after trebling)—almost 15 percent of the 3M Consumer and Office Business unit's operating income in 2000. The Court of Appeals for the Third Circuit rejected 3M's appeal and upheld the judgment. It concluded that rebate bundling, even if above cost, may exclude equally efficient competitors from offering product (in this case, tape). In the ruling, Judge Dolores K. Sloviter wrote that "they may foreclose portions of the market to a potential competitor who does not manufacture an equally diverse group of products and who therefore cannot make a comparable offer." Therefore, the bundled rebates were judged to be an exploitation of 3M's monopoly power.

Sources: Bush, D. & Gelb, B. D. 2005. When Marketing Practices Raise Antitrust Concerns. *MIT Sloan Management Review*, 46(4): 73–81; Campbell, C. 2006. Tale of the Tape. *Canadian Business.* April 24: 39–40; and Bergstrom, B. 2003. $68M Jury Award Upheld against 3M in Antitrust Case. *The Associated Press:* March 26.

ethics

Winnebago means "big RV" to most Americans. And the firm has a sterling reputation for great quality. The firm's huge northern Iowa factories do everything from extruding aluminum for body parts to molding plastics for water and holding tanks to dashboards. Such vertical integration at the factory may appear to be outdated and expensive, but it

Exhibit 6.3 Simplified Stages of Vertical Integration: Shaw Industries

strategy spotlight

6.3

Vertical Integration at Shaw Industries

Shaw Industries (now part of Berkshire Hathaway) is an example of a firm that has followed a very successful strategy of vertical integration. By relentlessly pursuing both backward and forward integration, Shaw has become the dominant manufacturer of carpeting products in the United States. According to CEO Robert Shaw, "We want to be involved with as much of the process of

Sources: White, J. 2003. Shaw to home in on more with Georgia Tufters deal. *HFN: The Weekly Newspaper for the Home Furnishing Network*, May 5: 32; Shaw Industries. 1993, 2000. Annual reports; and Server, A. 1994. How to escape a price war. *Fortune*, June 13: 88.

making and selling carpets as practical. That way, we're in charge of costs." For example, Shaw acquired Amoco's polypropylene fiber manufacturing facilities in Alabama and Georgia. These new plants provide carpet fibers for internal use and for sale to other manufacturers. With this backward integration, fully one-quarter of Shaw's carpet fiber needs are now met in-house. In early 1996 Shaw began to integrate forward, acquiring seven floor-covering retailers in a move that suggested a strategy to consolidate the fragmented industry and increase its influence over retail pricing. Exhibit 6.3 provides a simplified depiction of the stages of vertical integration for Shaw Industries.

guarantees excellent quality. The Recreational Vehicle Dealer Association started giving a quality award in 1996, and Winnebago has won it every year.

The *risks* of vertical integration include (1) the costs and expenses associated with increased overhead and capital expenditures to provide facilities, raw material inputs, and distribution channels inside the organization; (2) a loss of flexibility resulting from the inability to respond quickly to changes in the external environment because of the huge investments in vertical integration activities that generally cannot be easily deployed elsewhere; (3) problems associated with unbalanced capacities or unfilled demand along the value chain; and (4) additional administrative costs associated with managing a more complex set of activities. Exhibit 6.4 summarizes the benefits and risks of vertical integration.

In making vertical integration decisions, five issues should be considered.[31]

Exhibit 6.4
Benefits and Risks of Vertical Integration

Benefits
• A secure source of raw materials or distribution channels.
• Protection of and control over valuable assets.
• Access to new business opportunities.
• Simplified procurement and administrative procedures.

Risks
• Costs and expenses associated with increased overhead and capital expenditures.
• Loss of flexibility resulting from large investments.
• Problems associated with unbalanced capacities along the value chain.
• Additional administrative costs associated with managing a more complex set of activities.

1. *Is the company satisfied with the quality of the value that its present suppliers and distributors are providing?* If the performance of organizations in the vertical chain—both suppliers and distributors—is satisfactory, it may not, in general, be appropriate for a company to perform these activities themselves. Nike and Reebok have outsourced the manufacture of their shoes to countries such as China and Indonesia where labor costs are low. Since the strengths of these companies are typically in design and marketing, it would be advisable to continue to outsource production operations and continue to focus on where they can add the most value.

2. *Are there activities in the industry value chain presently being outsourced or performed independently by others that are a viable source of future profits?* Even if a firm is outsourcing value-chain activities to companies that are doing a credible job, it may be missing out on substantial profit opportunities. To illustrate, consider the automobile industry's profit pool. As you may recall from Chapter 5, there is much more potential profit in many downstream activities (e.g., leasing, warranty, insurance, and service) than in the manufacture of automobiles. Not surprisingly, carmakers such as Toyota and Honda are undertaking forward integration strategies to become bigger players in these high-profit activities.

3. *Is there a high level of stability in the demand for the organization's products?* High demand or sales volatility are not conducive to vertical integration. With the high level of fixed costs in plant and equipment as well as operating costs that accompany endeavors toward vertical integration, widely fluctuating sales demand can either strain resources (in times of high demand) or result in unused capacity (in times of low demand). The cycles of "boom and bust" in the automobile industry are a key reason why the manufacturers have increased the amount of outsourced inputs.

4. *Does the company have the necessary competencies to execute the vertical integration strategies?* As many companies would attest, successfully executing strategies of vertical integration can be very difficult. For example, Unocal, a major petroleum refiner, which once owned retail gas stations, was slow to capture the potential grocery and merchandise side of the business that might have resulted from customer traffic to its service stations. Unocal lacked the competencies to develop a separate retail organization and culture. The company eventually sold the assets and brand.

5. *Will the vertical integration initiative have potential negative impacts on the firm's stakeholders?* Managers must carefully consider the impact that vertical integration may have on existing and future customers, suppliers, and competitors. After Lockheed Martin, a dominant defense contractor, acquired Loral Corporation, an electronics supplier, for $9.1 billion, it had an unpleasant and unanticipated surprise. Loral, as a captive supplier of Lockheed, is now viewed as a rival by many of its previous customers. Thus, before Lockheed Martin can realize any net synergies from this acquisition, it must make up for the substantial business that it has lost.

Analyzing Vertical Integration: The Transaction Cost Perspective   Another approach that has proved very useful in understanding vertical integration is the **transaction cost perspective.**[32] According to this perspective, every market transaction involves some *transaction costs.* First, a decision to purchase an input from an outside source leads to *search* costs (i.e., the cost to find where it is available, the level of quality, etc.). Second, there are costs associated with *negotiating.* Third, a *contract* needs to be written spelling out future possible contingencies. Fourth, parties in a contract have to *monitor* each other. Finally, if a party does not comply with the terms of the contract, there are *enforcement* costs. Transaction costs are thus the sum of search costs, negotiation costs, contracting costs, monitoring costs, and enforcement costs. These transaction costs can be avoided by internalizing the activity, in other words, by producing the input in-house.

transaction cost perspective a perspective that the choice of a transaction's governance structure, such as vertical integration or market transaction, is influenced by transaction costs, including search, negotiating, contracting, monitoring, and enforcement costs, associated with each choice.

A related problem with purchasing a specialized input from outside is the issue of *transaction-specific investments*. For example, when an automobile company needs an input specifically designed for a particular car model, the supplier may be unwilling to make the investments in plant and machinery necessary to produce that component for two reasons. First, the investment may take many years to recover but there is no guarantee the automobile company will continue to buy from them after the contract expires, typically in one year. Second, once the investment is made, the supplier has no bargaining power. That is, the buyer knows that the supplier has no option but to supply at ever-lower prices because the investments were so specific that they cannot be used to produce alternative products. In such circumstances, again, vertical integration may be the only option.

Vertical integration, however, gives rise to a different set of costs. These costs are referred to as *administrative costs*. Coordinating different stages of the value chain now internalized within the firm causes administrative costs to go up. Decisions about vertical integration are, therefore, based on a comparison of transaction costs and administrative costs. If transaction costs are lower than administrative costs, it is best to resort to market transactions and avoid vertical integration. For example, McDonald's may be the world's biggest buyer of beef, but they do not raise cattle. The market for beef has low transaction costs and requires no transaction-specific investments. On the other hand, if transaction costs are higher than administrative costs, vertical integration becomes an attractive strategy. Most automobile manufacturers produce their own engines because the market for engines involves high transaction costs and transaction-specific investments.

>LO6.4
How corporations can use unrelated diversification to attain synergistic benefits through corporate restructuring, parenting, and portfolio analysis.

Unrelated Diversification: Financial Synergies and Parenting

unrelated diversification a firm entering a different business that has little horizontal interaction with other businesses of a firm.

With unrelated diversification, unlike related diversification, few benefits are derived from *horizontal relationships*—that is, the leveraging of core competencies or the sharing of activities across business units within a corporation. Instead, potential benefits can be gained from *vertical (or hierarchical) relationships*—the creation of synergies from the interaction of the corporate office with the individual business units. There are two main sources of such synergies. First, the corporate office can contribute to "parenting" and restructuring of (often acquired) businesses. Second, the corporate office can add value by viewing the entire corporation as a family or "portfolio" of businesses and allocating resources to optimize corporate goals of profitability, cash flow, and growth. Additionally, the corporate office enhances value by establishing appropriate human resource practices and financial controls for each of its business units.

Corporate Parenting and Restructuring

parenting advantage the positive contributions of the corporate office to a new business as a result of expertise and support provided and not as a result of substantial changes in assets, capital structure, or management.

We have discussed how firms can add value through related diversification by exploring sources of synergy *across* business units. Now, we discuss how value can be created *within* business units as a result of the expertise and support provided by the corporate office.

Parenting   The positive contributions of the corporate office are called the **"parenting advantage."**[33] Many firms have successfully diversified their holdings without strong evidence of the more traditional sources of synergy (i.e., horizontally across business units). Diversified public corporations such as BTR, Emerson Electric, and Hanson and leveraged buyout firms such as Kohlberg, Kravis, Roberts & Company, and Clayton, Dublilier & Rice are a few examples.[34] These parent companies create value through management expertise. How? They improve plans and budgets and provide especially competent central functions such as legal, financial, human resource management, procurement, and the like. They also help subsidiaries make wise choices in their own acquisitions, divestitures, and new internal development decisions. Such contributions often help business units to substantially increase their revenues and profits. Consider Texas-based Cooper Industries' acquisition of Champion International, the spark plug company, as an example of corporate parenting:[35]

> Cooper applies a distinctive parenting approach designed to help its businesses improve their manufacturing performance. New acquisitions are "Cooperized"—Cooper audits their manufacturing operations; improves their cost accounting systems; makes their planning, budgeting, and human resource systems conform with its systems; and centralizes union negotiations. Excess cash is squeezed out through tighter controls and reinvested in productivity enhancements, which improve overall operating efficiency. As one manager observed, "When you get acquired by Cooper, one of the first things that happens is a truckload of policy manuals arrives at your door." Such active parenting has been effective in enhancing the competitive advantages of many kinds of manufacturing businesses.

Restructuring   **Restructuring** is another means by which the corporate office can add value to a business.[36] The central idea can be captured in the real estate phrase "buy low and sell high." Here, the corporate office tries to find either poorly performing firms with unrealized potential or firms in industries on the threshold of significant, positive change. The parent intervenes, often selling off parts of the business; changing the management; reducing payroll and unnecessary sources of expenses; changing strategies; and infusing the company with new technologies, processes, reward systems, and so forth. When the restructuring is complete, the firm can either "sell high" and capture the added value or keep the business and enjoy financial and competitive benefits.[37]

Loews Corporation, a conglomerate with $15 billion in revenues competes in such industries as oil and gas, tobacco, watches, insurance, and hotels. It provides an exemplary example of how firms can successfully "buy low and sell high" as part of their corporate strategy.[38]

> Energy accounts for 33 percent of Loews' $30 billion in total assets. In the 1980s it bought six oil tankers for only $5 million each during a sharp slide in oil prices. The downside was limited. After all these huge hulks could easily have been sold as scrap steel. However, that didn't have to happen. Eight years after Loews purchased the tankers, they sold them for $50 million each.
>
> Loews was also extremely successful with its next energy play—drilling equipment. Although wildcatting for oil is very risky, selling services to wildcatters is not, especially if the assets are bought during a down cycle. Loews did just that. It purchased 10 offshore drilling rigs for $50 million in 1989 and formed Diamond Offshore Drilling. In 1995 Loews received $338 million after taking a 30 percent piece of this operation public!

For the restructuring strategy to work, the corporate management must have both the insight to detect undervalued companies (otherwise the cost of acquisition would be too high) or businesses competing in industries with a high potential for transformation.[39] Additionally, of course, they must have the requisite skills and resources to turn the businesses around, even if they may be in new and unfamiliar industries.

Restructuring can involve changes in assets, capital structure, or management.

- *Asset restructuring* involves the sale of unproductive assets, or even whole lines of businesses, that are peripheral. In some cases, it may even involve acquisitions that strengthen the core business.
- *Capital restructuring* involves changing the debt-equity mix, or the mix between different classes of debt or equity. Although the substitution of equity with debt is more common in buyout situations, occasionally the parent may provide additional equity capital.
- *Management restructuring* typically involves changes in the composition of the top management team, organizational structure, and reporting relationships. Tight

restructuring the intervention of the corporate office in a new business that substantially changes the assets, capital structure, and/or management, including selling off parts of the business, changing the management, reducing payroll and unnecessary sources of expenses, changing strategies, and infusing the new business with new technologies, processes, and reward systems.

financial control, rewards based strictly on meeting short- to medium-term performance goals, and reduction in the number of middle-level managers are common steps in management restructuring. In some cases, parental intervention may even result in changes in strategy as well as infusion of new technologies and processes.

Hanson, plc, a British conglomerate, made numerous such acquisitions in the United States in the 1980s, often selling these firms at significant profits after a few years of successful restructuring efforts. Hanson's acquisition and subsequent restructuring of the SCM group is a classic example of the restructuring strategy. Hanson acquired SCM, a diversified manufacturer of industrial and consumer products (including Smith-Corona typewriters, Glidden paints, and Durkee Famous Foods), for $930 million in 1986 after a bitter takeover battle. In the next few months, Hanson sold SCM's paper and pulp operations for $160 million, the chemical division for $30 million, Glidden paints for $580 million, and Durkee Famous Foods for $120 million, virtually recovering the entire original investment. In addition, Hanson also sold the SCM headquarters in New York for $36 million and reduced the headquarters staff by 250. They still retained several profitable divisions, including the titanium dioxide operations and managed them with tight financial controls that led to increased returns.[40]

Exhibit 6.5 summarizes the three primary types of restructuring activities.

Portfolio Management

During the 1970s and early 1980s, several leading consulting firms developed the concept of **portfolio management** to achieve a better understanding of the competitive position of an overall portfolio (or family) of businesses, to suggest strategic alternatives for each of the businesses, and to identify priorities for the allocation of resources. Several studies have reported widespread use of these techniques among American firms.[41]

Description and Potential Benefits   The key purpose of portfolio models is to assist a firm in achieving a balanced portfolio of businesses.[42] This consists of businesses whose profitability, growth, and cash flow characteristics complement each other and adds up to a satisfactory overall corporate performance. Imbalance, for example, could be caused either by excessive cash generation with too few growth opportunities or by insufficient cash generation to fund the growth requirements in the portfolio. Monsanto, for example, used portfolio planning to restructure its portfolio, divesting low-growth commodity chemicals businesses and acquiring businesses in higher-growth industries such as biotechnology.

The Boston Consulting Group's (BCG) growth/share matrix is among the best known of these approaches.[43] In the BCG approach, each of the firm's strategic business units (SBUs) is plotted on a two-dimensional grid in which the axes are relative market share and industry growth rate. The grid is broken into four quadrants. Exhibit 6.6 depicts the BCG matrix. Following are a few clarifications:

1. Each circle represents one of the corporation's business units. The size of the circle represents the relative size of the business unit in terms of revenues.

portfolio management a method of (a) assessing the competitive position of a portfolio of businesses within a corporation, (b) suggesting strategic alternatives for each business, and (c) identifying priorities for the allocation of resources across the businesses.

Exhibit 6.5
The Three Primary Types of Restructuring Activities

Asset Restructuring: The sale of unproductive assets, or even whole lines of businesses, that are peripheral.

Capital Restructuring: Changing the debt-equity mix, or the mix between different classes of debt or equity.

Management Restructuring: Changes in the composition of the top management team, organization structure, and reporting relationships.

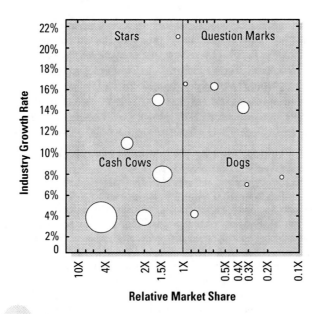

Exhibit 6.6 The Boston Consulting Group (BCG) Portfolio Matrix

2. Relative market share, measured by the ratio of the business unit's size to that of its largest competitor, is plotted along the horizontal axis.

3. Market share is central to the BCG matrix. This is because high relative market share leads to unit cost reduction due to experience and learning curve effects and, consequently, superior competitive position.

Each of the four quadrants of the grid has different implications for the SBUs that fall into the category:

- **Stars** are SBUs competing in high-growth industries with relatively high market shares. These firms have long-term growth potential and should continue to receive substantial investment funding.
- **Question Marks** are SBUs competing in high-growth industries but having relatively weak market shares. Resources should be invested in them to enhance their competitive positions.
- **Cash Cows** are SBUs with high market shares in low-growth industries. These units have limited long-run potential but represent a source of current cash flows to fund investments in "stars" and "question marks."
- **Dogs** are SBUs with weak market shares in low-growth industries. Because they have weak positions and limited potential, most analysts recommend that they be divested.

In using portfolio strategy approaches, a corporation tries to create shareholder value in a number of ways.[44] First, portfolio analysis provides a snapshot of the businesses in a corporation's portfolio. Therefore, the corporation is in a better position to allocate resources among the business units according to prescribed criteria (e.g., use cash flows from the "cash cows" to fund promising "stars"). Second, the expertise and analytical resources in the corporate office provide guidance in determining what firms may be attractive (or unattractive) acquisitions. Third, the corporate office is able to provide financial resources to the business units on favorable terms that reflect the corporation's overall ability to raise funds. Fourth, the corporate office can provide high-quality review and coaching for the individual businesses. Fifth, portfolio analysis provides a basis for developing strategic goals and reward/evaluation systems for business managers. For example, managers of cash cows would have lower targets for revenue growth than managers of stars, but the former would have higher threshold levels of profit targets on proposed projects than the managers of star businesses. Compensation systems would also reflect such realities. Cash cows understandably would be rewarded more on the basis of cash that their businesses generate than would managers of star businesses. Similarly, managers of star businesses would be held to higher standards for revenue growth than managers of cash cow businesses.

To see how companies can benefit from portfolio approaches, consider Ciba-Geigy.

> In 1994 Ciba-Geigy adopted portfolio planning approaches to help it manage its business units, which competed in a wide variety of industries, including chemicals, dyes, pharmaceuticals, crop protection, and animal health.[45] It placed each business unit in a category corresponding to the BCG matrix. The business unit's goals, compensation programs, personnel selection, and resource allocation were strongly associated with the category within which the business was placed. For example, business units classified as "cash cows" had much higher hurdles for obtaining financial resources (from the corporate office) for expansion than "question marks" since the latter were businesses for which Ciba-Geigy had high hopes for accelerated future growth and profitability. Additionally, the compensation of a business unit manager in a cash cow would be strongly associated with its success in generating cash to fund other businesses, whereas a manager of a question mark business would be rewarded on his or her ability to increase revenue growth and market share. The portfolio planning approaches appear to be working. In 2010, Ciba-Geigy's (now Novartis) revenues and net income stood at $45 billion and $8.5 billion, respectively. This represents a 110 percent increase in revenues and a most impressive 49 percent growth in net income over a six-year period.

Limitations   Despite the potential benefits of portfolio models, there are also some notable downsides. First, they compare SBUs on only two dimensions, making the implicit but erroneous assumption that (1) those are the only factors that really matter and (2) every unit can be accurately compared on that basis. Second, the approach views each SBU as a stand-alone entity, ignoring common core business practices and value-creating activities that may hold promise for synergies across business units. Third, unless care is exercised, the process becomes largely mechanical, substituting an oversimplified graphical model for the important contributions of the CEO's (and other corporate managers') experience and judgment. Fourth, the reliance on "strict rules" regarding resource allocation across SBUs can be detrimental to a firm's long-term viability. For example, according to one study, over one-half of all the businesses that should have been cash users (based on the BCG matrix) were instead cash providers.[46] Finally, while colorful and easy to comprehend, the imagery of the BCG matrix can lead to some troublesome and overly simplistic prescriptions. According to one author:

> The dairying analogy is appropriate (for some cash cows), so long as we resist the urge to oversimplify it. On the farm, even the best-producing cows eventually begin to dry up. The farmer's solution to this is euphemistically called "freshening" the cow: The farmer arranges a date for the cow with a bull, she has a calf, the milk begins flowing again. Cloistering the cow—isolating her from everything but the feed trough and the milking machines—assures that she will go dry.[47]

To see what can go wrong, consider Cabot Corporation.

> Cabot Corporation supplies carbon black for the rubber, electronics, and plastics industries. Following the BCG matrix, Cabot moved away from its cash cow, carbon black, and diversified into stars such as ceramics and semiconductors in a seemingly overaggressive effort to create more revenue growth for the corporation. Predictably, Cabot's return on assets declined as the firm shifted away from its core competence to unrelated areas. The portfolio model failed by pointing the company in the wrong direction in an effort to spur growth—away from their core business. Recognizing its mistake, Cabot Corporation

returned to its mainstay carbon black manufacturing and divested unrelated businesses. Today the company is a leader in its field with \$3 billion in 2010 revenues.[48]

Exhibit 6.7 summarizes the limitations of portfolio model analysis.

Caveat: Is Risk Reduction a Viable Goal of Diversification?

One of the purposes of diversification is to reduce the risk that is inherent in a firm's variability in revenues and profits over time. That is, if a firm enters new products or markets that are affected differently by seasonal or economic cycles, its performance over time will be more stable. For example, a firm manufacturing lawn mowers may diversify into snow blowers to even out its annual sales. Or a firm manufacturing a luxury line of household furniture may introduce a lower-priced line since affluent and lower-income customers are affected differently by economic cycles.

At first glance the above reasoning may make sense, but there are some problems with it. First, a firm's stockholders can diversify their portfolios at a much lower cost than a corporation, and they don't have to worry about integrating the acquisition into their portfolio. Second, economic cycles as well as their impact on a given industry (or firm) are difficult to predict with any degree of accuracy.

Notwithstanding the above, some firms have benefited from diversification by lowering the variability (or risk) in their performance over time. Consider Emerson Electronic.[49]

Emerson Electronic is a \$21 billion manufacturer that produces a wide variety of products, including measurement devices for heavy industry, temperature controls for heating

---

Exhibit 6.7
Benefits and Limitations of Portfolio Models

Benefits

- The corporation is in a better position to allocate resources to businesses according to explicit criteria.
- The corporate office can provide guidance on what firms may be attractive acquisitions.
- The corporate office can provide financial resources to businesses on favorable terms (that reflect the corporation's ability to raise funds).
- The corporate office can provide high-quality review and coaching for the individual businesses.
- It provides a basis for developing strategic goals and evaluation/reward systems for businesses.

Limitations

- They are overly simplistic, consisting of only two dimensions (growth and market share).
- They view each business as separate, ignoring potential synergies across businesses.
- The process may become overly largely mechanical, minimizing the potential value of managers' judgment and experience.
- The reliance on strict rules for resource allocation across SBUs can be detrimental to a firm's long-term viability.
- The imagery (e.g., cash cows, dogs) while colorful, may lead to troublesome and overly simplistic prescriptions.

and ventilation systems, and power tools sold at Home Depot. Recently, many analysts questioned Emerson's purchase of companies that sell power systems to the volatile telecommunications industry. Why? This industry is expected to experience, at best, minimal growth. However, CEO David Farr maintained that such assets could be acquired inexpensively because of the aggregate decline in demand in this industry. Additionally, he argued that the other business units, such as the sales of valves and regulators to the now-booming oil and natural gas companies, were able to pick up the slack. Therefore, while net profits in the electrical equipment sector (Emerson's core business) sharply decreased, Emerson's overall corporate profits increased 1.7 percent.

Risk reduction in and of itself is rarely viable as a means to create shareholder value. It must be undertaken with a view of a firm's overall diversification strategy.

The Means to Achieve Diversification

>LO6.5

The various means of engaging in diversification— mergers and acquisitions, joint ventures/strategic alliances, and internal development.

We have addressed the types of diversification (e.g., related and unrelated) that a firm may undertake to achieve synergies and create value for its shareholders. Now, we address the means by which a firm can go about achieving these desired benefits.

There are three basic means. First, through acquisitions or mergers, corporations can directly acquire a firm's assets and competencies. Although the terms *mergers* and *acquisitions* are used quite interchangeably, there are some key differences. With **acquisitions,** one firm buys another either through a stock purchase, cash, or the issuance of debt.[50] **Mergers,** on the other hand, entail a combination or consolidation of two firms to form a new legal entity. Mergers are relatively rare and entail a transaction among two firms on a relatively equal basis. Despite such differences, we consider both mergers and acquisitions to be quite similar in terms of their implications for a firm's corporate-level strategy.[51]

acquisitions the incorporation of one firm into another through purchase.

Second, corporations may agree to pool the resources of other companies with their resource base, commonly known as a joint venture or strategic alliance. Although these two forms of partnerships are similar in many ways, there is an important difference. Joint ventures involve the formation of a third-party legal entity where the two (or more) firms each contribute equity, whereas strategic alliances do not.

mergers the combining of two or more firms into one new legal entity.

Third, corporations may diversify into new products, markets, and technologies through internal development. Called corporate entrepreneurship, it involves the leveraging and combining of a firm's own resources and competencies to create synergies and enhance shareholder value. We address this subject in greater length in Chapter 12.

Mergers and Acquisitions

The rate of mergers and acquisitions (M&A) had dropped off beginning in 2001. This trend was largely a result of a recession, corporate scandals, and a declining stock market. However, the situation has changed dramatically. Over the past several years, several large mergers and acquisitions were announced. These include:[52]

- Kraft's acquisition of Cadbury for $19.4 billion.
- In Bev's acquisition of Anheuser-Busch for $52 billion.
- Pfizer's acquisition of Wyeth for $68 billion.
- Mittal Steel's acquisition of Arcelor for $33 billion.
- BellSouth's acquisition of AT&T for $86.0 billion.
- Sprint's merger with Nextel for $39 billion.
- Boston Scientific's $27 billion acquisition of medical device maker Guidant.
- Procter & Gamble's purchase of Gillette for $54 billion.
- Kmart Holding Corp.'s acquisition of Sears, Roebuck & Co. for $11 billion.

Exhibit 6.8 illustrates the dramatic increase in worldwide M&A activity in the U.S. up until 2008, when the global recession began. Several factors help to explain the rapid rise between 2002 and 2007. First, there was the robust economy and the increasing corporate profits that had boosted stock prices and cash. For example, the S&P 500 stock index companies, including financial companies, had a record of over $2 trillion in cash and other short-term assets.

Second, the weak U.S. dollar made U.S. assets less expensive relative to other countries. That is, from the perspective of a foreign acquirer, compared to any other period in recent memory, U.S. companies were "cheap." For example, a Euro, which was worth only 80 cents in 1999, was worth $1.35 by mid-2007. This made U.S. companies a relative bargain for a European acquirer.

Third, stricter governance standards were requiring poorly performing CEOs and boards of directors to consider unsolicited offers. In essence, top executives and board members were less likely to be protected by antitakeover mechanisms such as greenmail, poison pills, and golden parachutes (discussed at the end of the chapter).

2009 was a bad year for M&A activities due to the global recession. However, with the economy improving in 2010, the pace picked up again. The total value for M&A activity in 2010 was $2.8 trillion—a 17 percent increase over the previous year. Further, in the United States, companies sought approval on 1,166 M&A transactions in 2010 compared to only 716 in 2009—reflecting a 63 percent increase. (U.S. merger approval is required by the Federal Trade Commission for any deal valued at $63 million or more.)[53] According to Andrew Gavil, an antitrust law professor, "Merger activity is often associated with optimism, willingness to spend cash on hand, availability of credit and general levels of economic activity," though it may also indicate how difficult the recovery has been for some businesses (that is, assets can be acquired quite cheaply).

Motives and Benefits   Growth through mergers and acquisitions has played a critical role in the success of many corporations in a wide variety of high-technology and knowledge-intensive industries. Here, market and technology changes can occur very quickly and unpredictably.[54] Speed—speed to market, speed to positioning, and speed to becoming a viable company—is critical in such industries. For example, Alex Mandl, then

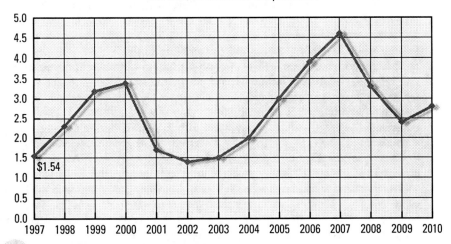

Exhibit 6.8 Global Value of Mergers and Acquisitions

Source: Bloomberg; Dealogic; personal communication with Meredith Leonard at Dealogic on January 27, 2009; and personal communication with Natalie Logan at Dealogic on January 27, 2011.

AT&T's president, was responsible for the acquisition of McCaw Cellular. Although many industry experts felt the price was too steep, he believed that cellular technology was a critical asset for the telecommunications business. Mandl claimed, "The plain fact is that acquiring is much faster than building."[55]

Mergers and acquisitions also can be a means of *obtaining valuable resources that can help an organization expand its product offerings and services.* For example, Cisco Systems, a dominant player in networking equipment, acquired more than 70 companies over a recent seven-year period.[56] This provides Cisco with access to the latest in networking equipment. Then it uses its excellent sales force to market the new technology to its corporate customers. Cisco also provides strong incentives to the staff of acquired companies to stay on. To realize the greatest value from its acquisitions, Cisco also has learned to integrate acquired companies efficiently and effectively.[57]

Mergers and acquisitions also can *provide the opportunity for firms to attain the three bases of synergy—leveraging core competencies, sharing activities, and building market power.* Consider Procter & Gamble's $57 billion acquisition of Gillette.[58] First, it helps Procter & Gamble to leverage its core competencies in marketing and product positioning in the area of grooming and personal care brands. For example, P&G has experience in repositioning brands such as Old Spice in this market (which recently passed Gillette's Right Guard brand to become No. 1 in the deodorant market). Gillette has very strong brands in razors and blades. Thus, P&G's marketing expertise enhances its market position. Second, there are opportunities to share value-creating activities. Gillette will benefit from P&G's stronger distribution network in developing countries where the potential growth rate for the industry's products remains higher than in the United States, Europe, or Japan. Consider the insight of A. F. Lafley, P&G's former CEO:

> When I was in Asia in the 90s, we had already gone beyond the top 500 cities in China. Today, we're way down into the rural areas. So we add three, four, five Gillette brands, and we don't even have to add a salesperson.

Third, the addition of Gillette increases P&G's market power. In recent years, the growth of powerful global retailers such as Walmart, Carrefour, and Costco has eroded much of the consumer goods industry's pricing power. A central part of P&G's recent strategy has been to focus its resources on enhancing its core brands. Today, 16 of its brands (each with revenues of over $1 billion) account for $30 billion of the firm's $51.4 billion in total revenues. Gillette, with $10.5 billion in total revenues, adds five brands which also have revenues of over $1 billion. P&G anticipates that its growing stable of "superbrands" will help it to weather the industry's tough pricing environment and enhance its power relative to large, powerful retailers such as Walmart and Target.

Merger and acquisition activity also can *lead to consolidation within an industry and can force other players to merge.*[59] In the pharmaceutical industry, the patents for many top-selling drugs are expiring and M&A activity is expected to heat up.[60] For example, many patents held by U.S. pharmaceutical companies (e.g., Pfizer's Lipitor) will expire in the next few years, which represents tens of billions of dollars in revenue. Clearly, this is an example of how the political—legal segment of the general environment (discussed in Chapter 2) can affect a corporation's strategy and performance. Although health care providers and patients are happy about the lower-cost generics that will arrive, drug firms are being pressed to make up for lost revenues. Combining top firms such as Glaxo Wellcome and SmithKline Beecham has many potential long-term benefits. They not only promise significant postmerger cost savings, but also the increased size of the combined companies brings greater research and development possibilities.

Corporations can also *enter new market segments by way of acquisitions.* Although Charles Schwab & Co. is best known for providing discount trading services for middle

America, it clearly is interested in other target markets.[61] In late 2000 Schwab surprised its rivals by paying $2.7 billion to acquire (divested in 2006) U.S. Trust Corporation, a 147-year-old financial services institution that is a top estate planner for the wealthy. However, Schwab is not ignoring its core market. The firm also purchased Cybercorp Inc., a Texas brokerage company, for $488 million. That firm offers active online traders sophisticated quotes and stock-screening tools. Exhibit 6.9 summarizes the benefits of mergers and acquisitions.

Potential Limitations   As noted in the previous section, mergers and acquisitions provide a firm with many potential benefits. However, at the same time, there are many potential drawbacks or limitations to such corporate activity.[62]

First, *the takeover premium that is paid for an acquisition typically is very high.* Two times out of three, the stock price of the acquiring company falls once the deal is made public. Since the acquiring firm often pays a 30 percent or higher premium for the target company, the acquirer must create synergies and scale economies that result in sales and market gains exceeding the premium price. Firms paying higher premiums set the performance hurdle even higher. For example, Household International paid an 82 percent premium to buy Beneficial, and Conseco paid an 83 percent premium to acquire Green Tree Financial. Historically, paying a high premium over the stock price has been a poor strategy.

Second, *competing firms often can imitate any advantages realized or copy synergies that result from the M&A.*[63] Thus, a firm can often see its advantages quickly erode. Unless the advantages are sustainable and difficult to copy, investors will not be willing to pay a high premium for the stock. Similarly, the time value of money must be factored into the stock price. M&A costs are paid up front. Conversely, firms pay for R&D, ongoing marketing, and capacity expansion over time. This stretches out the payments needed to gain new competencies. The M&A argument is that a large initial investment is worthwhile because it creates long-term advantages. However, stock analysts want to see immediate results from such a large cash outlay. If the acquired firm does not produce results quickly, investors often divest the stock, driving the price down.

Third, *managers' credibility and ego can sometimes get in the way of sound business decisions.* If the M&A does not perform as planned, managers who pushed for the deal find their reputation tarnished. This can lead them to protect their credibility by funneling more money, or escalating their commitment, into an inevitably doomed operation. Further, when a merger fails and a firm tries to unload the acquisition, they often must sell at a huge discount. These problems further compound the costs and erode the stock price.

Fourth, *there can be many cultural issues that may doom the intended benefits from M&A endeavors.* Consider, the insights of Joanne Lawrence, who played an important role in the merger between SmithKline and the Beecham Group.[64]

> The key to a strategic merger is to create a new culture. This was a mammoth challenge during the SmithKline Beecham merger. We were working at so many different cultural

---

Exhibit 6.9
Benefits of Mergers and Acquisitions

- Obtain valuable resources that can help an organization expand its product offerings.
- Provide the opportunity for firms to attain three bases of synergy: leveraging core competencies, sharing activities, and building market power.
- Lead to consolidation within an industry and force other players to merge.
- Enter new market segments.

strategy spotlight   6.4

Effectively Managing the Human Side of Acquisitions

When managing the human side of the merger and acquisition (M&A) process, firms face issues such as anxiety, employee shock, and protests. How companies manage such issues will reduce the volume of customer defections, supplier unrest, and government disapproval—as well as increase employee commitment.

In the follow-up to the P&G and Gillette merger, headhunters started targeting Gillette talent. P&G faced government disapproval and investigations in Gillette's home state of Massachusetts, as well as potential problems in India—where it intended to reduce the number of distributors. However, P&G was able to keep 90 percent of

Source: Kanter, R. M. 2009. Mergers That Stick. *Harvard Business Review*, 87(10): 121–125; and Neff, J. 2010. Why P&G's $57 Billion Bet on Gillette Hasn't Paid Off Big—Yet. *www.adage.com*. February 15: np.

Gillette employees who were offered jobs, which is much higher than the average in M&A situations.

P&G enlisted all Gillette employees in an active effort to keep customers, suppliers, and distributors happy, even employees who would eventually be let go. Former Gillette Chairman Jim Kilts said, "A lot of people who left were going to retire and leave anyway in the short term. And I think we seeded the company with some great talent down in the organization, so time will tell." In the instances when processes used by Gillette were deemed more efficient than P&G's, they were adopted. Overall, the company achieved its cost and revenue targets from the first year following the merger.

The best may be yet to come, as the company was able to make aggressive moves in key markets such as Brazil and India. In addition, there was a growing investment and expertise in sports marketing and faster internal decision making.

---

levels, it was dizzying. We had two national cultures to blend—American and British—that compounded the challenge of selling the merger in two different markets with two different shareholder bases. There were also two different business cultures: One was very strong, scientific, and academic; the other was much more commercially oriented. And then we had to consider within both companies the individual businesses, each of which has its own little culture.

Exhibit 6.10 summarizes the limitations of mergers and acquisitions.

Strategy Spotlight 6.4 addresses the human side of M&A activity—how they may be successfully managed.

Divestment: The Other Side of the "M&A Coin"   When firms acquire other businesses, it typically generates quite a bit of "press" in business publications such as *The Wall Street Journal, BusinessWeek,* and *Fortune.* It makes for exciting news, and one thing is for sure—large acquiring firms automatically improve their standing in the Fortune 500 rankings (since it is based solely on total revenues). However, managers must also carefully consider the strategic implications of exiting businesses.

Exhibit 6.10
Limitations of Mergers and Acquisitions

- Takeover premiums paid for acquisitions are typically very high.
- Competing firms often can imitate any advantages or copy synergies that result from the merger or acquisition.
- Managers' egos sometimes get in the way of sound business decisions.
- Cultural issues may doom the intended benefits from M&A endeavors.

6.5

strategy spotlight

Why Did Tyco International Sell a Majority Stake in One of Its Businesses?

Tyco International, with $17 billion in revenues, is the world's largest maker of security systems. On November 9, 2010, Tyco announced that it had agreed to sell a majority stake in its electrical and metal products unit to buyout firm Clayton Dubilier & Rice (CD&R) for $720 million. By taking this action, it withdrew its plans to spin off the division.

The proceeds from the sale of Tyco's 51 percent stake will help the firm accelerate its share buyback

program, which it had announced two months earlier. The unit, which had $1.4 billion in 2009 revenues, will operate as a standalone entity called Atkore International. It makes products such as metal-clad electrical cables and barbed razor ribbon. Tyco felt that it could profit more by selling the remaining 49 percent when markets improve.

The acquisition is very attractive to CD&R. According to Nathan K. Sleeper, a CD&R partner, "As a manufacturer and distributor of industrial products, Atkore is a leader in a market that CD&R knows very well. We look forward to working with the Atkore management team to build on the core strengths of the business—including an outstanding reputation, well-recognized brands, long-term customer relationships, and significant scale advantages—to create an even more successful independent enterprise."

Sources: Winter, C. 2010. Tyco International: Biding Time in Hope of Better Markets. *Bloomberg Businessweek.* November 15–22: 34; and Franco, T. C. 2010. Clayton, Dubilier & Rice to Acquire Tyco International's Electrical and Metal Products Business to Be Renamed Atkore International. *www.prnewswire.com.* November 9: np.

Divestments, the exit of a business from a firm's portfolio, are quite common. One study found that large, prestigious U.S. companies divested more acquisitions than they had kept.[65] Well-known divestitures in business history include (1) Novell's purchase of WordPerfect for stock valued at $1.4 billion and later sold to Corel for $124 million, and (2) Quaker Oats' unloading of the Snapple Beverage Company to Triarc for only $300 million in 1997—three years after it had bought it for $1.8 billion!

Divesting a business can accomplish many different objectives.* As the examples above demonstrate, it can be used to help a firm reverse an earlier acquisition that didn't work out as planned. Often, this is simply to help "cut their losses." Other objectives include: (1) enabling managers to focus their efforts more directly on the firm's core businesses,[66] (2) providing the firm with more resources to spend on more attractive alternatives, and (3) raising cash to help fund existing businesses. Strategy Spotlight 6.5 discusses another reason for a divestiture. Here, Tyco International sold part of one of its businesses to raise cash for its share buyback.

Divesting can enhance a firm's competitive position only to the extent that it reduces its tangible (e.g., maintenance, investments, etc.) or intangible (e.g., opportunity costs, managerial attention) costs without sacrificing a current competitive

divestment the exit of a business from a firm's portfolio.

---

* Firms can divest their businesses in a number of ways. Sell-offs, spin-offs, equity carve-outs, asset sales/dissolution, and split-ups are some such modes of divestment. In a sell-off, the divesting firm privately negotiates with a third party to divest a unit/subsidiary for cash/stock. In a spin-off, a parent company distributes shares of the unit/subsidiary being divested pro-rata to its existing shareholders and a new company is formed. Equity carve-outs are similar to spin-offs except that shares in the unit/subsidiary being divested are offered to new shareholders. Dissolution involves sale of redundant assets, not necessarily as an entire unit/subsidiary as in sell-offs but a few bits at a time. A split-up, on the other hand, is an instance of divestiture where the parent company is split into two or more new companies and the parent ceases to exist. Shares in the parent company are exchanged for shares in new companies and the exact distribution varies case by case.

advantage or the seeds of future advantages.[67] To be effective, divesting requires a thorough understanding of a business unit's current ability and future potential to contribute to a firm's value creation. However, since such decisions involve a great deal of uncertainty, it is very difficult to make such evaluations. In addition, because of managerial self-interests and organizational inertia, firms often delay divestments of underperforming businesses.

Successful divestment involves establishing objective criteria for determining divestment candidates.[68] Clearly, firms should not panic and sell for a song in bad times. Private equity firms and conglomerates naturally place great emphasis on value when it comes to assessing which business units to keep. In identifying which assets to sell, the management committee of $10 billion Textron, for example, applies three tests of value to the firm's diverse portfolio—which is composed of some 12 divisions and 72 strategic business units (SBUs). For Textron to retain a business unit:

- The unit's long-term fundamentals must be sound. The team gauges this by assessing the attractiveness of each SBU's market and the unit's competitive strength within that market.
- Textron must be able to grow the unit's intrinsic value by 15 percent or more annually. The team applies this screen by carefully analyzing each SBU's business plan each year and challenging its divisional management teams to assess the value-growth potential of each business objectively.
- The unit's revenues must reach a certain threshold. Textron seeks to hold a portfolio of relevant businesses, each with at least $1 billion in revenue. Businesses that are not generating $1 billion or more in sales—and are not likely to reach this watershed within the foreseeable future—are targets for divestiture.

Strategic Alliances and Joint Ventures

strategic alliance a cooperative relationship between two or more firms.

A **strategic alliance** is a cooperative relationship between two (or more) firms.[69] Alliances may be either informal or formal—that is, involving a written contract. **Joint ventures** represent a special case of alliances, wherein two (or more) firms contribute equity to form a new legal entity.

Strategic alliances and joint ventures are assuming an increasingly prominent role in the strategy of leading firms, both large and small.[70] Such cooperative relationships have many potential advantages.[71] Among these are entering new markets, reducing manufacturing (or other) costs in the value chain, and developing and diffusing new technologies.[72]

joint ventures new entities formed within a strategic alliance in which two or more firms, the parents, contribute equity to form the new legal entity.

Entering New Markets   Often a company that has a successful product or service wants to introduce it into a new market. However, it may not have the financial resources or the requisite marketing expertise because it does not understand customer needs, know how to promote the product, or have access to the proper distribution channels.[73]

The partnerships formed between Time-Warner, Inc., and three African American–owned cable companies in New York City are examples of joint ventures created to serve a domestic market. Time-Warner built a 185,000-home cable system in the city and asked the three cable companies to operate it. Time-Warner supplied the product, and the cable companies supplied the knowledge of the community and the know-how to market the cable system. Joining with the local companies enabled Time-Warner to win the acceptance of the cable customers and to benefit from an improved image in the black community.

Strategy Spotlight 6.6 discusses how a strategic alliance between two firms will help them crowdsource creative concepts.

6.6

Crowdsourcing: How a Strategic Alliance Will Benefit Both Parties

MRM Worldwide, a New York–based advertising firm, has entered into a strategic alliance with Aniboom, a "virtual" animation company. The alliance is designed to bring MRM's clients quicker and more cost-efficient animation services.

Aniboom, an Israeli company with offices in New York and San Francisco, was founded in 2006 by Uri Shinar, the former CEO of Israeli broadcaster Kesheet. It is a web-based platform that connects 8,000 animators in 70 countries around the world with clients in the TV, film, music, and video game sectors. Prospective clients submit Request for Proposals (RFPs) via the platform, and animators all over the world can respond. MRM global Chief Creative Officer Oren Frank believes that agencies are more likely to rely on this crowdsourcing approach

Sources: Van Hoven, M. 2009. Strategic Alliances: MRM and Aniboom Team Up, Crowdsource. *www.mediabistro.com.* August 31: np; and McClellan, S. 2009. MRM, Aniboom Team Up. *www.adweek.com.* August 31: np.

strategy spotlight

in the future as clients seek more efficient ways of doing business.

MRM's plans are to have animators compete for work: "MRMs clients can launch a content creation competition in the Aniboom community for advertising solutions and have the community at large or a panel of judges select the top finalists and ultimate winner of the assignment. Or the competition could be private, with only the final results exhibited to the public."

Such competitions are part of a group of highly volatile trends that have become increasingly popular. They breed competition and bolster the idea that capitalism weeds out the weak links. It also becomes harder (or more unappealing) for established industries to bid on business that's sought through these methods, because costs can outweigh profits. However, there is one thing that it has done: The playing field has been leveled somewhat for new players. May the best _____ win!

crowdsourcing

Reducing Manufacturing (or Other) Costs in the Value Chain Strategic alliances (or joint ventures) often enable firms to pool capital, value-creating activities, or facilities in order to reduce costs. For example, Molson Companies and Carling O'Keefe Breweries in Canada formed a joint venture to merge their brewing operations. Although Molson had a modern and efficient brewery in Montreal, Carling's was outdated. However, Carling had the better facilities in Toronto. In addition, Molson's Toronto brewery was located on the waterfront and had substantial real estate value. Overall, the synergies gained by using their combined facilities more efficiently added $150 million of pretax earnings during the initial year of the venture. Economies of scale were realized and facilities were better utilized.

Developing and Diffusing New Technologies Strategic alliances also may be used to build jointly on the technological expertise of two or more companies. This may enable then to develop products technologically beyond the capability of the companies acting independently.[74]

STMicroelectronics (ST) is a high-tech company based in Geneva, Switzerland, that has thrived—largely due to the success of its strategic alliances.[75] The firm develops and manufactures computer chips for a variety of applications such as mobile phones, set-top boxes, smart cards, and flash memories. In 1995 it teamed up with Hewlett-Packard to develop powerful new processors for various digital applications that are now nearing completion. Another example was its strategic alliance with Nokia to develop a chip that would give Nokia's phones a longer battery life. Here, ST produced a chip that tripled standby time to 60 hours—a breakthough that gave Nokia a huge advantage in the marketplace.

The firm's CEO, Pasquale Pistorio, was among the first in the industry to form R&D alliances with other companies. Now ST's top 12 customers, including HP, Nokia, and Nortel, account for 45 percent of revenues. According to Pistorio, "Alliances are in our DNA." Such relationships help ST keep better-than-average growth rates, even in difficult times. That's because close partners are less likely to defect to other suppliers.

Potential Downsides   Despite their promise, many alliances and joint ventures fail to meet expectations for a variety of reasons.[76] First, without the proper partner, a firm should never consider undertaking an alliance, even for the best of reasons.[77] Each partner should bring the desired complementary strengths to the partnership. Ideally, the strengths contributed by the partners are unique; thus synergies created can be more easily sustained and defended over the longer term. The goal must be to develop synergies between the contributions of the partners, resulting in a win–win situation. Moreover, the partners must be compatible and willing to trust each other.[78] Unfortunately, often little attention is given to nurturing the close working relationships and interpersonal connections that bring together the partnering organizations.[79]

internal development entering a new business through investment in new facilities, often called corporate enterpreneurship and new venture development.

Internal Development

Firms can also diversify by means of corporate entrepreneurship and new venture development. **In today's economy, internal development is such an important means by which companies expand their businesses that we have devoted a whole chapter to it (see Chapter 12).** Sony and the Minnesota Mining & Manufacturing Co. (3M), for example, are known for their dedication to innovation, R&D, and cutting-edge technologies. For example, 3M has developed its entire corporate culture to support its ongoing policy of generating at least 25 percent of total sales from products created within the most recent four-year period. During the 1990s, 3M exceeded this goal by achieving about 30 percent of sales per year from new internally developed products.

Zingerman's, a gourmet deli, has created a new business based on their core competence in human resource management. We discuss this new internal venture in Strategy Spotlight 6.7

Compared to mergers and acquisitions, firms that engage in internal development capture the value created by their own innovative activities without having to "share the wealth" with alliance partners or face the difficulties associated with combining activities across the value chains of several firms or merging corporate cultures.[80] Also, firms can often develop new products or services at a relatively lower cost and thus rely on their own resources rather than turning to external funding.[81]

>LO6.6
Managerial behaviors that can erode the creation of value.

There are also potential disadvantages. It may be time consuming; thus, firms may forfeit the benefits of speed that growth through mergers or acquisitions can provide. This may be especially important among high-tech or knowledge-based organizations in fast-paced environments where being an early mover is critical. Thus, firms that choose to diversify through internal development must develop capabilities that allow them to move quickly from initial opportunity recognition to market introduction.

managerial motives managers acting in their own self-interest rather than to maximize long-term shareholder value.

How Managerial Motives Can Erode Value Creation

Thus far in the chapter, we have implicitly assumed that CEOs and top executives are "rational beings"; that is, they act in the best interests of shareholders to maximize long-term shareholder value. In the real world, however, they may often act in their own self-interest. We now address some managerial motives that can serve to erode, rather than

6.7

strategy spotlight

A Gourmet Deli Firm Leverages Its Core Competence and Creates a New Business

In 1982, when Ari Weinzweig and Paul Saginaw opened Zingerman's Delicatessen in Ann Arbor, Michigan, their goal was to offer a world-class corned-beef sandwich. By 2003, Zingerman's was named "The Coolest Small Company in America" by *Inc.* magazine. Today, the Zingerman's Community of Businesses—including seven businesses—employs more than 500 people and generates annual sales of more than $35 million.

In 1994, the firm created a training arm, ZingTrain, to develop and deliver seminars on how to hire, fire, and inspire people. The program, mainly targeted at managers and small-business owners, promises "tips, tools, and techniques" to be more effective at every step—from hiring to the exit interview. At one session, the 15 participants included four managers from a pizza chain, a furniture store owner, two nonprofit executives, a co-owner of an Italian ice-cart business, and a journalist.

Source: Kanter, R. M. 2009. Mergers That Stick. *Harvard Business Review,* 87(10): 121–125; O'Brien, C. 2008. ZingTrain Keeps Retail Workers on the Right Track. *newhope360.com.* October 1: np; and *www.zingtrain.com.*

● Zingerman's, a delicatessen, leveraged its core competence in human resource management to create training programs.

During the session, the leaders drew on Zingerman's culture, discussing the "compact" in which employees take responsibility for their training's effectiveness. There were also tips for writing a great job description.

---

enhance, value creation. These include "growth for growth's sake," excessive egotism, and the creation of a wide variety of antitakeover tactics.

Growth for Growth's Sake

There are huge incentives for executives to increase the size of their firm. And these are not consistent with increasing shareholder wealth. Top managers, including the CEO, of larger firms typically enjoy more prestige, higher rankings for their firms on the Fortune 500 list (based on revenues, *not* profits), greater incomes, more job security, and so on. There is also the excitement and associated recognition of making a major acquisition. As noted by Harvard's Michael Porter, "There's a tremendous allure to mergers and acquisitions. It's the big play, the dramatic gesture. With one stroke of the pen you can add billions to size, get a front-page story, and create excitement in markets."[82]

In recent years many high-tech firms have suffered from the negative impact of their uncontrolled growth. Consider, for example, Priceline.com's ill-fated venture into an online service to offer groceries and gasoline.[83] A myriad of problems—perhaps most importantly, a lack of participation by manufacturers—caused the firm to lose more than $5 million a *week* prior to abandoning these ventures. Such initiatives are often little more than desperate moves by top managers to satisfy investor demands for accelerating revenues. Unfortunately, the increased revenues often fail to materialize into a corresponding hike in earnings.

growth for growth's sake managers' actions to grow the size of their firms not to increase long-term profitability but to serve managerial self-interest.

strategy spotlight   6.8

Cornelius Vanderbilt: Going to Great Lengths to Correct a Wrong

Cornelius Vanderbilt's legendary ruthlessness set a bar for many titans to come. Back in 1853, the commodore took his first vacation, an extended voyage to Europe aboard his yacht. He was in for a big surprise when he returned.

Source: McGregor, J. 2007. Sweet Revenge. *Business Week*, January 22: 64–70.

Two of his associates had taken the power of attorney that he had left them and sold his interest in his steamship concern, Accessory Transit Company, to themselves.

"Gentlemen," he wrote, in a classic battle cry, "you have undertaken to cheat me. I won't sue you for the law is too slow. I'll ruin you." He converted his yacht to a passenger ship to compete with them and added other vessels. He started a new line, appropriately named *Opposition*. Before long, he bought his way back in and regained control of the company.

At times, executives' overemphasis on growth can result in a plethora of ethical lapses, which can have disastrous outcomes for their companies. A good example (of bad practice) is Joseph Bernardino's leadership at Andersen Worldwide. Bernardino had a chance early on to take a hard line on ethics and quality in the wake of earlier scandals at clients such as Waste Management and Sunbeam. Instead, according to former executives, he put too much emphasis on revenue growth. Consequently, the firm's reputation quickly eroded when it audited and signed off on the highly flawed financial statements of such infamous firms as Enron, Global Crossing, and WorldCom. Bernardino ultimately resigned in disgrace in March 2002, and his firm was dissolved later that year.[84]

egotism managers' actions to shape their firms' strategies to serve their selfish interests rather than to maximize long-term shareholder value.

Egotism

A healthy ego helps make a leader confident, clearheaded, and able to cope with change. CEOs, by their very nature, are intensely competitive people in the office as well as on the tennis court or golf course. But, sometimes when pride is at stake, individuals will go to great lengths to win. Such behaviour, of course, is not a new phenomenon. We discuss the case of Cornelius Vanderbilt, one of the original Americans moguls, in Strategy Spotlight 6.8

Egos can get in the way of a "synergistic" corporate marriage. Few executives (or lower-level managers) are exempt from the potential downside of excessive egos. Consider, for example, the reflections of General Electric's former CEO Jack Welch, considered by many to be the world's most admired executive. He admitted to a regrettable decision: "My hubris got in the way in the Kidder Peabody deal. [He was referring to GE's buyout of the soon-to-be-troubled Wall Street firm.] I got wise advice from Walter Wriston and other directors who said, 'Jack, don't do this.' But I was bully enough and on a run to do it. And I got whacked right in the head."[85] In addition to poor financial results, Kidder Peabody was wracked by a widely publicized trading scandal that tarnished the reputations of both GE and Kidder Peabody. Welch ended up selling Kidder in 1994.

The business press has included many stories of how egotism and greed have infiltrated organizations.[86] Some incidents are considered rather astonishing, such as Tyco's former (and now convicted) CEO Dennis Kozlowski's well-chronicled purchase of a $6,000 shower curtain and vodka-spewing, full-size replica of Michaelangelo's David.[87]

6.9

strategy spotlight

How Antitakeover Measures May Benefit Multiple Stakeholders, Not Just Management

Antitakeover defenses represent a gray area, because management can often legitimately argue that such actions are not there solely to benefit themselves. Rather, they can benefit other stakeholders, such as employees, customers, and the community.

In the late 1980s, takeovers were very popular. The Dayton Hudson Corporation (now Target) even appealed to the Minnesota legislature to pass an antitakeover bill to help Dayton Hudson in its struggle with Hafts—the former owners of Dart, a drug store chain on the East Coast. History had shown that the Dayton Hudson management in place at the time was much better able to manage Dayton Hudson in the long run. In addition to Minnesota, many states now have laws that allow firms to take the interests of all stakeholders into account when considering a takeover bid.

In the summer of 2003, Oracle launched a hostile bid for PeopleSoft. Many charged that the tactics of Oracle CEO Larry Ellison had been unfair, and many of

PeopleSoft's customers took its side, indicating that Oracle ownership would not be of benefit to them. PeopleSoft was concerned that Oracle was merely seeking to buy PeopleSoft for its lucrative base of application software and was not interested in supporting the company's products. Oracle, on the other hand, sued PeopleSoft in an attempt to have the latter's so-called poison pill takeover defense removed.

In December 2004, Oracle struck a deal to buy PeopleSoft—ending a bitter 18-month hostile takeover battle. Oracle's $10.3 billion acquisition valued the firm at $26.50 a share—an increase of 66 percent over its initial offer of $16 a share. Noted analyst John DiFucci: "This is a financial acquisition primarily. Oracle is buying PeopleSoft for its maintenance stream." And, worth noting, PeopleSoft executives, including CEO and company founder David Duffield, did not join Oracle during the conference call announcing the acquisition. Oracle dropped its suit against PeopleSoft in which the former charged that PeopleSoft's "poison pill" takeover defense should be dismissed.

On moral grounds, some antitakeover defenses are not undertaken to entrench and protect management, but often they are. When such defenses are used simply to keep management in power, they are wrong. However, when they are used to defend the long-term financial health of the company and to protect broader stakeholder interests, they will be morally permissible.

Sources: Bowie, N. E. & Werhane, P. H. 2005. *Management Ethics.* Malden, MA: Blackwell Publishing; and La Monica, P. R. 2004. Finally, Oracle to Buy PeopleSoft. *CNNMoney.com*, December 13: np.

Other well-known examples of power grabs and extraordinary consumption of compensation and perks include executives at Enron, the Rigas family who were convicted of defrauding Adelphia of roughly $1 billion, former CEO Bernie Ebbers's $408 million loan from WorldCom, and so on.

A more recent example of excess and greed was exhibited by John Thain.[88] On January 22, 2009, he was ousted as head of Merrill Lynch by Bank of America's CEO, Ken Lewis:

> Thain embarrassingly doled out $4 billion in discretionary year-end bonuses to favored employees just before Bank of America's rescue purchase of failing Merrill. The bonuses amounted to about 10 percent of Merrill's 2008 losses.
>
> Obviously, John Thain believed that he was entitled. When he took over ailing Merrill in early 2008, he began planning major cuts, but he also ordered that his office be redecorated. He spent $1.22 million of company funds to make it "livable," which, in part, included $87,000 for a rug, $87,000 for a pair of guest chairs, $68,000 for a 19th-century credenza, and (what really got the attention of the press) $35,000 for a "commode with legs."

antitakeover tactics managers' actions to avoid losing wealth or power as a result of a hostile takeover

He later agreed to repay the decorating costs. However, one might still ask: What kind of person treats other people's money like this? And who needs a commode that costs as much as a new Lexus? Finally, a comment by Bob O'Brien, stock editor at Barrons.com clearly applies: "The sense of entitlement that's been engendered in this group of people has clearly not been beaten out of them by the brutal performance of the financial sector over the course of the last year."

Antitakeover Tactics

greenmail a payment by a firm to a hostile party for the firm's stock at a premium, made when the firm's management feels that the hostile party is about to make a tender offer.

Unfriendly or hostile takeovers can occur when a company's stock becomes undervalued. A competing organization can buy the outstanding stock of a takeover candidate in sufficient quantity to become a large shareholder. Then it makes a tender offer to gain full control of the company. If the shareholders accept the offer, the hostile firm buys the target company and either fires the target firm's management team or strips them of their power. Thus, antitakeover tactics are common, including greenmail, golden parachutes, and poison pills.[89]

The first, **greenmail,** is an effort by the target firm to prevent an impending takeover. When a hostile firm buys a large block of outstanding target company stock and the target firm's management feels that a tender offer is impending, they offer to buy the stock back from the hostile company at a higher price than the unfriendly company paid for it. Although this often prevents a hostile takeover, the same price is not offered to preexisting shareholders. However, it protects the jobs of the target firm's management.

golden parachute a prearranged contract with managers specifying that, in the event of a hostile takeover, the target firm's managers will be paid a significant severance package.

Second, a **golden parachute** is a prearranged contract with managers specifying that, in the event of a hostile takeover, the target firm's managers will be paid a significant severance package. Although top managers lose their jobs, the golden parachute provisions protect their income.

Third, **poison pills** are used by a company to give shareholders certain rights in the event of a takeover by another firm. They are also known as shareholder rights plans.

Clearly, antitakeover tactics can often raise some interesting ethical—and legal—issues. Strategy Spotlight 6.9 addresses how antitakeover measures can benefit multiple stakeholders—not just management.

poison pill used by a company to give shareholders certain rights in the event of takeover by another firm.

Reflecting on Career Implications . . .

- *Corporate-Level Strategy:* Be aware of your firm's corporate-level strategy. Can you come up with an initiative that will create value both within and across business units?
- *Core Competencies:* What do you see as your core competencies? How can you leverage them both within your business unit as well as across other business units?
- *Sharing Infrastructures:* What infrastructure activities and resources (e.g., information systems, legal) are available in the corporate office that would help you add value for your business unit—or other business units?
- *Diversification:* From your career perspective, what actions can you take to diversify your employment risk (e.g., coursework at a local university, obtain professional certification such as a C.P.A., networking through professional affiliation, etc.)? For example, in periods of retrenchment, such actions will provide you with a greater number of career options.

Summary

A key challenge for today's managers is to create "synergy" when engaging in diversification activities. As we discussed in this chapter, corporate managers do not, in general, have a very good track record in creating value in such endeavors when it comes to mergers and acquisitions. Among the factors that serve to erode shareholder values are paying an excessive premium for the target firm, failing to integrate the activities of the newly acquired businesses into the corporate family, and undertaking diversification initiatives that are too easily imitated by the competition.

We addressed two major types of corporate-level strategy: related and unrelated diversification. With *related diversification* the corporation strives to enter into areas in which key resources and capabilities of the corporation can be shared or leveraged. Synergies come from horizontal relationships between business units. Cost savings and enhanced revenues can be derived from two major sources. First, economies of scope can be achieved from the leveraging of core competencies and the sharing of activities. Second, market power can be attained from greater, or pooled, negotiating power and from vertical integration.

When firms undergo *unrelated diversification* they enter product markets that are dissimilar to their present businesses. Thus, there is generally little opportunity to either leverage core competencies or share activities across business units. Here, synergies are created from vertical relationships between the corporate office and the individual business units. With unrelated diversification, the primary ways to create value are corporate restructuring and parenting, as well as the use of portfolio analysis techniques.

Corporations have three primary means of diversifying their product markets—mergers and acquisitions, joint ventures/strategic alliances, and internal development. There are key trade-offs associated with each of these. For example, mergers and acquisitions are typically the quickest means to enter new markets and provide the corporation with a high level of control over the acquired business. However, with the expensive premiums that often need to be paid to the shareholders of the target firm and the challenges associated with integrating acquisitions, they can also be quite expensive. Not surprisingly, many poorly performing acquisitions are subsequently divested. At times, however, divestitures can help firms refocus their efforts and generate resources. Strategic alliances and joint ventures between two or more firms, on the other hand, may be a means of reducing risk since they involve the sharing and combining of resources. But such joint initiatives also provide a firm with less control (than it would have with an acquisition) since governance is shared between two independent entities. Also, there is a limit to the potential upside for each partner because returns must be shared as well. Finally, with internal development, a firm is able to capture all of the value from its initiatives (as opposed to sharing it with a merger or alliance partner). However, diversification by means of internal development can be very time-consuming—a disadvantage that becomes even more important in fast-paced competitive environments.

Finally, some managerial behaviors may serve to erode shareholder returns. Among these are "growth for growth's sake," egotism, and antitakeover tactics. As we discussed, some of these issues—particularly antitakeover tactics—raise ethical considerations because the managers of the firm are not acting in the best interests of the shareholders.

Summary Review Questions

1. Discuss how managers can create value for their firm through diversification efforts.
2. What are some of the reasons that many diversification efforts fail to achieve desired outcomes?
3. How can companies benefit from related diversification? Unrelated diversification? What are some of the key concepts that can explain such success?
4. What are some of the important ways in which a firm can restructure a business?
5. Discuss some of the various means that firms can use to diversify. What are the pros and cons associated with each of these?
6. Discuss some of the actions that managers may engage in to erode shareholder value.

Key Terms

corporate-level
  strategy, 202
diversification, 204
related diversification, 206
economies of scope, 206
core competencies, 206
sharing activities, 208
market power, 209
pooled negotiating
  power, 209
vertical integration, 210
transaction cost
  perspective, 213

unrelated
  diversification, 214
parenting advantage, 214
restructuring, 215
portfolio
  management, 216
acquisitions, 220
mergers, 220
divestment, 225
strategic alliance, 226
joint ventures, 226
internal
  development, 228

Application Questions & Exercises

1. What were some of the largest mergers and acquisitions over the last two years? What was the rationale for these actions? Do you think they will be successful? Explain.

2. Discuss some examples from business practice in which an executive's actions appear to be in his or her self-interest rather than the corporation's well-being.

3. Discuss some of the challenges that managers must overcome in making strategic alliances successful. What are some strategic alliances with which you are familiar? Were they successful or not? Explain.

4. Use the Internet and select a company that has recently undertaken diversification into new product markets. What do you feel were some of the reasons for this diversification (e.g., leveraging core competencies, sharing infrastructures)?

Ethics Questions

1. In recent years there has been a rash of corporate downsizing and layoffs. Do you feel that such actions raise ethical considerations? Why or why not?

2. What are some of the ethical issues that arise when managers act in a manner that is counter to their firm's best interests? What are the long-term implications for both the firms and the managers themselves?

Experiential Exercise

Time Warner (formerly AOL Time Warner) is a firm that follows a strategy of related diversification. Evaluate its success (or lack thereof) with regard to how well it has: (1) built on core competencies, (2) shared infrastructures, and (3) increased market power. (Fill answers in table below.)

Rationale for Related Diversification	Successful/Unsuccessful?	Why?
1. Build on core competencies		
2. Share infrastructures		
3. Increase market power		

References

1. Anonymous. 2010. Bebo sold by AOL after just two years. *www.bbc.co.uk.* June 17: np; Anonymous. 2010. AOL plans to sell or shut down Bebo. *www.bbc.co.uk.* April 7: np; Pimentel, B. 2008. AOL to buy Bebo for $850. *www.marketwatch.com.* October 25: np; Sarno, D. 2010. AOL posts loss but stock rises. *Los Angeles Times,* August 5: 3; Quinn, J. 2005. AOL losses top $1bn after write-downs. *The Daily Telegraph.* August 5: 3; Shearman, S. 2010. Returning to the fray. *Marketing.* October 13: 19;

Steel, E. & Worthen, B. 2010 With Bebo a no-go, AOL will unload the social site. *The Wall Street Journal,* June 17: B1; and Whitney, L. 2010. AOL sells off Bebo at last. *www.news.cnet.com.* October 25: np. We thank Ciprian Stan for his valued contribution.

2. Insights on measuring M&A performance are addressed in: Zollo, M. & Meier, D. 2008. What is M&A performance? *BusinessWeek,* 22(3): 55–77.

3. Insights on how and why firms may overpay for acquisitions are

addressed in: Malhotra, D., Ku, G., & Murnighan, J. K. 2008. When winning is everything. *Harvard Business Review,* 66(5); 78–86.

4. Pfizer deal helps lift stocks. 2009. online.wsy.com, January 26: np.

5. Dr. G. William Schwert, University of Rochester study cited in Pare, T. P. 1994. The new merger boom. *Fortune.* November 28: 96.

6. Lipin, S. & Deogun, N. 2000. Big mergers of the 1990's prove disappointing to shareholders. *The Wall Street Journal.* October 30: C1.

7. Rothenbuecher, J. & Schrottke, J. 2008. To get value from a merger, grow sales. *Harvard Business Review,* 86(5): 24–25; and Rothenbuecher, J. 2008. Personal communication, October 1.

8. Kyriazis, D. 2010. The long-term post acquisition performance of Greek acquiring firms. *International Research Journal of Finance and Economics.* 43: 69–79.

9. Pare, T. P. 1994. The new merger boom. *Fortune,* November 28: 96.

10. A discussion of the effects of director experience and acquisition performance is in: McDonald, M. L. & Westphal, J. D. 2008. What do they know? The effects of outside director acquisition experience on firm acquisition performance. *Strategic Management Journal,* 29(11): 1155–1177.

11. Ghosn, C. 2006. Inside the alliance: The win–win nature of a unique business mode. *Address to the Detroit Economic Club,* November 16.

12. For a study that investigates several predictors of corporate diversification, read: Wiersema, M. F. & Bowen, H. P. 2008. Corporate diversification: The impact of foreign competition, industry globalization, and product diversification. *Strategic Management Journal,* 29(2): 114–132.

13. Kumar, M. V. S. 2011. Are joint ventures positive sum games? The relative effects of cooperative and non-cooperative behavior. *Strategic Management Journal,* 32(1): 32–54.

14. Makri, M., Hitt, M. A., & Lane, P. J. 2010. Complementary technologies, knowledge relatedness, and invention outcomes in high technology mergers and acquisitions. *Strategic Management Journal,* 31(6): 602–628.

15. A discussion of Tyco's unrelated diversification strategy is in: Hindo, B. 2008. Solving Tyco's identity crisis. *BusinessWeek,* February 18: 62.

16. Our framework draws upon a variety of sources, including Goold, M. & Campbell, A. 1998. Desperately seeking synergy. *Harvard Business Review,* 76(5): 131–143; Porter, M. E. 1987. From advantage to corporate strategy. *Harvard Business Review,* 65(3): 43–59; and Hitt, M. A., Ireland,

R. D., & Hoskisson, R. E. 2001. *Strategic management: competitiveness and globalization* (4th ed.). Cincinnati, OH: South-Western.

17. Collis, D. J. & Montgomery, C. A. 1987. *Corporate strategy: Resources and the scope of the firm.* New York: McGraw-Hill.

18. This imagery of the corporation as a tree and related discussion draws on Prahalad, C. K. & Hamel, G. 1990. The core competence of the corporation. *Harvard Business Review,* 68(3): 79–91. Parts of this section also draw on Picken, J. C. & Dess, G. G. 1997. *Mission critical:* chap. 5. Burr Ridge, IL: Irwin Professional Publishing.

19. Graebner, M. E., Eisenhardt, K. M. & Roundy, P. T. 2010. Success and failure in technology acquisitions: Lessons for buyers and sellers. *The Academy of Management Perspectives,* 24(3): 73–92.

20. This section draws on Prahalad & Hamel, op. cit.; and Porter, op. cit.

21. A recent study that investigates the relationship between a firm's technology resources, diversification, and performance can be found in Miller, D. J. 2004. Firms' technological resources and the performance effects of diversification. A longitudinal study. *Strategic Management Journal,* 25: 1097–1119.

22. Collis & Montgomery, op. cit.

23. Fisher, A. 2008. America's most admired companies. *Fortune,* March 17: 74.

24. Henricks, M. 1994. VF seeks global brand dominance. *Apparel Industry Magazine,* August: 21–40; VF Corporation. 1993. First quarter corporate summary report. *1993 VF Annual Report.*

25. Hill, A. & Hargreaves, D. 2001. Turbulent times for GE-Honeywell deal. *Financial Times,* February 28: 26.

26. An interesting discussion of a merger in the Russian mining industry is in: Bush, J. 2008. Welding a new metals giant. *BusinessWeek,* July 14 & 21: 56.

27. Lowry, T. 2001. Media. *BusinessWeek,* January 8: 100–101.

28. This section draws on Hrebiniak, L. G. & Joyce, W. F. 1984. *Implementing*

strategy. New York: MacMillan; and Oster, S. M. 1994. *Modern competitive analysis.* New York: Oxford University Press.

29. The discussion of the benefits and costs of vertical integration draws on Hax, A. C. & Majluf, N. S. 1991. *The strategy concept and process: A pragmatic approach:* 139. Englewood Cliffs, NJ: Prentice Hall.

30. Fahey, J. 2005. Gray winds. *Forbes.* January 10: 143.

31. This discussion draws on Oster, op. cit.; and Harrigan, K. 1986. Matching vertical integration strategies to competitive conditions. *Strategic Management Journal,* 7(6): 535–556.

32. For a scholarly explanation on how transaction costs determine the boundaries of a firm, see Oliver E. Williamson's pioneering books *Markets and Hierarchies: Analysis and Antitrust Implications* (New York: Free Press, 1975) and *The Economic Institutions of Capitalism* (New York: Free Press, 1985).

33. Campbell, A., Goold, M., & Alexander, M. 1995. Corporate strategy: The quest for parenting advantage. *Harvard Business Review,* 73(2): 120–132; and Picken & Dess, op. cit.

34. Anslinger, P. A. & Copeland, T. E. 1996. Growth through acquisition: A fresh look. *Harvard Business Review,* 74(1): 126–135.

35. Campbell et al., op. cit.

36. This section draws on Porter, op. cit.; and Hambrick, D. C. 1985. Turnaround strategies. In Guth, W. D. (Ed.). *Handbook of business strategy:* 10-1–10-32. Boston: Warren, Gorham & Lamont.

37. There is an important delineation between companies that are operated for a long-term profit and those that are bought and sold for short-term gains. The latter are sometimes referred to as "holding companies" and are generally more concerned about financial issues than strategic issues.

38. Lenzner, R. 2007. High on Loews. *Forbes,* February 26: 98–102.

39. Casico. W. F. 2002. Strategies for responsible restructuring. *Academy of Management Executive,* 16(3): 80–91; and Singh, H. 1993. Challenges in

researching corporate restructuring. *Journal of Management Studies,* 30(1): 147–172.

40. Cusack, M. 1987. *Hanson Trust: A review of the company and its prospects.* London: Hoare Govett.

41. Hax & Majluf, op. cit. By 1979, 45 percent of Fortune 500 companies employed some form of portfolio analysis, according to Haspelagh, P. 1982. Portfolio planning: Uses and limits. *Harvard Busines Review,* 60: 58–73. A later study conducted in 1993 found that over 40 percent of the respondents used portfolio analysis techniques, but the level of usage was expected to increase to more than 60 percent in the near future: Rigby, D. K. 1994. Managing the management tools. *Planning Review,* September–October: 20–24.

42. Goold, M. & Luchs, K. 1993. Why diversify? Four decades of management thinking. *Academy of Management Executive,* 7(3): 7–25.

43. Other approaches include the industry attractiveness–business strength matrix developed jointly by General Electric and McKinsey and Company, the life-cycle matrix developed by Arthur D. Little, and the profitability matrix proposed by Marakon. For an extensive review, refer to Hax & Majluf, op. cit.: 182–194.

44. Porter, op. cit.: 49–52.

45. Collis, D. J. 1995. Portfolio planning at Ciba-Geigy and the Newport investment proposal. Harvard Business School Case No. 9-795-040. Novartis AG was created in 1996 by the merger of Ciba-Geigy and Sandoz.

46. Buzzell, R. D. & Gale, B. T. 1987. *The PIMS principles: Linking strategy to performance.* New York: Free Press; and Miller, A. & Dess, G. G. 1996. *Strategic management,* (2nd ed.). New York: McGraw-Hill.

47. Seeger, J. 1984. Reversing the images of BCG's growth share matrix. *Strategic Management Journal,* 5(1): 93–97.

48. Picken & Dess, op. cit.; Cabot Corporation. 2001. 10-Q filing, Securities and Exchange Commission, May 14.

49. Koudsi, S. 2001. Remedies for an economic hangover. *Fortune,* June 25: 130–139.

50. Insights on the performance of serial acquirers is found in: Laamanen, T. & Keil, T. 2008. Performance of serial acquirers: Toward an acquisition program perspective. *Strategic Management Journal,* 29(6): 663–672.

51. Some insights from Lazard's CEO on mergers and acquisitions are addressed in: Stewart, T. A. & Morse, G. 2008. Giving great advice. *Harvard Business Review,* 66(1): 106–113.

52. Coy, P., Thornton, E., Arndt, M., & Grow, B. 2005. Shake, rattle, and merge. *BusinessWeek,* January 10: 32–35; and Anonymous. 2005. Love is in the air. *Economist,* February 5: 9.

53. Silva, M. & Rovella, D. E. 2011. Intel is model to fight unfair competition, FTC chairman says. www.bloomberg.com. January 11: np.

54. For an interesting study of the relationship between mergers and a firm's product-market strategies, refer to Krisnan, R. A., Joshi, S., & Krishnan, H. 2004. The influence of mergers on firms' product-mix strategies. *Strategic Management Journal,* 25: 587–611.

55. Carey, D., moderator. 2000. A CEO roundtable on making mergers succeed. *Harvard Business Review,* 78(3): 146.

56. Shinal, J. 2001. Can Mike Volpi make Cisco sizzle again? *BusinessWeek,* February 26: 102–104; Kambil, A., Eselius, E. D., & Monteiro, K. A. 2000. Fast venturing: The quick way to start Web businesses. *Sloan Management Review,* 41(4): 55–67; and Elstrom, P. 2001. Sorry, Cisco: The old answers won't work. *BusinessWeek,* April 30: 39.

57. Like many high-tech firms during the economic slump that began in mid-2000, Cisco Systems experienced declining performance. On April 16, 2001, it announced that its revenues for the quarter closing April 30 would drop 5 percent from a year earlier—and a stunning 30 percent from the previous three months—to about $4.7 billion. Furthermore, Cisco announced that it would lay off 8,500 employees and take an enormous $2.5 billion charge to write down

inventory. By late October 2002, its stock was trading at around $10, down significantly from its 52-week high of $70. Elstrom, op. cit.: 39.

58. Coy, P., Thornton, E., Arndt, M., & Grow, B. 2005, Shake, rattle, and merge. *BusinessWeek,* January 10: 32–35; and, Anonymous. 2005. The rise of the superbrands. *Economist.* February 5: 63–65; and, Sellers, P. 2005. It was a no-brainer. *Fortune,* February 21: 96–102.

59. For a discussion of the trend toward consolidation of the steel industry and how Lakshmi Mittal is becoming a dominant player, read Reed, S. & Arndt, M. 2004. The Raja of steel. *BusinessWeek,* December 20: 50–52.

60. Barrett, A. 2001. Drugs. *BusinessWeek,* January 8: 112–113.

61. Whalen, C. J., Pascual, A. M., Lowery, T., & Muller, J. 2001. The top 25 managers. *BusinessWeek,* January 8: 63.

62. This discussion draws upon Rappaport, A. & Sirower, M. L. 1999. Stock or cash? The trade-offs for buyers and sellers in mergers and acquisitions. *Harvard Business Review,* 77(6): 147–158; and Lipin, S. & Deogun, N. 2000. Big mergers of 90s prove disappointing to shareholders. *The Wall Street Journal,* October 30: C1.

63. The downside of mergers in the airline industry is found in: Gimbel, B. 2008. Why airline mergers don't fly. *BusinessWeek,* March 17: 26.

64. Mouio, A. (Ed.). 1998. Unit of one. *Fast Company,* September: 82.

65. Porter, M. E. 1987. From competitive advantage to corporate strategy. *Harvard Business Review,* 65(3): 43.

66. The divestiture of a business which is undertaken in order to enable managers to better focus on its core business has been termed "downscoping." Refer to Hitt, M. A., Harrison, J. S., & Ireland, R. D. 2001. *Mergers and acquisitions: A guide to creating value for stakeholders.* Oxford Press: New York.

67. Sirmon, D. G., Hitt, M. A., & Ireland, R. D. 2007. Managing firm resources in dynamic environments to create value: Looking inside the black box. *Academy of Management Review,* 32(1): 273–292.

68. This discussion draws on: Mankins, M. C., Harding, D., & Weddigne, R-M. 2008. How the best divest. *Harvard Business Review,* 86(1): 92–99.

69. A study that investigates alliance performance is: Lunnan, R. & Haugland, S. A. 2008. Predicting and measuring alliance performance: A multidimensional analysis. *Strategic Management Journal,* 29(5): 545–556.

70. For scholarly perspectives on the role of learning in creating value in strategic alliances, refer to Anard, B. N. & Khanna, T. 2000. Do firms learn to create value? *Strategic Management Journal,* 12(3): 295–317; and Vermeulen, F. & Barkema, H. P. 2001. Learning through acquisitions. *Academy of Management Journal,* 44(3): 457–476.

71. For a detailed discussion of transaction cost economics in strategic alliances, read Reuer, J. J. & Arno, A. 2007. Strategic alliance contracts: Dimensions and determinants of contractual complexity. *Strategic Management Journal,* 28(3): 313–330.

72. This section draws on Hutt, M. D., Stafford, E. R., Walker, B. A., & Reingen, P. H. 2000. Case study: Defining the strategic alliance. *Sloan Management Review,* 41(2): 51–62; and Walters, B. A., Peters, S., & Dess, G. G. 1994. Strategic alliances and joint ventures: Making them work. *Business Horizons,* 4: 5–10.

73. A study that investigates strategic alliances and networks is: Tiwana, A. 2008. Do bridging ties complement strong ties? An empirical examination of alliance ambidexterity.

Strategic Management Journal, 29(3): 251–272.

74. Phelps, C. 2010. A longitudinal study of the influence of alliance network structure and composition on firm exploratory innovation. *Academy of Management Journal,* 53(4): 890–913.

75. Edmondson, G. & Reinhardt, A. 2001. From niche player to Goliath. *BusinessWeek,* March 12: 94–96.

76. For an institutional theory perspective on strategic alliances, read: Dacin, M. T., Oliver, C., & Roy, J. P. 2007. The legitimacy of strategic alliances: An institutional perspective. *Strategic Management Journal,* 28(2): 169–187.

77. A study investigating factors that determine partner selection in strategic alliances is found in: Shah, R. H. & Swaminathan, V. 2008. *Strategic Management Journal,* 29(5): 471–494.

78. Arino, A. & Ring, P. S. 2010. The role of fairness in alliance formation. *Strategic Management Journal,* 31(6): 1054–1087.

79. Greve, H. R., Baum, J. A. C., Mitsuhashi, H. & Rowley, T. J. 2010. Built to last but falling apart: Cohesion, friction, and withdrawal from interfirm alliances. *Academy of Management Journal,* 53(4): 302–322.

80. For an insightful perspective on how to manage conflict between innovation and ongoing operations in an organization, read: Govindarajan, V. & Trimble, C. 2010. *The other side of innovation: Solving the execution*

challenge. Boston, MA: Harvard Business School Press.

81. Dunlap-Hinkler, D., Kotabe, M. & Mudambi, R. 2010. A story of breakthrough versus incremental innovation: Corporate entrepreneurship in the global pharmaceutical industry. *Strategic Entrepreneurship Journal.* 4(2): 106–127.

82. Porter, op. cit.: 43–59.

83. Angwin, J. S. & Wingfield, N. 2000. How Jay Walker built WebHouse on a theory that he couldn't prove. *The Wall Street Journal,* October 16: A1, A8.

84. The fallen. 2003. *BusinessWeek,* January 13: 80–82.

85. The Jack Welch example draws upon Sellers, P. 2001. Get over yourself. *Fortune,* April 30: 76–88.

86. Li, J. & Tang, Y. 2010. CEO hubris and firm risk taking in China: The moderating role of managerial discretion. *Academy of Management Journal,* 53(1): 45–68.

87. Polek, D. 2002. The rise and fall of Dennis Kozlowski. *BusinessWeek,* December 23: 64–77.

88. John Thain and his golden commode. 2009. Editorial. Dallasnews .com, January 26: np; Task, A. 2009. Wall Street's $18.4B bonus: The sense of entitlement has not been beaten out. finance.yahoo.com, January 29: np; and Exit Thain. 2009. Newsfinancialcareers.com, January 22: np.

89. This section draws on Weston, J. F., Besley, S., & Brigham, E. F. 1996. *Essentials of managerial finance* (11th ed.): 18–20. Fort Worth, TX: Dryden Press, Harcourt Brace.

Chapter 7. International Strategy: Creating Value in Global Markets

chapter SEVEN

International Strategy:

Creating Value in Global Markets

After reading this chapter, you should have a good understanding of:

LO7.1 The importance of international expansion as a viable diversification strategy.

LO7.2 The sources of national advantage; that is, why an industry in a given country is more (or less) successful than the same industry in another country.

LO7.3 The motivations (or benefits) and the risks associated with international expansion, including the emerging trend for greater offshoring and outsourcing activity.

LO7.4 The two opposing forces—cost reduction and adaptation to local markets—that firms face when entering international markets.

LO7.5 The advantages and disadvantages associated with each of the four basic strategies: international, global, multidomestic, and transnational.

LO7.6 The difference between regional companies and truly global companies.

LO7.7 The four basic types of entry strategies and the relative benefits and risks associated with each of them.

LEARNING OBJECTIVES

The global marketplace provides many opportunities for firms to increase their revenue base and their profitability. Furthermore, in today's knowledge-intensive economy, there is the potential to create advantages by leveraging firm knowledge when crossing national boundaries to do business. At the same time, however, there are pitfalls and risks that firms must avoid in order to be successful. In this chapter we will provide insights on how to be successful and create value when diversifying into global markets.

After some introductory comments on the global economy, we address the question: What explains the level of success of a given industry in a given country? To provide a framework for analysis, we draw on Michael Porter's "diamond of national advantage," in which he identified four factors that help to explain performance differences.

In the second section of the chapter, we shift our focus to the level of the firm and discuss some of the major motivations and risks associated with international expansion. Recognizing such potential benefits and risks enables managers to better assess the growth and profit potential in a given country. We also address important issues associated with a topic of growing interest in the international marketplace—offshoring and outsourcing.

Next, in the third section—the largest in this chapter—we address how firms can attain competitive advantages in the global marketplace. We discuss two opposing forces firms face when entering foreign markets: cost reduction and local adaptation. Depending on the intensity of each of these forces, they should select among four basic strategies: international, global, multidomestic, and transnational. We discuss both the strengths and limitations of each of these strategies. We also present a recent perspective which posits that even the largest multinational firms are more regional than global even today.

The final section addresses the four categories of entry strategies that firms may choose in entering foreign markets. These strategies vary along a continuum from low investment, low control (exporting) to high investment, high control (wholly owned subsidiaries and greenfield ventures). We discuss the pros and cons associated with each.

▦ Learning from Mistakes

Carrefour is Europe's top retailer and ranks second in the world (behind Walmart). However, in late 2010, it decided to close up shop in much of Southeast Asia.[1] Its 44 stores in Thailand, 23 in Malaysia, and 2 in Singapore are up for sale. Potential buyers include Britain's Tesco, Japan's Aeon, and France's Casino.

Unfortunately, Carrefour's retreat may be ill-timed. Compared to Europe, the Southeast Asian economy is very strong. Thailand's modern retail sector is growing rapidly despite the country's political turmoil. Ditto for Malaysia. What went wrong?

Carrefour was one of the first foreign grocers to open shops in the region in the 1990s. However, Tesco, which arrived later, was far savvier in figuring out what consumers wanted. For example, when it found out that Thai shoppers traveled for miles to its "big-box" stores, it opened much smaller stores in rural towns. Carrefour, on the other hand, focused on Bangkok's big spenders and stuck to its hypermarket format. Toby Desforges, a marketing consultant, called this a "take it or leave it" approach. Unfortunately, Thai shoppers left it.

Another factor in Tesco's success in these markets was its choice of local partners. For example, in Thailand, it joined forces with CP Group, an agri-conglomerate, before going it alone. And its Malaysian partner, Sime Darby, was able to help it find properties that were suitable for its hypermarkets. Tesco also acquired eight stores in Malaysia from a rival in 2007. In contrast, Carrefour decided to go it alone in both markets and found itself boxed in by rivals.

Carrefour has operations in about 30 countries (twice as many as Tesco) and it may have overreached. In 2009, it pulled the plug on Russia—only months after opening its first store there. Tesco's outgoing chief executive, Sir Terry Leahy, felt that its rival entered emerging markets without a clear roadmap. He asserts, "Lots of retailers have begun international expansion, hit a problem, then retreated and lost market share." In the end, Carrefour ranked a distant fourth in Thailand and Malaysia; Tesco was first in both countries. Globally speaking, Carrefour still outranks Tesco in total revenues. But Tesco is more profitable.

In this chapter we discuss how firms create value and achieve competitive advantage in the global marketplace. Multinational firms are constantly faced with the dilemma of choosing between local adaptation—in product offerings, locations, advertising, and pricing—and global integration. We discuss how firms can avoid pitfalls such as those experienced by Carrefour in Southeast Asia. In addition, we address factors that can influence a nation's success in a particular industry. In our view, this is an important context in determining how well firms might eventually do when they compete beyond their nation's boundaries.

>LO7.1
The importance of international expansion as a viable diversification strategy.

The Global Economy: A Brief Overview

Managers face many opportunities and risks when they diversify abroad.[2] The trade among nations has increased dramatically in recent years and it is estimated that by 2015, the trade *across* nations will exceed the trade within nations. In a variety of industries such as semiconductors, automobiles, commercial aircraft, telecommunications, computers, and consumer electronics, it is almost impossible to survive unless firms scan the world for competitors, customers, human resources, suppliers, and technology.[3]

GE's wind energy business benefits by tapping into talent around the world. The firm has built research centers in China, Germany, India, and the U.S. "We did it," says CEO Jeffrey Immelt, "to access the best brains everywhere in the world." All four centers have played a key role in GE's development of huge 92-ton turbines:[4]

- Chinese researchers in Shanghai designed the microprocessors that control the pitch of the blade.

- Mechanical engineers from India (Bangalore) devised mathematical models to maximize the efficiency of materials in the turbine.
- Power-systems experts in the U.S. (Niskayuna, New York), which has researchers from 55 countries, do the design work.
- Technicians in Munich, Germany, have created a "smart" turbine that can calculate wind speeds and signal sensors in other turbines to produce maximum electricity.

The rise of **globalization**—meaning the rise of market capitalism around the world—has undeniably contributed to the economic boom in America's New Economy, where knowledge is the key source of competitive advantage and value creation.[5] It is estimated that it has brought phone service to about 300 million households in developing nations and a transfer of nearly $2 trillion from rich countries to poor countries through equity, bond investments, and commercial loans.[6]

There have been extremes in the effect of global capitalism on national economies and poverty levels around the world.[7] The economies of East Asia have attained rapid growth, but there has been comparatively little progress in other areas of the world.[8] For example, income in Latin America grew by only 6 percent in the past two decades when the continent was opening up to global capitalism. Average incomes in sub-Saharan Africa and the old Eastern European bloc have actually declined. The World Bank estimates that the number of people living on $1 per day has *increased* to 1.3 billion over the past decade.

Such disparities in wealth among nations raise an important question: Why do some countries and their citizens enjoy the fruits of global capitalism while others are mired in poverty? Or why do some governments make the best use of inflows of foreign investment and know-how and others do not? There are many explanations. Among these are the need of governments to have track records of business-friendly policies to attract multinationals and local entrepreneurs to train workers, invest in modern technology, and nurture local suppliers and managers. Also, it means carefully managing the broader economic factors in an economy, such as interest rates, inflation, and unemployment, as well as a good legal system that protects property rights, strong educational systems, and a society where prosperity is widely shared.

The above policies are the type that East Asia—in locations such as Hong Kong, Taiwan, South Korea, and Singapore—has employed to evolve from the sweatshop economies of the 1960s and 1970s to industrial powers today. On the other hand, many countries have moved in the other direction. For example, in Guatemala only 52.0 percent of males complete fifth grade and an astonishing 39.8 percent of the population subsists on less than $1 per day.[9] (By comparison, the corresponding numbers for South Korea are 98 percent and less than 2 percent, respectively.)

Strategy Spotlight 7.1 provides an interesting perspective on global trade—marketing to the "bottom of the pyramid."[10] This refers to the practice of a multinational firm targeting its goods and services to the nearly 5 billion poor people in the world who inhabit developing countries. Collectively, this represents a very large market with $14 trillion in purchasing power.

Next, we will address in more detail the question of why some nations and their industries are more competitive.[11] This establishes an important context or setting for the remainder of the chapter. After we discuss why some *nations and their industries* outperform others, we will be better able to address the various strategies that *firms* can take to create competitive advantage when they expand internationally.

globalization has two meanings. One is the increase in international exchange, including trade in goods and services as well as exchange of money, ideas, and information. Two is the growing similarity of laws, rules, norms, values, and ideas across countries.

Diamond of national advantage a framework for explaining why countries foster successful multinational corporations, consisting of four factors—factor endowments; demand conditions; related and supporting industries; and firm strategy, structure, and rivalry.

Factors Affecting a Nation's Competitiveness

Michael Porter of Harvard University conducted a four-year study in which he and a team of 30 researchers looked at the patterns of competitive success in 10 leading trading

strategy spotlight

Marketing to the "Bottom of the Pyramid"

Many executives wrongly believe that profitable opportunities to sell consumer goods exist only in countries where income levels are high. Even when they expand internationally, they often tend to limit their marketing to only the affluent segments within the developing countries. Such narrow conceptualizations of the market cause them to ignore the vast opportunities that exist at "the bottom of the pyramid," according to University of Michigan professor C. K. Prahalad. The *bottom of the pyramid* refers to the nearly 5 billion poor people who inhabit the developing countries. Surprisingly, they represent $14 trillion in purchasing power! And they are looking for products and services that can improve the quality of their lives such as clean energy, personal-care products, lighting, and medicines. Multinationals are missing out on growth opportunities if they ignore this vast segment of the market.

Unilever, the Anglo-Dutch maker of such brands as Dove, Lipton, and Vaseline, built a following among the world's poorest consumers by upending some of the basic rules of marketing. Instead of focusing on value for money, it shrunk packages to set a price even consumers living on $2 a day could afford. It helped people make money to buy its products. "It's not about doing good," but about tapping new markets, says Chief Executive Patrick Cescau.

Sources: Reingold, J. 2011. Can P&G Make Money in Places Where People Earn $2-A-Day? *Fortune*, January 17: 86–91; McGregor, J. 2008. The World's Most Influential Companies. *BusinessWeek*, December 22: 43–53; Miller, C. C. 2006. Easy Money. *Forbes*, November 27: 134–138; and Prahalad, C. K. 2005. *The Fortune at the Bottom of the Pyramid: Eradicating Poverty through Profits.* Philadelphia: Wharton School Publishing.

The strategy was forged about 25 years ago when Indian subsidiary Hindustan Lever (HL) found its products out of reach for millions of Indians. HL came up with a strategy to lower the price while making a profit: single-use packets for everything from shampoo to laundry detergent, costing pennies a pack. A bargain? Maybe not. But it put marquee brands within reach.

It has trained rural women to sell products to their neighbors. "What Unilever does well is get inside these communities, understand their needs, and adapt its business model accordingly," notes a professor at Barcelona's IESE Business School.

Similarly, Procter & Gamble, with $79 billion in annual revenues, has launched a skunkworks. It is staffed mostly by technical staff, rather than market researchers, to approach the $2-a-day consumer from a new perspective. Rather than try to invent products first or rely on market research alone, the group spends days or weeks in the field, visiting homes in Brazil, China, India, and elsewhere. It's the same approach the company uses in developed markets but requires much more effort, without the obvious potential payoff from consumers with disposable income. According to Robert McDonald, P&G's CEO and Chairman: "Our innovation strategy is not just diluting the top-tier product for the lower-end consumer. You have to discretely innovate for every one of those consumers on that economic curve, and if you don't do that, you'll fail."

No one is helped by viewing the poor as the wretched of the earth. Instead, they are the latest frontier of opportunity for those who can meet their needs. A vast market that is barely tapped, the bottom of the pyramid offers enormous opportunities.

---

factor endowments (national advantage) a nation's position in factors of production.

demand conditions (national advantage) the nature of home-market demand for the industry's product or service.

nations. He concluded that there are four broad attributes of nations that individually, and as a system, constitute what is termed "the diamond of national advantage." In effect, these attributes jointly determine the playing field that each nation establishes and operates for its industries. These factors are:

- *Factor endowments.* The nation's position in factors of production, such as skilled labor or infrastructure, necessary to compete in a given industry.
- *Demand conditions.* The nature of home-market demand for the industry's product or service.
- *Related and supporting industries.* The presence or absence in the nation of supplier industries and other related industries that are internationally competitive.
- *Firm strategy, structure, and rivalry.* The conditions in the nation governing how companies are created, organized, and managed, as well as the nature of domestic rivalry.

Factor Endowments[12,13]

Classical economics suggests that factors of production such as land, labor, and capital are the building blocks that create usable consumer goods and services.[14] However, companies in advanced nations seeking competitive advantage over firms in other nations *create* many of the factors of production. For example, a country or industry dependent on scientific innovation must have a skilled human resource pool to draw upon. This resource pool is not inherited; it is created through investment in industry-specific knowledge and talent. The supporting infrastructure of a country—that is, its transportation and communication systems as well as its banking system—are also critical.

Factors of production must be developed that are industry and firm specific. In addition, the pool of resources is less important than the speed and efficiency with which these resources are deployed. Thus, firm-specific knowledge and skills created within a country that are rare, valuable, difficult to imitate, and rapidly and efficiently deployed are the factors of production that ultimately lead to a nation's competitive advantage.

For example, the island nation of Japan has little land mass, making the warehouse space needed to store inventory prohibitively expensive. But by pioneering just-in-time inventory management, Japanese companies managed to create a resource from which they gained advantage over companies in other nations that spent large sums to warehouse inventory.

>LO7.2
The sources of national advantage; that is, why an industry in a given country is more (or less) successful than the same industry in another country.

Demand Conditions

Demand conditions refer to the demands that consumers place on an industry for goods and services. Consumers who demand highly specific, sophisticated products and services force firms to create innovative, advanced products and services to meet the demand. This consumer pressure presents challenges to a country's industries. But in response to these challenges, improvements to existing goods and services often result, creating conditions necessary for competitive advantage over firms in other countries.

Countries with demanding consumers drive firms in that country to meet high standards, upgrade existing products and services, and create innovative products and services. The conditions of consumer demand influence how firms view a market. This, in turn, helps a nation's industries to better anticipate future global demand conditions and proactively respond to product and service requirements.

Denmark, for instance, is known for its environmental awareness. Demand from consumers for environmentally safe products has spurred Danish manufacturers to become leaders in water pollution control equipment—products it successfully exported.

Related and Supporting Industries

Related and supporting industries enable firms to manage inputs more effectively. For example, countries with a strong supplier base benefit by adding efficiency to downstream activities. A competitive supplier base helps a firm obtain inputs using cost-effective, timely methods, thus reducing manufacturing costs. Also, close working relationships with suppliers provide the potential to develop competitive advantages through joint research and development and the ongoing exchange of knowledge.

Related industries offer similar opportunities through joint efforts among firms. In addition, related industries create the probability that new companies will enter the market, increasing competition and forcing existing firms to become more competitive through efforts such as cost control, product innovation, and novel approaches to distribution. Combined, these give the home country's industries a source of competitive advantage.

In the Italian footwear industry the supporting industries enhance national competitive advantage. In Italy, shoe manufacturers are geographically located near their suppliers. The manufacturers have ongoing interactions with leather suppliers and learn about new

related and supporting industries (national advantage) the presence, absence, and quality in the nation of supplier industries and other related industries that supply services, support, or technology to firms in the industry value chain.

textures, colors, and manufacturing techniques while a shoe is still in the prototype stage. The manufacturers are able to project future demand and gear their factories for new products long before companies in other nations become aware of the new styles.

Firm Strategy, Structure, and Rivalry

firm strategy, structure, and rivalry (national advantage) the conditions in the nation governing how companies are created, organized, and managed, as well as the nature of domestic rivalry.

Rivalry is particularly intense in nations with conditions of strong consumer demand, strong supplier bases, and high new entrant potential from related industries. This competitive rivalry in turn increases the efficiency with which firms develop, market, and distribute products and services within the home country. Domestic rivalry thus provides a strong impetus for firms to innovate and find new sources of competitive advantage.

This intense rivalry forces firms to look outside their national boundaries for new markets, setting up the conditions necessary for global competitiveness. Among all the points on Porter's diamond of national advantage, domestic rivalry is perhaps the strongest indicator of global competitive success. Firms that have experienced intense domestic competition are more likely to have designed strategies and structures that allow them to successfully compete in world markets.

In the U.S., for example, intense rivalry has spurred companies such as Dell Computer to find innovative ways to produce and distribute its products. This is largely a result of competition from IBM and Hewlett-Packard.

Strategy Spotlight 7.2 discusses India's software industry. It provides an integrative example of how Porter's "diamond" can help to explain the relative degree of success of an industry in a given country. Exhibit 7.1 illustrates India's "software diamond."

Concluding Comment on Factors Affecting a Nation's Competitiveness

Porter drew his conclusions based on case histories of firms in more than 100 industries. Despite the differences in strategies employed by successful global competitors, a common theme emerged: Firms that succeeded in global markets had first succeeded in intensely competitive home markets. We can conclude that competitive advantage for global firms typically grows out of relentless, continuing improvement, and innovation.[15]

International Expansion: A Company's Motivations and Risks

>LO7.3
The motivations (or benefits) and the risks associated with international expansion, including the emerging trend for greater offshoring and outsourcing activity.

Motivations for International Expansion

Increase Market Size   There are many motivations for a company to pursue international expansion. The most obvious one is to *increase the size of potential markets* for a firm's products and services.[16] By early 2009, the world's population exceeded 6.9 billion, with the U.S. representing less than 5 percent. Exhibit 7.2 lists the population of the U.S. compared to other major markets abroad.

Many multinational firms are intensifying their efforts to market their products and services to countries such as India and China as the ranks of their middle class have increased over the past decade. These include Procter & Gamble's success in achieving a 50 percent share in China's shampoo market as well as PepsiCo's impressive inroads in the Indian soft-drink market.[17] Let's take a brief look at China's emerging middle class:[18]

multinational firms firms that manage operations in more than one country.

- China's middle class has finally attained a critical mass—between 35 million and 200 million people, depending on what definition is used. The larger number is preferred by Fan Gong, director of China's National Economic Research Institute, who fixes the lower boundary of "middle" as a family income of $10,000.

7.2

strategy spotlight

India and the Diamond of National Advantage

Consider the following facts:

- SAP, the German software company, has developed new applications for notebook PCs at its 500-engineer Bangalore facility.

- General Electric plans to invest $100 million and hire 2,600 scientists to create the world's

Sources: Sachitanand, R. 2010. The New Face of IT. *Business Today,* 19:62; Anonymous. 2010. Training to Lead. *www.Dqindia.com.* October 5: np; Nagaraju, B.2011. India's Software Exports Seen Up 16–18 pct.in Fy12. *www. reuters.com.* February 2: np; Ghemawat, P. & Hout, T. 2008. Tomorrow's Global Giants. *Harvard Business Review,* 86(11): 80–88; Mathur, S. K. 2007. Indian IT Industry: A Performance Analysis and a Model for Possible Adoption. *ideas.repec.org,* January 1: np; Kripalani, M. 2002. Calling Bangalore: Multinationals Are Making It a Hub for High-Tech Research *BusinessWeek,* November 25: 52–54; Kapur, D. & Ramamurti, R. 2001. India's Emerging Competitive Advantage in Services. 2001. *Academy of Management Executive,* 15(2): 20–33; World Bank. *World Development Report:* 6. New York: Oxford University Press. Reuters. 2001. Oracle in India Push, Taps Software Talent. *Washington Post Online,* July 3.

largest research and development lab in Bangalore, India.

- Microsoft plans to invest $400 million in new research partnerships in India.

- Over one-fifth of Fortune 1000 companies outsource their software requirements to firms in India.

- Indian software exports have soared from $5.9 billion in 2000 to $23.6 billion in 2005 to a predicted $68 to $70 billion by 2012.

- For the past decade, the Indian software industry has grown at a 25 percent annual rate.

- More than 800 firms in India are involved in software services as their primary activity.

- Software and information technology firms in India employed 2.3 million people in 2010.

- The information technology industry accounted for 6 percent of India's Gross Domestic Product (GDP) in 2010—up from only 4.8 percent in 2007.

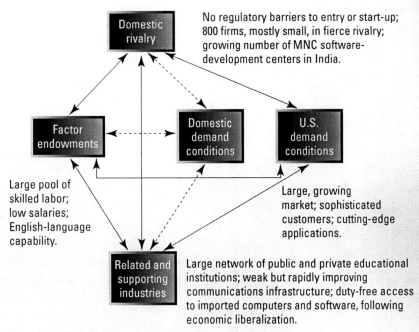

Note: Dashed lines represent weaker interactions.

Exhibit 7.1 India's Diamond in Software

Source: From Kampur D. and Ramamurti R., "India's Emerging Competition Advantage in Services," *Academy of Management Executive: The Thinking Manager's Source.* Copyright © 2001 by Academy of Management. Reproduced with permission of Academy of Management via Copyright Clearance Center.

(continued)

(continued)

What is causing such global interest in India's software services industry? Porter's diamond of national advantage helps clarify this question. See Exhibit 7.1.

First, *factor endowments* are conducive to the rise of India's software industry. Through investment in human resource development with a focus on industry-specific knowledge, India's universities and software firms have literally created this essential factor of production. For example, India produces the second largest annual output of scientists and engineers in the world, behind only the United States. In a knowledge-intensive industry such as software, development of human resources is fundamental to both domestic and global success.

Second, *demand conditions* require that software firms stay on the cutting edge of technological innovation. India has already moved toward globalization of its software industry; consumer demand conditions in developed nations such as Germany, Denmark, parts of Southeast Asia, and the United States created the consumer demand necessary to propel India's software makers toward sophisticated software solutions.*

Third, India has the *supplier base as well as the related industries* needed to drive competitive rivalry and

enhance competitiveness. In particular, information technology (IT) hardware prices declined rapidly in the 1990s. Furthermore, rapid technological change in IT hardware meant that latecomers like India were not locked into older-generation technologies. Thus, both the IT hardware and software industries could "leapfrog" older technologies. In addition, relationships among knowledge workers in these IT hardware and software industries offer the social structure for ongoing knowledge exchange, promoting further enhancement of existing products. Further infrastructure improvements are occurring rapidly.

Fourth, with over 800 firms in the software services industry in India, *intense rivalry forces firms to develop competitive strategies and structures.* Although firms like TCS, Infosys, and Wipro have become large, they were quite small less than a decade ago. And dozens of small and midsized companies are aspiring to catch up. This intense rivalry is one of the primary factors driving Indian software firms to develop overseas distribution channels, as predicted by Porter's diamond of national advantage.

It is interesting to note that the cost advantage of Indian firms may be eroding. For example, TCS's engineers' compensation has soared 13 percent in 2010. Other Asian companies are trying to steal its customers, and it is working hard to better understand overseas customers. Further, IBM and Accenture are aggressively building up their Indian operations, hiring tens of thousands of sought-after Indians by paying them more, thereby lowering their costs while raising those of TCS.

* Although India's success cannot be explained in terms of its home market demand (according to Porter's model), the nature of the industry enables software to be transferred among different locations simultaneously by way of communications links. Thus, competitiveness of markets outside India can be enhanced without a physical presence in those markets.

- The central government's emphasis on science and technology has boosted the rapid development of higher education, which is the incubator of the middle class.
- China may be viewed as a new example of economies of scale. Many American companies already have factories in China exporting goods. Now that there is a domestic market to go along with the export market, those factories can increase their output with little additional cost. That is one reason why many foreign companies' profits in China have been so strong in recent years.

Exhibit 7.2
Populations of Selected Nations and the World

Country	February 2011 (in est. millions)
China	1,334
India	1,182
United States	312
Japan	127
Germany	82
World Total	6,877

Source: *www.geohive.com/global/pop_data2.php.*

7.3

strategy spotlight

How Walmart Profits from Arbitrage

With sales of over $405 billion and net income of $14.8 billion, Walmart is considered one of the most successful companies in the world. In recent years, Walmart has embarked upon an ambitious international expansion agenda, opening stores in countries such as Mexico, China, Japan, and England. Walmart today has 4,122 stores outside the United States. Together they account for $100 billion in sales and $5 billion in operating income.

Walmart's above average industry profitability has been attributed to various factors, such as their superior logistics, strict control over overhead costs, and effective use of information systems. What is often lost sight

of is that their "everyday low pricing" strategy cannot work successfully unless they are able to procure the thousands of items they carry in each of their stores at the lowest possible prices. This is where their expertise in arbitraging plays a critical role. In 2004, Walmart bought $18 billion worth of goods directly from China. By 2006, this had grown to $26.7 billion. If one considers indirect imports through their other suppliers as well, Walmart's total imports from China could be anywhere between $50 billion and $70 billion each year. At a conservative estimate, this represents cost savings of approximately $16 billion to $23 billion! (These savings represent how much more these goods would have likely cost Walmart had the firm purchased them from the United States.) Clearly, the core of Walmart's international strategy is not their international store expansion strategy but their pursuit of worldwide arbitrage opportunities.

Sources: 2010 Walmart Annual Report; Ghemawat, P. 2007. *Redefining Global Strategy*. Boston: Harvard Business School Press; Scott, R.E. 2007. The WalMart Effect. *epi.org*, June 26: np; and Basker, E. & Pham, V.H. 2008. WalMart as Catalyst to U.S.-China Trade. *ssrn.com*; np.

Expanding a firm's global presence also automatically increases its scale of operations, providing it with a larger revenue and asset base.[19] As we noted in Chapter 5 in discussing overall cost leadership strategies, such an increase in revenues and asset base potentially enables a firm to *attain economies of scale*. This provides multiple benefits. One advantage is the spreading of fixed costs such as R&D over a larger volume of production. Examples include the sale of Boeing's commercial aircraft and Microsoft's operating systems in many foreign countries.

Filmmaking is another industry in which international sales can help amortize huge developmental costs.[20] For example, Tom Cruise found foreign buyers for his "Valkyrie" in 2008 and the film ultimately got about 59 percent of its $200 million in ticket sales abroad. And Sylvester Stallone's latest *Rambo* opened the same year and picked up $70 million, or 62 percent of its $113 million in total ticket sales from international markets.

Take Advantage of Arbitrage   *Taking advantage of arbitrage opportunities* is a second advantage of international expansion. In its simplest form, arbitrage involves buying something from where it is cheap and selling it somewhere where it commands a higher price. A big part of Walmart's success can be attributed to the company's expertise in arbitrage (see Strategy Spotlight 7.3). The possibilities for arbitrage are not necessarily confined to simple trading opportunities. It can be applied to virtually any factor of production and every stage of the value chain. For example, a firm may locate its call centers in India, its manufacturing plants in China, and its R&D in Europe, where the specific types of talented personnel may be available at the lowest possible price. In today's integrated global financial markets, a firm can borrow anywhere in the world where capital is cheap and use it to fund a project in a country where capital is expensive. Such arbitrage opportunities are even more attractive to global corporations because their larger size enables them to buy in huge volume, thus increasing their bargaining power with suppliers.

arbitrage opportunities an opportunity to profit by buying and selling the same good in different markets.

Extend a Product's Life Cycle   *Extending the life cycle of a product* that is in its maturity stage in a firm's home country but that has greater demand potential elsewhere is another benefit of international expansion. As we noted in Chapter 5, products (and industries) generally go through a four-stage life cycle of introduction, growth, maturity, and decline. In recent decades, U.S. soft-drink producers such as Coca-Cola and PepsiCo have aggressively pursued international markets to attain levels of growth that simply would not be available in the United States. Similarly, personal computer manufacturers such as Dell and Hewlett-Packard have sought out foreign markets to offset the growing saturation in the U.S. market.

Optimize the Location of Value-Chain Activities   *Optimizing the physical location for every activity in its value chain* is another benefit. Recall from our discussions in Chapters 3 and 5 that the value chain represents the various activities in which all firms must engage to produce products and services. They include primary activities, such as inbound logistics, operations, and marketing, as well as support activities, such as procurement, R&D, and human resource management. All firms have to make critical decisions as to where each activity will take place.[21] Optimizing the location for every activity in the value chain can yield one or more of three strategic advantages: performance enhancement, cost reduction, and risk reduction. We will now discuss each of these.

Performance Enhancement Microsoft's decision to establish a corporate research laboratory in Cambridge, England, is an example of a location decision that was guided mainly by the goal of building and sustaining world-class excellence in selected value-creating activities.[22] This strategic decision provided Microsoft with access to outstanding technical and professional talent. Location decisions can affect the quality with which any activity is performed in terms of the availability of needed talent, speed of learning, and the quality of external and internal coordination.

Cost Reduction Two location decisions founded largely on cost-reduction considerations are (1) Nike's decision to source the manufacture of athletic shoes from Asian countries such as China, Vietnam, and Indonesia, and (2) the decision of many multinational companies to set up production operations just south of the U.S.–Mexico border to access lower-cost labor. These operations are called *maquiladoras.* Such location decisions can affect the cost structure in terms of local manpower and other resources, transportation and logistics, and government incentives and the local tax structure.

Performance enhancement and cost-reduction benefits parallel the business-level strategies (discussed in Chapter 5) of differentiation and overall cost leadership. They can at times be attained simultaneously. Consider our example in the previous section on the Indian software industry. When Oracle set up a development operation in that country, the company benefited both from lower labor costs and operational expenses as well as from performance enhancements realized through the hiring of superbly talented professionals.

Risk Reduction Given the erratic swings in the exchange ratios between the U.S. dollar and the Japanese yen (in relation to each other and to other major currencies), an important basis for cost competition between Ford and Toyota has been their relative ingenuity at managing currency risks. One way for such rivals to manage currency risks has been to spread the high-cost elements of their manufacturing operations across a few select and carefully chosen locations around the world. Location decisions such as these can affect the overall risk profile of the firm with respect to currency, economic, and political risks.[23]

reverse innovation new products developed by developed country multination firms for emerging markets that have adequate functionality at a low cost.

Explore Reverse Innovation   Finally, *exploring possibilities for reverse innovation* has become a major motivation for international expansion. Many leading companies are discovering that developing products specifically for emerging markets can pay off in a big way. In the past, multinational companies typically developed products for their rich home markets and then tried to sell them in developing countries with minor adaptations.

However, as growth slows in rich nations and demand grows rapidly in developing countries such as India and China, this approach becomes increasingly inadequate. Instead, companies like GE have committed significant resources to developing products that meet the needs of developing nations, products that deliver adequate functionality at a fraction of the cost. Interestingly, these products have subsequently found considerable success in value segments in wealthy countries as well. Hence, this process is referred to as reverse innovation, a new motivation for international expansion.

As $3,000 cars, $300 computers, and $30 mobile phones bring what were previously considered as luxuries within the reach of the middle class of emerging markets, it is important to understand the motivations and implications of reverse innovation. *First,* it is impossible to sell first-world versions of products with minor adaptations in countries where average income per person is between $1,000 and $4,000, as is the case in most developing countries. To sell in these markets, entirely new products must be designed and developed by local technical talent and manufactured with local components. *Second,* although these countries are relatively poor, they are growing rapidly. For example, the Indian and Chinese economies are growing at double digit rates, and Brazil has achieved full employment. *Third,* if the innovation does not come from first-world multinationals, there are any number of local firms that are ready to grab the market with low-cost products. *Fourth,* as the consumers and governments of many first-world countries are rediscovering the virtues of frugality and are trying to cut down expenses, these products and services originally developed for the first world may gain significant market shares in developing countries as well.

Strategy Spotlight 7.4 describes several examples of reverse innovation.

Potential Risks of International Expansion

When a company expands its international operations, it does so to increase its profits or revenues. As with any other investment, however, there are also potential risks.[24] To help companies assess the risk of entering foreign markets, rating systems have been developed to evaluate political, economic, as well as financial and credit risks.[25] *Euromoney* magazine publishes a semiannual "Country Risk Rating" that evaluates political, economic, and other risks that entrants potentially face.[26] Exhibit 7.3 depicts a sample of country risk ratings, published by the World Bank, from the 178 countries that *Euromoney* evaluates. Note that the lower the score, the higher the country's expected level of risk.[27]

Next we will discuss the four main types of risk: political risk, economic risk, currency risk, and management risk.

Political and Economic Risk   Generally speaking, the business climate in the United States is very favorable. However, some countries around the globe may be hazardous to the health of corporate initiatives because of **political risk**.[28] Forces such as social unrest, military turmoil, demonstrations, and even violent conflict and terrorism can pose serious threats.[29] Consider, for example, the ongoing tension and violence in the Middle East between Israelis and Palestinians, and the social and political unrest in Indonesia.[30] Such conditions increase the likelihood of destruction of property and disruption of operations as well as nonpayment for goods and services. Thus, countries that are viewed as high risk are less attractive for most types of business.[31]

> **political risk** potential threat to a firm's operations in a country due to ineffectiveness of the domestic political system.

Another source of political risk in many countries is the absence of the rule of law. The absence of rules or the lack of uniform enforcement of existing rules leads to what might often seem to be arbitrary and inconsistent decisions by government officials. This can make it difficult for foreign firms to conduct business.

Consider Libya. The country is noted for its capricious government under the leadership of its ruler, Muammar Qaddafi, who has been in power for over 40 years. Here, business people often incur significant political risks. Let's look at a few examples:[32]

> **rule of law** a characteristic of legal systems where behavior is governed by rules that are uniformly enforced.

strategy spotlight   7.4

Reverse Innovation: How Developing Countries Are Becoming Hotbeds of Innovation

GE Healthcare's largest R&D facility is surprisingly located in Bangalore, India, thousands of miles away from its home country. Here, customers can hardly afford the sky-high prices of GE's medical devices. At 50,000 square feet and employing about 1,000 researchers and engineers, this facility recently developed a portable electrocardiogram that weighs only about two pounds, runs on batteries, and can do an electrocardiogram for 20 cents! Over the next six years, GE plans to spend $3 billion to create at least 100 healthcare innovations that would significantly lower costs, improve quality, increase access, and conquer the medical devices market in developing countries. Increasingly, many developing countries are becoming hotbeds of a new type of innovation often referred to as "reverse innovation" or "frugal innovation." Let us look at a few other examples of reverse innovation by GE as well as other companies:

- In the 1990s, GE attempted to sell ultrasound machines costing about $100,000 to high-end Chinese hospital imaging centers. But these expensive, bulky devices were poorly received by Chinese customers. Responding to this failure, a local GE team developed a cheap, portable ultrasound machine using a laptop computer enhanced with a probe which sold at a price between $30,000 and $40,000. By 2007, they were able to bring the price down to just $15,000. Today, these machines have found a worldwide market—both in developing economies as well as in the United States, where ambulance squads and emergency rooms are increasingly using them. Overall, sales of medical technology are exploding in China and India. China's market is expected to grow by 15 percent a year to 2015 and reach $43 billion by 2019. India's demand is growing at an even higher rate, 23 percent, and should top $10 billion by 2020.

- Moline, Illinois–based Deere & Co. opened a center in Pune, India, almost a decade ago with the intention to penetrate the Indian market. Many observers were skeptical about the ability of a company known for its heavy-duty farm equipment and big construction gear to succeed in a market where the majority of the farmers still used oxen-pulled plows. However, Deere saw potential and its engineers in Pune responded with four no-frills models. Though lacking first-world features like GPS and air conditioning, they were sturdy enough to handle the rigors of commercial farming. The tractors cost between $8400 and $11,600 in India. Subsequently, Deere targeted a segment of the home market that they had previously largely ignored—hobbyists as well as bargain hunters. These buyers do not care for advanced features but covet the same qualities as Indian farmers: affordability and maneuverability. Today, half of the no-frills models that Deere produces in India are exported to other countries. "These tractors are like Swiss Army knives. They get used for anything: mowing, transporting bales of hay, pushing dirt, and removing manure," claims Mike Alvin, a product manager at Deere.

- Narayana Hrudayalaya Hospital in Bangalore performs open heart surgeries at about $2000, which is a fraction of the $20,000 to $100,000 that it would cost in a U.S. hospital. How do they do it? By applying mass-production techniques pioneered by Henry Ford in the auto industry. The hospital has 1000 beds, roughly eight times the size of an American hospital, and performs 600 operations a week. The large volume allows the hospital to benefit from both economies of scale (that reduce cost) and, even more importantly, experience curve effects that improve the success rate. Today the hospital has established video and Internet links with hospitals not only in India, but in countries in Africa as well as in Malaysia. As the need to contain healthcare costs becomes more pressing in developed countries like the United States, techniques pioneered by Narayana Hrudayalaya Hospital may find acceptance in these countries.

Sources: Anonymous. 2011. Frugal healing. *The Economist.* January 22: 73–74; Immelt, J. R., Govindarajan, V., & Trimble, C. 2009. How GE Is Disrupting Itself. *Harvard Business Review,* 87 (10): 56–64; Chandran, R. 2010. Profiting from Treating India's Poor. *International Herald Tribune,* July 6: 17; Anonymous. 2010. The World Turned Upside Down. *The Economist,* April 17: 3–17; Mero, J. 2008. John Deere's Farm Team. *Fortune,* April 14: 119–124; and Anonymous. 2008. No-Frills IndianTtractors Find Favor with U.S. Farmers. *www.theindian.com,* April 29: np.

Exhibit 7.3   A Sample of International Country Risk Ratings: September 2010

Rank	Country	Overall Score (100)	Political Risk (30)	Economic Performance (30)	Infrastructure (10)	Total of Debt and Credit Indicators (20)	Access to Bank Finance/Capital Markets (10)
1	Norway	93.33	28.19	26.89	8.25	20.00	10.00
2	Switzerland	90.22	26.80	24.99	8.44	20.00	10.00
3	Sweden	88.93	28.04	22.65	8.24	20.00	10.00
4	Denmark	88.80	27.90	22.81	8.09	20.00	10.00
5	Finland	88.55	27.99	22.40	8.16	20.00	10.00
6	Luxembourg	88.27	27.54	21.71	9.03	20.00	10.00
7	Canada	88.26	27.80	22.12	8.34	20.00	10.00
8	Netherlands	88.20	27.71	22.85	7.64	20.00	10.00
9	Hong Kong	87.18	25.25	24.87	8.10	18.96	10.00
10	Australia	86.18	27.10	21.43	7.86	19.79	10.00
17	United States	82.10	26.26	17.91	7.92	20.00	10.00
36	China	72.60	17.37	22.31	6.81	17.45	8.67
110	Nigeria	37.80	11.25	12.12	5.25	2.19	7.00
120	Nicaragua	34.53	10.71	9.96	1.00	9.86	3.00
127	Iran	32.97	12.25	14.81	5.24	0.00	0.67
151	Afghanistan	20.95	8.26	8.31	3.38	0.00	1.00

Source: Country Risk September 2010: Full Results. *www.euromoney.com.*

- An Egyptian grocer spent years building a thriving business in Libya. Unfortunately, he made the mistake of going home during a holiday. Abrupt changes to visa rules meant that he could no longer return.
- The new manager of a hotel in Tripoli, an expatriate, fired some staff and switched suppliers. This prompted someone to make a telephone call. A sudden snap health inspection of the hotel revealed a few canned goods beyond their sell-by date. The manager is now in prison!
- A small Canadian oil firm, Verenex, joined the rush into Libya and struck an exciting find. Early in 2009, a Chinese company offered to buy Verenex, nearly all of whose assets are in Libya, for close to $450 million. The Libyan government blocked the sale but promised to match the price. After months of wrangling in the oil ministry, Libya's sovereign wealth fund slashed its offer to barely $300 million. Faced with further trouble if they failed to sell, Verenex shareholders reluctantly agreed.

The laws, and the enforcement of laws, associated with the protection of intellectual property rights can be a major potential **economic risk** in entering new countries.[33] Microsoft, for example, has lost billions of dollars in potential revenue through piracy of its software products in many countries, including China. Other areas of the globe, such as the former Soviet Union and some eastern European nations, have piracy problems as well.[34] Firms rich in intellectual property have encountered financial losses as imitations of their products have grown due to a lack of law enforcement of intellectual property rights.[35]

economic risk potential threat to a firm's operations in a country due to economic policies and conditions, including property rights laws and enforcement of those laws.

strategy spotlight   7.5

Counterfeiting: A Worldwide Problem

Although counterfeiting used to be a luxury goods problem, people are now trying to counterfeit items that have a wider effect on the economy, such as pharmaceuticals and computer parts. A new study by the U.S. Department of Commerce shows that fake goods have been infiltrating the army. The number of counterfeit parts in military electronics systems more than doubled between 2005 and 2008, potentially damaging high-tech weapons.

Counterfeiting can have health and safety implications as well. The World Health Organization says that up to 10 percent of medicines worldwide are counterfeit—a deadly hazard that could be costing the pharmaceutical industry $46 billion a year. "You won't die from purchasing a pair of counterfeit blue jeans or a counterfeit golf club. You can die from taking counterfeit pharmaceutical products. And there's no doubt that people have died in China from bad medicine," says John Theirault, head of global security for American pharmaceutical giant Pfizer.

The International Anti-Counterfeiting Coalition (IACC), a Washington D.C.–based nonprofit organization, estimates that the true figure for counterfeit and pirated goods is close to $600 billion and makes up about 5–7 percent of world trade. Several factors have contributed to the increase in counterfeiting in recent years. The shift of much of the world's manufacturing to countries with poor

protection of intellectual property rights has provided both technology and opportunity to make knock-offs. And the Internet and e-commerce sites like eBay have made it easier to distribute counterfeit goods. MarkMonitor, a firm that helps companies defend their brands online, estimates that sales of counterfeit goods via the Internet is about $135 billion.

The IACC provides some rather startling statistics relating to counterfeiting and its costs to business and society:

- Counterfeiting costs U.S. businesses $200 billion to $250 billion annually.

- Counterfeit merchandise is directly responsible for the loss of more than 750,000 American jobs.

- Since 1982, the global trade in illegitimate goods has increased from approximately $5.5 billion to $600 billion annually.

- U.S. companies suffer $9 billion in world trade losses due to international copyright piracy.

- Counterfeiting poses a threat to global health and safety.

The recent recession in the richer countries may have also given a boost to counterfeit goods. An anti-counterfeiting group has noticed a spike in knock-offs this recession, as consumers trade down from the real thing. Cost-cutting measures may have also made firms' supply chains more vulnerable to counterfeit parts. Lawsuits brought by companies are at an all-time high, says Kirsten Gilbert, a partner at a British law firm.

Source: Anonymous. 2010. Knock-offs Catch On. *The Economist*, March 6: 81–82; Balfour, F. 2005. Fake! *BusinessWeek*, February 7: 54–64; and Quinn, G. 2010. Counterfeiting Costs US Businesses $200 Billion Annually. *www.ipwatchdog.com*, August 30: np.

---

counterfeiting selling of trademarked goods without the consent of the trademark holder.

currency risk potential threat to a firm's operations in a country due to fluctuations in the local currency's exchange rate.

Strategy Spotlight 7.5 discusses a problem that is a severe threat to global trade—counterferting. Estimates are that counterfeiting accounts for between 5 to 7 percent of global merchandise trade—the equivalent of as much as $600 billion a year. And the potential corrosive effects include health and safety, not just economic, damage.[36]

Currency Risks   Currency fluctuations can pose substantial risks. A company with operations in several countries must constantly monitor the exchange rate between its own currency and that of the host country to minimize **currency risks.** Even a small change in the exchange rate can result in a significant difference in the cost of production or net profit when doing business overseas. When the U.S. dollar appreciates against other currencies, for example, U.S. goods can be more expensive to consumers in foreign countries. At the same time, however, appreciation of the U.S. dollar can have negative implications for American companies that have branch operations overseas. The reason for this is that profits from abroad must be exchanged for dollars at a more expensive rate of exchange, reducing the amount of profit when measured in dollars. For example, consider an American firm doing business in Italy. If this firm had a 20 percent profit in euros at its Italian center of operations, this profit would be totally wiped out when converted into U.S. dollars if the euro had depreciated 20 percent against the U.S. dollar. (U.S. multinationals typically engage in sophisticated "hedging strategies" to minimize currency risk. The discussion of this is beyond the scope of this section.)

It is important to note that even when government intervention is well intended, the macroeconomic effects of such action can be very negative for multinational corporations. Such was the case in 1997 when Thailand suddenly chose to devalue its currency, the baht, after months of trying to support it at an artificially high level. This, in effect, made the baht nearly worthless compared to other currencies. And in 1998 Russia not only devalued its ruble but also elected not to honor its foreign debt obligations.

Below, we discuss how Israel's strong currency—the shekel—forced a firm to reevaluate its strategy.

> For years O.R.T. Technologies resisted moving any operations outside of Israel. However, when faced with a sharp rise in the value of the shekel, the maker of specialized software for managing gas stations froze all local hiring and decided to transfer some developmental work to Eastern Europe. Laments CEO Alex Milner, "I never thought I'd see the day when we would have to move R&D outside of Israel, but the strong shekel has forced us to do so."[37]

Management Risks   **Management risks** may be considered the challenges and risks that managers face when they must respond to the inevitable differences that they encounter in foreign markets. These take a variety of forms: culture, customs, language, income levels, customer preferences, distribution systems, and so on.[38] As we will note later in the chapter, even in the case of apparently standard products, some degree of local adaptation will become necessary.[39]

Differences in cultures across countries can also pose unique challenges for managers.[40] Cultural symbols can evoke deep feelings.[41] For example, in a series of advertisements aimed at Italian vacationers, Coca-Cola executives turned the Eiffel Tower, Empire State Building, and the Tower of Pisa into the familiar Coke bottle. So far, so good. However, when the white marble columns of the Parthenon that crowns the Acropolis in Athens were turned into Coke bottles, the Greeks became outraged. Why? Greeks refer to the Acropolis as the "holy rock," and a government official said the Parthenon is an "international symbol of excellence" and that "whoever insults the Parthenon insults international culture." Coca-Cola apologized. Below are some cultural tips for conducting business in HongKong:

- Handshakes when greeting and before leaving are customary.
- After the initial handshake, business cards are presented with both hands on the card. Carefully read the card before putting it away.
- In Hong Kong, Chinese people should be addressed by their professional title (or Mr., Mrs., Miss) followed by their surname.
- Appointments should be made as far in advance as possible.
- Punctuality is very important and demonstrates respect.

management risk potential threat to a firm's operations in a country due to the problems that managers have making decisions in the context of foreign markets.

● Some of Hong Kong's customs are quite different from those of western countries.

- Negotiations in Hong Kong are normally very slow with much attention to detail. The same negotiating team should be kept throughout the proceedings.
- Tea will be served during the negotiations. Always accept and wait for the host to begin drinking before you partake.
- Be aware that "yes" may just be an indication that the person heard you rather than indicating agreement. A Hong Kong Chinese businessperson will have a difficult time saying "no" directly.

Below, we discuss a rather humorous example of how a local custom can affect operations at a manufacturing plant in Singapore.

> Larry Henderson, plant manager, and John Lichthental, manager of human resources, were faced with a rather unique problem. They were assigned by Celanese Chemical Corp. to build a plant in Singapore, and the plant was completed in July. However, according to local custom, a plant should only be christened on "lucky" days. Unfortunately, the next lucky day was not until September 3.
>
> The managers had to convince executives at Celanese's Dallas headquarters to delay the plant opening. As one might expect, it wasn't easy. But after many heated telephone conversations and flaming e-mails, the president agreed to open the new plant on a lucky day—September 3.[42]

Global Dispersion of Value Chains: Outsourcing and Offshoring

A major recent trend has been the dispersion of the value chains of multinational corporations across different countries; that is, the various activities that constitute the value chain of a firm are now spread across several countries and continents. Such dispersion of value occurs mainly through increasing offshoring and outsourcing.

A report issued by the World Trade Organization describes the production of a particular U.S. car as follows: "30 percent of the car's value goes to Korea for assembly, 17.5 percent to Japan for components and advanced technology, 7.5 percent to Germany for design, 4 percent to Taiwan and Singapore for minor parts, 2.5 percent to U.K. for advertising and marketing services, and 1.5 percent to Ireland and Barbados for data processing. This means that only 37 percent of the production value is generated in the U.S."[43] In today's economy, we are increasingly witnessing two interrelated trends: outsourcing and offshoring.

outsourcing using other firms to perform value-creating activities that were previously performed in-house.

Outsourcing occurs when a firm decides to utilize other firms to perform value-creating activities that were previously performed in-house.[44] It may be a new activity that the firm is perfectly capable of doing but chooses to have someone else perform for cost or quality reasons. Outsourcing can be to either a domestic or foreign firm.

offshoring shifting a value-creating activity from a domestic location to a foreign location.

Offshoring takes place when a firm decides to shift an activity that they were performing in a domestic location to a foreign location.[45] For example, both Microsoft and Intel now have R&D facilities in India, employing a large number of Indian scientists and engineers. Often, offshoring and outsourcing go together; that is, a firm may outsource an activity to a foreign supplier, thereby causing the work to be offshored as well.[46] Spending on offshore information technology will nearly triple between 2004 and 2010 to $60 billion, according to research firm Gartner.[47]

The recent explosion in the volume of outsourcing and offshoring is due to a variety of factors. Up until the 1960s, for most companies, the entire value chain was in one location. Further, the production took place close to where the customers were in order to keep transportation costs under control. In the case of service industries, it was generally believed that offshoring was not possible because the producer and consumer had to be present at the same place at the same time. After all, a haircut could not be performed if the barber and the client were separated!

For manufacturing industries, the rapid decline in transportation and coordination costs has enabled firms to disperse their value chains over different locations. For example, Nike's R&D takes place in the U.S., raw materials are procured from a multitude of countries, actual manufacturing takes place in China or Indonesia, advertising is produced in the U.S., and sales and service take place in practically all the countries. Each value-creating activity is performed in the location where the cost is the lowest or the quality is the best. Without finding optimal locations for each activity, Nike could not have attained its position as the world's largest shoe company.

The experience of the manufacturing sector was also repeated in the service sector by the mid-1990s. A trend that began with the outsourcing of low-level programming and data entry work to countries such as India and Ireland suddenly grew manyfold, encompassing a variety of white collar and professional activities ranging from call-centers to R&D. The cost of a long distance call from the U.S. to India has decreased from about $3 to $0.03 in the last 20 years, thereby making it possible to have call centers located in countries like India, where a combination of low labor costs and English proficiency presents an ideal mix of factor conditions.

Bangalore, India, in recent years, has emerged as a location where more and more U.S. tax returns are prepared. In India, U.S.–trained and licensed radiologists interpret chest X-rays and CT scans from U.S. hospitals for half the cost. The advantages from offshoring go beyond mere cost savings today. In many specialized occupations in science and engineering, there is a shortage of qualified professionals in developed countries, whereas countries, like India, China, and Singapore have what seems like an inexhaustible supply.[48]

For most of the 20th century, domestic companies catered to the needs of local populations. However, with the increasing homogenization of customer needs around the world and the institutionalization of free trade and investment as a global ideology (especially after the creation of the WTO), competition has become truly global. Each company has to keep its costs low in order to survive.[49] They also must find the best suppliers and the most skilled workers as well as locate each stage of the value chain in places where factor conditions are most conducive. Thus, outsourcing and offshoring are no longer mere options to consider, but an imperative for competitive survival.

While there is a compelling logic for companies to engage in offshoring, there can be many pitfalls. This has spurred many companies to outsource tech services to low-cost locations within the United States, instead of offshoring to foreign countries. We discuss this trend in Strategy Spotlight 7.6.

Achieving Competitive Advantage in Global Markets

We now discuss the two opposing forces that firms face when they expand into global markets: cost reduction and adaptation to local markets. Then we address the four basic types of international strategies that they may pursue: international, global, multidomestic, and transnational. The selection of one of these four types of strategies is largely dependent on a firm's relative pressure to address each of the two forces.

>LO7.4
The two opposing forces—cost reduction and adaptation to local markets—that firms face when entering international markets.

Two Opposing Pressures: Reducing Costs and Adapting to Local Markets

Many years ago, the famed marketing strategist Theodore Levitt advocated strategies that favored global products and brands. He suggested that firms should standardize all of their products and services for all of their worldwide markets. Such an approach would help a firm lower its overall costs by spreading its investments over as large a market as possible. Levitt's approach rested on three key assumptions:

strategy spotlight   7.6

A Small-Town Alternative to Offshoring Tech Services Work

These are great times for Cayuse Technologies, a 200-employee tech outsourcing firm. It is owned by the Confederated Tribes of the Umatilla Indian Reservation in northeast Oregon. In 2009 it had $7.7 million in revenues—seven times what it had in 2007, its first year in operation. And with its business from corporate clients like Accenture expected to soar next year, Cayuse plans to hire another 75 workers. Says Marc Benoist, the firm's general manager, "We still have capacity here at our facility, so we have plenty of room for growth."

Cayuse is one of many information technology companies in remote areas of the United States who position themselves as alternatives to offshore outsourcing. And the economics seem to make sense. On an hourly basis, these "rural outsourcers" charge much more than their overseas rivals. But when factors such as oversight and quality control of the offshore work are factored in, their rates are competitive. Their rates are also much lower than their domestic counterparts located in big cities, because they operate in areas that have lower living costs. "Their value proposition is, 'We cost less than the East or West Coast, and we're easier to deal with than India,'" says Mary Lacity, a professor at the University of Missouri at St. Louis, who studies outsourcing. Cayuse Technologies develops software, provides outsourcing of business processes, and serves as a contact for Accenture's clients, for example, processing and adjusting insurance claims. "It makes much more sense for Cayuse to perform those activities," according to Randall Willis, managing director of Accenture.

Sources: Lieber, N. 2010. 'Rural Outsourcers' vs. Bangalore. *Bloomberg Businessweek*, September 27–October 3: 52–53; Brickey, D. 2010. Rural Outsourcing Gains Favor; Cayuse Technologies as a Model. *www.eastoregonian.com*, October 13: np; and Alsever, J. 2010. Forget India, Outsource to Arkansas. *www.money.cnn.com*, July 8: np.

Consider the rationale behind Human Genome Sciences's (HGS) decision to use a rural outsourcing firm: HGS, a Rockville, Maryland biotech company with 900 employees, got bids from several outsourcers to handle the technical support for its back-office software. One of the bidders would have offshored the work to India. However, the idea of sending confidential company information overseas, outside the reach of the American intellectual property law, did not sit too well with David Evans, their IT director.

Instead, Evans hired Atlanta-based Rural Sourcing, Inc., and its team of software experts located in Jonesboro, Arkansas. HGS pays about $55 an hour for technical support from Rural Sourcing—a figure that is about 15 percent higher than the rates quoted by the Indian outsourcing firm that he considered. However, it is still about half of what it would cost for him to hire a software development firm located in the Washington, D.C., metro area.

Recently, IT research firm Gartner said in a report that while these firms make up a tiny portion of the market, they are an "attractive alternative" to offshore outsourcers because of language and other cultural factors. It is also easier for them to comply with U.S. data privacy regulations, according to the report.

Without a doubt, rural outsourcers won't replace the offshorers. After all, India has outsourcing revenues of about $50 billion, and that number is expected to triple by 2020, according to estimates by McKinsey & Company and an Indian trade group. In contrast, the rural outsourcing market is estimated to be less than $100 million. However, Lacity believes that this segment has growth potential—in part because of the efforts by federal policymakers to seek ways of creating jobs and as government outsourcing contracts increasingly require work to be done in the United States.

1. Customer needs and interests are becoming increasingly homogeneous worldwide.
2. People around the world are willing to sacrifice preferences in product features, functions, design, and the like for lower prices at high quality.
3. Substantial economies of scale in production and marketing can be achieved through supplying global markets.[50]

However, there is ample evidence to refute these assumptions.[51] Regarding the first assumption—the increasing worldwide homogeneity of customer needs and interests—consider the number of product markets, ranging from watches and handbags to soft drinks and fast foods. Companies have identified global customer segments and developed global products and brands targeted to those segments. Also, many other companies adapt lines to idiosyncratic country preferences and develop local brands targeted to local market segments. For example, Nestlé's line of pizzas marketed in the United Kingdom includes cheese with ham and pineapple topping on a French bread crust. Similarly, Coca-Cola in Japan markets Georgia (a tonic drink) as well as Classic Coke and Hi-C.

Consider the second assumption—the sacrifice of product attributes for lower prices. While there is invariably a price-sensitive segment in many product markets, there is no indication that this is increasing. In contrast, in many product and service markets—ranging from watches, personal computers, and household appliances, to banking and insurance—there is a growing interest in multiple product features, product quality, and service.

Finally, the third assumption is that significant economies of scale in production and marketing could be achieved for global products and services. Although standardization may lower manufacturing costs, such a perspective does not consider three critical and interrelated points. First, as we discussed in Chapter 5, technological developments in flexible factory automation enable economies of scale to be attained at lower levels of output and do not require production of a single standardized product. Second, the cost of production is only one component, and often not the critical one, in determining the total cost of a product. Third, a firm's strategy should not be product-driven. It should also consider other activities in the firm's value chain, such as marketing, sales, and distribution.

Based on the above, we would have a hard time arguing that it is wise to develop the same product or service for all markets throughout the world. While there are some exceptions, such as Harley-Davidson motorcycles and some of Coca-Cola's soft-drink products, managers must also strive to tailor their products to the culture of the country in which they are attempting to do business. Few would argue that "one size fits all" generally applies.

The opposing pressures that managers face place conflicting demands on firms as they strive to be competitive.[52] On the one hand, competitive pressures require that firms do what they can to *lower unit costs* so that consumers will not perceive their product and service offerings as too expensive. This may lead them to consider locating manufacturing facilities where labor costs are low and developing products that are highly standardized across multiple countries.

In addition to responding to pressures to lower costs, managers also must strive to be *responsive to local pressures* in order to tailor their products to the demand of the local market in which they do business. This requires differentiating their offerings and strategies from country to country to reflect consumer tastes and preferences and making changes to reflect differences in distribution channels, human resource practices, and governmental regulations. However, since the strategies and tactics to differentiate products and services to local markets can involve additional expenses, a firm's costs will tend to rise.

The two opposing pressures result in four different basic strategies that companies can use to compete in the global marketplace: international, global, multidomestic, and transnational. The strategy that a firm selects depends on the degree of pressure that it is facing for cost reductions and the importance of adapting to local markets. Exhibit 7.4 shows the conditions under which each of these strategies would be most appropriate.

It is important to note that we consider these four strategies to be "basic" or "pure"; that is, in practice, all firms will tend to have some elements of each strategy.

International Strategy

There are a small number of industries in which pressures for both local adaptation and lowering costs are rather low. An extreme example of such an industry is the "orphan" drug industry. These are medicines for diseases that are severe but affect only a small number of people. Diseases such as the Gaucher disease and Fabry disease fit into this category. Companies such as Genzyme and Oxford GlycoSciences are active in this segment of the drug

>LO7.5
The advantages and disadvantages associated with each of the four basic strategies: international, global, multidomestic, and transnational.

international strategy a strategy based on firms' diffusion and adaptation of the parent companies' knowledge and expertise to foreign markets, used in industries where the pressures for both local adaptation and lowering costs are low.

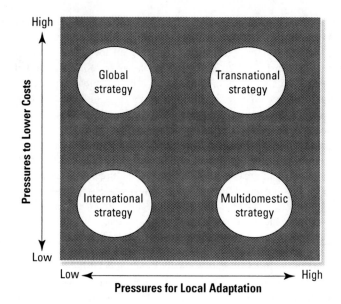

High

Pressures to Lower Costs

Global
strategy

Transnational
strategy

International
strategy

Multidomestic
strategy

Low

Low ← **Pressures for Local Adaptation** → High

Exhibit 7.4 Opposing Pressures and Four Strategies

industry. There is virtually no need to adapt their products to the local markets. And the pressures to reduce costs are low; even though only a few thousand patients are affected, the revenues and margins are significant, because patients are charged up to $100,000 per year. Legislation has made this industry even more attractive. The 1983 Orphan Drug Act provides various tax credits and exclusive marketing rights for any drug developed to treat a disease that afflicts fewer than 200,000 patients. Since 1983, more than 280 orphan drugs have been licensed and used to treat 14 million patients.[53]

An international strategy is based on diffusion and adaptation of the parent company's knowledge and expertise to foreign markets. Country units are allowed to make some minor adaptations to products and ideas coming from the head office, but they have far less independence and autonomy compared to multidomestic companies. The primary goal of the strategy is worldwide exploitation of the parent firm's knowledge and capabilities. All sources of core competencies are centralized.

The majority of large U.S. multinationals pursued the international strategy in the decades following World War II. These companies centralized R&D and product development but established manufacturing facilities as well as marketing organizations abroad. Companies such as McDonald's and Kellogg are examples of firms following such a strategy. Although these companies do make some local adaptations, they are of a very limited nature. With increasing pressures to reduce costs due to global competition, especially from low-cost countries, opportunities to successfully employ international strategy are becoming more limited. This strategy is most suitable in situations where a firm has distinctive competencies that local companies in foreign markets lack.

Risks and Challenges   Below, are some of the risks and challenges associated with an international strategy.

- Different activities in the value chain typically have different optimal locations. That is, R&D may be optimally located in a country with an abundant supply of scientists and engineers, whereas assembly may be better conducted in a low-cost location.

Nike, for example, designs its shoes in the United States, but all the manufacturing is done in countries like China or Thailand. The international strategy, with its tendency to concentrate most of its activities in one location, fails to take advantage of the benefits of an optimally distributed value chain.

- The lack of local responsiveness may result in the alienation of local customers. Worse still, the firm's inability to be receptive to new ideas and innovation from its foreign subsidiaries may lead to missed opportunities.

Exhibit 7.5 summarizes the strengths and weaknesses of international strategies in the global marketplace.

Global Strategy

As indicated in Exhibit 7.4, a firm whose emphasis is on lowering costs tends to follow a global strategy. Competitive strategy is centralized and controlled to a large extent by the corporate office. Since the primary emphasis is on controlling costs, the corporate office strives to achieve a strong level of coordination and integration across the various businesses.[54] Firms following a global strategy strive to offer standardized products and services as well as to locate manufacturing, R&D, and marketing activities in only a few locations.[55]

global strategy a strategy based on firms' centralization and control by the corporate office, with the primary emphasis on controlling costs, and used in industries where the pressure for local adaptation is low and the pressure for lowering costs is high.

A global strategy emphasizes economies of scale due to the standardization of products and services, and the centralization of operations in a few locations. As such, one advantage may be that innovations that come about through efforts of either a business unit or the corporate office can be transferred more easily to other locations. Although costs may be lower, the firm following a global strategy may, in general, have to forgo opportunities for revenue growth since it does not invest extensive resources in adapting product offerings from one market to another.

A global strategy is most appropriate when there are strong pressures for reducing costs and comparatively weak pressures for adaptation to local markets. Economies of scale becomes an important consideration.[56] Advantages to increased volume may come from larger production plants or runs as well as from more efficient logistics and distribution networks. Worldwide volume is also especially important in supporting high levels of investment in research and development. As we would expect, many industries requiring high levels of R&D, such as pharmaceuticals, semiconductors, and jet aircraft, follow global strategies.

Another advantage of a global strategy is that it can enable a firm to create a standard level of quality throughout the world. Let's look at what Tom Siebel, former chairman of Siebel Systems (now part of Oracle), the $2 billion developer of e-business application software, has to say about global standardization.

> Our customers—global companies like IBM, Zurich Financial Services, and Citicorp—expect the same high level of service and quality, and the same licensing policies, no matter where we do business with them around the world. Our human resources and legal

Exhibit 7.5
Strengths and Limitations of International Strategies in the Global Marketplace

Strengths	Limitations
• Leverage and diffusion of a parent firm's knowledge and core competencies. • Lower costs because of less need to tailor products and services.	• Limited ability to adapt to local markets. • Inability to take advantage of new ideas and innovations occurring in local markets.

departments help us create policies that respect local cultures and requirements worldwide, while at the same time maintaining the highest standards. We have one brand, one image, one set of corporate colors, and one set of messages, across every place on the planet. An organization needs central quality control to avoid surprises.[57]

Risks and Challenges   There are, of course, some risks associated with a global strategy.[58]

- A firm can enjoy scale economies only by concentrating scale-sensitive resources and activities in one or few locations. Such concentration, however, becomes a "double-edged sword." For example, if a firm has only one manufacturing facility, it must export its output (e.g., components, subsystems, or finished products) to other markets, some of which may be a great distance from the operation. Thus, decisions about locating facilities must weigh the potential benefits from concentrating operations in a single location against the higher transportation and tariff costs that result from such concentration.
- The geographic concentration of any activity may also tend to isolate that activity from the targeted markets. Such isolation may be risky since it may hamper the facility's ability to quickly respond to changes in market conditions and needs.
- Concentrating an activity in a single location also makes the rest of the firm dependent on that location. Such dependency implies that, unless the location has world-class competencies, the firm's competitive position can be eroded if problems arise. A European Ford executive, reflecting on the firm's concentration of activities during a global integration program in the mid-1990s, lamented, "Now if you misjudge the market, you are wrong in 15 countries rather than only one."

Many firms have learned through experience that products that work in one market may not be well received in other markets. Strategy Spotlight 7.7 describes the very different receptions that Pura, a cleaner-burning gasoline from Shell, received in Thailand and the Netherlands.

Exhibit 7.6 summarizes the strengths and weaknesses of global strategies.

Multidomestic Strategy

multidomestic strategy a strategy based on firms' differentiating their products and services to adapt to local markets, used in industries where the pressure for local adaptation is high and the pressure for lowering costs is low.

According to Exhibit 7.4, a firm whose emphasis is on differentiating its product and service offerings to adapt to local markets follows a multidomestic strategy.[59] Decisions evolving from a multidomestic strategy tend to be decentralized to permit the firm to tailor its products and respond rapidly to changes in demand. This enables a firm to expand its market and to charge different prices in different markets. For firms following this strategy, differences in language, culture, income levels, customer preferences, and distribution systems are only a few of the many factors that must be considered. Even in the case of relatively standardized products, at least some level of local adaptation is often necessary. Consider, for example, Honda motorcycles.

> While Honda uses a common basic technology, it must develop different types of motorcycles for different regions of the world. For example, North Americans primarily use motorcycles for leisure and sports; thus aggressive looks and high horsepower are key. Southeast Asians provide a counterpoint. Here, motorcycles are a basic means of transportation. Thus, they require low cost and ease of maintenance. And in Australia and New Zealand, shepherds use motorcycles to herd sheep. Therefore, they demand low-speed torque, rather than high speed and horsepower.[60]

In addition to the products themselves, how they are packaged must sometimes be adapted to local market conditions. Some consumers in developing countries are likely to have packaging preferences very different from Western consumers. For example, single-serve packets, or sachets, are very popular in India.[61] They permit consumers to purchase

7.7

strategy spotlight

Why Shell's Innovative Gasoline Product Backfired in Holland

Not every consumer wants eco-friendly goods, and relatively few will pay more for them. However, every day more customers are including environmental factors in their buying decisions. But what "sells" in one place might not in another.

Consider, for example, Shell Oil's (part of the Royal Dutch/Shell Group) experience in marketing Pura, a new, cleaner-burning gasoline in two very different countries. According to Mark Weintraub, Shell's director of sustainable development strategy, the firm used a "sustainable development lens" to identify a need for cleaner fuels in Thailand. As is the case in much of Asia, the combination of dense cities and high traffic volume was damaging air quality in Bangkok and elsewhere. A cleaner-burning fuel such as Pura, which produced less sulfur and other harmful emissions, seemed like a winner.

In an example of superior eco-design, Shell developed just such a fuel by converting natural gas to a zero-sulfur liquid and then mixing it with regular diesel. Shell

Source: Esty, D. C., & Winston, A. S. 2009. *Green to Gold.* Hoboken, NJ: Wiley; Peckham, J. 2002. Shell Spots "Premium Diesel" Opportunity for GTL Blend. *Diesel Fuel News.* February 4: np; and *www.showa-shell.co.jp.*

touted the blend as providing "more complete combustion to reduce smoke emissions and restore lost engine performance." Shell-Thailand Chairman Khun Vajrabhaya claimed, "Motorists should experience better performance of their vehicles within 2–3 tank-fulls of Shell Pura diesel. From our road tests on diesel-engine vehicles in both Thailand and the U.K., black smoke was satisfactorily reduced." Even though Shell charged a 7.5 cent a gallon premium, Pura gained market share and sales have been very strong. In short, the launch was a complete success.

Shell assumed that it could use the same pitch when it rolled out Pura in other countries. However, the launch in the Netherlands fell flat. Why? Shell later realized that emphasizing how cleaner-burning fuel protects a car's engine was not resonating in Holland. The message was more important in Thailand, where people are much more concerned about gasoline quality and the effect of impurities on engine performance and quality of life.

Clearly, the "green pitch" never went over well in Holland—even though the country is full of customers who say that they will buy green. It is just that the need to clean the local city air is not as pressing a concern as it is in Asia. Eventually, Shell relaunched Pura in Holland under the name V-Power and marketed it by stressing enhanced engine power.

---

only what they need, experiment with new products, and conserve cash. Products as varied as detergents, shampoos, pickles, and cough syrup are sold in sachets in India. It is estimated that they make up 20 to 30 percent of the total sold in their categories. In China, sachets are spreading as a marketing device for such items as shampoos. This reminds us of the importance of considering all activities in a firm's value chain (discussed in Chapters 3 and 5) in determining where local adaptations may be required.

Cultural differences may also require a firm to adapt its personnel practices when it expands internationally.[62] For example, some facets of Walmart stores have been easily

Strengths	Limitations
• Strong integration across various businesses.	• Limited ability to adapt to local markets.
• Standardization leads to higher economies of scale, which lowers costs.	• Concentration of activities may increase dependence on a single facility.
• Helps create uniform standards of quality throughout the world.	• Single locations may lead to higher tariffs and transportation costs.

Exhibit 7.6
Strengths and Limitations of Global Strategies

strategy spotlight 7.8

Dealing with Bribery Abroad

Most multinational firms experience difficult dilemmas when it comes to the question of adapting rules and guidelines, both formal and informal, while operating in foreign countries. A case in point is the Foreign Corrupt Practices Act of 1977, which makes it illegal for U.S. companies to bribe foreign officials to gain business or facilitate approvals and permissions. Unfortunately, in many parts of the world, bribery is a way of life, with large payoffs to government officials and politicians the norm to win government contracts. At a lower level, goods won't clear customs unless routine illegal, but well-accepted, payments, are made to officials. What is an American company to do in such situations?

Intel follows a strict rule-based definition of bribery as "a thing of value given to someone with the intent of obtaining favorable treatment from the recipient." The company strictly prohibits payments to expedite a shipment through customs if the payment did not "follow applicable rules and regulations, and if the agent gives money or payment in kind to a government official for personal benefit." Texas Instruments, on the other hand, follows a middle approach. They require employees to "exercise good judgment" in questionable circumstances "by avoiding activities that could create even the appearance that our decisions could be compromised." And Analog Devices has set up a policy manager as a consultant to overseas operations. The policy manager does not make decisions for country managers. Instead, the policy manager helps country managers think through the issues and provides information on how the corporate office has handled similar situations in the past.

Source: Begley, T. M., & Boyd, D. P. 2003. The Need for a Corporate Global Mind-Set. *MIT Sloan Management Review,* Winter: 25–32.

"exported" to foreign operations, while others have required some modifications.[63] When the retailer entered the German market in 1997, it took along the company "cheer"—Give me a W! Give me an A! Give me an L! Who's Number One? The Customer!—which suited German employees. However, Walmart's 10-Foot Rule, which requires employees to greet any customer within a 10-foot radius, was not so well received in Germany, where employees and shoppers alike weren't comfortable with the custom.

Strategy Spotlight 7.8 describes how U.S. multinationals have adapted to the problem of bribery in various countries while adhering to strict federal laws on corrupt practices abroad.

Risks and Challenges As you might expect, there are some risks associated with a multidomestic strategy. Among these are the following:

- Typically, local adaptation of products and services will increase a company's cost structure. In many industries, competition is so intense that most firms can ill afford any competitive disadvantages on the dimension of cost. A key challenge of managers is to determine the trade-off between local adaptation and its cost structure. For example, cost considerations led Procter & Gamble to standardize its diaper design across all European

● Australia is geographically distant from the United States. However, it is much closer when other dimensions are considered, such as income levels, language, culture, and political/legal systems.

markets. This was done despite research data indicating that Italian mothers, unlike those in other countries, preferred diapers that covered the baby's navel. Later, however, P&G recognized that this feature was critical to these mothers, so the company decided to incorporate this feature for the Italian market despite its adverse cost implications.

- At times, local adaptations, even when well intentioned, may backfire. When the American restaurant chain TGI Fridays entered the South Korean market, it purposely incorporated many local dishes, such as kimchi (hot, spicy cabbage), in its menu. This responsiveness, however, was not well received. Company analysis of the weak market acceptance indicated that Korean customers anticipated a visit to TGI Fridays as a visit to America. Thus, finding Korean dishes was inconsistent with their expectations.

- The optimal degree of local adaptation evolves over time. In many industry segments, a variety of factors, such as the influence of global media, greater international travel, and declining income disparities across countries, may lead to increasing global standardization. On the other hand, in other industry segments, especially where the product or service can be delivered over the Internet (such as music), the need for even greater customization and local adaptation may increase over time. Firms must recalibrate the need for local adaptation on an ongoing basis; excessive adaptation extracts a price as surely as underadaptation.

Some films and TV programs may cross country boundaries rather successfully, while others are less successful. Let's consider an effort by Disney that fell far short:

> Remember *The Alamo,* not the nineteenth-century battle between Mexican forces and Texas rebels, but the 2004 movie? The film definitely met the big-budget criterion—it cost Disney nearly $100 million. It did not generate strong box-office receipts in English. But what was surprising was Disney's attempt to create crossover appeal to Latinos. These efforts included more balanced treatment of Anglos versus Mexicans, prominently featuring Tejano folk heroes in the film, and running a separate Spanish-language marketing effort. But such efforts were doomed to fail. Why? According to one authority, the Alamo is "such an open wound among American Hispanics."[64]

Exhibit 7.7 summarizes the strengths and limitations of multidomestic strategies.

Transnational Strategy

A *transnational strategy* strives to optimize the trade-offs associated with efficiency, local adaptation, and learning.[65] It seeks efficiency not for its own sake, but as a means to achieve global competitiveness.[66] It recognizes the importance of local responsiveness but as a tool for flexibility in international operations.[67] Innovations are regarded as an outcome of a larger process of organizational learning that includes the contributions of everyone in the firm.[68] Also, a core tenet of the transnational model is that a firm's assets and capabilities

transnational strategy a strategy based on firms' optimizing the trade-offs associated with efficiency, local adaptation, and learning, used in industries where the pressures for both local adaptation and lowering costs are high.

Strengths	Limitations
• Ability to adapt products and services to local market conditions.	• Decreased ability to realize cost savings through scale economies.
• Ability to detect potential opportunities for attractive niches in a given market, enhancing revenue.	• Greater difficulty in transferring knowledge across countries.
	• May lead to "overadaptation" as conditions change.

Exhibit 7.7
Strengths and Limitations of Multidomestic Strategies

are dispersed according to the most beneficial location for each activity. Thus, managers avoid the tendency to either concentrate activities in a central location (a global strategy) or disperse them across many locations to enhance adaptation (a multidomestic strategy). Peter Brabeck, Chairman of Nestlé, the giant food company, provides such a perspective.

> We believe strongly that there isn't a so-called global consumer, at least not when it comes to food and beverages. People have local tastes based on their unique cultures and traditions—a good candy bar in Brazil is not the same as a good candy bar in China. Therefore, decision making needs to be pushed down as low as possible in the organization, out close to the markets. Otherwise, how can you make good brand decisions? That said, decentralization has its limits. If you are too decentralized, you can become too complicated—you get too much complexity in your production system. The closer we come to the consumer, in branding, pricing, communication, and product adaptation, the more we decentralize. The more we are dealing with production, logistics, and supply-chain management, the more centralized decision making becomes. After all, we want to leverage Nestlé's size, not be hampered by it.[69]

The Nestlé example illustrates a common approach in determining whether or not to centralize or decentralize a value-chain activity. Typically, primary activities that are "downstream" (e.g., marketing and sales, and service), or closer to the customer, tend to require more decentralization in order to adapt to local market conditions. On the other hand, primary activities that are "upstream" (e.g., logistics and operations), or further away from the customer, tend to be centralized. This is because there is less need for adapting these activities to local markets and the firm can benefit from economies of scale. Additionally, many support activities, such as information systems and procurement, tend to be centralized in order to increase the potential for economies of scale.

A central philosophy of the transnational organization is enhanced adaptation to all competitive situations as well as flexibility by capitalizing on communication and knowledge flows throughout the organization.[70] A principal characteristic is the integration of unique contributions of all units into worldwide operations. Thus, a joint innovation by headquarters and by one of the overseas units can lead potentially to the development of relatively standardized and yet flexible products and services that are suitable for multiple markets.

Asea Brown Boveri (ABB) is a firm that successfully follows a transnational strategy. ABB, with its home bases in Sweden and Switzerland, illustrates the trend toward cross-national mergers that lead firms to consider multiple headquarters in the future. It is managed as a flexible network of units, and one of management's main functions is the facilitation of information and knowledge flows between units. ABB's subsidiaries have complete responsibility for product categories on a worldwide basis. Such a transnational strategy enables ABB to benefit from access to new markets and the opportunity to utilize and develop resources wherever they may be located.

Risks and Challenges   As with the other strategies, there are some unique risks and challenges associated with a transnational strategy.

- *The choice of a seemingly optimal location cannot guarantee that the quality and cost of factor inputs (i.e., labor, materials) will be optimal.* Managers must ensure that the relative advantage of a location is actually realized, not squandered because of weaknesses in productivity and the quality of internal operations. Ford Motor Co., for example, has benefited from having some of its manufacturing operations in Mexico. While some have argued that the benefits of lower wage rates will be partly offset by lower productivity, this does not always have to be the case. Since unemployment in Mexico is higher than in the United States, Ford can be more selective in its hiring practices for its Mexican operations. And, given the lower turnover among its Mexican employees, Ford can justify a high level of investment in training and development. Thus, the net result can be not only lower wage rates but also higher productivity than in the United States.

- *Although knowledge transfer can be a key source of competitive advantage, it does not take place "automatically."* For knowledge transfer to take place from one subsidiary to another, it is important for the source of the knowledge, the target units, and the corporate headquarters to recognize the potential value of such unique know-how. Given that there can be significant geographic, linguistic, and cultural distances that typically separate subsidiaries, the potential for knowledge transfer can become very difficult to realize. Firms must create mechanisms to systematically and routinely uncover the opportunities for knowledge transfer.

Exhibit 7.8 summarizes the relative advantages and disadvantages of transnational strategies.

Global or Regional? A Second Look at Globalization

Thus far, we have suggested four possible strategies from which a firm must choose once it has decided to compete in the global marketplace. In recent years, many writers have asserted that the process of globalization has caused national borders to become increasingly irrelevant.[71] However, some scholars have recently questioned this perspective, and they have argued that it is unwise for companies to rush into full scale globalization.[72]

Before answering questions about the extent of firms' globalization, let's try to clarify what "globalization" means. Traditionally, a firm's globalization is measured in terms of its foreign sales as a percentage of total sales. However, this measure can be misleading. For example, consider a U.S. firm that has expanded its activities into Canada. Clearly, this initiative is qualitatively different from achieving the same sales volume in a distant country such as China. Similarly, if a Malaysian firm expands into Singapore or a German firm starts selling its products in Austria, this would represent an expansion into a geographically adjacent country. Such nearby countries would often share many common characteristics in terms of language, culture, infrastructure, and customer preferences. In other words, this is more a case of regionalization than globalization.

Extensive analysis of the distribution data of sales across different countries and regions led Alan Rugman and Alain Verbeke to conclude that there is a stronger case to be made in favor of regionalization than globalization. According to their study, a company would have to have at least 20 percent of its sales in each of the three major economic regions—North America, Europe, and Asia—to be considered a global firm. However, they found that only nine of the world's 500 largest firms met this standard! Even when they relaxed the criterion to 20 percent of sales each in at least two of the three regions, the number only increased to 25. *Thus, most companies are regional or, at best, biregional— not global—even today.* Exhibit 7.9 provides a listing of the large firms that met each of these two criteria.

> **>LO7.6**
> The difference between regional companies and truly global companies.

regionalization
increasing international exchange of goods, services, money, people, ideas, and information; and the increasing similarity of culture, laws, rules, and norms within a region such as Europe, North America, or Asia.

Strengths	Limitations
• Ability to attain economies of scale.	• Unique challenges in determining optimal locations of activities to ensure cost and quality.
• Ability to adapt to local markets.	
• Ability to locate activities in optimal locations.	• Unique managerial challenges in fostering knowledge transfer.
• Ability to increase knowledge flows and learning.	

Exhibit 7.8
Strengths and Limitations of Transnational Strategies

Exhibit 7.9
Global or Regional?
Sales Distribution of the
***Fortune* Global 500 Firms**

Firms with at least 20 percent sales in Asia, Europe, and North America each but with less than 50 percent sales in any one region:

IBM	Nokia	Coca-Cola
Sony	Intel	Flextronics
Philips	Canon	LVMH

Firms with at least 20 percent sales in at least two of the three regions (Asia, Europe, North America) but with less than 50 percent sales in any one region:

BP Amoco	Alstom	Michelin
Toyota	Aventis	Kodak
Nissan	Daigeo	Electrolux
Unilever	Sun Microsystems	BAE
Motorola	Bridgestone	Alcan
GlaxoSmithKline	Roche	L'Oreal
EADS	3M	Lafarge
Bayer	Skanska	
Ericsson	McDonald's	

Firms with at least 50 percent of their sales in one of the three regions—other than their home region:

Daimler Chrysler	Santander	Sodexho Alliance
ING Group	Delhaize "Le Lion"	Manpower
Royal Ahold	Astra Zeneca	Wolseley
Honda	News Corporation	

Sources: Peng, M.W. 2010. *Global Strategy* 2nd ed. Mason, OH: Thomson Southwestern; and Rugman, A.M., & Verbeke, A. 2004. A Perspective on Regional and Global Strategies of Multinational Enterprises. *Journal of International Business Studies,* 35: 3–18.

In a world of instant communication, rapid transportation, and governments that are increasingly willing to open up their markets to trade and investment, why are so few firms "global"? The most obvious answer is that distance still matters. After all, it is easier to do business in a neighboring country than in a far away country, all else being equal. Distance, in the final analysis, may be viewed as a concept with many dimensions, not just a measure of geographical distance. For example, both Canada and Mexico are the same distance from the U.S. However, U.S. companies find it easier to expand operations into Canada than into Mexico. Why? Canada and the U.S. share many commonalities in terms of language, culture, economic development, legal and political systems, and infrastructure development. Thus, if we view distance as having many dimensions, the U.S. and Canada are very close, whereas there is greater distance between the U.S. and Mexico. Similarly, when we look at what we might call the "true" distance between the U.S. and China, the effects of geographic distance are multiplied by distance in terms of culture, language, religion, and legal and political systems between the two countries. On the other hand, although U.S. and Australia are geographically distant, the "true" distance is somewhat less when one considers distance along the other dimensions.

Another reason for regional expansion is the rise of the trading blocs. The European Union originally started in the 1950s as a regional trading bloc. However, recently it has

**trading
blocs** groups of countries agreeing to increase trade between them by lowering trade barries.

achieved a large degree of economic and political integration in terms of common currency and common standards that many thought infeasible, if not impossible, only 20 years ago. The resulting economic benefits have led other regions also to consider similar moves. For example, the North American Free Trade Agreement (NAFTA) has the eventual abolition of all barriers to the free movement of goods and services among Canada, the U.S., and Mexico as its goal. Other regional trading blocks include MERCOSUR (consisting of Argentina, Brazil, Paraguay, and Uruguay) and the Association of Southeast Asian Nations (ASEAN) (consisting of about a dozen Southeast Asian countries).

Regional economic integration has progressed at a faster pace than global economic integration and the trade and investment patterns of the largest companies reflect this reality. After all, regions represent the outcomes of centuries of political and cultural history that results not only in commonalities but also mutual affinity. For example, stretching from Algeria and Morocco in the West to Oman and Yemen in the East, more than 30 countries share the Arabic language and the Muslim religion, making these countries a natural regional bloc. Similarly, the countries of South and Central America share the Spanish language (except Brazil), Catholic religion, and a shared history of Spanish colonialism. No wonder firms find it easier and less risky to expand within their region than to other regions.

Entry Modes of International Expansion

>LO7.7
The four basic types of entry strategies and the relative benefits and risks associated with each of them.

A firm has many options available to it when it decides to expand into international markets. Given the challenges associated with such entry, many firms first start on a small scale and then increase their level of investment and risk as they gain greater experience with the overseas market in question.[73]

Exhibit 7.10 illustrates a wide variety of modes of foreign entry, including exporting, licensing, franchising, joint ventures, strategic alliances, and wholly owned subsidiaries.[74] As the exhibit indicates, the various types of entry form a continuum ranging from exporting (low investment and risk, low control) to a wholly owned subsidiary (high investment and risk, high control).[75]

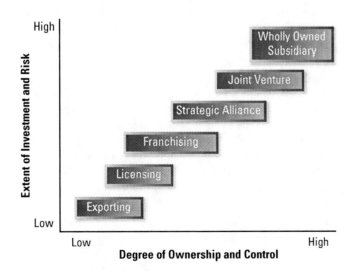

Exhibit 7.10 **Entry Modes for International Expansion**

There can be frustrations and setbacks as a firm evolves its international entry strategy from exporting to more expensive types, including wholly owned subsidiaries. For example, according to the CEO of a large U.S. specialty chemical company:

> In the end, we always do a better job with our own subsidiaries; sales improve, and we have greater control over the business. But we still need local distributors for entry, and we are still searching for strategies to get us through the transitions without battles over control and performance.[76]

Exporting

exporting
producing goods in one country to sell to residents of another country.

Exporting consists of producing goods in one country to sell in another.[77] This entry strategy enables a firm to invest the least amount of resources in terms of its product, its organization, and its overall corporate strategy. Many host countries dislike this entry strategy because it provides less local employment than other modes of entry.[78]

Multinationals often stumble onto a stepwise strategy for penetrating markets, beginning with the exporting of products. This often results in a series of unplanned actions to increase sales revenues. As the pattern recurs with entries into subsequent markets, this approach, named a "beachhead strategy," often becomes official policy.[79]

Benefits   Such an approach definitely has its advantages. After all, firms start from scratch in sales and distribution when they enter new markets. Because many foreign markets are nationally regulated and dominated by networks of local intermediaries, firms need to partner with local distributors to benefit from their valuable expertise and knowledge of their own markets. Multinationals, after all, recognize that they cannot master local business practices, meet regulatory requirements, hire and manage local personnel, or gain access to potential customers without some form of local partnership.

Multinationals also want to minimize their own risk. They do this by hiring local distributors and investing very little in the undertaking. In essence, the firm gives up control of strategic marketing decisions to the local partners—much more control than they would be willing to give up in their home market.

Risks and Limitations   Exporting is a relatively inexpensive way to enter foreign markets. However, it can still have significant downsides. In a study of 250 instances in which multinational firms used local distributors to implement their exporting entry strategy, the results were dismal. In the vast majority of the cases, the distributors were bought (to increase control) by the multinational firm or fired. In contrast, successful distributors shared two common characteristics:

- They carried product lines that complemented, rather than competed with, the multinational's products.
- They behaved as if they were business partners with the multinationals. They shared market information with the corporations, they initiated projects with distributors in neighboring countries, and they suggested initiatives in their own or nearby markets. Additionally, these distributors took on risk themselves by investing in areas such as training, information systems, and advertising and promotion in order to increase the business of their multinational partners.

licensing a contractual arrangement in which a company receives a royalty or fee in exchange for the right to use its trademark, patent, trade secret, or other valuable intellectual property.

The key point is the importance of developing collaborative, win–win relationships.

To ensure more control over operations without incurring significant risks, many firms have used licensing and franchising as a mode of entry. Let's now discuss these and their relative advantages and disadvantages.

Licensing and Franchising

Licensing and franchising are both forms of contractual arrangements. **Licensing** enables a company to receive a royalty or fee in exchange for the right to use its trademark, patent, trade secret, or other valuable item of intellectual property.[80]

Franchising contracts generally include a broader range of factors in an operation and have a longer time period during which the agreement is in effect. Franchising remains a primary form of American business. According to a recent survey, more than 400 U.S. franchisers have international exposure.[81] This is greater than the combined totals of the next four largest franchiser home countries—France, the United Kingdom, Mexico, and Austria.

Benefits   In international markets, an advantage of licensing is that the firm granting a license incurs little risk, since it does not have to invest any significant resources into the country itself. In turn, the licensee (the firm receiving the license) gains access to the trademark, patent, and so on, and is able to potentially create competitive advantages. In many cases, the country also benefits from the product being manufactured locally. For example, Yoplait yogurt is licensed by General Mills from Sodima, a French cooperative, for sale in the United States. The logos of college and professional athletic teams in the United States are another source of trademarks that generate significant royalty income domestically and internationally.

Franchising has the advantage of limiting the risk exposure that a firm has in overseas markets. At the same time, the firm is able to expand the revenue base of the company.

> **franchising** a contractual arrangement in which a company receives a royalty or fee in exchange for the right to use its intellectual property; it usually involves a longer time period than licensing and includes other factors, such as monitoring of operations, training, and advertising.

Risks and Limitations   The licensor gives up control of its product and forgoes potential revenues and profits. Furthermore, the licensee may eventually become so familiar with the patent and trade secrets that it may become a competitor; that is, the licensee may make some modifications to the product and manufacture and sell it independently of the licensor without having to pay a royalty fee. This potential situation is aggravated in countries that have relatively weak laws to protect intellectual property. Additionally, if the licensee selected by the multinational firm turns out to be a poor choice, the brand name and reputation of the product may be tarnished.[82]

With franchising, the multinational firm receives only a portion of the revenues, in the form of franchise fees. Had the firm set up the operation itself (e.g., a restaurant through direct investment), it would have had the entire revenue to itself.

Companies often desire a closer collaboration with other firms in order to increase revenue, reduce costs, and enhance their learning—often through the diffusion of technology. To achieve such objectives, they enter into strategic alliances or joint ventures, two entry modes we will discuss next.

Strategic Alliances and Joint Ventures

Joint ventures and strategic alliances have recently become increasingly popular.[83] These two forms of partnership differ in that joint ventures entail the creation of a third-party legal entity, whereas strategic alliances do not. In addition, strategic alliances generally focus on initiatives that are smaller in scope than joint ventures.[84]

Benefits   As we discussed in Chapter 6, these strategies have been effective in helping firms increase revenues and reduce costs as well as enhance learning and diffuse technologies.[85] These partnerships enable firms to share the risks as well as the potential revenues and profits. Also, by gaining exposure to new sources of knowledge and technologies, such partnerships can help firms develop core competencies that can lead to competitive advantages in the marketplace.[86] Finally, entering into partnerships with host country firms can provide very useful information on local market tastes, competitive conditions, legal matters, and cultural nuances.[87]

Strategic alliances can be between firms in totally different industries. Strategy Spotlight 7.9 discusses a collaboration between the Italian automaker Lamborghini and Callaway, the U.S. golf equipment manufacturer.

strategy spotlight 7.9

Lamborghini and Callaway Form a High-Tech Alliance

Lamborghini's Sesto Elemento concept car was the hit at the 2010 Paris Auto Show. It would not seem to have much in common with Callaway's new Diablo Octane and Octane Tour drivers. However, both are made using an ingenious new material called Forged Composite that the companies developed together. The material is much stronger than titanium but weighs only one-third as much.

The partnership between Lamborghini and Callaway began in 2008. Researchers from the two companies met at a materials science conference and found that they had much in common. Says Callaway's CEO George Fellows, "The collaboration has been great. The DNA of both companies, pushing for a technological edge in performance-oriented consumer products, is very similar." In short, both firms are engaged in developing lighter and stronger composite materials for their products. And most would agree that the markets that they serve are dissimilar enough to make full cooperation feasible.

Source: Newport, J. P. 2010. Drive the Ball Like It's a Lamborghini, Maybe. *Wall Street Journal.* November 13–14: A14; *www.callaway.com*; and Anonymous. 2010. Automobili Lamborghini and Callaway Golf Form Strategic Partnership. *autonewscast.com*, September 30: np.

Let's look at how each company has benefited from their joint development of Forged Composite.

The weight-savings in Callaway's new drivers, which deploy Forged Composite only in the crowns (the bottom half of the clubheads is still made of titanium), is only 10 grams. Although 10 grams might seem insignificant, such weight loss up top gives designers much more flexibility in how they distribute mass around the bottom. This helps to create more desirable ball flight characteristics and improve forgiveness on off-center hits.

For Lamborghini, Forged Composite enhances a car's power-to weight ratio and acceleration capability. To illustrate, the Sesto Elemento can accelerate from zero to 60 miles per hour in an astonishing 2.5 seconds. This is almost a full second faster than the Italian automaker's speed champ—the $240,000 Superleggera. The difference is entirely due to weight, in part because both cars use the same 570-horsepower, four-wheel-drivetrain. But by building the chassis almost entirely of Forged Composite, engineers were able to reduce the curb weight by nearly a third—to an anorexic 2,072 pounds. "The power-to-weight ratio is more like a motorcycle's," claims Lamborghini's CEO Stephan Winkelmann. After further testing, he expects Forged Composite to begin working its way into production within a few years.

Risks and Limitations Managers must be aware of the risks associated with strategic alliances and joint ventures and how they can be minimized.[88] First, there needs to be a clearly defined strategy that is strongly supported by the organizations that are party to the partnership. Otherwise, the firms may work at cross-purposes and not achieve any of their goals. Second, and closely allied to the first issue, there must be a clear understanding of capabilities and resources that will be central to the partnership. Without such clarification, there will be fewer opportunities for learning and developing competencies that could lead to competitive advantages. Third, trust is a vital element. Phasing in the relationship between alliance partners permits them to get to know each other better and develop trust. Without trust, one party may take advantage of the other by, for example, withholding its fair share of resources and gaining access to privileged information through unethical (or illegal) means. Fourth, cultural issues that can potentially lead to conflict and dysfunctional behaviors need to be addressed. An organization's culture is the set of values, beliefs, and attitudes that influence the behavior and goals of its employees.[89] Thus, recognizing cultural differences as well as striving to develop elements of a "common culture" for the partnership is vital. Without a unifying culture, it will become difficult to combine and leverage resources that are increasingly important in knowledge-intensive organizations (discussed in Chapter 4).[90]

Finally, the success of a firm's alliance should not be left to chance.[91] To improve their odds of success, many companies have carefully documented alliance-management knowledge by creating guidelines and manuals to help them manage specific aspects of the entire alliance life cycle (e.g., partner selection and alliance negotiation and contracting). For example, Lotus Corp. (part of IBM) created what it calls its "35 rules of thumb" to manage each phase of an alliance from formation to termination. Hewlett-Packard developed 60 different tools and templates, which it placed in a 300-page manual for guiding decision making. The manual included such tools as a template for making the business case for an alliance, a partner evaluation form, a negotiation template outlining the roles and responsibilities of different departments, a list of the ways to measure alliance performance, and an alliance termination checklist.

When a firm desires the highest level of control, it develops wholly owned subsidiaries. Although wholly owned subsidiaries can generate the greatest returns, they also have the highest levels of investment and risk. We will now discuss them.

Wholly Owned Subsidiaries

A **wholly owned subsidiary** is a business in which a multinational company owns 100 percent of the stock. Two ways a firm can establish a wholly owned subsidiary are to (1) acquire an existing company in the home country or (2) develop a totally new operation (often referred to as a "greenfield venture").

wholly owned subsidiary a business in which a multinational company owns 100 percent of the stock.

Benefits   Establishing a wholly owned subsidiary is the most expensive and risky of the various entry modes. However, it can also yield the highest returns. In addition, it provides the multinational company with the greatest degree of control of all activities, including manufacturing, marketing, distribution, and technology development.[92]

Wholly owned subsidiaries are most appropriate where a firm already has the appropriate knowledge and capabilities that it can leverage rather easily through multiple locations. Examples range from restaurants to semiconductor manufacturers. To lower costs, for example, Intel Corporation builds semiconductor plants throughout the world—all of which use virtually the same blueprint. Knowledge can be further leveraged by hiring managers and professionals from the firm's home country, often through hiring talent from competitors.

Risks and Limitations   As noted, wholly owned subsidiaries are typically the most expensive and risky entry mode. With franchising, joint ventures, or strategic alliances, the risk is shared with the firm's partners. With wholly owned subsidiaries, the entire risk is assumed by the parent company. The risks associated with doing business in a new country (e.g., political, cultural, and legal) can be lessened by hiring local talent.

For example, Wendy's avoided committing two blunders in Germany by hiring locals to its advertising staff.[93] In one case, the firm wanted to promote its "old-fashioned" qualities. However, a literal translation would have resulted in the company promoting itself as "outdated." In another situation, Wendy's wanted to emphasize that its hamburgers could be prepared 256 ways. The problem? The German word that Wendy's wanted to use for "ways" usually meant "highways" or "roads." Although such errors may sometimes be entertaining to the public, it is certainly preferable to catch these mistakes before they confuse the consumer or embarrass the company.

We have addressed entry strategies as a progression from exporting through the creation of wholly owned subsidiaries. However, we must point out that many firms do not follow such an evolutionary approach. For example, because of political and regulatory reasons, Pepsi entered India through a joint venture with two Indian firms in 1998. As discussed in Strategy Spotlight 7.10, this provided Pepsi with a first-mover advantage within the Indian market, where it remains well ahead of its archrival, Coca-Cola.

strategy spotlight   7.10

Pepsi's First-Mover Advantage in India Has Paid Off

Pepsi (pronounced "Pay-psee") became a common synonym for cola in India's most widely spoken language after having the market to itself in the early 1990s. PepsiCo's linguistic advantage translates into higher sales for its namesake product. Although Atlanta-based Coke has larger total beverage sales in India because it owns several non-cola drink brands, Pepsi's 4.5 percent of the soft drink market outshines Coke's 2.6 percent, according to Euromonitor. That's a notable exception to much of the rest of the world, where Coke's cola soundly beats its main rival.

What explains Pepsi's success in India? Coke pulled out of the market in 1977 after new government regulations forced it to partner with an Indian company and share the drink's secret formula. In contrast, Pepsi formed a joint venture in 1988 with two Indian companies and introduced products under the Lehar brand. (Lehar Pepsi

Source: Srivastava, M. 2010. For India's Consumers, Pepsi Is the Real Thing. *Bloomberg Businessweek.* September 20–26: 26–27; Bhushan, R. 2010. Pepsi India Touches Eco Watershed, First Unit to Achieve Positive Water Balance. *www.indiatimes.com.* May 27: np; and *www.pepsicoindia.*

was introduced in 1990.) Coke then re-entered the market in 1993 after Indian regulations were changed to permit foreign brands to operate without Indian partners.

Coke's time out of India cost it dearly. "Pepsi got here sooner, and got to India just as it was starting to engage with the West and with Western products," said Lalita Desai, a linguist at Jadavpur University who studies how English words enter Indian languages. "And with no real international competition, 'Pepsi' became the catch-all for anything that was bottled, fizzy, and from abroad."

PepsiCo has also been very successful in promoting water conservation in India. Its Indian operation became the first of its global units (and probably the only one in the beverage industry) to conserve and replenish more water that it consumed in 2009. Its rival, Coca Cola, on the other hand, is facing a serious situation in India as it has been fined Rs 216 crore ($4.7 million) as compensation for groundwater pollution and depletion.

Today, PepsiCo is the fourth largest consumer products company in India. The firm also has invested more than $1 billion in India, created direct and indirect employment to 150,000 people in the country, and has 13 company-owned bottling plants, according to its website.

Reflecting on Career Implications . . .

- *International Strategy:* Be aware of your organization's international strategy. What percentage of the total firm activity is international? What skills are needed to enhance your company's international efforts? How can you get more involved in your organization's international strategy? For your career, what conditions in your home country might cause you to seek careers abroad?
- *Outsourcing and Offshoring:* What activities in your organization can/should be outsourced or offshored? Be aware that you are competing in the global marketplace for employment and professional advancement. Continually take inventory of your talents, skills, and competencies.
- *International Career Opportunities:* Work assignments in other countries can often provide a career boost. Be proactive in pursuing promising career opportunities in other countries. Anticipate how such opportunities will advance your short- and long-term career aspirations.
- *Management Risks:* Develop cultural sensitivity. This applies, of course, to individuals from different cultures in your home-based organization as well as in your overseas experience.

Summary

We live in a highly interconnected global community where many of the best opportunities for growth and profitability lie beyond the boundaries of a company's home country. Along with the opportunities, of course, there are many risks associated with diversification into global markets.

The first section of the chapter addressed the factors that determine a nation's competitiveness in a particular industry. The framework was developed by Professor Michael Porter of Harvard University and was based on a four-year study that explored the competitive success of 10 leading trading nations. The four factors, collectively termed the "diamond of national advantage," were factor conditions, demand characteristics, related and supporting industries, and firm strategy, structure, and rivalry.

The discussion of Porter's "diamond" helped, in essence, to set the broader context for exploring competitive advantage at the firm level. In the second section, we discussed the primary motivations and the potential risks associated with international expansion. The primary motivations included increasing the size of the potential market for the firm's products and services, achieving economies of scale, extending the life cycle of the firm's products, and optimizing the location for every activity in the value chain. On the other hand, the key risks included political and economic risks, currency risks, and management risks. Management risks are the challenges associated with responding to the inevitable differences that exist across countries such as customs, culture, language, customer preferences, and distribution systems. We also addressed some of the managerial challenges and opportunities associated with offshoring and outsourcing.

Next, we addressed how firms can go about attaining competitive advantage in global markets. We began by discussing the two opposing forces—cost reduction and adaptation to local markets—that managers must contend with when entering global markets. The relative importance of these two factors plays a major part in determining which of the four basic types of strategies to select: international, global, multidomestic, or transnational. The chapter covered the benefits and risks associated with each type of strategy. We also presented a recent perspective by Alan Rugman who argues that despite all the talk of globalization, most of the large multinationals are regional or at best biregional (in terms of geographical diversification of sales) rather than global.

The final section discussed the four types of entry strategies that managers may undertake when entering international markets. The key trade-off in each of these strategies is the level of investment or risk versus the level of control. In order of their progressively greater investment/risk and

control, the strategies range from exporting to licensing and franchising, to strategic alliances and joint ventures, to wholly owned subsidiaries. The relative benefits and risks associated with each of these strategies were addressed.

Summary Review Questions

1. What are some of the advantages and disadvantages associated with a firm's expansion into international markets?
2. What are the four factors described in Porter's diamond of national advantage? How do the four factors explain why some industries in a given country are more successful than others?
3. Explain the two opposing forces—cost reduction and adaptation to local markets—that firms must deal with when they go global.
4. There are four basic strategies—international, global, multidomestic, and transnational. What are the advantages and disadvantages associated with each?
5. What is the basis of Alan Rugman's argument that most multinationals are still more regional than global? What factors inhibit firms from becoming truly global?
6. Describe the basic entry strategies that firms have available when they enter international markets. What are the relative advantages and disadvantages of each?

Key Terms

globalization, 241
diamond of national
   advantage, 241
factor endowments
   (national
   advantage), 242
related and supporting
   industries (national
   advantage), 243
firm strategy, structure,
   and rivalry (national
   advantage), 244
multinational firms, 244
arbitrage
   opportunities, 247
reverse innovation, 248
political risk, 249
rule of law, 249
economic risk, 251

counterfeiting, 252
currency risk, 252
management risk, 253
outsourcing, 254
offshoring, 254
international
   strategy, 257
global strategy, 259
multidomestic
   strategy, 260
transnational
   strategy, 263
regionalization, 265
trading blocs, 266
exporting, 268
licensing, 268
franchising, 269
wholly owned
   subsidiary, 271

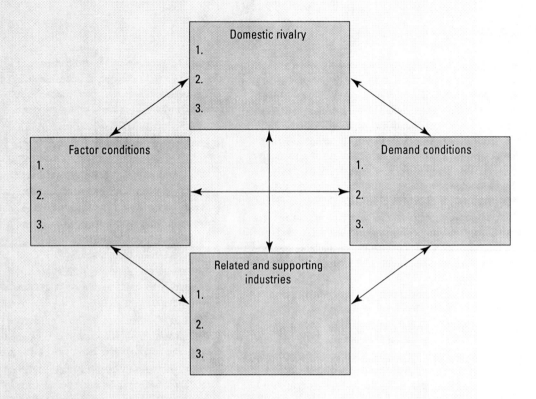

Experiential Exercise

The United States is considered a world leader in the motion picture industry. Using Porter's diamond framework for national competitiveness, explain the success of this industry.

Application Questions & Exercises

1. Data on the "competitiveness of nations" can be found at *www.imd.ch/wcy/ranking/*. This website provides a ranking on a 331 criteria for 59 countries. How might Porter's diamond of national advantage help to explain the rankings for some of these countries for certain industries that interest you?

2. The Internet has lowered the entry barriers for smaller firms that wish to diversify into international markets. Why is this so? Provide an example.

3. Many firms fail when they enter into strategic alliances with firms that link up with companies based in other countries. What are some reasons for this failure? Provide an example.

4. Many large U.S.–based management consulting companies such as McKinsey and Company and the BCG Group have been very successful in the international marketplace. How can Porter's diamond explain their success?

Ethics Questions

1. Over the past few decades, many American firms have relocated most or all of their operations from the United States to countries such as Mexico and China that pay lower wages. What are some of the ethical issues that such actions may raise?

2. Business practices and customs vary throughout the world. What are some of the ethical issues concerning payments that must be made in a foreign country to obtain business opportunities?

References

1. Anonymous. 2010. Exit Carrefour. *The Economist.* September 23: 77; Thomas, D. & Fuse, T. 2010. Retailers jump in for Carrefour SE Asia assets. *www.reuters.com.* September 1: np; and Chan, C. 2010. Carrefour said to list Tesco, Casino as potential unit buyers. *www.businessweek.com.* September 9: np.

2. For a recent discussion on globalization by one of international business's most respected authors, read Ohmae, K. 2005. *The next global stage: Challenges and opportunities in our borderless world.* Philadelphia: Wharton School Publishing.

3. Our discussion of globalization draws upon Engardio, P. & Belton, C. 2000. Global capitalism: Can it be made to work better? *Business Week,* November 6: 72–98.

4. Sellers, P. 2005. Blowing in the wind. *Fortune,* July 25: 63.

5. An interesting and balanced discussion on the merits of multinationals to the U.S. economy is found in: Mandel, M. 2008. Multinationals: Are they good for America? *BusinessWeek,* March 10: 41–64.

6. Engardio & Belton, op. cit.

7. For insightful perspectives on strategy in emerging economies, refer to the article entitled: Strategy research in emerging economies: Challenging the conventional wisdom in the January 2005 issue of *Journal of Management Studies,* 42(1).

8. Black, J. S. & Morrison, A. J. 2010. A cautionary tale for emerging market giants. *Harvard Business Review,* 88(9): 99–105.

9. The above discussion draws on Clifford, M. L., Engardio, P., Malkin, E., Roberts, D., & Echikson, W. 2000. Up the ladder. *BusinessWeek,* November 6: 78–84.

10. A recent discussion of the "bottom of the pyramid" is: Akula, V. 2008. Business basics at the bottom of the pyramid. *Harvard Business Review,* 86(6): 53–59.

11. Some insights into how winners are evolving in emerging markets are addressed in: Ghemawat, P. & Hout, T. 2008. Tomorrow's global giants:

Not the usual suspects. *Harvard Business Review,* 66(11): 80–88.

12. For another interesting discussion on a country perspective, refer to Makino, S. 1999. MITI Minister Kaora Yosano on reviving Japan's competitive advantages. *Academy of Management Executive,* 13(4): 8–28.

13. The following discussion draws heavily upon Porter, M. E. 1990. The competitive advantage of nations. *Harvard Business Review,* March–April: 73–93.

14. Landes, D. S. 1998. *The wealth and poverty of nations.* New York: W. W. Norton.

15. A recent study that investigates the relationship between international diversification and firm performance is Lu, J. W. & Beamish, P. W. 2004. International diversification and firm performance: The s-curve hypothesis. *Academy of Management Journal,* 47(4): 598–609.

16. Part of our discussion of the motivations and risks of international expansion draws upon Gregg, F. M. 1999. International strategy. In Helms, M. M. (Ed.). *Encyclopedia of management:* 434–438. Detroit: Gale Group.

17. These two examples are discussed, respectively, in Dawar, N. & Frost, T. 1999. Competing with giants: Survival strategies for local companies in emerging markets. *Harvard Business Review,* 77(2): 119–129; and Prahalad, C. K. & Lieberthal, K. 1998. The end of corporate imperialism. *Harvard Business Review,* 76(4): 68–79.

18. Meredith, R. 2004. Middle kingdom, middle class. *Forbes,* November 15: 188–192; and Anonymous. 2004. Middle class becomes rising power in China. *www.Chinadaily.com.* November 6.

19. Eyring, M. J., Johnson, M. W. & Nair, H. 2011. New business models in emerging markets. *Harvard Business Review,* 89 (1/2): 88–98.

20. Cieply, M. & Barnes, B. 2010. After rants, skepticism over Gibson bankability grows in non-U.S. markets. *International Herald Tribune,* July 23: 1.

21. This discussion draws upon Gupta, A. K. & Govindarajan, V. 2001. Converting global presence into global competitive advantage. *Academy of Management Executive,* 15(2): 45–56.

22. Stross, R. E. 1997. Mr. Gates builds his brain trust. *Fortune,* December 8: 84–98.

23. For a good summary of the benefits and risks of international expansion, refer to Bartlett, C. A. & Ghoshal, S. 1987. Managing across borders: New strategic responses. *Sloan Management Review,* 28(5): 45–53; and Brown, R. H. 1994. *Competing to win in a global economy.* Washington, DC: U.S. Department of Commerce.

24. For an interesting insight into rivalry in global markets, refer to MacMillan, I. C., van Putten, A. B., & McGrath, R. G. 2003. Global gamesmanship. *Harvard Business Review,* 81(5): 62–73.

25. It is important for firms to spread their foreign operations and outsourcing relationships with a broad, well-balanced mix of regions and countries to reduce risk and increase potential reward. For example, refer to Vestring, T., Rouse, T., & Reinert, U. 2005. Hedge your offshoring bets. *MIT Sloan Management Review,* 46(3): 27–29.

26. An interesting discussion of risks faced by Lukoil, Russia's largest oil firm is in: Gimbel, B. 2009. Russia's king of crude. *Fortune,* February 2: 88–92.

27. Some insights on how Africa has improved as a potential source of investment is in: Collier, P. & Warnholz, J-L. 2009. Now's the time to invest in Africa. *Harvard Business Review,* 87(2): 23.

28. For a discussion of some of the challenges associated with government corruption regarding entry strategies in foreign markets, read Rodriguez, P., Uhlenbruck, K., & Eden, L. 2005. Government corruption and entry strategies of multinationals. *Academy of Management Review,* 30(2): 383–396.

29. For a discussion of the political risks in China for United States companies,

refer to Garten, J. E. 1998. Opening the doors for business in China. *Harvard Business Review*, 76(3): 167–175.

30. Shari, M. 2001. Is a holy war brewing in Indonesia? *BusinessWeek,* October 15: 62.

31. Insights on how forensic economics can be used to investigate crimes and wrongdoing are in: Fisman, R. 2009. The rise of forensic economics. *Harvard Business Review,* 87(2): 26.

32. Anonymous. 2010. Libya: Why it is still stuck. *The Economist,* April 10: 49.

33. For an interesting perspective on the relationship between diversification and the development of a nation's institutional environment, read Chakrabarti, A., Singh, K., & Mahmood, I. 2007. Diversification and performance: Evidence from East Asian firms. *Strategic Management Journal,* 28(2): 101–120.

34. A study looking into corruption and foreign direct investment is: Brouthers, L. E., Gao, Y., & McNicol, J. P. 2008. *Strategic Management Journal,* 29(6): 673–680.

35. Gikkas, N. S. 1996. International licensing of intellectual property: The promise and the peril. *Journal of Technology Law & Policy,* 1(1): 1–26.

36. Insights into bribery in the international context are addressed in: Martin, K. D., Cullen, J. B., Johnson, J. L., & Parboteeah, P. 2008. Deciding to bribe: A cross-level analysis of firm and home country influences on bribery activity. *Academy of Management Journal,* 50(6): 1401–1422.

37. Sandler, N. 2008. Israel: Attack of the super-shekel. *BusinessWeek,* February 25: 38.

38. For an excellent theoretical discussion of how cultural factors can affect knowledge transfer across national boundaries, refer to Bhagat, R. S., Kedia, B. L., Harveston, P. D., & Triandis, H. C. 2002. Cultural variations in the cross-border transfer of organizational knowledge: An integrative framework. *Academy of Management Review,* 27(2): 204–221.

39. An interesting discussion on how local companies compete effectively with large multinationals is in: Bhatacharya, A. K. & Michael, D. C.

2008. *Harvard Business Review,* 66(3): 84–95.

40. To gain insights on the role of national and regional cultures on knowledge management models and frameworks, read Pauleen, D. J. & Murphy, P. 2005. In praise of cultural bias. *MIT Sloan Management Review,* 46(2): 21–22.

41. Berkowitz, E. N. 2000. *Marketing* (6th ed.). New York: McGraw-Hill.

42. Harvey, M. & Buckley, M. R. 2002. Assessing the "conventional wisdoms" of management for the 21st century organization. *Organization Dynamics,* 30 (4): 368–378.

43. World Trade Organization. *Annual Report 1998.* Geneva: World Trade Organization.

44. Lei, D. 2005. Outsourcing. In Hitt, M. A. & Ireland, R. D. (Eds.). *The Blackwell encyclopedia of management.* Entrepreneurship: 196–199. Malden, MA: Blackwell.

45. Future trends in offshoring are addressed in: Manning, S., Massini, S., & Lewin, A. Y. 2008. A dynamic perspective on next-generation offshoring: The global sourcing of science and engineering talent. *Academy of Management Perspectives,* 22(3): 35–54.

46. An interesting perspective on the controversial issue regarding the offshoring of airplane maintenance is in: Smith, G. & Bachman, J. 2008. Flying in for a tune-up overseas. *Business Week.* April 21: 26–27.

47. Dolan, K.A. 2006. Offshoring the offshorers. *Forbes.* April 17: 74–78.

48. The discussion above draws from Colvin, J. 2004. Think your job can't be sent to India? Just watch. *Fortune,* December 13: 80; Schwartz, N. D. 2004. Down and out in white collar America. *Fortune,* June 23: 321–325; Hagel, J. 2004. Outsourcing is not just about cost cutting. *The Wall Street Journal,* March 18: A3.

49. Insightful perspectives on the outsourcing of decision making are addressed in: Davenport, T. H. & Iyer, B. 2009. Should you outsource your brain? *Harvard Business Review.* 87 (2): 38. (7)

50. Levitt, T. 1983. The globalization of markets. *Harvard Business Review,* 61(3): 92–102.

51. Our discussion of these assumptions draws upon Douglas, S. P. & Wind, Y. 1987. The myth of globalization. *Columbia Journal of World Business,* Winter: 19–29.

52. Ghoshal, S. 1987. Global strategy: An organizing framework. *Strategic Management Journal,* 8: 425–440.

53. Huber, P. 2009. Who pays for a cancer drug? *Forbes,* January 12: 72.

54. For insights on global branding, refer to Aaker, D. A. & Joachimsthaler, E. 1999. The lure of global branding. *Harvard Business Review,* 77(6): 137–146.

55. For an interesting perspective on how small firms can compete in their home markets, refer to Dawar & Frost, op. cit.: 119–129.

56. Hout, T., Porter, M. E., & Rudden, E. 1982. How global companies win out. *Harvard Business Review,* 60(5): 98–107.

57. Fryer, B. 2001. Tom Siebel of Siebel Systems: High tech the old-fashioned way. *Harvard Business Review,* 79(3): 118–130.

58. The risks that are discussed for the global, multidomestic, and transnational strategies draw upon Gupta & Govindarajan, op. cit.

59. A discussion on how McDonald's adapts its products to overseas markets is in: Gumbel, P. 2008. Big Mac's local flavor. *Fortune,* May 5: 115–121.

60. Sigiura, H. 1990. How Honda localizes its global strategy. *Sloan Management Review,* 31: 77–82.

61. Prahalad & Lieberthal, op. cit.: 68–79. Their article also discusses how firms may have to reconsider their brand management, costs of market building, product design, and approaches to capital efficiency when entering foreign markets.

62. Hofstede, G. 1980. *Culture's consequences: International differences in work-related values.* Beverly Hills, CA: Sage; Hofstede, G. 1993. Cultural constraints in management theories. *Academy of Management Executive,* 7(1): 81–94; Kogut, B. & Singh, H. 1988. The effect of national culture on the choice of entry mode. *Journal of International Business Studies,* 19: 411–432; and

Usinier, J. C. 1996. *Marketing across cultures.* London: Prentice Hall.

63. McCune, J. C. 1999. Exporting corporate culture. *Management Review.* December: 53–56.

64. Ghemawat, P. 2007. *Redefining global strategy.* Boston: Harvard School Press.

65. Prahalad, C. K. & Doz, Y. L. 1987. *The multinational mission: Balancing local demands and global vision.* New York: Free Press.

66. For an insightful discussion on knowledge flows in multinational corporations, refer to: Yang, Q., Mudambi, R., & Meyer, K. E. 2008. Conventional and reverse knowledge flows in multinational corporations. *Journal of Management,* 34(5): 882–902.

67. Kidd, J. B. & Teramoto, Y. 1995. The learning organization: The case of Japanese RHQs in Europe. *Management International Review,* 35 (Special Issue): 39–56.

68. Gupta, A. K. & Govindarajan, V. 2000. Knowledge flows within multinational corporations. *Strategic Management Journal,* 21(4): 473–496.

69. Wetlaufer, S. 2001. The business case against revolution: An interview with Nestlé's Peter Brabeck. *Harvard Business Review,* 79(2): 112–121.

70. Nobel, R. & Birkinshaw, J. 1998. Innovation in multinational corporations: Control and communication patterns in international R&D operations. *Strategic Management Journal,* 19(5): 461–478.

71. Chan, C. M., Makino, S., & Isobe, T. 2010. Does subnational region matter? Foreign affiliate performance in the United States and China. *Strategic Management Journal,* 31 (11): 1226–1243.

72. This section draws upon Ghemawat, P. 2005. Regional strategies for global leadership. *Harvard Business Review.* 84(12): 98–108; Ghemawat, P. 2006. Apocalypse now? *Harvard Business Review.* 84(12): 32; Ghemawat, P. 2001. Distance still matters: The hard reality of global expansion. *Harvard Business Review,* 79(8): 137–147; Peng, M.W. 2006. *Global strategy:* 387. Mason, OH: Thomson Southwestern; and Rugman, A. M. & Verbeke, A. 2004. A perspective on regional and global strategies of multinational enterprises. *Journal of International Business Studies.* 35: 3–18.

73. For a rigorous analysis of performance implications of entry strategies, refer to Zahra, S. A., Ireland, R. D., & Hitt, M. A. 2000. International expansion by new venture firms: International diversity, modes of entry, technological learning, and performance. *Academy of Management Journal,* 43(6): 925–950.

74. Li, J. T. 1995. Foreign entry and survival: The effects of strategic choices on performance in international markets. *Strategic Management Journal,* 16: 333–351.

75. For a discussion of how home-country environments can affect diversification strategies, refer to Wan, W. P. & Hoskisson, R. E. 2003. Home country environments, corporate diversification strategies, and firm performance. *Academy of Management Journal,* 46(1): 27–45.

76. Arnold, D. 2000. Seven rules of international distribution. *Harvard Business Review,* 78(6): 131–137.

77. Sharma, A. 1998. Mode of entry and ex-post performance. *Strategic Management Journal,* 19(9): 879–900.

78. This section draws upon Arnold, op. cit.: 131–137; and Berkowitz, op. cit.

79. Salomon, R. & Jin, B. 2010. Do leading or lagging firms learn more from exporting? *Strategic Management Journal,* 31(6): 1088–1113.

80. Kline, D. 2003. Strategic licensing. *MIT Sloan Management Review,* 44(3): 89–93.

81. Martin, J. 1999. Franchising in the Middle East. *Management Review.* June: 38–42.

82. Arnold, op. cit.; and Berkowitz, op. cit.

83. An in-depth case study of alliance dynamics is found in: Faems, D., Janssens, M., Madhok, A., & Van Looy, B. 2008. Toward an integrative perspective on alliance governance: Connecting contract design, trust dynamics, and contract application. *Academy of Management Journal,* 51(6): 1053–1078.

84. Knowledge transfer in international joint ventures is addressed in: Inkpen, A. 2008. Knowledge transfer and international joint ventures. *Strategic Management Journal,* 29(4): 447–453.

85. Wen, S. H. & Chuang, C.-M. 2010. To teach or to compete? A strategic dilemma of knowledge owners in international alliances. *Asia Pacific Journal of Management,* 27(4): 697–726.

86. Manufacturer–supplier relationships can be very effective in global industries such as automobile manufacturing. Refer to Kotabe, M., Martin, X., & Domoto, H. 2003. Gaining from vertical partnerships: Knowledge transfer, relationship duration, and supplier performance improvement in the U.S. and Japanese automotive industries. *Strategic Management Journal,* 24(4): 293–316.

87. For a good discussion, refer to Merchant, H. & Schendel, D. 2000. How do international joint ventures create shareholder value? *Strategic Management Journal,* 21(7): 723–738.

88. This discussion draws upon Walters, B. A., Peters, S., & Dess, G. G. 1994. Strategic alliances and joint ventures: Making them work. *Business Horizons,* 37(4): 5–11.

89. Some insights on partnering in the global area are discussed in: MacCormack, A. & Forbath, T. 2008. *Harvard Business Review,* 66(1): 24, 26.

90. For a rigorous discussion of the importance of information access in international joint ventures, refer to Reuer, J. J. & Koza, M. P. 2000. Asymmetric information and joint venture performance: Theory and evidence for domestic and international joint ventures. *Strategic Management Journal,* 21(1): 81–88.

91. Dyer, J. H., Kale, P., & Singh, H. 2001. How to make strategic alliances work. *MIT Sloan Management Review,* 42(4): 37–43.

92. For a discussion of some of the challenges in managing subsidiaries, refer to O'Donnell, S. W. 2000. Managing foreign subsidiaries: Agents of headquarters, or an independent network? *Strategic Management Journal,* 21(5): 525–548.

93. Ricks, D. 2006. *Blunders in international business* (4th ed.). Malden, MA: Blackwell Publishing.

Chapter 9. Strategic Control and Corporate Governance

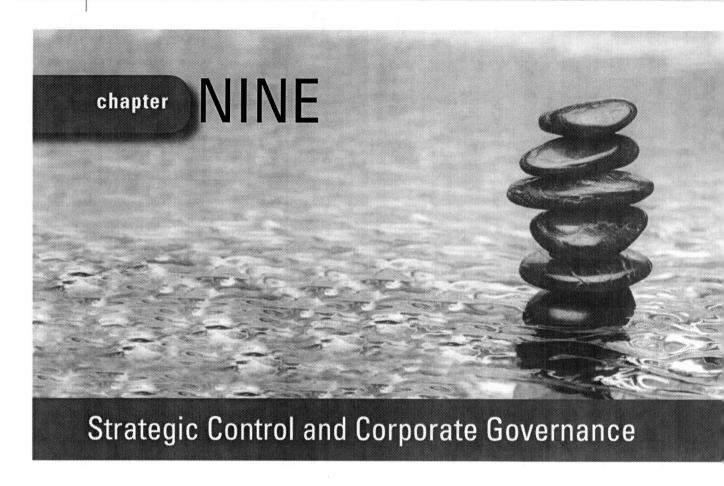

chapter NINE

Strategic Control and Corporate Governance

After reading this chapter, you should have a good understanding of:

LO9.1   The value of effective strategic control systems in strategy implementation.

LO9.2   The key difference between "traditional" and "contemporary" control systems.

LO9.3   The imperative for "contemporary" control systems in today's complex and rapidly changing competitive and general environments.

LO9.4   The benefits of having the proper balance among the three levers of behavioral control: culture; rewards and incentives; and, boundaries.

LO9.5   The three key participants in corporate governance: shareholders, management (led by the CEO), and the board of directors.

LO9.6   The role of corporate governance mechanisms in ensuring that the interests of managers are aligned with those of shareholders from both the United States and international perspectives.

LEARNING OBJECTIVES

Organizations must have effective strategic controls if they are to successfully implement their strategies. This includes systems that exercise both informational control and behavioral control. Controls must be consistent with the strategy that the firm is following. In addition, a firm must promote sound corporate governance to ensure that the interests of managers and shareholders are aligned.

In the first section, we address the need to have effective informational control, contrasting two approaches to informational control. The first approach, which we call "traditional," is highly sequential. Goals and objectives are set, then implemented, and after a set period of time, performance is compared to the desired standards. In contrast, the second approach, termed "contemporary," is much more interactive. Here, the internal and external environments are continually monitored, and managers determine whether the strategy itself needs to be modified. Today the contemporary approach is required, given the rapidly changing conditions in virtually all industries.

Next, we discuss behavioral control. Here the firm must strive to maintain a proper balance between culture, rewards, and boundaries. We also argue that organizations that have strong, positive cultures and reward systems can rely less on boundaries, such as rules, regulations, and procedures. When individuals in the firm internalize goals and strategies, there is less need for monitoring behavior, and efforts are focused more on important organizational goals and objectives.

The third section addresses the role of corporate governance in ensuring that managerial and shareholder interests are aligned. We provide examples of both effective and ineffective corporate governance practices. We discuss three governance mechanisms for aligning managerial and shareholder interests: a committed and involved board of directors, shareholder activism, and effective managerial rewards and incentives. Public companies are also subject to external control. We discuss several external control mechanisms, such as the market for corporate control, auditors, banks and analysts, the media, and public activists. We close with a discussion of corporate governance from an international perspective.

Learning from Mistakes

Chesapeake Energy had a terrible year in 2008. Its net income dropped about 50 percent from the previous year and its stock plummeted from 39 to 17 during the year—a loss of 56 percent.[1] Its board of directors, however, fared much better than its shareholders. In fact, its directors were among the highest paid corporate directors in 2008. For example, one of the eight "independent" directors, 80-year-old Breene Kerr, received $784,687 in total compensation. He's considered independent only because he is not a member of Chesapeake's management, but he just happens to be the cousin of the CEO, Aubrey McClendon. The other directors did almost as well, receiving an average of about $670,000 each. Let's take a look and see what possible reasons there may be for why the directors have been compensated so well.

CEO Aubrey McClendon aggressively bought Chesapeake's stock in July 2008, mostly on margin, at prices as high as $72 a share. Unfortunately, the stock began to sharply drop. In September, margin calls forced McClendon to sell almost all of his position at a price between $13.60 and $24 a share, depleting his net worth.

The board rushed to the rescue! It promptly awarded McClendon a $75 million "special bonus" for 2008. As if such enormous (and undeserved) compensation were not sufficient, the board felt it necessary to justify another use of corporate funds. In December 2008, the company purchased McClendon's extensive collection of antique historic maps of the American Southwest for $12.1 million.

But that is not all. At a cost of $3.5 million, the company became a founding sponsor of the Oklahoma City Thunder, a National Basketball Association franchise owned and operated by The Professional Basketball Club, LLC ("PBC"). McClendon had a 19.2 percent equity interest in the franchise.

The company's compensation committee did provide a rationale for McClendon's huge bonus: it stressed the board's wish to keep him as CEO. And McClendon reciprocated when asked why Chesapeake pays its directors so much, "We have a very large and complex company and we value our directors' time."

---

strategic control the process of monitoring and correcting a firm's strategy and performance.

We first explore two central aspects of **strategic control:**[2] (1) *informational control,* which is the ability to respond effectively to environmental change, and (2) *behavioral control,* which is the appropriate balance and alignment among a firm's culture, rewards, and boundaries. In the final section of this chapter, we focus on strategic control from a much broader perspective—what is referred to as *corporate governance.*[3] Here, we direct our attention to the need for a firm's shareholders (the owners) and their elected representatives (the board of directors) to ensure that the firm's executives (the management team) strive to fulfill their fiduciary duty of maximizing long-term shareholder value. As we just saw in the Chesapeake Energy example, clearly there was a breakdown in corporate governance. This gave the CEO seemingly unlimited power at the expense of the shareholders.

>LO9.1
The value of effective strategic control systems in strategy implementation.

Ensuring Informational Control: Responding Effectively to Environmental Change

We discuss two broad types of control systems: "traditional" and "contemporary." As both general and competitive environments become more unpredictable and complex, the need for contemporary systems increases.

A Traditional Approach to Strategic Control

The **traditional approach to strategic control** is sequential: (1) strategies are formulated and top management sets goals, (2) strategies are implemented, and (3) performance is measured against the predetermined goal set, as illustrated in Exhibit 9.1.

Control is based on a feedback loop from performance measurement to strategy formulation. This process typically involves lengthy time lags, often tied to a firm's annual planning cycle. Such traditional control systems, termed "single-loop" learning by Harvard's Chris Argyris, simply compare actual performance to a predetermined goal.[4] They are most appropriate when the environment is stable and relatively simple, goals and objectives can be measured with a high level of certainty, and there is little need for complex measures of performance. Sales quotas, operating budgets, production schedules, and similar quantitative control mechanisms are typical. The appropriateness of the business strategy or standards of performance is seldom questioned.[5]

James Brian Quinn of Dartmouth College has argued that grand designs with precise and carefully integrated plans seldom work.[6] Rather, most strategic change proceeds incrementally—one step at a time. Leaders should introduce some sense of direction, some logic in incremental steps.[7] Similarly, McGill University's Henry Mintzberg has written about leaders "crafting" a strategy.[8] Drawing on the parallel between the potter at her wheel and the strategist, Mintzberg pointed out that the potter begins work with some general idea of the artifact she wishes to create, but the details of design—even possibilities for a different design—emerge as the work progresses. For businesses facing complex and turbulent business environments, the craftsperson's method helps us deal with the uncertainty about how a design will work out in practice and allows for a creative element.

Mintzberg's argument, like Quinn's, questions the value of rigid planning and goal-setting processes. Fixed strategic goals also become dysfunctional for firms competing in highly unpredictable competitive environments. Strategies need to change frequently and opportunistically. An inflexible commitment to predetermined goals and milestones can prevent the very adaptability that is required of a good strategy.

Even organizations that have been extremely successful in the past can become complacent or fail to adapt their goals and strategies to the new conditions. An example of such a firm is General Motors (GM). For many decades, it was the leading firm in the automotive industry. As recently as 2006, it was recognized by Morgan Stanley as the top car producer. However, GM suffered from many underlying problems that were aggravated by the recent worldwide recession, which eroded demand for automobiles. In Strategy Spotlight 9.1, we address what may be considered one of their key underlying problems—a lack of informational control.

A Contemporary Approach to Strategic Control

Adapting to and anticipating both internal and external environmental change is an integral part of strategic control. The relationships between strategy formulation, implementation, and control are highly interactive, as suggested by Exhibit 9.2. It also illustrates two different types of strategic control: informational control and behavioral control. **Informational control** is primarily concerned with whether or not the organization is "doing the right

traditional approach to strategic control a sequential method of organizational control in which (1) strategies are formulated and top management sets goals, (2) strategies are implemented, and (3) performance is measured against the predetermined goal set.

> **>LO9.2**
> The key difference between "traditional" and "contemporary" control systems.

> **>LO9.3**
> The imperative for "contemporary" control systems in today's complex and rapidly changing competitive and general environments.

informational control a method of organizational control in which a firm gathers and analyzes information from the internal and external environment in order to obtain the best fit between the organization's goals and strategies and the strategic environment.

Exhibit 9.1 Traditional Approach to Strategic Control

strategy spotlight   9.1

What Did General Motors Do Wrong?

General Motors (GM), which was founded in 1908, had been ruling the automotive industry for more than half a century. GM provided a broad range of vehicles, reflecting the company's promise to offer "a car for every purse and purpose." As recently as 2007, their stock was trading above $40 a share. And then just few months after celebrating its 100th anniversary in 2008, GM filed for bankruptcy. On May 29, 2009, GM's stock closed at 75 cents a share, which was a historic low for the company. The government funded a $50 billion bailout to save GM and took a 60 percent ownership stake in the company when they exited bankruptcy in 2010.

GM's market dominance grew out of its abilities to mass manufacture, market, and distribute cars for all customer types. While their advantage initially was based on automotive design and manufacturing prowess, over time, GM became rigid and lost its feel for reading the American car market that it helped create. They were not manufacturing competitive vehicles and increasingly relied on volume and the profits from financing auto sales for their success. At the same time, GM faced increasing competition from Japanese automakers, but they were slow to respond to this competitive entry due to their bureaucratic culture and complacency driven by the profitability of their financing operations. The Japanese competitors developed competencies to design world-class vehicles and produced them more efficiently than GM. As a result, they lured away many of GM's customers. GM's management failed to respond to changes in customer needs and automotive technologies as well as the evolving competitive landscape.

GM did have vast numbers of loyal buyers, but lost many of them through a series of strategic and cultural missteps. Trying to balance the competing needs of seven major brands, GM often resorted to a practice (sarcastically) called "launch and leave"—spending billions upfront to bring vehicles to market, but then failing to keep supporting them with sustained advertising. They also failed to differentiate the brands. Originally, each brand was designed to meet the needs of a different customer segment. However, GM's brand identities became muddled as they sold essentially the same car for different brands. According to Jim Wangers, a retired advertising

● A 1957 Cadillac—a successful product that reflects General Motors' glory days.

executive, "Nobody gave any respect to this thing called image because it wasn't in the business plan. It was all about, 'When is this going to earn a profit?'"

Faced with a declining market position, GM executives did not address the need for changes. Instead, they fell prey to two common biases. First, they exhibited *attribution bias*. When their performance started to fall, they attributed their struggles to outside forces, such as the weak Japanese yen, unfair trade practices, and higher costs from their unionized workers. In short, they became expert at the art of explaining away their problems, attributing blame to everyone but themselves. Second, they exhibited *confirmation bias*—the tendency of managers to filter out information that does not match up with their preconceived notions. GM rewarded people who followed the old way of doing things, and those who challenged that thinking were marginalized—causing them to lose opportunities for promotion. So the smart thing for those seeking promotion within GM was to praise the CEO's wisdom and carry out his orders. This confirmation bias syndrome kept GM from viewing the threat from Japanese automakers as significant, contributed to its decision to pull its electric car off the market, and more recently led it to ignore the effect of higher gas prices and a collapse in credit markets on consumers' willingness to buy profitable gas guzzlers like the Hummer or tricked-out Escalades and SUVs. In falling prey to these biases, GM's management failed to recognize the need for change in response to changes in the market, in technology, and in customers' demands.

Sources: Maynard, M. 2009. After Many Stumbles, the Fall of a Giant. *The New York Times.* June 1: A1; Smith, A. 2009. GM Stock Falls below $1. *money. cnn.com.* May 29: np; Maynard, M. 2009. After 93 Years, GM Shares Go Out on a Low Note. *dealbook.nytimes.com.* May 29: np; Holstein, W. J. 2009. Who's to Blame for GM's Bankruptcy? *www.businessweek.com.* June 1: np; and Cohan, P. 2009. After 101 Years, Why GM Failed. *www.dailyfinance.com.* May 31: np.

Exhibit 9.2 Contemporary Approach to Strategic Control

things." **Behavioral control,** on the other hand, asks if the organization is "doing things right" in the implementation of its strategy. Both the informational and behavioral components of strategic control are necessary, but not sufficient, conditions for success. What good is a well-conceived strategy that cannot be implemented? Or what use is an energetic and committed workforce if it is focused on the wrong strategic target?

> **behavioral control** a method of organizational control in which a firm influences the actions of employees through culture, rewards, and boundaries.

John Weston is the former CEO of ADP Corporation, the largest payroll and tax-filing processor in the world. He captures the essence of contemporary control systems.

> At ADP, 39 plus 1 adds up to more than 40 plus 0. The 40-plus-0 employee is the harried worker who at 40 hours a week just tries to keep up with what's in the "in" basket. . . . Because he works with his head down, he takes zero hours to think about what he's doing, why he's doing it, and how he's doing it. . . . On the other hand, the 39-plus-1 employee takes at least 1 of those 40 hours to think about what he's doing and why he's doing it. That's why the other 39 hours are far more productive.[9]

Informational control deals with the internal environment as well as the external strategic context. It addresses the assumptions and premises that provide the foundation for an organization's strategy. Do the organization's goals and strategies still "fit" within the context of the current strategic environment? Depending on the type of business, such assumptions may relate to changes in technology, customer tastes, government regulation, and industry competition.

This involves two key issues. First, managers must scan and monitor the external environment, as we discussed in Chapter 2. Also, conditions can change in the internal environment of the firm, as we discussed in Chapter 3, requiring changes in the strategic direction of the firm. These may include, for example, the resignation of key executives or delays in the completion of major production facilities.

In the contemporary approach, information control is part of an ongoing process of organizational learning that continuously updates and challenges the assumptions that underlie the organization's strategy. In such "double-loop" learning, the organization's assumptions, premises, goals, and strategies are continuously monitored, tested, and reviewed. The benefits of continuous monitoring are evident—time lags are dramatically shortened, changes in the competitive environment are detected earlier, and the organization's ability to respond with speed and flexibility is enhanced.

Contemporary control systems must have four characteristics to be effective.[10]

1. Focus on constantly changing information that has potential strategic importance.
2. The information is important enough to demand frequent and regular attention from all levels of the organization.
3. The data and information generated are best interpreted and discussed in face-to-face meetings.
4. The control system is a key catalyst for an ongoing debate about underlying data, assumptions, and action plans.

An executive's decision to use the control system interactively—in other words, to invest the time and attention to review and evaluate new information—sends a clear signal

strategy spotlight   9.2

Google's Interactive Control System

Google has tried typical hierarchical control systems typically found in large firms. However, the firm reverted to its interactive control system within weeks. All of Google's roughly 5,000 product developers work in teams of three engineers. Larger projects simply assemble several teams of three workers. Within teams, there is a rotating "über-tech leader" depending on the project. Engineers tend to work in more than one team and do not need permission to switch teams. According to Shona Brown, VP for operations, "If at all possible, we want people to commit to things rather than be assigned to things." At Google "employees don't need a lot of signoffs to try something new, but they won't get much in the way of resources until they've accumulated some positive user feedback."

Google's executives regularly review projects with project leaders and analyze data about projects. Google uses some of its own web page ranking technology in the review of software and other business projects. Using their own employees as mini test markets, managers often solicit employee opinions and analyze usage patterns of new product features and technologies. This interactive control of corporate information allows Google to make faster decisions about its business, including:

- Compare performance of customer usage and feedback among all components of the Google business in real time.
- Quickly discover shortfalls before major problems arise.

Sources: Hamel, G. 2007. Break Free. *Fortune*, October 1, 156(7): 119–126; Iyer, B. and Davenport, T. 2008. Reverse Engineering Google's Innovation Machine. *Harvard Business Review*, April: 59–68; Pham, A. 2008. Google to End Virtual World, Lively, Launched by the Internet Giant Less Than Five Months Ago. *Los Angeles Times*, November 21: C3; and Helft, M. 2009. Google Ends Sale of Ads in Papers after 2 Years. *New York Times*, January 21: B3.

- Become aware of unexpected successes that have often led to innovations.
- Discontinue failing products and services in a timely manner to save the company money.

These manager meetings return significant rewards for Google. Innovations that have been implemented as a result of high information control include:

- Gmail, an e-mail system that utilizes Google's core search features to help users organize and find e-mail messages easily.
- Google News, a computer-generated news site that aggregates headlines from more than 4,500 English-language news sources worldwide, groups similar stories together, and displays them according to each reader's personalized interests.
- Google AdSense, a service that matches ads to a website's content and audience and operates on a revenue-sharing business model.

Google managers are able to quickly analyze user feedback and revenue data to discontinue projects that are not working out as originally intended. This information control allows managers to reallocate resources to more promising projects in a timely manner.

- Google Lively, a virtual world simulation, was launched and shut down after five months in 2008 after management determined that the service was not competitive.
- Google Print Ads, Google's automated method of selling ads through auctions to the newspaper industry, was terminated in early 2009 when managers analyzed the data and determined that the revenue stream was negligible compared to the costs of the program.

---

to the organization about what is important. The dialogue and debate that emerge from such an interactive process can often lead to new strategies and innovations. Strategy Spotlight 9.2 discusses how executives at Google use an interactive control process.

>LO9.4
The benefits of having the proper balance among the three levers of behavioral control: culture, rewards and incentives, and boundaries.

Attaining Behavioral Control: Balancing Culture, Rewards, and Boundaries

Behavioral control is focused on implementation—doing things right. Effectively implementing strategy requires manipulating three key control "levers": culture, rewards, and boundaries (see Exhibit 9.3). There are two compelling reasons for an increased emphasis on culture and rewards in a system of behavioral controls.[11]

First, the competitive environment is increasingly complex and unpredictable, demanding both flexibility and quick response to its challenges. As firms simultaneously downsize and face the need for increased coordination across organizational boundaries, a control system based primarily on rigid strategies, rules, and regulations is dysfunctional. The use of rewards and culture to align individual and organizational goals becomes increasingly important.

Second, the implicit long-term contract between the organization and its key employees has been eroded.[12] Today's younger managers have been conditioned to see themselves as "free agents" and view a career as a series of opportunistic challenges. As managers are advised to "specialize, market yourself, and have work, if not a job," the importance of culture and rewards in building organizational loyalty claims greater importance.

Each of the three levers—culture, rewards, and boundaries—must work in a balanced and consistent manner. Let's consider the role of each.

Building a Strong and Effective Culture

Organizational culture is a system of shared values (what is important) and beliefs (how things work) that shape a company's people, organizational structures, and control systems to produce behavioral norms (the way we do things around here).[13] How important is culture? Very. Over the years, numerous best sellers, such as *Theory Z, Corporate Cultures, In Search of Excellence,* and *Good to Great,*[14] have emphasized the powerful influence of culture on what goes on within organizations and how they perform.

Collins and Porras argued in *Built to Last* that the key factor in sustained exceptional performance is a cultlike culture.[15] You can't touch it or write it down, but it's there in every organization; its influence is pervasive; it can work for you or against you.[16] Effective leaders understand its importance and strive to shape and use it as one of their important levers of strategic control.[17]

> **organizational culture** a system of shared values and beliefs that shape a company's people, organizational structures, and control systems to produce behavioral norms.

The Role of Culture   Culture wears many different hats, each woven from the fabric of those values that sustain the organization's primary source of competitive advantage. Some examples are:

- Federal Express and Southwest Airlines focus on customer service.
- Lexus (a division of Toyota) and Hewlett-Packard emphasize product quality.
- Newell Rubbermaid and 3M place a high value on innovation.
- Nucor (steel) and Emerson Electric are concerned, above all, with operational efficiency.

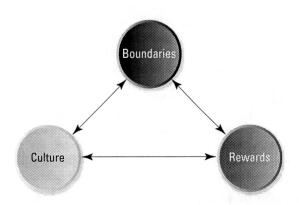

Exhibit 9.3 Essential Elements of Behavioral Control

Culture sets implicit boundaries—unwritten standards of acceptable behavior—in dress, ethical matters, and the way an organization conducts its business.[18] By creating a framework of shared values, culture encourages individual identification with the organization and its objectives. Culture acts as a means of reducing monitoring costs.[19]

Sustaining an Effective Culture   Powerful organizational cultures just don't happen overnight, and they don't remain in place without a strong commitment—both in terms of words and deeds—by leaders throughout the organization.[20] A viable and productive organizational culture can be strengthened and sustained. However, it cannot be "built" or "assembled"; instead, it must be cultivated, encouraged, and "fertilized."[21]

Storytelling is one way effective cultures are maintained. Many are familiar with the story of how Art Fry's failure to develop a strong adhesive led to 3M's enormously successful Post-it Notes. Perhaps less familiar is the story of Francis G. Okie.[22] In 1922 Okie came up with the idea of selling sandpaper to men as a replacement for razor blades. The idea obviously didn't pan out, but Okie was allowed to remain at 3M. Interestingly, the technology developed by Okie led 3M to develop its first blockbuster product: a waterproof sandpaper that became a staple of the automobile industry. Such stories foster the importance of risk taking, experimentation, freedom to fail, and innovation—all vital elements of 3M's culture.

Rallies or "pep talks" by top executives also serve to reinforce a firm's culture. The late Sam Walton was known for his pep rallies at local Walmart stores. Four times a year, the founders of Home Depot—former CEO Bernard Marcus and Arthur Blank—used to don orange aprons and stage Breakfast with Bernie and Arthur, a 6:30 a.m. pep rally, broadcast live over the firm's closed-circuit TV network to most of its 45,000 employees.[23]

Southwest Airlines' "Culture Committee" is a unique vehicle designed to perpetuate the company's highly successful culture. The following excerpt from an internal company publication describes its objectives:

> The goal of the Committee is simple—to ensure that our unique Corporate Culture stays alive. . . . Culture Committee members represent all regions and departments across our system and they are selected based upon their exemplary display of the "Positively Outrageous Service" that won us the first-ever Triple Crown; their continual exhibition of the "Southwest Spirit" to our Customers and to their fellow workers; and their high energy level, boundless enthusiasm, unique creativity, and constant demonstration of teamwork and love for their fellow workers.[24]

Motivating with Rewards and Incentives

Reward and incentive systems represent a powerful means of influencing an organization's culture, focusing efforts on high-priority tasks, and motivating individual and collective task performance.[25] Just as culture deals with influencing beliefs, behaviors, and attitudes of people within an organization, the **reward system**—by specifying who gets rewarded and why—is an effective motivator and control mechanism.[26] Consider how Starbucks uses its stock option plan as an incentive to motivate its employees.[27] By introducing a stock option plan called "bean stock" to managers, baristas, and other employees, Starbucks has turned every employee into a partner. Starbucks' managers began referring to all employees as *partners,* an appropriate title because all staff, including part-timers working at least 20 hours per week, were eligible for stock options after six months with the company. By turning employees into partners, Starbucks gave them a chance to share in the success of the company and make the connection between their contributions and the company's market value very clear. There was a pronounced effect on the attitudes and performance of employees because of the bean stock program. They began coming up with many innovative ideas about how to cut costs, increase sales, and create value.

The Potential Downside   Generally speaking, people in organizations act rationally, each motivated by their personal best interest.[28] However, the collective sum of individual

reward system
policies that specify who gets rewarded and why.

behaviors of an organization's employees does not always result in what is best for the organization; individual rationality is no guarantee of organizational rationality.

As corporations grow and evolve, they often develop different business units with multiple reward systems. They may differ based on industry contexts, business situations, stage of product life cycles, and so on. Subcultures within organizations may reflect differences among functional areas, products, services, and divisions. To the extent that reward systems reinforce such behavioral norms, attitudes, and belief systems, cohesiveness is reduced; important information is hoarded rather than shared, individuals begin working at cross-purposes, and they lose sight of overall goals.

Such conflicts are commonplace in many organizations. For example, sales and marketing personnel promise unrealistically quick delivery times to bring in business, much to the dismay of operations and logistics; overengineering by R&D creates headaches for manufacturing; and so on. Conflicts also arise across divisions when divisional profits become a key compensation criterion. As ill will and anger escalate, personal relationships and performance may suffer.

Creating Effective Reward and Incentive Programs To be effective, incentive and reward systems need to reinforce basic core values, enhance cohesion and commitment to goals and objectives, and meet with the organization's overall mission and purpose.[29]

At General Mills, to ensure a manager's interest in the overall performance of his or her unit, half of a manager's annual bonus is linked to business-unit results and half to individual performance.[30] For example, if a manager simply matches a rival manufacturer's performance, his or her salary is roughly 5 percent lower. However, if a manager's product ranks in the industry's top 10 percent in earnings growth and return on capital, the manager's total pay can rise to nearly 30 percent beyond the industry norm.

Effective reward and incentive systems share a number of common characteristics.[31] (see Exhibit 9.4). The perception that a plan is "fair and equitable" is critically important. The firm must have the flexibility to respond to changing requirements as its direction and objectives change. In recent years many companies have begun to place more emphasis on growth. Emerson Electric has shifted its emphasis from cost cutting to growth. To ensure that changes take hold, the management compensation formula has been changed from a largely bottom-line focus to one that emphasizes growth, new products, acquisitions, and international expansion. Discussions about profits are handled separately, and a culture of risk taking is encouraged.[32]

Setting Boundaries and Constraints

In an ideal world, a strong culture and effective rewards should be sufficient to ensure that all individuals and subunits work toward the common goals and objectives of the whole organization.[33] However, this is not usually the case. Counterproductive behavior can arise because of motivated self-interest, lack of a clear understanding of goals and objectives, or outright malfeasance. **Boundaries and constraints** can serve many useful purposes for organizations, including:

> **boundaries and constraints** rules that specify behaviors that are acceptable and unacceptable.

- Objectives are clear, well understood, and broadly accepted.
- Rewards are clearly linked to performance and desired behaviors.
- Performance measures are clear and highly visible.
- Feedback is prompt, clear, and unambiguous.
- The compensation "system" is perceived as fair and equitable.
- The structure is flexible; it can adapt to changing circumstances.

Exhibit 9.4
Characteristics of Effective Reward and Evaluation Systems

- Focusing individual efforts on strategic priorities.
- Providing short-term objectives and action plans to channel efforts.
- Improving efficiency and effectiveness.
- Minimizing improper and unethical conduct.

Focusing Efforts on Strategic Priorities   Boundaries and constraints play a valuable role in focusing a company's strategic priorities. A well-known example of a strategic boundary is Jack Welch's (former CEO of General Electric) demand that any business in the corporate portfolio be ranked first or second in its industry. Similarly, Eli Lilly has reduced its research efforts to five broad areas of disease, down from eight or nine a decade ago.[34] This concentration of effort and resources provides the firm with greater strategic focus and the potential for stronger competitive advantages in the remaining areas.

Norman Augustine, Lockheed Martin's former chairman, provided four criteria for selecting candidates for diversification into "closely related" businesses.[35] They must (1) be high tech, (2) be systems-oriented, (3) deal with large customers (either corporations or government) as opposed to consumers, and (4) be in growth businesses. Augustine said, "We have found that if we can meet most of those standards, then we can move into adjacent markets and grow."

Boundaries also have a place in the nonprofit sector. For example, a British relief organization uses a system to monitor strategic boundaries by maintaining a list of companies whose contributions it will neither solicit nor accept. Such boundaries are essential for maintaining legitimacy with existing and potential benefactors.

Providing Short-Term Objectives and Action Plans   In Chapter 1 we discussed the importance of a firm having a vision, mission, and strategic objectives that are internally consistent and that provide strategic direction. In addition, short-term objectives and action plans provide similar benefits. That is, they represent boundaries that help to allocate resources in an optimal manner and to channel the efforts of employees at all levels throughout the organization.[36] To be effective, short-term objectives must have several attributes. They should:

- Be specific and measurable.
- Include a specific time horizon for their attainment.
- Be achievable, yet challenging enough to motivate managers who must strive to accomplish them.

Research has found that performance is enhanced when individuals are encouraged to attain specific, difficult, yet achievable, goals (as opposed to vague "do your best" goals).[37]

Short-term objectives must provide proper direction and also provide enough flexibility for the firm to keep pace with and anticipate changes in the external environment, new government regulations, a competitor introducing a substitute product, or changes in consumer taste. Unexpected events within a firm may require a firm to make important adjustments in both strategic and short-term objectives. The emergence of new industries can have a drastic effect on the demand for products and services in more traditional industries.

Action plans are critical to the implementation of chosen strategies. Unless action plans are specific, there may be little assurance that managers have thought through all of the resource requirements for implementing their strategies. In addition, unless plans are specific, managers may not understand what needs to be implemented or have a clear time frame for completion. This is essential for the scheduling of key activities that must be implemented. Finally, individual managers must be held accountable for the implementation. This helps to provide the necessary motivation and "sense of ownership" to implement action plans on a timely basis. Strategy Spotlight 9.3 illustrates how action

9.3

strategy spotlight

Developing Meaningful Action Plans: Aircraft Interior Products, Inc.

MSA Aircraft Interior Products, Inc., is a manufacturing firm based in San Antonio, Texas, that was founded in 1983 by Mike Spraggins and Robert Plenge. The firm fulfills a small but highly profitable niche in the aviation industry with two key products. The Accordia line consists of patented, lightweight, self-contained window-shade assemblies. MSA's interior cabin shells are state-of-the-art assemblies that include window panels, side panels, headliners, and suspension system structures. MSA's products have been installed on a variety of aircraft, such as the Gulfstream series; the Cessna Citation; and Boeing's 727, 737, 757, and 707.

Much of MSA's success can be attributed to carefully articulated action plans consistent with the firm's mission and objectives. During the past five years, MSA has increased its sales at an annual rate of 15 to 18 percent. It has also succeeded in adding many prestigious companies to its customer base. Below are excerpts from MSA's mission statement and objectives as well as the action plans to achieve a 20 percent annual increase in sales.

Mission Statement

- Be recognized as an innovative and reliable supplier of quality interior products for the high-end, personalized transportation segments of the aviation, marine, and automotive industries.

- Design, develop, and manufacture interior fixtures and components that provide exceptional value to

Source: For purposes of confidentiality, some of the information presented in this spotlight has been disguised. We would like to thank company management and Joseph Picken, consultant, for providing us with the information used in this application.

the customer through the development of innovative designs in a manner that permits decorative design flexibility while retaining the superior functionality, reliability, and maintainability of well-engineered, factory-produced products.

- Grow, be profitable, and provide a fair return, commensurate with the degree of risk, for owners and stockholders.

Objectives

1. Achieve sustained and profitable growth over the next three years:
   - 20 percent annual growth in revenues
   - 12 percent pretax profit margins
   - 18 percent return on shareholder's equity

2. Expand the company's revenues through the development and introduction of two or more new products capable of generating revenues in excess of $8 million a year by 2014.

3. Continue to aggressively expand market opportunities and applications for the Accordia line of window-shade assemblies, with the objective of sustaining or exceeding a 20 percent annual growth rate for at least the next three years.

Exhibit 9.5 details an "Action Plan" for Objective 3.

MSA's action plans are supported by detailed month-by-month budgets and strong financial incentives for its executives. Budgets are prepared by each individual department and include all revenue and cost items. Managers are motivated by their participation in a profit-sharing program, and the firm's two founders each receive a bonus equal to three percent of total sales.

Description	Primary Responsibility	Target Date
1. Develop and implement 2010 marketing plan, including specific plans for addressing Falcon 20 retrofit programs and expanded sales of cabin shells.	R. H. Plenge (V.P. Marketing)	December 15, 2011
2. Negotiate new supplier agreement with Gulfstream Aerospace.	M. Spraggins (President)	March 1, 2012
3. Continue and complete the development of the UltraSlim window and have a fully tested and documented design ready for production at a manufacturing cost of less than $900 per unit.	D. R. Pearson (V.P. Operations)	June 15, 2012
4. Develop a window design suitable for L-1011 and similar wide-body aircraft and have a fully tested and documented design ready for production at a manufacturing cost comparable to the current Boeing window.	D. R. Pearson (V.P. Operations)	September 15, 2012

Exhibit 9.5   Action Plan for Objective Number 3

plans fit into the mission statement and objectives of a small manufacturer of aircraft interior components. Exhibit 9.5 provides details of an action plan to fulfill one of the firm's objectives.

Improving Operational Efficiency and Effectiveness   Rule-based controls are most appropriate in organizations with the following characteristics:

* Environments are stable and predictable.
* Employees are largely unskilled and interchangeable.
* Consistency in product and service is critical.
* The risk of malfeasance is extremely high (e.g., in banking or casino operations).[38]

McDonald's Corp. has extensive rules and regulations that regulate the operation of its franchises.[39] Its policy manual states, "Cooks must turn, never flip, hamburgers. If they haven't been purchased, Big Macs must be discarded in 10 minutes after being cooked and French fries in 7 minutes. Cashiers must make eye contact with and smile at every customer."

Guidelines can also be effective in setting spending limits and the range of discretion for employees and managers, such as the $2,500 limit that hotelier Ritz-Carlton uses to empower employees to placate dissatisfied customers. Regulations also can be initiated to improve the use of an employee's time at work.[40] Computer Associates restricts the use of e-mail during the hours of 10 a.m. to noon and 2 p.m. to 4 p.m. each day.[41]

Minimizing Improper and Unethical Conduct   Guidelines can be useful in specifying proper relationships with a company's customers and suppliers.[42] Many companies have explicit rules regarding commercial practices, including the prohibition of any form of payment, bribe, or kickback. Cadbury Schweppes has followed a simple but effective step in controlling the use of bribes by specifying that all payments, no matter how unusual, are recorded on the company's books. Its former chairman, Sir Adrian Cadbury, contended that such a practice causes managers to pause and consider whether a payment is simply a bribe or a necessary and standard cost of doing business.[43]

Regulations backed up with strong sanctions can also help an organization avoid conducting business in an unethical manner. After the passing of the Sarbanes-Oxley Act (which provides for stiffer penalties for financial reporting misdeeds), many chief financial officers (CFOs) have taken steps to ensure ethical behavior in the preparation of financial statements. For example, Home Depot's CFO, Carol B. Tomé, strengthened the firm's code of ethics and developed stricter guidelines. Now all 25 of her subordinates must sign personal statements that all of their financial statements are correct—just as she and her CEO, have to do now.[44]

● McDonald's relies on extensive rules and regulations to maintain efficient operations at its restaurants.

Behavioral Control in Organizations: Situational Factors

Here, the focus is on ensuring that the behavior of individuals at all levels of an organization is directed toward achieving organizational goals and objectives. The three fundamental types of control are culture, rewards and incentives, and boundaries and constraints. An organization may pursue one or a combination of them on the basis of a variety of internal and external factors.

Not all organizations place the same emphasis on each type of control.[45] In high-technology firms engaged in basic research, members may work under high levels of autonomy. An individual's performance is generally quite difficult to measure accurately because of the long lead times involved in R&D activities. Thus, internalized norms and values become very important.

When the measurement of an individual's output or performance is quite straightforward, control depends primarily on granting or withholding rewards. Frequently, a sales manager's compensation is in the form of a commission and bonus tied directly to his or her sales volume, which is relatively easy to determine. Here, behavior is influenced more strongly by the attractiveness of the compensation than by the norms and values implicit in the organization's culture. The measurability of output precludes the need for an elaborate system of rules to control behavior.[46]

Control in bureaucratic organizations is dependent on members following a highly formalized set of rules and regulations. Most activities are routine and the desired behavior can be specified in a detailed manner because there is generally little need for innovative or creative activity. Managing an assembly plant requires strict adherence to many rules as well as exacting sequences of assembly operations. In the public sector, the Department of Motor Vehicles in most states must follow clearly prescribed procedures when issuing or renewing driver licenses.

Exhibit 9.6 provides alternate approaches to behavioral control and some of the situational factors associated with them.

Evolving from Boundaries to Rewards and Culture

In most environments, organizations should strive to provide a system of rewards and incentives, coupled with a culture strong enough that boundaries become internalized. This reduces the need for external controls such as rules and regulations.

First, hire the right people—individuals who already identify with the organization's dominant values and have attributes consistent with them. We addressed this issue in Chapter 4; recall the "Bozo Filter" developed by Cooper Software (pages 129–130). Microsoft's David Pritchard is well aware of the consequences of failing to hire properly.

Exhibit 9.6
Organizational Control: Alternative Approaches

Approach	Some Situational Factors
Culture: A system of unwritten rules that forms an internalized influence over behavior.	• Often found in professional organizations. • Associated with high autonomy. • Norms are the basis for behavior.
Rules: Written and explicit guidelines that provide external constraints on behavior.	• Associated with standardized output. • Tasks are generally repetitive and routine. • Little need for innovation or creative activity.
Rewards: The use of performance-based incentive systems to motivate.	• Measurement of output and performance is rather straightforward. • Most appropriate in organizations pursuing unrelated diversification strategies. • Rewards may be used to reinforce other means of control.

If I hire a bunch of bozos, it will hurt us, because it takes time to get rid of them. They start infiltrating the organization and then they themselves start hiring people of lower quality. At Microsoft, we are always looking for people who are better than we are.

Second, training plays a key role. For example, in elite military units such as the Green Berets and Navy SEALs, the training regimen so thoroughly internalizes the culture that individuals, in effect, lose their identity. The group becomes the overriding concern and focal point of their energies. At firms such as FedEx, training not only builds skills, but also plays a significant role in building a strong culture on the foundation of each organization's dominant values.

Third, managerial role models are vital. Andy Grove, former CEO and co-founder of Intel, didn't need (or want) a large number of bureaucratic rules to determine who is responsible for what, who is supposed to talk to whom, and who gets to fly first class (no one does). He encouraged openness by not having many of the trappings of success—he worked in a cubicle like all the other professionals. Can you imagine any new manager asking whether or not he can fly first class? Grove's personal example eliminated such a need.

Fourth, reward systems must be clearly aligned with the organizational goals and objectives. Where do you think rules and regulations are more important in controlling behavior—Home Depot, with its generous bonus and stock option plan, or Walmart, which does not provide the same level of rewards and incentives?

The Role of Corporate Governance

> **>LO9.5**
>
> The three key participants in corporate governance: shareholders, management (led by the CEO), and the board of directors.

We now address the issue of strategic control in a broader perspective, typically referred to as "corporate governance." Here we focus on the need for both shareholders (the owners of the corporation) and their elected representatives, the board of directors, to actively ensure that management fulfills its overriding purpose of increasing long-term shareholder value.[47]

> **corporate governance** the relationship among various participants in determining the direction and performance of corporations. The primary participants are (1) the shareholders, (2) the management, and (3) the board of directors.

Robert Monks and Nell Minow, two leading scholars in **corporate governance,** define it as "the relationship among various participants in determining the direction and performance of corporations. The primary participants are (1) the shareholders, (2) the management (led by the CEO), and (3) the board of directors."* Our discussion will center on how corporations can succeed (or fail) in aligning managerial motives with the interests of the shareholders and their elected representatives, the board of directors.[48] As you will recall from Chapter 1, we discussed the important role of boards of directors and provided some examples of effective and ineffective boards.[49]

Good corporate governance plays an important role in the investment decisions of major institutions, and a premium is often reflected in the price of securities of companies that practice it. The corporate governance premium is larger for firms in countries with sound corporate governance practices compared to countries with weaker corporate governance standards.[50]

Sound governance practices often lead to superior financial performance. However, this is not always the case. For example, practices such as independent directors (directors who are not part of the firm's management) and stock options are generally assumed to result in

---

*Management cannot ignore the demands of other important firm stakeholders such as creditors, suppliers, customers, employees, and government regulators. At times of financial duress, powerful creditors can exert strong and legitimate pressures on managerial decisions. In general, however, the attention to stakeholders other than the owners of the corporation must be addressed in a manner that is still consistent with maximizing long-term shareholder returns. For a seminal discussion on stakeholder management, refer to Freeman, R. E. 1984. *Strategic Management: A Stakeholder Approach.* Boston: Pitman.

9.4

strategy spotlight

The Relationship between Recommended Corporate Governance Practices and Firm Performance

A significant amount of research has examined the effect of corporate governance on firm performance. Some research has shown that implementing good corporate governance structures yields superior financial performance. Other research has not found a positive relationship between governance and performance. Results of a few of these studies are summarized below.

1. *A positive correlation between corporate governance and different measures of corporate performance.* Recent studies show that there is a strong positive correlation between effective corporate governance and different indicators of corporate performance such as growth, profitability, and customer satisfaction. Over a recent three-year period, the average return of large capitalized firms with the best governance practices was more than five times higher than the performance of firms in the bottom corporate governance quartile.

Sources: Dalton, D. R., Daily, C. M., Ellstrand, A. E., & Johnson, J. L., 1998. Meta-analytic reviews of board composition, leadership structure, and financial performance. *Strategic Management Journal*, 19(3): 269–290; Sanders, W. G. & Hambrick, D. C. 2007. Swinging for the fences: The effects of CEO stock options on company risk-taking and performance. *Academy of Management Journal*, 50(5): 1055–1078; Harris, J. & Bromiley, P. 2007. Incentives to cheat: The influence of executive compensation and firm performance on financial misrepresentation. *Organization Science*, 18(3): 350–367; Bauwhede, H. V. 2009. On the relation between corporate governance compliance and operating performance. *Accounting and Business Research*. 39(5): 497–513; Gill, A. 2001. Credit Lyonnais Securities (Asia). *Corporate governance in emerging markets: Saints and sinners*, April; and Low, C. K. 2002. *Corporate governance: An Asia-Pacific critique*. Hong Kong: Sweet & Maxwell Asia.

2. *Compliance with international best practices leads to superior performance.* Studies of European companies show that greater compliance with international corporate governance best practices concerning board structure and function has significant and positive relationships with return on assets (ROA). In 10 of 11 Asian and Latin American markets, companies in the top corporate governance quartile for their respective regions averaged 10 percent greater return on capital employed (ROCE) than their peers. In a study of 12 emerging markets, companies in the lowest corporate governance quartile had a much lower ROCE than their peers.

3. *Many recommended corporate governance practices do not have a positive relationship with firm performance.* In contrast to these studies, there is also a body of research suggesting that corporate governance practices do not have a positive influence on firm performance. With corporate boards, there is no evidence that including more external directors on the board of directors of U.S. corporations has led to substantially higher firm performance. Also, giving more stock options to CEOs to align their interests with stakeholders may lead them to take high-risk bets in firm investments that have a low probability to improve firm performance. Rather than making good decisions, CEOs may "swing for the fences" with these high-risk investments. Additionally, motivating CEOs with large numbers of stock options appears to increase the likelihood of unethical accounting violations by the firm as the CEO tries to increase the firm's stock price.

ethics

better performance. But in many cases, independent directors may not have the necessary expertise or involvement, and the granting of stock options to the CEO may lead to decisions and actions calculated to prop up share price only in the short term. Strategy Spotlight 9.4 presents some research evidence on governance practices and firm performance.

At the same time, few topics in the business press are generating as much interest (and disdain!) as corporate governance.

Some recent notable examples of flawed corporate governance include:[51]

- Satyam Computer Services, a leading Indian outsourcing company that serves more than a third of the Fortune 500 companies, significantly inflated its earnings and assets for years. The chairman, Ramalinga Raju, resigned and admitted he had cooked the books. Mr. Raju said he had overstated cash on hand by $1 billion and inflated profits and revenues in the September 2008 quarter. Satyam shares sank 78 percent, and the benchmark Sensex index lost 7.3 percent that day (January 7, 2009).

- Former Brocade CEO Gregory Reyes was sentenced to 21 months in prison and fined $15 million for his involvement in backdating stock option grants. Mr. Reyes was the first executive to go on trial and be convicted over the improper dating of stock-option awards, which dozens of companies have acknowledged since the practice came to light (January 17, 2008).
- In October 2010, Angelo Mozilo, the co-founder of Countrywide Financial, agreed to pay $67.5 million to the Securities and Exchange Commission (SEC) to settle fraud charges. He was charged with deceiving the home loan company's investors while reaping a personal windfall. He was accused of hiding risks about Countrywide's loan portfolio as the real estate market soured. Former Countrywide President David Sambol and former Chief Financial Officer Eric Sieracki were also charged with fraud, as they failed to disclose the true state of Countrywide's deteriorating mortgage portfolio. The SEC accused Mozilo of insider trading, alleging that he sold millions of dollars worth of Countrywide stock after he knew the company was doomed.
- Bernard L. Madoff, a former stock broker, investment advisor, and nonexecutive chairman of the NASDAQ stock market, was sentenced to 150 years of prison in June 2009 for a massive Ponzi scheme that defrauded thousands of investors of billions of dollars. Mr. Madoff pleaded guilty to 11 felony counts and admitted to managing the largest Ponzi scheme in history and concealing it from federal authorities and investors for more than a decade.

Because of the many lapses in corporate governance, we can see the benefits associated with effective practices.[52] However, corporate managers may behave in their own self-interest, often to the detriment of shareholders. Next we address the implications of the separation of ownership and management in the modern corporation, and some mechanisms that can be used to ensure consistency (or alignment) between the interests of shareholders and those of the managers to minimize potential conflicts.

The Modern Corporation:
The Separation of Owners (Shareholders) and Management

Some of the proposed definitions for a *corporation* include:

- "The business corporation is an instrument through which capital is assembled for the activities of producing and distributing goods and services and making investments. Accordingly, a basic premise of corporation law is that a business corporation should have as its objective the conduct of such activities with a view to enhancing the corporation's profit and the gains of the corporation's owners, that is, the shareholders." (Melvin Aron Eisenberg, *The Structure of Corporation Law*)
- "A body of persons granted a charter legally recognizing them as a separate entity having its own rights, privileges, and liabilities distinct from those of its members." (*American Heritage Dictionary*)
- "An ingenious device for obtaining individual profit without individual responsibility." (Ambrose Bierce, *The Devil's Dictionary*)[53]

corporation a mechanism created to allow different parties to contribute capital, expertise, and labor for the maximum benefit of each party.

All of these definitions have some validity and each one reflects a key feature of the corporate form of business organization—its ability to draw resources from a variety of groups and establish and maintain its own persona that is separate from all of them. As Henry Ford once said, "A great business is really too big to be human."

Simply put, a **corporation** is a mechanism created to allow different parties to contribute capital, expertise, and labor for the maximum benefit of each party.[54] The shareholders (investors) are able to participate in the profits of the enterprise without taking direct responsibility for the operations. The management can run the company without the responsibility of personally providing the funds. The shareholders have limited liability as well as rather limited involvement in the company's affairs. However, they reserve the right to elect directors who have the fiduciary obligation to protect their interests.

Over 70 years ago, Columbia University professors Adolf Berle and Gardiner C. Means addressed the divergence of the interests of the owners of the corporation from the professional managers who are hired to run it. They warned that widely dispersed ownership "released management from the overriding requirement that it serve stockholders." The separation of ownership from management has given rise to a set of ideas called "agency theory." Central to agency theory is the relationship between two primary players—the *principals* who are the owners of the firm (stockholders) and the *agents*, who are the people paid by principals to perform a job on their behalf (management). The stockholders elect and are represented by a board of directors that has a fiduciary responsibility to ensure that management acts in the best interests of stockholders to ensure long-term financial returns for the firm.

Agency theory is concerned with resolving two problems that can occur in agency relationships.[55] *The first is the agency problem that arises (1) when the goals of the principals and agents conflict, and (2) when it is difficult or expensive for the principal to verify what the agent is actually doing.*[56] The board of directors would be unable to confirm that the managers were actually acting in the shareholders' interests because managers are "insiders" with regard to the businesses they operate and thus are better informed than the principals. Thus, managers may act "opportunistically" in pursuing their own interests—to the detriment of the corporation.[57] Managers may spend corporate funds on expensive perquisites (e.g., company jets and expensive art), devote time and resources to pet projects (initiatives in which they have a personal interest but that have limited market potential), engage in power struggles (where they may fight over resources for their own betterment and to the detriment of the firm), and negate (or sabotage) attractive merger offers because they may result in increased employment risk.[58]

The second issue is the problem of risk sharing. This arises when the principal and the agent have different attitudes and preferences toward risk. The executives in a firm may favor additional diversification initiatives because, by their very nature, they increase the size of the firm and thus the level of executive compensation.[59] At the same time, such diversification initiatives may erode shareholder value because they fail to achieve some synergies that we discussed in Chapter 6 (e.g., building on core competencies, sharing activities, or enhancing market power). Agents (executives) may have a stronger preference toward diversification than shareholders because it reduces their personal level of risk from potential loss of employment. Executives who have large holdings of stock in their firms were more likely to have diversification strategies that were more consistent with shareholder interests—increasing long-term returns.[60]

At times, top-level managers engage in actions that reflect their self-interest rather than the interests of shareholders. We provide two examples below:[61]

- Micky M. Arison is chief executive of Carnival, the big cruise line. He is also chief executive and owner of the Miami Heat of the National Basketball Association. Carnival paid the Heat $675,000 for sponsorship, advertising, and season tickets. Although that may be a rather small sum—given Carnival's $2.2 billion in net income for the period—we could still ask whether the money would have been spent on something else if Arison didn't own the team.
- Alliance Semiconductor CEO N. Damodar Reddy has committed $20 million to Solar Ventures, a venture capital company run by his brother, C. N. Reddy. Other unnamed insiders purchased undisclosed stakes in Solar. However, Alliance won't disclose whether its CEO is one of them. To date, it has invested $12.5 million in

agency theory a theory of the relationship between principals and their agents, with emphasis on two problems: (1) the conflicting goals of principals and agents, along with the difficulty of principals to monitor the agents, and (2) the different attitudes and preferences toward risk of principals and agents.

Solar. Beth Young, senior research associate of the Corporate Library poses an interesting question: "Is Reddy using shareholder capital just to keep afloat his brother's fund and the insiders' investment?"

Governance Mechanisms: Aligning the Interests of Owners and Managers

>LO9.6
The role of corporate governance mechanisms in ensuring that the interests of managers are aligned with those of shareholders from both the United States and international perspectives.

As noted above, a key characteristic of the modern corporation is the separation of ownership from control. To minimize the potential for managers to act in their own self-interest, or "opportunistically," the owners can implement some governance mechanisms.[62] First, there are two primary means of monitoring the behavior of managers. These include (1) a committed and involved *board of directors* that acts in the best interests of the shareholders to create long-term value and (2) *shareholder activism,* wherein the owners view themselves as share*owners* instead of share*holders* and become actively engaged in the governance of the corporation. Finally, there are managerial incentives, sometimes called "contract-based outcomes," which consist of *reward and compensation agreements.* Here the goal is to carefully craft managerial incentive packages to align the interests of management with those of the stockholders.[63]

We close this section with a brief discussion of one of the most controversial issues in corporate governance—duality. Here, the question becomes: Should the CEO also be chairman of the board of directors? In many Fortune 500 firms, the same individual serves in both roles. However, in recent years, we have seen a trend toward separating these two positions. The key issue is what implications CEO duality has for firm governance and performance.

board of directors a group that has a fiduciary duty to ensure that the company is run consistently with the long-term interests of the owners, or shareholders, of a corporation and that acts as an intermediary between the shareholders and management.

A Committed and Involved Board of Directors The **board of directors** acts as a fulcrum between the owners and controllers of a corporation. They are the intermediaries who provide a balance between a small group of key managers in the firm based at the corporate headquarters and a sometimes vast group of shareholders.[64] In the United States, the law imposes on the board a strict and absolute fiduciary duty to ensure that a company is run consistent with the long-term interests of the owners—the shareholders. The reality, as we have seen, is somewhat more ambiguous.[65]

The Business Roundtable, representing the largest U.S. corporations, describes the duties of the board as follows:

1. Select, regularly evaluate, and, if necessary, replace the CEO. Determine management compensation. Review succession planning.
2. Review and, where appropriate, approve the financial objectives, major strategies, and plans of the corporation.
3. Provide advice and counsel to top management.
4. Select and recommend to shareholders for election an appropriate slate of candidates for the board of directors; evaluate board processes and performance.
5. Review the adequacy of the systems to comply with all applicable laws/regulations.[66]

Given these principles, what makes for a good board of directors?[67] According to the Business Roundtable, the most important quality is a board of directors who are active, critical participants in determining a company's strategies.[68] That does not mean board members should micromanage or circumvent the CEO. Rather, they should provide strong oversight going beyond simply approving the CEO's plans. A board's primary responsibilities are to ensure that strategic plans undergo rigorous scrutiny, evaluate managers against high performance standards, and take control of the succession process.[69]

Although boards in the past were often dismissed as CEO's rubber stamps, increasingly they are playing a more active role by forcing out CEOs who cannot deliver on performance.[70] According to the consulting firm Booz Allen Hamilton, the rate of CEO departures for performance reasons more than tripled, from 1.3 percent to 4.2 percent, between 1995 and 2002.[71] And today's CEOs are not immune to termination. In September 2010, Jonathan Klein, the president of the CNN/U.S. cable channel, was fired because CNN's ratings had suffered.[72] Don Blankenship, CEO of coal mining giant Massey Energy, resigned in December 2010 after a deadly explosion in Massey's Upper Big Branch mine in West Virginia, a mine that had received numerous citations for safety violations in the last few years. The blast was the worst mining disaster in the United States in 40 years and resulted in criminal as well as civil investigations and lawsuits. Tony Hayward, CEO of oil and energy company British Petroleum (BP), was forced to step down in October 2010 after the Deepwater Horizon oil spill in the Gulf of Mexico led to an environmental disaster and a $20 billion recovery fund financed by BP.

Interestingly, CEO turnover declined during the recent financial crisis—going from 12.7 percent in 2007 to only 9.4 percent in 2010. One likely reason: Boards were reluctant to change leadership during the recession, concerned that if a CEO departed, investors might think that the company was coming unglued. However, with the economy recovering, Peter Crist, chairman of an executive search firm, predicts a return to double-digit turnover at big companies. He says, "We are going into a 24-month cycle of CEO volatility." "Deliver or depart" will clearly become a stronger message from boards.

Increasing CEO turnover could, however, pose a major problem for many organizations. Why? It appears that boards of directors are not typically engaged in effective succession planning. For example, only 35 percent of 1,318 executives surveyed by Korn/Ferry International in December 2010 said their companies had a succession plan. And 61 percent of respondents to a survey (conducted by Heidrick & Struggles and Stanford University's Rock Center for Corporate Governance) claimed their companies had *no* viable internal candidates.

Another key component of top-ranked boards is director independence.[73] Governance experts believe that a majority of directors should be free of all ties to either the CEO or the company.[74] That means a minimum of "insiders" (past or present members of the management team) should serve on the board, and that directors and their firms should be barred from doing consulting, legal, or other work for the company.[75] Interlocking directorships—in which CEOs and other top managers serve on each other's boards—are not desirable. But perhaps the best guarantee that directors act in the best interests of shareholders is the simplest: Most good companies now insist that directors own significant stock in the company they oversee.[76]

Such guidelines are not always followed. At times, the practices of the boards of directors are the antithesis of such guidelines. Consider the Walt Disney Co. Over a five-year period, former CEO Michael Eisner pocketed an astonishing $531 million. He likely had very little resistance from his board of directors:

> Many investors view the Disney board as an anachronism. Among Disney's 16 directors is Eisner's personal attorney—who for several years was chairman of the company's compensation committee! There was also the architect who designed Eisner's Aspen home and his parents' apartment. Joining them are the principal of an elementary school once attended by his children and the president of a university to which Eisner donated $1 million. The board also includes the actor Sidney Poitier, seven current and former Disney executives, and an attorney who does business with Disney. Moreover, most of the outside directors own little or no Disney stock. "It is an egregiously bad board—a train wreck waiting to happen," warns Michael L. Useem, a management professor at the University of Pennsylvania's Wharton School.[77]

This example also shows that "outside directors" are only beneficial to strong corporate governance if they are vigilant in carrying out their responsibilities.[78] As humorously suggested by Warren Buffett, founder and chairman of Berkshire Hathaway: "The ratcheting up of compensation has been obscene. . . . There is a tendency to put cocker spaniels on compensation committees, not Doberman pinschers."[79]

Many firms do have exemplary board practices. Below we list some of the excellent practices at Intel Corp., the world's largest semiconductor chip manufacturer, with $35 billion in revenues:[80]

- *Mix of inside and outside directors.* The board believes that there should be a majority of independent directors on the board. However, the board is willing to have members of management, in addition to the CEO, as directors.
- *Board presentations and access to employees.* The board encourages management to schedule managers to be present at meetings who: (1) can provide additional insight into the items being discussed because of personal involvement in these areas, or (2) have future potential that management believes should be given exposure to the board.
- *Formal evaluation of officers.* The Compensation Committee conducts, and reviews with the outside directors, an annual evaluation to help determine the salary and executive bonus of all officers, including the chief executive officer.

Exhibit 9.7 shows how boards of directors can improve their practices.

Shareholder Activism   As a practical matter, there are so many owners of the largest American corporations that it makes little sense to refer to them as "owners" in the sense of

Exhibit 9.7   Best Practice Ideas: The New Rules for Directors

Issue	Suggestion
Pay	**Know the Math**
Companies will disclose full details of CEO payouts. Activist investors are already drawing up hit lists of companies where CEO paychecks are out of line with performance.	Before okaying any financial package, directors must make sure they can explain the numbers. They need to adopt the mindset of an activist investor and ask: What's the harshest criticism someone could make about this package?
Strategy	**Make It a Priority**
Boards have been so focused on compliance that duties like strategy and leadership oversight too often get ignored. Only 59 percent of directors in a recent study rated their board favorably on setting strategy	To avoid spending too much time on compliance issues, move strategy up to the beginning of the meeting. Annual one-, two- or three-day offsite meetings on strategy alone are becoming standard for good boards.
Financials	**Put in the Time**
Although 95 percent of directors in the recent study said they were doing a good job of monitoring financials, the number of earnings restatements hit a new high in 2006, after breaking records in 2004 and 2005.	Even nonfinancial board members need to monitor the numbers and keep a close eye on cash flows. Audit committee members should prepare to spend 300 hours a year on committee responsibilities.
Crisis Management	**Dig in**
Some 120 companies are under scrutiny for options backdating, and the 100 largest companies have replaced 56 CEOs in the past five years—nearly double the terminations in the prior five years.	The increased scrutiny on boards means that a perfunctory review will not suffice if a scandal strikes. Directors can no longer afford to defer to management in a crisis. They must roll up their sleeves and move into watchdog mode.

Source: From No Byrnes and J. Sassen, "Board of Hard Knocks," *BusinessWeek*, January 22, 2007, pp. 36–39. Used with permission of *Bloomberg BusinessWeek*. copyright © 2007. All rights reserved.

individuals becoming informed and involved in corporate affairs.[81] However, even an individual shareholder has several rights, including (1) the right to sell the stock, (2) the right to vote the proxy (which includes the election of board members), (3) the right to bring suit for damages if the corporation's directors or managers fail to meet their obligations, (4) the right to certain information from the company, and (5) certain residual rights following the company's liquidation (or its filing for reorganization under bankruptcy laws), once creditors and other claimants are paid off.[82]

Collectively, shareholders have the power to direct the course of corporations.[83] This may involve acts such as being party to shareholder action suits and demanding that key issues be brought up for proxy votes at annual board meetings.[84] The power of shareholders has intensified in recent years because of the increasing influence of large institutional investors such as mutual funds (e.g., T. Rowe Price and Fidelity Investments) and retirement systems such as TIAA-CREF (for university faculty members and school administrative staff).[85] Institutional investors hold approximately 50 percent of all listed corporate stock in the United States.[86]

Shareholder activism refers to actions by large shareholders, both institutions and individuals, to protect their interests when they feel that managerial actions diverge from shareholder value maximization.

Many institutional investors are aggressive in protecting and enhancing their investments. They are shifting from traders to owners. They are assuming the role of permanent shareholders and rigorously analyzing issues of corporate governance. In the process they are reinventing systems of corporate monitoring and accountability.[87]

Consider the proactive behavior of CalPERS, the California Public Employees' Retirement System, which manages over $200 billion in assets and is the third largest pension fund in the world. Every year CalPERS reviews the performance of U.S. companies in its stock portfolio and identifies those that are among the lowest long-term relative performers and have governance structures that do not ensure full accountability to company owners. This generates a long list of companies, each of which may potentially be publicly identified as a CalPERS "Focus Company"—corporations to which CalPERS directs specific suggested governance reforms. CalPERS meets with the directors of each of these companies to discuss performance and governance issues. The CalPERS Focus List contains those companies that continue to merit public and market attention at the end of the process.

The 2009 CalPERS Focus List named four companies for poor economic and governance practices: *Eli Lilly* of Indianapolis, Indiana; *Hill-Rom Holdings* of Batesville, Indiana; *Hospitality Properties Trust* of Newton, Massachusetts; and *IMS Health* of Norwalk, Connecticut.[88] In addition to the four firms performing below their peer group for the past five years, CalPERS has expressed the following specific concerns about these firms:

- Eli Lilly, the big drug manufacturer, continues to deny shareowners any opportunity to amend bylaws.
- Hill-Rom Holdings, a medical technology provider, refuses to remove its staggered board structure and to allow shareowners to amend its bylaws.
- Hospitality Properties Trust, a real estate investment fund in hotels and trade centers, refuses to terminate its "classified" board, where directors serve staggered terms rather than standing for election each year.
- IMS Health, a provider of intelligence to the pharmaceutical and health care industries, denies the right of shareowners to call a special meeting or act by written consent and to adopt annual nonbinding advisory votes on executive compensation practices.

While appearing punitive to company management, such aggressive activism has paid significant returns for CalPERS (and other stockholders of the "Focused" companies). A Wilshire Associates study of the "CalPERS Effect" of corporate governance examined the performance of 62 targets over a five-year period: while the stock of these companies

shareholder activism actions by large shareholders to protect their interests when they feel that managerial actions of a corporation diverge from shareholder value maximization.

trailed the Standard & Poor's Index by 89 percent in the five-year period before CalPERS acted, the same stocks outperformed the index by 23 percent in the following five years, adding approximately $150 million annually in additional returns to the fund.

Perhaps no discussion of shareholder activism would be complete without mention of Carl Icahn, a famed activist with a personal net worth of about $13 billion:

> The bogeyman I am now chasing is the structure of American corporations, which permit managements and boards to rule arbitrarily and too often receive egregious compensation even after doing a subpar job. Yet they remain accountable to no one.[89]

Managerial Rewards and Incentives   As we discussed earlier in the chapter, incentive systems must be designed to help a company achieve its goals.[90] From the perspective of governance, one of the most critical roles of the board of directors is to create incentives that align the interests of the CEO and top executives with the interests of owners of the corporation—long-term shareholder returns.[91] Shareholders rely on CEOs to adopt policies and strategies that maximize the value of their shares.[92] A combination of three basic policies may create the right monetary incentives for CEOs to maximize the value of their companies:[93]

1. Boards can require that the CEOs become substantial owners of company stock.
2. Salaries, bonuses, and stock options can be structured so as to provide rewards for superior performance and penalties for poor performance.
3. Threat of dismissal for poor performance can be a realistic outcome.

In recent years the granting of stock options has enabled top executives of publicly held corporations to earn enormous levels of compensation. In 2007, the average CEO in the Standard & Poor's 500 stock index took home 433 times the pay of the average worker—up from 40 times the average in 1980. The counterargument, that the ratio is down from the 514 multiple in 2000, doesn't get much traction.[94] It has been estimated that there could be as many as 50 or more companies with CEO pay packages over $150 million.[95]

Many boards have awarded huge option grants despite poor executive performance, and others have made performance goals easier to reach. In 2002 nearly 200 companies swapped or repriced options—all to enrich wealthy executives who are already among the country's richest people. However, stock options can be a valuable governance mechanism to align the CEO's interests with those of the shareholders. The extraordinarily high level of compensation can, at times, be grounded in sound governance principles.[96] For example, Howard Solomon, CEO of Forest Laboratories, received total compensation of $148.5 million in 2001.[97] This represented $823,000 in salary, $400,000 in bonus, and $147.3 million in stock options that were exercised. However, shareholders also did well, receiving gains of 40 percent. The firm has enjoyed spectacular growth over the past ten years, and Solomon has been CEO since 1977. Thus, huge income is attributed largely to gains that have built up over many years. As stated by compensation committee member Dan Goldwasser, "If a CEO is delivering substantial increases in shareholder value, . . . it's only appropriate that he be rewarded for it."

However, the "pay for performance" principle doesn't always hold.[98] In addition to the granting of stock options, boards of directors are often failing to fulfill their fiduciary responsibilities to shareholders when they lower the performance targets that executives need to meet in order to receive millions of dollars. At Ford, for example, its "profit" goal for 2007 was to *lose* $4.9 billion. Ford beat the target, however, and lost *only* $3.9 billion. CEO Alan Mulally was rewarded $12 million in compensation, including a $7 million bonus for exceeding the profit goal. Ford's stock price fell 10 percent in 2007.

TIAA-CREF has provided several principles of corporate governance with regard to executive compensation (see Exhibit 9.8).[99] These include the importance of aligning the rewards of all employees—rank and file as well as executives—to the long-term performance of the corporation; general guidelines on the role of cash compensation, stock, and "fringe benefits"; and the mission of a corporation's compensation committee.[100]

Exhibit 9.8
TIAA-CREF's Principles on the Role of Stock in Executive Compensation

Stock-based compensation plans are a critical element of most compensation programs and can provide opportunities for managers whose efforts contribute to the creation of shareholder wealth. In evaluating the suitability of these plans, considerations of reasonableness, scale, linkage to performance, and fairness to shareholders and all employees also apply. TIAA-CREF, the largest pension system in the world, has set forth the following guidelines for stock-based compensation. Proper stock-based plans should:

- Allow for creation of executive wealth that is reasonable in view of the creation of shareholder wealth. Management should not prosper through stock while share-holders suffer.

- Have measurable and predictable outcomes that are directly linked to the company's performance.

- Be market oriented, within levels of comparability for similar positions in companies of similar size and business focus.

- Be straightforward and clearly described so that investors and employees can understand them.

- Be fully disclosed to the investing public and be approved by shareholders.

Source: *www.tiaa-cref.org/pubs.*

CEO Duality: Is It Good or Bad?

CEO duality is one of the most controversial issues in corporate governance. It refers to the dual leadership structure where the CEO acts simultaneously as the chair of the board of directors.[101] Scholars, consultants, and executives who are interested in determining the best way to manage a corporation are divided on the issue of the roles and responsibilities of a CEO. Two schools of thought represent the alternative positions:

Unity of Command   Advocates of the unity of command perspective believe when one person holds both roles, he or she is able to act more efficiently and effectively. CEO duality provides firms with a clear focus on both objectives and operations as well as eliminates confusion and conflict between the CEO and the chairman. Thus, it enables smoother, more effective strategic decision making. Holding dual roles as CEO/chairman creates unity across a company's managers and board of directors and ultimately allows the CEO to serve the shareholders even better. Having leadership focused in a single individual also enhances a firm's responsiveness and ability to secure critical resources. This perspective maintains that separating the two jobs—that of a CEO and that of the chairperson of the board of directors—may produce all types of undesirable consequences. CEOs may find it harder to make quick decisions. Ego-driven chief executives and chairmen may squabble over who is ultimately in charge. The shortage of first-class business talent may mean that bosses find themselves second-guessed by people who know little about the business.[102] Companies like Coca-Cola, JPMorgan Chase, and Time Warner have refused to divide the CEO's and chairman's jobs and support this duality structure.

Agency Theory   Supporters of agency theory argue that the positions of CEO and chairman should be separate. The case for separation is based on the simple principle of the separation of power. How can boards discharge their basic duty—monitoring the boss—if the boss is chairing its meetings and setting its agenda? How can a board act as a safeguard against corruption or incompetence when the possible source of that corruption and incompetence is sitting at the head of the table? CEO duality can create a conflict of interest that could negatively affect the interests of the shareholders.

Duality also complicates the issue of CEO succession. In some cases, a CEO/chairman may choose to retire as CEO but keep his or her role as the chairman. Although this splits up the roles, which appeases an agency perspective, it nonetheless puts the new CEO in a difficult position. The chairman is bound to question some of the new changes put in place, and the board as a whole might take sides with the chairman they trust and with whom they have a history. This conflict of interest would make it difficult for the new CEO to institute any changes, as the power and influence would still remain with the former CEO.[103]

Duality also serves to reinforce popular doubts about the legitimacy of the system as a whole and evokes images of bosses writing their own performance reviews and setting their own salaries. One of the first things that some of America's troubled banks, including Citigroup, Washington Mutual, Wachovia, and Wells Fargo, did when the financial crisis hit in 2007–2008 was to separate the two jobs. Firms like Siebel Systems, Disney, Oracle, and Microsoft have also decided to divide the roles between CEO and the chairman and eliminate duality.

The increasing pressures for effective corporate governance have led to a sharp decline in duality. Firms now routinely separate the jobs of chairman and chief executive. For example, in 2009, fewer than 12 percent of incoming CEOs were also made chairman— compared with 48 percent in 2002.

These same pressures have led to other changes in corporate governance practices. For example, the New York Stock Exchange and NASDAQ have demanded that companies should have a majority of independent directors. Also, CEOs are held accountable for their performance and tossed out if they fail to perform, with the average length of tenure dropping from 8.1 years in 2000 to 6.3 years in 2009. Finally, more than 90 percent of S&P 500 companies with CEOs who also serve as chairman of the board have appointed "lead" or "presiding" directors to act as a counterweight to a combined chairman and chief executive.

External Governance Control Mechanisms

Thus far, we've discussed internal governance mechanisms. Internal controls, however, are not always enough to ensure good governance. The separation of ownership and control that we discussed earlier requires multiple control mechanisms, some internal and some external, to ensure that managerial actions lead to shareholder value maximization. Further, society-at-large wants some assurance that this goal is met without harming other stakeholder groups. Now we discuss several **external governance control mechanisms** that have developed in most modern economies. These include the market for corporate control, auditors, governmental regulatory bodies, banks and analysts, media, and public activists.

external governance control mechanisms methods that ensure that managerial actions lead to shareholder value maximization and do not harm other stakeholder groups that are outside the control of the corporate governance system.

The Market for Corporate Control   Let us assume for a moment that internal control mechanisms in a company are failing. This means that the board is ineffective in monitoring managers and is not exercising the oversight required of them and that shareholders are passive and are not taking any actions to monitor or discipline managers. Under these circumstances managers may behave opportunistically.[104] Opportunistic behavior can take many forms. First, they can *shirk* their responsibilities. Shirking means that managers fail to exert themselves fully, as is required of them. Second, they can engage in *on the job consumption*. Examples of on the job consumption include private jets, club memberships, expensive artwork in the offices, and so on. Each of these represents consumption by managers that does not in any way increase shareholder value. Instead, they actually diminish shareholder value. Third, managers may engage in *excessive product-market diversification*.[105] As we discussed in Chapter 6, such diversification serves to reduce only the employment risk of the managers rather than the financial risk of the shareholders, who can more cheaply diversify their risk by owning a portfolio of investments. Is there any external mechanism to stop managers from shirking, consumption on the job, and excessive diversification?

The **market for corporate control** is one external mechanism that provides at least some partial solution to the problems described. If internal control mechanisms fail and the management is behaving opportunistically, the likely response of most shareholders will be to sell their stock rather than engage in activism.[106] As more stockholders vote with their feet, the value of the stock begins to decline. As the decline continues, at some point the market value of the firm becomes less than the book value. A corporate raider can take over the company for a price less than the book value of the assets of the company. The first thing that the raider may do on assuming control over the company will be to fire the underperforming management. The risk of being acquired by a hostile raider is often referred to as the **takeover constraint.** The takeover constraint deters management from engaging in opportunistic behavior.[107]

Although in theory the takeover constraint is supposed to limit managerial opportunism, in recent years its effectiveness has become diluted as a result of a number of defense tactics adopted by incumbent management (see Chapter 6). Foremost among them are poison pills, greenmail, and golden parachutes. Poison pills are provisions adopted by the company to reduce its worth to the acquirer. An example would be payment of a huge one-time dividend, typically financed by debt. Greenmail involves buying back the stock from the acquirer, usually at an attractive premium. Golden parachutes are employment contracts that cause the company to pay lucrative severance packages to top managers fired as a result of a takeover, often running to several million dollars.

market for corporate control an external control mechanism in which shareholders dissatisfied with a firm's management sell their shares.

takeover constraint the risk to management of the firm being acquired by a hostile raider.

Auditors   Even when there are stringent disclosure requirements, there is no guarantee that the information disclosed will be accurate. Managers may deliberately disclose false information or withhold negative financial information as well as use accounting methods that distort results based on highly subjective interpretations. Therefore, all accounting statements are required to be audited and certified to be accurate by external auditors. These auditing firms are independent organizations staffed by certified professionals who verify the firm's books of accounts. Audits can unearth financial irregularities and ensure that financial reporting by the firm conforms to standard accounting practices.

Recent developments leading to the bankruptcy of firms such as Enron and World-Com and a spate of earnings restatements raise questions about the failure of the auditing firms to act as effective external control mechanisms. Why did an auditing firm like Arthur Andersen, with decades of good reputation in the auditing profession at stake, fail to raise red flags about accounting irregularities? First, auditors are appointed by the firm being audited. The desire to continue that business relationship sometimes makes them overlook financial irregularities. Second, most auditing firms also do consulting work and often have lucrative consulting contracts with the firms that they audit. Understandably, some of them tend not to ask too many difficult questions, because they fear jeopardizing the consulting business, which is often more profitable than the auditing work.

The recent restatement of earnings by Xerox is an example of the lack of independence of auditing firms. The SEC filed a lawsuit against KPMG, the world's third largest accounting firm, in January 2003 for allowing Xerox to inflate its revenues by $3 billion between 1997 and 2000. Of the $82 million that Xerox paid KPMG during those four years, only $26 million was for auditing. The rest was for consulting services. When one of the auditors objected to Xerox's practice of booking revenues for equipment leases earlier than it should have, Xerox asked KPMG to replace him. It did.[108]

Banks and Analysts   Commercial and investment banks have lent money to corporations and therefore have to ensure that the borrowing firm's finances are in order and that the loan covenants are being followed. Stock analysts conduct ongoing in-depth studies of the firms that they follow and make recommendations to their clients to buy, hold, or sell. Their rewards and reputation depend on the quality of these recommendations. Their access to information, knowledge of the industry and the firm, and the insights they gain from interactions with the management of the company enable them to alert the investing community of both positive and negative developments relating to a company.

It is generally observed that analyst recommendations are often more optimistic than warranted by facts. "Sell" recommendations tend to be exceptions rather than the norm. Many analysts failed to grasp the gravity of the problems surrounding failed companies such as Enron and Global Crossing till the very end. Part of the explanation may lie in the fact that most analysts work for firms that also have investment banking relationships with the companies they follow. Negative recommendations by analysts can displease the management, who may decide to take their investment banking business to a rival firm. Otherwise independent and competent analysts may be pressured to overlook negative information or tone down their criticism. A recent settlement between the Securities and Exchange Commission and the New York State Attorney General with 10 banks requires them to pay $1.4 billion in penalties and to fund independent research for investors.[109]

Regulatory Bodies The extent of government regulation is often a function of the type of industry. Banks, utilities, and pharmaceuticals are subject to more regulatory oversight because of their importance to society. Public corporations are subject to more regulatory requirements than private corporations.[110]

All public corporations are required to disclose a substantial amount of financial information by bodies such as the Securities and Exchange Commission. These include quarterly and annual filings of financial performance, stock trading by insiders, and details of executive compensation packages. There are two primary reasons behind such requirements. First, markets can operate efficiently only when the investing public has faith in the market system. In the absence of disclosure requirements, the average investor suffers from a lack of reliable information and therefore may completely stay away from the capital market. This will negatively impact an economy's ability to grow. Second, disclosure of information such as insider trading protects the small investor to some extent from the negative consequences of information asymmetry. The insiders and large investors typically have more information than the small investor and can therefore use that information to buy or sell before the information becomes public knowledge.

The failure of a variety of external control mechanisms led the U.S. Congress to pass the Sarbanes-Oxley Act in 2002. This act calls for many stringent measures that would ensure better governance of U.S. corporations. Some of these measures include:[111]

- *Auditors* are barred from certain types of nonaudit work. They are not allowed to destroy records for five years. Lead partners auditing a client should be changed at least every five years.
- *CEOs* and *CFOs* must fully reveal off-balance-sheet finances and vouch for the accuracy of the information revealed.
- *Executives* must promptly reveal the sale of shares in firms they manage and are not allowed to sell when other employees cannot.
- *Corporate lawyers* must report to senior managers any violations of securities law lower down.

Strategy Spotlight 9.5 addresses one of the increased expenses that many companies now face in complying with the Sarbanes-Oxley Act—higher compensation for more involved and committed directors.

Media and Public Activists The press is not usually recognized as an external control mechanism in the literature on corporate governance. There is no denying that in all developed capitalist economies, the financial press and media play an important indirect role in monitoring the management of public corporations. In the United States, business magazines such as *Bloomberg Businessweek* and *Fortune,* financial newspapers such as

9.5

strategy spotlight

The Impact of the 2002 Sarbanes-Oxley Act on Corporate Directors

The cost of outside directors has been rising. Not only are well-qualified directors in short supply but also the Sarbanes-Oxley Act has increased the demands of the job. According to compensation consultants Pearl Meyer & Partners, the typical director of a large corporation earned $216,000 in 2009, up from $129,667 in 2003. For some, total compensation, including cash payments, stock grants, and other perks, has climbed above seven figures. Even during the recession of 2008–2009, corporate directors' paychecks seemed to be soaring. For example, in 2008 Anthony P. Terracciano made $4.8 million as the chairman of student loan giant SLM and Jack P. Randall made $1.5 million from XTO Energy, an oil and natural gas producing company.

Directors can thank the Sarbanes-Oxley Act for the continuing generosity. The Act was created to protect shareholders by restricting the power of corporate executives. In the past, many boards had become little more

Sources: Byrnes, N. 2010. The Gold-Plated Boardroom. *Bloomberg Business-week.* February 22: 72–73; and Hilburn, W. 2010. Trends in Director Compensation. *www.businessweek.com.* October 19: np.

than rubber stamps for everything from merger strategy to executive compensation. This led to disaster in cases such as Enron, WorldCom, and Tyco. Sarbanes-Oxley and other regulatory efforts sought to protect shareholders by empowering directors and making them more accountable.

Following the Sarbanes-Oxley Act, there were several years of 20 percent to 30 percent annual increases as director compensation rose to reflect the new realities of expanded responsibilities for directors as well as the increased demand for directors who met independence rules. The pay increases came at a time when the supply of new directors was declining due to the additional risks—real or perceived—of serving as a director.

One consequence of Sarbanes-Oxley is that many directors work harder. A decade ago a typical director attended four board meetings a year and spent about 100 hours a year on board tasks, according to the National Association of Corporate Directors. Now, directors attend an average of six board meetings a year, spend an average of 225 hours a year on board duties, and convene at other times for committee meetings. In fact, corporate directors can log as many as 400 hours a year when corporations are financially distressed or reorganizing.

The Wall Street Journal and *Investors Business Daily,* as well as television networks like Financial News Network and CNBC are constantly reporting on companies. Public perceptions about a company's financial prospects and the quality of its management are greatly influenced by the media. Food Lion's reputation was sullied when ABC's *Prime Time Live* in 1992 charged the company with employee exploitation, false package dating, and unsanitary meat handling practices. Bethany McLean of *Fortune* magazine is often credited as the first to raise questions about Enron's long-term financial viability.[112]

Similarly, consumer groups and activist individuals often take a crusading role in exposing corporate malfeasance.[113] Well-known examples include Ralph Nader and Erin Brockovich, who played important roles in bringing to light the safety issues related to GM's Corvair and environmental pollution issues concerning Pacific Gas and Electric Company, respectively. Ralph Nader has created over 30 watchdog groups, including:[114]

- *Aviation Consumer Action Project.* Works to propose new rules to prevent flight delays, impose penalties for deceiving passengers about problems, and push for higher compensation for lost luggage.
- *Center for Auto Safety.* Helps consumers find plaintiff lawyers and agitate for vehicle recalls, increased highway safety standards, and lemon laws.
- *Center for Study of Responsive Law.* This is Nader's headquarters. Home of a consumer project on technology, this group sponsored seminars on Microsoft remedies and pushed for tougher Internet privacy rules. It also took on the drug industry over costs.
- *Pension Rights Center.* This center helped employees of IBM, General Electric, and other companies to organize themselves against cash-balance pension plans.

strategy spotlight   9.6

Two Examples of Powerful External Control Mechanisms

McDonald's

After years of fending off and ignoring critics, McDonald's has begun working with them. In 1999, People for the Ethical Treatment of Animals (PETA) launched its "McCruelty" campaign asking the company to take steps to alleviate the suffering of animals killed for its restaurants. Since then, PETA has switched tactics and is cooperating with the burger chain to modernize the company's animal welfare standards and make further improvements. Following pressure from PETA, McDonald's used its influence to force egg suppliers to improve the living conditions of hens and cease debeaking them. PETA has publicly lauded the company for its efforts. Recently, McDonald's also has required beef and pork processors to improve their handling of livestock prior to slaughter. The company conducts regular audits of the packing plants to determine whether the animals are being treated humanely and will suspend purchases from slaughterhouses that don't meet the company's standards. The company's overall image appears to have improved. According to the global consulting firm Reputation Institute, McDonald's score, on a scale of 100, has climbed 8 points to 63 since 2007—a dramatic improvement.

Sources: Kiley, D. & Helm, B. 2009. The Great Trust Offensive. *Bloomberg Businessweek*, September 28: 38–42; Brasher, P. 2010. McDonald's Orders Improvements in Treatment of Hens. *abcnews.com*, August 23: np; Glover, K. 2009. PETA vs. McDonald's: The Nicest Way to Kill a Chicken. *www.bnet.com*. February 20: np; *www.mccruelty.com*; Greenhouse, S. 2010. Pressured, Nike to Help Workers in Honduras. *The New York Times*, July 27: B1; Padgett, T. 2010. Just Pay It: Nike Creates Fund for Honduran Workers. *www.time.com*, July 27: np; and Bustillo, M. 2010. Nike to Pay Some $2 Million to Workers Fired by Subcontractors. *www.online.wsj.com*, July 26: np.

Nike

In January 2009, 1,800 laborers lost their jobs in Honduras when two local factories that made shirts for the U.S. sports-apparel giant Nike suddenly closed their doors and did not pay workers the $2 million in severance and other unemployment benefits they were due by law. Following pressure from U.S. universities and student groups, Nike announced that it was setting up a $1.5 million "workers' relief fund" to assist the workers. Nike also agreed to provide vocational training and finance health coverage for workers laid off by the two subcontractors.

The relief fund from Nike came after pressure by groups such as the Worker Rights Consortium, which informed Nike customers of the treatment of the workers. The Worker Rights Consortium also convinced scores of U.S. universities whose athletic programs and campus shops buy Nike shoes and clothes to threaten cancellation of those lucrative contracts unless Nike did something to address the plight of the Honduran workers. Another labor watchdog, United Students Against Sweatshops, staged demonstrations outside Nike shops while chanting "Just Pay It," a play on Nike's commercial slogan, "Just Do It." The University of Wisconsin cancelled its licensing agreement with the company over the matter and other schools, including Cornell University and the University of Washington, indicated they were thinking of following suit. The agreement is the latest involving overseas apparel factories in which an image-conscious brand like Nike responded to campaigns led by college students, who often pressure universities to stand up to producers of college-logo apparel when workers' rights are threatened.

As we have noted above, some public activists and watchdog groups can exert a strong force on organizations and influence decisions that they may make. Strategy Spotlight 9.6 provides two examples of this phenomenon.

Corporate Governance: An International Perspective

The topic of corporate governance has long been dominated by agency theory and based on the explicit assumption of the separation of ownership and control.[115] The central conflicts are principal–agent conflicts between shareholders and management. However, such an underlying assumption seldom applies outside of the United States and the United Kingdom. This is particularly true in emerging economies and continental Europe. Here, there is often concentrated ownership, along with extensive family ownership and control, business group structures, and weak legal protection for minority shareholders. Serious conflicts tend to exist between two classes of principals: controlling shareholders and minority shareholders. Such conflicts can be called **principal–principal (PP) conflicts,** as opposed to *principal–agent* conflicts (see Exhibits 9.9 and 9.10).

Strong family control is one of the leading indicators of concentrated ownership. In East Asia (excluding China), approximately 57 percent of the corporations have board chairmen and CEOs from the controlling families. In continental Europe, this number is 68 percent. A very common practice is the appointment of family members as board chairmen, CEOs, and other top executives. This happens because the families are controlling (not necessarily majority) shareholders. In 2003, 30-year-old James Murdoch was appointed CEO of British Sky Broadcasting (BSkyB), Europe's largest satellite broadcaster. There was very vocal resistance by minority shareholders. Why was he appointed in the first place? James's father just happened to be Rupert Murdoch, who controlled 35 percent of BSkyB and chaired the board. Clearly, this is a case of a PP conflict.

In general, three conditions must be met for PP conflicts to occur:

- A dominant owner or group of owners who have interests that are distinct from minority shareholders.
- Motivation for the controlling shareholders to exercise their dominant positions to their advantage.
- Few formal (such as legislation or regulatory bodies) or informal constraints that would discourage or prevent the controlling shareholders from exploiting their advantageous positions.

principal–principal conflicts conflicts between two classes of principals— controlling shareholders and minority shareholders— within the context of a corporate governance system.

	Principal–Agent Conflicts	Principal–Principal Conflicts
Goal Incongruence	Between shareholders and professional managers who own a relatively small portion of the firm's equity.	Between controlling shareholders and minority shareholders.
Ownership Pattern	Dispersed—5%–20% is considered "concentrated ownership."	Concentrated—Often greater than 50% of equity is controlled by controlling shareholders.
Manifestations	Strategies that benefit entrenched managers at the expense of shareholders in general (e.g., shirking, pet projects, excessive compensation, and empire building).	Strategies that benefit controlling shareholders at the expense of minority shareholders (e.g., minority shareholder expropriation, nepotism, and cronyism).
Institutional Protection of Minority Shareholders	Formal constraints (e.g., judicial reviews and courts) set an upper boundary on potential expropriation by majority shareholders. Informal norms generally adhere to shareholder wealth maximization.	Formal institutional protection is often lacking, corrupted, or un-enforced. Informal norms are typically in favor of the interests of controlling shareholders ahead of those of minority investors.

Exhibit 9.9
Traditional Principal– Agent Conflicts versus Principal–Principal Conflicts: How They Differ along Dimensions

Source: Adapted from Young, M., Peng, M. W., Ahlstrom, D., & Bruton, G. 2002. Governing the Corporation in Emerging Economics: A Principal–Principal Perspective. *Academy of Management Best Papers Proceedings,* Denver.

Exhibit 9.10 **Principal–Agent Conflicts and Principal–Principal Conflicts: A Diagram**

Source: Young, M. N., Peng, M. W., Ahlstrom, D., Bruton, G. D., & Jiang, 2008. Principal–Principal Conflicts in Corporate Governance. *Journal of Management Studies* 45(1):196–220; and Peng, M. V. 2006. *Global Strategy.* Cincinnati: Thomson South-Western. We are very appreciative of the helpful comments of Mike Young of Hong Kong Baptist University and Mike Peng of the University of Texas at Dallas.

expropriation of minority shareholders activities that enrich the controlling shareholders at the expense of the minority shareholders.

The result is often that family managers, who represent (or actually are) the controlling shareholders, engage in **expropriation of minority shareholders,** which is defined as activities that enrich the controlling shareholders at the expense of minority shareholders. What is their motive? After all, controlling shareholders have incentives to maintain firm value. But controlling shareholders may take actions that decrease aggregate firm performance if their personal gains from expropriation exceed their personal losses from their firm's lowered performance.

Another ubiquitous feature of corporate life outside of the United States and United Kingdom are *business groups* such as the keiretsus of Japan and the chaebols of South Korea. This is particularly dominant in emerging economies. A **business group** is "a set of firms that, though legally independent, are bound together by a constellation of formal and informal ties and are accustomed to taking coordinated action."[116] Business groups are especially common in emerging economies, and they differ from other organizational forms in that they are communities of firms without clear boundaries.

business groups a set of firms that, though legally independent, are bound together by a constellation of formal and informal ties and are accustomed to taking coordinated action.

Business groups have many advantages that can enhance the value of a firm. They often facilitate technology transfer or intergroup capital allocation that otherwise might be impossible because of inadequate institutional infrastructure such as excellent financial services firms. On the other hand, informal ties—such as cross-holdings, board interlocks, and coordinated actions—can often result in intragroup activities and transactions, often at very favorable terms to member firms. Expropriation can be legally done through *related transactions,* which can occur when controlling owners sell firm assets to another firm they own at below market prices or spin off the most profitable part of a public firm and merge it with another of their private firms.

Strategy Spotlight 9.7 provides examples from Latin America of effective corporate governance.

9.7

strategy spotlight

Effective and Ineffective Corporate Governance among "Multilatinas"

Latin-owned companies, such as Mexico's Cemex, Argentina's Arcor, and Brazil's Embraer, have been successful in their home markets against U.S. and European competitors. Several of these companies have become "multilatinas," pursuing a strategy of regional and international expansion. Recently, 82 percent of merger and acquisition deals in Latin America were originated by Latin companies. However, while the rise of these Latin firms is promising, it is not enough to ensure they will be competitive globally against large industrialized multinational firms. Access to international capital markets necessary for the "multilatinas" to grow has created a need for a new openness in corporate governance and transparency for these firms.

There are three components emerging-market multinational firms need to implement to succeed:

Sources: Pigorini, P., Ramos, A., & de Souza, I. 2008. Pitting Latin Multinationals against Established Giants. *Strategy + Business*, November 4: *www. strategy-business.com/media/file/leading_ideas-20081104.pdf*; Martinez, J., Esperanca, J., & de la Torre, J. 2005. Organizational Change among Emerging Latin American Firms: From "Multilatinas" to Multinationals. *Management Research*, 3(3): 173–188; Krauss, C. 2007. Latin American Companies Make Big U.S. Gains. *New York Times*, May 2: *www.nytimes.com/2007/05/02/-business/worldbusiness/02latin.html*.

- **Shareholder rights.** Minority shareholders must be protected through clear and fair dividend distribution and fair valuation in the event of mergers and acquisitions.

- **Compliance.** The audit committee of the board must be empowered to evaluate the financial statements of the firm and interact with both internal and external auditors.

- **Board and management composition.** Because many multilatinas are still in the process of building effective governance systems, it is important that the board members and top managers have credible professional backgrounds and experience.

These firms need to set up the right board and manager dynamics both to improve access to capital and to implement international management. Many multilatinas were or still are family-owned firms. Boards of these firms tend to be filled with members who have a strong loyalty to the controlling family, but not necessarily exposure to global strategic initiatives and strategies. Many of these firms still use centralized information control systems. In order to grow, some firms may have to consider giving local country managers more authority to make decisions.

Reflecting on Career Implications . . .

- *Behavioral Control:* What sources of behavioral control does your organization employ? In general, too much emphasis on rules and regulations may stifle initiative and be detrimental to your career opportunities.

- *Rewards and Incentives:* Is your organization's reward structure fair and equitable? Does it effectively reward outstanding performance? If not, there may be a long-term erosion of morale which may have long-term adverse career implications for you.

- *Culture:* Consider the type of organization culture that would provide the best work environment for your career goals. How does your organization's culture deviate from this concept? Does your organization have a strong and effective culture? If so, professionals are more likely to develop strong "firm specific" ties, which further enhances collaboration.

- *Corporate Governance:* Does your organization practice effective corporate governance? Such practices will enhance a firm's culture and it will be easier to attract top talent. Operating within governance guidelines is usually a strong indicator of organizational citizenship which, in turn, should be good for your career prospects.

Summary

For firms to be successful, they must practice effective strategic control and corporate governance. Without such controls, the firm will not be able to achieve competitive advantages and outperform rivals in the marketplace.

We began the chapter with the key role of informational control. We contrasted two types of control systems: what we termed "traditional" and "contemporary" information control systems. Whereas traditional control systems may have their place in placid, simple competitive environments, there are fewer of those in today's economy. Instead, we advocated the contemporary approach wherein the internal and external environment are constantly monitored so that when surprises emerge, the firm can modify its strategies, goals, and objectives.

Behavioral controls are also a vital part of effective control systems. We argued that firms must develop the proper balance between culture, rewards and incentives, and boundaries and constraints. Where there are strong and positive cultures and rewards, employees tend to internalize the organization's strategies and objectives. This permits a firm to spend fewer resources on monitoring behavior, and assures the firm that the efforts and initiatives of employees are more consistent with the overall objectives of the organization.

In the final section of this chapter, we addressed corporate governance, which can be defined as the relationship between various participants in determining the direction and performance of the corporation. The primary participants include shareholders, management (led by the chief executive officer), and the board of directors. We reviewed studies that indicated a consistent relationship between effective corporate governance and financial performance. There are also several internal and external control mechanisms that can serve to align managerial interests and shareholder interests. The internal mechanisms include a committed and involved board of directors, shareholder activism, and effective managerial incentives and rewards. The external mechanisms include the market for corporate control, banks and analysts, regulators, the media, and public activists. We also addressed corporate governance from both a United States and an international perspective.

Summary Review Questions

1. Why are effective strategic control systems so important in today's economy?
2. What are the main advantages of "contemporary" control systems over "traditional" control systems? What are the main differences between these two systems?

3. Why is it important to have a balance between the three elements of behavioral control—culture; rewards and incentives; and, boundaries?
4. Discuss the relationship between types of organizations and their primary means of behavioral control.
5. Boundaries become less important as a firm develops a strong culture and reward system. Explain.
6. Why is it important to avoid a "one best way" mentality concerning control systems? What are the consequences of applying the same type of control system to all types of environments?
7. What is the role of effective corporate governance in improving a firm's performance? What are some of the key governance mechanisms that are used to ensure that managerial and shareholder interests are aligned?
8. Define principal–principal (PP) conflicts. What are the implications for corporate governance?

Key Terms

strategic control, 318	agency theory, 333
traditional approach to strategic control, 319	board of directors, 334
informational control, 319	shareholder activism, 337
behavioral control, 321	external governance control mechanisms, 340
organizational culture, 323	market for corporate control, 341
reward system, 324	takeover constraint, 341
boundaries and constraints, 325	principal–principal conflicts, 345
corporate governance, 330	expropriation of minority shareholders, 346
corporation, 332	business groups, 346

Experiential Exercise

McDonald's Corporation, the world's largest fast-food restaurant chain, with 2010 revenues of $24 billion, has recently been on a "roll." Its shareholder value has more than doubled between February 2006 and February 2011. Using the Internet or library sources, evaluate the quality of the corporation in terms of management, the board of directors, and shareholder activism. Are the issues you list favorable or unfavorable for sound corporate governance?

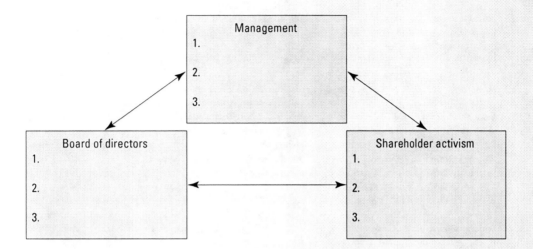

Application Questions & Exercises

1. The problems of many firms may be attributed to a "traditional" control system that failed to continuously monitor the environment and make necessary changes in their strategy and objectives. What companies are you familiar with that responded appropriately (or inappropriately) to environmental change?

2. How can a strong, positive culture enhance a firm's competitive advantage? How can a weak, negative culture erode competitive advantages? Explain and provide examples.

3. Use the Internet to research a firm that has an excellent culture and/or reward and incentive system. What are this firm's main financial and nonfinancial benefits?

4. Using the Internet, go to the website of a large, publicly held corporation in which you are interested. What evidence do you see of effective (or ineffective) corporate governance?

Ethics Questions

1. Strong cultures can have powerful effects on employee behavior. How does this create inadvertent control mechanisms? That is, are strong cultures an ethical way to control behavior?

2. Rules and regulations can help reduce unethical behavior in organizations. To be effective, however, what other systems, mechanisms, and processes are necessary?

References

1. Loomis, C. J. 2010. Directors: Feeding at the trough. *Fortune*, January 18: 20; Schonberger, J. 2009. Why you should care about corporate governance, *www.fool.com*. November 10: np; Hood, H. J. 2009. *Chesapeake Energy Corporation* Schedule 14A; and *www.sec.gov*. November 10: np. We thank Zia Shakir for his valued contributions.

2. This chapter draws upon Picken, J. C. & Dess, G. G. 1997. *Mission critical*. Burr Ridge, IL: Irwin Professional Publishing.

3. For a unique perspective on governance, refer to: Carmeli, A. & Markman, G. D. 2011. Capture, governance, and resilience: Strategy implications from the history of Rome. *Strategic Management Journal*, 32(3):332–341.

4. Argyris, C. 1977. Double-loop learning in organizations. *Harvard Business Review*, 55: 115–125.

5. Simons, R. 1995. Control in an age of empowerment. *Harvard Business Review*, 73: 80–88. This chapter draws on this source in the discussion of informational control.

6. Goold, M. & Quinn, J. B. 1990. The paradox of strategic controls. *Strategic Management Journal*, 11: 43–57.

7. Quinn, J. B. 1980. *Strategies for change*. Homewood, IL: Richard D. Irwin.

8. Mintzberg, H. 1987. Crafting strategy. *Harvard Business Review*, 65: 66–75.

9. Weston, J. S. 1992. Soft stuff matters. *Financial Executive*, July–August: 52–53.

10. This discussion of control systems draws upon Simons, op. cit.

11. Ryan, M. K., Haslam, S. A., & Renneboog, L. D. R. 2011. Who gets the carrot and who gets the stick? Evidence of gender discrimination in executive remuneration. *Strategic Management Journal*, 32(3): 301–321.

12. For an interesting perspective on this issue and how a downturn in the economy can reduce the tendency toward "free agency" by managers and professionals, refer to Morris, B. 2001. White collar blues. *Fortune,* July 23: 98–110.

13. For a colorful example of behavioral control in an organization, see: Beller, P. C. 2009. Activision's unlikely hero. *Forbes.* February 2: 52–58.

14. Ouchi, W. 1981. *Theory Z.* Reading, MA: Addison-Wesley; Deal, T. E. & Kennedy, A. A. 1982. *Corporate cultures.* Reading, MA: Addison-Wesley; Peters, T. J. & Waterman, R. H. 1982. *In search of excellence.* New York: Random House; Collins, J. 2001. *Good to great.* New York: HarperCollins.

15. Collins, J. C. & Porras, J. I. 1994. *Built to last: Successful habits of visionary companies.* New York: Harper Business.

16. Lee, J. & Miller, D. 1999. People matter: Commitment to employees, strategy, and performance in Korean firms. *Strategic Management Journal,* 6: 579–594.

17. For an insightful discussion of IKEA's unique culture, see Kling, K. & Goteman, I. 2003. IKEA CEO Anders Dahlvig on international growth and IKEA's unique corporate culture and brand identity. *Academy of Management Executive,* 17(1): 31–37.

18. For a discussion of how professionals inculcate values, refer to Uhl-Bien, M. & Graen, G. B. 1998. Individual self-management: Analysis of professionals' self-managing activities in functional and cross-functional work teams. *Academy of Management Journal,* 41(3): 340–350.

19. A perspective on how antisocial behavior can erode a firm's culture can be found in Robinson, S. L. & O'Leary-Kelly, A. M. 1998. Monkey see, monkey do: The influence of work groups on the antisocial behavior of employees. *Academy of Management Journal,* 41(6): 658–672.

20. An interesting perspective on organizational culture is in: Mehta, S. N. 2009. UnderArmour reboots. *Fortune,* February 2: 29–33.

21. For insights on social pressure as a means for control, refer to: Goldstein, N. J. 2009. Harnessing social pressure. *Harvard Business Review,* 87(2): 25.

22. Mitchell, R. 1989. Masters of innovation. *BusinessWeek,* April 10: 58–63.

23. Sellers, P. 1993. Companies that serve you best. *Fortune,* May 31: 88.

24. Southwest Airlines Culture Committee. 1993. *Luv Lines* (company publication), March–April: 17–18; for an interesting perspective on the "downside" of strong "cultlike" organizational cultures, refer to Arnott, D. A. 2000. *Corporate cults.* New York: AMACOM.

25. Kerr, J. & Slocum, J. W., Jr. 1987. Managing corporate culture through reward systems. *Academy of Management Executive,* 1(2): 99–107.

26. For a unique perspective on leader challenges in managing wealthy professionals, refer to Wetlaufer, S. 2000. Who wants to manage a millionaire? *Harvard Business Review,* 78(4): 53–60.

27. *www.starbucks.com*; Wood, Z. 2010. Starbucks' staff set to get free shares in incentive schemes. *www.guardian.co.uk*; December 19: np; and Hammers, M. 2003. Starbucks is pleasing employees and pouring profits. *Workforce Management.* October: 58–59.

28. These next two subsections draw upon Dess, G. G. & Picken, J. C. 1997. *Beyond productivity.* New York: AMACOM.

29. For a discussion of the benefits of stock options as executive compensation, refer to Hall, B. J. 2000. What you need to know about stock options. *Harvard Business Review,* 78(2): 121–129.

30. Tully, S. 1993. Your paycheck gets exciting. *Fortune,* November 13: 89.

31. Carter, N. M. & Silva, C. 2010. Why men still get more promotions than women. *Harvard Business Review,* 88(9): 80–86.

32. Zellner, W., Hof, R. D., Brandt, R., Baker, S., & Greising, D. 1995. Go-go goliaths. *BusinessWeek,* February 13: 64–70.

33. This section draws on Dess & Picken, op. cit.: chap. 5.

34. Simons, op. cit.

35. Davis, E. 1997. Interview: Norman Augustine. *Management Review,* November: 11.

36. This section draws upon Dess, G. G. & Miller, A. 1993. *Strategic management.* New York: McGraw-Hill.

37. For a good review of the goal-setting literature, refer to Locke, E. A. & Latham, G. P. 1990. *A theory of goal setting and task performance.* Englewood Cliffs, NJ: Prentice Hall.

38. For an interesting perspective on the use of rules and regulations that is counter to this industry's (software) norms, refer to Fryer, B. 2001. Tom Siebel of Siebel Systems: High tech the old fashioned way. *Harvard Business Review,* 79(3): 118–130.

39. Thompson, A. A. Jr. & Strickland, A. J., III. 1998. *Strategic management: Concepts and cases* (10th ed.): 313. New York: McGraw-Hill.

40. Ibid.

41. Teitelbaum, R. 1997. Tough guys finish first. *Fortune,* July 21: 82–84.

42. Weaver, G. R., Trevino, L. K., & Cochran, P. L. 1999. Corporate ethics programs as control systems: Influences of executive commitment and environmental factors. *Academy of Management Journal,* 42(1): 41–57.

43. Cadbury, S. A. 1987. Ethical managers make their own rules. *Harvard Business Review,* 65: 3, 69–73.

44. Weber, J. 2003. CFOs on the hot seat. *BusinessWeek,* March 17: 66–70.

45. William Ouchi has written extensively about the use of clan control (which is viewed as an alternate to bureaucratic or market control). Here, a powerful culture results in people aligning their individual interests with those of the firm. Refer to Ouchi, op. cit. This section also draws on Hall, R. H. 2002. *Organizations: Structures, processes, and outcomes* (8th ed.). Upper Saddle River, NJ: Prentice Hall.

46. Poundstone, W. 2003. *How would you move Mount Fuji?* New York: Little, Brown and company, page 59.

47. Interesting insights on corporate governance are in: Kroll, M., Walters, B. A., & Wright, P. 2008. Board vigilance, director experience, and

corporate outcomes. *Strategic Management Journal,* 29(4): 363–382.

48. For a brief review of some central issues in corporate governance research, see: Hambrick, D. C., Werder, A. V., & Zajac, E. J. 2008. New directions in corporate governance research. *Organization Science,* 19(3): 381–385.

49. Monks, R. & Minow, N. 2001. *Corporate governance* (2nd ed.). Malden, MA: Blackwell.

50. Pound, J. 1995. The promise of the governed corporation. *Harvard Business Review,* 73(2): 89–98.

51. Maurer, H. & Linblad, C. 2009. Scandal at Satyam. *BusinessWeek,* January 19: 8; Scheck, J. & Stecklow, S. 2008. Brocade ex-CEO gets 21 months in prison. *The Wall Street Journal,* January 17: A3; Levine, D. & Graybow, M. 2010. Mozilo to pay millions in Countrywide settlement. *finance.yahoo.com.* October 15: np; Ellis, B. 2010. Countrywide's Mozilo to pay $67.5 million settlement. *cnnmoney.com.* October 15: np; Frank, R., Efrati, A., Lucchetti, A. & Bray, C. 2009. Madoff jailed after admitting epic scam. *The Wall Street Journal.* March 13: A1; and Henriques, D. B. 2009. Madoff is sentenced to 150 years for Ponzi scheme. *www.nytimes.com.* June 29: np.

52. Corporate governance and social networks are discussed in: McDonald, M. L., Khanna, P., & Westphal, J. D. 2008. *Academy of Management Journal.* 51(3): 453–475.

53. This discussion draws upon Monks & Minow, op. cit.

54. For an interesting perspective on the politicization of the corporation, read: Palazzo, G. & Scherer, A. G. 2008. Corporate social responsibility, democracy, and the politicization of the corporation. *Academy of Management Review,* 33(3): 773–774.

55. Eisenhardt, K. M. 1989. Agency theory: An assessment and review. *Academy of Management Review,* 14(1): 57–74. Some of the seminal contributions to agency theory include Jensen, M. & Meckling, W. 1976. Theory of the firm: Managerial behavior, agency costs, and ownership

structure. *Journal of Financial Economics,* 3: 305–360; Fama, E. & Jensen, M. 1983. Separation of ownership and control. *Journal of Law and Economics,* 26: 301, 325; and Fama, E. 1980. Agency problems and the theory of the firm. *Journal of Political Economy,* 88: 288–307.

56. Nyberg, A. J., Fulmer, I. S., Gerhart, B. & Carpenter, M. 2010. Agency theory revisited: CEO return and shareholder interest alignment. *Academy of Management Journal,* 53(5): 1029–1049.

57. Managers may also engage in "shirking"—that is, reducing or withholding their efforts. See, for example, Kidwell, R. E., Jr. & Bennett, N. 1993. Employee propensity to withhold effort: A conceptual model to intersect three avenues of research. *Academy of Management Review,* 18(3): 429–456.

58. For an interesting perspective on agency and clarification of many related concepts and terms, visit *www.encycogov.com.*

59. The relationship between corporate ownership structure and export intensity in Chinese firms is discussed in: Filatotchev, I., Stephan, J., & Jindra, B. 2008. Ownership structure, strategic controls and export intensity of foreign-invested firms in transition economies. *Journal of International Business,* 39(7): 1133–1148.

60. Argawal, A. & Mandelker, G. 1987. Managerial incentives and corporate investment and financing decisions. *Journal of Finance,* 42: 823–837.

61. The Carnival and Alliance Semiconductor examples draw upon: MacDonald, E. 2004. Crony capitalism. *Forbes,* June 21: 140–146.

62. For an insightful, recent discussion of the academic research on corporate governance, and in particular the role of boards of directors, refer to Chatterjee, S. & Harrison, J. S. 2001. Corporate governance. In Hitt, M. A., Freeman, R. E., & Harrison, J. S. (Eds.). *Handbook of strategic management:* 543–563. Malden, MA: Blackwell.

63. For an interesting theoretical discussion on corporate governance in

Russia, see: McCarthy, D. J. & Puffer, S. M. 2008. Interpreting the ethicality of corporate governance decisions in Russia: Utilizing integrative social contracts theory to evaluate the relevance of agency theory norms. *Academy of Management Review,* 33(1): 11–31.

64. Haynes, K. T. & Hillman, A. 2010. The effect of board capital and CEO power on strategic change. *Strategic Management Journal,* 31(110): 1145–1163.

65. This opening discussion draws on Monks & Minow, op. cit. 164, 169; see also Pound, op. cit.

66. Business Roundtable. 1990. *Corporate governance and American competitiveness,* March: 7.

67. The director role in acquisition performance is addressed in: Westphal, J. D. & Graebner, M. E. 2008. What do they know? The effects of outside director acquisition experience on firm acquisition performance. *Strategic Management Journal,* 29(11): 1155–1178.

68. Byrne, J. A., Grover, R., & Melcher, R. A. 1997. The best and worst boards. *BusinessWeek,* November 26: 35–47. The three key roles of boards of directors are monitoring the actions of executives, providing advice, and providing links to the external environment to provide resources. See Johnson, J. L., Daily, C. M., & Ellstrand, A. E. 1996. Boards of directors: A review and research agenda. *Academy of Management Review,* 37: 409–438.

69. Pozen, R. C. 2010. The case for professional boards. *Harvard Business Review,* 88(12): 50–58.

70. The role of outside directors is discussed in: Lester, R. H., Hillman, A., Zardkoohi, A., & Cannella, A. A. Jr. 2008. Former government officials as outside directors: The role of human and social capital. *Academy of Management Journal,* 51(5): 999–1013.

71. McGeehan, P. 2003. More chief executives shown the door, study says. *New York Times,* May 12: C2.

72. The examples in this paragraph draw upon Helyar, J. & Hymowitz,

C. 2011. The recession is gone, and the CEO could be next. *Bloomberg Businessweek.* Februrary 7–February 13: 24–26; Stelter, B. 2010. Jonathan Klein to leave CNN. *mediadecoder. blogs.nytimes.com.* September 24: np; Silver, A. 2010. Milestones. *TIME Magazine.* December 20: 28; *www. bp.com* and Mouawad, J. & Krauss, C. 2010. BP is expected to replace Hayward as chief with American. *The New York Times.* July 26: A1.

73. For an analysis of the effects of outside directors' compensation on acquisition decisions, refer to Deutsch, T., Keil, T., & Laamanen, T. 2007. Decision making in acquisitions: The effect of outside directors' compensation on acquisition patterns. *Journal of Management,* 33(1): 30–56.

74. Director interlocks are addressed in: Kang, E. 2008. Director interlocks and spillover effects of reputational penalties from financial reporting fraud. *Academy of Management Journal,* 51(3): 537–556.

75. There are benefits, of course, to having some insiders on the board of directors. Inside directors would be more aware of the firm's strategies. Additionally, outsiders may rely too often on financial performance indicators because of information asymmetries. For an interesting discussion, see Baysinger, B. D. & Hoskisson, R. E. 1990. The composition of boards of directors and strategic control: Effects on corporate strategy. *Academy of Management Review,* 15: 72–87.

76. Hambrick, D. C. & Jackson, E. M. 2000. Outside directors with a stake: The linchpin in improving governance. *California Management Review,* 42(4): 108–127.

77. Ibid.

78. Disney has begun to make many changes to improve its corporate governance, such as assigning only independent directors to important board committees, restricting directors from serving on more than three boards, and appointing a lead director who can convene the board without approval by the CEO. In recent years, the Disney Co. has shown up on some

"best" board lists. In addition Eisner has recently relinquished the chairman position.

79. Talk show. 2002. *BusinessWeek,* September 30: 14.

80. Ward, R. D. 2000. *Improving corporate boards.* New York: Wiley.

81. A discussion on the shareholder approval process in executive compensation is presented in: Brandes, P., Goranova, M., & Hall, S. 2008. Navigating shareholder influence: Compensation plans and the shareholder approval process. *Academy of Management Perspectives,* 22(1): 41–57.

82. Monks and Minow, op. cit.: 93.

83. A discussion of the factors that lead to shareholder activism is found in Ryan, L. V. & Schneider, M. 2002. The antecedents of institutional investor activism. *Academy of Management Review,* 27(4): 554–573.

84. For an insightful discussion of investor activism, refer to David, P., Bloom, M., & Hillman, A. 2007. Investor activism, managerial responsiveness, and corporate social performance. *Strategic Management Journal,* 28(1): 91–100.

85. There is strong research support for the idea that the presence of large block shareholders is associated with value-maximizing decisions. For example, refer to Johnson, R. A., Hoskisson, R. E., & Hitt, M. A. 1993. Board of director involvement in restructuring: The effects of board versus managerial controls and characteristics. *Strategic Management Journal,* 14: 33–50.

86. For a discussion of institutional activism and its link to CEO compensation, refer to: Chowdhury, S. D. & Wang, E. Z. 2009. Institutional activism types and CEO compensation. *Journal of Management,* 35(1): 5–36.

87. For an interesting perspective on the impact of institutional ownership on a firm's innovation strategies, see Hoskisson, R. E., Hitt, M. A., Johnson, R. A., & Grossman, W. 2002. *Academy of Management Journal,* 45(4): 697–716.

88. *www.calpers.ca.gov;*

89. Icahn, C. 2007. Icahn: On activist investors and private equity run wild.

BusinessWeek, March 12: 21–22. For an interesting perspective on Carl Icahn's transition (?) from corporate raider to shareholder activist, read Grover, R. 2007. Just don't call him a raider. *BusinessWeek,* March 5: 68–69. The quote in the text is part of Icahn's response to the article by R. Grover.

90. For a study of the relationship between ownership and diversification, refer to Goranova, M., Alessandri, T. M., Brandes, P., & Dharwadkar, R. 2007. Managerial ownership and corporate diversification: A longitudinal view, *Strategic Management Journal,* 28(3): 211–226.

91. Jensen, M. C. & Murphy, K. J. 1990. CEO incentives—It's not how much you pay, but how. *Harvard Business Review,* 68(3): 138–149.

92. For a perspective on the relative advantages and disadvantages of "duality"—that is, one individual serving as both Chief Executive Office and Chairman of the Board, see Lorsch, J. W. & Zelleke, A. 2005. Should the CEO be the chairman? *MIT Sloan Management Review,* 46(2): 71–74.

93. A discussion of knowledge sharing is addressed in: Fey, C. F. & Furu, P. 2008. Top management incentive compensation and knowledge sharing in multinational corporations. *Strategic Management Journal,* 29(12): 1301–1324.

94. Sasseen, J. 2007. A better look at the boss's pay. *BusinessWeek,* February 26: 44–45; and Weinberg, N., Maiello, M., & Randall, D. 2008. Paying for failure. *Forbes,* May 19: 114, 116.

95. Byrnes, N. & Sasseen, J. 2007. Board of hard knocks. *BusinessWeek,* January 22: 36–39.

96. Research has found that executive compensation is more closely aligned with firm performance in companies with compensation committees and boards dominated by outside directors. See, for example, Conyon, M. J. & Peck, S. I. 1998. Board control, remuneration committees, and top management compensation. *Academy of Management Journal,* 41: 146–157.

97. Lavelle, L., Jespersen, F. F., & Arndt, M. 2002. Executive pay. *Business-Week,* April 15: 66–72.

98. A perspective on whether or not CEOs are overpaid is provided in: Kaplan, S. N. 2008. Are U.S. CEOs overpaid: A response to Bogle and Walsh, J. P. *Academy of Management Perspectives.* 22(3): 28–34.

99. *www.tiaa-cref.org/pubs.*

100. Some insights on CEO compensation— and the importance of ethics—are addressed in: Heineman, B. W. Jr. 2008. The fatal flaw in pay for performance. *Harvard Business Review.* 86(6): 31, 34.

101. Chahine, S. & Tohme, N. S. 2009. Is CEO duality always negative? An exploration of CEO duality and ownership structure in the Arab IPO context. *Corporate Governance: An International Review.* 17(2): 123–141; and McGrath, J. 2009. How CEOs work. *HowStuffWorks.com.* January 28: np.

102. Anonymous. 2009. Someone to watch over them. *The Economist.* October 17: 78; Anonymous. 2004. Splitting up the roles of CEO and Chairman: Reform or red herring? *Knowledge@Wharton.* June 2: np; and Kim, J. 2010. Shareholders reject split of CEO and chairman jobs at JPMorgan. *FierceFinance.com.* May 18: np.

103. Tuggle, C. S., Sirmon, D. G., Reutzel, C. R. & Bierman, L. 2010. Commanding board of director attention: Investigating how organizational performance and CEO duality affect board members' attention to monitoring. *Strategic Management Journal.* 31: 946–968; Weinberg, N. 2010. No more lapdogs. *Forbes.* May 10: 34–36; and Anonymous. 2010. Corporate constitutions. *The Economist.* October 30: 74.

104. Such opportunistic behavior is common in all principal-agent relationships. For a description of agency problems, especially in the context of the relationship between shareholders and managers, see Jensen, M. C. & Meckling, W. H. 1976. Theory of the firm: Managerial behavior, agency costs, and ownership structure. *Journal of Financial Economics,* 3: 305–360.

105. Hoskisson, R. E. & Turk, T. A. 1990. Corporate restructuring: Governance and control limits of the internal market. *Academy of Management Review,* 15: 459–477.

106. For an insightful perspective on the market for corporate control and how it is influenced by knowledge intensity, see Coff, R. 2003. Bidding wars over R&D-intensive firms: Knowledge, opportunism, and the market for corporate control. *Academy of Management Journal,* 46(1): 74–85.

107. Walsh, J. P. & Kosnik, R. D. 1993. Corporate raiders and their disciplinary role in the market for corporate control. *Academy of Management Journal,* 36: 671–700.

108. Gunning for KPMG. 2003. *Economist,* February 1: 63.

109. Timmons, H. 2003. Investment banks: Who will foot their bill? *BusinessWeek,* March 3: 116.

110. The role of regulatory bodies in the banking industry is addressed in: Bhide, A. 2009. Why bankers got so reckless. *BusinessWeek,* February 9: 30–31.

111. Wishy-washy: The SEC pulls its punches on corporate-governance rules. 2003. *Economist,* February 1: 60.

112. McLean, B. 2001. Is Enron overpriced? *Fortune,* March 5: 122–125.

113. Swartz, J. 2010. Timberland's CEO on standing up to 65,000 angry activists. *Harvard Business Review,* 88 (9): 39–43.

114. Bernstein, A. 2000. Too much corporate power. *BusinessWeek,* September 11: 35–37.

115. This section draws upon Young, M. N., Peng, M. W., Ahlstrom, D., Bruton, G. D., & Jiang, Y. 2005. Principal–principal conflicts in corporate governance (un-published manuscript); and, Peng, M. W. 2006. *Globalstrategy.* Cincinnati: Thomson South-Western. We appreciate the helpful comments of Mike Young of Hong Kong Baptist University and Mike Peng of the University of Texas at Dallas.

116. Khanna, T. & Rivkin, J. 2001. Estimating the performance effects of business groups in emerging markets. *Strategic Management Journal,* 22: 45–74.

appendix

CASE 2

Whole Foods Market in 2010: Vision, Core Values, and Strategy

Arthur A. Thompson
The University of Alabama

ounded in 1980, Whole Foods Market had evolved from a local supermarket for natural and health foods in Austin, Texas, into the world's largest chain of natural and organic foods supermarkets. The company had 2009 sales revenues of $8 billion and, in early 2010, had 289 stores in the United States, Canada, and Great Britain. Over the course of its 30-year history, Whole Foods Market had emerged as a leader in the natural and organic foods movement across the United States, helping the industry gain acceptance among growing numbers of consumers concerned about the food they ate. The company sought to offer the highest quality, least processed, most flavorful naturally preserved and fresh foods available, and it marketed them in appealing store environments that made shopping at Whole Foods interesting and enjoyable. John Mackey, the company's cofounder and CEO, believed that marketing high-quality natural and organic foods to more and more customers in more and more communities would gradually transform the diets of individuals in a manner that would help them live longer, healthier, more pleasurable lives.

Mackey's vision was for Whole Foods to become an international brand synonymous with carrying the highest quality natural and organic foods available and being the best food retailer in every community in which Whole Foods stores were located. He wanted Whole Foods Market to set the standard for excellence in food retailing. But the company's mission—summarized in the slogan "Whole Foods, Whole People, Whole Planet"—extended well beyond food retailing (see Exhibit 1). Mackey was convinced that Whole

Foods' rapid growth and market success had much to do with its having "remained a uniquely mission-driven company—highly selective about what we sell, dedicated to our core values and stringent quality standards, and committed to sustainable agriculture."

While Mackey's growth objectives for Whole Foods had been to have 400 stores and sales of $12 billion by the end of fiscal year 2010, the economic downturn in the United States that accelerated swiftly in 2008 hit Whole Foods hard and forced a number of strategy changes in 2008–2009.

THE NATURAL AND ORGANIC FOODS INDUSTRY

Foods labeled "natural" and "organic" generated estimated retail sales across North America of $30 to $35 billion in 2009. *Natural foods* are defined as foods that are (1) minimally processed; (2) largely or completely free of artificial ingredients, preservatives, and other non–naturally occurring chemicals; and (3) as near to their whole, natural state as possible. The U.S. Department of Agriculture's Food and Safety Inspection Service defines *natural food* as "a product containing no artificial ingredient or added color and that is minimally processed." Organic foods were a special subset of the natural foods category and, to earn the label "organic," had to be grown and processed without the use of pesticides, antibiotics,

Exhibit 1 **Whole Foods' Mission: Whole Foods, Whole People, Whole Planet**

Whole Foods

We obtain our products locally and from all over the world, often from small, uniquely dedicated food artisans. We strive to offer the highest quality, least processed, most flavorful and naturally preserved foods. We believe that food in its purest state, unadulterated by artificial additives, sweeteners, colorings and preservatives, is the best tasting and most nutritious food available.

Whole People

We recruit the best people we can to become part of our team. We empower them to make many operational decisions, creating a respectful workplace where team members are treated fairly and are highly motivated to succeed. We look for team members who are passionate about food, but also well-rounded human beings who can play a critical role in helping to build our Company into a profitable and beneficial part of every community we serve.

Whole Planet

We believe companies, like individuals, must assume their share of responsibility for our planet. We actively support organic farming on a global basis because we believe it is the best method for promoting sustainable agriculture and protecting the environment and farm workers. We also assist our global neighbors through our Whole Planet Foundation's microlending operations. On a local basis, we are actively involved in our communities by supporting food banks, sponsoring neighborhood events, and contributing at least 5% of our after-tax profits in the form of cash or products to not-for-profit organizations.

Source: Whole Foods, 2009 10-K report, p. 5.

hormones, synthetic chemicals, artificial fertilizers, preservatives, dyes or additives, or genetic engineering. Organic foods included fresh fruits and vegetables, meats, and processed foods that had been produced using:

1. Agricultural management practices that promoted a healthy and renewable ecosystem that used no genetically engineered seeds or crops; petroleum-based fertilizers; fertilizers made from sewage sludge; or long-lasting pesticides, herbicides, or fungicides.

2. Livestock management practices that involved organically grown feed, fresh air and outdoor access for the animals, and no use of antibiotics or growth hormones.

3. Food-processing practices that protected the integrity of the organic product and disallowed the use of radiation, genetically modified ingredients, or synthetic preservatives.

According to the Nielsen Company's "Healthy Eating Report for 2008," food labeled as "natural" generated $22.3 billion in sales in the United States in 2008, up 10 percent from 2007, and up 37 percent from 2004; UPC-coded organic foods accounted for $4.9 billion in sales, up 16 percent from the year before, and up 132 percent since 2004.[1] A study sponsored by the Organic Trade Association found that U.S. sales of organic food

and nonfood products in 2008 totaled $24.6 billion. *Nutrition Business Journal,* a provider of marketing research data for the nutrition industry, estimated that sales of natural and organic foods in the United States totaled $31 billion in 2009. Organic food sales were said to represent 3.5 percent of total U.S. retail sales of food and beverages and about 1 percent of total retail sales of food and beverages in Canada.[2] Global sales of organic products were estimated to be $52 billion in 2008 and to have grown at a compound rate of 13 percent since 2004.[3]

In 1990, passage of the Organic Food Production Act started the process of establishing national standards for organically grown products in the United States, a movement that included farmers, food activists, conventional food producers, and consumer groups. In October 2002, the U.S. Department of Agriculture (USDA) officially established labeling standards for organic products, overriding both the patchwork of inconsistent state regulations for what could be labeled as organic and the different rules of some 43 agencies for certifying organic products. The new USDA regulations established four categories of food with organic ingredients, with varying levels of organic purity:

1. *100 percent organic products:* Such products were usually whole foods, such as fresh

fruits and vegetables, grown by organic methods—which meant that the product had been grown without the use of synthetic pesticides or sewage-based fertilizers; had not been subjected to irradiation; and had not been genetically modified or injected with bioengineered organisms, growth hormones, or antibiotics. Products that were 100 percent organic could carry the green USDA organic certification seal, provided the merchant could document that the food product had been organically grown (usually by a certified organic producer).

2. *Organic products:* Such products, often processed, had to have at least 95 percent organically certified ingredients. These could also carry the green USDA organic certification seal.

3. *Made with organic ingredients:* Such products had to have at least 70 percent organic ingredients; they could be labeled "made with organic ingredients" but could not display the USDA seal.

4. *All other products with organic ingredients:* Products with less than 70 percent organic ingredients could not use the word *organic* on the front of a package, but organic ingredients could be listed among other ingredients in a less prominent part of the package.

The USDA's labeling standards were intended to enable shoppers who were ingredient-conscious or wanted to buy pesticide-free food or support sustainable agricultural practices to evaluate product labels where the word *organic* appeared. The standards were not meant to imply anything about the health or safety of organic products (because there was no credible scientific evidence that organic products were more nutritious or safer to eat than conventionally grown products). The USDA also issued regulations requiring documentation on the part of growers, processors, exporters, importers, shippers, and merchants to verify that they were certified to grow, process, or handle organic products carrying the USDA's organic seal. In 2003, Whole Foods was designated as the first national "Certified Organic" grocer by Quality Assurance International, a federally recognized, independent third-party certification organization.

Major food-processing companies like Kraft, General Mills, Groupe Danone (the parent of yogurt-maker Dannon), Dean Foods, and Kellogg had all purchased organic food producers in an effort to capitalize on growing consumer interest in organic foods. Heinz had introduced an organic ketchup and bought a 19 percent stake in Hain Celestial Group, one of the largest organic and natural foods producers. Campbell Soup had introduced organic tomato juice. Starbucks, Green Mountain Coffee Roasters, and several other premium coffee marketers were marketing organically grown coffees; Coca-Cola's Odwalla juices were organic; Del Monte and Hunt's were marketing organic canned tomatoes; and Tyson Foods and several other chicken producers had introduced organic chicken products. Producers of organically grown beef were selling all they could produce; in 2009, the market share of natural/organic beef was about 2.7 percent based on dollars and 1.8 percent based on volume.[4]

According to the most recent data from the USDA, there were 4.1 million acres of organic farmland in the United States (about 1.7 million acres of cropland and 2.4 million acres of rangeland and pasture) in 2005, up from a total of 2.1 million acres in 2001.[5] There were approximately 13,000 certified organic producers in the United States in 2007, and perhaps another 9,000 small farmers growing organic products. All 50 states had some certified organic farmland, with California, North Dakota, Montana, Minnesota, Wisconsin, Texas, and Idaho having the largest amount of certified organic cropland.

While less than 1 percent of U.S. farmland was certified organic in 2005, farmers were becoming increasingly interested in and attracted to organic farming, chiefly because of the substantially higher prices they could get for organically grown fruits, vegetables, and meats. Since 2005, health-conscious chefs at many fine restaurants had begun sourcing ingredients for their dishes from local organic farmers and touting the use of organically grown products on their menus. Growing restaurant use of organically grown herbs, vegetables, and fruits, as well as organic cheeses and meats, was spurring the growth of organic farming (since supplying local restaurants gave organic producers a ready market for their crops).

RETAILING OF ORGANIC FOODS

Organic foods and beverages were available in nearly every food category in 2010 and were available in more than 80 percent of U.S. retail food stores. Close to 70 percent of overall organic sales in 2009 were through mainstream supermarkets/ grocery stores and leading organic and natural food supermarket chains such as Whole Foods, Trader Joe's, and Fresh Market. Roughly 20 percent of organic sales were through small, independent chain natural grocery stores.

In recent years, mainstream supermarkets had gradually expanded their offerings of natural and organic products for two reasons. One was that mounting consumer enthusiasm for organic products allowed retailers to earn attractively high profit margins on organics (compared with other grocery items, where intense price competition among rival supermarket chains on general food products limited profit margins). The other was that consumer demand for organics was growing at double-digit rates (compared with growth rates of only 2–3 percent for traditional grocery products). Several factors had combined to transform organic foods retailing, once a niche market, into the fastest-growing segment of U.S. food sales:

- A "wellness," or health-consciousness, trend among people of many ages and ethnic groups.
- Heightened awareness of the role that food, nutrition, and good eating patterns played in long-term health. Among those most interested in organic products were aging, affluent people concerned about their health.
- Increasing consumer concerns over the purity and safety of food due to the presence of pesticide residues, growth hormones, artificial ingredients and other chemicals, and genetically engineered ingredients.
- Growing belief that organic farming had positive environmental effects, particularly in contributing to healthier soil and water conditions and to sustainable agricultural practices.

Organic food products were anywhere from to 10 to 40 percent more expensive than non-organic foods, chiefly because of higher production, distribution, and marketing costs for organic products.

Such higher prices were the primary barrier for most consumers in trying or using organic products.

By 2010, most supermarket chains stocked a selection of natural and organic food items— including fresh produce, canned and frozen fruits and vegetables, milk, cheeses, yogurt, vinegars, salad dressings, cereals, pastas, and meats—and the number and variety of organic items on supermarket shelves was growing. Fresh fruits and vegetables accounted for close to 40 percent of total organic food sales, with organic lettuce, spinach, broccoli, cauliflower, celery, carrots, and apples among the biggest sellers. Meat, dairy, bread and grains, and snack foods were among the fastest-growing organic product categories.

Leading supermarket chains like Walmart, Kroger, Publix, Safeway, and Supervalu/Save-a-Lot had created special "organic and health food" sections for nonperishable natural foods and organics in most of their stores. Kroger, Publix, and several other chains also had special sections for fresh organic fruits and vegetables in their produce cases in most all of their stores. Walmart, Target, Safeway, Publix, and Kroger were stocking organic beef and chicken in many of their stores. Whole Foods was struggling to find organic beef and chicken suppliers that were big enough to supply all its stores. Two chains— upscale Harris Teeter in the southeastern United States and Whole Foods Market—had launched their own private-label brands of organics. Exhibit 2 shows the leading supermarket retailers in North America in 2009. Whole Foods Market was ranked 21st in 2009, up from 26th in 2004.

WHOLE FOODS MARKET

Whole Foods Market was founded in Austin, Texas, when John Mackey, the current CEO, and two other local natural foods grocers in Austin decided the natural foods industry was ready for a supermarket format. The original Whole Foods Market opened in 1980 with a staff of only 19. It was an immediate success. At the time, there were less than half a dozen natural foods supermarkets in the United States. By 1991, the company had 10 stores, revenues of $92.5 million, and net income of $1.6 million; over the next 18 years, sales grew at a compound annual rate of approximately 28 percent, to just over $8 billion. Whole Foods

Exhibit 2   **Leading North American Supermarket Chains, 2009**

Rank/Company	Number of Stores	2009 Estimated Sales of Food and Grocery Products in North America (in billions)	Estimated Share of Total Grocery Sales in North America ($894 billion)
1. Walmart	2,751	$125.3[a]	14.0%
2. Kroger	2,477	77.2[b]	8.6
3. Supervalu	2,491	45.0[c]	5.0
4. Safeway	1,743	44.8	5.0
5. Costco	527	39.1[d]	4.4
6. Loblaw[f]	1,036	31.5	3.5
7. Sam's Club	599	25.7[e]	2.9
8. Publix Supermarkets	990	24.0	2.7
9. Ahold USA[g]	704	21.8	2.4
10. Delhaize America[h]	1,544	19.2	2.1
11. Whole Foods Market	284	8.0	0.9

[a] Sales revenue numbers are an estimate of sales of food, grocery, and supermarket-related items only for all Walmart Discount Stores and Supercenters in the United States; such sales represented about 49 percent of total sales at these stores.

[b] The sales revenue number for Kroger includes sales at all of the company's retail outlets (including fuel centers, drugstores, apparel, and jewelry), not just those at its several supermarket chains (Kroger, City Market, King Sooper, Ralph's, and 11 other small chains).

[c] Sales data for Supervalu include 1,279 conventional supermarkets (including stores recently acquired from Albertson's), 317 corporate-owned Save-A-Lots, 863 licensed Save-A-Lots, and 32 licensed Cub Foods stores.

[d] The sales revenue number for Costco includes only the sales of grocery and supermarket-related items (food, sundries, fresh produce) rather than sales of all products sold at Costco stores.

[e] The sales number for Sam's Club includes only those items related to food and sundries (snack foods, tobacco, alcoholic and nonalcoholic beverages, paper goods, laundry and home care, and other consumables) but is for all Sam's Club stores worldwide; food and sundries items accounted for 67% of total sales of approximately $46.7 billion at all Sam's Club locations worldwide in 2009.

[f] Loblaw is a Canadian chain that operates 628 corporate stores and supplies 408 franchised stores. The sales revenue numbers are in U.S. dollars.

[g] Ahold USA, the U.S. division of Netherlands-based Ahold, includes 376 Stop & Shops, 180 Giant Foods (Landover, Md.), and 148 Giant Foods (Carlisle, Pa.).

[h] Delhaize includes 1,148 Food Lion stores, 167 Hannaford Bros. stores, 108 Sweetbay Supermarkets, 69 Harvey's stores, 61 Bloom units, and 18 Bottom Dollar Food stores.

Source: Wal-Mart's 2009 10-K report, Costco's 2009 10-K report, and Top 75 North American Food Retailers, www.supermarketnews.com, accessed March 29, 2010.

became a public company in 1992, with its stock trading on the NASDAQ. As of March 2010, Whole Foods operated 278 stores in 38 U.S. states and the District of Columbia, 6 stores in Canada, and 5 in Great Britain. Just over 97 percent of Whole Foods' sales were in the United States. Its stores averaged approximately 37,000 square feet in size and $29 million in sales annually.

Core Values

In 1997, when Whole Foods developed the "Whole Foods, Whole People, Whole Planet" slogan to symbolize its mission, John Mackey, known as a

go-getter with a "cowboy way of doing things," said:

This slogan taps into perhaps the deepest purpose of Whole Foods Market. It's a purpose we seldom talk about because it seems pretentious, but a purpose nevertheless felt by many of our team members and by many of our customers (and hopefully many of our shareholders too). Our deepest purpose as an organization is helping support the health, well-being, and healing of both people (customers and Team Members) and of the planet (sustainable agriculture, organic production and environmental sensitivity). When I peel away the onion of my personal consciousness down to its core in trying to understand what has driven me to create and grow this company, I come to my desire to promote the general well-being of everyone on earth as well as the earth itself. This is my personal greater purpose with the company and the slogan perfectly reflects it.

Complementing the "Whole Foods, Whole People, Whole Planet" mission was a statement of seven core values that governed how the company endeavored to conduct its business (see Exhibit 3).

Whole Foods' managers and, just as important, employees (referred to as team members) took pride in "walking the talk" when it came to the seven core values. The prevailing philosophy at Whole Foods was that the company's success and long-term profitability depended on its ability to simultaneously satisfy the needs and desires of its customers, team members, investors, and suppliers, while also demonstrating a genuine concern for the communities in which it operated and the environment.

Exhibit 3   Whole Foods Market's Seven Core Values

Our Core Values

The following list of core values reflects what is truly important to us as an organization. These are not values that change from time to time, situation to situation or person to person, but rather they are the underpinning of our company culture. Many people feel Whole Foods is an exciting company of which to be a part and a very special place to work. These core values are the primary reasons for this feeling, and they transcend our size and our growth rate. By maintaining these core values, regardless of how large a company Whole Foods becomes, we can preserve what has always been special about our company. These core values are the soul of our company.

1. **Selling the Highest Quality Natural and Organic Products Available**
   - **Passion for Food**—We appreciate and celebrate the difference natural and organic products can make in the quality of one's life.
   - **Quality Standards**—We have high standards and our goal is to sell the highest quality products we possibly can. We define quality by evaluating the ingredients, freshness, safety, taste, nutritive value and appearance of all of the products we carry. We are buying agents for our customers and not the selling agents for the manufacturers.

2. **Satisfying and Delighting Our Customers**
   - **Our Customers**—They are our most important stakeholders in our business and the lifeblood of our business. Only by satisfying our customers first do we have the opportunity to satisfy the needs of our other stakeholders.
   - **Extraordinary Customer Service**—We go to extraordinary lengths to satisfy and delight our customers. We want to meet or exceed their expectations on every shopping trip. We know that by doing so we turn customers into advocates for our business. Advocates do more than shop with us, they talk about Whole Foods to their friends and others. We want to serve our customers competently, efficiently, knowledgeably and with flair.
   - **Education**—We can generate greater appreciation and loyalty from all of our stakeholders by educating them about natural and organic foods, health, nutrition and the environment.
   - **Meaningful Value**—We offer value to our customers by providing them with high quality products, extraordinary service and a competitive price. We are constantly challenged to improve the value proposition to our customers.
   - **Retail Innovation**—We value retail experiments. Friendly competition within the company helps us to continually improve our stores. We constantly innovate and raise our retail standards and are not afraid to try new ideas and concepts.
   - **Inviting Store Environments**—We create store environments that are inviting and fun, and reflect the communities they serve. We want our stores to become community meeting places where our customers meet their friends and make new ones.

3. **Team Member Happiness and Excellence**
   - **Empowering Work Environments**—Our success is dependent upon the collective energy and intelligence of all of our Team Members. We strive to create a work environment where motivated Team Members can flourish and succeed to their highest potential. We appreciate effort and reward results.
   - **Self-Responsibility**—We take responsibility for our own success and failures. We celebrate success and see failures as opportunities for growth. We recognize that we are responsible for our own happiness and success.
   - **Self-Directed Teams**—The fundamental work unit of the company is the self-directed Team. Teams meet regularly to discuss issues, solve problems and appreciate each others' contributions. Every Team Member belongs to a Team.

(Continued)

Our Core Values

- **Open & Timely Information**—We believe knowledge is power and we support our Team Members' right to access information that impacts their jobs. Our books are open to our Team Members, including our annual individual compensation report. We also recognize everyone's right to be listened to and heard regardless of their point of view.

- **Incremental Progress**—Our company continually improves through unleashing the collective creativity and intelligence of all of our Team Members. We recognize that everyone has a contribution to make. We keep getting better at what we do.

- **Shared Fate**—We recognize there is a community of interest among all of our stakeholders. There are no entitlements; we share together in our collective fate. To that end we have a salary cap that limits the compensation (wages plus profit incentive bonuses) of any Team Member to nineteen times the average total compensation of all full-time Team Members in the company.

4. Creating Wealth Through Profits & Growth

- **Stewardship**—We are stewards of our shareholders' investments and we take that responsibility very seriously. We are committed to increasing long term shareholder value.

- **Profits**—We earn our profits every day through voluntary exchange with our customers. We recognize that profits are essential to creating capital for growth, prosperity, opportunity, job satisfaction and job security.

5. Caring About Our Communities & Our Environment

- **Sustainable Agriculture**—We support organic farmers, growers and the environment through our commitment to sustainable agriculture and by expanding the market for organic products.

- **Wise Environmental Practices**—We respect our environment and recycle, reuse, and reduce our waste wherever and whenever we can.

- **Community Citizenship**—We recognize our responsibility to be active participants in our local communities. We give a minimum of 5% of our profits every year to a wide variety of community and non-profit organizations.

- **Integrity in All Business Dealings**—Our trade partners are our allies in serving our stakeholders. We treat them with respect, fairness and integrity at all times and expect the same in return.

6. Creating Ongoing Win-Win Partnerships With Our Suppliers

- **Integrity in All Business Dealings**—Our supplier partners are our allies in serving the interests of our other stakeholders in bringing to market the safest highest quality products available. We treat them with respect, fairness and integrity at all times and expect the same in return. We seek supplier partnerships that share our concern for social responsibility and the environment.

- **Honesty and Communication**—We are committed to honesty, timeliness and clarity in communicating with our suppliers and we expect the same in return.

- **Transparency**—We seek to create transparency from "farm to fork" with respect to production, planning, sourcing, ingredients, product safety and efficacy in order to bring to market the safest highest quality products available. We work with our supplier partners in eliminating all unnecessary production and distribution costs to help ensure the best possible price.

- **Education**—We partner with our suppliers to educate, inspire and communicate the outstanding quality and benefits of our products to promote a lifestyle of health, balance and well-being.

- **Innovation/Differentiation**—We foster supplier partnerships that enable us to remain at the forefront of the retail food industry, by creating new, unique and innovative products.

7. Promoting the health of our stakeholders through healthy eating education

These core values speak to our belief in a balanced way of doing business. They very succinctly express the purpose of our business, which is not only to make profits, but to create value for all of our major stakeholders—our customers, team members, suppliers, investors, and the community and environment. All are linked interdependently.

Source: Whole Foods Market, www.wholefoodsmarket.com, accessed March 11, 2010.

Growth Strategy

Since going public in 1991, Whole Foods had maintained a growth strategy of expanding via a combination of opening its own new stores and acquiring small, owner-managed chains that had capable personnel and were located in desirable markets—the company's most significant acquisitions are shown in Exhibit 4. But attractive acquisition candidates were hard to find because

Exhibit 4   Major Acquisitions by Whole Foods Market, 1992–2009

Year	Company Acquired	Location	Number of Stores	Acquisition Costs
1992	Bread & Circus	U.S. Northeast	6	$20 million plus $6.2 million in common stock
1993	Mrs. Gooch's	Southern California	7	2,970,596 shares of common stock
1996	Fresh Fields Markets	East Coast and Chicago area	22	4.8 million shares of stock plus options for 549,000 additional shares
1997	Merchant of Vino	Detroit area	6	Approximately 1 million shares of common stock
1997	Bread of Life	South Florida	2	200,000 shares of common stock
1999	Nature's Heartland	Boston area	4	$24.5 million in cash
2000	Food for Thought (Natural Abilities, Inc)	Sonoma County, California	3	$25.7 million in cash, plus assumption of certain liabilities
2001	Harry's Farmer's Market	Atlanta	3	Approximately $35 million in cash
2004	Fresh & Wild	Great Britain	7	$20 million in cash plus 239,000 shares of common stock
2007	Wild Oats Natural Marketplace	United States and Canada	74 (after sale of 35 stores)	$565 million plus the assumption of $137 million in debt; however, Whole Foods received approximately $166 million for the 35 stores that were subsequently sold (out of the total of 109 stores that were acquired)

Source: Investor relations section of www.wholefoodsmarket.com, accessed November 18, 2004, and March 21, 2008.

most retailers of natural and organic foods were one-store operations or small, regional chains having stores in the 5,000- to 20,000-square-foot range. Starting in 2002, Whole Food's management decided to drive growth by opening 10 to 15 decidedly bigger stores in metropolitan areas each year—stores that ranged from 40,000 square feet to as much as 80,000 square feet and were on the same scale or larger than the conventional supermarkets operated by Kroger, Safeway, Publix, and other chains.

Then, in 2007, Whole Foods began what proved to be a largely successful, but contentious, two-and-a-half-year battle to purchase the struggling Wild Oats Market—Whole Foods' biggest competitor in natural and organic foods—for an acquisition price of $700 million. Wild Oats operated 109 older and smaller stores (averaging 24,000 square feet in size) in 23 states under the Wild Oats Market, Henry's Farmer's Market, and Sun Harvest brands and had total annual sales of about $1.2 billion. The Federal Trade Commission (FTC) opposed the acquisition on the grounds that competition in the organic foods retailing segment would be weakened; however, a U.S. district court ruled that the FTC's position lacked merit. When the district court's ruling was upheld on appeal, Whole Foods went forward and completed its acquisition of Wild Oats in late August 2007. Acquiring Wild Oats gave Whole Foods entry into 5 new states and 14 new metropolitan markets. Whole Foods then quickly sold 35 Henry's and Sun Harvest stores in California and Texas previously acquired by Wild

Oats, along with a California distribution center, to Los Angeles food retailer Smart & Final, realizing approximately $165 million from the sale and reducing its net purchase price for Wild Oats Market to about $535 million (which included the assumption of $148 million in Wild Oats' debt).[6] In addition, Whole Foods immediately closed nine Wild Oats stores that did not fit with its brand strategy or real estate strategy and began planning to relocate seven smaller Wild Oats stores to existing or soon-to-be-opened Whole Foods locations. In fiscal 2008, Whole Foods launched a program to spend close to $45 million renovating Wild Oats stores and rebranding them as Whole Foods stores.

Then, in a surprising move in July 2008, the U.S. Court of Appeals for the District of Columbia reversed the lower court's order allowing Whole Foods to acquire Wild Oats and directed the U.S. district court to reopen proceedings for further evidentiary hearings. Separately, the FTC reopened its administrative actions challenging the acquisition on antitrust grounds. To resolve the dispute, the FTC and Whole Foods entered into a consent agreement in March 2009 whereby Whole Foods would sell:

- Twelve of the former Wild Oats stores it was currently operating and one Whole Foods store.
- The leases and related fixed assets for 19 former Wild Oats stores (10 of which were closed by Wild Oats prior to the acquisition and 9 of which were closed by Whole Foods Market).
- Wild Oats trademarks and other intellectual property associated with the Wild Oats stores.

The divestiture period was later extended until 2010 to allow for the finalization of good-faith offers for 6 of the 13 operating stores and 2 of the closed stores, as well as Wild Oats' trademark and intellectual property; Whole Foods was allowed to keep the 7 remaining operating stores without further obligation to attempt to divest them. In 2010, there were 51 former Wild Oats stores operating under the Whole Foods name. In his "Letter to Stakeholders" in the company's 2009 annual report, John Mackey expressed confidence that sales and profits at these stores would continue to improve in coming years, enabling the company to realize a solid return for shareholders on

the Wild Oats acquisition. However, management stated that, going forward, Whole Foods' growth strategy would be based primarily on opening new stores rather than on making acquisitions.[7]

Store Location Strategy

In March 2010, Whole Foods had 290 stores in 38 states; it planned to open an additional 9 stores by the end of fiscal year 2010, 17 new stores in fiscal year 2011, and 17 new stores in fiscal 2012 (Whole Foods' fiscal year ended the last Sunday in September). Whole Foods favored store locations in the upscale areas of urban metropolitan areas. Most stores were in high-traffic shopping locations on premier real estate sites; some were freestanding, some were in strip centers; and some were in high-density mixed-use projects. The company's "sweet spot" for most markets it had entered during 2001–2009 was a store footprint between 45,000 and 60,000 square feet (the new stores of supermarket chains like Safeway and Kroger averaged around 55,000 square feet). All told, in 2010, Whole Foods had more than 90 stores that were 40,000 square feet or larger—the biggest was a 99,800-square-foot store in London, England. Whole Foods had the two largest supermarkets in New York City: a 58,000-square-foot store on Columbus Circle in Manhattan and a 71,000-square-foot store in the Bowery area. Whole Foods had a 74,500-square-foot store in Columbus, Ohio; a flagship 78,000-square-foot store in Austin, Texas; a 77,000-square-foot store in Pasadena, California; a 75,000-square-foot store in Chicago; and two 75,000-square-foot stores in the suburbs of Atlanta, Georgia. It had more than 13 stores in excess of 65,000 square feet and an additional 4 of that size in development.

But the economic slowdown that began in 2007 and then quickly accelerated into a deep recession in 2008–2009 forced a major overhaul of Whole Foods' store expansion strategy. In November 2007, when Whole Foods had 87 new stores in varying stages of development, the company announced it was scaling back its store expansion program. The leases for 14 of the new stores were downsized by an average of 12,000 square feet each, and planned openings of some stores were delayed, prompting a reduction in the gross square footage of stores in development from 4.5 million in November 2007 to 3.3 million in November 2008 and 2.4 million in 2009. Then in 2008–2009, when the recession in the United States hit full force, management terminated 18 leases for stores in development and downsized others, determining that planned store openings during 2010–2012 would be reduced and that the majority of its new stores would be in the range of 35,000–50,000 square feet. The leases that Whole Foods had for its 51 stores in varying stages of development (some of which were for relocations of existing stores) in February 2010 averaged about 44,000 square feet (down from an average of 56,000 square feet for the 88 stores in development in November 2006). In addition, the construction and store development teams for Whole Foods' new stores adopted a leaner and more disciplined approach to design and building, including plans for smaller stores with simpler decor and smaller, less labor-intensive perishable departments; these moves were expected to result in lower costs on both a per-store and per-square-foot basis. Exhibit 5 provides store-related statistics.

Exhibit 5   Number of Stores in the Whole Foods Markets Chain, 1991–2007, and Selected Store Operating Statistics, 2000–2007

Year	Number of Stores at End of Fiscal Year	Year	Number of Stores End of Fiscal Year
1991	10	2001	126
1992	25	2002	135
1993	42	2003	145
1994	49	2004	163
1995	61	2005	175
1996	68	2006	186
1997	75	2007	276
1998	87	2008	275
1999	100	2009	284
2000	117	Jan. 2010	289

	Fiscal Years Ending the Last Sunday in September					
	2000	**2005**	**2006**	**2007**	**2008**	**2009**
Store sales (000s)	$1,838,630	$4,701,289	$5,607,376	$6,591,773	$7,953,912	$ 8,031,620
Average weekly sales	$ 324,710	$ 536,986	$ 593,439	$ 616,706	$ 570,000	$ 549,000
Comparable store sales growth*	8.6%	12.8%	11.0%	7.1%	4.9%	−3.1%
Total square footage of all stores, end of year	3,180,000	5,820,000	6,377,000	9,312,000	9,895,000	10,566,000
Average store size, end of year, in square feet	27,000	33,000	34,000	34,000	36,000	37,000
Gross margin, all-store average	34.5%	34.6%	34.2%	35.1%	34.9%	34.8%
Store contribution, all-store average**	9.4%	9.6%	9.3%	9.6%	9.6%	8.9%

* Defined as average annual sales increases at stores open a full year or more; represents the rate at which sales at existing stores are increasing annually on average.

** Defined as gross profit minus direct store expenses, where gross profit equals store revenues less cost of goods sold.

Sources: Whole Foods Market's 2005 10-K report and 2009 10-K report. Investor relations section of www.wholefoodsmarket.com, accessed November 18, 2004, and March 21, 2008.

The cash investment needed to get a new Whole Foods Market site ready for opening varied with the metropolitan area, store size, amount of work performed by the landlord, and the complexity of site development issues—the average capital cost for new stores was projected to be about $8 million in 2010–2012 (in 2007, capital costs averaged $15.1 million per new store).[8] In addition to the capital cost of a new store, it took about $850,000 to stock a store with inventory, a portion of which was financed by vendors. Pre-opening expenses (including rent) averaged $3 million for the 15 new stores opened or relocated in fiscal 2009.

Whole Foods had its own internally developed model to analyze potential markets according to education levels, population density, and income within certain drive times. After picking a target metropolitan area, the company's store development group did a comprehensive site study and developed sales and profit projections for several potential locations; before entering into a lease for a site, the projections had to pass specified profitability hurdles over and above a return on the capital invested in a store. During the 2007–2009 period, because of both the uncertain economic environment and internally constrained cash flows, Whole Foods' management instituted lease approval requirements for new store sites that entailed conservative sales projections and the expectation of a cumulative profit in five years or less (after deducting a return on Whole Foods' cash investment in the store). New stores opened 12 to 24 months after a lease was signed.

Product Line Strategy

Because Whole Foods stores were different sizes and had different shopper clienteles, the product and brand selections varied from 20,000 items in small stores to 50,000 items in the largest stores. Whole Foods' product line included natural, organic, and gourmet food and nonfood items in the following principal categories:

- Fresh produce—fruits; vegetables; displays of fresh-cut fruits; and a selection of seasonal, exotic, and specialty products like cactus pears, cippolini onions, and Japanese eggplant.
- Meat and poultry—natural and organic meats, house-made sausages, turkey, and chicken products from animals raised on wholesome grains, pastureland, and well water (and not grown with the use of by-products, hormones, or steroids).
- Fresh seafoods, some wild-caught and some farmed using safe and environmentally responsible practices. A portion of the fresh fish selections came from the company's four seafood processing and distribution facilities (Pigeon Cove, Select Fish, South Seafood, and Mid-Atlantic Seafood). Seafood items coming from distant supply sources were flown in to stores to ensure maximum freshness.
- A selection of daily baked goods—breads, cakes, pies, cookies, bagels, muffins, and scones.
- Prepared foods—soups, packaged salads and sandwiches, oven-ready meals, rotisserie meats, hearth-fired pizza, pastas, salad bars, a sandwich station, and a selection of entrées and side foods prepared daily.
- Fine-quality cheeses, olives (up to 40 varieties in some stores), chocolates, and confections.
- Frozen foods, juices, yogurt and dairy products, smoothies, and bottled waters.
- A wide selection of dried fruits, nuts, and spices (either prepackaged or dispensed from bins).
- Beer and wines.
- Coffees and teas. The company's Allegro coffee subsidiary supplied all stores with specialty and organic coffees that spanned the roasting spectrum from light to extra-dark roast. The tea selections included only fine and exotic teas from all the major tea-growing regions of the world.
- Grocery and household products—canned and packaged goods, pastas, soaps, cleaning products, and other conventional household items that helped make Whole Foods' larger stores a one-stop grocery shopping destination where people could get everything on their shopping list.
- A body care and nutrition department with natural and organic body care and cosmetics products, vitamin supplements, homeopathic remedies, and aromatherapy products. All items entailed the use of non-animal testing methods and contained no artificial ingredients.

- A family of private-label offerings led by its "365 Everyday Value" and "365 Organic" brands that spanned many product categories and were less expensive than comparable name brands. Whole Foods had also created private-label branding with consistent logos and packaging for specific departments and product categories (examples included "Whole Body" for personal care and nutrition products; "Whole Baby" for baby foods and baby care products; "Whole Pantry" for herbs, spices, and condiments; and "Whole Catch" for prepackaged fresh and frozen seafood items). In addition, Whole Foods had a grouping of "exclusive" and "control brand" products that outside suppliers produced and packaged exclusively for sale in Whole Foods stores. Altogether, Whole Foods' private-label lineup included 2,400 individual stock-keeping units (SKUs).

- Natural and organic pet foods (including the company's own private-label line), treats, toys, and pest control remedies.

- A floral department with sophisticated flower bouquets and a selection of plants for inside and outside the home.

- Educational materials and books related to healthy eating, cooking, healing and alternative healthcare, and lifestyle.

Whole Foods was the world's biggest seller of organic produce. Prepared foods, fresh produce, and fresh meats and seafood accounted for about 67 percent of Whole Foods' sales in 2007–2009, considerably higher than the 40–50 percent that such perishables represented at conventional supermarkets. The 2001 acquisition of the Harry's Market superstores in Atlanta, where 75 percent of sales were perishables, had provided the company with personnel having valuable intellectual capital in creatively merchandising all major perishables categories. Management believed that the company's emphasis on fresh fruits and vegetables, bakery goods, meats, seafood, and other perishables differentiated Whole Foods stores from other supermarkets and attracted a broader customer base. According to John Mackey:

> First-time visitors to Whole Foods Market are often awed by our perishables. We devote more space to fresh fruits and vegetables, including an extensive selection of organics, than most of our competitors. Our meat and poultry products are natural—no artificial ingredients, minimal processing, and raised without the use of artificial growth hormones, antibiotics or animal by-products in their feed. Our seafood is either wild-caught or sourced from aquaculture farms where environmental concerns are a priority. Also, our seafood is never treated with chlorine or other chemicals, as is common practice in the food retailing industry. With each new store or renovation, we challenge ourselves to create more entertaining, theatrical, and scintillatingly appetizing prepared foods areas. We bake daily, using whole grains and unbleached, unbromated flour and feature European-style loaves, pastries, cookies and cakes as well as gluten-free baked goods for those allergic to wheat. We also offer many vegetarian and vegan products for our customers seeking to avoid all animal products. Our cheeses are free of artificial flavors, colors, and synthetic preservatives, and we offer an outstanding variety of both organic cheeses and cheeses made using traditional methods.[9]

Whole Foods' three-story showcase Union Square store in Manhattan carried locally made New York offerings, seasonal items from the nearby Greenmarket farmer's market, and numerous exotic and gourmet items. A 28-foot international section featured such items as Lebanese fig jam, preserved lemons from Morocco, Indian curries, Thai rice, stuffed grape leaves from Greece, and goulash from Hungary. The prepared foods section had a Grilling Station where shoppers could get grilled-to-order dishes such as swordfish in red pepper Romesco sauce and steak with a mushroom demi-glace.

One of Whole Foods Market's foremost commitments to its customers was to sell foods that met strict standards and that were of high quality in terms of nutrition, freshness, appearance, and taste—Exhibit 6 shows the company's quality standards. Whole Foods guaranteed 100 percent satisfaction on all items purchased and went to great lengths to live up to its core value of satisfying and delighting customers. Buyers personally visited the facilities of many of the company's suppliers and were very picky about the items they chose and the ingredients they contained. For the benefit of prospective food suppliers, the company maintained a list of ingredients it considered unacceptable in food products.

Exhibit 6 Whole Foods Market's Product Quality Standards and Customer Commitments

Our business is to sell the highest quality foods we can find at the most competitive prices possible. We evaluate quality in terms of nutrition, freshness, appearance, and taste. Our search for quality is a never-ending process involving the careful judgment of buyers throughout the company.

- We carefully evaluate each and every product we sell.
- We feature foods that are free of artificial preservatives, colors, flavors, sweeteners, and hydrogenated fats.
- We are passionate about great tasting food and the pleasure of sharing it with others.
- We are committed to foods that are fresh, wholesome and safe to eat.
- We seek out and promote organically grown foods.
- We provide food and nutritional products that support health and well-being.

Whole Foods Market's Quality Standards team maintains an extensive list of unacceptable ingredients (see below). However, creating a product with no unacceptable ingredients does not guarantee that Whole Foods Market will sell it. Our buyers are passionate about seeking out the freshest, most healthful, minimally processed products available. In 2008, there were 81 chemicals on Whole Foods' list of unacceptable ingredients, including artificial colors, artificial flavors, aspartame, bleached flour, cyclamates, hydrogenated fats, irradiated foods, nitrates and nitrites, saccharin, sorbic acid, sucralose, and sulfites (sulfur dioxide).

Source: Whole Foods Market, "Our Quality Standards," www.wholefoodsmarket.com, accessed March 24, 2008, and March 16, 2010.

Pricing Strategy

Whole Foods' strategy was to sell at the most competitive prices possible. While the majority of the company's private-label products and some of its other offerings were "value-priced," prices at Whole Foods were normally higher than at conventional supermarkets. This was in part because the costs of growing, distributing, and marketing organic products were 10 to 40 percent more than those of non-organic items and in part because Whole Foods' strategy was to carry the highest-quality natural and organic foods available. Likewise, the earth-friendly detergents, toilet papers, and other household items that Whole Foods merchandised frequently had higher price tags than did the name brands of comparable products found in traditional supermarkets. The higher prices that Whole Foods charged for many of its products had prompted some media critics to dub the stores "Whole Paycheck," a term that resonated with price-sensitive grocery shoppers who had visited a Whole Foods store. Nonetheless, Whole Foods' clientele was sufficiently enchanted with the company's product offerings and shopping experience that they overlooked the pricing and patronized Whole Foods stores in increasing numbers.

Sales revenues at Whole Foods grew a robust 20 percent annually during 2000–2007. Average weekly sales at Whole Foods stores rose steadily from $324,700 in fiscal 2000 to $616,700 in fiscal 2007, a compound increase of 9.6 percent annually. Observers attributed this to several factors. One grocery industry analyst said, "If people believe that the food is healthier and they are doing something good for themselves, they are willing to invest a bit more, particularly as they get older. It's not a fad."[10] Another analyst noted that while Whole Foods served a growing niche, it had managed to attract a new kind of customer, one who was willing to pay a premium to dabble in health food without being totally committed to vegetarianism or an organic lifestyle.[11] Shopping at Whole Foods was also attractive to food lovers and fine-food connoisseurs who saw food as being about pleasurable taste and indulgence and were willing to pay a premium for what they saw as a high-quality gourmet experience.

However, despite all the attractions of a Whole Foods shopping event, sales growth at Whole Foods stores unexpectedly evaporated when the U.S. economy collapsed in the fall of 2008, a deep recession ensued, and concerned consumers cut back on spending. Average weekly sales at Whole Foods stores dropped from $616,700 in fiscal 2007 to $569,700 in fiscal 2008 and to $549,500 in 2009. Annual sales per square foot of store space fell from $879 in fiscal 2006 to $804 in fiscal 2008 and to $760 in fiscal 2009.[12] The company's 1 percent increase in sales revenues from $7.95 billion in fiscal 2008 to just $8.03 billion in fiscal 2009 was far and away the smallest annual revenue gain since Whole Foods became a public company in 1991. According to John Mackey, "We knew that 2009 was going to be a tough year but did not predict just how challenging the economic environment would be. For the first time in 30 years, we experienced a decline in our comparable store sales."[13] As was the case with the company's store expansion strategy, the great recession of 2008–2009 caused Mackey and other Whole Foods executives to act swiftly and decisively to change the company's strategy to better match the economic climate and allay customer concerns about the higher costs of doing their grocery shopping at Whole Foods.

Among the company's early strategic moves was an aggressive campaign to emphasize the number of value-priced items that were available at Whole Foods, to better communicate to customers how Whole Foods' prices stacked up against those of rivals, and to improve the perception of customers about the value of shopping at Whole Foods—or, as Mackey put it, to "stress our 'value' along with our 'values.'" The new pricing strategy campaign to improve shopper perceptions of Whole Foods regarding value had several elements:

- Drawing upon new pricing research capabilities to monitor the prices of its supermarket rivals, Whole Foods trimmed the prices of items it considered as "key" to boosting the value perceptions of shoppers. Signs were placed on store shelves calling attention to items with price reductions and to hundreds of value-priced items, many of which were at such popular price points as $0.99, $1.09, $1.49, $1.99, and $2.99. In a number of areas (like cheeses and packaged nuts), Whole Foods instituted programs to get deals from suppliers that enabled it to provide better values for customers without sacrificing its gross margins. The goal was to strike the right balance between spurring higher sales and maintaining profit margins.
- To help put good value front and center, the company began using aisle displays with accompanying signage to feature weekly hot deals, everyday-low-priced products, budget-priced cheeses and wines, and

out-of-the-ordinary products with budget prices; formerly, the practice was to use most aisle displays to promote gourmet cheeses, upscale wines, exotic fresh produce, and novel but premium-priced items. In addition, grocery bags at checkout counters had such printed messages as "365 Everyday Value Products. Cut Costs. Not Quality" and "365 Everyday Value Products. Comparison Shopping Strongly Encouraged."

- Stores began featuring new family-sized prepared food selections for $17.99, prepared food items in "sizes for every budget," and family-sized value packs of fruits, vegetables, meats, and chicken.
- An in-store value guide, *The Whole Deal*, was created that contained cents-off coupons, highlighted products with everyday low prices, and offered low-budget recipes and meal-planning advice to help shoppers stretch their food dollars. *The Whole Deal* proved quite popular among customers, prompting the company to increase its printing from 800,000 copies quarterly to 1.3 million copies bimonthly and to begin a *Whole Deal* e-newsletter (which enabled shoppers to see the specials and print out the coupons before they left home). In the months following its introduction, *The Whole Deal* spurred increased redemption rates for the coupons, along with increases in basket size and number of items per basket. Whole Foods had about 500,000 e-newsletter subscribers as of early 2010.
- The company took advantage of opportunity buys offered by suppliers and lower costs in several product categories, including fresh produce and meat, using those to push strong promotions and pass the savings on to customers in the form of lower prices. In-store signs announced "Great Buys" and "More of the good stuff for less than you think!"

In February 2010, Whole Foods' management was pleased with the results of its new pricing strategy and emphasis on value, believing that it had changed the dialogue about Whole Foods prices and improved customer perceptions about the value of doing their grocery shopping at Whole Foods. Sales growth per store for the first quarter of fiscal 2010 was 3.5 percent (versus −4.0

percent in the first quarter of fiscal 2009), and total revenues were up 7.0 percent over the first quarter of fiscal 2009. John Mackey said,

> Early last year, we made the shift from being fairly reactionary on pricing to being much more strategic. We have seen this strategy successfully play out over the last several quarters, as we produced strong year-over-year improvement in gross margin and comparable store sales growth. While many of our competitors have gone back and forth on their pricing strategies, we remain focused on continuing to strike the right balance between driving sales over the long term by improving our value offerings while maintaining margin.
>
> Our first quarter results exceeded our own expectations on both the top line and bottom line. Given the strong sales momentum we are seeing, there are many reasons to be bullish about our future results.[14]

Management said its outlook for full-year fiscal 2010 was sales growth of 8.5 to 10.5 percent and comparable store sales growth (for stores open at least 12 months) of 3.5 to 5.5 percent. Mackey indicated that the company would continue to press forward on its value-pricing strategy, endeavoring to be aggressive in seeking out good prices from suppliers and keeping its prices on key items as competitive as possible. Mackey indicated that Whole Foods could not match the prices charged by either Walmart or Costco (neither of which stocked many organic products). However, it was Whole Foods' policy for the prices on its 365 private-label products to match the prices of comparable items at Trader Joe's, one of its principal competitors in organic foods, unless there was a significant difference in quality. Many Whole Foods customers also shopped at Trader Joe's in communities where both companies had stores.

New Strategic Moves to Control Expenses in 2008–2009

When the sharp economic downturn began in September 2008, Whole Foods' management also moved swiftly to institute a series of cost-containment measures relating to cost of goods sold, direct store expenses, and general and administrative expenses. Purchases from suppliers were scrutinized for possible cost savings. A hiring and salary freeze was imposed and remained in effect until July 2009. In order to trim back on labor costs at its stores, the company used a set of tools on a daily basis to monitor and adjust the work hours of some store employees according to hourly shopper traffic and sales volumes. The size of the company's overall workforce was reduced by normal attrition (as team members retired or left the company), but there were no involuntary layoffs. Team members joined forces with managers throughout the company to find ways to operate the business more frugally.

Management was pleased with the success of its cost-containment initiatives. Gross profit (sales minus cost of goods sold) as a percentage of sales improved from 34.03 percent in fiscal 2008 to 34.29 percent in fiscal 2009 and 34.34 percent in the first quarter of fiscal 2010. Direct store expenses as a percent of sales held steady at 26.5 percent in fiscal 2008, 26.7 percent in fiscal 2009, and 26.6 percent in the first quarter of fiscal 2010. General and administrative expenses dropped from $270.4 million in fiscal 2008 to $243.7 million in fiscal 2009; in the first quarter of 2010, they were 8.1 percent below the level of the prior-year first quarter.

Merchandising Strategy

The layout of each Whole Foods store was customized to fit the particular site and building configuration and to best show off the particular product mix chosen for that store's target clientele. The driving concept of Whole Foods' merchandising strategy was to create an inviting and interactive store atmosphere that turned shopping for food from a chore into a fun, pleasurable experience. Stores had colorful decor, and products were displayed in an attractive manner that both welcomed close inspection and stimulated purchases (see Exhibit 7). The effect was to project Whole Foods as an authentic retailer of natural and organic products, a lifestyle brand, and a supermarket playground with both a unique environment and unusually appealing food selections (some wholesome and safe to eat, some "must try," and some definitely calorific with mouthwatering eye appeal). According to one industry analyst, Whole Foods had "put together the ideal model for the foodie who's a premium gourmet and the natural foods buyer. When you walk into a Whole Foods store, you're overwhelmed by a desire to look at everything you see."[15]

Case 2   Whole Foods Market in 2010: Vision, Core Values, and Strategy   **C-21**

Exhibit 7   Scenes from Whole Foods Stores

Most stores featured hand-stacked produce, appealing displays of fresh seafood and meats, open kitchens with teams of in-store chefs, scratch bakeries, prepared foods stations, salad bars, gourmet food sections with items from around the world, multiple opportunities to sample products, and ever-changing merchandise displays. To further a sense of community and interaction with customers, Whole Foods stores typically included sit-down eating areas, a healthy-eating center where shoppers could speak with trained store personnel about healthy eating choices, customer comment boards, and customer service booths. There were "Take Action" centers for customers who wanted information on such topics as sustainable agriculture, organics, the sustainability of seafood supplies and overfishing problems, food safety, product quality, the environment, and similar issues. Cooking classes were offered at 39 stores, and 30 Whole Foods stores had state-of-the art culinary centers equipped with instructional kitchens that offered hands-on cooking classes, tastings, demonstration dinners, and workshops. A few stores offered valet parking, massages, personal shopping, and home delivery. Management's intent was for Whole Foods stores to play a unique role as a third place, besides the home and office, where its customers could gather, interact, and learn while at the same time discovering the many joys of eating and sharing food.

Whole Foods' 78,000-square-foot flagship Austin store was a top Central Texas tourist destination and downtown Austin landmark; it had an intimate village-style layout; six mini-restaurants within the store; a raw food and juice bar; more than 600 varieties of cheese and 40 varieties of olives; a selection of 1,800 wines; a Candy Island with handmade lollipops and popcorn balls; a hot nut bar with an in-house nut roaster; a world foods section; a walk-in beer cooler with 800 selections; 14 pastry chefs making a variety of items; a natural home section with organic cotton apparel and household linens; an extensive meat department with an in-house smoker and 50 oven-ready items prepared by in-house chefs; and a theater-like seafood department with more than 150 fresh seafood items and on-the-spot shucking, cooking, smoking, slicing, and frying to order. The Columbus Circle store in Manhattan had a 248-seat café where shoppers could enjoy restaurant-quality prepared foods while relaxing in a comfortable community setting; a Jamba Juice smoothie station that served freshly blended-to-order fruit smoothies and juices; a full-service sushi bar by Genji Express where customers sat on bar stools enjoying fresh-cut sushi wrapped in organic nori; a walk-in greenhouse showcasing fresh-cut and exotic flowers; a wine shop with more than 700 varieties of wine from both large and small vineyards and family estates; and a chocolate enrobing station in the bakery where customers could request just about anything covered in chocolate. The two-story store in Pasadena, California (Whole Foods' largest store west of the Rocky Mountains), had a wine and tapas lounge, a seafood bar, a sandwich bar, an Italian trattoria, 1,200 selections of wine, fresh donuts made hourly, a 6,000-square-foot produce department that featured more than 500 items daily, and free wireless Internet access. The three-floor, 99,800-square-foot store in London, England, had 55 in-store chefs, 13 dining venues (including a tapas bar, a champagne and oyster bar, a pub, and a sushi and dim sum eatery) that accommodated 350 diners, a self-service bulk foods center with 100 selections, and a 12-meter display of fresh seafood (many of the seafood selections were hook-and-line caught off the shores of the UK). Management believed that the extensive and attractive displays of fresh produce, seafood, meats and house-made sausages, baked goods, and prepared foods in its larger stores appealed to a broader customer base and were responsible for the fact that Whole Foods stores bigger than 35,000 square feet had performed better than the company's smaller stores (up until 2008–2009 when the full forces of a deep recession hit the company's largest stores particularly hard).

Whole Foods got very high marks from merchandising experts and customers for its presentation—from the bright colors of the produce displays, to the quality of the foods and customer service, to the wide aisles and cleanliness. Management was continually experimenting with new merchandising concepts to keep stores fresh and exciting for customers. According to a Whole Foods regional manager, "We take the best ideas from each of our stores and try to incorporate them in all our other stores. We're constantly making our stores better."[16] Whole Foods' merchandising skills were said to be a prime factor in its success in luring shoppers back time and again—sales per square foot at Whole Foods stores tended to run about double the sales per square foot of Kroger and Safeway.

Marketing and Customer Service

Whole Foods spent less than other supermarkets on advertising and marketing—about 0.4 percent of its revenues in fiscal 2009—preferring instead to rely primarily on word-of-mouth recommendations and testimonials from customers. The corporate marketing budget was divided among national and regional programs, *The Whole Deal* in-store value guide and e-newsletter, and activities for individual stores. Stores spent most of their marketing budgets on in-store promotional signage and events such as local farmers' markets, taste fairs, classes, store tours, and product samplings. Store personnel were encouraged to extend company efforts to encourage the adoption of a natural and organic lifestyle by going out into the community and conducting a proactive public relations campaign. Each store also had a separate budget for making contributions to philanthropic activities and community outreach programs in an effort to maintain a high profile in the local community.

Since one of its core values was to satisfy and delight customers, Whole Foods Market empowered team members to exert their best efforts to meet or exceed customer expectations on every shopping trip. Store personnel were personable and chatty with shoppers. Customers could get personal attention in every department of the store. When customers asked where an item was located, team members often took them to the spot, making conversation along the way and offering to answer any questions. Team members were quite knowledgeable and enthusiastic about the products in their particular department and tried to take advantage of opportunities to inform and educate customers about natural foods, organics, healthy eating, and food-related environmental issues. They took pride in helping customers navigate the extensive variety to make the best choices. Seafood and meat department personnel provided customers with custom cuts, cooking instructions, and personal recommendations.

Management wanted competent, knowledgeable, and friendly service to be a hallmark of shopping at a Whole Foods Market. The aim was to turn highly satisfied customers into advocates for Whole Foods who talked to close friends and acquaintances about their positive experiences shopping at Whole Foods.

Store Operations and Work Environment

Whole Foods employed a team approach to store operations. Depending on store size and traffic volume, Whole Foods stores employed between 25 and 620 team members, who were organized into as many as 13 self-managed teams per store, each led by a team leader. Each team within a store was responsible for a different product category or aspect of store operations such as customer service, prepared foods, produce, and customer checkout stations. Teams were empowered to make many decisions at the store level pertaining to merchandising, departmental operations, and efforts to please customers. Each year, Whole Foods asked team members to give their leaders constructive feedback by completing a confidential team leader survey.

Whole Foods' commitment to team-based management of store operations stemmed from the conviction that the company's long-term success was dependent on the collective efforts of energetic and intelligent team members who were motivated to (1) go to great lengths to satisfy and delight customers and (2) operate the store as efficiently and profitably as possible. The team approach, complemented by a strong emphasis on empowering employees and tying a part of their compensation to store profitability and stock option awards, was seen as promoting a strong corporate culture and contributing to a work environment where motivated team members could flourish, build a career, and reach their highest potential. Management also believed that team members were further motivated and inspired by the company's strategic vision—many team members felt good about their jobs and had a greater sense of purpose because the work they did contributed to better diets and eating habits on the part of Whole Foods shoppers and to the overall well-being of society at large. Indeed, many job candidates were drawn to interview at Whole

Foods because their personal philosophy and lifestyle matched well with the company's "Whole Foods, Whole People, Whole Planet" mission of selling natural and organic foods, advancing the cause of long-term sustainable agricultural practices, and promoting a cleaner environment. Management believed that voluntary turnover of full-time team members at Whole Foods, which fell from 23 percent in fiscal year 2008 to 12 percent in fiscal year 2009, was very low for the food retailing industry and helped the company do a better job of satisfying its customers and operating its stores efficiently.

Top executives at Whole Foods were acutely aware that the company's decentralized team approach to store operations—where many personnel, merchandising, and operating decisions were made by teams at the individual store level—made it critical to have an effective store team leader. The store team leader worked with one or more associate store team leaders, as well as with all the department team leaders, to operate the store as efficiently and profitably as possible. Team leaders screened candidates for job openings on their team, but a two-thirds majority of the team had to approve a new hire—approval came only after a 30-day trial for the candidate. Store team leaders reported directly to one of twelve regional presidents.

All the teams at each store were continuously evaluated on measures relating to sales, operations, and morale; the results were made available to team members and to headquarters personnel.[17] Teams competed not only against the goals they had set for themselves but also against other teams at their stores or in their region—competition among teams was encouraged. In addition, stores went through two review processes—a store tour and a "customer snapshot." Each store was toured periodically and subjected to a rigorous evaluation by a group of 40 personnel from another region; the group included region heads, store team leaders, associate team leaders, and leaders from two operating teams. Customer snapshots involved a surprise inspection by a headquarters official or regional president who rated the store on 300 items; each store had 10 surprise inspections annually, with the results distributed to every store and included in the reward system. Rewards were team-based and tied to performance metrics.

Whole Foods promoted from within as much as possible, with team members often moving up to assume positions at stores soon to be opened or at stores in other regions. Whole Foods had created the intranet Whole Foods Market University (WFM-U) to provide team members with information and education on a vast array of topics and better connect them to the company's core values, aspects of the company's operations, and the organic food and supermarket industries. There were self-paced courses available on such subjects as organic products, dietary supplements and the law, the company's numerous quality standards, and how the gain-sharing program worked. All stores had budgets for enhancing team member job skills and performance.

Every year, management gave team members an opportunity to complete a morale survey covering job satisfaction, opportunity and empowerment, pay, training, and benefits. In 2004, the overall participation rate was 63 percent (versus 71 percent in 2003). Of the team members responding in 2004, 86 percent said they almost always or frequently enjoyed their job (the same percentage as in 2003), and 82 percent said they almost always or frequently felt empowered to do their best work at Whole Foods Market (up slightly from 81 percent in 2003). Common responses to the question "What is the best thing about working at Whole Foods Market?" included "my coworkers," "the customers," "flexibility," "the work environment," "growth and learning opportunities," "the products Whole Foods sells," "the employee benefits," "the team concept," and "the culture of empowerment."

A team member at Whole Foods' store in Austin, Texas, said, "I really feel like we're a part of making the world a better place. When I joined the company 17 years ago, we only had four stores. I have always loved—as a customer and now as a Team Member—the camaraderie, support for others, and progressive atmosphere at Whole Foods Market."[18] A team member at a New York store said, "I love working for Whole Foods Market because you have a better chance of advancing and great benefits. I've worked for a lot of companies, and I have to say that this feels more like a family than a group of co-workers. Everyone gets credit for what they do, not just leadership."[19] According to the company's vice president of human resources, "Team members who love to take initiative, while enjoying working as part of a team and being rewarded through shared fate, thrive here."

Whole Foods Market had approximately 52,500 team members in 2009, including approximately 43,000 full-time, 7,500 part-time, and 2,000 temporary team members; 45 percent were minorities and 44 percent were women.[20] None were represented by unions, although there had been a couple of unionization attempts. John Mackey was viewed as fiercely anti-union and had once said: "The union is like having herpes. It doesn't kill you, but it's unpleasant and inconvenient and it stops a lot of people from becoming your lover."[21] When workers at a Whole Foods Market in Madison, Wisconsin, voted to unionize in 2002, John Mackey spent more than nine months going to all of the company's stores to speak with store employees personally, listen to what was on their minds, and gather suggestions for improving working conditions. Unionization efforts had never made any headway at Whole Foods, and the company was widely regarded as very progressive and genuinely committed to creating a positive, satisfying work environment.

Whole Foods had made *Fortune* magazine's "100 Best Companies to Work For" list for 13 consecutive years (1998–2010), one of only 13 companies to make the list every year since its inception. It ranked 18th in 2010, 22nd in 2009, 16th in 2008, 5th in 2007, and 15th in 2006; only in 2000 did it rank lower than 50th on the list. In scoring companies, *Fortune* placed two-thirds weight on responses to a 57-question survey of approximately 400 randomly selected employees and one-third on *Fortune*'s own evaluation of a company's demographic makeup, pay and benefits, and culture.

Compensation, Incentives, Benefits, and the Use of Economic Value Added (EVA) Measures of Performance

Whole Foods' management wanted the company's compensation, incentive and reward programs, and benefits package to be perceived as fair to all stakeholders. Compensation levels were attractive. In early 2010, Whole Foods said its average hourly wage was $16.98.[22] Wages and salary differentials between store employees and executives reflected a philosophy of egalitarianism. Whole Foods had a salary cap that limited the compensation (wages plus profit incentive bonuses) of any team member or officer to 19 times the average total compensation of all full-time team members in the company—a policy mandated in the company's core values. The salary cap was raised from 14 to 19 times the average total compensation in 2007—it had been 8 times in 2003; the increases stemmed from the need to attract and retain key executives. Thus, if the average total compensation of a Whole Foods team member was $35,000, then a cap of 19 times the average meant that an executive could not be paid more than $665,000. All team members had access to the company's financial books, including an annual compensation report listing the gross pay of each team member and company executive. Cofounder and CEO John Mackey had recently set his annual salary at $1 and received no cash bonuses or stock option awards.

In addition, Whole Foods strived to create a "shared-fate consciousness" on the part of team members by uniting the self-interests of team members with those of shareholders. One way management reinforced this concept was through a "gain-sharing program" (which was equivalent to profit-sharing plans that some companies employed) based on an economic value added (EVA) management and incentive system adopted by Whole Foods in 1999. EVA is defined as company net operating profits after taxes minus a charge for the cost of capital necessary to generate that profit. Senior executives managed the company with the goal of improving EVA at the store level and company-wide; they believed that an EVA-based bonus system was the best financial framework for team members to use in helping make decisions that created sustainable shareholder value. At Whole Foods, EVA at the store level was based on store contribution (store revenues minus cost of goods sold minus store operating expenses) relative to store investment over and above a weighted-average cost of capital of 9 percent—average store contribution percentages for 2000–2009 are shown in the last line of Exhibit 5. The teams in all stores were challenged to find ways to boost store contribution and store EVA, and all gain-sharing bonuses for store-level team members (except store leaders and assistant store leaders) were tied to these two measures of store performance. Typically, gain-sharing distributions added 5–7 percent to team member wages.

In 2009, approximately 1,000 senior executives, regional managers, store team leaders, and assistant store team leaders throughout the company were also on an EVA-based incentive compensation plan. The primary measure determining the payout for these officers and team leaders was EVA improvement. The company's overall EVA climbed from a negative $30.4 million in fiscal 2001 to a positive $2.6 million in fiscal 2003, $15.6 million in fiscal 2004, $25.8 million in 2005, and $64.4 million in 2006, but then dropped sharply to $35.4 million in 2007. The company did not publicly report overall EVA data for fiscal years 2008 and 2009. (Note: In addition to using EVA measures for its incentive system, Whole Foods used EVA calculations [1] to determine whether the sales and profit projections for new stores would yield a positive and large enough EVA to justify the investment, [2] to guide decisions on store closings, and [3] to evaluate new acquisitions.) Whole Foods executives believed that the emphasis on empowered teams and EVA-based incentives helped harness the collective energy and intelligence of team members to operate their departments effectively and efficiently—thereby enabling Whole Foods to manage its stores better than rival supermarket chains managed their stores.

A second way that Whole Foods endeavored to link the interests of team members with those of shareholders was through three kinds of stock ownership programs:

1. *A team member stock option plan*—All full-time and part-time team members were eligible to receive stock option grants each year based on their leadership performance and their length of service; the number of shares available for these grants was determined annually by the company's board of directors. Stock-option grants based on outstanding leadership performance were awarded on the basis of the recommendation of a team member's regional president. Stock-option grants based on length of service were made to full- or part-time nonseasonal team members with more than 6,000 service hours. Options were

granted at a price equal to the market value of the stock at the grant date and were exercisable over a four-year period beginning one year from the date of the grant. Since the inception of the plan in 1992, approximately 94 percent of the stock options granted were to team members who were not executive officers. The share-based expenses associated with these stock-option awards to team members (which were based on the Black-Scholes multiple option pricing model and were reported on the company's consolidated statement of operations in accordance with generally accepted accounting principles) totaled $12.8 million in fiscal 2009, $10.5 million in 2008, and $13.2 million in 2007.[23] The company had recently instituted a policy limiting the number of shares granted in any one year so that annual earnings-per-share dilution due to share-based payment expenses would not exceed 10 percent.

2. *A team member stock purchase plan*—Through payroll deductions, all full-time team members with a minimum of 400 hours of service could purchase shares of Whole Foods common stock at 95 percent of the market price on the purchase date. Approximately 194,000 shares were purchased by team members in fiscal 2009.

3. *A team member 401(k) retirement savings plan*—Team members with a minimum of 1,000 service hours in any one year were eligible to participate in a "Growing Your Future" 401(k) plan. Team members were automatically enrolled unless they opted out of the plan. In fiscal 2009, Whole Foods made matching contributions totaling $3.7 million to the 401(k) plan. Whole Foods Market stock was one of the investment options in the 401(k) plan.

In fiscal 2009, Whole Foods issued a total of $52.9 million in common stock pursuant to its various stock plans for team members, as compared to $119.5 million in fiscal 2008 and $110.3 million in fiscal 2007.[24]

The Benefits Package for Team Members Starting in 2002, team members across the company were encouraged to actively contribute ideas about the benefits they would like the company to offer. The suggestions were compiled and put into a choice of packages, and the choices were submitted to team members for a vote. The benefits plan that was adopted for 2003 through 2006 was approved by 83 percent of the 79 percent of the team members participating in the benefits vote. Under the adopted plan, team members could select their own benefits package. The resulting health insurance plan that the company put in place in January 2003 involved the company paying 100 percent of the premium for full-time employees and the establishment of company-funded "personal wellness accounts," which team members could use to pay the higher deductibles; any unused balances in a team member's account could roll over and accumulate for future expenses.

A second company-wide benefits vote was held in fiscal 2006 to determine the benefits program that would be in place from 2007 through 2009. One outcome of the second vote, in which approximately 77 percent of eligible team members participated, was that the company again provided health insurance at no cost to eligible full-time employees (defined as those who worked 30 or more hours per week and had worked a minimum of 800 hours); the cost of dependent health insurance premiums was shared between the company and the team member, with the percentage paid by the team member declining as years of service with the company increased.

A third vote, in which 84 percent of Whole Foods employees participated, was taken in fiscal 2009 to establish the benefit package for 2010 through 2012. This vote resulted in a continuation of company-paid health insurance at no cost to eligible full-time team members, defined in this instance as those who worked 30 or more hours per week and had worked a minimum of 10,000 service hours (approximately five years of employment). Team members who had worked a minimum of 800 service hours and less than 10,000 service hours paid a medical insurance premium of $10 per biweekly period. Dependent health insurance premiums were generally shared between the company and the team member, with the percentage paid by the team member declining as years of service with the company increased; dependent premiums for health insurance became 100 percent company-paid when a

team member reached 10,000 service hours. As in the two prior voting periods, the benefits package for 2010–2012 called for Whole Foods to provide each team member with a personal wellness account (from $300 up to $1,800 per year, based on years of service) to help cover the cost of deductibles and other allowable out-of-pocket health care expenses not covered by insurance; unused balances in a team member's personal wellness account rolled forward at the end of the year.

Other key benefits included:

- Paid time off based on hours worked. The paid time off could be used for vacations, holidays, illness, and personal days, as a team member saw fit.
- A 20 percent discount on all purchases at Whole Foods. This benefit became available on a team member's first day of employment.
- Dental and eye care plans. Coverage was available for both team members and their dependents.
- Life insurance and disability insurance plans.
- A dependent care reimbursement plan that allowed team members to contribute pretax funds to pay for anticipated day care expenses incurred while at work.
- Assistance for unforeseeable emergencies. This benefit was funded by voluntary team member paycheck deductions (usually $1), by paid-time-off donations (from team member to team member), and by the company (in situations where there was a major disaster).

Purchasing and Distribution

Whole Foods' buyers purchased most of the items retailed in the company's stores from local, regional, and national wholesale suppliers and vendors. Much of the buying responsibility was located at the regional and national levels in order to put the company in a better position to negotiate volume discounts with major vendors and distributors. Whole Foods Market was the largest account for many suppliers of natural and organic foods. United Natural Foods was the company's biggest supplier, accounting for about 28 percent of Whole Foods' total purchases in fiscal 2009; United was the company's primary supplier of dry grocery and frozen food products.

However, regional and store managers had discretionary authority to source from local organic farmers and suppliers that met the company's quality standards. In 2007–2008, the company's buyers began to place stronger emphasis on buying directly from producers and manufacturers.

Whole Foods owned two produce procurement centers that facilitated the procurement and distribution of the majority of the produce Whole Foods sold. However, where feasible, local store personnel sourced produce items from local organic farmers as part of the company's commitment to promote and support organic farming methods. Recently, Whole Foods had instituted its Local Producer Loan Program, which provided up to $10 million in low-interest loans to small local producers; the purpose of this loan program was to make it easier for small organic farmers and start-up entrepreneurs to bring more locally produced organic foods to market. Loans ranged from $1,000 to $100,000 and could be used for purchasing more animals, investing in new equipment, or converting to organic production. Whole Foods kept the fees, interest rates, and paperwork to a minimum so as not to discourage a small local farm or business from taking steps to expand its operations. Whole Foods hosted farmers' markets in the parking lots of some of its stores.

The company operated 10 regional distribution centers to supply its stores. Eight regional bake houses and five regional commissary kitchens supplied area stores with various prepared foods. A central coffee-roasting operation supplied stores with the company's Allegro brand of coffees.

Whole Foods' Social Responsibility Strategy and Community Citizenship Initiatives

Whole Foods was pursuing a comprehensive social responsibility strategy. Key elements of this strategy included standards relating to animal welfare, support for organic farming and sustainable agriculture, healthy eating education, a loan program to support local producers of organic products, actions to promote responsible and sustainable seafood practices, the Green Action program to implement wise environmental practices,

a policy of donating at least 5 percent of after-tax profits (in cash or products) to nonprofit or educational organizations, the Whole Trade Guarantee program, the activities of the company's Whole Planet Foundation, and a variety of community citizenship activities. The loan program to support small organic farmers was mentioned earlier. Other elements of Whole Foods' social responsibility strategy included the following:

- Whole Foods had implemented a system called Five-Step Animal Welfare Rating, which laid out a set of "animal compassionate" standards expected of Whole Foods' meat and poultry suppliers. These standards entailed a requirement of humane living conditions for animals, prohibited the use antibiotics and growth hormones, prohibited the use of feeds containing animal by-products, and specified other permissible and prohibited production and handling techniques (e.g., prohibitions against raising animals in crates, cages, or crowded facilities). Whole Foods ceased selling live lobsters in 2006 because the process of handling live lobsters throughout the supply chain (from capture to in-store tank conditions) was not in line with the company's commitment to humane treatment. In early 2008, Whole Foods created the Global Animal Partnership, a foundation for the purpose of working with farms, ranches, and others to foster continuous improvement of the environment and conditions for each species that supported the animal's natural physical, emotional, and behavioral well-being. Whole Foods refused to sell commercial veal from tethered calves, foie gras from force-fed geese, and eggs from caged hens.

- Whole Foods' Green Mission Task Force promoted environmentally sound practices for every aspect of store and facility operations, including paperless ordering systems, use of biodegradable supplies for food and wine sampling, composting, use of recycled paper, holding company and community recycling drives for electronics, providing receptacles for glass and plastic recycling in dining areas, the use of Green Seal products for cleaning and maintenance, and installation of flushless urinals (each of which saved an average of 40,000 gallons of water annually). Starting in

2006, Whole Foods began purchasing renewable energy credits from wind farms to offset 100 percent of the electricity used in all of its stores and facilities in the United States and Canada; a growing number of Whole Foods stores had installed solar panels to supply a portion of their electricity requirements. In early 2008, Whole Foods began using all-natural fiber packaging at its salad and food bars. As of Earth Day 2008 (April 22), Whole Foods ended the use of disposable plastic bags at the checkout lanes of all its stores, chiefly because such bags did not break down in landfills. Company officials said the move would eliminate use of 100 million plastic bags annually—customers were instead offered reusable paper bags made of 100 percent recycled paper (at a cost of 10 cents each) and an opportunity to purchase stylish long-life canvas bags for 99 cents (80 percent of the content of the canvas bags came from recycled plastic bottles). Whole Foods' distribution vehicles had been converted to the use of biodiesel fuel.

- In October 2005, Whole Foods established the not-for-profit Whole Planet Foundation, charged with combating poverty and promoting self-sufficiency in third-world countries that supplied Whole Foods with some of the products it sold. Most of the foundation's efforts involved providing loans, training, and other financial services to aspiring entrepreneurs and the self-employed poor. So far, Whole Foods had made grants and microloans in excess of $11 million to more than 60,000 recipients (98 percent of whom were women) in 17 countries; the average loan size was $185, and the loan repayment rate was running about 98 percent.[25] In 2010, the Whole Planet Foundation initiated a $1.5 million campaign to help empower poor women in developing countries to create prosperity for themselves; shoppers could donate $1 to the program at the checkout registers in all Whole Foods stores or make a donation at the company's website. In the days following the January 2010 earthquake disaster in Haiti, the foundation also committed $1 million to enable its partner organization in Haiti, Fonkoze Financial Services, to rebuild its infrastructure and reopen its

branch offices; Fonkoze served more than 55,000 women borrowers and 1 million families who received monies from relatives and friends abroad. The funding allowed Fonkoze to be the first bank in Haiti to reopen after the earthquake and get needed cash to customers and make microloans to members to reestablish their businesses.

- In March 2007, Whole Foods launched its Whole Trade Guarantee, a program that committed the company to paying small-scale producers (chiefly in impoverished, low-wage countries where living standards were low) a price for their products that more than covered the producer's costs. The goal was to make sure that the producers of products meeting Whole Foods' quality standards could always afford to create, harvest, or grow their product so that they did not have to abandon their work or jeopardize the well-being of their family to make ends meet. The commitment to paying such producers a premium price was viewed as an investment in them and their communities as well as a way for producers to be able to put money back into their operations, enable them to invest in training and education for their workers, and have sufficient take-home pay to help support a better life. In 2010, the Whole Trade Guarantee label was featured on more than 1,350 items at Whole Foods stores. Whole Foods donated 1 percent of the retail sales of all Whole Trade Guarantee products sold to the Whole Planet Foundation (such donations amounted to $762,000 in fiscal 2009).

- A renewed drive to make customers more aware of healthy-eating choices began in 2009 and was in full force in 2010. The company had partnered with Eat Right America and the creator of the Engine 2 Diet to create Getting Started programs. In addition, there were in-store healthy eating areas, new healthy prepared foods selections, an educational booth where team members dispensed information and provided healthy eating materials, signs and brochures explaining how to use the Aggregate Nutrient Density Index (ANDI) scoring system as a guide to selecting healthy foods, and Health Starts Here logos and signs adjacent to items considered to be good healthy eating choices.

During 2010, John Mackey planned to launch a program to better engage the company's team members in the healthy eating campaign (because they were the ones who interfaced with customers) by giving them a monetary incentive to get healthier. All team members received a standard 20 percent discount on their purchases at Whole Foods. Mackey's plan was for team members who scored well on three of four biomarkers of good health (having a low body mass index, not being a smoker, having a good cholesterol count, and having good blood pressure) to receive a 25 percent silver discount card; team members with acceptable scores on all four markers were to receive a 30 percent gold discount card. Mackey believed that a silver or gold discount card would become a status symbol among team members. He also envisioned instituting competitions for the healthiest team in a store, the healthiest store in each region, and the healthiest region in the company. Mackey said, "I fully expect that I am going to get a gold card. I see in my mind's eye how this is going to play out. I'm into it."[26]

• Team members at every Whole Foods store were heavily involved in such community citizenship activities as sponsoring blood donation drives, preparing meals for seniors and the homeless, holding fund-raisers to help the disadvantaged, growing vegetables for a domestic violence shelter, participating in housing renovation projects, and working as delivery people for Meals on Wheels. Each store donated food to area food banks and shelters. Several times a year, individual Whole Foods stores held events called 5% Days (or CommUnity Giving Days), during which 5 percent of that day's sales were donated to a local nonprofit or educational organization. Each store had latitude in deciding what activities it would undertake to support the local community.

Most Whole Foods stores had signs alerting customers to the company's various social responsibility initiatives; brochures were available at all stores containing more detailed information about the various programs discussed above. Exhibit 8 presents Whole Foods' efforts to support responsible and sustainable seafood practices.

In 2010, Ethisphere Institute named Whole Foods as one of the world's most ethical companies; Ethisphere is a leading research-based international think tank dedicated to the creation, advancement, and sharing of best practices in business ethics, corporate social responsibility, anticorruption, and environmental sustainability.

Mackey's Ethics Are Called into Question.

Business Ethics named Whole Foods Market to its "100 Best Corporate Citizens" list in 2004, 2006, and 2007. However, during 2007, CEO John Mackey was the center of attention in two ethics-related incidents. The first involved a discovery that, over a seven-year period, Mackey had typed out more than 1,100 entries on Yahoo Finance's message board touting his company's stock and occasionally making uncomplimentary remarks about rival Wild Oats Markets. Mackey's postings stopped several months prior to Whole Foods' offer to buy Wild Oats Market. In making his postings, Mackey used the alias Rahodeb—a variation of Deborah, his wife's name. *The Wall Street Journal* reported that in January 2005 Rahodeb posted that no one would buy Wild Oats at its current price of $8 per share and that Whole Foods had nothing to gain by buying Wild Oats because the latter's stores were too small.[27] A *New York Times* article reported that, on March 28, 2006, Rahodeb wrote, "OATS has lost their way and no longer has a sense of mission or even a well-thought-out theory of the business. They lack a viable business model that they can replicate. They are floundering around hoping to find a viable strategy that may stop their erosion. Problem is they lack the time and the capital now."[28] The *New York Times* article quoted Mackey as saying, "I posted on Yahoo! under a pseudonym because I had fun doing it. I never intended any of those postings to be identified with me." Mackey's postings, which came to light in June–July 2007 and spurred calls for his resignation on grounds that he breached his fiduciary responsibility, were first discovered by the Federal Trade Commission in Whole Foods documents that the FTC obtained in the course of challenging the Wild Oats acquisition. According to Mackey, some of the views he expressed in his Rahodeb postings represented his personal beliefs and others represented his playing the role

Exhibit 8   **Whole Foods' Position on Seafood Sustainability**

It's pretty clear that our oceans are in trouble. The world's fish stocks are disappearing due to overfishing and bad harvesting practices and fish farming is not yet the solution we thought it would be.

The good news is that there's hope, but we all have to pitch in so our favorite seafood remains available for us and for future generations. As a shopper, you have the power to turn the tide. Buying seafood from responsible, certified fisheries is the way to go. You reward their actions and encourage other fisheries to be responsible too. Looking for the blue Marine Stewardship Council sticker on seafood packaging is a good place to start.

As a company, we're committed to responsible seafood practices, including:

- Supporting fishing practices that ensure the ecological health of the ocean and the abundance of marine life.
- Partnering with groups who encourage responsible practices and provide the public with accurate information about the issue.
- Operating our own well-managed seafood facilities.
- Helping educate our customers on the importance of practices that can make a difference now and well into the future.
- Promoting and selling the products of well-managed fisheries.

As the largest retailer of natural and organic food, we want to be able to continue over the long-term to provide our customers with fish to buy. However, at the same time, we want to support ecological health and the abundance of marine life. We believe the Marine Stewardship Council's "Fish Forever" certified sustainably managed seafood program accomplishes both.

A global independent, not-for-profit organization, the Marine Stewardship Council promotes sustainable fisheries and responsible fishing practices world-wide to help preserve fish stocks for future generations. Whole Foods Market Inc. was one of the first American companies to support and participate in the Marine Stewardship Council.

Accredited, independent certifying agencies measure compliance to the principles and criteria of sustainability developed by the Marine Stewardship Council. Certified fisheries are rewarded the right to use the "Fish Forever" eco-label to signify to consumers that the product was caught using environmentally sound, economical and socially responsible management practices.

Source: Whole Foods Market, www.wholefoodsmarket.com, accessed March 24, 2010.

of devil's advocate. He said that no proprietary information about Whole Foods was disclosed.[29] In the days following the media reports of the postings, Mackey expressed remorse for his postings, apologized for his behavior, and asked stakeholders to forgive him for exercising bad judgment. Nonetheless, the content of certain Mackey postings were cited in court documents filed by the FTC as reasons why Whole Foods' acquisition of Wild Oats should be blocked. On July 17, 2007, the Securities and Exchange Commission (SEC) announced that it had begun an investigation of the postings. That same day, Whole Foods announced that the company's board of directors had formed a special committee to investigate the postings and retained legal counsel to advise it during the investigation. Whole Foods said it would cooperate fully with the SEC inquiry.

In October 2007, Whole Foods announced that the special committee had completed its investigation of Mackey's message board postings and that the board of directors affirmed its support of the CEO; the company indicated that the special committee's findings would be turned over to the SEC and that the company would have no further comment pending the SEC investigation.[30] In April 2008, the SEC closed its investigation into Mackey's online chat activities and took no actions against Mackey or Whole Foods.

A second controversy-stirring incident involved a Mackey-authored blog entitled "Whole Foods, Wild Oats and the FTC" that appeared on the company's website on June 19, 2007. Mackey, who objected strenuously to the grounds on which the Federal Trade Commission was trying to block Whole Foods' acquisition of Wild Oats, dedicated the blog to providing updates and information regarding the FTC proceeding and to making the case for why the company's acquisition of Wild Oats Market should be allowed to go forward. Mackey explained the basis for the blog:

My blog posting provides a detailed look into Whole Foods Market's decision-making process regarding the merger, as well as our company's experience interacting with the FTC staff assigned to this merger. I provide explanations of how I think the FTC, to date, has neglected to do its homework appropriately, especially given the statements made regarding prices, quality, and service levels in its complaint. I also provide a glimpse into the bullying tactics used against Whole Foods Market by this taxpayer-funded agency. Finally, I provide answers in my FAQ section to many of the questions that various Team Members have fielded from both the media and company stakeholders. As previously announced, we set an intention as a company to be as transparent as possible throughout this legal process, and this blog entry is my first detailed effort at transparency.

The blog by Mackey included the following post titles:

- Why Whole Foods Market Wants to Buy Wild Oats
- Whole Foods Market's Objections to the FTC's Investigation
- What the FTC Is Claiming in Its Objections to the Merger
- FAQs

Critics of Mackey's blog said it was inappropriate for a CEO to publicly air the company's position, to take issue with the FTC, and to make the company's case for why the acquisition should be allowed to proceed. At the least, some critics opined, the blog should be toned down.[31] When the SEC announced on July 17, 2007, that it would investigate John Mackey's financial message board postings, Mackey put a hold on further blog postings regarding the FTC's actions to try to block the Wild Oats acquisition.

Whole Foods Market's Financial Performance

Since 1991, Whole Foods Market had been profitable every year except 2000, when it reported a net loss of $8.5 million, owing to divestiture of its NatureSmart nutritional supplement business and losses in two affiliated dot-com enterprises in which Whole Foods owned a minority interest. However, the company quickly returned to profitability, with earnings rising from $67.8 million in fiscal year 2001 to a peak of $203.8 million in fiscal year 2006. Even though Whole Foods' revenues grew from $5.6 billion in fiscal 2006 to $8.0 billion in fiscal 2009, profitability suffered because of a combination of three factors:

1. The rising costs associated with opening a larger number of new stores (many of which were also bigger and entailed larger pre-opening costs) in 2007 and 2008.

2. The expenses associated with acquiring Wild Oats in 2007 and trying to make its stores profitable in 2008. The additional debt to finance the Wild Oats acquisition drove interest expenses up from a mere $32,000 in fiscal 2007 to $36.5 million in fiscal 2008. Store relocations, closures, and lease termination costs (much of was directly related to the Wild Oats stores) jumped from $5.3 million in fiscal 2006 to $10.9 million in fiscal 2007 and to $36.5 million in fiscal 2008.

3. The sudden and deep economic recession in 2008–2009, which prompted a drop in average weekly sales at Whole Foods stores.

Whole Foods' net profits declined to $182.7 million in fiscal 2007 and to $114.5 million in fiscal 2008 before rebounding slightly to $118.8 million in fiscal 2009. Exhibits 9, 10, and 11 present the company's recent statements of operations, consolidated balance sheets, and selected cash flow data.

Whole Foods had very strong cash flows from operations prior to the Wild Oats acquisition, enabling it to fund its capital requirements (which were mainly for new store development and store relocations) and avoid incurring much, if any, long-term debt. The company began paying dividends in January 2004, raising them several times, and paying a special dividend of $1.60 per share in fiscal 2006. But the Wild Oats acquisition triggered a cash flow crunch. To aid in financing the Wild Oats acquisition and continue fast-paced opening of new stores, Whole Foods took on long-term debt of more than $700 million and negotiated a $250 million revolving line of credit with its banks during the last quarter of fiscal 2007; the revolving line of credit was later increased to $350 million. Starting in fiscal 2009, the company's board of directors suspended dividend payments on common shares for the foreseeable future.

In November–December 2008 (the first quarter of Whole Foods' fiscal year 2009), the cash shortage became so severe that Whole Foods negotiated the issuance of 425,000 shares of preferred stock to Leonard Green & Partners for approximately

Exhibit 9   **Whole Foods Market, Statement of Operations, Fiscal Years 2005–2009 ($ thousands)**

	Fiscal Year 2009	Fiscal Year 2008	Fiscal Year 2007	Fiscal Year 2006	Fiscal Year 2005
Sales	$8,031,620	$7,953,912	$6,591,773	$5,607,376	$4,701,289
Cost of goods sold and occupancy costs	5,277,310	5,247,207	4,295,170	3,647,734	3,052,184
Gross profit	2,754,310	2,706,705	2,296,603	1,959,642	1,649,105
Direct store expenses	2,145,809	2,107,940	1,711,229	1,421,968	1,223,473
Store contribution	608,501	598,765	585,374	537,674	425,632
General and administrative expenses	243,749	270,428	217,743	181,244	158,864
Pre-opening and relocation costs	80,403	92,099	70,180	37,421	37,035
Operating income	284,349	236,238	297,451	319,009	229,733
Interest expense, net	(36,856)	(36,416)	(4,208)	(32)	(2,223)
Investment and other income	3,449	6,697	11,324	20,736	9,623
Income before income taxes	250,942	206,519	304,567	339,713	237,133
Provision for income taxes	104,138	91,995	121,827	135,885	100,782
Net income	$ 146,804	$ 114,524	$ 182,740	$ 203,828	$ 136,351
Basic earnings per share	$0.85	$0.82	$1.30	$1.46	$1.05
Weighted average shares outstanding	140,414	139,886	140,088	139,328	130,090
Diluted earnings per share	$0.85	$0.82	$1.29	$1.41	$0.99
Weighted average shares outstanding, diluted basis	140,414	140,011	141,836	145,082	139,950
Dividends declared per share	—	$0.60	$0.87	$2.45	$0.47

Note: Whole Foods' fiscal year ends the last Sunday in September.
Source: Whole Foods Market, 2009 10-K report, p. 24.

$413.1 million, net of closing and issuance costs of $11.9 million. The preferred shares called for an 8.0 percent annual dividend payment and included a provision restricting Whole Foods' ability to pay cash dividends on its common stock without prior written consent of the holders of a majority of the preferred shares. Two Leonard Green partners were subsequently elected to membership on Whole Foods' board of directors. The agreement also gave Leonard Green the option to convert its shares of preferred stock into shares of Whole Foods common stock at any time prior to November 27, 2009 (the earliest date at which Whole Foods could opt to redeem the 425,000 shares of preferred stock). On October 23, 2009, because of rapidly improving internal cash flows from operations, Whole

Foods announced its intention to redeem all 425,000 preferred shares on November 27, 2009. Leonard Green & Partners then proceeded to exercise its conversion option and received 29.7 million shares of Whole Foods common stock in return for its 425,000 preferred shares, which boosted the total number of common shares outstanding to about 170.3 million. At the time of the conversion, Whole Foods' common stock price was trading at about $25.90, making the value of the conversion to Leonard Green & Partners worth approximately $770 million, far above the $425 million redeemable value of the preferred shares. Because of the conversion to common stock, Whole Foods did not have to use any cash to redeem the $425 million in preferred stock.

Exhibit 10   Whole Foods Market, Consolidated Balance Sheet, Fiscal Years 2008–2009 ($ thousands)

	Year Ending Sept. 27, 2009	Year Ending Sept. 28, 2008
Assets		
Current assets:		
Cash and cash equivalents	$ 430,130	$ 30,534
Restricted cash	71,023	617
Accounts receivable	104,731	115,424
Merchandise inventories	310,602	327,452
Deferred income taxes	87,757	80,429
Prepaid expenses and other current assets	51,137	68,150
Total current assets	1,055,380	622,606
Property and equipment, net of accumulated depreciation and amortization	1,897,853	1,900,117
Goodwill	658,254	659,559
Intangible assets, net of accumulated amortization	73,035	78,499
Deferred income taxes	91,000	109,002
Other assets	7,866	10,953
Total assets	$3,783,388	$3,380,736
Liabilities and Shareholders' Equity		
Current liabilities:		
Current installments of long-term debt and capital lease obligations	$ 389	$ 380
Accounts payable	189,597	183,134
Accrued payroll, bonus and other benefits due team members	207,983	196,233
Dividends payable	8,217	—
Other current liabilities	277,838	286,430
Total current liabilities	684,024	666,177
Long-term debt and capital lease obligations, less current installments	738,848	928,790
Deferred lease liabilities	250,326	199,635
Other long-term liabilities	69,262	80,110
Total liabilities	1,742,460	1,874,712
Series A redeemable preferred stock, $0.01 par value, 425 and no shares authorized, issued and outstanding in 2009 and 2008, respectively	413,052	—
Shareholders' equity:		
Common stock, no par value, 300,000 shares authorized; 140,542 and 140,286 shares issued and outstanding in 2009 and 2008, respectively	1,283,028	1,266,141
Accumulated other comprehensive income (loss)	(13,367)	422
Retained earnings	358,215	239,461
Total shareholders' equity	1,627,876	1,506,024
Commitments and contingencies		
Total liabilities and shareholders' equity	$3,783,388	$3,380,736

Source: Whole Foods Market, 2009 10-K report, p. 40.

Exhibit 11   **Whole Foods Market, Selected Cash Flow Data, Fiscal Years 2007–2009 ($ thousands)**

	Fiscal Year ending Sept. 27, 2009	Fiscal Year ending Sept. 28, 2008	Fiscal Year ending Sept. 30, 2007
Net cash provided by operating activities	$ 587,721	$ 334,992	$ 391,486
Cash flows from investing activities			
Development costs of new store locations	(247,999)	(357,520)	(388,759)
Other property, plant and equipment expenditures	(66,616)	(171,952)	(135,772)
Purchase of available-for-sale securities	—	(194,316)	(277,283)
Sale of available-for-sale securities	—	194,316	475,625
Payment for purchase of acquired entities, net of cash acquired	—	(5,480)	(596,236)
Proceeds received from divestiture, net	—	163,913	—
Other items	32,595	(36,167)	32,595
Net cash used in investing activities	$(386,283)	$(372,721)	$(890,373)
Cash flows from financing activities			
Dividends paid	—	$(109,072)	$ (96,742)
Issuance of common stock	4,286	18,019	54,383
Purchase of treasury stock	—	—	(99,997)
Excess tax benefit related to exercise of tem member stock options	42	5,686	12,839
Proceeds from issuance of redeemable preferred stock, net	413,042	—	—
Proceeds form long-term borrowing	123,000	317,000	717,000
Payments on long-term debt and capital lease obligations	(318,370)	(161,151)	(93,360)
Net cash provided by (used in) financing activities	$ 199,455	$ (69,830)	$ 494,123
Other cash flow data			
Cash and cash equivalents at beginning of year	$ 30,534	—	$ 2,252
Cash and cash equivalents at end of year	430,130	30,534	—
Net change in cash and cash equivalents	399,596	30,534	(2,252)
Interest paid	43,685	36,155	4,561
Federal and state income taxes paid	69,701	118,366	152,626

Source: Whole Foods Market, 2009 10-K report, p. 43.

Whole Foods' strategy changes at the beginning of fiscal 2009—particularly the cost-containment and value-pricing initiatives—helped produce very strong cash flows from operations of $587.7 million for fiscal year 2009, well above the $335 million in fiscal 2008 and $391.5 million in fiscal 2007. This allowed Whole Foods to internally fund its development costs for new stores ($248 million) and other capital projects ($66.6 million). Cash flows were sufficient to pay down the company's total long-term debt by $190 million and increase cash and cash equivalents to $430.1 million (versus only $30.5 million at the end of fiscal 2008). Management expressed confidence in being able to cover the long-term debt maturing in 2012. Capital expenditures during fiscal 2010 were expected to be in the range of $350–$400 million, with about 65 percent of this amount being for new-store development. In March 2010, Whole Foods announced that it was forecasting diluted earnings per share of $1.20 to $1.25 for fiscal 2010. As of December 31, 2009, the company had further boosted its cash and short-term investments to $569.6 million; total debt was $734.1 million.[32]

COMPETITORS

The food retailing business was intensely competitive. The degree of competition Whole Foods faced varied from locality to locality, and to some extent from store location to store location within a given locale depending on the proximity of stores of its two closest competitors in the natural foods and organics segment of the food retailing industry, Fresh Market and Trader Joe's. Other competitors included conventional supermarkets, small chains, local independent retailers of natural and health foods, and regional and national supermarkets, a number of which had a growing selection of natural and organic foods. Whole Foods also faced competition in parts of its product line from specialty grocery stores (with upscale delicatessen offerings and prepared foods), small-scale health food stores, and retailers of vitamins and nutritional supplements. Whole Foods' executives had said it was to the company's benefit for conventional supermarkets to offer natural and organic foods for two reasons: first, it helped fulfill the company's mission of improving the health and well-being of people and the planet, and, second, it helped create new customers for Whole Foods by providing a gateway experience. They contended that as more people were exposed to natural and organic products, they were more likely to become a Whole Foods customer because Whole Foods was the category leader for natural and organic products, offered the largest selection at competitive prices, and provided the most-informed customer service.

Fresh Market

Fresh Market, headquartered in Greensboro, North Carolina, was a family-owned 94-store chain operating in 18 states in the Southeast, Midwest, Mid-Atlantic, and Northeast. Founded by Ray Berry, a former vice president with Southland Corporation who had responsibility over some 3,600 7-Eleven stores, the first Fresh Market store opened in 1982 in Greensboro. Berry's concept was to develop a small neighborhood store with the feel and atmosphere of an open European-style market that was service-oriented and focused on perishable goods (particularly fresh produce and meats and seafood displayed in glass-front refrigerated cases). All fixtures and display pieces were purchased used, as the store was financed entirely with the family's savings. The Greensboro store, which had low-level lighting and classical music playing in the background, was a hit with customers, and Berry began to open similar stores in other locales. During the 1982–2000 period, Fresh Market's sales revenues grew at a 25.2 percent compound rate, reaching $193 million in 2000; revenues were an estimated $655 million in 2009. The company had almost 7,000 employees in early 2010. Management planned to open 9 to 12 new stores annually, gradually expanding into more states. Expansion was funded by internal cash flows and bank debt. Financial data were not available because the company was privately owned, but Fresh Market's profitability was believed to be above the industry average.

Fresh Market stores were typically in the range of 18,000 to 25,000 square feet and were located in neighborhood shopping areas near educated, high-income residents. Newer stores had an open-air design that evoked "old-world European charm, artful sophistication, old-fashioned retail sentiment, and a warm and friendly atmosphere." Warm lights, classical background music, and terra-cotta-colored tiles made Fresh Market stores a cozier place to shop than a typical supermarket. Fresh Market's product line included meats, seafood, 400 fresh produce items (that included a growing organic selection), fresh-baked goods (30 breads, 15 pies, cakes, cookies, and fruit tarts), prepared foods and meals to-go, 30 varieties of coffees, a small selection of grocery and dairy items, bulk products, 200 varieties of domestic and imported cheeses, deli items (including rotisserie meats, sandwiches, wraps, soups, and sandwiches), wine and beer, and a small assortment of cookbooks, gift cards, baskets, cutting boards, and gift baskets. The emphasis was on variety, freshness, and quality.

Aside from inviting store ambience and the atmosphere of an old-world European market, Fresh Market differentiated itself from natural foods stores and traditional supermarkets with what management considered to be superlative service, attractive fresh produce displays, daily product sampling (including freshly brewed coffee for shoppers), and "upscale grocery boutique" items such as pick-and-pack spices; gourmet chocolates; hard-to-get H&H bagels from New York City; Ferrara's New York cheesecake; fresh Orsini parmesan cheese; Acqua della Madonna bottled water; and an extended selection of olive oils, mustards, bulk products (granolas, nuts, beans, dried fruits, spices, and snack mixes), wine, and beer. Each department had at least one employee in the area constantly to help shoppers and answer questions—the idea was to force interaction between store employees and shoppers. From time to time, stores had cooking classes, wine tastings, and food sampling events. Each Fresh Market store had an annual sidewalk sale to raise funds for the Juvenile Diabetes Research Foundation where root beer floats, hot dogs, and gourmet cookies were offered in exchange for a donation.

Stores had 75 to 100 employees, resulting in labor costs that were about double those of supermarket chains. Whenever possible, Fresh Market offered promotions and transfers to people from within the company; all store managers had been promoted from within the company. After 90 days, all full-time employees were eligible to enroll in plans providing medical, prescription medication, dental, vision, life, and disability coverage; coverage could be extended to spouses or domestic partners and children. There were also low-cost medical, prescription, life, dental, and vision insurance plans for new and part-time employees. In addition, there were annual bonus programs for all employees, 20 percent employee discounts on most products, a paid annual leave program, a 401(k) plan with 50 percent company matching of employee contributions, an employee assistance program, and a flexible spending account program.

Trader Joe's

Founded in 1967 and based in Pasadena, California, Trader Joe's was a specialty supermarket chain with more than 339 stores in 25 states as well as Washington, D.C.; about half of the stores were in California. The company had an ongoing strategy to open additional stores. A privately owned company, Trader Joe's had seen its sales increase from an estimated $2.1 billion in 2003 (with 210 stores) to approximately $8.0 billion in 2009, roughly equal to sales at Whole Foods; Trader Joe's was ranked 21st on *Supermarket News'* 2010 list of the top 75 retailers (based on 2009 sales estimates).

Management described the company's mission and business as follows:

> At Trader Joe's, our mission is to bring our customers the best food and beverage values and the information to make informed buying decisions. There are more than 2,000 unique grocery items in our label, all at honest everyday low prices. We work hard at buying things right: Our buyers travel the world searching for new items and we work with a variety of suppliers who make interesting products for us, many of them exclusive to Trader Joe's. All our private label products have their own "angle," i.e., vegetarian, Kosher, organic or just plain decadent, and all have minimally processed ingredients.
>
> Customers tell us, "I never knew food shopping could be so much fun!" Some even call us "The home of cheap thrills!" We like to be part of our neighborhoods and get to know our customers. And where else do you shop that even the CEO, Dan Bane, wears a loud Hawaiian shirt.
>
> Our tasting panel tastes every product before we buy it. If we don't like it, we don't buy it. If customers don't like it, they can bring it back for a no-hassle refund.
>
> We stick to the business we know: good food at the best prices! Whenever possible we buy direct from our suppliers, in large volume. We bargain hard and manage our costs carefully. We pay in cash, and on time, so our suppliers like to do business with us.
>
> Trader Joe's Crew Members are friendly, knowledgeable and happy to see their customers. They taste our items too, so they can discuss them with their customers. All our stores regularly cook up new and interesting products for our customers to sample.[33]

Prices and product offerings varied somewhat by region and state. There were no weekly specials or cents-off coupons or glitzy promotional discounts. Customers could choose from an eclectic and somewhat upscale variety of baked goods, organic foods, fresh fruits and vegetables, imported and domestic cheeses, gourmet chocolates and candies, coffees, fresh salads, meatless entrées and other vegan products, low-fat and low-carbohydrate foods, frozen fish and seafood, heat-and-serve entrées, packaged meats, juices, wine and beer, snack foods, energy bars, vitamins, nuts and trail mixes, and whatever other exotic items the company's buyers had come upon. About 20–25 percent of Trader's Joe's products were imported. There were very few brand-name items; some 2,000 items carried the Trader Joe's label and its other quirky labels for particular foods: Trader Jose's (Mexican food), Trader Ming's (Chinese food), Trader Giotto's (Italian food), Pilgrim Joe's (seafood), Trader Jacques' (imported French soaps), Joe's Diner (certain frozen entrées), and Joe's Kids (children's food); these accounted for about 70 percent of total sales. Items with a Trader Joe's logo contained no artificial flavors, colors, preservatives, trans fats, MSG, or genetically modified ingredients. About 10 to 15 new, seasonal, or one-time-buy items were introduced each week. Products that weren't selling well were dropped. Trader Joe's was the exclusive retailer of Charles Shaw wine, popularly known as "Two Buck Chuck" because of its $1.99 price tag in California (outside California, the price ranged as high as $3 because of higher liquor taxes and transportation costs). In its early days, the company had been built on its large selection of California wines and hard liquors; later, when the company's founder, Joe Coulombe, realized that Trader Joe's stores appealed to the highly educated and to lower-income people, food items sold at low everyday prices were added.[34]

Stores were open, with wide aisles, appealing displays, cedar plank walls, and a nautical decor; employees ("crew members") wore colorful Hawaiian shirts. Given the combination of low prices, an emporium-like atmosphere, intriguing selections, and friendly service, customers viewed shopping at Trader Joe's as an enjoyable experience. The company was able to keep the prices of its unique products attractively low (relative to those at Whole Foods and Fresh Market) because of (1) buyers who were always on the lookout for exotic items they could buy at a discount (all products had to pass a taste test and a cost test), (2) less expensive store locations and decor, (3) lower labor costs (there were fewer employees per store), (4) big private-label sales, and (5) very high sales volumes per square foot of store space (said to be $1,132 in 2003).[35]

Trader Joe's crew members were well paid; wages at the non-union company were said to average $21 per hour in 2004 (versus an average of $17.90 paid to unionized grocery chains); pay for first-year supervisors averaged $40,000 per year and entry-level part-timers earned $8 to $12 per hour.[36] The benefits package for employees was considered quite good and included a company-paid retirement plan; a 10 percent employee discount; flexible work hours; free Trader Joe's shirts (which were required on-the-job attire); disability insurance; an employee assistance program; and medical, dental, and vision insurance. Part-time crew members were eligible for medical, dental, and vision coverage after meeting the eligibility requirements; most crew members qualified after working two to three months.

Full-time employees were scheduled to work 40 or 47.5 hours a week and were supervisors. Full-time positions included three levels of hourly supervisors (Novitiate, Specialist, and Merchant) and two levels of salaried management—First Mate (assistant store manager) and Captain (store manager). About 80 percent of Trader Joe's Novitiates began their employment as part-time crew members; individuals outside the company who had strong retail/grocery experience were also considered for the position of Novitiate (supervisor-in-training). The company had a retail management training program designed to take experienced candidates from the level of Novitiate to Second Mate (assistant manager) in about 15 months. Part-time employees worked up to 40 hours a week and did not supervise other crew members; the performance of part-time crew members was reviewed twice a year. All appointments as Captains and First Mates came from the ranks of crew members currently employed at Trader Joe's, including those chosen for newly opened stores. When a new store was scheduled to open, the store Captain and First Mate were responsible for hiring crew members.

Fresh & Easy Neighborhood Markets

In 2007, a new chain, Fresh & Easy Neighborhood Market, emerged as a competitor in the natural and organic segment of the retail grocery industry. Fresh & Easy was a newly established subsidiary of British supermarket giant

Tesco, the world's third-largest retailer (sales of £59.4 billion for fiscal year ending February 23, 2008, equivalent to about $95 billion). Tesco did extensive research on 60 American families and had numerous focus groups in California provide comments on store prototypes before opening its first 21 stores in Phoenix, followed quickly by an additional 38 stores in Las Vegas, San Diego, and Los Angeles. Some of the stores were located in low-income central-city neighborhoods, while others were adjacent to medium- and upper-income residential areas. Tesco's ambitious growth strategy called for opening Fresh & Easy locations at the rate of 3 stores per week, with 200 stores open by February 2009 and as many as 500 stores by 2011. The company opened an 820,000-square-foot distribution center (big enough to supply about 400 stores) in a Los Angeles suburb that was used both to create and package prepared foods and to supply area stores; a warehouse for northern California was being planned for when store expansion moved northward.

The Fresh & Easy concept called for stores to be in readily accessible neighborhood locations, have about 10,000 square feet of shopping space (about the size of an average Walgreens), stock around 3,500 items (versus about 60,000 at a typical supermarket), and convey a theme of fresh, wholesome, and easy-to-prepare foods in a convenient and pleasant setting. Product offerings ranged from gourmet items to everyday staples and included natural and organic foods; fruits and vegetables; meats, fish, and poultry; and a selection of prepared foods and grab-and-go products—all intended to convey a theme of fresh, wholesome, and easy-to-prepare. About 45 percent of the products on the shelves were house-branded Fresh & Easy items—one of the biggest-selling private-label items was a $1.99 bottle of Fresh & Easy "Big Kahuna" Australian wine (an idea said to be an imitation of Trader Joe's Two-Buck Chuck).[37] Other key features of Fresh & Easy stores included:

- Low prices (around 20–25 percent below traditional supermarkets and on a par with the prices at Walmart Supercenters).
- Locally sourced and mostly packaged fresh produce with expiration dates.
- Wide aisles and simple store layouts.

- Low shelves that allowed shoppers to see all across the store.
- All self-checkout.
- Energy-efficient store designs, lighting, and equipment (and the 820,000-square-foot distribution center had the largest solar panel roof in California).
- Packages, particularly for Fresh & Easy brand prepared foods, that let shoppers see what was inside.
- A taste-before-you-buy policy that encouraged shoppers to take almost any product to the "Kitchen Table" area of the store, where a staff person would open it or cook it and dole out samples.

However, in April 2008, top executives at Fresh & Easy announced that the company would put a three-month hold on further new store openings "to kick the tires, smooth out any wrinkles and make some improvements customers have asked for."[38] Management had already corrected a problem of stores frequently running out of certain items and responded to unexpectedly high demand for prepared foods by adding more than 100 new selections. But there was also thought to be a more fundamental strategic issue about whether the Fresh & Easy concept of offering a limited selection of organic and natural foods at relatively cheap prices was really working. One analyst estimated that weekly sales at Fresh & Easy stores had only been about $170,000 instead of the projected $200,000.[39] A research report by another analyst was considerably more downbeat, suggesting that weekly sales could be averaging as little as $60,000.[40] Skeptics of the Fresh & Easy format believed that health-conscious food shoppers could find a far wider, more appealing selection at Whole Foods stores (and to a lesser extent at Trader Joe's), and the shopping ambience was much superior at both Whole Foods and Trader Joe's. Inexpensive packaged foods were commonplace at supermarkets and full-range superstores.

However, Tesco was widely viewed as a formidable retailer with ample resources to fine-tune Fresh & Easy's business concept and strategy and to eventually generate a return on its $700 million–plus investment in Fresh & Easy. In commenting on the Fresh & Easy venture in the United States, Tesco CEO Sir

Terry Leahy said, "Clearly, it is high risk. If it fails it's embarrassing. . . . If it succeeds then it's transformational."[41] In April 2008, Leahy announced that sales at the 115 Fresh & Easy stores in Arizona, California, and Nevada were "ahead of budget" and that the best-performing stores were exceeding $20 in sales per square foot per week—a typical new grocery store in the U.S. was said to average $9 to $10 in weekly sales per square foot during the first year of operations.[42] He indicated that the company planned to have 200 Fresh & Easy stores open in the United States by mid-2009. However, as of March 2010, Fresh & Easy had only 146 stores in three states (California, Arizona, and Nevada). Tesco reported a loss of approximately $220 million on its Fresh & Easy business for fiscal 2009, up from a loss of about $124 million in fiscal 2008.[43]

Independent and Small Chain Retailers of Natural and Organic Products

In 2009 there were approximately 12,250 independent and small chain retailers of natural and organic foods, vitamins/supplements, and natural personal care products. Combined sales of independent natural and organic product retailers were an estimated $20.9 billion in 2008.[44] There were a number of small regional chains like Sunflower Farmers Market (30 stores in six states) and Sprouts Farmers Markets (53 stores in four states), but the majority were single-store, owner-managed enterprises serving small to medium-size communities and particular neighborhoods in metropolitan areas. Product lines and range of selection at the stores of independent natural and health foods retailers varied from narrow to moderately broad, depending on a store's market focus and the shopper traffic it was able to generate. Two vitamin/supplement chains, General Nutrition and Vitamin World, dominated the $9.3 billion vitamin/supplement segment with about 5,700 store locations; vitamin/supplement chains were an alternative source for many of the products that Whole Foods stocked in the vitamin/supplement section of its stores.

Over half of the independent stores had less than 2,500 square feet of retail sales space and generated revenues of less than $1 million annually; the core product offerings of these retailers were vitamins and mineral/herbal supplements, complemented by a selection of organic and natural foods and certain prepared foods—some 5,000 items in total. But there were roughly 1,000 natural and health foods retailers with store sizes exceeding 6,000 square feet and sales per store of about $10 million annually. Sales of vitamins and mineral/herbal supplements at many small independent stores were beginning to flatten, chiefly because conventional supermarket chains and most large drugstore chains now carried a sizable selection of vitamins/supplements. Sales at small retailers of natural and organic foods were also under pressure because conventional supermarkets had a growing selection of organic and natural foods, while chains like Whole Foods and Trader Joe's had a far wider selection of organic and natural products of all types. One industry expert noted that "shoppers can pick up a bag of mixed organic salad greens, a half-gallon of organic milk, some hormone-free chicken, trans fat–free cookies and crackers, non-dairy beverages and—brace yourself—even gluten-free foods, right in the aisles of their regular supermarkets."[45]

Sunflower Farmers Market Sunflower Farmers Market, headquartered in Boulder, Colorado, began operations in 2003 with four stores—two in Phoenix, one in Albuquerque, and one in Denver.[46] In late 2007, Sunflower raised $30 million in equity financing from PCG Capital Partners (in return for one-third ownership of the company) to fund its store expansion initiative; plans called for opening about eight new locations annually. The founding partner and CEO of Sunflower Farmers Market was Mark Gilliland, formerly a cofounder and president of Wild Oats Market who had been forced out at Wild Oats when his aggressive expansion strategy put the company in dire financial straits. Gilliland's vision was for Sunflower to have 50 locations in 2013 and annual sales of $500 million. By 2010, the company had grown to 30 stores in Arizona, New Mexico, Colorado, California, Nevada, and Utah; it also operated a distribution center in Phoenix. Revenues were roughly $200 million in 2008. About 90 percent of Sunflower's management team was comprised of former Wild Oats managers.

Sunflower's strategic objective was to establish a discount niche in organic and natural foods using a strategy with elements borrowed from Trader Joe's and small farmer's market-type stores. The company's mission statement described its four-pronged strategic approach:

- **We Will Always Offer the Best Quality Food at the Lowest Prices in Town.** "Better-than-supermarket quality at better-than-supermarket prices" is our motto.

- **We Keep Our Overhead Low.** No fancy fixtures or high rent. No corporate headquarters . . . just regular people, like you, looking for the best deals we can find.

- **We Buy Big.** We source directly, we pay our vendors quickly and we buy almost everything by the pallet or truckload. That buying power means big savings for you!

- **We Keep It Simple.** We don't charge our vendors "slotting allowances" or shelf space fees. Just honest-to-goodness negotiating for the lowest possible price and we pass the savings on to you.

Sunflower's tag line was "Serious Food . . . Silly Prices." The company targeted budget-conscious consumers who wanted to eat healthy or were interested in natural and organic foods but were averse to paying premium prices. According to Gilliland, "There's nothing fancy about us. In terms of atmosphere, we're comparable to Trader Joe's, but with a few more bells and whistles and a higher level of finish. For instance, we have a service meat department and offer lots more produce. . . . We try to kill everyone on price, especially on produce. It's our loss leader. We even beat Walmart when it comes to produce prices."[47] The chain had been described as a more-affordable, downsized, no-frills version of Whole Foods.[48] Management strived to locate new stores on recycled real estate sites, keep store build-out costs low, and use basic store fixtures and furnishings, thus enabling a new store to be built and equipped for less than $2 million.

Sunflower's stores had an average footprint of 20,000 square feet and a bright, colorful warehouse-like atmosphere. Stores stocked about 6,000 different items, a number of which were one-of-a-kind products purchased in large lots from brokers. The product focus was on organic,

natural, and minimally processed food items. Pallets of goods were placed wherever there was floor space available. Each store stocked fresh produce; meats and seafood; cereals; nutrition bars; canned goods; pastas; frozen meals; premium roasted coffees; gluten-free foods; bulk foods; cheeses; breads; deli selections (sliced meats, soups, salads, sandwiches, sushi, and a fresh olive and antipasto bar); beer and wine; and an assortment of health, wellness, and personal care items. Private-label items accounted for about 20 percent of sales. Each store had a weekly sales flyer (also available by e-mail), and an events calendar for each store could be viewed online at the company's website (www.sfmarkets.com). Stores also served the community by organizing activities, lectures, and events that emphasized the value of good nutrition and a healthy lifestyle.

Sprouts Farmers Market

Founded in 2002, Sprouts was a regional chain with stores in Arizona, Texas, California, and Colorado. It specialized in fresh produce but also offered a large selection of vitamins and supplements, all-natural meats, fresh seafood, 200 bins of bulk food items, a selection of natural and organic grocery products, 1,500 gluten-free products, dairy products (including rBST-free milk), imported cheeses, deli meats, bakery items, and beer and wine. Its mission was "helping America eat healthier, live longer, and spend less." Its vision was to operate stores throughout the United States and "strive to create value for the customer, maintain a fun and unique environment for our customers and employees, be the employer of choice, and create an environment where new ideas and risk taking are encouraged." In 2010, the company, headquartered in Phoenix, had 50 stores in four states (Arizona, California, Colorado, and Texas) and more than 4,000 employees. Twelve new stores were planned for 2010. Revenues were expected to approach $500 million in 2010, up from an estimated $110 million in 2005. Sprouts Farmers Market, owned by the Boney family, was the 13-largest privately held company in Arizona and the seventh-fastest-growing privately held company in the state. The Boney family had sold its Henry's Market chain to Wild Oats in 1999.

Existing Sprouts stores ranged from 23,000 to 37,000 square feet and were bright and cheery, with wide aisles and low shelves that allowed shoppers to see all parts of the store. Each store had weekly specials; Wednesdays were promoted as "Double Ad Day" because the previous week's ad prices overlapped the current week's ad prices (which began on Wednesdays); weekly specials, as well as a calendar of events at each store, could be accessed at the company's website (www.sprouts.com). A magazine issued every two months, *Sprouts Farmers Market,* had feature articles on various subjects, health and wellness information, recipes, menus, and a news and notes section, as well as ads featuring products available at the company's stores.

The company had been referred to as "Whole Foods Lite" because, while using fresh produce as a primary sales driver, stores carried less organic produce and items were sold at lower price points.[49] It targeted educated, health-oriented, value-conscious grocery shoppers.

ENDNOTES

[1] The Nielsen Company, "Healthy Eating Report for 2008," January 21, 2009, posted at http://blog.nielsen.com/nielsenwire/consumer, accessed March 10, 2010.

[2] Lieberman Research Group, *2009 Organic Industry Survey,* a study conducted for the Organic Trade Association and posted at www.environmentalleader.com/2009/05/06/us-organic-sales-up-by-171/, accessed March 10, 2010; Anne Macey, "Retail Sales of Certified Organic Food Products, in Canada, in 2006," a study commissioned and published by the Organic Agriculture Centre of Canada, May 2007.

[3] Datamonitor, "Food: Global Industry Guide," www.researchandmarkets.com/research/18f9c2/food_global_indus, accessed March 11, 2010.

[4] Based on data in "Organic Beef Profile," Iowa State University Extension, www.agmrc.org, accessed on March 10, 2010.

[5] Economic Research Service, U.S. Department of Agriculture, data accessed at www.ers.usda.gov on March 25, 2008.

[6] Whole Foods Market, 2009 10-K report, p. 51.

[7] Whole Foods Market, 2009 10-K report, p. 10.

[8] Company press releases, February 19, 2008, and February 16, 2010.

[9] Whole Foods Market, "Letter to Shareholders," 2003 annual report.

[10] Hollie Shaw, "Retail-Savvy Whole Foods Opens in Canada," *National Post,* May 1, 2002, p. FP9.

[11] See Karin Schill Rives, "Texas-Based Whole Foods Market Makes Changes to Cary, N.C., Grocery Store," *News and Observer,* March 7, 2002.

[12] Calculated from data in Exhibit 5.

[13] Whole Foods Market, "Letter to Stakeholders," 2009 annual report.

[14] Company press release, February 16, 2010.

[15] As quoted in Marilyn Much, "Whole Foods Markets: Austin, Texas Green Grocer Relishes Atypical Sales," *Investors Business Daily,* September 10, 2002.

[16] As quoted in "Whole Foods Market to Open in Albuquerque, N.M.," *Santa Fe New Mexican,* September 10, 2002.

[17] Information contained in John R. Wells and Travis Haglock, "Whole Foods Market, Inc.," Harvard Business School case study 9-705-476.

[18] Company press release, January 21, 2003.

[19] Company press release announcing Whole Foods Market's inclusion on *Fortune*'s "The 100 Best Companies to Work For" list, January 21, 2010.

[20] Whole Foods Market, 2009 10-K report, p. 14, and company press release, January 21, 2010.

[21] As quoted in John K. Wilson, "Going Whole Hog with Whole Foods," Bankrate.com, posted December 23, 1999, and accessed March 21, 2010. Mackey made the statement in 1991 when efforts were being made to unionize the company's store in Berkeley, California.

[22] Company press release, January 21, 2010.

[23] Whole Foods Market, 2009 10-K report, pp. 28 and 34.

[24] Whole Foods Market, 2009 10-K report, p. 42; 2008 10-K report, p. 48; and 2007 10-K report, p. 43.

[25] Slide presentation at Whole Foods Market's annual shareholders meeting, March 8, 2010.

[26] "Frank Talk from Whole Foods' John Mackey," *Wall Street Journal,* August 4, 2009, http://online.wsj.com, accessed March 13, 2010.

[27] David Kesmodel and John R. Wilke, "Whole Foods Is Hot, Wild Oats a Dud—So Said Rahodeb," *Wall Street Journal,* July 12, 2007, http://online.wsj.com/article/SB118418782959963745.html, accessed April 7, 2007.

[28] Andrew Martin, "Whole Foods Executive Used Alias," *New York Times,* July 12, 2007, http://www.nytimes.com/2007/07/12/business/12foods.html, accessed April 7, 2008.

[29] Ibid.

[30] Company press release, October 5, 2007.

[31] According to a July 13, 2007, posting on a *BusinessWeek* message board, http://www.businessweek.com/careers/managementiq/archives/2007/07/who_advises_joh.html, accessed March 26, 2010.

[32] Company press release, February 16, 2010, p. 1.

[33] Trader Joe's, www.traderjoes.com, accessed December 1, 2005.

[34] In 1977, Coulombe sold the company to German billionaire Theo Albrecht (who had since put the company in a trust); Albrecht was a cofounder of German supermarket chain Aldi.

[35] "Trader Joe's: The Trendy American Cousin," *Business Week,* April 26, 2004, www.businessweek.com, accessed March 29, 2010.

[36] "The American Way of Aldi," *Deutsche Welle,* January 16, 2004, www.dw-world.de, accessed March 29, 2010.

[37] Matthew Boyle, "Tesco Needs a Fresh Start in the U.S.," *Fortune,* December 4, 2007, www.cnnmoney.com, accessed April 7, 2008.

[38] As quoted in Bruce Horovitz, "British Invasion Hits Grocery Stores," *USA Today,* April 7, 2008, p. B2.

[39] Ibid.

[40] Ibid.

[41] As quoted in "Fresh, But Far from Easy," *The Economist,* June 21, 2007, www.economist.com, accessed April 7, 2008.

[42] Company press release, April 15, 2008.

[43] "Tesco Faces Growing Losses in US," *Daily Mail,* April 21, 2009, www.thisismoney.co.uk, accessed March 30, 2010.

[44] *National Foods Merchandiser,* June 2009, p. 12, www.naturalfoodmerchandiser.com, accessed March 31, 2010.

[45] Jay Jacobwitz, "Independent Retailers Need New Customers: The New 'Integrated' Foods Shopper," *Merchandising Insights,* November 2009, http://wfcgreenbook.com, accessed March 30, 2010.

[46] This section is based on information posted at the Sunflower Markets website (www.sunflowermarkets.com) and in Joe Lewandowski, "Naturals Stores Freshen Their Strategies," *Natural Foods Merchandiser,* January 1, 2004, www.naturalfoodsmerchandiser.com, accessed November 19, 2004.

[47] Connie Gentry, Katherine Field, and Marianne Wilson, "Forty Under 40: Small Chains Flourish," *Chain Store Age,* January 2009, www.sfmarkets.com, accessed March 31, 2010.

[48] Ibid.

[49] David Giddens, "Sprouts Growing in Texas," *Dallas Business Journal,* June 10, 2005, www.dallas.bizjournals.com, accessed March 31, 2010.